Scottish
Highlands & Islands

THE ROUGH GUIDE

There are more than one hundred and fifty Rough Guide titles
covering destinations from Amsterdam to Zimbabwe

Forthcoming titles include
Beijing • Cape Town • Croatia • Ecuador • Switzerland

Rough Guide Reference Series
Classical Music • Drum 'n' Bass • English Football • European Football
House • The Internet • Jazz • Music USA • Opera • Reggae
Rock Music • Techno • World Music

Rough Guide Phrasebooks
Czech • Dutch • Egyptian Arabic • European Languages • French • German
Greek • Hindi & Urdu • Hungarian • Indonesian • Italian • Japanese
Mandarin Chinese • Mexican Spanish • Polish • Portuguese • Russian
Spanish • Swahili • Thai • Turkish • Vietnamese

Rough Guides on the Internet
www.roughguides.com

ROUGH GUIDE CREDITS

Text editor: Geoff Howard
Series editor: Mark Ellingham
Editorial: Martin Dunford, Jonathan Buckley, Jo Mead, Kate Berens, Amanda Tomlin, Ann-Marie Shaw, Paul Gray, Helena Smith, Judith Bamber, Orla Duane, Olivia Eccleshall, Ruth Blackmore, Sophie Martin, Claire Saunders, Gavin Thomas, Alexander Mark Rogers, Polly Thomas, Joe Staines, Lisa Nellis, Andrew Tomičić, Claire Fogg, Richard Lim, Duncan Clark, Peter Buckley (UK); Andrew Rosenberg, Mary Beth Maioli (US)
Production: Susanne Hillen, Andy Hilliard, Link Hall, Helen Ostick, Julia Bovis, Michelle Draycott, Katie Pringle, Robert Evers, Neil Cooper

Cartography: Melissa Baker, Maxine Repath, Nichola Goodliffe, Ed Wright
Picture research: Louise Boulton, Sharon Martins
Online editors: Kelly Cross, Loretta Chilcoat (US)
Finance: John Fisher, Gary Singh, Edward Downey, Mark Hall, Tim Bill
Marketing & Publicity: Richard Trillo, Niki Smith, David Wearn, Jemima Broadbridge (UK); Jean-Marie Kelly, Myra Campolo, Simon Carloss (US)
Administration: Tania Hummel, Charlotte Marriott, Demelza Dallow

ACKNOWLEDGEMENTS

The authors would like to thank: the National Trust for Scotland; Historic Scotland; Caledonian MacBrayne, P&O Scottish Ferries and Orkney Ferries for help getting around the islands.

Rob Humphreys would also like to thank: Alasdair Enticknap for helpful hints on updating the Outer Hebs; Dick and Sue Courchee for B&B tips; Val and Gordon for enthusiastic updates for Skye and elsewhere; Val (again) for further trips beyond the call of duty; Kate, Stan and Josh for groundwork in the snow and sun in Islay, Mull and Orkney; and Geoff Howard for his calm, relaxed approach to life.

Donald Reid would also like to thank all those who smoothed the way with information, assistance, opinions, good leads, beds, meals and enthusiasm, particularly Sally Munro of the Highlands & Islands Tourist Board; Beverley Tricker of Aberdeen & Grampian Tourist Board; Fran & Chris at Rua Reidh; Gavin & Nicola at Aite Cruinnichidh; Frank & Kate at Rogat; Rob for his steady eye, insight and motivation; Geoff for pulling it together; and Mo for being prepared to wander where it was all about.

The editor would like to thank Nikky Twyman for proofreading; Helen Ostick for typesetting; and Ed Wright for cartography.

PUBLISHING INFORMATION

This first edition published February 2000 by Rough Guides Ltd, 62–70 Shorts Gardens, London, WC2H 9AB.
Distributed by the Penguin Group:
Penguin Books Ltd, 27 Wrights Lane, London W8 5TZ
Penguin Books USA Inc., 375 Hudson Street, New York 10014, USA
Penguin Books Australia Ltd, 487 Maroondah Highway, PO Box 257, Ringwood, Victoria 3134, Australia
Penguin Books Canada Ltd, 10 Alcorn Avenue, Toronto, Ontario, Canada M4V 1E4
Penguin Books (NZ) Ltd, 182–190 Wairau Road, Auckland 10, New Zealand
Typeset in Linotron Univers and Century Old Style to an original design by Andrew Oliver.
Printed in England by Clays Ltd, St Ives PLC
Illustrations in Part One and Part Three by Edward Briant.
Illustrations on p.1 & p.427 by Henry Iles
© Rob Humphreys and Donald Reid 2000

Scottish
Highlands & Islands

THE ROUGH GUIDE

written and researched by

Rob Humphreys and Donald Reid

with additional research by

Pete Heywood, Colin Irwin, Helena Smith and Paul Tarrant

THE ROUGH GUIDES

THE ROUGH GUIDES

TRAVEL GUIDES • PHRASEBOOKS • MUSIC AND REFERENCE GUIDES

 We set out to do something different when the first Rough Guide was published in 1982. Mark Ellingham, just out of university, was travelling in Greece. He brought along the popular guides of the day, but found they were all lacking in some way. They were either strong on ruins and museums, but went on for pages without mentioning a beach or taverna, or they were so conscious of the need to save money that they lost sight of Greece's cultural and historical significance. Also, none of the books told him anything about Greece's contemporary life – its politics, its culture, its people, and how they lived.

So, with no job in prospect, Mark decided to write his own guidebook, one which aimed to provide practical information that was second to none, detailing the best beaches and the hottest clubs and restaurants, while also giving hard-hitting accounts of every sight, both famous and obscure, and providing up-to-the-minute information on contemporary culture. It was a guide that encouraged independent travellers to find the best of Greece, and was a great success, getting shortlisted for the Thomas Cook travel guide award, and

encouraging Mark, along with three friends, to expand the series.

The Rough Guide list grew rapidly and the letters flooded in, indicating a much broader readership than had been anticipated, but one which uniformly appreciated the Rough Guide mix of practical detail and humour, irreverence and enthusiasm. Things haven't changed. The same four friends who began the series are still the caretakers of the Rough Guide mission today: to provide the most reliable, up-to-date and entertaining information to independent-minded travellers of all ages, on all budgets.

We now publish more than 150 titles and have offices in London and New York. The travel guides are written and researched by a dedicated team of more than a hundred authors, based in Britain, Europe, the USA and Australia. We have also created a unique series of phrasebooks to accompany the travel series, along with an acclaimed series of music guides, and a best-selling pocket guide to the Internet and World Wide Web. We also publish comprehensive travel information on our Web site:

www.roughguides.com

HELP US UPDATE

THE AUTHORS

Rob Humphreys joined the Rough Guides in 1989, having worked as a failed actor, taxi driver and male model. He has spent some part of every year in Scotland since he was nowt but a lad in rural Yorkshire. He has also travelled extensively in central and eastern Europe, writing guides to Prague, the Czech and Slovak republics, and St Petersburg, as well as London.

Donald Reid was born and brought up in Glasgow, studied Law at Edinburgh University, and left the country soon after-wards to avoid the threat of an office. Having worked on an island in the Caribbean and as a trawler fisherman in Australia, he floated into Cape Town one misty December morning in 1993 and took a notion to hang around, working on books, magazines and newspapers in South Africa for the next three years. He returned to Scotland and now lives in Edinburgh working as a freelance writer and editor. He is the co-author of the *Rough Guide to Scotland* and the *Rough Guide to South Africa*.

CONTENTS

Introduction x

PART THREE CONTEXTS 427

LIST OF MAPS

MAP SYMBOLS

▬▬	Railway	🏛	Abbey
M74	Motorway	🏛	Stately home
▬▬	Road	♦	Museum
▬▬	Dirt road	⌖	Gardens
)-----(	Tunnel	✕	Battlefield
▬▬	Pedestrianized street	⌂	Cairn
→▬	One-way street	🗿	Standing stones
⊔⊔⊔⊔	Steps	⁘	Stone circle
- - - - -	Footpath	◎	Cup- and ring-marked rocks
– – –	Ferry route	⚠	Campsite
▬▬	Waterway	◉	Accommodation
▬ ▬ ▬	Chapter division boundary	⌂	Hostel
♦	Point of interest	✈	Airport
▲	Peak	🅿	Parking
☼	Hill	ⓘ	Tourist office
�▽	Viewpoint	⊠	Post office
☀	Rocks	🍾	Whisky distillery
☀	Lighthouse	■	Building
☀	Waterfall	⊞	Church (town maps)
◠	Cave	▨	Park
∴	Ruins/archeological site	▦	National park
♔	Castle/tower	🌲	Forest
✝	Church (regional maps)	▨	Beach
⛳	Golf course	⊡	Cemetery
⛷	Ski area		

INTRODUCTION

L ocated on the northwest fringe of Europe, the remote **Scottish Highlands and Islands** are one of the continent's most unspoilt, scenic areas, a rugged region of imposing mountain ranges bounded by scattered island groups and wild seas. Shaped over thousands of years by geological faults, scouring glaciers and the hostile weather systems of the North Atlantic, the magnificent land- and seascapes of the region have themselves moulded its rich history, producing some of Europe's best-preserved Stone Age settlements, centuries of warring clansmen, romantic heroes such as Rob Roy and Bonnie Prince Charlie, and the recurring themes of precarious existence and determined survival.

The **Highlands** – the massed ranks of hills rising to over four thousand feet, and the glens and lochs between them – begin north of the **Highland Boundary Fault**, a geological divide separating the northern two-thirds of Scotland from its more populous central belt. While for many these bare-topped mountains represent the very essence of Scotland, they are only half the picture. In the west, the soaring peaks are complemented by a savagely indented coastline, where empty beaches and spectacular cliffs are interspersed with patches of unexpectedly lush vegetation. Off the west coast, arrayed like scattered jigsaw pieces, are the **Hebrides**, whose five hundred wind-swept islands comprise the largest of Scotland's archipelagos. Meanwhile, off the north coast of the mainland lie the fertile, treeless islands of **Orkney** and, halfway across the North Sea to Norway, the bleak and rugged **Shetland** islands.

Strictly speaking, the Highland Boundary Fault runs from the Firth of Clyde to Stonehaven, just south of Aberdeen, but its significance goes beyond mere geology. Communication with the rest of Scotland across this geographic divide has always been patchy, and remains difficult in places even today. As a result, the **history** of the Highlands and Islands is quite distinct from the rest of Scotland, with its deeply embedded clan structure and the influence of Norse rule, which continued in some of the islands until as late as the fifteenth century. And, while the Jacobite defeat at Culloden in 1746 was a blow to Scottish pride, it was an unmitigated disaster for the Highlands and Islands, signalling the destruction of the Highland clan system, and the ultimately the entire Highland way of life. The **Clearances** that followed in the nineteenth century more than halved the population, and even today the Highland landscape is littered with the crumbling shells of pre-Clearance crofting communities.

The Highlands and Islands remain a sparsely populated area – the largest centre, Inverness, is little more than a large town. In contrast to the rest of Scotland, there is little heavy industry, leaving the **economy** extremely fragile, with depopulation a constant threat, particularly in the islands. In some cases, only the arrival of settlers from outside the region has stemmed the dwindling numbers. Nowadays, the traditional Highland industries of farming, crofting, fishing and whisky distilling are no longer enough to provide jobs for the younger generation, and have had to be supplemented by forestry, fish-farming and the oil industry. However, all three of these tend to have a detrimental effect on the environment, whose health is of paramount importance to the region's other growth industry, **tourism**. All in all, it's a tricky juggling act that the region is still stuggling to master, balancing the importance of grabbing new opportunities with the will to maintain traditional values.

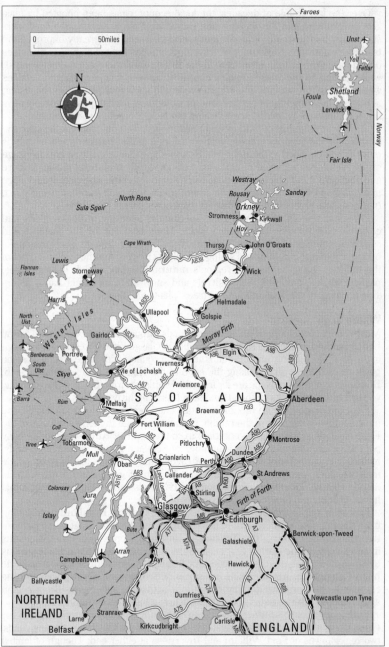

Over the last couple of decades, the local economy has been boosted by massive government and European Union subsidies. Such funding has helped kick-start many businesses (not all of them successful), and has greatly improved the **transport** network. Nevertheless, travelling remains time-consuming: distances on land are greater than elsewhere in the Britain (and there are no motorways), while getting to the islands means coordinating with ferry or plane timetables whilst hoping the weather doesn't intervene and spoil your plans. For the visitor, of course, the difficulty of getting around is no great hardship, as most journeys are accompanied by terrific scenery, and the lack of urgency soon seduces.

The Norse language of Orkney and Shetland has died out, and Gaelic, once the language of the majority of those living in the rest of the Highlands and Islands, is more or less confined to the Hebrides. However, the unique **culture and heritage** of the region has survived remarkably well, especially traditional music, folklore and literature, all of which continue to be championed enthusiastically, from village pub *ceilidhs* to dedicated centres. In other aspects too, such as religion and sport, traditions and practices remain distinct from other parts of Scotland.

For most visitors, though, it's the spectacular **scenery** of peaks, glens and coastline that remains the primary draw. Many also opt for the plentiful and rewarding **outdoor activities**, particularly hillwalking, though good mountain-biking, canoeing, climbing and skiing can all be enjoyed. Another valuable part of the outdoor experience is the region's **natural history**, which boasts eagles, puffins, whales, dolphins, red squirrels and snow-white mountain hares, along-side an array of precious indigenous trees, plants and flowers.

Where to go

Most visitors come to the Highlands and Islands through the gateway of the Central Belt of Scotland, dominated by the major cities of Glasgow in the west and Edinburgh in the east. The majority of routes into the region connect with these centres at some point, or with those strung along the edge of the Highland fault – Stirling, Perth, Dundee and Aberdeen. None are far from the Highlands: from Glasgow, for example, you can be by the banks of Loch Lomond in less than thirty minutes.

West of Glasgow, a rich mix of mountains and sea can be found in **Argyll**, the most southwesterly part of the region. Gathered around the long sea-lochs of the Firth of Clyde and the zigzag coastline from the **Mull of Kintyre** up to the busy port of **Oban**, Argyll includes a number of Scotland's most accessible islands, including craggy **Arran** in the Firth of Clyde, **Islay**, famous for its peaty single malt whiskies and its huge wintering population of geese, and **Mull**, with its moody volcanic mountains and intriguing off-lying islands, including the spiritual haven of **Iona** and the geological wonders of **Staffa**.

East of Argyll, in the heart of Scotland, are the **Central Highlands**, stretching from the first rise of hills north of the Highland Fault to the Great Glen. Here, in the nineteenth century, the **Trossachs**' forested slopes and sparkling lochs inspired some of the world's first mass tourism, while **Deeside** was made famous by Queen Victoria's attachment to its wild beauty. To the north of the region is the huge **Cairngorm** massif, which has many of Scotland's highest peaks and the Highland's best-organized array of outdoor activities, plus **Speyside**, a region synonymous with two icons of Scottish leisure: whisky and salmon-fishing.

Cutting a dramatic southwest–northeast swath through northern Scotland is the **Great Glen**, a string of lochs interlinked by the Caledonian Canal, with the Highlands' two major towns of **Fort William** and **Inverness** at either end. Though of limited appeal in their own right, both are useful bases for exploring the Glen, which includes two of Scotland's best-known (if slightly disappointing) sights: **Loch Ness**, speculative home of the eponymous monster; and **Ben Nevis**, the very highest of the Highland peaks. You don't have to look hard to find evidence of the thickly layered history of the region: near Inverness is the battlesite of **Culloden**, where Bonnie Prince Charlie's Jacobite rebellion ended in 1746; on the shores of Loch Ness is **Urquhart Castle**, one of the most dramatic ruins in the Highlands; and south of Fort William is the beautiful **Glen Coe**, poignant scene of an infamous seventeenth-century clan massacre.

The Great Glen sees the largest concentration of visitors to the Highlands and Islands, but many also take in the island of **Skye** – effortlessly reached by a controversial bridge but also, more romantically, by ferry from Mallaig or Glenelg. A deeply indented coastline, dark sea-lochs and the towering Cullin peaks make for some of the west coast's fiercest scenery, good for touring, walking and mountaineering. Beyond Skye, across a body of water known as the Minch, lie the Outer Hebrides or **Western Isles**, a string of islands forming a barrier between the mainland and the North Atlantic. The largest and most populated of this Gaelic-speaking archipelago is the dual island of **Lewis** and **Harris**, where you'll the prehistoric standing stones at **Calanais** (Callanish), a sight to rival England's Stonehenge. To the south lies the "Long Island" of the **Uists**, **Benbecula** and **Barra**, fringed by an almost uninterrupted series of golden beaches.

Back on the mainland, the wildest and remotest parts of the country are found in the **north and northwest Highlands**, which include three very different coastlines and a memorable array of landscapes. Along the west coast, the mountain ranges of **Torridon** and **Assynt** are most popular with walkers, while the stunning coastal scenery of Wester Ross and its lively main town, **Ullapool**, make this one of the Highlands' most celebrated corners. The stormy north coast, from **Cape Wrath** to **John O'Groats**, harbours a poignant history of villages forcibly cleared in the nineteenth century, as well as the ecological treasure of the flat, boggy **Flow Country**. The east coast, from the **Black Isle** immediately north of Inverness to the town of **Wick**, is often passed over, but offers a rich heritage, including prehistoric remains and memories of fast-disappearing fishing communities.

From Thurso and John O'Groats, boats leave for the cluster of islands that make up the **Orkney Islands**. By far the most picturesque town here is the port of Stromness, the main point of arrival for those coming by boat, while the capital, Kirkwall, boasts a magnificent medieval cathedral. Further north, now two hundred miles from Aberdeen, are the **Shetland Islands**, where the bustling and historic harbour at Lerwick shelters craft from every corner of the North Atlantic. Orkney and Shetland, both with a rich Norse heritage, differ not only from each other but are also quite distinct from other islands and the Highlands in both dialect and culture. Far-flung and weather-buffeted, they offer some of the country's wildest scenery, finest birdwatching and stunning archeological remains.

When to go

Pressure systems rolling in off the North Atlantic mean that the weather changes a lot in the Highlands and Islands – notoriously, it can transform from bright and sunny to wet and miserable (and back again) in the space of an hour or two. It's worth being prepared for both at any time of year, particularly if you're planning to be outdoors.

In general, however, the west coast and Hebrides are wetter than the Central Highlands and east coast all year round, but also a little warmer. In **winter**, the air temperature rarely drops below freezing along the western seaboard, although a

CLIMATE IN THE HIGHLANDS AND ISLANDS

Average daily maximum temperatures in °C and monthly rainfall in mm

	Jan	Feb	Mar	April	May	June	July	Aug	Sept	Oct	Nov	Dec
Oban												
°C	6	7	9	11	14	16	17	17	15	12	9	7
mm	146	109	83	90	72	87	120	116	141	169	146	172
Tiree												
°C	7	7	8	10	13	15	16	16	15	13	10	8
mm	120	71	77	60	56	66	79	83	123	123	125	123
Braemar												
°C	4	4	6	9	13	16	17	17	14	11	6	5
mm	93	59	59	51	65	55	58	76	73	87	87	96
Nairn												
°C	6	6	9	11	14	17	18	17	16	13	8	7
mm	48	34	33	36	43	46	62	75	50	54	60	52
Fort William												
°C	6	7	9	11	14	17	17	17	15	13	9	7
mm	200	132	152	111	103	124	137	150	199	215	220	238
Wick												
°C	6	6	7	9	11	14	15	15	14	12	8	7
mm	81	58	55	45	47	49	61	74	68	73	90	82
Shetland												
°C	5	5	6	8	10	13	14	14	13	10	7	6
mm	127	93	93	72	64	64	67	78	113	119	140	147

sharp wind and damp air can make it feel bitterly cold. Inland, much lower temperatures and snow are common on most of the hills and the glens during the winter months, when skiing takes places at various resorts in the Highlands. In many parts of the Highlands and Islands, however, and especially the remoter parts, travellers are scarce in winter and many places close.

Spring and **autumn** often prove attractive times to visit, with rich colours appearing in the glens, bursts of good weather and less of the bustle of the tourist trail than summer. May is consistently the driest month of the year across the region, and average temperatures in both May and October are still in the mid-teens (°C). However, the **summer** months remain the most appealing time to be here, not simply for the chance of better weather (with temperatures nudging 20°C), but also for the longer days, which can see dusk lingering well into late evening – in fact, in the far north, Orkney and Shetland, darkness scarcely falls in June and July. The warmer weather does have its drawbacks, however – most significantly, the clouds of **midges**, tiny biting insects which frequently appear around dusk, dawn and in dank conditions, and can drive even the most committed outdoors type scurrying indoors.

GETTING THERE FROM THE USA AND CANADA

The majority of airlines fly from the USA and Canada to London with connections to any number of Scottish airports (see p.11). However, if you are planning on travelling throughout the British Isles you might want to fly into London and take a slower, more scenic route up to Scotland, either by rail or road.

Only **Glasgow** is served by nonstop direct flights from North America. Flights to **Edinburgh** tend to route through London or Dublin; to get to **Aberdeen** or **Inverness** you can fly to London or Manchester and hop on a British Airways, British Midland, or Air UK shuttle. Aberdeen is also well served with flights from Paris, Amsterdam and Scandinavia. For the **Scottish Islands** there are many internal flights from Glasgow and Edinburgh, or you can take any of a number of ferries from the west coast or from Aberdeen. See p.10 for the full picture on flying to the Highlands and Islands from other parts of Britain.

Figure on seven hours' flying time nonstop from New York to Glasgow, or seven hours to London with an extra hour and a quarter to Glasgow or Edinburgh (not including stopover time). Add an extra four or five hours to travel from the West Coast. Most eastbound flights cross the Atlantic overnight, reaching Britain the next morning, although a few flights from the East Coast leave early in the morning, landing late the same evening.

SHOPPING FOR TICKETS

Barring special offers, the absolute cheapest of the airlines' published fares is a winter **SuperApex** ticket, sometimes known as a "Eurosaver". However, these are only available at certain times of the year and on certain routes, and your stay is limited to between seven and 21 days. You're more likely, therefore, to get an **Apex** ticket, which also carries certain restrictions: you have to book – and pay – at least 21 days before departure, spend at least seven days abroad (maximum stay three months), and you tend to get penalized if you change your schedule. Some airlines also issue **Special Apex** tickets to people younger than 24, often extending the maximum stay to a year. In addition, many airlines offer youth or student fares to **under-26s**; a passport or driving licence are sufficient proof of age, though these tickets are subject to availability and can have eccentric booking conditions. It's worth remembering that most cheap return fares involve spending at least one Saturday night away and that many tickets will only permit you a percentage refund if you need to cancel or alter your journey, so make sure you check the restrictions carefully before buying a ticket.

You can normally cut costs further by going through a **specialist flight agent** – either a **consolidator**, who buys up blocks of tickets from the airlines and sells them at a discount, or a **discount agent**, who, in addition to selling discounted flights, may also offer special student and youth fares and a range of other travel-related services such as insurance, rail passes, car rentals, tours and the like. Bear in mind, though, that these companies make their money by dealing in bulk – don't expect them to answer lots of questions, and remember that the penalties for changing your plans can be stiff. Some agents specialize in **charter flights**, which may be cheaper than anything available on a scheduled flight, but again departure dates are fixed and withdrawal penalties are high (check the refund policy). If you travel a lot, **discount travel clubs** are another option – the annual membership fee may be worth it for benefits such as cut-price air tickets and car rental.

However, you shouldn't automatically assume that tickets purchased through a travel specialist will be cheapest – once you get a quote, check with the airlines and you may turn up an even better deal. **Students** might be able to find cheaper flights through the major student travel agencies, such as STA Travel, Nouvelles Frontières and, for Canadian students, Travel CUTS.

A further possibility is to see if you can arrange a **courier flight**, although the hit-or-miss nature of these makes them most suitable for the single traveller who travels light and has a very flexible schedule. In return for shepherding a parcel through customs and possibly giving up your baggage allowance, you can expect to get a heavily discounted ticket. For information about courier flights, you could contact Now Voyager (☎212/431-1616) in New York. For more options, consult *A Simple Guide to Courier Travel* (Pacific Data Sales Publishing).

If you are travelling to Scotland as part of a much longer journey, you might want to consider buying a **Round-the-World (RTW) ticket**. Some travel agents can sell you an "off-the-shelf" RTW ticket that will have you touching down in about half a dozen cities (London is easily arranged, but a Scottish connection will probably have to be added on separately); others will have to assemble one for you, which can be tailored to your needs but is likely to be more expensive.

The newest tool for finding low price air fares is the **World Wide Web**. There are a number of new sites, where you can look up fares and even book tickets. You can search in the travel sections of your Web browser, or try one of the following locations: Travelocity at www.travelocity.com; Travel Information Service at www.ibm.tiss.com; or FLIFO Cyber Travel Agent at www.flifo.com. In addition, you could link up with Discount Airfares Worldwide On-Line at www.etn.nl/discount.htm, which is a hub of consolidator and discount agent Web links, maintained by the non-profit European Travel Network.

Regardless of where you buy your ticket, **fares** will depend on the season. Fares to Scotland are highest from around early June to mid-September, when the weather is best; they drop during the "shoulder" seasons – mid-September to early November, and mid-April to early June – and you'll get the best prices during the low season, November through to April, when only a few hardy souls feel like vacationing in Scotland (excluding Christmas and New Year, when prices are hiked up and seats are at a premium). Note also that flying at the weekend ordinarily adds up to $50 to the round-trip fare; price ranges quoted below assume midweek travel.

FLIGHTS FROM THE USA

There are several daily **nonstop flights to Glasgow** from US cities: British Airways flies from New York, American from Chicago, and Northwest from Boston. You can also fly to London on any of those airlines, as well as on Virgin, TWA, Continental and Delta, and take a connecting flight to Scotland.

Low-season **Apex** fares to Glasgow from New York and other East Coast cities cost US $400–500; and from the West Coast, US$500–600. During the shoulder season, prices rise to US$500–550 from New York, US$700–800

DISCOUNT TRAVEL AGENTS IN THE USA AND CANADA

Air Brokers International, 323 Geary St, Suite 411, San Francisco, CA 94102 (☎1-800/883-3273 or 415/397-1383, www.airbrokers.com). Consolidator and specialist in RTW and Circle Pacific tickets.

Air Courier Association, 15000 W 6th Ave., Suite 203, Golden, CO 80401 (☎1-800/282-1202 or 303/278-8810, www.aircourier.org). Courier flight broker. Annual fee $64 ($25 membership fee plus $39 annual fee).

Airhitch, 2641 Broadway, New York, NY 10025 (☎1-800/326-2009 or 212/864-2000, www.airhitch.org). Standby-seat broker: For a set price, they guarantee to get you on a flight as close to your preferred destination as possible, within a week.

Council Travel, 205 E 42nd St, New York, NY 10017 (☎1-888-COUNCIL, www.counciltravel.com), and branches in many other US cities. Student/budget travel agency.

Discount Airfares Worldwide On-Line (www.etn.nl/discount.htm). A hub of consolidator and discount agent Web links, maintained by the non-profit European Travel Network.

Educational Travel Centre, 438 N Frances St, Madison, WI 53703 (☎1-800/747-5551 or 608/256-5551, www.edtrav.com). Student/youth and consolidator fares.

High Adventure Travel, 442 Post St, Suite 400, San Francisco, CA 94102 (☎1-800/350-0612 or 415/912-5600, www.highadv.com). Round-the-world and Circle Pacific tickets. The Web site features an interactive database called "Farebuilder", which lets you build your own RTW itinerary.

International Association of Air Travel Couriers, 220 S Dixie Hwy, #3, Lake Worth, FL 33460 (☎561/582-8320, www.courier.org). Courier flight broker. Membership $45 per year.

International Travel Network/Airlines of the Web (www.itn.net/airlines). Online air travel info and reservations site.

New Frontiers/Nouvelles Frontières, 12 E 33rd St, New York, NY 10016 (☎1-800/366-6387 or 212/779-0600, www.new-frontiers.com); 1000 Sherbrook East, Suite 720, Montréal, H2L 1L3 (☎514/526-8444); and other branches in LA, San Francisco and Québec City. French discount travel firm.

Now Voyager, 74 Varick St, Suite 307, New York, NY 10013 (☎212/431-1616, www.nowvoyagertravel.com). Lesbian and gay-friendly courier flight broker and consolidator.

Skylink, 265 Madison Ave, 5th Floor, New York, NY 10016 (☎1-800/AIR-ONLY or 212/599-0430), with branches in Chicago, Los Angeles, Montréal, Toronto and Washington DC. Consolidator.

STA Travel, Head Office: 5900 Wiltshire Blvd, Suite 2110, Los Angeles, CA 90036 (☎1-800/777-0112, www.sta-travel.com), and other branches in the New York, San Francisco, Boston, Miami, Chicago, Seattle, Philadelphia and Washington, DC areas. Worldwide discount travel firm specializing in student/youth fares; also student IDs, travel insurance, car rental, rail passes, etc.

Student Flights, 5010 E Shea Blvd, Suite 104A, Scottsdale, AZ 85254 (☎1-800/255-8000 or 602/951-1177, www.isecard.com). Student/youth fares, student IDs.

TFI Tours International, 34 W 32nd St, 12th Floor, New York, NY 10001 (☎1-800/745-8000 or 212/736-1140). Consolidator.

Travac Tours, 989 6th Ave, 16th Floor, New York NY 10018 (☎1-800/872-8800 or 212/563-3303, www.travac.com). Consolidator and charter broker. They will fax current fares from their fax line: 1/888-872-8327.

Travel Avenue, 10 S Riverside Plaza, Suite 1404, Chicago, IL 60606 (☎1-800/333-3335 or 312/876-6866, www.tipc.com). Full-service travel agent that offers discounts in the form of rebates.

Travel CUTS, 187 College St, Toronto, ON M5T 1P7 (☎1-800/667-2887 or 416/979-2406, www.travelcuts.com), and other branches all over Canada, including San Francisco (415/247-1800). Organization specializing in student fares, IDs and other travel services.

Travelocity (www.travelocity.com). Online consolidator.

UniTravel, 11737 Administration Drive, Suite 120, St Louis, MO 63146 (☎1-800/325-2222 or 314/569-2501, www.unitravel.com). Consolidator.

Worldtek Travel, 111 Water St, New Haven, CT 06511 (☎1/800-243-1723, www.worldtek.com). Discount travel agency for worldwide travel.

Worldwide Discount Travel Club, 1674 Meridian Ave, Suite 206, Miami Beach, FL 33139 (☎305/534-2082) Discount travel club.

from Los Angeles, and in the summer fares can reach US$700–950 from New York and up to US$1100 from Los Angeles.

For direct flights to London, British Airways, British Midland, Air UK, EasyJet and Ryanair offer the greatest selection of onward connections to Scotland (see p.11). Aer Lingus also serves Edinburgh, and United can ticket you straight through to several Scottish destinations on British Midland. Flying to Manchester in the north of England is another possibility, though this won't be any cheaper than the direct Apex fare to Glasgow.

FLIGHTS FROM CANADA

Air Canada flies daily nonstop to **Glasgow from Toronto** in summer (four times a week in winter). From other Canadian cities you can fly via London on Air Canada or British Airways (see p.11 for details of onward travel to the Highlands and Islands), or alternatively fly to Chicago, New York or Boston and pick up a nonstop flight to Glasgow from there. In addition, Air Canada also has direct flights from Toronto to Manchester.

Low-season midweek Apex fares from Toronto and Montréal to Glasgow should set you back CAN$600–700, and from Vancouver CAN$800–900. During the shoulder seasons fares are CAN$650–750 from Toronto, CAN$850–950 from Vancouver, and in high season expect to pay CAN$750–950 from Toronto and CAN$950–1150 from Vancouver.

PACKAGES AND INCLUSIVE TOURS

Although you may want to see Scotland at your own speed, you shouldn't dismiss out of hand the idea of a **package deal**. Many agents and airlines put together very flexible deals, sometimes amounting to no more than a flight plus car or train pass and accommodation, which can actually work out to be better value than the same arrangements made on arrival, especially in the case of fly-drive deals, as car rental is expensive in Britain.

There are also many tour operators that specialize in travel to Scotland. Most can do packages of the standard highlights, and many also organize **walking or cycling trips** through the countryside, with any number of theme tours based around Scotland's literary heritage, history, pubs, gardens, golf – you name it. A few possibilities are listed in the box below, and a good travel agent will be able to point out others. For further listings, contact the British Tourist Authority (☎1-800/462-2748) or check out the Scottish Tourist Board's Web site at www.holiday.scotland.net. Be sure to examine the fine print of any deal, and make sure the operator is a member of the United States Tour Operator Association (USTOA) or approved by the American Society of Travel Agents (ASTA).

NORTH AMERICAN TOUR OPERATORS TO SCOTLAND

Abercrombie & Kent (☎1-800/323-7308, www.abercrombiekent.com). Land and rail tours of Scotland.

Above the Clouds Trekking (☎1-800/233-4499, www.gorp.com/abvclds.htm). Week-long walking tours of the Highlands.

British Coastal Trails (☎1-800/473-1210, www.bctwalk.com). Walking trips in the Borders and Western Isles.

British Travel International (☎1-800/327-6097). Offers self-catering country cottages and B&B accommodation in Scotland and can arrange air tickets, rail and bus passes.

CIE Tours International (☎1-800/243-8687 or 973/292-3899, www.cietours.com). Escorted bus tours and deluxe castle tours of Scotland.

Especially Britain (☎1-800/869-0538). Fly-drives and independent rail tours with accommodation in B&Bs, country houses and castles.

Golf International Inc (☎800/833-1389). Scottish golf vacation specialist.

Himalayan Travel (☎1-800/225-2380, www.gorp.com/himtravel.htm). Hiking and walking tours of Scotland.

Home At First (☎1-800/523-5842). Rents out cottages and flats in Scotland.

Jerry Quinlan's Celtic Golf (☎1-800/535-6148 or 609/884-8090, www.jqcelticgolf.com). Customized golf tours of Scotland's best links.

Lord Addison Travel (☎1-800/326-0170, www.lordaddison.com). Small escorted specialist tours, including garden tours and history tours, such as the "Bonnie Prince Charlie tour".

Prestige Tours (☎1-800/890-7375). A variety of Scottish tours.

Sterling Tours (☎1-800/727-4359, www.sterlingtours.com). Scottish specialist offering various independent itineraries, some packages.

GETTING THERE FROM AUSTRALIA & NEW ZEALAND

There are no direct flights to Scotland from Australia or New Zealand, and mostly you will have to route through London then get an onward flight north. Travelling time is nearly 24 hours, so you might be better off including a stopover – and a good night's sleep – in your itinerary. Fares obviously depend on the time of the year: low-season rates run from mid-January to the end of February, and October to mid-November; high season is mid-May to August, and December to mid-January; and shoulder season is the rest of the year. Tickets purchased direct from the airlines tend to be more expensive, while travel agents can offer better deals and have the latest information on special offers and stopovers – the best discounts are often available through Flight Centres, STA and Travel.com.au, who can also advise on visa regulations. Students and under-26s can usually get a further ten percent off published prices.

All the fares quoted below are from Australia's east coast, unless otherwise stated, to London. From Perth you'll pay A$200–400 less on flights routed through Asia and Africa, and the same amount more for flights via the Americas. In addition, you'll need to add on an extra A$80–200, depending on the season, for the flight to Glasgow or Edinburgh; most travel agents will be able to book this leg for you in advance, though you may find it cheaper to wait and pick up a low-cost flight in London (see p.11

for details). Alternatively, you may prefer to travel overland from London by bus or train. BritRail train passes can be good value if you intend to do a lot of travelling in the UK, but must be bought before you leave home (see p.12 for full details).

The cheapest scheduled flights to London are **via Asia** with Gulf Air or Thai Airways, which charge A$1350–1500 in low season, and A$1760 in high season, and involve a transfer in the carrier's hub city. For A$1600 in low season to A$1815 in peak season, you can fly with Virgin Atlantic and either Malaysia Airlines via Kuala Lumpur or Ansett via Hong Kong. In the mid-range, Lufthansa and Singapore Airlines all fly direct to London for A$1700–1900, while British Airways and Qantas quote published through-fares to Edinburgh or Glasgow of A$1760 in low season up to A$2195 in high season. From Perth, Royal Brunei Airlines offer a fare to London of A$1455 year-round. Many of the airlines also offer fly-drive packages and stopovers in their hub cities for no extra cost; Qantas, for example, flies from all major Australian cities daily, including a stopover in Asia and thirteen-day car rental in London, with fares starting at A$1799 in low season to A$2199 in peak season.

Via Africa, the lowest fares start at A$1999, with South African Airways via Johannesburg to London. Qantas/British Airways include a free stopover in Perth and Johannesburg or Harare on the way out, and Asia on the return, for A$2019–2600.

Flights are pricier **via North America**, with United Airlines offering the cheapest deal via Los Angeles and either New York, Washington or Chicago for A$1950–2430, while Air New Zealand via Auckland and Los Angeles, and Canadian Airlines via Toronto or Vancouver, both charge around A$1975–2450.

Currently the best fare of all on offer is the Britannia Airways or Airtours **charter flights**, which run several times a month to Gatwick and Manchester via Singapore and Bahrain. Fares start at A$1099 in low season and range up to A$1759 in high season, though the flight only runs between November and March and is definitely a "no-frills" service. For extra money they offer the option of upgrading to a better quality of in-flight meals.

AIRLINES IN AUSTRALIA AND NEW ZEALAND

Air New Zealand, Australia ☎132476; New Zealand ☎09/357 3000; *www.airnz.co.nz*. Daily direct flights to London Heathrow from major Australian cities via Asia and from major New Zealand cities via Los Angeles.

Airtours/Britannia Airways, Australia ☎02/9247 4833. Several flights a month from Sydney, Adelaide, Brisbane, Melbourne, Perth and Auckland to London Gatwick, and once a week from Sydney to Manchester via Singapore and Bahrain; flights only run between November and March.

British Airways, Australia ☎02/8904 8800; New Zealand ☎09/356 8690; *www.british-airways.com*. Daily direct flights from Sydney to London Heathrow via Singapore/Los Angeles, and twice-weekly via Harare or Johannesburg; daily flights from Auckland via Los Angeles, with onward connections to Scotland.

Canadian Airlines, Australia ☎1300/655 767; New Zealand ☎09/309 0735; *www.british-airways.com*. Several flights a week to London Heathrow via Vancouver/Toronto from Sydney, Melbourne and Auckland.

Cathay Pacific, Australia ☎131747; New Zealand ☎09/379 0861; *www.british-airways.com*. Several flights a week to London and Manchester from Brisbane, Sydney, Melbourne, Perth, Cairns and Auckland, via Hong Kong.

Gulf Air, Australia ☎02/9244 2199, *www.british-airways.com*. Several flights weekly from Sydney to London via Singapore and Bahrain or Abu Dhabi.

Japanese Airlines (JAL), Australia ☎02/9272 1111; New Zealand ☎09/379 9906. Daily flights to London Heathrow via Tokyo or Osaka from Brisbane and Sydney, and several weekly flights from Cairns and Auckland: onward connections to Edinburgh on British Midland.

KLM, Australia ☎02/9231 6333 or 1-800/505 747; *www.klm.om*. Twice-weekly flights from Sydney to London Heathrow via Amsterdam and Singapore.

Korean Air, Australia ☎02/9262 6000; New Zealand ☎09/307 3687. Several flights a week to London from Sydney, Brisbane, Auckland and Christchurch, via Seoul.

Malaysia Airlines (MAS), Australia ☎132627; New Zealand ☎09/373 2741. Several flights a week to London Heathrow from Sydney, Melbourne, Perth and Auckland, via Kuala Lumpur.

Qantas, Australia ☎131313; New Zealand ☎09/357 8900 or 0800/808 767; *www.qantas.com.au*. Daily flights from major Australian and New Zealand cities to London Heathrow, via Singapore, Bangkok or Hong Kong.

Royal Brunei Airlines, Australia ☎07/3221 7757. Three flights weekly to London from Brisbane, and two weekly from Darwin and Perth, via Abu Dhabi and Brunei.

Singapore Airlines, Australia ☎131011; New Zealand ☎09/379 3209. Daily flights to London Heathrow, and Manchester from Brisbane, Sydney, Melbourne, Perth and Auckland, via Singapore.

South African Airways (SAA), Australia ☎02/9223 4402; New Zealand ☎09/309 9132; *www.qantas.com.au*. Flights to London from major Australian cities via Perth and Johannesburg/Harare.

Thai Airways, Australia ☎1300/651960; New Zealand ☎09/377 3886; *www.thaiair.om*. Several flights a week to London Heathrow, via Bangkok from Brisbane, Sydney, Melbourne, Perth and Auckland.

United Airlines, Australia ☎131777; New Zealand ☎09/379 3800; *www.ual.com*. Daily flights to London Heathrow and Manchester, via Los Angeles, Chicago, New York or Washington from Sydney, Melbourne and Auckland.

Virgin Atlantic, Australia ☎02/9244 2747, *www.flyvirgin.com/atlantic/*. Daily flights to London Heathrow via Kuala Lumpur from Sydney, Melbourne and Adelaide.

From New Zealand, the cheapest scheduled flights to London Heathrow (with an extra NZ$150–250 for flights to Edinburgh and Glasgow) are with Korean Air, Thai Airways (in conjunction with KLM) or JAL, all of whom fly via their respective home cities for around NZ$2050–2280. British

Airways' daily flight from Auckland costs from NZ$2780 (low season) to NZ$3170 (high season), including a connecting flight to Edinburgh or Glasgow. The most direct route to London is via North America with United Airlines, stopping in Los Angeles and Chicago, for NZ$2770 (low sea-

DISCOUNT AGENTS IN AUSTRALIA AND NEW ZEALAND

Anywhere Travel, 345 Anzac Parade, Kingsford, Sydney (☎02/9663 0411; *anywhere@ozemail.com.au*).

Budget Travel, 16 Fort St, Auckland, plus branches around the city (☎09/366 0061 or 0800/808 040).

Destinations Unlimited, 3 Milford Rd, Auckland (☎09/373 4033).

Flight Centres, 82 Elizabeth St, Sydney, plus branches nationwide (☎13 1600); 205 Queen St, Auckland (☎09/309 6171), plus branches nationwide.

STA Travel (*www.statravelaus.com.au*), 702 Harris St, Ultimo, Sydney; 256 Flinders St, Melbourne, plus offices in state capitals and major universities (fastfare telesales ☎1300/360 960; nearest branch 131776); 10 High St, Auckland, plus branches in Wellington, Christchurch, Dunedin, Palmerston North, Hamilton and at major universities (telesales ☎09/366 6673).

Status Travel, 22 Cavenagh St, Darwin (☎08/8941 1843).

Student Uni Travel, 92 Pitt St, Sydney (☎02/9232 8444), plus branches in Melbourne, Darwin, Brisbane, Cairns and Perth.

Thomas Cook, 175 Pitt St, Sydney; 257 Collins St, Melbourne; plus branches in other state capitals (telesales ☎1800/063 913; nearest branch 131771); Level 5, Telstra Business Centre, Auckland (☎09/359 5200).

Trailfinders, 8 Spring St, Sydney (☎02/9247 7666).

Travel.com.au (*www.travel.com.au*), 80 Clarence St, Sydney (☎02/9290 1500).

Usit Beyond, cnr Shortland and Jean Batten Place, Auckland (☎09/379 4224), plus branches in Christchurch, Hamilton, Palmerston North and Wellington.

UK Flight Shop (*www.ukflightshop.com.au*), 7 Macquarie Place, Sydney (☎02/9247 4833), plus branches in Melbourne and Perth.

SPECIALIST TOUR AGENTS

Adventure Specialists, 69 Liverpool St, Sydney (☎02/9261 2927). Offers a selection of walking and cycling holidays throughout Scotland.

Adventure Travel Company, 164 Parnell Rd, Parnell, East Auckland (☎09/379 9755). New Zealand agents for Peregrine Adventures.

Adventure World, 73 Walker St, North Sydney (☎02/9956 7766 and 1800/221 931), plus branches in Adelaide, Brisbane, Melbourne and Perth; 101 Great South Rd, Remuera, Auckland (☎09/524 5118). Based in London, but with an extensive variety of tours throughout Scotland.

Best of Britain, 352a Military Rd, Cremorne, Sydney (☎02/9909 1055). Can arrange flights, accommodation, car rental, tours, canal boats and B&Bs throughout Scotland.

Explore Holidays, 55 Blaxland Rd, Ryde, NSW 2112 (☎02/9857 6200). Wholesaler of guest-house, B&B and hotel accommodation throughout Scotland, as well as Military Tattoo packages.

Peregrine Adventures (*www.peregrine.net.au*), 258 Lonsdale St, Melbourne (☎03/9663 8611), plus offices in Brisbane, Sydney, Adelaide and Perth. Adventure travel company specializing in small-group walking and cycling holidays in Scotland, with travel between main points by minibus.

Sundowners, Suite 15, 600 Lonsdale St, Melbourne (☎03/9600 1934 or 1800/337 089). Russian and Trans-Siberian Railway specialists; escorted group tours and independent travel by train to Scotland via Moscow.

Wiltrans/Maupintour, Level 10, 189 Kent St, Sydney (☎02/9255 0899). Fully escorted tours around Scotland's historic homes and gardens, staying in upmarket accommodation.

YHA Travel Centre, 422 Kent St, Sydney (☎02/9261 1111); 205 King St, Melbourne (☎03/9670 9611); 38 Sturt St, Adelaide (☎08/8231 5583); 154 Roma St, Brisbane (☎07/3236 1680); 236 William St, Perth (☎08/9227 5122); 69 Mitchell St, Darwin (☎08/8981 2560); 28 Criterion St, Hobart (☎03/6234 9617). Organizes budget accommodation throughout England, Wales and Scotland for YHA members.

son) to NZ$3170 (high season). As with Australia, the cheapest fare of all is on Britannia Airways' charter flight from Auckland to Gatwick and Manchester, which runs several times a month from November to March. Fares from Auckland are NZ$1620 low season to NZ$2110 in high season.

If you're visiting Scotland as part of a longer trip, a **round-the-world (RTW) ticket** can work out very good value. Currently the best deals on offer are the Qantas/British Airways "Global Explorer" or "One World" tickets allowing four stops (including Glasgow or Edinburgh), costing from A$1895/NZ$3070. The "Star Alliance" between Ansett, Air New Zealand, United Airlines, Thai Airways, Varig, SAS, Lufthansa and Air Canada allows at least six stopovers worldwide, and starts at A$2699/NZ$3300. Note that, while it's easy enough to include London on a round-the-world itinerary, a stop in Scotland may involve backtracking and can be harder to arrange; you may find it cheaper to buy the London to Scotland leg separately, or to travel overland (see p.12 for details).

GETTING THERE FROM BRITAIN, IRELAND & EUROPE

Crossing the border from England into Scotland is straightforward, with train and bus services forming part of the British national network. Trains from London to Glasgow or Edinburgh take between four and six hours, while buses take at least eight hours. Flying will obviously save you an enormous amount of time, depending on where you're heading out to in the Highlands and Islands, though fares are only really competitive on popular routes such as London to Edinburgh. You can also reach mainland Scotland direct by ferry, in under an hour from Ireland, and in 24 hours from Norway. On the whole, the cheapest and quickest way to reach Scotland from the rest of Europe is by plane.

BY PLANE

You can fly direct to Scotland's **main airports** – Edinburgh, Glasgow and Aberdeen – in an hour or so, from all three major London airports (Heathrow, Gatwick and Stansted), as well as from Luton and various other provincial airports. There are also direct flights from Belfast, Dublin and numerous other major European airports. However, in order to fly to any of the smaller airports in the Highlands and Islands, you'll need to change planes (see p.30 for more details on flights within Scotland).

There are flights almost hourly to Edinburgh and Glasgow from **London**, and nearly as many to Aberdeen. As a broad guide to what you're likely to pay, reckon on around £30 for a rock-bottom one-way ticket and £50 for a return, from airlines such as EasyJet or Ryanair. These flights tend to leave from airports such as Luton and Stansted, and are often subject to rigid restrictions, but the savings can make the extra effort well worthwhile. Go, British Airways' low-cost airline, also fly from Stansted to Edinburgh, and offer competitive fares, from £70 return. The other three main carriers – British Airways, British Midland and KLM Air UK – all have special offer fares from time to time. Again, ticket prices depend very much on the restrictions. The cheaper tickets usually have to be bought at least a week in advance, apply to only a very few mid-week flights, must include a Saturday-night stayover, and are either non-refundable or only partially refundable, and non-exchangeable. For a flexible, refundable fare, you're looking £100 one-way London to Glasgow, and double that for a return.

Note, too, that **airport tax**, currently £10, is levied for each single or return ticket on all domestic flights to Scotland. The tax may or may not be included in the price, and you'll almost certainly have to pay a passenger surcharge (£10) on

AIRLINES IN BRITAIN AND IRELAND

Aer Lingus (Eire ☎01/844 4777, UK ☎0645/737747; www.aerlingus.ie). Dublin to Edinburgh or Glasgow.

British Airways (UK ☎0345/222111; Eire ☎0141/222 2345; www.british-airways.com). BA fly direct to Edinburgh, Glasgow and Aberdeen from all three London airports, as well as Belfast, Birmingham, Bristol, Cardiff, Manchester and Southampton. They also fly Gatwick to Inverness, Leeds/Bradford to Aberdeen, and from Jersey to Edinburgh and Glasgow, plus they handle flights to the Hebrides, Orkney and Shetland, which are operated by BA's franchises.

British Midland (UK ☎0345/554554; Eire ☎01/283 8833; www.iflybritishmidland.com). East Midlands to Edinburgh, Glasgow and

Aberdeen; Heathrow to Edinburgh and Glasgow; and Amsterdam to Edinburgh.

EasyJet (☎01582/702900 or 0870/600 0000; www.easyjet.com). Luton to Edinburgh, Glasgow, Aberdeen and Inverness.

Go (☎0845/605 4321; www.go-fly.com). BA's low-cost airline currently offers direct flights from Stansted to Edinburgh.

KLM Air UK (UK ☎0990/074074; Eire ☎0345/445588; www.klm.com). Amsterdam to Edinburgh, Glasgow and Aberdeen; Stansted to Glasgow and Aberdeen; London City to Edinburgh; and Norwich to Aberdeen.

Ryanair (Eire ☎01/609 7800; UK ☎0541/569569). Dublin and Stansted to Glasgow (Prestwick).

AGENTS AND OPERATORS IN BRITAIN AND IRELAND

Council Travel, 28a Poland St, London W1V 3DB; (☎0171/437 7767, www.destination-group.com). Flights and student discounts.

North South Travel, Moulsham Mill Centre, Parkway, Chelmsford CM2 7PX (☎01245/492882). Friendly, competitive travel agency, whose profits are used to support projects in the developing world.

STA Travel (www.statravel.co.uk), 86 Old Brompton Rd, London SW7 3LH; 117 Euston Rd, London NW1 2SX; 38 Store St, London WC1E 7BZ; 11 Goodge St, London W1P 1FE (UK/Europe ☎0171/ 361 6161); 38 North St, Brighton, BN1 1RH (☎01273/728282); 25 Queens Rd, Bristol BS8 1QE (☎0117/929 4399); 38 Sidney St, Cambridge CB2 3HX (☎01223/366966); 75 Deansgate, Manchester M3 2BW (☎0161/834 0668); 88 Vicar Lane, Leeds LS1 7JH (☎0113/244 9212); 9 St Mary's Place, Newcastle-upon-Tyne NE1 7PG (☎0191/233 2111); 36 George St, Oxford OX1 2OJ (☎01865/792800); and branches on university campuses in London, Birmingham, Brighton, Bristol, Cambridge, Canterbury, Cardiff, Coventry, Durham, Leicestershire, Leeds, Loughborough, Nottingham, Manchester, Oxford, Sheffield and Warwick. Specialists in low-cost

flights and tours for students and under-26s, though other customers welcome.

Usit Campus (www.campustravel.co.uk), 52 Grosvenor Gardens, London SW1W 0AG (UK/Europe ☎0171/730 3402); 541 Bristol Rd, Selly Oak, Birmingham B29 6AU (☎0121/414 1848); 61 Ditchling Rd, Brighton BN1 4SD (☎01273/570226); 37–39 Queens Rd, Clifton, Bristol BS8 1QE (☎0117/929 2494); 5 Emmanuel St, Cambridge CB1 1NE (☎01223/324283); 166 Deansgate, Manchester M3 3FE (☎0161/833 2046, telesales 273 1721); 105–106 St Aldates, Oxford OX1 1BU (☎01865/242067); Fountain Centre, College St, Belfast BT1 6ET (☎01232/324 073); 10–11 Market Parade, Patrick St, Cork (☎021/270 900); 33 Ferryquay St, Derry (☎01504/371 888); 19 Aston Quay, Dublin 2 (☎01/602 1777 or 677 8117; Europe and UK 01/602 1600 or 679 8833, long-haul 01/602 1700); Victoria Place, Eyre Square, Galway (☎091/565 177); Central Buildings, O'Connell St, Limerick (☎061/415 064); 36–37 Georges St, Waterford (☎051/872 601). Student/youth travel specialists, with branches also in YHA shops and on university campuses all over Britain.

top of that. Anyone under 26 should also check out specialist agencies such as Usit Campus or STA Travel, who offer **youth deals**, including Domestic Air Passes (also known as Hopper Passes) on British Airways flights, which can get

you to Inverness and the Hebrides for a fraction of the published fare. Addresses for discount agents are listed in the box above.

Coming from **Ireland**, the best deals are with Ryanair, who operate three flights a day from

Dublin to Glasgow Prestwick (actually situated near Ayr). Their cheapest fares are around IR£60 return (with an additional IR£20 airport tax), though special offers for less crop up from time to time. A fully flexible fare with Aer Lingus can cost three or four times that amount, but will allow you to change your ticket or claim a refund. From **Belfast**, your only option is British Airways, who have several daily flights to Edinburgh, Glasgow and Aberdeen; the cheapest fare is around £70 return.

BY TRAIN

The only **direct train services** to the Scottish Highlands and Islands from south of the border are to Fort William and Inverness. From **London to Inverness**, you have a choice of taking the daytime service run by GNER, which departs from King's Cross and takes eight hours, or catching the overnight sleeper train from Euston, run by ScotRail. The direct **London to Fort William** route is only served by the overnight sleeper service, which is also available to Aberdeen, Dundee, Edinburgh and Glasgow.

In most other cases, you'll need to **change trains** in Edinburgh or Glasgow, both of which are served by frequent direct services from London, and are easily reached from other main English towns and cities, though this may also involve changing trains en route. Apart from GNER, whose trains from King's Cross run up the east coast to Edinburgh and beyond, there's also Virgin, whose trains depart from Euston and go to Glasgow via the west coast. The **fares** of both companies are fiendishly complex; the restrictions and conditions are outlined in detail below.

Journey times from London can be as little as four and a half hours to Edinburgh and five hours to Glasgow; from Manchester, reckon on around two and a half hours to Edinburgh and three hours to Glasgow. From either of these two points, allow another two and a half hours to Aberdeen and three and a half hours to Inverness. Edinburgh, Glasgow, Aberdeen, Inverness and Fort William are all served by the overnight **sleeper trains** from London Euston, run by ScotRail. The GNER London King's Cross to Inverness service takes eight hours.

Eurostar operates frequent train services through the **Channel Tunnel** to London Waterloo from Lille (2hr), Paris (3hr) and Brussels (2hr 40min). You then have to change trains, and stations, to Euston or King's Cross for the onward journey. If you are driving from mainland Europe,

RAIL ENQUIRIES

Eurostar ☎0990/186186
Eurotunnel ☎0990/353535
GNER ☎0345/225225
National Rail Enquiries ☎0345/484950
Rail Europe ☎0990/848848
ScotRail ☎08457/550033
Virgin ☎08457/222333

you might want to take the frequent train service – **Eurotunnel** – that carries you and your car from Calais to Folkestone in 35 minutes; fares range from £84 to £169 per carload, and depend on whether you book in advance, and whether you're prepared to travel at antisocial hours.

TICKETS AND PASSES

The most flexible ticket is a **Saver** return, which can be used on all trains on the outward and return journeys. **SuperSavers**, which cost slightly less, cannot be used on Fridays (nor on a dozen other specified days of the year), and are not valid for any peak-hour services. Saver and SuperSaver tickets are valid for a month (outward travel has to be on the date of issue), and can be used to cross from one mainline station to another via the London Underground. A variety of advance purchase tickets are issued in limited numbers on certain services: **SuperAdvance** tickets must be booked before 2pm, the day before the date of travel; **Apex** tickets have to be booked at least seven days before travelling; and **SuperApex** tickets have to be booked at least fourteen days in advance. Each of the train companies also offer various other promotional fares from time to time, or offer the above tickets under a different name.

To take the **GNER London–Edinburgh service** as an example: a Saver return costs £79, a SuperSaver £69, a SuperAdvance £59, an Apex £49, and a SuperApex just £36. For **London–Inverness**, a Saver return is £92, a SuperSaver £83, a SuperAdvance £77 and an Apex £64; note that there's no SuperApex on this route, but GNER occasionally offer a **Bargain** ticket at around £50 return. For all these tickets you should book as far in advance as you possibly can – many Apex and SuperApex are sold out weeks before the travel date, especially around Christmas and Easter. A **seat reservation** is included in all advance purchase tickets, but not with Savers and SuperSavers, though one can be booked in advance for £1 a seat. If you find yourself without a seat on a weekend or bank holiday long-distance service, you can often upgrade to first class by paying a £10 supplement.

If you're travelling up from London it's definitely worth considering taking one of the **Caledonian Sleepers**, run by ScotRail, daily except Saturday nights from Euston. A sample Apex return fare to Fort William or Inverness is £99, which includes a bed in a two-person berth; first-class customers enjoy the luxury of a single-berth cabin. Note, however, that there are no discounts for railcard holders on Apex tickets. Children pay full price, unless you go for a Family Ticket, which costs £209 return to Fort William or Inverness for one adult and three children, or two adults and two children. You can usually board the train an hour before departure.

Although it is still theoretically possible to have your car transported via **Motorail** (☎0990/502309), the price is prohibitive. To have your car transported from London to Glasgow, for example, costs £165 one way and £295 return (Caledonian Sleeper customers get a £50 discount). It's also extremely inconvenient, as pickup and delivery takes place at the airports and not at the train stations.

Three discount **passes**, all valid for a year, are available in Britain to nationals and foreign visitors alike. The **Young Person's Railcard** costs £18 and gives reductions of a third on all standard, Saver and SuperSaver fares to full-time students studying in Britain and anyone who is between 16 and 26 years of age. A **Senior Citizens' Railcard**, also £18 and offering reductions of a third on many tickets, is available to all those aged 60 or over. For both passes you'll need to show proof of age (for foreign visitors, your passport is preferred) and provide two passport-size photographs. Foreign students will need to show proof of full-time study in Britain.

Children aged 5–15 pay half the adult fare on most journeys, but there are no discounts on Apex and SuperApex tickets. Under-5s travel free, but are not entitled to their own seat on crowded trains. The best option if you're travelling with kids is to buy a **Family Railcard**, which costs £20 and gives a variety of discounts (from a fifth to a third) for up to four adults, travelling with children (visitors will need to show their passports). Even more enticingly, it allows up to four children aged 5–15 to travel anywhere in the

country for a flat fare of £2 each (which includes a seat reservation). If all your children are under 5, you must buy at least one £2 fare to qualify for the discount.

If you've been resident in a European country other than the UK for at least six months, an **InterRail** pass might be a cost-effective way to travel, if Scotland is part of a longer European trip. If bought outside the UK, the passes offer a month's unlimited train travel within Britain, plus discounts on cross-Channel ferries and Eurostar – the only restriction is that they are not valid in the country of purchase. InterRail passes are now zonal: an all-zone pass costs £349 for a month (£259 for under-26s); three zones cost £309 (£229 for under-26s); two zones cost £279 (£209 for under-26s); and one zone costs £229 (£159 for under-26s), but is only valid for 22 days.

BY BUS

Inter-town **bus** services (known as **coaches** in Scotland and the rest of Britain) duplicate many train routes, often at half the price or less. The frequency of service is usually comparable to the train, and in some instances the difference in journey time isn't that great; buses are also reasonably comfortable, and on longer routes often have drinks and sandwiches available on board.

Two of the main operators between England and Scotland are National Express (☎0990/808080) and its sister company, Scottish Citylink (☎0990/505050). If you're a full-time student, under 25 or over 50, you can buy a **Coach Card** for £8, valid for one year, which will get you a thirty percent discount on all fares. Children normally travel for half-price, but if you buy a **Lone Parent Coach Card**, which costs £8 and lasts for a year, one child can travel for free; the £15 **Family Card** allows two children to travel for free with two adults. See "Getting around" (p.25) for details of bus and train passes for within Scotland.

Direct buses run from most provincial British cities to **Edinburgh**, **Glasgow**, **Aberdeen** and **Inverness**. Tickets are widely available from bus stations and hundreds of agents throughout England. Typical fares from London to Glasgow and Edinburgh (journeys of around 8hr) are £30 return on National Express. You can travel during the day or overnight, thus saving you the cost of overnight accommodation. The journeys to Aberdeen and Inverness take around eleven and twelve hours respectively, with the ticket to both costing under £50 return. There's also a 25 percent **discount** on bookings made seven days in advance.

If you're going to do quite a bit of travelling by bus, it might be worth buying a **Tourist Trail Pass**, which gives you unlimited travel within Britain on National Express and Scottish Citylink coaches. Passes start at £49 for two days' travel out of three; £85 for five days out of ten; £120 for seven days out of twenty-one; £187 for fourteen days out of thirty. Coach Card holders can get discounts on these prices. The passes can be bought both from major travel agents, at Gatwick and Heathrow airports and at the British Travel Centre, 1 Regent St, London W1 (walk-in service only). In Scotland, outlets include St Andrew Square Bus Station, Edinburgh, and Buchanan Street Bus Station, Glasgow, as well as other local bus stations. In **North America** these passes are available from British Travel International (☎1-800/327-6097, *www.britishtravel.com*) and US National Express (☎540/298-1395).

A fun alternative for travellers wishing to take in some of the highlights of England and Wales en route to Scotland is the popular Haggis Backpackers' London to Edinburgh **minibus tour**. Beginning in London, the bus takes three to six days to reach Edinburgh, via Bath, Stratford, Snowdonia, Chester, York and the Lake District. Tickets cost £75 for the three-day tour and £119 for the six-day jaunt, and cover only the travel and guided tours, but not accommodation or entry to attractions. There are up to two departures a week in summer, departing from outside the OVC (Overseas Visitors' Club), 41 Longridge Rd, London SW5. For more details, contact Haggis in Edinburgh (☎0131/557 9393, *www.haggis-backpackers.com*).

BY CAR

If you're **driving** to Scotland from the south, the two main routes are up the east of England on the A1, or up the west side of the country using the M6, A74 and M74. The latter route offers at least dual-carriageway driving the whole way. It takes the best part of a day to get from London to Edinburgh or Glasgow by car. If you drive flat out and encounter no roadwork delays, you can get to either city in around eight hours. If you prefer a slower, more scenic route, head off the A1 up the A68, which takes the hilly but scenic route over the border at Carter Bar, and adds an hour or so to the journey time. To reach Aberdeen, add

another two hours' motorway driving from Edinburgh; to reach Inverness, reckon on slightly longer, depending on the traffic. All other roads in the Highlands and Islands are fairly slow going, so calculate your journey time, using 40mph (65kph) as a very rough indicator of average speed.

BY FERRY

The only way to get to Scotland direct by **ferry from Europe** is on the Smyril Line service, which links Shetland with Norway, the Faroe Islands and Iceland (mid-May to early Sept only). The most direct route is from **Bergen (Norway)** to Lerwick in Shetland and then on to Aberdeen with P&O Scottish Ferries. The first leg of the journey to Lerwick (1 weekly) takes twelve hours, with the crossing to Aberdeen (6 weekly) taking fourteen hours. Special through-fares from Bergen to Aberdeen are available for around £100 single for each passenger and another £100 if you want to take a car, plus another £50 per person if you want a berth in a cabin.

There's a greater choice of ferry services from Europe to ports in England, the most convenient being those to Newcastle, less than an hour's drive from the Scottish border, or Hull in the northeast, two hours' drive from Scotland. Tariffs on the ferries are bewilderingly complex: prices vary with the month, day or even hour at certain times of the year, not to mention how long you're staying and the size of your car. The highest prices are usually for daytime sailings in July and August; the lowest, for night journeys out of season. You can often get further reductions through special offers, or by booking in advance – a sensible precaution in any case, as ferries can get booked solid in peak months. Prices given below are for one-way peak-period daytime sailings.

P&O North Sea Ferries sail daily to Hull from **Rotterdam and Zeebrugge** (14–15hr; £50 single for foot passengers, £120 with a small car). From Scandinavia, Fjord Line sail to Newcastle from **Bergen** and/or **Stavanger** (1–3 times weekly; 20–27hr depending on whether it's direct).

Scandinavian Seaways runs one service a week all year round from **Gothenburg (Sweden)** to Newcastle (26hr), costing £115 per person, with an extra £65 for a car. From May to September, they also operate a **Hamburg** to Newcastle service (21hr), four times a week, costing around £85 per person, plus another £50 for cars. The same company also runs from **Ijmuiden**

FERRY COMPANIES

Argyll & Antrim Steam Packet Company (UK ☎0990/523523). Ballycastle to Campbeltown.

Fjord Line (☎0191/296 1313; Bergen ☎5554 8600; Stavanger ☎5152 4545). Bergen and Stavanger to Newcastle.

Hoverspeed (UK ☎0990/240241; France ☎0800/901777). Dieppe to Newhaven; Boulogne to Folkestone; and Calais or Ostend to Dover.

P&O European Ferries (Portsmouth Services ☎0870/600 3300; Irish services ☎0870/242 4777; Cherbourg ☎02/3388 6570). Bilbao, Cherbourg or Le Havre to Portsmouth; Larne to Cairnryan.

P&O North Sea Ferries (Hull ☎01482/377177; Rotterdam ☎01812/55555; Zeebrugge ☎050/543 430). Rotterdam or Zeebrugge to Hull.

P&O Scottish Ferries (Aberdeen ☎01224/572615). Lerwick and Stromness to Aberdeen.

P&O Stena Line (UK ☎0990/980222; Calais ☎03/21.46.04.40). Calais to Dover.

Scandinavian Seaways (Harwich ☎0191/293 6262; Amsterdam ☎25/553 4546; Gothenburg ☎031/650650; Hamburg ☎040/389 0371). Gothenburg or Ijmuiden (Amsterdam) to Newcastle; and Hamburg to Newcastle or Harwich.

SeaCat (UK ☎0990/523523). Belfast to Stranraer or Troon.

Smyril Line (Aberdeen ☎01224/572615; Torshavn, Faroe ☎01/5900). Bergen or Faroe to Lerwick.

Stena Line (Belfast ☎01232/747747). Belfast to Stranraer.

(**Amsterdam**) to Newcastle (14hr), which costs roughly £55 per person and £60 for a car.

A further alternative is to take Eurotunnel (see p.12), or one of the very frequent ferries to England from the **French ports**; there's a greater choice of sailings this way, though the drive up to Scotland from the south coast can easily take a full day. Hoverspeed and P&O Stena Line offer regular sailings from Calais to Dover (the shortest route), for which the lowest fare for a foot passenger is £25 single (or £100 and upwards for small car). For full details of ferry routes and prices, call the ferry companies direct; telephone numbers are listed in the box above.

From Ireland, P&O European Ferries runs several crossings daily from **Larne to Cairnryan** (2hr by ferry, 1hr by jetliner); fares for foot passengers are £20–25 single, and £100–120 with a car.

Stena Line operates numerous conventional ferries and a high-speed service daily on the **Belfast to Stranraer** route (1hr 45min–3hr 15min), at £25 single for foot passengers, and £85–130 for a car. In addition, there are daily SeaCat catamarans on this route (just 1hr 30min), and costing £25 single for foot passengers, £85 with a car. SeaCat also run catamarans from Belfast to Troon, just outside Ayr (2hr 30min), with prices only very slightly higher. There's also a new ferry link run by the Argyll & Antrim Steam Packet Company from **Ballycastle to Campbeltown** (mid-June to Sept only; 2hr 45min), which runs twice daily. Single fares are roughly £25 for a foot passenger, and £90 for a small car. All the ferry companies also offer much cheaper five-day return fares, as well as rock-bottom day-return fares. For more details, call the companies.

RED TAPE

Citizens of all European countries – except **Albania, Bosnia, Bulgaria, Macedonia, Romania, Slovakia, Yugoslavia** and all the former Soviet republics (other than the Baltic States) – can enter Britain with just a passport, generally for up to three months. US, Canadian, Australian and New Zealand citizens can stay for up to six months, providing they have a return ticket and adequate funds to cover their stay. Citizens of most other countries require a visa, obtainable from the British consular or mission office in the country of application. All overseas consulates in the Highlands and Islands are detailed in the listings sections for Kirkwall (p.363) and Lerwick (p.396).

Details of British immigration and visa requirements are listed on the Foreign and Commonwealth Office's **Web site** (*www.fco.gov.uk*), from which you can download the full range of application forms and information leaflets. In addition, an independent charity, the **Immigration Advisory Service (IAS)**, County House, 190 Great Dover St, London SE1 4YB (☎0171/357 6917, *www.vois.org.uk*), offers free and confidential advice to anyone applying for Entry Clearance into the UK.

LONG STAYS AND WORK PERMITS

For stays of longer than six months, US, Canadian, Australian and New Zealand citizens can apply to the British Embassy (see box opposite) in person or by post for an **Entry Clearance Certificate**. Unless you're a resident of an EU country, you need a **permit** to work legally in the UK, although without the backing of an established employer or company this can be very difficult to obtain. People aged between 17 and 27 may, however, apply for a **Working Holiday-Maker Entry Certificate**, which entitles you to stay in the UK for up to two years and to do casual work. The certificates are only available abroad, from British embassies and consulates, and when you apply you must have proof of a valid return or onward ticket, and the means to support yourself while you're in Britain. Note, too, that the certificates are valid from the date of entry into Britain – you won't be able to recoup time spent out of the country during the two-year period.

In North America, full-time, bona fide college students can get temporary work or study permits through the **Council of International Education Exchange (CIEE)**, 205 E 42nd St, New York, NY 10017 (☎212/822 2600, *www.ciee.org*). In addition, Commonwealth citizens with a parent or grandparent born in the UK can apply for a **Certificate of Entitlement to the Right of Abode**, which permits them to work in Britain. If you're unsure about whether or not you may eligible for one of these, contact your nearest British Mission (embassy, high commission or consulate), or the Foreign and Commonwealth Office in London (☎0171/270 1500 or 238 4633).

CUSTOMS AND TAX

Travellers from **EU countries** coming into Britain do not have to make a declaration to customs at their place of entry. The current limits for duty-paid goods from within the EU are 800 cigarettes or 1kg of tobacco, 110 litres of beer, 90 litres of wine, 20 litres of fortified wine and 10 litres of spirits. Duty-free shopping was phased out in 1999. **Travellers from non-EU countries** are only allowed to bring in 200 cigarettes or 250g of tobacco, 2 litres of wine, plus 1 litre of spirits or 2 litres of fortified wine.

There are **import restrictions** on a variety of articles and substances, from firearms to furs derived from endangered species, none of which should bother the average tourist. However, if you need any clarification on British import regulations, contact HM Customs and Excise, Dorset

---

BRITISH EMBASSIES ABROAD

Australia (High Commission) Commonwealth Ave, Yarralumla, Canberra, ACT 2600 (☎1902/941555, www.uk.emb.gov.au).

Canada (High Commission) 80 Elgin St, Ottawa K1P 5K7 (☎613/237-1530, www.bis-canada.org).

Ireland 29 Merrion Rd, Ballsbridge, Dublin 4 (☎01/205 3822).

Netherlands Koningslaan 44, 1075AE Amsterdam (☎676 4343).

New Zealand (High Commission) 44 Hill St, Wellington (☎04/472 6049, www.brithigh-comm.org.nz).

South Africa (High Commission) 91 Parliament St, Cape Town 8001 (☎461 7220).

USA 3100 Massachusetts Ave NW, Washington, DC 20008 (☎202/462-1340, http://britain-info.org).

House, Stamford St, London SE1 9PJ (☎0171/928 3344, www.hmce.gov.uk). You cannot bring pets into Britain on holiday, as tight quarantine restrictions apply to animals brought from overseas (except for Ireland).

Many goods in Britain, with the chief exceptions of books and food, are subject to **Value Added Tax** (**VAT**), which currently increases the cost of an item by 17.5 percent. Visitors from non-EU countries can save a lot of money through the Retail Export Scheme, which allows a refund of VAT on goods to be taken out of the country. EU nationals will usually save very little, if anything, however, because of their own VAT rates. Note that not all shops participate in this scheme – those doing so display a sign to this effect – and that you cannot reclaim VAT charged on hotel bills or other services.

MONEY, BANKS AND COSTS

The basic unit of currency in Britain is the pound sterling (£), divided into 100 pence (p). Coins come in denominations of 1p, 2p, 5p, 10p, 20p, 50p, £1 and £2. Bank of England banknotes are legal tender in Scotland; in addition, the Bank of Scotland, the Royal Bank of Scotland and the Clydesdale Bank issue their own banknotes in denominations of £1, £5, £10, £20, £50 and £100 – legal tender in the rest of Britain, no matter what shopkeepers south of the border might say. Shopkeepers will carefully scrutinize any £20 or £50 notes, as forgeries are widespread, and you'd be well advised to do the same. The quickest test is to hold the note up to the light to make sure there's a thin wire filament running from top to bottom; this is by no means foolproof, but it will catch most fakes.

CARRYING MONEY

There are no exchange controls in Britain, so you can bring in as much money as you like. The easiest and safest way to carry your money is in **travellers' cheques**, available for a small commission (usually one percent) from any major bank. The most commonly accepted travellers' cheques are American Express (Amex), followed by Visa and Thomas Cook – most cheques issued by banks will be one of these brands. You'll usually pay commission again when you cash each cheque, normally another one percent or so, or a flat rate, though no commission is payable on Amex cheques exchanged at Amex offices. Make sure you keep a record of the cheques as you cash them, so that you'll be able to get the value of all uncashed cheques refunded immediately if you lose them.

Most hotels, shops and restaurants in Scotland accept the major **credit cards** (Access/ MasterCard, Visa and Amex), although they're less useful in remote rural areas; smaller establishments all over the country, such as B&Bs, will often accept cash only. You can get cash advances from certain **ATMs** – call the issuing bank or credit company to get a list of locations in Scotland. In addition, you may be able to make withdrawals using your ATM cash card, if you have a **PIN number** designed to work overseas.

Visa and Access/MasterCard holders can then use Bank of Scotland, Clydesdale and Royal Bank of Scotland ATMs – known in Britain as **cashpoint** machines. If you have an account with a highstreet bank in England or Wales, you can simply take your cashpoint card with you. Bank of Scotland and Royal Bank of Scotland cashpoints take Lloyds and Barclays cash cards, while Clydesdale takes HSBC/Midland and National Westminster cards. Bank of Scotland, Clydesdale and most building society cashpoints are in the Link network and accept all affiliated cards.

BANKS

In every sizeable town in the Highlands and Islands, and in some surprisingly small places, you'll find a branch of at least one of the big highstreet **banks**: Bank of Scotland, Royal Bank of Scotland, Clydesdale and TSB Scotland. However, on the smaller islands, and in remoter parts of the Highlands, you may find there is only a mobile bank that runs to a timetable, usually available from the local post office; remember that only one customer is allowed in a mobile bank at any one time. General opening hours for banks are Monday to Friday from between 9am and 9.30am to between 4pm and 5pm, though some branches are open until slightly later on Thursdays. Almost everywhere, banks are the best places in which to change money and cheques. Outside banking hours you'll have to use a **bureau de change**, found in most city centres and often at train stations or airports, but in much of the Highlands and Islands you'll have

to try the local **tourist office**, or **hotel**, where the rates are normally very poor.

If, as a foreign visitor, you run out of money or there is some kind of emergency, the quickest way to get money sent out is to have the cash **wired** to the nearest bank via Western Union (☎0800/833833) or Moneygram (☎0800/894887). Both charge on a sliding scale: for example, it will cost you around £15 to wire out £100, but only £80 to wire out £2500. You should get the money within twenty minutes. You can do the same thing through Thomas Cook or American Express if there's a branch nearby, but it usually takes a day or two. Your bank may also have reciprocal arrangements with a Scottish bank, but again the money transfer will take a day or so.

COSTS

Scotland is an expensive place to visit, although in general it is marginally less pricey than England. The minimum expenditure, if you're camping, cycling or hitching and preparing most of your own food, is in the region of £15 a day, rising to around £30 a day if you're using the hostelling network, some public transport and eating the odd meal out. Couples staying at budget B&Bs, eating at unpretentious restaurants and visiting a fair number of tourist attractions, are looking at £30 each per day minimum; if you're renting a car, staying in comfortable B&Bs or hotels and eating well, you should reckon on over £60 a day per person. Single travellers should budget on spending around sixty percent of what a couple would spend (single rooms cost more than half a double). Note that the price of petrol rises steadily but surely the further you venture into the Highlands and Islands, and can easily top 80p a litre.

TIPPING

There are no fixed rules for **tipping** in Scotland. If you think you've received good service, particularly in restaurants or cafés, you may want to leave a tip of ten to fifteen percent, but check first that service has not already been included. It is not normal, however, to leave tips in pubs, although bar staff are sometimes offered drinks, which they may accept in the form of money (the assumption is they'll spend this on a drink after closing time). Taxi drivers, on the other hand, will expect tips on long journeys – ten percent is the norm. The other occasion when you'll be expected to tip is in upmarket hotels, where many folk rely on being tipped to bump up their often dismal wages.

YOUTH AND STUDENT DISCOUNTS

Various official youth/student ID cards are widely available and most will soon pay for themselves in savings. Full-time students are eligible for the **International Student ID Card** (**ISIC**), which entitles the bearer to special fares on local transport, and discounts at museums, theatres and other attractions. For Americans, there's also a health benefit, providing up to US$3000 in emergency medical coverage and US$100 a day for sixty days in the hospital, plus a 24-hour hotline to call in the event of a medical, legal or financial emergency. The card, which costs $20 for Americans, CAN$30 for Canadians, A$15 for Australians and NZ$17 in New Zealand, is available from branches of Council Travel, STA and Travel CUTS (see p.5 and p.11 for addresses).

You only have to be 25 or younger to qualify for the **Go-25 Card**, which costs the same as the ISIC and carries the same benefits. It can be purchased through Council Travel in the US and around the world, Hostelling International in Canada (see "Accommodation", p.32) and STA in Australia and New Zealand.

INSURANCE AND HEALTH

Wherever you're travelling from, it's a good idea to have some kind of travel insurance, which covers you for loss of possessions and money, as well as the cost of all medical and dental treatment. If you're travelling to Scotland from elsewhere in Britain, you may well be covered by your domestic insurance policy.

The amount of cover you get varies according to the premium, but a standard policy should always cover the cost of cancellation and curtailment of flights, medical expenses, travel delay, accident, missed departures, lost baggage, lost passport, personal liability and legal expenses. Policies tend to weigh in at under £30 per month, though it's always worth shopping around to get the best price. Good companies to phone for quotes include Columbus Direct (☎0171/375 0011) or Endsleigh Insurance (☎0171/436 4451). Some companies refuse to cover travellers over 65, or stop at 69 or 74 years of age, and most that do charge hefty premiums. The best policies for **older travellers**, with no upper age limit, are offered by Age Concern (☎01883/346964).

Whatever your policy, if you have anything stolen, get a copy of the police report of the incident, as this is essential to substantiate your claim.

NORTH AMERICAN COVER

Before buying an insurance policy, check that you're not already covered. **Canadian provincial health plans** typically provide some overseas medical coverage, although they're unlikely to pick up the full tab in the event of a mishap. Holders of official **student/teacher/youth cards** (see above) are covered for accident coverage and hospital inpatient benefits, and the annual membership fee is far less than the cost of comparable insurance. **Students** may also find that their student health coverage extends during the vacations and for one term beyond the date of last enrolment. Bank and **credit cards** (particularly American Express) often provide certain levels of medical or other insurance, and travel insurance may also be included if you use a major

TRAVEL INSURANCE COMPANIES IN NORTH AMERICA

Access America ☎1-800/284-8300.
Carefree Travel Insurance ☎1-800/323-3149.
Council Travel ☎1/888-COUNCIL,
www.counciltravel.com
Desjardins Travel Insurance Canada only ☎1-800/463-7830.
International Student Insurance Service
(ISIS), available through STA Travel
☎1-800/777-0112, *www.sta-travel.com*.

Travel Assistance International
☎1-800/821-2828.
Travel Guard ☎1-800/826-1300,
www.noelgroup.com.
Travel Insurance Services ☎1-800/937-1387.
Worldwide Assistance ☎1-800/821-2828.

credit or charge card to pay for your trip. In addition, **homeowners' or renters'** insurance often covers theft or loss of documents, money and valuables while overseas.

If you do need to purchase a separate travel insurance **policy**, be aware that they can vary hugely: some are comprehensive, while others cover only certain risks (accidents, illnesses, delayed or lost luggage, cancelled flights and so on). In particular, ask whether the policy pays medical costs up front or reimburses you later, and whether it provides for medical evacuation to your home country. For policies that include lost or stolen luggage, check exactly what is and isn't covered, and make sure the per-article limit will cover your most valuable possessions. A specialist travel insurance company (see the box above) can give you advice about various policies and ensure that you get one suited to your needs.

The lowest **premiums** are usually available through student/youth travel agencies: for example, ISIS policies (for students of any age) for eight to fifteen days cost US$60 with medical coverage, and US$45 without; for a month you'll pay US$110 and US$85 respectively; and for two months the charge is US$165 with medical coverage, US$135 without. Non-students will pay a bit more: Travel Assistance International, for example, offers a fifteen-day policy including medical cover for US$75–95, and a thirty-day plan for US$105–130. If you're planning to do any "dangerous sports" (skiing and mountaineering for example), check whether these activities are covered, as some companies levy a surcharge.

Most North American travel policies apply only to items lost, stolen or damaged while in the custody of an identifiable, responsible third party such as a hotel porter, an airline or luggage consignment. Even in these cases you will have to

contact the local police within a certain time limit to have a complete report made out so that your insurer can process the claim.

AUSTRALIAN AND NEW ZEALAND COVER

Travel insurance policies in Australia and New Zealand tend to be put together by airlines and travel agent groups, and are all fairly similar in terms of coverage and price. A typical policy for the UK covering medical costs, lost baggage and personal liability will cost around A$140/NZ$150 for two weeks, A$190/NZ$210 for one month, and A$300/NZ$330 for two months.

The following companies offer some of the widest cover available and can be arranged direct or through most travel agents: Ready Plan, 141 Walker St, Dandenong, Melbourne (☎03/9791 5077 or 1300/555 017) and 10/63 Albert St, Auckland (☎09/300 5333); and Cover More, Level 9, 32 Walker St, North Sydney (☎02/9202 8000 or 1800/251 881), with branches also in Victoria, Queensland, and at 57 Simon St, Auckland (☎09/377 5958).

HEALTH

No vaccinations are required for entry into Britain. **EU** citizens are entitled to free medical treatment at National Health Service hospitals on production of an **E111** form. Australia, New Zealand and several non-EU European countries have reciprocal health-care arrangements with Britain. Citizens of other countries will be charged for all medical services except those administered by Accident and Emergency units at National Health Service hospitals. In other words, if you've just been hit by a car, you would not be charged if the injuries simply required stitching and setting in the emergency unit, but you would if admission to a hospital ward were necessary. Health insurance is therefore extremely advisable for all non-EU nationals.

Pharmacists can dispense only a limited range of drugs without a doctor's prescription. Most are open standard shop hours, though in large towns some may close as late as 10pm – local newspapers carry lists of late-opening pharmacies. In large towns, pharmacies stay open late on a rota basis; contact the local police for current details. **Doctors' surgeries** tend to be open from about 9am to noon and then for a couple of hours in the evening; outside surgery hours, you can turn up at the Casualty department of the local hospital for complaints that require immediate attention – unless it's an emergency; in which case, ring for an ambulance on ☎999.

EMERGENCIES

For the most part the Scottish police are approachable and helpful to visitors. If you're lost in a major town, asking a police officer is generally the quickest way to get help – alternatively, you could ask a traffic warden, a much-maligned species of law enforcer responsible for parking restrictions and other vehicle-related matters.

EMERGENCIES

For **police**, **fire brigade**, **ambulance**, **mountain rescue** or **coastguard**, dial ☎**999**.

Traditionally their uniform includes a flat cap with a yellow band, though a variety of different uniforms have been introduced during the 1990s. Police officers on street duty wear a peaked flat hat with a black-and-white-chequered band, and are generally armed with a truncheon (baton).

The Scottish Highlands and Islands have the lowest crime rate in the country – in fact, you could travel for days without ever seeing a police officer. Drink-driving, drug smuggling and poaching are probably the most common crimes. Most acts of petty vandalism tend to take place on a Friday or Saturday night after a heavy evening's drinking. Should you have anything stolen or be involved in some incident that requires reporting, go to the local police station; the ☎999 number should only be used in emergencies.

INFORMATION AND MAPS

If you want to do a bit of research before arriving in Scotland, you should contact the British Tourist Authority (BTA) in your country or write direct to the main office of the Scottish Tourist Board (STB), marking your letter "Information Department" – the addresses are given below – or email the STB (*info@stb.gov.uk*). The BTA and STB will send you a wealth of free literature, some of it just rose-tinted advertising copy, but much of it extremely useful – especially the maps, city guides and event calendars. If you want more hard facts on a particular area, approach the area tourist boards, which are listed opposite or visit one of the Web sites suggested below.

Tourist offices (sometimes called Tourist Information Centres) exist in virtually every major town in the Scottish Highlands and Islands, though not on some of the smaller, remoter islands, where you'll have to rely on locals for advice. Tourist office phone numbers and opening hours can be found in the relevant sections of the guide. Opening hours vary from month to month, with offices in many areas closing completely in the winter season. All centres offer information on accommodation (and can usually book rooms – see p.31), local public transport, attractions and restaurants, as well as selling books, local guides, maps and souvenirs. In many cases their services are free, though some offices make a small charge for an accommodation list or a town guide with an accompanying street plan.

MAPS

Many bookshops will have a selection of maps of Scotland and Britain in general, but see the box on p.24 for a list of travel specialists. Virtually every service station in Scotland stocks one or more of the big **road atlases**. The best of these are the large-format ones produced by the AA, RAC, Collins and Ordnance Survey, which cover all of Britain at around three miles to one inch, and include larger-scale plans of major towns. You could also invest in the excellent **fold-out maps** published by Michelin and Bartholomew; the latter includes clear town plans of the major cities. Another option is the official tourist map series published by Estate Publications; perfect if you're driving or cycling round one particular region since it marks all the major tourist sights as well as youth hostels and campsites. These are available from just about every tourist office in Scotland.

If you're after more detail, the most comprehensive **maps** of the Highlands and Islands are produced by the **Ordnance Survey** series – renowned for its accuracy and clarity. The 204 maps in their 1:50,000 (a little over a mile to an inch) Landranger series cover the whole of Britain and show enough detail to be useful for most walkers. There's more detail still in the 1:25,000 Pathfinder series, which also covers the whole of Britain, though it is currently being replaced by the new improved Explorer series, drawn to the same scale. The full Ordnance Survey range is only available at a few big-city stores, although in the Highlands and Islands you'll find the relevant maps for the local area in local shops or tourist offices.

HIGHLANDS AND ISLANDS ONLINE

TOURISM

www.aboutscotland.co.uk
Useful for accommodation, easy to use and linked to holiday activities.

www.holiday.scotland.net
The official Scottish Tourist Board site, with sections on transport, accommodation, sightseeing and outdoor activities.

SCOTTISH TOURIST BOARD OFFICES

Scotland 23 Ravelston Terrace, Edinburgh EH4 3EU (☎0131/332 2433).

England 19 Cockspur St, London SW1 5BL (☎0171/930 8661, 930 8662 or 930 8663).

BRITISH TOURIST AUTHORITY OFFICES ABROAD

Australia Level 16, Gateway, 1 Macquarie Place, Sydney, NSW 2000 (☎02/9377 4400).

Canada 5915 Airport Rd, Suite 120, Mississauga, Toronto, ON L4V 1T1 (☎905/405 1840 or 1-888-VISIT-UK).

Netherlands Aurora Gebouw (5e), Stadhouderskade 2, 1054 ES Amsterdam (☎020/607 0002).

New Zealand 17th Floor, Fay Richwhite Building, 151 Queen St, Auckland 1 (☎09/303 1446).

South Africa Lancaster Gate, Hyde Park Lane, Hyde Park 2196, Johannesburg (☎011/325 0342).

USA 7th Floor, 551 Fifth Ave, New York, NY 10176-0799 (☎ 212/986 2200 or 1-800-GO-2-BRITAIN); 10880 Wilshire Blvd, Suite 570, Los Angeles, CA 90024 (☎310/470 2782).

REGIONAL TOURIST BOARDS IN THE HIGHLANDS & ISLANDS

Aberdeen & Grampian Tourist Board, 27 Albyn Place, Aberdeen AB10 1YL (☎01224/632727).

Argyll, The Isles, Loch Lomond, Stirling & Trossachs Tourist Board, Old Town Jail, St John St, Stirling (☎01786/470945).

Ayrshire & Arran Tourist Board, Burns House, Burns Statue Square, Ayr KA7 1UT (☎01292/288688).

Highlands of Scotland Tourist Board, Peffery House, Strathpeffer IV14 9HA (☎01463/421160).

Orkney Tourist Board, 6 Broad St, Kirkwall, Orkney KW15 1NX (☎01856/872856).

Perthshire Tourist Board, Lower City Mills, West Mill St, Perth PH1 5QP (☎01738/627958).

Shetland Island Tourism, Market Cross, Lerwick, Shetland ZE1 0LU (☎01595/693434).

Western Isles Tourist Board, 4 South Beach, Stornoway, Isle of Lewis HS1 2XY (☎01851/703088).

www.nts.org.uk

Web site of the National Trust for Scotland, which is constantly updated; you can check current opening hours and events.

www.rampantscotland.co.uk

Well worth looking at its index of links to everything Scottish if you're searching for something specific.

www.scotland-info.co.uk

A big site covering the whole of the country, with a commercial bent – links to shops, hotels and so on – but good on information for individual areas.

www.travelscotland.co.uk

Run in association with the STB, this is a lively magazine-format site, with features and reviews.

THE ISLANDS

www.hebrides.com

Absorbing site on the islands off the west coast of Scotland, with masses of pages and links.

www.orknet.co.uk

Run by the Orkney tourist board and council, covering tourism, business, community and heritage. Lots of information and easy to use.

www.shetland-tourism.co.uk

Excellent Shetland tourist board site, covering almost everything you could possibly want to know – well linked and well illustrated.

SPORT

http://aviemore.org

Site run by local chamber of commerce with good information on skiing holidays and facilities, accommodation and outdoor sports, from trout fishing to four-wheel, off-road driving.

www.golfscotland.co.uk

A real must for golf fanatics: it lists all the courses and gives their details, organizes tours for the Open and is updated with the latest golfing news.

MAP OUTLETS

ENGLAND

Blackwell's Map and Travel Shop, 53 Broad St, Oxford OX1 3BQ (☎01865/792792, *bookshop.blackwell.co.uk*).

Heffers Map Shop, 3rd Floor, in Heffers Stationery Department, 19 Sidney St, Cambridge CB2 3HL (☎01223/568467, *www.heffers.co.uk*).

The Map Shop, 30a Belvoir St, Leicester LE1 6QH (☎0116/2471400).

Newcastle Map Centre, 55 Grey St, Newcastle upon Tyne NE1 6EF (☎0191/261 5622).

Stanfords, 12–14 Long Acre, London WC2E 9LP (☎0171/836 1321, *sales@stanfords.co.uk*). Other branches within Campus Travel at 52 Grosvenor Gardens, London SW1W 0AG (☎0171/730 1314); within the British Airways offices at 156 Regent St, London W1R 5TA (☎0171/434 4744); and at 29 Corn St, Bristol BS1 1HT (☎0117/929 9966).

IRELAND

Easons Bookshop, 40 O'Connell St, Dublin 1 (☎01/873 3811).

Fred Hanna's Bookshop, 27–29 Nassau St, Dublin 2 (☎01/677 1255).

Hodges Figgis Bookshop, 56–58 Dawson St, Dublin 2 (☎01/677 4754).

Waterstone's, Queens Building, 8 Royal Ave, Belfast BT1 1DA (☎01232/247 355); 7 Dawson St, Dublin 2 (☎01/679 1415); 69 Patrick St, Cork (☎021/276 522).

NORTH AMERICA

Adventurous Traveler Bookstore, PO Box 1468, Williston, VT 05495 (☎1-800/282-3963, *www.AdventurousTraveler.com*).

Book Passage, 51 Tamal Vista Blvd, Corte Madera, CA 94925 (☎415/927-0960).

The Complete Traveler Bookstore, 199 Madison Ave, New York, NY 10016 (☎212/685-9007); 3207 Fillmore St, San Francisco, CA 94123 (☎415/923-1511); 28 Church St, Cambridge, MA 02138 (☎617/497-6277); 500 Bolyston St, Boston, MA 02116.

Map Link, 30 S La Petera Lane, Unit #5, Santa Barbara, CA 93117 (☎805/692-6777).

The Map Store Inc, 1636 1st St, Washington, DC 20006 (☎202/628-2608).

Open Air Books and Maps, 25 Toronto St, Toronto, ON M5R 2C1 (☎416/363-0719).

Phileas Fogg's Books & Maps, #87 Stanford Shopping Center, Palo Alto, CA 94304 (☎1-800/533-FOGG).

Rand McNally, 444 N Michigan Ave, Chicago, IL 60611 (☎312/321-1751); 150 E 52nd St, New York, NY 10022 (☎212/758-7488); 595 Market St, San Francisco, CA 94105 (☎415/777-3131); call ☎1-800/234-0679 for other locations, or for maps by mail order.

Sierra Club Bookstore, 6014 College Ave, Oakland, CA 94618 (☎510/658-7470).

Travel Books & Language Center, 4931 Cordell Ave, Bethesda, MD 20814 (☎1-800/220-2665).

Traveler's Bookstore, 22 W 52nd St, New York, NY 10019 (☎212/664-0995).

Ulysses Travel Bookshop, 4176 St-Denis, Montréal (☎514/843-9447).

World Wide Books and Maps, 736 Granville St, Vancouver, BC V6Z 1E4 (☎604/687-3320).

AUSTRALIA AND NEW ZEALAND

Mapland, 372 Little Bourke St, Melbourne, VIC 3000 (☎03/9670 4383).

The Map Shop, 16a Peel St, Adelaide, SA 5000 (☎08/8231 2033).

Perth Map Centre, 891 Hay St, Perth, WA 6000 (☎08/9322 5733).

Speciality Maps, 58 Albert St, Auckland (☎09/307 2217).

Travel Bookshop, Shop 3, 175 Liverpool St, Sydney, NSW 2000 (☎02/9261 8200).

Worldwide Maps and Guides, 187 George St, Brisbane, Queensland (☎07/3221 4330).

THE ENVIRONMENT

www.geo.ed.ac.uk/home/scotland/scotland/html

Produced by the Geography Department of Edinburgh University – an introduction to all things Scottish, history, geography and politics. Excellent background information with a myriad of links.

www.scotlandthegreen.co.uk

Green travel, accommodation and shopping; as yet it's not very comprehensive, but it's getting there.

MUSIC

www.ceolas.org

A very informative Celtic music site, both historical and contemporary, with lots of music to listen to.

GETTING AROUND

There's no getting away from the fact that getting around the Highlands and Islands is a time-consuming business: off the main routes, public transport services are few and far between, particularly in more remote parts of Argyll, and the Highlands and Islands. With careful planning, however, practically everywhere is accessible and you'll have no trouble getting to the main tourist destinations. In most parts of Scotland, especially if you take the scenic backroads, the low level of traffic makes driving wonderfully unstressful.

BY TRAIN

There are no proper **railways** in the Scottish islands, and the railway network in the Highlands is minimal, with only three lines reaching the west coast, at Oban, Mallaig and Kyle of Lochalsh. Fort William and Inverness are both served by train, but they are no longer connected

with each other, and there's just one line north of Inverness. That said, travelling by rail in the Highlands is an experience not to be missed, with some lines rated among the great scenic routes of the world. For a rundown of the different fares available in getting to Scotland by train, see p.12.

ScotRail runs all train services in the Highlands, and you can buy **tickets** at most large stations, from major travel agents, or over the phone with a credit card. **Seat reservations** to Inverness are included in the price of the ticket if you book in advance. The ticket offices at many rural and commuter stations are closed in the evenings and at weekends; in these instances there's sometimes a **ticket machine** on the platform. If the machine isn't working, or there simply isn't one, you can buy your ticket on board. However, if you've embarked at a station that does have a ticket office open or a machine, and you haven't bought a ticket, there's a spot fine of £10.

In addition to the British Rail passes outlined on p.13, ScotRail offers a couple of **travel passes** worth considering. The most flexible is the **Freedom of Scotland Travelpass**, which gives unlimited train travel within Scotland. It's also valid on all CalMac ferry links on the west coast (see ferry information on p.29), as well as on various buses in the remoter regions where the railway network is nonexistent. You also get up to a third off P&O ferries to Orkney and Shetland. The pass currently costs £69/A$205/NZ$246 for four out of eight days' travel, £99/A$295/NZ$354 for eight days out of fifteen, or £119/A$354/NZ$424 for twelve days out of fifteen, and comes complete with timetables, a map and a card giving

RAIL CONTACTS

BRITAIN

National Rail Enquiries ☎0345/484950, *www.railtrack.co.uk*. Gives details of timetables, fares and other information on rail travel within Scotland.

ScotRail ☎08457/550033, *www.scotrail.co.uk*. For booking tickets and seats on all trains within Scotland, and sleeper trains to Scotland.

NORTH AMERICA

BritRail Travel International
☎1-888/274-8724 or 212/575-2667, *www.britrail.com/us*
CIT Eurail ☎1-800/223-7987
DER Travel Services ☎1-800/421-2929

McFarland Ltd ☎1-800/437-2687, *www.reveretvl.com*
Online Travel ☎1-800/660-5300, *www.online@eurorail.com*
Rail Europe USA, ☎1-800/438-7245; Canada, ☎1-800/361-7245; *www.raileurope.com*

AUSTRALIA AND NEW ZEALAND

Rail Plus (Australia) ☎1300/555 003.

Rail Plus (New Zealand) ☎09/303 2484.

discounts at tourist attractions, shops and restaurants throughout Scotland.

The **Highland Rover** allows unlimited travel on trains within the Highland region, plus the West Highland Line (Glasgow–Oban), and travel between Aberdeen and Aviemore. It also allows free travel on buses between Oban, Fort William and Inverness. However, it does not cover travel from Glasgow to Inverness or Aberdeen, so you have to be canny about your route planning. The Highland Rover currently costs £49 and is valid for four out of eight consecutive days. The Freedom of Scotland and the Highland Rover passes are both available from ScotRail telesales (see box above).

If you plan to do a lot of travelling around the UK, your best bet is to buy one of the range of passes which allow unlimited travel in Scotland, England and Wales. The only one of these passes that can be bought in the UK is the **All-Line Rail Rover**, which costs £275 for seven consecutive days' travel, or £450 for fourteen days. All other BritRail passes are only available for purchase before you leave your home country, through local travel agents or the specialist companies listed below. The **BritRail Consecutive Pass** allows unlimited standard-class travel for four consecutive days from around US$190/A$268/NZ$321; eight days costs US$265/A$383/NZ$459; fifteen days costs US$400/A$574/NZ$688; 22 days costs US$505/ A$727/NZ$872; and one month comes to US$600/A$861/NZ$1033. Under-26s pay US$150/

A$215/NZ$258 for four days; US$215/A$307/ NZ$368 for eight days; US$280/A$402/NZ$482 for fifteen days; US$355/A$509/NZ$610 for 22 days; or US$420/ A$603/NZ$723 for one month. Seniors (over 60s and only available for first-class travel) pay US$240/A$342/NZ$410 for four days, US$340/A$488/NZ$585 for eight days, US$510/ A$732/NZ$878 for fifteen days, US$645/A$927/ NZ$1112 for 22 days, or US$765/A$1098/ NZ$1317 for one month.

Better value if you're not travelling every day is the **BritRail Flexipass**, which allows four days of travel within a two-month period for US$235/A$336/NZ$403; eight days out of two months for US$340/A$487/NZ$584; or fifteen days out of two months for US$515/A$739/ NZ$886. Under-26s pay US$185/A$269/NZ$323 for four days out of two months, US$240/A$341/ NZ$409 for eight days in two months, or US$360/ A$517/NZ$620 for fifteen days out of two months. For seniors (over 60s and only available for first-class travel), the prices are US$300/ A$428/NZ$513 for four days out of two months; US$435/ A$621/NZ$745 for eight days in two months; and US$655/A$942/NZ$1130 for fifteen days in a two-month period.

A great bargain for **travellers with children** allows one free child pass for each paying adult, and, if four adults are travelling together on a BritRail Pass, two of the four can purchase the pass for half-price. BritRail Pass holders can also get special rates on the London to Paris Eurostar, and the passes are valid on Airport Links services plus the Heathrow Express service.

BY BUS

Travelling around Scotland by **bus** may take a little longer than using the train, but works out considerably cheaper. There's a plethora of regional companies, but by far the biggest national operator is **Scottish Citylink** (☎0990/505050), a subsidiary company of National Express. With train travel being so expensive, bus services have become very popular, so for busy routes and at weekends and holidays it's a good idea to buy a "reserved-journey ticket", which guarantees you a seat.

If you're under 26, a full-time student, or 50 and over, it's worth buying a **Smart Card**, which costs £5 for a year, £12 for three, giving you thirty percent on all adult fares. Children normally pay half-fare, but with a **Parent & Child Saver Card** (£5 a year) one child can travel free; the **Family Saver Card** (£10 a year) allows two children to travel free with two adults.

If you plan to do a lot of travelling by bus, it may be worth buying a **Explorer Pass**, which offers unlimited travel on the Scottish Citylink network: it costs £30 for three consecutive days; £60 for any five days within ten; £90 for any eight within sixteen; and £120 for any fifteen within thirty. Smart Card holders can get a third off the above prices. However, If you're travelling a lot in England and Wales, too, you might be better off with a National Express Tourist Trail Pass, details of which appear on p.14.

The SYHA also sells its own **Explore Scotland** bus pass, which allows free travel on Citylink buses. You also get a Historic Scotland Scottish Explorer Pass (see p.40), free SYHA membership and several nights of free hostel accommodation. The pass costs £165 for five out of ten days' travel, with seven nights' accommodation, or £280 for eight days' travel out of sixteen, with fourteen nights' accommodation.

Local bus services are run by a bewildering array of companies, but the local tourist office should be able provide you with up-to-date timetables and telephone numbers. As a general rule, the further away from urban areas you get, the less frequent and more expensive bus services become – in most places, you'll find little or no transport running on a Sunday. However, even on the smallest islands, where there is no scheduled bus service, there's usually someone on the island who operates a minibus that will at least take you to and from the ferry terminal to your final destination.

Some parts of the Highlands and Islands are only served by the **postbus** network, which operates minibuses (and a few cars) carrying mail and three to ten fare-paying passengers. They often set off early in the morning from the main post office and collect mail (or deliver it) from/to the nether regions. It's a sociable, though excruciatingly slow, way to travel, and may well be the only means of reaching hidden-away B&Bs and the like. You can get a booklet of routes and timetables from the Royal Mail Communications (☎0131/228 7407), or the Scottish Tourist Board (see p.23).

BUS TOURS

If you're backpacking, a cheap, flexible and fun way of travelling around the Highlands and Islands is on one of the popular "**jump-on-jump-off**" **minibus** services that operate out of Edinburgh. The leading operator at the moment is Haggis Backpackers, whose minibus calls at Pitlochry, Inverness, Loch Ness, Ullapool, Kyleakin and Isle of Skye, Fort William, Oban, Loch Lomond and Glasgow before returning to Edinburgh. It runs every day except Sunday, throughout the year, stopping at independent hostels along the route – which saves you the hassle of lugging your bags around – and you can spend as long as you like at each place. The Flexitour pass for one complete circuit costs £85: for further details, contact Haggis Backpackers, at 11 Blackfriars St, Edinburgh EH1 1NB (☎0131/557 9393, *www.haggis-backpackers.com*).

Haggis also run backpackers' **minibus tours** of Scotland. Prices start at £75 for a three-day round-trip from Edinburgh, taking in Loch Ness, Skye, Glen Coe and other Highland highlights, while a six-day guided tour, combining most of Scotland's main tourist destinations, costs £139; these fares do not include food and accommodation, but the tour companies can help with hostel booking. Several other companies run similar guided tours, including the popular Rabbie's Trail Burners tours, which also start in Edinburgh (207 High St, ☎0131/226 3133, *www.rabbies.com*), and offer a range of tours led by knowledgeable driver-guides. If you're pushed for time and want to do a whistlestop tour of England and Wales en route to Scotland, another option worth considering is the

Haggis Backpackers London to Edinburgh trip, outlined in "Getting there from Britain, Ireland & Europe" on p.14.

BY CAR

If you want to cover a lot of the country in a short time, or just want more flexibility, you'll need your own transport. In order to **drive** in Scotland you must have a current driving licence; foreign nationals will need to supplement this with an international driving permit, available from state and national motoring organizations for a small fee. If you're bringing your own car into the country, you should also carry your vehicle registration or ownership document at all times. Furthermore, you must be adequately insured, so check your existing policy.

DRIVING ORGANIZATIONS

American Automobile Association (**AAA**; *www.aaa.com*). Each state has its own club – check the phone book for local addresses and phone numbers. The AAA can refer members to overseas auto associations, and can provide international drivers' licences and *carnets de passage* (for those planning to transport cars across certain international boundaries).

Australian Automobile Association, 212 Northbourne Ave, Canberra ACT 2601 (☎02/6247 7311).

Automobile Association, PO Box 126, Basingstoke, RG21 4BA (☎0990/448866, *www.theaa.co.uk*).

Canadian Automobile Association (**CAA**). Each region has its own club – check the phone book for local addresses and phone numbers. Benefits are comparable to the AAA's (see above), and membership rates vary.

New Zealand Automobile Association, PO Box 5, Auckland (☎09/377 4660).

Royal Automobile Club (**RAC**), RAC House, PO Box 700, Bristol BS99 1RB (☎0800/550550, *www.rac.co.uk*).

CAR RENTAL FIRMS

BRITAIN

Avis ☎0990/900500.
Budget ☎0800/181181.
Europcar ☎0345/222525.
Hertz ☎0990/996699.

Holiday Autos ☎0990/300400.
National Car Rental ☎0990/365365.
Thrifty ☎0990/168238.

AUSTRALIA

Avis ☎1800/225533.

Budget ☎1300/362848.

Hertz ☎1800/550067.

NEW ZEALAND

Avis ☎09/526 2847.

Budget ☎09/375 2222.

Hertz ☎09/367 6350.

NORTH AMERICA

Alamo ☎1-800/522-9696, *www.goalamo.com*
Auto Europe ☎1-800/223-5555, *www.wrld.com/ae*
Avis ☎1-800/331-1084, *www.avis.com*
Budget ☎1-800/527-0700, *www.budgetrentacar.com*
Dollar ☎1-800/421-6868, *www.dollarcar.com*
Enterprise Rent-a-Car ☎1-800/325-8007, *www.pickenterprise.com*

Europe by Car ☎1-800/223-1516, *www.europebycar.com*
Hertz ☎1-800/654-3001; in Canada ☎1-800/263-0600; *www.hertz.com*
Holiday Autos ☎1-800/422-7737, *www.holiday/colauto.com*
National ☎1-800/CAR-RENT, *www.nationalcar.com*
Thrifty ☎1-800/367-2277, *www.thrifty.com*
US Rent-a-Car ☎1-800/777-9377.
Value ☎1-800/468-2583.

In Scotland, as in England, you drive on the left, which can lead to a few tense days of acclimatization for many overseas drivers. **Speed limits** are 30 or 40mph (50 or 65kph) in built-up areas, 70mph (110kph) on motorways and dual carriageways, and 60mph (100kph) on most other roads. As a rule, assume that in any area with street lighting the speed limit is 30mph (50kph), unless otherwise stated. In the Highlands and Islands, there are still plenty of **single-track roads** with passing places, indicated either by a white diamond- or square-shaped signpost or by a black-and-white striped pole. Not only should you stop in a passing place on your left, in order to allow approaching traffic to pass, but you should also do so to enable cars behind to overtake. In much of the region, the roads are littered with sheep, which are entirely oblivious to cars, so slow down and edge your way past – should you kill one, it is your duty to inform the local farmer.

The three major motoring organizations, the Automobile Association (AA), the Royal Automobile Club (RAC) and Green Flag Emergency Assistance, all operate 24-hour emergency **breakdown** services. The AA and RAC also provide many other motoring services, including a reciprocal arrangement for free assistance through many overseas motoring organizations – check the situation with yours before setting out. On motorways, the AA and RAC can be called from roadside booths. Elsewhere, ring ☎0800/887766 for the AA; ☎0800/828282 for the RAC; and ☎0800/400600 for Green Flag. You can ring these emergency numbers even if you are not a member of the respective organization, although a substantial fee will be charged. In theory, you should be attended to within an hour; however, in the Highlands and Islands, you may have a long wait for assistance. When assistance does arrive, it may well be a local garage affiliated to one of the above organizations, and not someone in an offical AA or RAC van.

It may also be worth investing in a policy with **home relay**, as spare parts can be hard to get hold of in the Highlands and Islands, and most standard policies will only get you to the nearest garage, where you can find yourself stranded for days until the part you need is sent from Inverness or Glasgow. Bear in mind, too, that the remoter regions of the Highlands and Islands have comparatively few garages and petrol stations – there are even a few islands with no public petrol station or garage.

On the whole, it's inadvisable for anyone travelling alone to **hitch** in Scotland. However, in the Highlands and Islands, there's a long-established tradition of giving lifts, though you may have to wait a long time before you're picked up, simply because of the low volume of traffic.

CAR RENTAL

Car rental in Scotland is expensive, and, especially if you're travelling from North America, you'll probably find it cheaper to arrange things in advance through one of the multinational chains. If you do rent a car, the least you can expect to pay is around £135 a week – the rate for a small hatchback from Holiday Autos, one of the most competitive rental agencies. The multinationals charge around £40 per day, and you may well find that you can save a considerable sum by using a local firm, particularly over the course of a week.

Most companies prefer you to pay with a credit card; otherwise you may have to leave a deposit of over £100. There are very few automatics at the lower end of the price scale – if you want one, you should book well ahead. To rent a car you need to show your driving licence; few companies will rent to drivers with less than a year's experience and most will only rent to people between 21 and 70 years of age.

Motorbike rental is ludicrously expensive, at around £50 a day/£220 a week for a 500cc machine, and around £90/£325 for a one-litre tourer, including insurance, helmets and luggage.

BY FERRY

Scotland has 61 inhabited islands, according to the last census, and 49 of them have scheduled ferries. Ferries, therefore, play an immensely important part in travelling around the islands. Most ferries carry cars and vans, and the vast majority can be booked in advance. In fact, if you're taking a vehicle on a ferry, you should book ahead as far in advance as possible, whatever the time of year, as places can get filled up months in advance.

Caledonian MacBrayne (abbreviated by most people, and throughout this book, to **CalMac**) has a virtual monopoly on services on the River Clyde and those to the Inner and Outer Hebrides, sailing to 21 islands altogether. They aren't cheap, but they do have two types of reduced-fare pass. The **Island Hopscotch** offers a range of economy fares for cars and passengers on a number of preset routes and is valid for one

---

CAR FERRY COMPANIES IN SCOTLAND

Caledonian MacBrayne, The Ferry Terminal, Gourock PA19 1QP (☎0990/650000, *reservations@calmac.co.uk*).

Orkney Ferries, Shore St, Kirkwall KW15 1LG (☎01856/872044).

P&O Scottish Ferries, PO Box 5, Jamieson's Quay, Aberdeen AB11 5NP (☎01224/572615, *passenger@poscottishferries.co.uk*).

Western Ferries, Hunter's Quay, Dunoon, Argyll PA23 8HG (☎01369/704452).

---

month from the date of the first journey. It's the best option for anyone planning to make several short ferry trips between islands, though you do have to follow a set itinerary. Much more flexible is the **Island Rover**, which entitles you to eight or fifteen consecutive days' unlimited ferry travel. It does not, however, guarantee you a place on any ferry, so you still need to book ahead if you're taking a car. The eight-day pass costs £41 for passengers and £199 for cars, while the fifteen-day pass costs £59 and £299 respectively. CalMac schedules are highly complicated, but you can get details from the address given in the box above.

P&O Scottish Ferries run car ferries to Orkney and Shetland. For Orkney, you can depart either from Aberdeen (1–2 weekly; 8–10hr) or from Scrabster, near Thurso (1–3 daily; 2hr). Fares from Aberdeen are roughly £80 return for a foot passenger, plus £140 for a car; from Scrabster, passengers pay £30 return, plus £80 for a car. There's also a summer-only passenger ferry from John O'Groats to Orkney (May–Sept 2–4 daily; 45min), run by **John O'Groats Ferries** (see p.346). P&O run an overnight ferry from Aberdeen to Shetland (14–20hr), which runs daily except Saturday night in summer. Fares work out around

£115 return for a foot passenger, plus £175 return for a small car. On all routes you should book in advance if you are taking a vehicle.

The various Orkney islands are linked to each other by services run by **Orkney Ferries**; Shetland's inter-island ferries are run in conjunction with the local council, so contacting the local tourist board (see p.23) is your best bet. There are also numerous small operators round the Scottish coast, some of whom run additional passenger-only services to the smaller islands, and run day-excursion trips; their phone numbers are listed in the relevant chapters of this guide.

It's possible to book ferry tickets in advance in **North America**, if you're organized enough to know exactly when you'll be making the crossing. For sailings to/from France, Belgium or the Netherlands, contact BritRail Travel International (☎1-888/274-8724) or Scots American (☎1-201/768-1187); to/from Scandinavia, contact Bergen Line (☎1-800/323-7436) or Scandinavian Seaways (☎1-800/533-3755). In **Australia** and **New Zealand**, you can book ferry tickets in advance at branches of Thomas Cook (see p.9).

BY PLANE

Apart from the three major Scottish airports of Glasgow, Edinburgh and Aberdeen, there are numerous minor airports in the Highlands and Islands, some little more than gravel airstrips or even airfields. If you're thinking of travelling on an internal flight, make sure you book as far in advance as possible, as seats are limited, with as few as eight available on inter-island flights within Orkney and Shetland. Be prepared, too, for your flight to be delayed or even cancelled, as weather conditions can prevent planes taking off at any time of the year.

Internal flights are pretty expensive on the whole: a single fare from Glasgow to Islay will set

---

AIRPORTS SERVING THE HIGHLANDS AND ISLANDS

Aberdeen	☎01224/722331	**Kirkwall**	☎01856/872421
Barra	☎01871/890283	**Stornoway**	☎01851/702256
Benbecula	☎01870/602310	**Sumburgh**	☎01950/460654
Campbeltown	☎01586/552571	**Tingwall**	☎01595/840246
Edinburgh	☎0131/333 1000	**Tiree**	☎01879/220456
Glasgow	☎0141/887 1111	**Unst**	☎01957/711620
Inverness	☎01463/232471	**Wick**	☎01955/602215
Islay	☎01496/302361		

you back around £75, and there are very few discounted tickets available. However, if you are short on time, the extra expense may well be worth it. Most flights are operated by British Airways, British Regional Airlines or Loganair, though the majority of flights can be booked directly through British Airways (☎0345/222111). For inter-island flights in Shetland (excluding Fair Isle), you need to book direct through Loganair (☎01595/840246).

The main airports serving the Highlands and Islands are listed below; call them, or British Airways, for timetable information, or pick up a BA schedule from a travel agent. BA should also be able to fill you in on any cost-cutting special tickets available. The **Highland Rover**, for example, costs just £169, and allows you to take any five flights within seven days (flights to and between Orkney and Shetland are covered, but not services within either of those two archipelagos).

ACCOMMODATION

In common with the rest of Britain, accommodation in the Scottish Highlands and Islands is expensive. Budget travellers are well catered for with numerous hostels, and those with money to spend will relish the more upmarket hotels, many of which are converted feudal seats. Just about every tourist office can help you find the right sort of accommodation to suit, whatever your budget. This can be easily arranged on arrival, but you'll find a much greater choice if you book in advance; tourist offices usually make a small fee for booking rooms. In some areas you will pay a deposit that's deducted from your first night's bill (usually ten percent), while in others the office will take a percentage or flat-rate commission – on average, around £3. Another useful service operated by the majority of tourist offices is the "Book-a-Bed-Ahead" service,

which reserves accommodation for you in your next port of call, and costs £3 per booking.

HOTELS AND B&BS

The STB operates a nationwide system for grading **hotels**, **guest houses** and **B&Bs**, which is updated annually. Although the STB cover a huge number of places, by no means everyone participates, and you shouldn't assume that a particular B&B is no good simply because it's not on the STB books. Within the STB system, the most important element is the new **star awards**, from one to five. These aim to reflect the quality of welcome, service and hospitality, and not simply the level of facilities – these can be assesed from the categorization of the establishment as a hotel, guesthouse, B&B and so on, in addition to the star rating. The AA and the RAC have their own star system, independent of, and slightly more subjective than, the STB.

Hotels come in all shapes and sizes, and, at the lower end of the scale, merge almost imperceptibly into B&Bs and guest houses. The latter range from private houses with a couple of bedrooms set aside for paying guests and a dining room for the consumption of a rudimentary breakfast, to rooms as well furnished as those in hotels costing twice as much, with delicious home-prepared breakfasts, and an informal hospitality that a larger place couldn't match.

There's no hard-and-fast correlation between standards and price. However, at the bottom end of the **price scale** (though not necessarily the quality scale) you'll probably pay around £30 per

ACCOMMODATION PRICE CODES

Throughout this book, accommodation **prices** have been graded with the numbers below, according to the cost of the least expensive double room in high season. Although costs will rise slightly overall within the life of this edition, the relative comparisons should remain valid. The bulk of the recommendations will fall in categories ② to ⑤; those in the highest categories are limited to places that are especially attractive. Bear in mind that many of the chain hotels slash their tariffs at the weekend, and that many of the cheaper places will also have more expensive rooms. Note that, in our accommodation listings, price codes are not given for youth hostels – all youth hostel accommodation costs under £10 per person per night, except in the odd rare case, where we have quoted the price in the review.

① under £40	④ £60–70	⑦ £110–150
② £40–50	⑤ £70–90	⑧ £150–200
③ £50–60	⑥ £90–110	⑨ over £200

night for a double room at a B&B, rising to around £60 in a comfortable guest house, and from £90 and upwards in an established, award-winning hotel. For a full explanation of the price codes used in this book, see the box above.

Many B&Bs, even the pricier ones, have only a few rooms, so **advance booking** is recommended. This is especially true in the islands, where the number of options is limited. You might also want to book in for dinner, bed and breakfast (not to mention packed lunch), as many islands have limited, or no, eating and drinking options, and some don't even have a shop. Another important point to remember is that, outside of the main towns and cities, many places are only open for the summer season, roughly from Easter to October. You'll always find somewhere to stay outside this period, but the choice may be pretty limited.

HOSTELS

The network of the **Scottish Youth Hostels Association** (**SYHA**) consists of some eighty properties, usually offering bunk-bed accommodation in single-sex dormitories or smaller rooms. Most youth hostels have moved away from the ethic of former days, when you had to perform chores before leaving. However, the more rural hostels retain some of the old ways – you're certainly expected to leave the place looking spick and span, and an 11.30pm curfew is still the norm.

All the hostels referred to as "youth hostels" in the guide are official SYHA properties unless stated otherwise. For Scottish residents, adult membership costs £6, and can be obtained either via the **SYHA National Office** (see box oppo-

site), or at the first SYHA hostel you book into. SYHA membership gives you automatic membership to **Hostelling International** (**HI**), as does membership of any of the seventy HI-affiliated hostelling associations around the world. Don't worry if you arrive in Scotland without HI membership, as you can join up at virtually any SYHA hostel. HI membership costs £9, though you can pay in £1.50 instalments, spread out over the first six nights – that way it makes no odds if you only end up staying in a couple of nights in hostels. It's also worth noting that youth hostel members are entitled to half-price entry to all National Trust for Scotland properties (see p.39).

Hostels in the Highlands and Islands are generally cheaper than those in the rest of Britain: the majority charge between £6.50 and £10 a night. The cost of hostel **meals**, where available, is low: breakfast is around £2.50, and evening meals start at £5. Nearly all hostels have kitchen facilities, for those who prefer self-catering. If you need to check any tariffs in advance, phone the hostel, or consult the current *SYHA Handbook*, which comes free when you pay your membership subscription.

At any time of the year, **advance booking** is a good idea, particularly at Easter, Christmas and from May to August. You can book by post, telephone or, sometimes, fax, and your bed will be held until 6pm on the day of arrival. If you have a credit card, you can also use HI's **International Booking Network** (**IBN**) to book beds as far as six months in advance – there is a small booking fee for this service which varies from country to country. Even if you haven't booked, always phone ahead – phone numbers are given in the guide. Not all hostels are open all year round, and many close during the day, so it's worth getting hold of

YOUTH HOSTEL ASSOCIATIONS

Australia Australian Youth Hostels Association, 422 Kent St, Sydney (☎02/9261 1111).

Canada Hostelling International Canada, Room 400, 205 Catherine St, Ottawa, ON K2P 1C3 (☎1-800/663-5777 or 613/237-7884). Annual membership adults $26.75, free for under-18s when accompanied by parents; two-year memberships cost $35.

England and Wales Youth Hostel Association (YHA), Trevelyan House, 8 St Stephen's Hill, St Albans AL1 2DY (☎01727/855215, www.yha/england/wales.org.uk).

Ireland An Óige, 61 Mountjoy St, Dublin 7 (☎01/830 4555, www.irelandyha.org).

New Zealand Youth Hostels Association of New Zealand, PO Box 436, Christchurch 1 (☎03/379 9970).

Northern Ireland Youth Hostel Association of Northern Ireland, 22 Donegal Rd, Belfast BT12 5JN (☎01232/324733).

Scotland Scottish Youth Hostel Association (SYHA), 7 Glebe Crescent, Stirling FK8 2JA (☎01786/891400, central reservations ☎0541/553255, www.syha.org.uk).

USA Hostelling International-American Youth Hostels (HI-AYH), 733 15th St NW, Suite 840, PO Box 37613, Washington, DC 20005 (☎202/783-6161, www.hostel.com). Annual membership adults US$25, youths (under 18) US$10, seniors (55 or over) US$15, families $35.

a copy of the current *SYHA Handbook* in order to check the details.

Allied to the SYHA is the **Gatliff Hebridean Hostels Trust** (**GHHT**), a charitable organization that rents out very simple croft accommodation in the Western Isles. Accommodation is very basic, almost primitive, and most of these hostels have no phone (and therefore no advance booking system) but the settings are invariably spectacular, and you can also camp by them. In Shetland, camping böds, operated by the **Shetland Amenity Trust**, offer similarly simple accommodation: you need all your usual camping equipment, except, of course, a tent. For more details about Gatliff hostels and camping böds, see the relevant chapters in the guide.

In addition, there are numerous independent hostels, bunkhouses and bothies, which vary enormously in the quality and range of facilities they offer. However, these are usually laid-back places with no membership, fewer rules and no curfew. Some belong to **Highland Hostels** (*info@highland-hostels.co.uk*), which has a variety of bunkhouses and bothies in the Highlands; others belong to **Independent Backpackers Hostels Scotland** (**IBHS**), an association of independent hostels in the Highlands and Islands. Housed in buildings ranging from croft houses to converted churches, they all have dormitories, hot showers, common rooms and self-catering kitchens, while many organize a range of outdoor activities. Prices hover at around £10 per person per night. Detailed reviews of most independent hostels in Scotland are featured in the relevant sections of this book,

and in more detail in the excellent *Independent Hostels Guide* by Sam Dalley, which is updated annually and published by Backpacker Press (for details, contact the distributors, Cordee Books and Maps, 3a De Montfort St, Leicester LE1 7HD; ☎0116/254 3579).

CAMPING AND SELF-CATERING

There are a fair few **campsites** in the Highlands and Islands, most of which are open from April to October. The most expensive sites, which charge about £10 to pitch a tent, are usually well equipped, with shops, a restaurant, a bar and, occasionally, sports facilities. At the other end of the scale, farmers sometimes offer pitches on their land for as little as £2.50 per night. The AA lists and grades campsites in its publication *Camping and Caravanning in Britain and Ireland*, and the area tourist boards can all supply lists of their recommended sites.

In the Highlands and Islands, tents often have to share space with **caravans** at official campsites. The great majority of these are permanently moored nose-to-tail in the vicinity of some of Scotland's finest scenery; others are positioned singly in back gardens or amidst farmland. Some can be booked as self-catering caravans, either by the week, or for shorter periods. With prices hovering around £100 a week, this can work out as one of the cheapest options if you're travelling with kids in tow.

In many parts of the Highlands and Islands, it's also possible to do **rough camping**, though

SELF-CATERING ACCOMMODATION

Finlayson Hughes, 45 Church St, Inverness IV1 1DR (☎01463/224343). Fifty or so properties mainly in the Highlands and Islands, everything from castles to bothies, from around £200 a week upwards.

Forest Holidays, Forestry Commission, 231 Corstorphine Rd, Edinburgh EH12 7AT (☎0131/334 0303). Only two sites, at Loch Awe, and Strathyre near Callander: purpose-built cabins in beautiful woodland areas, sleeping five or six people. Prices start from around £150 for three nights in June, though during school holidays you must book the cabins for at least a week.

Highland Hideways, 5/7 Stafford St, Oban, Argyll PA34 5NJ (☎01631/526056). A range of self-catering properties, mainly on the Highlands and Islands, which range from a former bank in Oban to a converted boathouse on Loch Awe. Free colour brochure.

Landmark Trust, Shottesbrook, Maidenhead SL6 3SW (☎01628 825925). The Landmark Trust has fifteen upmarket historical properties in Scotland. Their brochure costs £9.50, which is redeemable when you book a holiday.

National Trust for Scotland, 5 Charlotte Square, Edinburgh EH2 4DU (☎0131/226 5922). The NTS owns 34 converted historic cottages and houses around Scotland, with prices starting at around £250 week in high season.

you should always ask permission from the local landowner, crofter or farmer before pitching your tent. On some of the remoter islands, there are toilets and shower blocks by beaches, or in the main town. Wherever you decide to camp, it's worth bearing in mind the spectre that haunts all camping in Scotland – the midge (see p.44).

For **North Americans** planning to do a lot of camping, an international camping carnet is a sound investment, available from home motoring organizations, or from Family Campers and RVers (FCRV), 4804 Transit Rd, Building 2, Depew, NY 14043 (☎1-800/245-9755). The carnet is good for discounts at member sites and serves as useful identification. FCRV annual membership costs US$25, and the carnet is an additional US$10.

You may prefer more robust **self-catering** accommodation, and there are thousands of STB-approved properties for rent by the week, ranging from city penthouses to secluded cottages. The least you can expect to pay for four-berth self-catering accommodation in summer is around £150 per week, but for something special – such as a well-sited coastal cottage – you should budget for more than twice that amount. In the guide we give summer rates for self-catering accommodation, but note that rates can be as little as half that amount out of season. A good source of accommodation is the STB's self-catering guide. Updated annually, this full-colour brochure lists over 1200 properties, ranging from cottages and chalets to luxurious apartments, with colour photographs of most places included. Copies can be bought or ordered through any Scottish tourist office (see p.23).

FOOD AND DRINK

The quality of Scottish food has improved by leaps and bounds in recent years. Scottish produce – particularly the country's meat, fish, seafood and game – is of outstanding quality and has to some extent been rediscovered of late. Bear in mind, too, that even in the Highlands and Islands the larger towns usually have at least a couple of ethnic restaurants. If you fancy trying your hand at some traditional cooking, we've included a few recipes on p.463.

In many hotels and B&Bs you'll be offered a **Scottish breakfast**, similar to its English counterpart of sausage, bacon and egg, but with the addition of black pudding (blood and gristle) and potato scones. Porridge is another likely option – properly made, with genuine oatmeal and traditionally cooked with salt and eaten without sugar, though the latter is always on offer. You may also be served kippers (smoked herring) or Arbroath smokies (smoked haddock), or a large piece of haddock eaten with a poached egg on top. Oatcakes (plain, slightly salty biscuits) and a "buttery" – a butter-enriched bread related to the French croissant – might feature. Scotland's staple drink, like England's, is **tea**, drunk strong and with milk, though **coffee** is just as readily available everywhere.

The quintessential Scots dish is **haggis**, a sheep's stomach bag stuffed with spiced liver, offal, oatmeal and onion, and traditionally eaten with bashed neeps (mashed turnips) and chappit tatties (mashed potatoes). The humble haggis has become rather trendy in recent years, and you can, in the big cities, get a vegetarian version. Other staples include steak and kidney pie and shepherd's pie (minced beef covered with mashed potato and baked), as well as **stovies**, a tasty mash of onion and fried potato heated up with minced beef. In this cold climate, home-made soup is often welcome; try **Scots broth**, made with combinations of lentil, split pea, mutton stock or vegetables and barley.

Scots **beef** is delicious, especially the Aberdeen Angus breed; menus will specify if your steak falls into that fine category. **Venison**, the meat of the red deer, also features large – low in cholesterol and very tasty, it's served roasted or in casseroles, often flavoured with juniper or with a whisky sauce. If you like **game** and can afford it, splash out on grouse, the most highly prized of all game birds, strong, dark and succulent, best eaten with bread sauce. Pheasant is also worth a try and is less rich than other game, more like a tasty chicken – you can eat it stuffed with oatmeal or with a mealie pudding, a kind of vegetarian black pudding made from onion, oatmeal and spices.

The Highlands and Islands have a huge variety of fresh **fish** to choose from. In the coastal towns, prawns, mussels, oysters, crab and scallops are always available, while inland salmon is a must, especially the more delicately flavoured wild salmon – though this will always cost more than the farmed variety. Both are served either hot with melted butter, small new potatoes and a creamy Hollandaise sauce, or cold in a salad. Trout is also farmed in Scotland, often fried in oatmeal and eaten with bacon. Look out especially for the wild brown trout, whose firm pink flesh is almost as prized as salmon.

Puddings, often smothered in butterscotch sauce or syrup, are taken very seriously in Scotland. One traditional favourite is Cranachan, made with toasted oatmeal steeped in whisky and folded into whipped cream flavoured with fresh raspberries; on the same lines, Atholl Brose, related to English syllabub, is made with oatmeal, whisky and cream. For the ultimate dessert decadence, try the clootie dumpling, a sweet, stodgy fruit pudding soaked in a cloth for hours. If it all sounds a bit rich, you might prefer the black bun, a peppery fruitcake encased in a thin pastry and

HIGHLANDS AND ISLANDS CHEESES

Scotland is never going to compete with France in the cheese stakes, but the Highlands and Islands do produce a few distinctive **cheeses** that beat the average Scottish cheddar for taste. **Crowdie**, originally made with left-over milk, is a young, soft cheese which can be found locally in many places. The Islands, in particular, produce some very palatable cheeses. On **Arran** there's a mild, creamy blue called Brodick Blue, as well as Dunlop, of the cheddar family, but with a softer texture (also produced on the Isle of Islay); on the **Isle of Bute**, there's Drumleish, a young, mild cheese with a buttery flavour, and one actually named Isle of Bute, a hard cheddar-like cheese; the **Isle of Mull** produces one bearing its name, which is a traditional unpasteurized farmhouse cheddar, made in Tobermory; the **Orkney islands** produce Orkney, a distinctive cheddar, produced for two hundred years, as well as several local crofting cheeses; Inverloch, from the **Isle of Gigha**, is a pasteurized goat's cheese covered in brightly coloured wax, often in the shape of fruit; **Mull of Kintyre** is a small truckle of mature Scottish cheddar coated in black wax (also available smoked); Highland is a mature cheese from **Campbeltown** with a distinctive aftertaste.

traditionally eaten at New Year, or the many home-made shortbreads – far superior to the commercial varieties.

One Scottish institution that satisfies the Scots' sweet tooth is **high tea**, consisting of a cooked main course and a plethora of cakes, washed down with tea or coffee and eaten between about 5pm and 6.30pm.

As for **fast food**, fish and chips is as popular in Scotland as in England and "**chippies**" abound, serving battered fish (invariably known as a "fish supper", even if eaten at lunchtime), haggis and oatmeal-based numbers such as black and mealie puddings.

WHERE TO EAT

For **budget food** in the Highlands and Islands you'll need to head for a **café**, ranging from the most basic "greasy spoons" to a more refined **tearoom**, where you can sample Scottish home-baking. Some of the cheapest places to eat in are the **pubs** or **hotel bars** – indeed, in the more remote villages and islands this might be your only option. Bar food ranges from the very ordinary – anything from the freezer with chips – to food that equals the à la carte dishes served in the adjacent hotel restaurant.

As for **restaurants**, standards vary enormously. At their worst, restaurants in the Highlands and Islands can charge over £15 a head for a three-course meal that's little better than your average bar meal. At their best, you'll get a top-class chef producing superb freshly prepared dishes with a Scottish slant. Most restaurants are situated in hotels but are happy to serve non-residents. However, you could easily end up paying £25 a head. Except in places with imaginative menus, **vegetarians** are still looked on somewhat askance, though the situation is slowly improving.

The restaurant listings in the guide include a mix of high-quality and budget establishments. (If you're primarily on a culinary pilgrimage, you might consider getting hold of a copy *of A Taste of Scotland*, the country's top annual foodie guide.) To help give an idea of costs, each place listed in this guide is placed in one of three **price categories**: inexpensive (under £10 a head), moderate (£10–20) and expensive (£20–30). Prices do not include alcohol. For those who'd like to try their hand at a few Scottish dishes, there are some **Scottish recipes** on p.463.

DRINKING

As in the rest of Britain, Scottish **pubs**, which originated as travellers' hostelries and coaching inns, are *the* great social institution. The focal points of any community, Scottish pubs vary hugely, from old-fashioned inns, with heaps of atmosphere and open fires, to raucous theme pubs, with jukeboxes and satellite TV. Out in the less populated Islands, pubs are few and far between, with most drinking taking place in the local hotel bar.

Scotland has all-day **opening hours**, and pubs are generally open from Monday to Saturday 11am to 11pm, with "last orders" called by the bar staff about fifteen minutes before closing time. On Sunday the hours are reduced; many pubs are closed in the afternoon and last orders are called at 10.30pm. In general, you have to be 16 to enter a pub unaccompanied, though some places have special family rooms for people with children, and beer gardens where younger kids can run free. The legal drinking age is 18.

BEER

Beer is the staple drink in Scotland's pubs, the indigenous variety a thick, dark ale, known as **heavy**, served at room temperature with a full head in pints or half-pints. Scottish beers are graded by the shilling: a system used since the 1870s and indicating the level of potency – the higher the shilling mark, the stronger or "heavier" the beer. A pint costs anything from £1.50 to £2.20, depending on the brew and the locale of the pub.

Scotland's biggest-name breweries are McEwan's and Younger's, part of the mighty Scottish and Newcastle group, and Tennents, owned by the English firm Bass. The beers produced by these companies tend to be heavier, smoother and stronger than their English equivalents: look out for McEwan's Export and Tennant's Special, two of the most popular brands, while the 80 shilling ales produced by both companies are strong, smooth, flavoursome drinks.

Out in the Highlands and Islands, the quality of the beer served tends to deteriorate. There are, however, a couple of relatively new, small **local breweries** that have sprung up in the Highlands and Islands, that can be real life-savers in a region where good beer can be hard to come by: the dry, fruity Alice Ale, brewed in Inverness, and the Orkney Brewery's Raven Ale, are ones to seek out, as are the real ales produced by Skye's own microbrewery, based in Uig.

WHISKY

Scotland's national drink is **whisky** – *uisge beatha*, or the "water of life" in Gaelic – sometimes drunk in pubs as a sort of chaser with a half-pint of beer on the side, a combination known as a "nip and a hauf". A standard single measure is 50ml.

Whisky has been produced in Scotland since the fifteenth century, but only really took off in popularity after the 1780 tax on claret made wine too expensive for most people. The taxman soon caught up with whisky distilling, however, and drove the stills underground. Today, many distilleries operate on the site of simple cottages that once distilled the stuff illegally. In 1823, Parliament revised its Excise Laws, in the process legalizing whisky production, and today the drink is Scotland's chief export. There are two types of whisky: single malt, made from malted barley, and grain whisky, which (relatively cheap to produce) is made from maize and a small amount of malted barley in a continuous still. **Blended**, which accounts for more than ninety percent of all sales, is, as the name suggests, a blend of the two types.

Grain whisky forms about seventy percent of the average bottle of blended whisky, but the distinctive flavour of the different blends comes from the malt whisky which is added to the grain in different quantities. The more expensive the blend, the higher the proportion of skilfully chosen and aged malts that have gone into it. Among many brand names, Johnnie Walker, Bells, Teachers and The Famous Grouse are some of the most widely available. All have a similar flavour, and are often drunk with mixers such as lemonade or mineral water.

Despite the dominance of the blended whiskies, **single malt whiskies** are infinitely superior, and best drunk neat (or with a little water) to appreciate their distinctive flavours. Malt whisky is made by soaking barley in water for two or three days until it swells, after which it is left to germinate for up to twelve days, allowing the starch in the barley seed to become soluble. The malted barley is dried with peat, mashed with hot water and fermented with yeast to convert the sugar into crude alcohol, which is then twice distilled and the vapours condensed as a spirit, aged for a minimum of three years (usually much longer) in oak casks. Single malts vary enormously depending on the peat used for drying, the water used for mashing, and the type of oak cask used in the maturing process, but they fall into four distinct groups: Highland, Lowland, Campbeltown and Islay, with the majority in the Highland category and being produced largely on Speyside. You can get the best-known whiskies – among them Glenlivet, Glenmorangie, MacAllan, Talisker, Laphroaig, Highland Park, and Glenfiddich, the top seller – in most pubs.

Most distilleries have a highly developed nose for PR and offer guided tours that range from slick and streamlined to small and friendly. All of them offer visitors a "wee dram" as a finale, and those distilleries that charge an entrance fee often give you your money back if you buy a bottle at the end – though prices are no lower at source than in the shops.

NON-ALCOHOLIC DRINKS

Scotland produces a prodigious amount of **natural mineral water**, mostly for export, as the country's tap water tends to be chill and clean. However, Scotland has the distinction of being the only country in the world where neither Coke nor Pepsi is the most popular fizzy drink. That accolade belongs to Irn-Bru, a fizzy, orange, sickly sweet concoction sold in just about every shop in the country.

POST AND PHONES

In most towns across the Highlands and Islands, post offices are open Monday to Friday 9am to 5.30pm and Saturday 9am to 12.30pm or 1pm. However, in smaller communities you'll find sub-post offices operating out of a shop, shed, or even a private house. Hours can vary enormously – and can often be very short indeed – but the post office counter won't be open longer hours even if the shop is.

Stamps can be bought at post office counters, from vending machines outside, or from an increasing number of newsagents. A first-class letter to anywhere in the UK currently costs 26p and should – in theory – arrive the next day; second-class letters cost 19p, and take from two to four days. Airmail letters of less than 20g (0.7oz) cost 30p to EU and non-EU countries. Letters to other overseas destinations cost from 44p for 10g, and 63p for 20g. Pre-stamped aerogrammes conforming to overseas airmail weight limits of under 10g can be bought for 37p only from post offices. For more information about Royal Mail postal services, phone ☎0345/740740.

Most public **payphones** in the Highlands and Islands are still operated by British Telecom (BT) and are dotted across the countryside – the more remote ones are marked on OS maps. Many BT payphones take all coins from 10p upwards, although some only accept **phonecards**, available from post offices and newsagents displaying the BT logo. These cards come in denominations

---

OPERATOR SERVICES AND PHONE CODES

Operator ☎100
Directory assistance ☎192

International operator ☎155
Overseas directory assistance ☎153

INTERNATIONAL CALLS

To **telephone Scotland** from overseas, dial ☎011 from the US and Canada, ☎0011 from Australia and ☎00 from New Zealand, followed in all cases by 44, then the area code minus its initial zero, and then the number.

To call **overseas from Scotland**, dial ☎00, followed by the country code, the area code (minus the zero if there is one), and then the number. Country codes include:

Australia ☎61   Ireland ☎353   New Zealand ☎64   South Africa ☎27   USA and Canada ☎1

of £2, £3, £5, £10 and £20. Calls are cheapest between 6pm and 8am from Monday to Friday and all day on Saturday and Sunday, though for Australia and New Zealand calls are cheapest daily between midnight and 7am, and between 2.30pm and 7.30pm. Throughout this guide, every phone number is prefixed by the area code, separated from the subscriber number by an oblique slash. You don't have to dial the prefix if you're in the same area code. Any number with the prefix ☎0800 is free; ☎0345 numbers are charged at the local rate; ☎0990 numbers, at the national rate.

OPENING HOURS, HOLIDAYS & ENTRANCE CHARGES

New Year's Day, January 1, is the only fixed **public holiday**, but all Scottish towns and cities have a one-day holiday in both spring and autumn – dates vary from place to place but normally fall on a Monday. If you want to know the exact dates, you can get a booklet detailing them from the Glasgow Chamber of Commerce, 30 George Square, Glasgow G2 1EQ.

MUSEUMS AND MONUMENTS

The **tourist season** in the Highlands and Islands runs from Easter to October, and outside this period many indoor attractions are shut – though ruins, parks and gardens are normally accessible year-round. We've given full details of opening hours and admission charges in the guide.

Shop hours in Scotland are generally Monday to Saturday 9am to 5.30pm or 6pm. In large towns like Inverness, Fort William and Oban, you'll find quite a few shops and supermarkets open on Sundays and late at night, with Thursday or Friday the favoured evenings. However, outside the larger towns, you'll find precious little open on a Sunday, with many small towns also retaining an "early closing day" when shops close at 1pm – Wednesday is the favourite. In Lewis, Harris and North Uist, you will find absolutely nowhere open on a Sunday.

Unlike in England, Scotland's **bank holidays** mean just that: they are literally days when the banks are closed, rather than general public holidays, and they vary from year to year. They include January 2; the Friday before Easter; the first and last Monday in May; the last Monday in August; St Andrew's Day (November 30); Christmas Day (December 25); and Boxing Day (December 26).

A fair few sights in the area – ranging from castles and country houses to islands, gardens and tracts of protected landscape – come under the control of the privately run **National Trust for Scotland**, 5 Charlotte Square, Edinburgh EH2 4DU (☎0131/226 5922), or the state-run **Historic Scotland**, Longmore House, Salisbury Place, Edinburgh EH9 1SH (☎0131/668 8600), shown respectively as the "NTS" or "HS" in the guide. Both organizations charge an entry fee for most places, and these can be quite high, especially for the more grandiose NTS estates. If you think you'll be visiting more than half a dozen owned by the NTS, or more than a dozen owned by HS, it's worth taking **annual membership** (NTS £26, family £42; HS £24, one-parent family £27, two-parent family £42), which allows free entry to their properties.

In addition, both the NTS and HS offer short-term passes that give discounts on admission prices. The **National Trust Touring Pass**, which costs £16 for an adult and £26 for a family, is valid for seven days and gives free admission to all

NTS properties; the fourteen-day pass costs £24 and £42 respectively. The HS **Scottish Explorer** seven-day ticket allows free entry to seventy monuments, castles and other properties, and costs £13.50 or £28 for a family; a two-week equivalent costs £18 and £36 respectively. **HI members** (see p.32) are automatically eligible for half-price entry into all NTS properties.

A lot of Scottish **stately homes** remain in the hands of the landed gentry, who tend to charge around £5 for admission to edited highlights of their domain. Many other old buildings, albeit rarely the most momentous structures, are owned by local authorities, and admission is often cheap and sometimes free.

The majority of fee-charging attractions in Scotland give 25–50 percent **reductions** for senior citizens, the unemployed, full-time stu-dents and children under 16, with under-5s being admitted free almost everywhere. Proof of age will be required in most cases. The entry charges quoted in the guide are the full adult charges.

North Americans can buy the Scottish Explorer and National Trust Touring passes at travel agents or directly from Especially Britain (see p.6). A further option, only open to overseas visitors, is the **Great British Heritage Pass**, which gives free admission to some 600 sites throughout Britain, including many which are not run by the NTS or HS. Costing US$45 for seven days, around US$70 for fifteen days and US$90 for a month, it can be purchased through most travel agents at home, on arrival at any large UK airport, from British Airways offices, and the British Travel Centre, 1 Regent St, London W1 (walk-in service only).

THE MEDIA

The provincial daily press is more widely read in the Highlands and Islands than any-where else in Britain, with biggest-selling regional title being Aberdeen's famously parochial *Press and Journal*, which has special editions for each area of the Highlands and Islands. For an insight into life in the Highlands and Islands, there's the staid weekly *Oban Times*. More entertaining and more radical is the campaigning week-ly *West Highland Free Press*, printed on Skye. All carry articles in Gaelic as well as English. Further north, the lively *Shetland Times* and Orkney's sedate *Orcadian* are essential weekly reads for anyone living in or just visiting those islands.

The principal **British daily newspapers** are also usually available in the Highlands and Islands, though distances can delay (and weather conditions sometimes prevent) their arrival in the Islands. The **tabloids** are as popular as in England, and many appear in a specific Scottish edition; the downmarket *Daily Record*, from the same stable as the *Daily Mirror*, is Scotland's biggest-selling daily paper. All the national "qual-ities", however, from the *Guardian* to the *Daily Telegraph* are justifiably seen in Scotland as being London newspapers. The **Scottish press** produces two major serious daily newspapers: Edinburgh's liberal-left *Scotsman* and the Glasgow's centre-right *Daily Herald*. Both offer good coverage of the current issues affecting Scotland, along with British and foreign news, sport, arts and lifestyle pages. Many national **Sunday newspapers** have a Scottish edition north of the border, although again Scotland has its own Sunday "heavies": *Scotland on Sunday*, from the *Scotsman* stable, and the *Sunday Herald*, complementing its eponymous daily. Both have heavyweight political analysis bulked out by exhaustive sports sections, and energetic arts and lifestyle supplements. Scottish **monthlies** include the *Scottish Field*, a lowbrow version of England's *Tatler*, covering the interests and pur-suits of the landed gentry, and the widely read *Scots Magazine*, an old-fashioned middle-of-the-road publication which promotes family values and lots of good fresh air.

TELEVISION AND RADIO

In Scotland there are five main **television chan-nels**: the state-owned BBC1 and BBC2, and the independent commercial channels, ITV, Channel Four and Channel 5. Though assailed by govern-

RADIO STATIONS IN THE HIGHLANDS AND ISLANDS

BBC Radio Scotland 92–95FM, 810MW. Nationwide news, sport, music, current affairs and arts.

BBC Radio nan Gaidheal 103.4FM. Broadcasts news, phone-ins and great traditional music for much of the day, all in Gaelic.

Lochbroom FM 102.2FM. Britain's smallest radio station, broadcasting to the world and the Ullapool area.

Moray Firth 99.4FM, 1107MW. Award-winning independent station for the Inverness area.

Nevis Radio 96.6FM. From the slopes of Ben Nevis, all that's happening in Fort William and its surrounds.

SIBC 96.2FM Shetland's very own independent radio station.

ment critics of late, the **BBC** is just about maintaining its worldwide reputation for in-house quality productions, ranging from expensive costume dramas to intelligent documentaries – split between the avowedly mainstream BBC1 and the more rarefied fare of BBC2. In northwest Scotland, there are also regular programmes broadcast by BBC Gaelic TV. Three companies – the populist STV, which serves most of southern Scotland and parts of the West Highlands, the Aberdeen-based Grampian; and Border Television which transmits from Carlisle – form the **ITV** network in Scotland. This is complemented by the more eclectic and less mainstream broadcasting of the partly subsidized **Channel Four**, and downmarket **Channel 5**, which can't yet be received in many parts of Scotland. A plethora of **satellite** and, in the cities, **cable stations**, are also available, though the dominant force is still Rupert Murdoch's **Sky**, which offers unlimited news, movies, soaps, home shopping and game shows, along with increasing amounts of British sport, which plays wall-to-wall in pubs the length of the country. For the time being, however, the old terrestrial stations still attract the majority of viewers.

Market forces are also eating away at the **BBC radio** network, which broadcasts six main channels in Scotland, though most of them originate largely from London. Radio One plays almost exclusively mainstream pop music; Radio Two specializes in MOR music; Radio Three broadcasts predominantly classical music; Radio Four is a blend of current affairs, arts and drama; and Radio Five Live, the newest station, transmits a mix of sport and news. The award-winning BBC Radio Scotland offers a Scottish perspective on news, politics, arts, music, travel and sport, and provides a Gaelic network in the northwest with local programmes in Shetland, Orkney, and the north.

A web of **local commercial radio** stations stretches north as far as Shetland, mostly mixing rock and pop music with news, but a few tiny community-based stations such as Lochbroom FM in Ullapool – famed for its daily midge count – transmit documentaries and discussions on local issues. The most populated areas of Scotland also receive UK commercial radio: Classic FM lures listeners from Radios Two and Three, Virgin Radio competes head to head with Radio One, and Talk Radio UK competes with Radio Five Live for sports coverage, phone-ins and chat.

EVENTS AND SPECTATOR SPORTS

There's a huge range of organized annual events on offer in the Highlands and Islands, reflecting both vibrant contemporary culture and well-marketed heritage. Many tourists will want to home straight in on Highland Games and other tartan-draped theatricals, but it's worth bearing in mind that there's more to the region than this: numerous local celebrations perpetuate ancient customs, and traditional music is still alive and kicking in places such as the Hebrides and the Northern Isles.

A few of the smaller, more obscure events, particularly those with a pagan bent, are in no way created for tourists, and indeed do not always welcome the casual visitor. If in doubt, check at the local tourist office. The STB publishes a weighty and complete list of Scottish events in December: it's free and you can get it from area tourist offices or direct from their headquarters.

HIGHLAND GAMES

Despite their name, **Highland Games** are held all over Scotland, from May until mid-September: they vary in size and differ in the range of events they offer. Although the most famous are at Oban, Cowal and especially Braemar, often the smaller ones are more fun. They probably originated in the fourteenth century as a means of recruiting the best fighting men for the clan chiefs, and were popularized by Queen Victoria to encourage the traditional dress, music, games and dance of the Highlands; various royals still attend the Games at Braemar. The most distinctive events are known as the "**heavies**" – tossing the caber, putting the stone, and tossing the weight over the bar – all of which require prodigious strength and skill. Tossing the caber is the most spectacular, when the athlete must run carrying an entire tree trunk and attempt to heave it end over end in a perfect, elegant throw. Just as important as the sporting events are the **piping competitions** – for individuals and bands – and **dancing competitions**, where you'll see girls as young as three tripping the quick, intricate steps of dances such as the Highland Fling.

SHINTY

Although **football** (soccer) is far and away Scotland's most popular spectator sport, it is only played on a local level in the Highlands and Islands. **Scottish Rugby**, too, has its heartland elsewhere, in Edinburgh and the Borders. The one sport that has its stronghold in the West Highlands and Speyside, is the game of **shinty** (the word derives from the Gaelic *sinteag*, meaning "leap") arrived in the country from Ireland around 1500 years ago. Until the latter part of the nineteenth century, it was played on an informal basis and teams from neighbouring villages had to come to an agreement about rules before matches could begin. However, in 1893, the sport's governing body, the **Camanachd Association** – from the Gaelic word for "shinty", *camanachd* – was set up to formalize the rules. The first **Camanachd Cup Final** was held in Inverness in 1896, with Glasgow Cowal going down 2–0 to Kingussie.

Today, shinty is still fairly close to its Irish roots in the game of hurling, with each team having twelve players including a goalkeeper, and each goal counting for a point. The game, sometimes described as "hockey with injuries", isn't for the faint-hearted; it's played at a furious pace, with sticks – called camans or cammocks – flying alarmingly in all directions. Support is enthusiastic and vocal, and if you're in the Highlands during the season – roughly parallel with the soccer season – it's well worth trying to catch a match: check with tourist offices or the local paper to see if there are any local fixtures.

CURLING

The one winter sport which enjoys a strong Scottish identity is **curling**, occasionally still played on a frozen outdoor rink, or "pond", though most commonly these days seen in indoor ice rinks found in many sizeable Scottish towns. The game, which involves sliding smooth-bottomed eighteen-kilogramme discs of granite called "stones" across the ice towards a target circle, is said to have been invented in Scotland, although its earliest representation is in a sixteenth-century Flemish painting. Played by two teams of four, curling is a highly tactical and skilful sport, enlivened by team members using brushes to sweep the ice in front of a moving stone to help it travel further and straighter. If you're interested in seeing curling being played, go along to the ice rink in places such as Perth, Hamilton or Aviemore on a winter evening.

EVENTS CALENDAR

December 31 and January 1: Hogmanay and Ne'er Day. Traditionally more important to the Scots than Christmas, known for the custom of "first-footing", when groups of revellers troop into neighbours' houses at midnight bearing gifts – the first foot should ideally be a dark-haired stranger carrying coal and salt (so the house won't lack for warmth or food), and a bottle of whisky (for obvious reasons). More popular these days are huge and highly organized street parties.

January 1: Kirkwall Boy's and Men's Ba' Games, Orkney. Mass, drunken football game through the streets of the town, with the castle and the harbour the respective goals – as a grand finale, the players jump into the harbour.

January 11: Burning of the Clavie, Burghead, Moray. A burning tar barrel is carried through the town and then rolled down Doorie Hill. Charred fragments of the Clavie offer protection against the evil eye.

Last Tuesday in January: Up-Helly-Aa, Lerwick, Shetland. Norse fire festival culminating in the burning of a specially built Viking longship. Visitors will need an invite from one of the locals, or you can buy a ticket for the Town Hall celebrations; see p.393.

January 25: Burns Night. Burns suppers all over Scotland. Dinners held to commemorate Scotland's greatest poet, involving haggis, whisky and lots of poetry recital.

February: Scottish Curling Championship held in a different (indoor) venue each year.

April: Spirit of Speyside Scotch Whisky Festival.

April: Shetland Folk Festival.

April: Traditional Music Festival, Tobermoray.

May Bank Holiday Isle of Bute Jazz Festival.

Early May Western Isles Challenge. A three-day team race from Barra to Lewis, featuring hill-running, mountain-biking and sea canoeing.

Late May Tarbert Scottish Series. A week of yacht races based at the port on the Loch Fyne side of Kintyre.

Late May Orkney Folk Festival takes place over four days, centred on Stromness.

Late May Bergen–Shetland Yacht Race. Annual yacht race across the North Sea that takes place on Norwegian Whitsun holiday.

Late May Week-long Islay Festival (Feis Ile).

Late May: Atholl Highlanders Parade at Blair Castle, Perthshire. The annual parade and inspection of Britain's last private army by their colonel-in-chief, the Duke of Atholl.

Late May: Scottish Hebridean Islands Peak Race. The biggest combined sailing and fell-running competition in the world.

June: Shinty Camanachd Cup Final. The climax of the season for Scotland's own stick-and-ball game, normally held in one of the main Highland towns.

June: Beginning of the Highland Games season across the Highlands, northeast and Argyll.

June: St Magnus Festival, Orkney. Classical and folk music, drama, dance and literature celebrating the Orkney Islands.

July: Mendelssohn on Mull Festival.

July: Scottish Open Golf Championship, held at a different venue each year.

July: Highland Games at Caithness, Elgin, Glengarry, North Uist, Inverness, Inveraray, Mull, Lewis, Durness, Lochaber, Dufftown, Halkirk.

July Hebridean Celtic Festival. A four-day Celtic music and culture festival held in Stornoway.

July Feis and Eilean. A ten-day celebration of Gaelic culture centred on Sabhal Mor Ostaig on Skye.

August: Annual ploughing match on South Ronaldsay in Orkney. Small children dress as horses and drag decorative wooden ploughs along the beach in a competition to turn the straightest furrows.

August: Mull of Kintyre Music & Arts Festival.

August: Highland Games at Dunoon (Cowal), Mallaig, Skye, Dornoch, Aboyne, Strathpeffer, Assynt, Bute, Glenfinnan, Argyllshire, Glenurquhart and Invergordon.

Early September: Highland Games at Braemar.

Early September Orkney Science Festival takes place over the course of a week.

September: Ben Nevis Race (for amateurs), to the top of the highest mountain in Scotland and back again.

October: The National Mod Competitive festival of all aspects of Gaelic performing arts, held in various venues.

October: Glenfiddich Piping Championships at Blair Atholl for the world's top ten solo pipers.

October Accordion and Fiddle Festival in Shetland.

OUTDOOR PURSUITS

Many visitors come to the Highlands and Islands specifically to enjoy a landscape that's perfect for outdoor pursuits at all levels of fitness and ambition: vast stretches of glens and moorland and spectacular mountains, which in winter can provide great skiing. Throughout the country, numerous marked trails range from hour-long ambles to coast-to-coast treks. The shoreline, lochs and rivers give opportuni-

ties for fishing as well as sailing and watersports, including surfing, and there are plenty of fine beaches. Scotland, of course, is also the "home of golf": it's relatively cheap to play here, and there are proportionally more courses than anywhere else in the world.

WALKING AND CLIMBING

The whole of the Highlands and Islands offers superb opportunities for **hillwalking**, and there are two **Long Distance Footpaths** (**LDPs**) which will take days to walk, though you can, of course, just do a section of them. The better known is the **West Highland Way**, a 95-mile hike from Glasgow to Fort William via Loch Lomond and Glen Coe. The gentler **Speyside Way**, in Aberdeenshire, leads for 45 miles from the Cairngorms to the Moray Firth past a number of whisky distilleries. The green signposts of the Scottish Rights of Way Society point to these and many other cross-country routes, which include "drove roads", long-established paths through the hills along which clansmen once led their cattle to or from markets held in the larger settlements.

The **Highlands** are Scotland's main climbing area and boast many challenging peaks as well

THE MIDGE

Despite being only just over a millimetre long, and enjoying a life span on the wing of just a few weeks, the **midge** (*culicoides*) – a tiny biting fly prevalent in the Highlands (mainly the west coast) and Islands – is considered to be second only to the weather as the major deterrent to tourism in Scotland. There are more than thirty varieties of midge, though only half of these actually bite humans. Ninety percent of all midge bites are down to the female *culicoides impunctatus* or Highland midge (the male does not bite). With two sets of jaws and twenty teeth in each, the female needs a good meal of blood in order to produce eggs.

To some, these persistent creatures are merely a nuisance; others have a violent allergic reaction when bitten. The easiest way to avoid midges is to visit in the winter, since they only appear between April and October. Midges also favour still, damp,

overcast or shady conditions and are at their meanest around sunrise and sunset. Direct sunlight, heavy rain, noise and smoke discourage them to some degree, though the most effective deterrent is, undoubtedly, wind. You'll soon notice if they're near; cover up arms and legs and try to avoid wearing dark colours, which attract the creatures. Various **repellents** are worth a try. Recommendations include Autan and Jungle Formula (widely available from pharmacists), the herbal remedy citronella, and Skin So Soft by Avon, which is said to be very effective, despite not being designed to fend off midges. An alternative to repellents for protecting your face, especially if you are walking or camping, is the midge net, which you secure by tucking under your hat. Although they appear ridiculous at first, midge nets are commonplace and extremely useful.

USEFUL ADDRESSES FOR WALKERS

Assynt Guided Holidays, Birchbank, Knockan, Elphin, Sutherland (☎ & fax 1854/666215). Mountain walks, and glen and lochside ambles, and fishing trips, with one of Scotland's most knowledgeable guides.

C-N-Do Scotland WS, Unit 32, Stirling Enterprise Park, Stirling FK7 7RP (☎01786/445703, *cndo.scotland@btinternet.com*). Munro-bagging for novices and experts, in small groups and with qualified leaders, as well as day-long winter skills and navigation courses.

Cordee (Book Distributors), 3a de Montfort St, Leicester LE1 7HD (☎0116/254 3579). Produces extensive lists of walking books, and distributes all Scottish Mountaineering Club publications.

Glencoe Mountain Sport, 37 Park Rd, Ballachulish, Glencoe, Argyll PA39 4JB (☎01855/811472, *www.glencoe-mountain-sport.co.uk*). Year-round programme of gentle walks and scrambles on Skye, and around Glen Coe and Ben Nevis.

John Muir Trust, Freepost, Musselburgh, Midlothian EH21 7BR (☎0131/665 0596). An organization that purchases land for conservation and public access and can give details of public rights of way.

Mountaineering Council of Scotland, 4a St Catherine's Rd, Perth PH1 5SE (☎01738/638227). The representative body for all mountain activities, which publishes details of estate boundaries and contact phone numbers to help climbers and walkers check on estate activities before setting out.

National Trust for Scotland, 5 Charlotte Square, Edinburgh EH2 4DU (☎0131/226 5922). Guided ranger walks in Torridon and Glencoe.

North-West Frontiers, 18a Braes, Ullapool, Ross-shire IV26 2SZ (☎ & fax 01854/612628, *www.nwfrontiers.com*). Guided mountain trips with small groups in the northwest Highlands, starting in Inverness; May to October only.

Ossian Guides, Sanna, Newtonmore, Inverness-shire PH20 1DG (☎01540/673402). Walking, scrambling and photo-treks with qualified leaders throughout the Highlands.

Ramblers Association Scotland, 23 Crusader House, Haig Business Park, Markinch, Fife KY7 6AQ (☎01592/611177).

Rua Reidh Lighthouse, Melvaig, Gairloch, Wester Ross (☎01445/771263, *ruaheidh@netcomuk.co.uk*). Accompanied and self-guided wilderness walks on the west coast, from three-night to one-week itineraries. Family multi-activity holidays also available.

Scottish Rights of Way Society, John Cotton Business Centre, 10–12 Sunnyside, Edinburgh EH7 5RA (☎0131/652 2937). A campaigning organization which is strong on providing access for walkers.

Scottish Youth Hostel Association, 7 Glebe Crescent, Stirling FK8 2JA (☎01786/451181).

Walkabout Scotland, 2 Rossie Place, Edinburgh EH7 5SG (☎0774/703 2300). A great way to get a taste of walking in the Highlands, with guided day-trips from Edinburgh – they tackle a different hill, of different grades, for each day of the week. All transport included in the price (£30 per person).

---

as great hill walks. There are 284 mountains over 3000ft (914m) in Scotland, known as **Munros** after the man who first classified them: many walkers "collect" or "bag" them, and it's possible to chalk up several in a day. Serious climbers will probably head for **Glen Coe** or **Torridon**, which offer difficult routes in spectacular surroundings. These and some of the other finest Highland areas (Lawers, Kintail, West Affric) are in the ownership of the National Trust for Scotland, while Blaven on Skye and Ladhar Bheinn (Knoydart) are John Muir Trust properties; both allow year-round access. Elsewhere, the accepted freedom to roam in wilder parts of the countryside allows extensive walking and climbing, although

there may be restricted access during lambing (dogs are particularly unwelcome in April and May) and deerstalking seasons (mid-August to the third week in October). The booklet *Heading for the Scottish Hills* (published by the Scottish Mountaineering Club or SMC) provides such information on all areas.

Numerous short walks (from accessible towns and villages) and several major walks are touched on this guide. However, you should only use these notes as general outlines and always in conjunction with a good map. Where possible, we have given details of the best maps to use – in most cases one of the excellent and reliable Ordnance Survey (OS) series (see p.22). You should never attempt walks beyond your abilities and always follow the guidelines below. Other useful sources for information on walks are listed in the box on p.45. If you decide to follow one of the walks and haven't got a map with you, head for the nearest tourist office, which will usually supply OS and other local maps, safety advice and guidebooks/leaflets, as will shops in most areas. Among the many **guidebooks** available for serious walking and climbing, the SMC's series of District Guides offer blow-by-blow accounts of climbs written by professional mountaineers – for other good walking guides, see the "Books" section of Contexts (p.461). These, as well as a wide range of maps, are available from most of the good **outdoor stores** scattered around the country. These shops are normally staffed by experienced climbers and walkers, who are a good source of candid advice about the equipment you'll need and favourite hiking areas. The best stores for this are Tiso and Nevisport, which have various branches in Scotland.

MOUNTAIN SAFETY

The mountains of the Scottish Highlands, while not nearly as high or as steep as the Alps, are sufficiently far north and exposed to the Atlantic that weather conditions often change rapidly. Even in summer you can experience **blizzards** and icy **winds** of up to 100mph on the high tops, and Scottish mountain-rescue teams are kept busy by inexperienced walkers who did not realize the levels of danger involved – in an average year there are more fatalities on Ben Nevis than on Mount Everest.

It's essential to be properly prepared, even for what appears to be an easy expedition in settled weather. Take layers of **warm clothing**, with a brightly coloured and waterproof outer layer; the appropriate 1:50,000 (or even smaller-scale) **maps**; a **compass** (which you should know how to use); and **food** and **water**. **Footwear** is important, too – while you'll often start out along a forest track or well-maintained footpath, paths often peter out and it's bound to get wet underfoot somewhere along the way. If you're making any sort of ascent, you should have boots which have a good grip and offer a degree of ankle support. It's a good idea to know the **weather forecast** before you set out, and take time to **plan your route** using a map and, if possible, a good guidebook. Make sure, too, that someone knows

where you have gone and when you expect to be back (and remember to contact them again on your return).

Once you're on the hill, always put safety first: never underestimate just how fast the **weather** can change (or how extreme the changes can be). If it looks as if it's closing in, get down fast. In **winter**, all the dangers are magnified. Shorter daylight hours means darkness closes in rapidly, so take extra warm clothing, gloves, a hat and a torch, and, unless you're experienced, stick to lower-level walks. To go hillwalking where there's snow or ice on the ground, you must have specialized **equipment** such as crampons and ice axes. In **summer**, carry sun protection and at least a litre of water.

WINTER SPORTS

Skiing, including **snowboarding**, takes place at five different locations in the Highlands – Glencoe, the Nevis Range beside Fort William, Glenshee, the Lecht and the Cairngorms near Aviemore – but as none of these can offer anything even vaguely approaching an Alpine experience it is as well not to come with high expectations. They can go for months on end through the winter with insufficient snow, then see the approach roads suddenly made impassable by a glut of the stuff.

All the resorts have a combination of chairlifts and tows – Nevis Range boasts a gondola – and equipment can always be rented nearby. Expect to pay up to £20 for a standard day pass at one of the resorts, or £55 for a three-day pass; rental of skis or snowboard comes in at around £15 per day, with reductions for multi-day rental. At weekends, in good weather with decent snow, expect the slopes to be packed with trippers from the Central Belt, although midweek usually sees queues dissolving and the experience improving immeasurably. We've given details for each of the resorts in the appropriate place in the text, including telephone numbers to use to find out ski conditions; for more general information, contact Snowsport Scotland in Edinburgh (☎0131/317 7280) or get hold of the STB's Ski Scotland brochure (*www.ski.scotland.net*).

Nordic, or cross-country, skiing, is found in a few places, notably around Braemar near Glenshee and the Cairngorms. This can be a great way to free yourself from the crowds of the resorts and explore the Highland wilderness made pristine by the snow, although the demands on fitness and navigational abilities are higher. The best way to get started or to find out about good routes is to contact an outdoor pursuits company who offer Nordic rental and instruction – try Cairnwell Ski School in Glenshee (☎01250/885255) or Huntly Nordic Ski Centre in Huntly, Aberdeenshire (☎01466/794428, *hnsc@rocketmail.com*).

PONY TREKKING AND HORSE RIDING

Pony trekking as an organized leisure activity originated in Scotland; the late Lieutenant Commander Jock Kerr Hunter set up the first **riding school** here fifty or so years ago, to encourage people to explore the country via its old drove roads. Since then, equestrian centres have mushroomed, and miles of the most beautiful lochsides, heather-clad moorland and long sandy beaches are now accessible on horseback, to novices as well as experienced riders.

The Scottish Tourist Board produces a glossy brochure listing around sixty **riding centres** across the country, all of them approved by either the Trekking and Riding Society of Scotland (TRSS) or the British Horse Society (BHS). Membership of these schemes ensures that the centre is inspected each year, the horses are well looked after, and the staff are properly qualified. As a rule, any centre will offer the option of **pony trekking** (leisurely ambles on sure-footed Highland ponies), **hacking** (for experienced riders who want to go for a short ride at a fastish pace), and **trail riding** (over longer distances, for riders who feel secure at a canter). In addition, a network of special **horse and rider B&Bs** in Scotland means you can ride independently on your own horse.

CYCLING AND MOUNTAIN-BIKING

Despite the recent boom in the sale of mountain bikes, **cyclists** are still treated with notorious neglect by many motorists and by the people who plan the country's traffic systems. Very few of Scotland's towns have proper cycle routes, but the rural back roads are infinitely more enjoyable, particularly in the gentle landscape of Argyll or the West Highlands, where generally amiable gradients and a decent density of pubs and B&Bs make it a perfect area for cycle touring. Your main problem out in the countryside will be finding spare parts – anything more complex than inner tubes or tyres can be very hard to come by.

Cycling is popular in the Highland walking areas, but cyclists should always keep to tracks where a right to cycle exists, and pass walkers at considerate speeds. Footpaths, unless otherwise marked, are for pedestrian use only. The Forestry Commission has recently established 1150 miles of excellent off-road routes all over the country, which are detailed in numerous *Cycling in the Forest* leaflets (available from Forest Enterprise offices listed below, and from most tourist offices). Waymarked and graded, these are best attempted on **mountain bikes** with multi-gears, although many of the gentler routes may be tackled on hybrid and standard road cycles.

Transporting your bike by train is a good way of getting to the interesting parts of Scotland without a lot of hard pedalling. Bikes are allowed on the main GNER and Virgin trains (subject to availability of space) for a £3 charge; you should book the space as far in advance as possible. Bikes are carried free on ScotRail services, but again, subject to availability (call ScotRail bookings on ☎08457/550033). Bus and coach companies, including National Express and Scottish Citylink, rarely accept cycles unless they are dismantled and boxed. One notable exception is the Bike Bus Company (☎0131/229 6274), which operates a minibus and trailer service out of Edinburgh for cyclists.

Bike rental is available at shops in many tourist centres, although only a few more enlightened establishments offer much more than pretty heavy and basic standard models – okay for a brief spin, but not for any serious touring. Expect to pay £10–20 per day; most rental outlets also give good discounts for multi-day rental.

Another option is to shell out on a **cycling holiday package**. These take many forms, but generally include transport of your luggage to each stop, prebooked accommodation, detailed route instructions, a packed lunch and backup support. Most holiday companies offer some budget packages, with hostel instead of hotel or B&B accommodation, and the cost-cutting option of using your own bike. A week-long tour starts at around £250 per person for hostel accommodation, including bike rental. For a list of recommended cycling holiday specialists, see the box on p.48.

Britain's biggest **cycling organization**, the Cyclists' Touring Club or CTC (see box on p.48), provides lists of tour operators and rental outlets in Scotland, and supplies members with touring and technical advice, as well as insurance. As a general introduction, the Scottish Tourist Board's *Cycling in Scotland* brochure is worth sending off for, with practical advice and suggestions for itineraries around the country. The STB's recently introduced "Cyclists Welcome" scheme gives guest houses and B&Bs around the country a chance to advertise that they're cyclist-friendly, and able to provide such things as an overnight laundry service, a late meal or a packed lunch. Recommended as a more detailed guide is *Cycling in Scotland & North East England* by Philip Routledge (available from Sigma Leisure, 1 South Oak Lane, Wilmslow, Cheshire SK9 6AR; £7.95 plus £2 p&p), which crams dozens of maps, route details and general information into 220 pages.

GOLF

There are over 400 **golf courses** in Scotland, where the game is less elitist and more accessible than anywhere else in the world. Golf in its present form took shape in the fifteenth century on the dunes of Scotland's east coast, and today you'll find some of the oldest courses in the world on these early coastal sites, known as "links". If you want a round of golf, it's often possible just to turn up and play, though it's sensible to phone ahead and book, and essential for the championship courses (see below).

Public courses are owned by the local council, while **private** courses belong to a club. You can play on both – occasionally the private cours-

es require that you are a member of another club, and the odd one asks for introductions from a member, but these rules are often waived for overseas visitors and all you need to do is pay a one-off fee. The cost of one round will set you back around £10 on a small nine-hole course, and more than £40 for eighteen holes. Simply pay as you enter and play. In remote areas the courses are sometimes unstaffed – just put the admission fee into the honour box. Most courses have **resident professionals** who give lessons, and some rent equipment at reasonable rates. Renting a caddie car will add an extra few pounds to the cost.

Scotland's **championship** courses, which often host the British Open tournament, are renowned for their immaculately kept greens and challenging holes and, though they're favoured by serious players, anybody with a valid handicap certificate can enjoy them. The most famous one in the Highlands and Islands is **Royal Dornoch** in Sutherland (☎01862/810219; £45). Worth shelling out for if you're coming to Scotland primarily to play golf is a ticket which gives you access to a number of courses in any one region – **Golf Pass Scotland** (☎0990/133206) covers four different Tourist Board areas.

FISHING

Scotland's serrated coastline – with the deep-sea lochs of the west and the myriad offshore islands – encompasses the full gamut of marine habitats, and ranks among the cleanest coasts in Europe. Combine this with an abundance of **salmon**, **sea trout**, **brown trout** and **pike**, acres of open space and easy access, and you have an angler's paradise. Whether you're into game-, coarse- or sea-fishing, you'll be spoilt for choice. The only element in short supply is company; Scotland may offer wonderful fishing, but its unpolluted, open waters don't attract anywhere near the numbers of anglers you'd expect.

Nor will you get bogged down in fishing bureaucracy. No licence is needed to fish in Scotland, although nearly all land is privately owned and its fishing therefore controlled by a landlord/lady or his/her agent. Permission, however, is usually easy to obtain: **permits** can be bought without hassle at local tackle shops, or through fishing clubs in the area – if in doubt, ask at the nearest tourist office. The other thing to bear in mind is that salmon and sea trout have strict **seasons**, which vary between districts but usually stretch from late August to late February. Once again, individual tourist offices will know the precise dates, or you can check in the Scottish Tourist Board's excellent *Fish Scotland* brochure (free from any tourist office or by post; see p.23). It provides a rough introduction to game-, coarse- and sea-angling, with tips on how to find the famous sea marks and salmon beats, and a rundown of less-well-known fishing spots. Other sources of useful information are the Scottish Federation of Sea Anglers, Brian Burn, Flat 2, 16 Bellevue Rd, Ayr KA7 2SA (☎01292/264735), and the Scottish Anglers National Association, Caledonia House, South Gyle, Edinburgh EH12 9DQ (☎0131/339 8808).

BEACHES

The Highlands and Islands boast some very fine **beaches** and bays, most of them clean and many of them deserted even in high summer – perhaps hardly surprising, given the bracing winds and chilly water. Few people come here for a beach holiday, but it's worth sampling one or two, even if you never shed as much as a sweater. Bizarrely enough, given the low temperature of the water, the beaches in the north are beginning to figure on surfers' itineraries, attracting enthusiasts from all over Europe (see below). Perhaps the most beautiful beaches of all are to be found on the islands: endless, isolated stretches that on a sunny day can be paradisal.

In order to comply with EU directives on bathing-water quality, Scotland's 23 dirtiest beaches have been monitored over the past decade for pollution, and measures implemented to ensure they clean up their act. In 1999 the Tidy Britain Group awarded their top award, a Blue Flag, to only one Scottish beach, Silver Sands at Aberdour, and, while great strides have been made over the past few years, a handful of bathing beaches remain on the blacklist.

SURFING

Unlikely though it may seem, Scotland is fast gaining a reputation as a **surfing** destination, with a good selection of excellent quality breaks. It may not have the sunshine of Hawaii, and the water is generally steely-grey rather than turquoise-blue, but there are world-class waves to be found. **Thurso** is the number-one spot on the **north coast**, and boasts one of the finest reef breaks in Europe. In addition, the rest of this coastline – Sango Bay, Torrisdale, Farr Bay and Armadale, in particular – offers waves comparable to those in Hawaii, Australia and Indonesia. However, Scotland's northern coastline lies on the same latitude as Alaska and Iceland, so the water temperature is very low: even in midsummer it rarely exceeds 15°C, and in winter can drop to as low as to 7°C. The one vital accessory, therefore, is a good wet suit (ideally a 5/3mm steamer), wetsuit boots and, outside of summer, gloves and a hood, too.

In addition to Thurso, the beaches of the **Moray Firth** also offer a good North Sea swell. Of the islands, the west coasts of **Coll**, **Tiree** and **Islay** get great swell from the Atlantic and have good beaches, while the spectacular west coast offers numerous possibilities, in particular one of Britain's most isolated beaches, **Sandwood Bay**. In the Outer Hebrides, the best breaks are to be found along the northern coastline of **Lewis**, near Carloway and Bragar.

Many of these beaches are surrounded by stunning scenery, and you'd be unlucky to encounter another surfer for miles. However, this isolation – combined with the cold water and big, powerful waves – means that, in general, much of Scottish surf is best left to **experienced surfers** (see box on p.50). If you're a beginner, get local advice before you go in, and be aware of your limitations. Remember: if you get caught in a current off the west coast, the next stop might be Iceland.

The popularity of surfing in Scotland has led to a spate of **surf shops** opening up, all of which rent or sell equipment, and provide good informa-

TOP BREAKS IN THE HIGHLANDS AND ISLANDS

*Thurso East, just below the castle; see p.258. One of the best right-hand reef breaks in Europe.

*Brimm's Ness, five miles west of Thurso; see p.258. A selection of reef breaks that pick up the smallest of swells.

*Skirza Harbour, three miles south of John O'Groats; see p.261. An excellent left-hand reef break on the far northeast tip of Scotland.

Sandside Bay, on the north coast, ten miles west of Thurso; see p.258. Reef and beach breaks, but dubious water quality due to the proximity of the Dounreay nuclear power station.

*Torrisdale Bay, Bettyhill, on the north coast of the Highlands; see p.257. An excellent right-hand river-mouth break.

Sandwood Bay, a day's hike south of Cape Wrath in Sutherland; see p.254. Beach breaks on one of the most scenic and remote shorelines in Britain, only accessible on foot.

Machrihanish Bay, Mull of Kintyre; see p.110. Four miles of beach breaks on one of Scotland's loneliest peninsulas.

*Valtos, on the Uig peninsula, Lewis; see p.319. A break on one of the Outer Hebrides' most exquisite shell-sand beaches.

*Experienced surfers only.

---

tion about the local breaks and events on the surfing scene (the last two listed also offer surfing lessons): Clan, 45 Hyndland St, Partick, Glasgow (☎0141/339 6523); Boardwise, 1146 Argyle St, Glasgow (☎0141/334 5559); ESP, 6 Greyfriars St, Elgin (☎01343/550129); Granite Reef, 45 Justice St, Aberdeen (☎01224/621193); and Momentum,

22 Bruntsfield Place, Edinburgh (☎0131/229 6665). Two further sources of information are *Surf UK* by Wayne "Alf" Alderson (Fernhurst Books; £13.95), with details on over 400 breaks around Britain, and the bimonthly *Surf* magazine (£3), which is good for grassroots information on the Scottish surfing scene.

TRAVELLERS WITH DISABILITIES

Scotland has numerous specialist tour operators catering for disabled travellers, and the number of non-specialist operators who welcome clients with disabilities is increasing. For more information on these operators, you should get in touch with Disability Scotland, Princes House, 5 Shandwick Place, Edinburgh EH2 4RG (☎0131/229 8632, *dis_scot.gcal.ac.uk*). It has a comprehensive computer database covering all aspects of disabled holidays in Scotland and publishes a full directory. See also the box opposite for other useful organizations in Britain.

Should you go it alone, you'll find that Scottish attitudes towards travellers are far behind advances towards independence made in North America and Australia. Access to theatres, cinemas and other public places has improved recently, but **public transport** companies rarely make

any effort to help disabled people, though some ScotRail InterCity services now accommodate wheelchair-users in comfort. Wheelchair-users and blind or partially sighted people are automatically given thirty to fifty percent reductions on train fares, and people with other disabilities are eligible for the **Disabled Persons Railcard** (£14 per year), which gives a third off most tickets. There are no bus discounts for the disabled, and of the major **car rental** firms only Hertz offers models with hand controls at the same rate as conventional vehicles, and even these are only available in the more expensive categories. Its the same story for **accommodation**, with modified suites for people with disabilities available only at higher-priced establishments and perhaps the odd B&B.

Useful **publications** include RADAR's annually updated *Holidays in the British Isles: A Guide for Disabled People*. Another publication to look

ACCESS FOR TRAVELLERS WITH DISABILITIES

BRITAIN AND IRELAND

Access Travel, 16 Haweswater Ave, Astley, Lancashire M29 7BL (☎01942/888844). Tour operator that can arrange flights, transfer and accommodation. This is a small business, which personally checks out places before recommendation.

Disability Action Group, 2 Annadale Ave, Belfast BT7 3JH (☎01232/491011).

Holiday Care Service, 2nd Floor, Imperial Building, Victoria Rd, Horley, Surrey RH6 7PZ (☎01293/774535, Minicom 01293/776943). Provides free lists of accessible accommodation abroad – European, American and long-haul destinations – plus a list of accessible attractions in the UK. Information on financial help for holidays also available.

Irish Wheelchair Association, Blackheath Drive, Clontarf, Dublin 3 (☎01/833 8241, *iwa@iol.ie*).

RADAR (Royal Association for Disability and Rehabilitation), 12 City Forum, 250 City Rd, London EC1V 8AF (☎0171/250 3222, Minicom 0171/250 4119, *www.radar.org.uk*). A good source of advice on holidays and travel. They produce an annual holiday guide for the UK (£7.50, includes p&p), which contains some information on Scotland.

Tripscope, The Courtyard, Evelyn Rd, London W4 5JL (☎0181/994 9294). This registered charity provides a national telephone information service, offering free advice on UK and international transport and travel for those with a mobility problem.

NORTH AMERICA

Directions Unlimited, 720 N Bedford Rd, Bedford Hills, NY 10507 (☎1-800/533-5343). Tour operator specializing in custom tours for people with disabilities.

Jewish Rehabilitation Hospital, 3205 Place Alton Goldbloom, Chomedy, Laval H7V 1RT Canada (☎514/688-9550; *axis@musica.mcgill.ca*). Friendly service providing general advice about travelling abroad with disabilities. Will reply to email queries.

Mobility International USA, PO Box 10767, Eugene, OR 97440 (voice and TDD ☎503/343-1284). Information and referral services, access guides, tours and exchange programmes. Annual membership $25 (includes quarterly newsletter).

Society for the Advancement of Travel for the Handicapped (SATH), 347 5th Ave, Suite 610, New York, NY 10016 (☎212/447-7284). Non-profit travel-industry referral service that passes queries onto its members as appropriate;

allow plenty of time for a response.

Travel Information Service, Moss Rehabilitation Hospital, 1200 W Tabor Rd, Philadelphia, PA 19141 (☎215/456-9600; TTY for the hearing impaired 215/456-9602, *www.moss-resourcenet.com*). Telephone information and referral service.

Twin Peaks Press, Box 129, Vancouver, WA 98666 (☎360/694-2462 or 1-800/637-2256). Publisher of the *Directory of Travel Agencies for the Disabled* (US$19.95), listing more than 370 agencies worldwide; *Travel for the Disabled* (US$19.95); the *Directory of Accessible Van Rentals* (US$9.95); and *Wheelchair Vagabond* (US$14.95), loaded with personal tips.

Wheels Up! (☎1-800/389-4335). Provides discounted air-fare, tour and cruise prices for disabled travelers, and also publishes a free monthly newsletter.

AUSTRALIA AND NEW ZEALAND

ACROD, PO Box 60, Curtin, ACT 2605 (☎02/6282 4333). Compiles lists of organizations, accommodation, travel agencies and tour operators.

Barrier Free Travel, 36 Wheatley St, North Bellingen, NSW 2454 (☎02/6655 1733).

Disabled Persons Assembly, 173–175 Victoria St, Wellington (☎04/811 9100).

out for is *The World Wheelchair Traveller* by Susan Abbott and Mary Ann Tyrrell (AA Publications), which includes basic hints and useful advice.

DIRECTORY

Electricity In Britain the current is 240V AC. North American appliances need a transformer and adapter; Australasian appliances need only an adapter.

Gaelic In many areas of the Highlands and Hebrides, road signs are bilingual English/Gaelic. In the guide, the Gaelic translation is given (in italics and parentheses) the first time any village or island is mentioned, after which the English name is used. The main exception to this rule is in the Western Isles, where signposting is often exclusively in Gaelic – we've reflected this in the main text by giving the Gaelic first and putting the English in parentheses. Thereafter, we've used the Gaelic, except for the islands and ferry ports, which are more familiar in the English, as they appear on CalMac timetables.

Laundry Coin-operated laundries are found in nearly all large towns in the Highlands and Islands (with the notable exception of Shetland), and are open about twelve hours a day from Monday to Friday, less on weekends. A wash followed by a spin or tumble dry costs about £2.50; a "service wash" (your laundry done for you in a few hours) costs about £1 extra. In the remoter regions of Scotland, you'll have to rely on hostel and campsite laundry facilities.

Smoking The last decade has seen a dramatic change in attitudes towards smoking, and a significant reduction in the consumption of cigarettes. Smoking is now outlawed from just about all public buildings and on public transport, and many restaurants and hotels have become totally non-smoking. Smokers are advised, when booking a table or a room, to check that their vice is tolerated there.

Time Greenwich Mean Time (GMT) is used from late October to late March, after which the clocks go forward an hour for British Summer Time (BST). GMT is five hours ahead of the US Eastern Standard Time, and ten hours behind Australian Eastern Standard Time.

Toilets Public loos are found at most train and bus stations and signposted on town highstreets; a fee of 10p or 20p is sometimes charged.

Videos Visitors from North America planning to use their video cameras in Britain should note that Betamax videocassettes are less easy to obtain in Scotland, where VHS is the commonly used format, so bring a supply with you.

PART TWO

THE

GUIDE

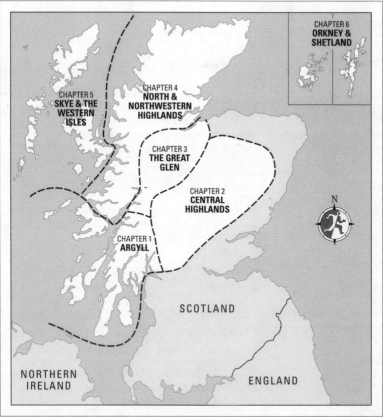

CHAPTER 6
ORKNEY & SHETLAND

CHAPTER 5
SKYE & THE WESTERN ISLES

CHAPTER 4
NORTH & NORTHWESTERN HIGHLANDS

CHAPTER 3
THE GREAT GLEN

CHAPTER 2
CENTRAL HIGHLANDS

CHAPTER 1
ARGYLL

N

SCOTLAND

NORTHERN IRELAND

ENGLAND

CHAPTER ONE

ARGYLL

C ut off for centuries from the rest of Scotland by the mountains and sea lochs that characterize the region, **Argyll** remains remote, its scatter of offshore islands forming part of the Inner Hebridean archipelago (the remaining Hebrides are dealt with in the "Skye and the Western Isles" chapter). Geographically, as well as culturally, this is a transitional area between Highland and Lowland, boasting a rich variety of scenery, from lush, subtropical gardens warmed by the Gulf Stream to flat and treeless islands on the edge of the Atlantic. It's in the folds and twists of the countryside and the views out to the islands that the strengths and beauties of mainland Argyll lie – the one area of man-made sights you shouldn't miss is the cluster of **Celtic** and **prehistoric sites** near Kilmartin. The overall population is tiny; even **Oban**, Argyll's chief ferry port, has just seven thousand inhabitants, while the prettiest, **Inveraray**, boasts a mere four hundred.

The eastern duo of **Bute** and **Arran** are the most popular of Scotland's more southerly islands, the latter – now strictly speaking part of North Ayrshire – justifiably so, with spectacular scenery ranging from the granite peaks of the north to the Lowland pasture of the south. Of the Hebridean islands covered in this chapter, mountainous **Mull** is the most visited, though it is large enough to absorb the crowds, many of whom are only passing through en route to the tiny isle of **Iona**, a centre of Christian culture since the sixth century. **Islay**, best known for its distinctive malt whiskies, is fairly quiet even in the height of summer, as is neighbouring **Jura**, which offers excellent walking opportunities. And, for those seeking further solitude, there's the island of **Colonsay**, with its golden sands, and the more remote islands of **Tiree** and **Coll**, which, although swept with fierce winds, boast more sunny days than anywhere else in Scotland.

The region's name derives from *Aragaidheal*, which translates as "Boundary of the Gaels", the Irish Celts who settled here in the fifth century AD, and whose **kingdom of Dalriada** embraced much of what is now Argyll. Known to the Romans as *Scotti* – hence "Scotland" – it was the Irish Celts who promoted Celtic Christianity, and whose Gaelic language eventually became the national tongue. After a brief period of Norse invasion and settlement, the islands (and the peninsula of Kintyre) fell to the immensely powerful Somerled, who became King of the Hebrides and Lord of Argyll in the twelfth century. Somerled's successors, the MacDonalds, established Islay as their headquarters in the 1200s, but were in turn dislodged by Robert the Bruce. Of Bruce's allies, it was the **Campbells** who benefited most from the MacDonalds' demise and, eventually, as the dukes of Argyll, gained control of the entire area – even today, they remain one of the largest landowners in the region.

In the aftermath of the Jacobite uprisings, Argyll, like the rest of the Highlands, was devastated by the **Clearances**, with thousands of crofters evicted from their homes in order to make room for profitable sheep farming – "the white plague" –

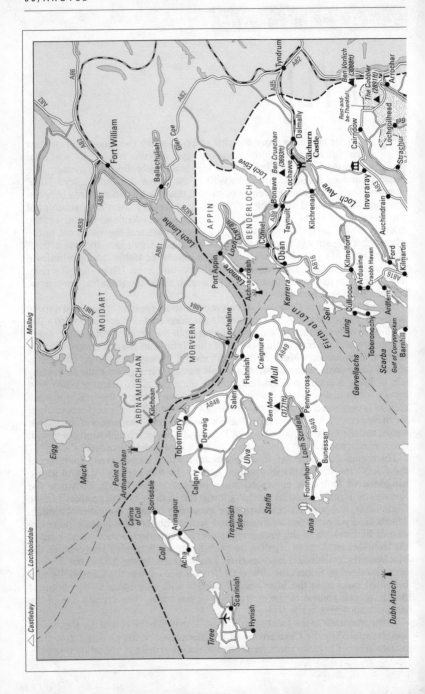

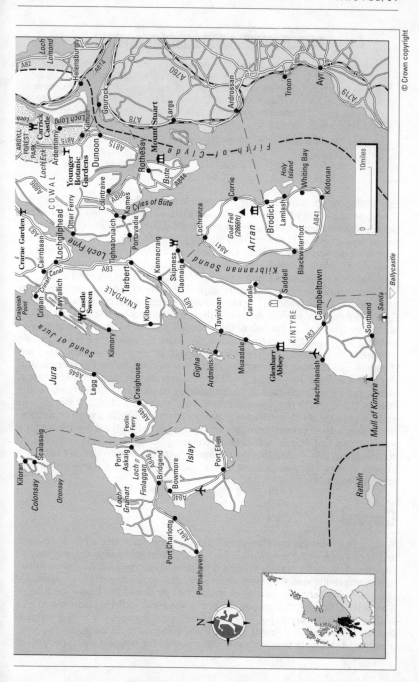

© Crown copyright

ACCOMMODATION PRICE CODES

Throughout this book, accommodation **prices** have been graded with the codes below, according to the cost of the least expensive double room in high season. Price codes are not given for campsites, most of which charge under £10 per person. Almost all hostels charge less than £10 a night for a bed – the few exceptions to this rule have the prices quoted in the text. For a full account of the accommodation price codes, see p.32.

① under £40	④ £60–70	⑦ £110–150
② £40–50	⑤ £70–90	⑧ £150–200
③ £50–60	⑥ £90–110	⑨ £200 and over

---

and cattle-rearing. More recently forestry plantations have dramatically altered the landscape of Argyll, while purpose-built marinas have sprouted all around the heavily indented coastline. Today the traditional industries of fishing and farming are in deep crisis, as is the modern industry of fish-farming, leaving the region ever more dependent on tourism, EU grants and a steady influx of new settlers to keep things going, while Gaelic, once the language of the majority in Argyll, retains only a tenuous hold on the outlying islands of Islay, Coll and Tiree.

It's on Argyll's west coast that the unpredictability of the **weather** can really affect your holiday. If you can, avoid July and August, when the crowds on Mull, Iona and Arran are at their densest – there's no guarantee the weather will be any better than during the rest of the year, and you might have more chance of avoiding the persistent Scottish midge (for more on which, see p.44). **Public transport** throughout Argyll is minimal, though buses do serve most major settlements, and the train line reaches all the way to Oban. In the remoter parts of the region and on the islands, you'll have to rely on a combination of walking, shared taxis and the postbus. If you're planning to take a car across to one of the islands, it's essential that you book both your outward and return journeys as early as possible, as the ferries get very booked up. And lastly, a word on **accommodation**: a large proportion of visitors to this part of Scotland come here for a week or two and stay in self-catering cottages. On some islands and in more remote areas, this is often the most common form of accommodation available – in peak season, you should book several months in advance (for more on self-catering, see p.33).

Cowal

West of Helensburgh, the claw-shaped **Cowal peninsula**, formed by Loch Fyne and Loch Long, is the most-visited part of Argyll, largely due to its proximity to Glasgow. The area's seaside resorts developed along the eastern shores in the nineteenth century, as they were easily accessible by steamer from Glasgow. It's still quicker to get to Cowal via the ferries that ply across the Clyde; car drivers have a long, though exhilarating drive through some rich Highland scenery in order to reach the same spot. The Cowal landscape is extremely varied, ranging from the Munros of the **Argyll Forest Park** in the north, to the gentle low-lying coastline of the southwest, but most visitors – and the majority of the population

– confine themselves to the area around **Dunoon** (which has Cowal's chief tourist office) in the east, leaving the rest of the countryside relatively undisturbed.

Argyll Forest Park

The **Argyll Forest Park** stretches from the western shores of Loch Lomond south as far as Holy Loch, providing the most exhilarating scenery on the peninsula. The park includes the **Arrochar Alps**, north of Glen Croe and Glen Kinglas, whose Munros offer some of the best climbing in Argyll: Ben Ime (3318ft) is the tallest of the range, and Ben Arthur or "The Cobbler" (2891ft) easily the most distinctive. All are for experienced walkers only. Less threatening are the peaks south of Glen Croe, between Loch Long and Loch Goil (branching off Loch Long), known as **Argyll's Bowling Green** – no ironic nickname, but an English corruption of the Gaelic *Baile na Greine* (Sunny Hamlet). At the other end of the scale, there are several gentle forest walks clearly laid out by the Forestry Commission and helpful leaflets available from tourist offices.

Arrochar and around

Approaching from Glasgow along the A83, you enter the park from **ARROCHAR**, at the head of Loch Long. The village itself is ordinary enough, but the setting is dramatic, and it makes a convenient base for exploring the northern section of the park. There's a **train station**, a mile or so east, off the A83 to Tarbet, and numerous **hotels** and **B&Bs** – try the very friendly *Lochside Guest House* (☎01301/702467; ①), on the main road, which rents out bikes, or the *Mansefield Hotel* (☎01301/702282; ②), a little to the south on the quieter A814 to Garelochhead. If you want a bite **to eat**, head for the *Village Inn*, near the *Mansefield*; the local nightlife revolves around *Callum's Bar*, two doors down from *Lochside Guest House*.

Two miles beyond Arrochar at **ARDGARTAN**, there's a lochside Forestry Commission **campsite** (☎01301/702293; Easter–Oct), an SYHA **youth hostel** (☎01301/702362; closed Jan) and, a little further down the road, a **visitor centre** (daily: April–June, Sept & Oct 10am–5pm; July & Aug 10am–6pm; ☎01301/702432), run jointly by the tourist board and the Forestry Commission. It's a great source of advice on weather conditions and wildlife, and organizes var-

---

CLIMBING THE COBBLER

The jagged, triple-peaked ridge of Ben Arthur (2891ft) – better known as **The Cobbler** because it is supposed to look like a cobbler bent over his work – is easily the most enticing of the peaks within the Argyll Forest Park. It's surprisingly accessible, with the most popular route starting from the car park at Succoth, halfway between Arrochar and Ardgartan. Skirting the woods, you eventually join the Allt a' Bhalachain, which climbs steeply up to the col between the northern peak (known as The Cobbler's Wife) and The Cobbler itself. Traversing the ridge in order to ascend one or all of the three peaks is a tricky business, and the climb should only be attempted by experienced hikers. The total distance of the climb is only five miles, but the return trip will probably take you between five and six hours. For more on safety precautions, see p.46.

ious nature activities, ranging from hill-climbing to deer-spotting, though advance booking is essential. There are also waymarked walks starting from the centre.

Rest-and-be-Thankful, Cairndow and Lochgoilhead

Approaching Cowal from the east, you're forced to climb **Glen Croe**, a strategic hill pass whose saddle is called – for obvious reasons – **Rest-and-be-Thankful**. Here the road forks, with the single-track B828 heading down to **LOCHGOIL-HEAD**, overlooking Loch Goil. The setting is difficult to beat, but the village has been upstaged by the *Drimsynie Holiday Resort*, whose triangular chalets pock-mark the landscape for a mile to the west. A road tracks the west side of the loch, petering out after five miles at the ruins of **Carrick Castle**, a classic tower-house castle built around 1400 and used as a hunting lodge by James IV.

If you'd rather skip Lochgoilhead, continue along the A83 from the Rest-and-be-Thankful down the grand Highland sweep of Glen Kinglas to **CAIRNDOW**, at the head of Loch Fyne. Just behind the village, off the main road, you'll find the **Ardkinglas Woodland Garden** (daily dawn–dusk; £2), which contains exotic rhododendrons, azaleas and a superb collection of conifers, some of which rise to over 200ft. A mile or so further along on the A83 around the head of the loch at Clachan is the famous **Loch Fyne Oyster Bar** (☎01499/600264), which sells more oysters than anywhere else in the country, plus lots of other fish and seafood treats. You can easily assemble a gourmet picnic here, and the moder-ately expensive restaurant is excellent.

Loch Eck and around

If you're heading south into Cowal from Cairndow, take the A815 which follows the loch southwest to **STRACHUR**, where the church has medieval grave slabs set into its walls and there's a restored smiddy. Just to the north of the village stands the famous *Creggans Inn*, belonging to the son of Sir Fitzroy Maclean (☎01369/860279; ⑥); even if the rooms and restaurant are too pricey, you can pop into the bar or the all-day coffee shop.

The road divides at Strachur, with the A815 heading inland to **Loch Eck**, an exceptionally narrow freshwater loch, squeezed between steeply banked woods, and a favourite spot for trout fishing. At the southern tip of Loch Eck are the beau-tifully laid-out **Younger Botanic Gardens** (mid-March to mid-Oct daily 10am–6pm; £3), an offshoot of Edinburgh's Royal Botanic Gardens, famed for their rhododendrons and especially striking for their avenue of Great Redwoods, planted in 1863 and now over 100ft high. There's an excellent inexpensive café by the entrance, open in the season, with an imaginative menu – you can eat there without visiting the gardens if trees aren't your thing. If you're feeling energetic, you could combine a visit here with one of the most popular of the local **forest walks**, a leisurely stroll up the rocky ravine of **Puck's Glen**; the walk begins from the car park a mile south of the gardens (1hr 30min round-trip). The *Stratheck* **campsite** at the southern end of Loch Eck (☎01369/840472; March–Dec) enjoys a nice situation.

Before heading south to Dunoon, it's worth taking a trip down the north shores of Holy Loch, the former site of the US nuclear submarine base which closed in 1992, to **KILMUN**, where there's a fascinating church with a mausoleum where many a Duke of Argyll is buried – alas closed to the public – several good stained-glass windows and an organ driven by tap water (teas and tours in the summer). There's also an arboretum at Kilmun, through which the Forestry Commission has laid out several walks, which make for a pleasant stroll. You can get some good **food** in the village at the *Fern Grove Bistro*, which does takeaway and a couple of **rooms** as well (☎01369/840334; ②; April–Oct). Further up the coast, round the corner and overlooking **LOCH LONG**, there's more choice of accommodation: the *Gairletter Caravan Park* **campsite** (☎01369/810208; April–Oct), at **BLAIRMORE**, which enjoys an idyllic lochside spot, and, further on still, *Ardentinny* (☎01369/810209; ④), a whitewashed eighteenth-century **hotel** on a spit of land jutting out into the loch.

Dunoon

In the nineteenth century, Cowal's capital, **DUNOON**, grew from a mere village to a major Clyde seaside resort and favourite holiday spot for Glaswegians. Nowadays, tourists tend to arrive by ferry from Gourock and, though their numbers are smaller, Dunoon remains by far the largest town in all Argyll, with 13,000 inhabitants. Apart from its practical uses and its fine pier, however, there's little to tempt you to linger in Dunoon.

The centre of town is dominated by a grassy lump of rock known as **Castle Hill**, crowned by Castle House, built in the 1820s by a wealthy Glaswegian, and the subject of a bitter dispute with the local populace over closure of the common land around his house. The people eventually won, and the grounds remain open to the public to this day, as does the house, which is now home to the local **museum** (June–Oct Mon–Sat 10am–4.30pm; £1.50). There's some good hands-on nature stuff for kids, an excellent section on the Clyde steamers and details about **Highland Mary**, whose statue is in the grounds. Betrothed to Robbie Burns, who seems conveniently to have ignored the fact that he already had a pregnant wife, Highland Mary nursed the poet through typhus while they planned to elope to the West Indies, only to die tragically from the disease herself. Another more violent scene in local history is commemorated by a memorial on a nearby rock: at least 36 men of the Lamont clan were executed by their rivals, the Campbells, who hanged them from "a lively, fresh-growing ash tree" in 1646. The tree couldn't take the strain, and had to be cut down two years later – tradition has it that blood gushed from the roots when it was felled.

With an hour or so to spare, you could visit the **Cowal Bird Garden** (April–Oct daily 10.30am–6pm; £3), one mile northwest along the A885 to Sandbank, and wander through their woodland amid exotic caged birds as well as free-roaming peacocks, macaws and pot-bellied pigs. If the weather's fine, take the **Ardnadam Heritage Trail**, a mile further up the road, to the wonderful Dunan viewpoint looking out to the Firth of Clyde; if the weather's bad, you could head for Dunoon Ceramics, on Hamilton Street, which produces various styles of high-quality porcelain and bone china, and offers tours around the factory (Mon–Thurs 10am–4pm, Fri 10am–3pm).

Practicalities

It's a good idea to take advantage of Dunoon's **tourist office** (the main one in Cowal) on Alexandra Parade (April & Oct Mon–Fri 9am–5.30pm, Sat 10am–5.30pm, Sun 11am–3pm; May, June & Sept Mon–Fri 9am–5.30pm, Sat & Sun 10am–5pm; July & Aug Mon–Fri 9am–7pm, Sat 10am–7pm, Sun 10am–5pm; Nov–March Mon–Thurs 9am–5.30pm, Fri 9am–5pm; ☎01369/703785). The shorter, more frequent of the two **ferry crossings** across the Clyde from Gourock to

Dunoon is the half-hourly Western Ferries service to Hunter's Quay, a mile north of the town centre; CalMac has the prime position, however, on the main pier, and has better transport connections if you're on foot.

If you need to **stay** the night, there's an enormous choice of B&Bs: try *Cedars* (☎01369/702425; ②), which is better than average and central, or the town's landmark *Argyll Hotel*, opposite the pier (☎01369/702059; ②), which is not as plush as you might expect. For real class, though, head for the highly reputable *Ardfillayne House*, West Bay (☎01369/702267; ③), its welcoming next-door neighbour *Abbot's Brae* (☎01369/705021, *enquiry@abbotsbrae.ndirect.co.uk*; ③), or, topping the lot, the luxurious *Enmore Hotel* (☎01369/702230, *enmorehotel@btinternet.com*; ⑤), an eighteenth-century villa on Marine Parade, near Hunter's Quay. The good news for hostellers is that there's a **hostel** due to open in 2000 on Alexandra Parade, run by the Baptist Church (for the latest, phone ☎01369/706665).

Chatters, 58 John St (March–Dec Wed–Sat), is Dunoon's best **restaurant**, offering delicious Loch Fyne seafood and Scottish beef; for something a bit less pricey, the *Argyll* does decent, filling bar snacks. Dunoon boasts a two-screen cinema (a rarity in Argyll) on John Street, but the town's most famous entertainment by far is the **Cowal Highland Gathering**, the largest of its kind in the world, held here on the last weekend in August, and culminating in the awesome spectacle of the massed pipes and drums of more than 150 bands marching through the streets. For **bike rental**, head for the Highland Stores on Argyll Street, or the *Argyll Hotel*; for **pony trekking**, contact the Velvet Path Riding and Trekking Centre (☎01369/830580) at Inellan, four miles south of Dunoon.

Southwest Cowal

The mellower landscape of **southwest Cowal**, in complete contrast to the bustle of Dunoon or the Highland grandeur of the Argyll Forest Park, becomes immediate as soon as you head west along the scenic B836 to Loch Striven, and then on to Loch Soch Riddon, where, from either side, there are few more beautiful sights than the **Kyles of Bute**, the thin slithers of water that separate the bleak bulk of north Bute from Cowal, and constitute some of the best sailing territory in Scotland.

COLINTRAIVE, on the eastern Kyle, marks the narrowest point in the Kyles – barely more than a couple of hundred yards – and is the place from which the small CalMac car ferry departs to Bute (possibly the most expensive ferry journey in the world, mile for mile). However, the most popular spot from which to appreciate the Kyles is the A8003 as it rises dramatically above the sea lochs before descending to the peaceful, lochside village of **TIGHNABRUAICH**, best known for its excellent **sailing school** (☎01700/811396), which offers week-long courses from beginners to advanced. Boat trips still call at the pier and the village is thriving, boasting a bank, a post office and several shops as well as a good inexpensive place to eat – the *Burnside Bistro*. The *Royal Hotel* (☎01700/811239, *royalhotel@btinternet.com*; ⑤), by the waterside, serves exceptionally good bar meals, but it's a lot cheaper to stay in neighbouring **KAMES** at the *Kames Hotel* (☎01700/811489; ②), which has wonderful views over the Kyles. Close by Kames pier is the tank landing site where troops practised for the D-day invasion of France in the World War II.

The Kyles can get busy in July and August, but you can escape the crowds by heading for Cowal's deserted west coast, overlooking Loch Fyne. The one brief glimpse of habitation en route is the luxurious, whitewashed *Kilfinan Hotel* (☎01700/821201; ⑨; closed Feb), set back from a sandy bay seven miles along the B8000 from Tighnabruaich. The road rejoins the coast at **OTTER FERRY**, which has a small sandy beach, a wonderful pub and an oyster restaurant, *The Oystercatcher*, with tables outside if the weather's good. There was once a ferry link to Lochgilphead from here, though the "otter" part is not derived from the furry beast but from the Gaelic *an oitir* (sandbank), which juts out a mile or so into Loch Fyne. If you're heading for Kintyre, Islay or Jura, you can avoid the long haul around Loch Fyne – some seventy miles or so – by using the **ferry service to Tarbert** from Portavadie, three miles southwest of Kames.

The faster road north from Portavadie and the Kyles is the A886, which runs through the lovely forested Glendaruel. En route, the road passes the pretty village of **CLACHAN OF GLENDARUEL**, whose riverside churchyard preserves several medieval grave slabs. **Accommodation** is available at the homely *Glendaruel Hotel* (☎01369/820274; ③), which does the unusual bar snacks, and there's a prize-winning **campsite** in the forest just up the road (☎01369/820267; April–Oct) at *Glendaruel Caravan Park*.

Isle of Bute

The island of **Bute** is in many ways simply an extension of the Cowal peninsula, from which it is separated by the merest slither of water. Until 1975, it formed its own county, along with the Isle of Arran, to the south, but it's now been thrown in with Argyll. Thanks to its consistently mild climate and its ferry link with Wemyss Bay, Bute has been a popular holiday and convalescence spot for Clydesiders – particularly the elderly – for over a century. Its chief town, **Rothesay**, rivals Dunoon as the major seaside resort on the Clyde, and easily surpasses the latter, thanks to the two superb castles in its vicinity. Most of Bute's inhabitants are centred around the two wide bays on the east coast of the island, which resembles one long seaside promenade. Consequently, it's easy enough to escape the crowds by heading for the sparsely populated west coast, which, in any case, has much the sandiest beaches.

Rothesay

Bute's one and only town, **ROTHESAY** is a handsome Victorian resort, set in a wide sweeping bay, backed by green hills, with a classic palm-tree promenade and 1920s pagoda-style Winter Gardens. It creates a much better general impression than Dunoon, with its period architecture and the occasional flourishes of wrought-ironwork. Even if you're just passing through, you must pay a visit to the ornate **Victorian toilets** (daily: Easter–Oct 8am–9pm; Nov–Easter 9am–5pm; 10p) on the pier, which were built by Twyfords in 1899 and have since been declared a national treasure. Men have the best time, as the porcelain urinals steal the show, but women can ask for a guided tour, if the coast is clear, and learn about the haunted cubicle. While you're on the harbourfront, look out for the wrought-iron arch marking the **Highland Boundary Fault**, which cuts the island (and Rothesay) in two: the view in one direction looks out on the Highlands and in the other to the Lowlands.

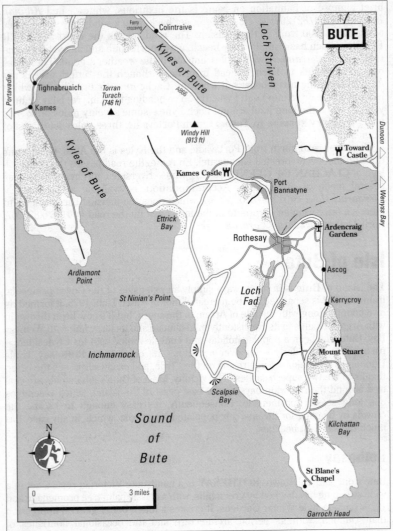

Rothesay also boasts the militarily useless, but architecturally impressive, moated ruins of **Rothesay Castle** (April–Sept daily 9.30am–6.30pm; Oct–March Mon–Wed 9.30am–4.30pm, Thurs 9.30am–noon, Sat 9.30am–4.30pm; £1.80), hidden amid the town's backstreets but signposted from the pier. Built around the twelfth century, it was twice captured by the Vikings in the 1200s; such vulnerability was the reasoning behind the unusual, almost circular curtain wall, with its four big drum towers, only one of which remains fully intact.

In rainy weather you could hide inside the **Bute Museum** (Oct–March Tues–Sat 2.30–4.30pm; April–Sept Mon–Sat 10.30am–4.30pm, Sun 2–4.30pm; £1.20) behind the castle, whose local history section has some shining imperial weights and measures and a triple mousetrap. More interesting, though, is the fourteenth-century **St Mary's Chapel**, beside the High Kirk on the outskirts of town up the High Street; it houses a couple of impressive canopied medieval tombs and, in the churchyard, the mausoleum of the Marquesses of Bute and the grave of Napoleon's niece, who married a Sheriff of Lancaster.

A real little gem in summer is **Ardencraig Gardens** (May–Sept Mon–Fri 10am–4.30pm, Sat & Sun 1–4.30pm; free), up the hill opposite Craigmore Pier, where the Victorian hothouses are a riot of blooms and the garden is techni-colour, with flowers in the midst of aviaries full of exotic birds; there is even a decent tearoom with mouthwatering home-made cakes. More horticultural delights are to be found out along the road to Mount Stuart (see p.66) at the **Ascog Fernery and Garden** (April to mid-Oct Wed–Sun 10am–5pm; £2.50), an unusual Victorian fernery that has been lovingly restored and still boasts an ancient fern, reputed to be a thousand years old.

Practicalities

Rothesay's **tourist office**, opposite the pier at 15 Victoria St (April & Oct Mon–Fri 9am–5.30pm, Sat 10am–5.30pm, Sun 11am–3pm; May, June & Sept Mon–Fri 9am–5.30pm, Sat & Sun 10am–5pm; July & Aug Mon–Fri 9am–7pm, Sat 10am–7pm, Sun 10am–5pm; Nov–March Mon–Thurs 9am–5.30pm, Fri 9am–5pm; ☎01700/502151), can help with **accommodation**, though there's no shortage of B&Bs all along the seafront from Rothesay north to Port Bannatyne. One of the most attractive hotels on the bay is *Cannon House* (☎01700/502819; ④), close to the pier on Battery Place, while the nearby *Commodore* (☎01700/502178; ②) is a more modest choice. Another very comfortable option, set in its own grounds out in Ardbeg, is *Ardmory House* (☎01700/502346; ⑤), which is also one of the best places to eat in town. At the quiet end of town on Mountstuart Road, try the very friendly *Bayview Hotel* (☎01700/505411; ②), or, further out in Ascog, the B&B at *Ascog Farm* (☎01700/503372; ①), which is exceptionally good value. Finally, *New Farm* (☎01700/831646; ②), just one mile from Mount Stuart, has a few rooms in a lovely converted farmhouse, above a moderately expensive **restaurant** which uses local ingredients and produces its own delicious bread; it's popular, so be sure to make a reservation. A good **self-catering** option at Port Ballantyne is the six Victorian cottages in the grounds of *Kames Castle* (☎01700/504500, *kames-castle@easynet.co.uk*).

The best **food** options in Rothesay itself are *Oliver's*, on Victoria Street, which serves decent pasta and steak (and occasionally local seafood), and the water-front bistro, *Fowlers* (closed Tues), in the Winter Gardens, which offers a good-value menu and a superb view of the bay. For Rothesay's finest fish and chips, head for the *West End Café* on Gallowgate. You can't miss the many Zavaroni cafés, part of the subculture of Italian cafés in the Clyde area; the most famous member of the family was, of course, Lena, a teenage pop star in the 1970s. If you want to check your email, the *Harbour Café* on the seafront combines coffee and cakes and surfing.

It's worth noting that Rothesay has a **cinema** in the Winter Gardens. Bute also holds its own **Highland Games** on the last weekend in August – Prince Charles, as Duke of Rothesay, occasionally attends – plus an international **folk festival** on the third weekend in July, and a (mainly trad) **jazz festival** during May Bank Holiday. There are several golf courses, **pony trekking** at Kingarth Trekking Centre (☎01700/831673), near Kilchattan Bay, and **bike rental** from the Mountain Bike Centre, 24 East Princes St, or *Calder Bros*, 7 Bridge St, both of which are open daily.

Mount Stuart

One very good reason for coming to Bute is to visit **Mount Stuart** (Easter & May to mid-Oct Mon, Wed & Fri–Sun 11am–5pm; £6 house and gardens), a fantasy Gothic house set amidst acres of lush woodland gardens, overlooking the Firth of Clyde just three miles south of Rothesay. Home of the obscenely wealthy seventh Marquess of Bute, the building was created by the marvellously eccentric third Marquess after a fire in 1877 had destroyed the family seat. With little regard for expense, the marquess shipped in tons of Italian marble, building a railway line to transport it down the coast and employing craftsmen who had worked with the great William Burges on the marquess's earlier medieval concoctions at Cardiff Castle. The building was by no means finished when the third Marquess died in 1900, and work continues even today, though subsequent family members haven't had quite the inspirational taste of their predecessor.

A bus runs from Rothesay approximately every 45 minutes to the gates of the Mount Stuart, while the house itself is a pleasant fifteen-minute walk through the gardens from the ticket office; if it's raining it might be worth taking the shuttle service provided. Inside the building, the showpiece is the columned **Marble Hall**, its vaulted ceiling and stained-glass windows decorated with the signs of the zodiac, reflecting the marquess's taste for mysticism. The marquess was equally fond of animal and plant imagery, hence you'll find birds feeding on berries in the dining-room frieze and monkeys reading (and tearing up) books and scrolls in the library. Look out also for the unusual heraldic plaster ceiling in the drawing room. After the heavy furnishings of the ground-floor rooms, you can seek aesthetic relief in the **Marble Chapel**, built entirely out of dazzling white Carrara marble, with a magnificent Cosmati floor pattern. Upstairs is less interesting, with the notable exception of the **Horoscope Room**, where you can see a fine astrological ceiling and adjacent observatory.

Although the sumptuous interior of Mount Stuart is not to everyone's taste, it's worth coming here if only to picnic and explore the wonderfully mature **gardens** (same hours as house, but open at 10am; £3 gardens only), established in the eighteenth century by the third Earl of Bute, who had a hand in London's Kew Gardens. Before you leave Mount Stuart, take a look at the planned village of **Kerrycroy**, just beyond the main exit, built by the second Marquess in the early nineteenth century for the estate workers. Semi-detached houses – alternately mock-Tudor and whitewashed stone – form an crescent overlooking a pristine village green and, beyond, the sea.

The rest of Bute

The Highland–Lowland dividing line passes through the middle of Bute, which is all but sliced in two by the freshwater Loch Fad. As a result, the northern half of the island is hilly, uninhabited and little-visited, while the southern half is made up of Lowland-style farmland. The two highest peaks on the island are **Windy**

Hill (913ft) and **Torran Turach** (746ft), both in the north; from the latter, there are fine views of the Kyles, but for a gentler overview of the island you can simply walk up to the **viewpoint**, on a hill a few miles east of Rothesay.

A site well worth visiting, which recalls Bute's early monastic history, is **St Blane's Chapel**, a twelfth-century ruin beautifully situated in open countryside on the west coast, close to the island's southernmost tip. The medieval church stands amidst the foundations of an earlier Christian settlement established in the sixth century by St Catan, uncle to the local-born St Blane. In a rather peculiar arrangement, the upper graveyard was reserved for the men of the parish while the women were consigned to the lower one.

Four miles up the west coast is the sandy strand of **Scalpsie Bay** while, further on, beyond the village of Straad, lies **St Ninian's Point**, where the ruins of a sixth-century chapel overlook another fine sandy strand and the uninhabited island of **Inchmarnock**, to which, according to tradition, alcoholics were banished in the last century. Bute's finest sandy beach, however, is **Ettrick Bay**, with an excellent tearoom (April–Oct) at the north end. On the road from Ettrick Bay to Rothesay, you can still see traces of the tramlines which used to bring visitors to the beach in its heyday.

Inveraray and around

A classic example of an eighteenth-century planned town, **INVERARAY** was built on the site of a ruined fishing village in 1745 by the third Duke of Argyll, head of the powerful Campbell clan, in order to distance his newly rebuilt castle from the hoi polloi in the town and to establish a commercial and legal centre for the region. Today Inveraray, an absolute set piece of Scottish Georgian architecture, has a truly memorable setting, the brilliant white arches of Front Street reflected in the still waters of Loch Fyne, which separate it from the Cowal peninsula.

The Town

Squeezed onto a promontory some distance from the duke's new castle, there's not much more to Inveraray's "New Town" than its distinctive **Main Street** (set at a right angle to Front Street), flanked by whitewashed terraces, whose window casements are picked out in black. At the top of the street, the road divides to circumnavigate the town's Neoclassical church, originally built in two parts: the southern half served the Gaelic-speaking community, while the northern half – still in use and worth a peek for its period wood-panelled interior – served those who spoke English.

East of the church is **Inveraray Jail** (daily: April–Oct 9.30am–6pm; Nov–March 10am–5pm; £4.50), whose attractive Georgian courthouse and grim prison blocks ceased to function in the 1930s. The jail is now an imaginative and thoroughly enjoyable museum, which graphically recounts prison conditions from medieval times up until the nineteenth century – and even brings it up to date by including a picture of life in Barlinnie Prison. You can also sit in the beautiful semicircular courthouse and listen to the trial of a farmer accused of fraud.

Moored at the town pier is the **Arctic Penguin** (daily: April–Oct 9.30am–6pm; Nov–March 10am–5pm; £3), a handsome, triple-masted schooner built in Dublin in 1911 – it has some nautical knick-knacks and displays on the maritime history of the Clyde, but is only really worth a wander round in wet weather. During the replanning of the town, the fifteenth-century **Inveraray Cross** was moved to its present position on Front Street by the loch; a more interesting cross (from the island of Tiree) can be found in the castle gardens (see below), featuring a crucifixion scene on one side, and a stag-hunting scene on the reverse.

For a panoramic view of the town, castle and loch, you can climb the **Bell Tower** (May–Sept daily 10am–1pm & 2–5pm; £1.50) of All Saints' Church, accessible via the peaceful avenue of trees through the screen arches on Front Street. Built after World War I as a memorial to the fallen Campbells by the tenth Duke of Argyll, the tower contains a ringing peal of ten bells, which are apparently the second heaviest in the world – it takes four hours to ring a complete peal.

Inveraray Castle

A ten-minute walk north of the New Town, the neo-Gothic **Inveraray Castle** (April–June, Sept & Oct Mon–Thurs & Sat 10am–1pm & 2–6pm, Sun 1–6pm; July & Aug Mon–Sat 10am–6pm, Sun 1–6pm; £4) remains the family home of the Duke of Argyll. Built in 1745 by the third duke, it was given a touch of the Loire with the addition of dormer windows and conical roofs in the nineteenth century. Inside, the most startling feature is the armoury hall, whose displays of weaponry – supplied to the Campbells by the British government to put down the Jacobites – rise through several storeys (look out for Rob Roy's rather sad-looking sporran and dirk handle, the traditional dagger worn in Highland dress).

Gracing the extensive **castle grounds** (daily dawn–dusk; free) is the aforementioned Celtic cross from Tiree, and one of three elegant bridges built during the re-landscaping of Inveraray (the other two are on the road from Cairndow). Of the walks marked out in the grounds, the most strenuous takes you to the tower atop **Dùn na Cuaiche** (813ft), from which there's a spectacular view over the castle, town and loch. Back at sea level, in the old stables, the **Combined Operations Museum** (April–Oct Mon–Thurs & Sat 11am–6pm, Sun 1–6pm; £1.25), in the old stables, recalls the intriguing wartime role of Inveraray as a training centre for the D-day landings, during which over half a million troops practised secret amphibious manoeuvres around Loch Fyne.

Around Inveraray

If you've got children in tow, the **Argyll Wildlife Park** (daily 10am–5pm; £3.50), two miles south of Inveraray, along the A83 to Campbeltown, provides some light relief, allowing children to come face to face with Scotland's indigenous fauna, from sika deer to wildcats.

Three miles further on, the **Auchindrain Folk Museum** (April–Sept daily 10am–5pm; £3) is in fact a fascinating old township of around twenty thatched buildings, which give an idea of life here before the Clearances, and before the planning of towns like neighbouring Inveraray. Original furniture, straw on the floors, and hens wandering in and out of the houses, give the place a lived-in feel, and the informative visitor centre has a good bookshop and a tearoom, whose water comes from the same spring that served the original township.

Another four miles down the road is **Crarae Garden** (daily: March–Oct 9am–6pm; Nov–Feb dawn–dusk; £2.50), laid out earlier this century as a "Himalayan ravine" in a deep glen that tumbles down into Loch Fyne. It is this dramatic setting that sets Crarae apart from the innumerable other gardens of Argyll, and provides the scenic backdrop for the gardens, with over 400 rhododendrons, azaleas and wide variety of eucalyptus and conifers. There's also a visitor centre and tearoom open in summer.

Practicalities

Inveraray's **tourist office** is on Front Street (April & mid-Sept to Oct Mon–Sat 9am–5pm, Sun noon–5pm; May & June Mon–Sat 9am–5pm, Sun 11am–5pm; July to mid-Sept daily 9am–6pm; Nov–March Mon–Fri 11am–4pm, Sat & Sun noon–4pm; ☎01499/302063), as is the town's chief **hotel**, the historic and very comfortable *Argyll* (☎01499/302466; ④), formerly the *Great Inn*, where Dr Johnson and Boswell stayed. A cheaper, but equally well-appointed alternative is the Georgian *Fernpoint Hotel* (☎01499/302170; ①), round by the pier; otherwise there's a convenient **B&B** called *Lorona* (☎01499/302258; ①; April–Oct), on Main Street, *Creag Dhubh* (☎01499/302430; ①; March–Nov) is set in a large garden overlooking Loch Fyne, up the Lochgilphead road, or, for a more secluded position, try *Breagha Lodge* (☎01499/302061; ③) by the golf course. Four miles south of the town, try the friendly farm cottages or house of *Kilean House* (☎01499/302474; ①). The **youth hostel** (☎01499/302454; mid-March to Oct) is in a modern building just up Dalmally Road (A819), while the old Royal Navy base, two miles down the A83, is now the excellent, fully equipped *Argyll Caravan Park* (☎01499/302285; April–Oct). The **bar** of the *George Hotel* in the middle of town is the liveliest spot, while for tea and cakes head for *The Poacher*. However, by far the best place to sample Loch Fyne's delicious fresh fish and seafood is the superb, moderately priced restaurant of the *Loch Fyne Oyster Bar* (see p.60), six miles back up the A83 towards Glasgow.

Loch Awe and Taynuilt

Legend has it that **Loch Awe** – at more than 25 miles in length, the longest stretch of fresh water in the country – was created by a witch and inhabited by a monster even more gruesome than the one at Loch Ness. The northwestern shores of the loch are the most peaceful, with gentle hills and the magnificent **Inverliever Forest**, where the Forestry Commission has laid out a series of none-too-strenuous **forest walks** around Dalavich. The most spectacular of these is the hour-long circular walk from Inverinan up to the Royal Engineers' wooden footbridge, which takes you over a pretty waterfall.

Dotted around the north of the loch, where it's joined by the A819 from Inveraray, the A85 from Tyndrum and the railway from Glasgow, are several tiny islands sporting picturesque ruins. On **Inishail** you can see a crumbling thirteenth-century chapel which once served as a burial ground for the MacArthur clan; the ruined castle on **Fraoch Eilean** dates from the same period. Fifteenth-century **Kilchurn Castle**, strategically situated on a rocky spit – once an island – at the head of the loch and once a Campbell stronghold, has been abandoned to the elements since being struck by lightning in the 1760s, and is now one of Argyll's most photogenic lochside ruins.

During the summer you can sail around Kilchurn Castle as part of an hour-long steamboat cruise that sets off from the pier at **LOCHAWE**, right by the village's train station. A mile further along the A85, it's worth pausing at **St Conan's Kirk**, an unusual architectural work fashioned in a sort of home-made Norman/Gothic style. The original church was built in the 1880s, but the version you see now was begun in 1907 by Walter Campbell and completed by his sister Helen. The church contains a fair amount of historical bric-a-brac, from a piece of Robert the Bruce to fragments from Iona Abbey and Eton College, but by far the finest sections are the ambulatory, with its tall, clear windows overlooking Loch Awe, and the dinky lead-roofed cloisters.

Further west, gorged into the giant granite bulk of Ben Cruachan (3695ft), is the underground **Cruachan Power Station** (daily: Easter–June & Sept–Nov 9.30am–5pm; July & Aug 9.30am–6pm; £3), built in 1965. Half-hour guided tours set off every hour from the newly refurbished **visitor centre** by the loch, taking you to a viewing platform above the generating room deep inside the "hollow mountain". Using the water from an artificial loch high up on Ben Cruachan to drive the turbines, the power station can become fully operational in less than two minutes, supplying electricity during surges on the National Grid. Sadly it takes ten percent more electricity to pump the water back up into the artificial loch, so the station only manages to make a profit by buying cheap off-peak power and selling during daytime peak demand. If you're keen to go, make sure you get there before the queues start to form, particularly in summer.

In order to maintain the right level of water in Loch Awe itself, a dam was built at the mouth of the loch, which then had to be fitted with a special lift to transport the salmon – for which the loch is justly famous – upriver to spawn. From the dam, the River Awe squeezes through the mountains via the gloomy rock-walled **Pass of Brander** (which means "ambush" in Gaelic), where Robert the Bruce put to flight the MacDougall clan in 1308, cutting them down as they fought with one another to cross the river and escape.

There are two particularly luxurious **hotels** on the northwestern shores of Loch Awe: the *Taychreggan Hotel* (☎01866/833211; ⑥), an old drovers' inn by the loch, to the southeast of Kilchrenan, and the *Ardanaiseig Hotel* (☎01866/833333; ⑦; closed Jan), a palatial Scottish Baronial pile four miles to the northeast down a dead-end track. Both these hotels have superb, though expensive, restaurants, and the *Ardanaiseig* also has its own glorious gardens (daily 9.30am–dusk), worth visiting even if you're not staying here. Considerably easier to reach is the *Loch Awe Hotel* (☎01838/200261; ⑤; closed Jan), another Scots Baronial hotel, on the busy A85, along the north shore of the loch. The nicest **B&Bs** are on the more peaceful western shores: try the comfortable *Thistle-Doo* (☎01866/833339; ③) at Kilchrenan. Further south, at Dalavich, there are Forestry Commission **chalets** for rent by the loch; you must stay a minimum of three nights, and book through Forest Holidays (☎0131/334 0303). Loch Awe is stocked full of trout, pike and salmon, and there are **boats to rent** (and fishing tackle) from Donald Wilson (☎01866/833256), based at Ardbrecknish, southwest of Cladich on the east shore, though he will deliver boats to any other point on the loch for a fee.

Taynuilt and Loch Etive

TAYNUILT, where the River Awe flows into **Loch Etive**, is a small but sprawling village, best known for its iron-smelting works. To reach this industrial heritage site, follow the signpost off the A85 to **Bonawe Iron Furnace** (April–Sept Mon–Sat 9.30am–6.30pm, Sun 2–6.30pm; £2.50; HS), which was originally founded by Cumbrian ironworkers in 1753. It was clearly cheaper, in those days, to import iron ore from south of the border, rather than transport charcoal to the

Lake District, since several iron furnaces were established in the area, of which Bonawe was the most successful. A whole series of buildings in various states of repair are scattered across the factory site, which employed 600 people at its height, and eventually closed down in 1876.

From the pier beyond the iron furnace, **boat cruises** (May–Sept Mon–Fri 10.30am & 2pm, Sat & Sun 2pm; April & early Oct daily 2pm; £8) explore the otherwise inaccessible reaches of Loch Etive; phone Loch Etive Cruises (☎01866/822430) for more details. Before you reach Taynuilt from Loch Awe, a sign to the right invites you to visit the **Inverawe Fisheries and Smokery** (March–Dec daily 8am–dusk), where you can buy traditionally smoked local fish and mussels, learn how to fly-fish, check out the exhibition on traditional smoking techniques, or go for a stroll down to nearby Loch Etive with your picnic.

Oban and around

The solidly Victorian resort of **OBAN** enjoys a superb setting – the island of Kerrera providing its bay with a natural shelter – distinguished by a bizarre granite amphitheatre, dramatically lit at night, on the hilltop above the town. Despite a population of just 8500, it's by far the largest port in northwest Scotland, the second-largest town in Argyll, and the main departure point for ferries to the Hebrides. If you arrive late, or are catching an early boat, you may have to spend the night here (there's no real need otherwise); if you're staying elsewhere, it's a useful base for wet-weather activities and shopping, although it does get uncomfortably crowded in the summer.

Oban lies at the centre of the coastal region known as Lorn, named after the Irish Celt Loarn, who, along with his brothers Fergus and Oengus, settled here around 500 AD. Given the number of tourists that pass through or stay in the area, it's hardly surprising that a few out-and-out tourist attractions have developed, which can be handy to know about if it's raining and/or you have children with you. The mainland is very picturesque, although its beauty is no secret – to escape the crowds, head off and explore the islands, like **Lismore** or **Kerrera**, just offshore.

Arrival, information and accommodation

Arriving in Oban **by car** can be a bit of a nightmare in the summer. If you're heading straight for the ferry, either make sure you leave an extra hour to allow for sitting in the tailbacks, which can stretch for more than a mile back along the A85, or try and approach the town from the south along the A816. If you're just coming in to town to look around, use one of the park-and-ride or supermarket car parks. The CalMac **ferry terminal** (☎01631/566688) for the islands is on Railway Pier, is a stone's throw from the train station (☎01631/563083), which is itself adjacent to the bus stops on Station Square. The **tourist office** (April Mon–Fri 9am–5pm, Sat & Sun noon–5pm; May to mid-June Mon–Sat 9am–5.30pm, Sun 10am–5pm; mid- to late June, early Sept Mon–Sat 9am–6.30pm, Sun 10am–5pm; July & Aug Mon–Sat 9am–9pm, Sun 9am–7pm; late Sept to Oct Mon–Sat 9am–5.30pm, Sun 10am–4pm; Nov–March Mon–Fri 9.30am–5pm, Sat & Sun noon–4pm; ☎01631/563122) is housed in a converted church on Argyll Square, and has a visually attractive, interactive exhibition where the altar used to be, useful for whiling away half an hour in wet weather.

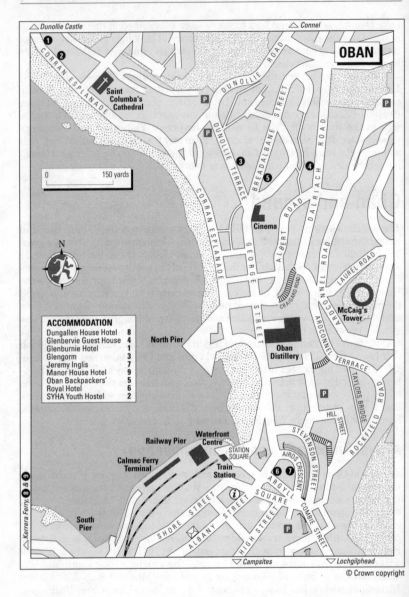

△ Dunollie Castle   △ Connel

OBAN

Saint Columba's Cathedral

DUNOLLIE ROAD

BREADALBANE STREET

DALRIACH ROAD

DUNOLLIE TERRACE

CORRAN ESPLANADE

Cinema

GEORGE STREET

ALBERT ROAD

ARDCONNEL ROAD

LAUREL ROAD

McCaig's Tower

CRAIGARD ROAD

ARDCONNEL TERRRACE

TAYLORS BRIDGE

0   150 yards

N

ACCOMMODATION

Dungallen House Hotel	8
Glenbervie Guest House	4
Glenburnie Hotel	1
Glengorm	3
Jeremy Inglis	7
Manor House Hotel	9
Oban Backpackers'	5
Royal Hotel	6
SYHA Youth Hostel	2

North Pier

Oban Distillery

ROCKFIELD ROAD

HILL STREET

STEVENSON STREET

Railway Pier

Waterfront Centre

STATION SQUARE

Calmac Ferry Terminal

Train Station

AIROS CRESCENT

ARGYLL SQUARE

COMBIE STREET

◁ Kerrera Ferry, 8 & 9

South Pier

SHORE STREET

ALBANY STREET

HIGH STREET

▽ Campsites   ▽ Lochgilphead

© Crown copyright

Oban is positively heaving with **hotels** and **B&Bs**, most of them very reasonably priced and many of them on or near the quayside. Although it's easy enough to search out a vacancy, in high season it might be wise to pay the small fee charged by the tourist office for finding you a room. If you're catching the 6am ferry to Coll or Tiree, you might want to consider staying overnight in one of the two- or four-bed berths on board the ferry, a cheaper option than a local B&B and one which allows you a longer lie-in – you can book your berth from any CalMac office, as long as you do so before 6pm on the evening before departure.

Hotels and B&Bs

Dungallen House Hotel, Gallanach Road (☎01631/563799). Solid Victorian vila hotel set in its own woodland grounds, hidden away on the Gallanach Road, with great views across the Sound of Kerrera. ⑤. Closed Feb & Nov.

Glenbervie Guest House, Dalriach Road (☎01631/564770). Superior Victorian guest house set slightly above the town on a quiet road heaving with accommodation. ①.

Glenburnie Hotel, Corran Esplanade (☎01631/562089, *glenburnie8@hotmail.com*). Efficiently run medium-sized Victorian hotel on the quieter section of the Esplanade, beyond the Cathedral. ③. April–Oct.

Glengorm, Dunollie Road (☎01631/565361). If you want a cheap B&B in the centre of town, this is as good a bet as any, on a busy street replete with similarly priced B&Bs. ①. March–Nov.

Manor House Hotel, Gallanach Road (☎01631/562087). Beautiful eighteenth-century manor house, peacefully located by the shores of the Sound of Kerrera, with a topnotch restaurant attached. ④. Closed Jan.

Royal Hotel, Argyll Square (☎01631/563021). The best of Oban's big central hotels, the *Royal* is pleasantly plush and has been recently refurbished; all rooms are en suite. ⑤.

Hostels and campsites

Jeremy Inglis, 21 Airds Crescent (☎01631/565065 or 563064). Halfway between a hostel and a B&B, with an eccentric proprietor who also runs *McTavish's Kitchens*. Shared rooms, doubles or family rooms available, plus kitchen facilities; breakfast included.

Oban Backpackers, Breadalbane Street (☎01631/562107, *hostels@scotlands-top-hostels.com*). Friendliest, cheapest and most central of Oban's hostels, with a pool table, real fire and a communal kitchen.

Oban Caravan & Camping Park, Gallanachmore Farm, Gallanach Road (☎01631/566425). Bigger of the two sites, with caravans to rent, plus ten pitches, situated two miles southwest of Oban along the Gallanach Road beside the Sound of Kerrera. Open April to mid-Oct.

Oban Divers Caravan Park, Glenshellach Road (☎01631/562755). A mile and a half south of the ferry terminal. Kids' playground, but no dogs allowed. Open March–Nov.

SYHA Youth Hostel, Corran Esplanade (☎01631/562025, *reservations@syha.org.uk*). Converted Victorian house, with the purpose-built Oban Lodge annexe behind, both a fair trek from the ferry terminal along the Corran Esplanade, just beyond the Catholic Cathedral. Breakfast included.

The Town

The only truly remarkable sight in Oban is the town's landmark, **McCaig's Folly**, a stiff ten-minute climb from the quayside. Built in imitation of Rome's Colosseum, it was the brainchild of a local businessman a century ago, who had the twin aims of alleviating off-season unemployment among the local stonemasons and creating a museum, art gallery and chapel. Originally, the plan was to add a 95-foot central tower, but work never progressed further than the exterior granite walls before McCaig died. In his will, McCaig gave instructions for the lancet windows to be filled with bronze statues of the family, though no such work was ever undertaken. Instead, the folly has been turned into a sort of walled garden, and simply provides a wonderful seaward panorama, particularly at sunset.

Down in the centre of town, you can pass a few hours admiring the boats in the harbour and looking out for scavenging seals in the bay. If the weather's bad, you can shelter in the ugly **Waterfront Centre**, beside the equally cheerless new train station (the Victorian one was demolished in 1988). Caithness Glass have a shop outlet and small exhibition in the centre, though you can no longer watch glass-blowing demonstrations. Another option is to take a forty-minute guided tour of the **Oban Distillery** (Mon–Fri 9.30am–5pm; Easter–Oct also Sat; July–Sept Sat until 8.30pm; £3), in the centre of town off George Street, which ends with a dram of whisky (and a refund of the admission fee if you buy a bottle).

A pleasant half-hour evening stroll can be had by walking north along the Corran Esplanade, past the modern, Roman Catholic **Cathedral of St Columba** – built in the 1920s by Sir Giles Gilbert Scott, architect of Battersea Power Station – to the rocky ruins of **Dunollie Castle**, a MacDougall stronghold on a very ancient site, successfully defended by the laird's Jacobite wife during the 1715 uprising but abandoned after 1745.

Anyone looking for the **World in Miniature** (April–Oct daily 10am–6pm; £2.50), which used to reside on Oban's North Pier, now has to travel seven miles south along the A816 to view the museum's assortment of minute "dolls' house" rooms. However, folks with kids would probably be better off heading just a couple of miles out of Oban, east along Glencruitten Road, to the **Oban Rare Breeds Farm Park** (daily: late March to Oct 10am–5.30pm; mid-June to Aug 10am–7.30pm; £4), which displays rare but indigenous species of deer, cattle, sheep and so forth – they can meet the baby animals at the children's corner.

A host of private boat operators can be found around the harbour, on the North, South and Railway piers: their **trips and tours** – to Mull, Iona, Staffa, Seal Island and the Treshnish Isles – are worth considering, particularly if you're pushed for time, or have no transport. Gordon Grant Tours (☎01681/700338), on Oban's Railway Pier, offers a whole range of trips, including an entire day's cruise around the Treshnish Isles. Other operators include the Mull Experience (May–Sept; ☎01680/812421), who give you a day-trip taking in Mull Rail, plus Torosay and Duart castles. Those with a bit more stamina can take one of the circular day tours from Oban offered by Bowman's, 3 Stafford St (☎01631/563221), either taking in Iona and a boat trip to Staffa, or Tobermory and a bit of Mull scenery. **Boat rental** is available from Borro Boats, on the Gallanach Road (☎01631/563292), and you can **rent bikes** from Oban Cycles, 9 Craigard Rd (☎01631/566996).

Eating, drinking and nightlife

Oban doesn't hold a lot of treats for visitors or locals. If you're only here to catch a ferry, you might as well grab a quick bite to eat at the excellent **takeaway** seafood counter by the side of the CalMac terminal. Venturing further into town, you can't miss *McTavish's Kitchens*, on George Street, a local institution serving unexceptional soups, burgers, grills and sandwiches. More promising is the nearby *Kitchen Garden* deli's mezzanine **café**, or *F'Eats*, a new place on John Street offering delicious toasted panini and good cappuccino. Oban's best **restaurant** is, without doubt, *The Gathering* (☎01631/565421; Easter–Christmas daily from 5pm) on Breadalbane Street, which excels in, among other things, moderately expensive local fish and seafood. The inexpensive *Box Tree* restaurant, on George

Street, is your next best bet, with a wide choice of veggie dishes and seafood on offer. And, of course, there's always fish and chips: try *Onorio's*, 86 George St (closed Sun).

Oban's only half-decent **pub** is the *Oban Inn* opposite the North Pier, with a classic dark-wood-flagstone-and-brass bar downstairs and lounge bar with stained glass upstairs. The town's nightlife doesn't bear thinking about (though you can read all about it in the *Oban Times*). It's worth noting, however, that Oban is one of the few places in Argyll with a **cinema**, confusingly known as The Highland Theatre (☎01631/562444), at the north end of George Street. You should be able to catch some **live music** at the weekend at *O'Donnell's* Irish pub, underneath *The Gathering*, or in the bar of the *Royal Hotel*, on Argyll Square, and occasionally (concert-style) at the Corran Halls, along the Esplanade. The annual **Argyllshire Gathering** takes place on the last weekend in August, featuring piping competitions and Highland Games.

Isle of Kerrera

One of the best places to escape from the crowds that plague Oban is the low-lying island of **Kerrera**, which shelters Oban Bay from the worst of the westerly winds. Measuring just five miles by two, the island is easily explored on foot, and gives panoramic views from its highest point, Càrn Breugach (620ft), over to Mull, the Slate Islands, Lismore, Jura and beyond.

The ferry lands by the lobster factory, roughly halfway down the east coast, at the north end of **Horseshoe Bay**, where King Alexander II died in 1249. If the weather's fine and you feel like lazing by the sea, head for the island's finest sandy beach, **Slatrach Bay**, on the west coast, one mile northwest of the ferry jetty. Otherwise, the most rewarding trail is down to **Gylen Castle**, a clifftop ruin on the south coast, built in 1582 by the MacDougalls and burnt to the ground by the Covenanter General Leslie in 1647. You can head back to the ferry via the Drove Road, where cattle from Mull and other islands were once herded to be swum across the sound to the market in Oban.

The passenger and bicycle **ferry** departs daily from the mainland two miles down the Gallanach road from Oban (phone ☎01631/563665 for the latest schedule; £3 return). Kerrera has a total population of fewer than thirty – and no shop – so if you're day-tripping make sure you bring enough supplies with you. Alternatively, you can eat at the *Kerrera Teagarden* (daily 10am–5pm), in Lower Gylen, which serves home-made, often organic, veggie snacks. You can also stay at Lower Gylen in the *Kerrera Bothy*, a converted eighteenth-century stable building (☎01631/570223, *email@landlign.demon.co.uk*; April–Oct) – ring ahead if you need transport from the ferry.

Dunstaffnage Castle and Connel

Just beyond the northern satellite suburbs of Oban, on a strategic promontory overlooking the important water crossroads at the mouth of Loch Etive, lie the ruins of **Dunstaffnage Castle** (April–Sept daily 9.30am–6.30pm; Oct–March Mon–Wed, Sat & Sun 9am–4pm, Thurs; £1.80; HS). Originally built as a thirteenth-century MacDougall fort, the castle was captured by Robert the Bruce in 1309, and remained in royal hands until it was handed over to the Campbells in 1470. Garrisoned by government forces during the 1745 rebellion, it served as a temporary prison for Flora MacDonald, and was eventually destroyed by fire in 1810. The approach, through a housing estate, is a bit unsettling, but, with the castle's substantial curtain wall battlements partially intact, Dunstaffnage makes for a fun and safe place to explore, and gives great views across to Lismore and Morvern.

A couple of miles further up the A85, at **CONNEL**, you can't fail to admire the majestic steel cantilever **Connel Bridge**, built in 1903 to take the old branch railway line across the sea cataract at the mouth of Loch Etive, north to Fort William. The name "Connel" comes from the Gaelic *conghail* (tumultuous flood), which refers to the rapids, clearly visible from the bridge, and caused by the water at low ebb rushing over a ledge of rock between the two shores of the loch. The A828 now crosses Connel Bridge to take you onto Benderloch (see below).

Benderloch

On the north side of the Connel Bridge lies the hammerhead peninsula of **Benderloch** (from *beinn eadar da loch*, "hill between two lochs"), on whose northern shores you'll find **Barcaldine Castle** (Easter & late May to Sept daily 11am–5.30pm; £3.25), an early seventeenth-century Campbell tower house. The house was abandoned by the Campbells in favour of Barcaldine House, three miles northeast, and eventually sold in 1842. Bought back by the family as a ruin in 1896 and restored, it is now occupied and run by the current heir, London-born and bred Roderick, and his wife Caroline. There are no real treasures here, but the castle has a pleasant, lived-in feel, and is fun to explore, with dungeons and hidden staircases. To help balance the books, the Campbells also offer **B&B** at the castle (☎01631/720598; ③). Those with rather larger budgets might prefer to stay at Argyll's most exclusive hotel, the *Isle of Eriska*, a luxury, turreted, Scottish Baronial pile, run by the Buchanan-Smiths on their own 300-acre island, off the northern point of Benderloch (☎01631/720371, *office@eriska-hotel.co.uk*; ⑨; March–Dec), with an acclaimed and very expensive dining room (open to non-residents in the evening).

Since the weather in this part of Scotland can be bad at almost any time of the year, it's as well to know about the **Oban Sea Life Centre** (April–June daily 9am–6pm; July & Aug daily 9am–7pm; call ☎01631/720386 for winter opening times; £5.50), which is, in actual fact, to be found on the A828, along the southern shores of Loch Creran. Here you can see locally caught sea creatures at close quarters – look out for the octopus and stingray, and the wonderful "herring ring" – before they are returned to the sea at the end of the season. The centre's self-service *Shoreline* restaurant features a small oyster bar.

Appin

With the new Creagan Bridge in place – the old wrought-iron railway bridge sadly having been demolished – there's no need to circumnavigate Loch Creran in order to reach the district of **Appin**, best known as the setting for Robert Louis Stevenson's *Kidnapped*, a fictionalized account of the "Appin Murder" of 1752, when Colin Campbell was shot in the back, allegedly by one of the disenfranchised Stewart clan. However, the new bridge also means than the eastern reaches of the loch, and **Glen Creran** itself, are now even more peaceful and secluded. The lovely dead-end single-track road through the woods to Fasnacloich shelters several wonderful B&B retreats such as *Lochside Cottage* (☎01631/730216; ②), a large white house with a garden sloping down to a freshwater loch. At the end of the road there's a seven-mile forest walk over to Ballachulish (see p.194).

The name "Appin" derives from the Gaelic *abthaine*, meaning "Lands belonging to the Abbey", in this case the one on the island of Lismore (see below), which is linked to the peninsula by passenger ferry from **PORT APPIN**, a pretty little fishing village at the westernmost tip of the peninsula. Overlooking a host of tiny little islands, dotted around Loch Linnhe, with Lismore and the mountains Morvern and Mull in the background, this is, without doubt, one of Argyll's most picturesque spots. The *Pierhouse Hotel* (☎01631/730302; ⑦), nicely situated right by the ferry, has a popular bar, and an expensive, but excellent and very popular seafood restaurant (prices are slightly lower at lunchtimes). Alternatively, you could eat at the *Pierhouse*, but stay in the friendly *Rhugarbh Croft* (☎01631/730309; ②), up the road in North Shian, and enjoy home-made bread and free-range eggs for breakfast.

One of Argyll's most romantic ruined castles, the much-photographed **Castle Stalker**, occupies a tiny rock island to the north of Port Appin. Built by the Stewarts of Appin in the sixteenth century and gifted to King James IV as a hunting lodge, it inevitably fell into the hands of the Campbells after 1745. The current owners open the castle to the public for a very short period only each year; ring ☎01631/730234 or ask at Oban tourist office for this year's opening times. If you're looking for **outdoor pursuits** in Appin, head for the Linnhe Marine Water Sports Centre (☎01631/730401; May–Sept) in Lettershuna (just north of Castle Stalker), which rents out boats of all shapes and sizes, offers sailing and windsurfing lessons, not to mention waterskiing, clay-pigeon shooting and even pony trekking.

Isle of Lismore

Lying in the middle of Loch Linnhe, to the north of Oban, and barely rising above a hillock, the narrow island of **Lismore** offers wonderful gentle walking or cycling opportunities, with unrivalled views, in fine weather, across to the mountains of Morvern, Lochaber and Mull. Legend has it that SS Columba and Moluag both fancied the skinny island as a missionary base, but as they raced towards it Moluag cut off his finger and threw it ashore ahead of Columba, claiming the land for himself. Of Moluag's sixth-century foundation nothing remains, but from 1236 until 1507 the island served as the seat of the Bishop of Argyll. It was a judicious choice, as Lismore is undoubtedly one of the most fertile of the Inner Hebrides – its name, coined by Moluag himself, derives from the Gaelic *lios mór*, meaning "great garden" – and at one time it supported nearly 1400 inhabitants; the population today is around a tenth of that figure.

The ferry from Oban lands at **ACHNACROISH**, roughly halfway along the eastern coastline. To get to grips with the history of the island and its Gaelic culture (and have a cup of tea), head inland until you catch the signs for the nearby **Comann Eachdraidh Lios Mór**, or Lismore Historical Society (Easter & May–Sept Mon–Sat 10am–5pm; £1). The island post office and shop are along the main road between Achnacroish and **CLACHAN**, a couple of miles northeast, where the diminutive, whitewashed former **Cathedral of St Moluag** stands. All that remains of the fourteenth-century cathedral is the choir, which was reduced in height and converted into the parish church in 1749; inside you can see a few

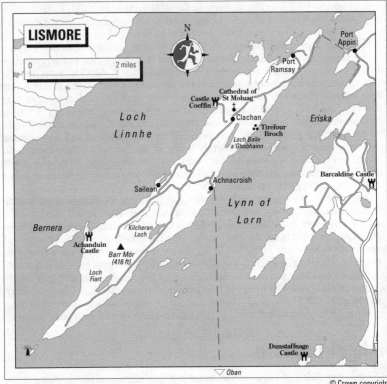

© Crown copyright

of the original seats for the upper clergy, a stone basin in the south wall, and several medieval doorways. Due east of the church – head north up the road and take the turning signposted on the right – the circular **Tirefour Broch**, over two thousand years old, occupies a commanding position and boasts walls almost ten feet thick in places. West of Clachan are the much more recent ruins of **Castle Coeffin**, a twelfth-century MacDougall fortress once believed to have been haunted by the ghost of Beothail, sister of the Norse prince Caiffen. A few other places worth exploring are **Sailean**, an abandoned quarry village further south along the west coast, with its disused kilns and cottages; the ruins of **Achanduin Castle**, in the southwest, where the bishops are thought to have resided; and Barr Mór (416ft), the island's highest point.

Two **ferries** serve Lismore: a small CalMac car ferry from Oban to Achnacroish (Mon–Sat 2–4 daily; 50min), and a shorter passenger- and bicycle-only crossing from Port Appin to the island's north point (daily every 2hr; 5min). There's a **postbus** round the island (Mon–Sat; pick up a timetable from Oban tourist office). **Accommodation** on the island is limited to a handful of B&Bs: try the budget B&B at *Clachan Farm* (☎0631/760271; ①), or the *Schoolhouse* (☎01631/760262; ①), north of Clachan, which also serves evening meals. **Bike rental** is available from Island Bike Hire (☎01631/760213) for around £10 a day.

Isle of Mull

The second largest of the Inner Hebrides, **Mull** is by far the most accessible: just forty minutes from Oban by ferry. As so often, first impressions largely depend on the weather – it is the wettest of the Hebrides (and that's saying something) – for without the sun the large tracts of moorland, particularly around the island's highest peak, Ben More (3196ft), can appear bleak and unwelcoming. There are, however, areas of more gentle pastoral scenery around **Dervaig** in the north and **Salen** on the east coast, and the indented west coast varies from the sandy beaches around **Calgary** to the cliffs of Loch na Keal. The most common mistake is to try and "do" the island in a day or two: flogging up the main road to the picturesque capital of **Tobermory**, then covering the fifty-odd miles between there and Fionnphort, in order to visit **Iona**. Mull is a place that will grow on you only if you have the time and patience to explore.

Historically, crofting, whisky distilling and fishing supported the islanders (*Muileachs*), but the population – which peaked at 10,000 – decreased dramatically in the nineteenth century due to the Clearances and the 1846 potato famine. On Mull, it is a trend that has been reversed, mostly due to the large influx of settlers from elsewhere in the country which has brought the current population up to over 2500. One of the main reasons for this resurgence is, of course, tourism –

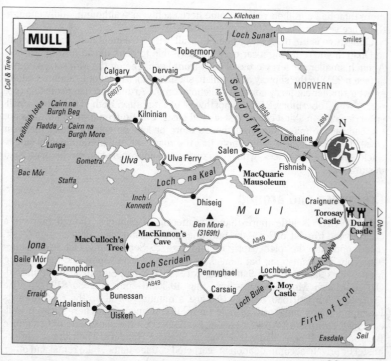

© Crown copyright

TRIPS AND TOURS AROUND MULL

Among the Hebrides, Mull is perhaps second only to Skye when it comes to the number of **coach tours** that clog up the island's single-track roads. Exploring the place by yourself is, frankly, the most enjoyable way to see it, though if you fancy visiting one of the offshore islands or seeing some wildlife, but don't quite know how to go about it, there's plenty of choice. If you're based in Oban and time is limited, the Mull Experience (see p.74) gives you a day-trip taking in Mull Rail, plus Torosay and Duart castles for around £16, or there's Bowman's (see p.74), who offer circular day tours taking in either Iona and a boat trip to Staffa or Tobermory and a bit of Mull scenery, from £16 to £34.

On Mull itself, there's a huge choice of land-based, **wildlife tours**, many heading off in pursuit of the island's two most elusive creatures, the otter and the golden eagle: try Explore Mull Wildlife, based in Dervaig (see p.84), who offer half- or full days from £15 to £20; or Island Encounter (☎01680/300441), based in Aros, near Salen, who do full days at around £22. Various boat trips to Staffa and the Treshnish Isle are detailed on p.87, but there are also two very good operators who offer wildlife trips on the sea, usually combining whale- and dolphin-watching, with a bit of bird- and seal-watching: Inter-Island Cruises, based in Dervaig (see p.84), go to Staffa and the Treshnish Isles; and Sea Life Surveys, based in the offices of the Hebridean Whale and Dolphin Trust (see p.82) in Tobermory. Sea outings start at around £35.

---

more than half a million visitors come here each year – although, oddly enough, there are very few large hotels or campsites.

Craignure is the main entry point to Mull, with a frequent daily **car ferry** link to Oban; if you're taking a car over, it's advisable to book ahead for this service. A much smaller car ferry crosses daily from Lochaline on the Morvern peninsula (see p.221) to the slipway at Fishnish, six miles northwest of Craignure; another even smaller car ferry connects Kilchoan on the Ardnamurchan peninsula (see p.222) with Tobermory, 24 miles northwest of Craignure. Both of these two smaller ferries run on a first-come, first-served basis. **Public transport** on Mull is not too bad on the main A849, but there's more or less no service along the west coast. Those with **cars** should note that the roads are still predominantly single-track, with passing places, which can cause serious congestion on the main road in summer.

Craignure and around

CRAIGNURE is little more than a scattering of cottages, though there is a CalMac and **tourist office** – the only one on the island open all year round – situated opposite the pier (April to mid-June & Sept to mid-Oct Mon–Thurs 9am–7pm, Fri 9am–5pm, Sat 9am–6.30pm, Sun 10.30am–5pm; mid-June to Aug Mon–Thurs 9am–7pm, Fri 9am–5pm, Sat 9am–8.15pm, Sun 10.30am–7pm; mid-Oct to March Mon–Sat 9am–5pm, Sun 10.30am–5pm; ☎01680/812377). The *Craignure Inn* (☎01680/812305; ③), just a minute's stroll up the road towards Fionnphort, is a snug **pub** to hole up in, if you need one. There's also a well-equipped **campsite** (☎01680/812496; April–Oct) on the south side of Craignure Bay, behind the new village hall, run by Sheiling Holidays. The campsite offers hostel or private accommodation in "carpeted cottage tents", bike rental and other outdoor activities. The best **guest house** in the area, *Old Mill Cottage* (☎01680/812442; ③), is three miles south in Lochdon; it also has a small and highly recommended restaurant attached.

Bus connections with Fionnphort (Mon–Sat 3–4 daily, Sun 1 daily; 1hr 10min) and Tobermory (Mon–Sat 4–5 daily, Sun 3 daily; 50min) are infrequent, so check with Oban tourist office before you catch the ferry. The other method of transport available at Craignure is the diminutive, narrow-gauge Mull & West Highland Railway, commonly known as **Mull Rail** (Easter to mid-Oct; phone ☎01680/812494 for full details; £3.30 return), the only working railway in the Scottish Islands. The Craignure station is situated beyond the Sheiling Holidays campsite, and the line stretches southeast for about a mile and a half to Torosay Castle (see below). If you prefer to take the train one-way only, it's an easy half-hour walk along the coast. The company use diesel and steam locomotives, so ring ahead if you want to be sure of a steam-driven train.

Torosay and Duart castles

Two castles lie immediately southeast of Craignure. The first, **Torosay Castle** (Easter to mid-Oct daily 10.30am–5pm; £4.50), is a full-blown Scottish Baronial creation. The house itself is stuffed with memorabilia relating to the present owners, the Guthries, all of it amusingly captioned but of no great import, with the possible exception of the belongings of the late David Guthrie-James, who was something of an adventurer and a POW in Colditz. Torosay's real highlight, however, is the magnificent **gardens** (open all year daily 10.30am–5.30pm; gardens only £3.50) with their avenue of eighteenth-century Venetian statues, Japanese section, and views over to neighbouring Duart. If the admission price puts you off Torosay, head for the silversmiths or the workshop of the **Mull Weavers** (Mon–Sat 9am–5pm; April–Oct also Sun; free), in the castle grounds, where you can watch the old-fashioned dobby loom in the workshop weave tartan.

Lacking the gardens, but on a picturesque spit of rock a couple of miles east of Torosay, **Duart Castle** (May to mid-Oct daily 10.30am–6pm; £3.50) is clearly visible from the Oban–Craignure ferry. Headquarters of the once-powerful MacLean clan from the thirteenth century, it was burnt down by the Campbells and confiscated after the 1745 rebellion. Finally in 1911, the 26th clan chief, Fitzroy MacLean (1835–1936) – not to be confused with the Scottish writer of the same name – managed to buy it back and restore it. You can peek at the dungeons, climb up to the ramparts, study the family photos, and learn about the world scout movement – the 27th clan chief became Chief Scout in 1959. After your visit, you can enjoy home-made cakes and tea at the castle's excellent tearoom.

Tobermory

Mull's chief town, **TOBERMORY**, is easily the most attractive fishing port on the west coast of Scotland, its clusters of brightly coloured houses and boats sheltering in a bay backed by a steep bluff. Founded in 1788 by the British Society for Encouraging Fisheries, it never really took off as a fishing port and only survived due to the steady influx of crofters evicted from other parts of the island during the Clearances. With a population of more than 700, it is, without doubt, the capital of Mull, and if you're staying any length of time on the island you're bound to end up here, not least because it has a Womble named after it.

Information and accommodation

The **tourist office** (April & mid-Sept to Oct Mon–Sat 9am–5pm, Sun 10.30am–5pm; May & June daily 9am–5pm; July to mid-Sept daily 9am–6pm; ☎01688/302182) is in the same building as the CalMac ticket office at the far end of Main Street. If you want to rent a **bike**, head for the youth hostel (see below), or Tom-a'Mhuillin (☎01688/302164) on the Salen road. The island's only permanent **bank**, the Clydesdale, is on Main Street (a mobile one tours the island; ask at the tourist office for details).

The tourist office can book you into a **B&B** for a small fee – not a bad idea in high season, when the places on Main Street tend to get booked up fast, and the rest are a stiff climb from the harbour. The small, friendly **SYHA hostel** is on Main Street (☎01688/302481; late Feb to Oct) and has laundry facilities. The nearest **campsite** is *Newdale* (☎01688/302306; April–Nov), nicely situated one and a half miles outside Tobermory on the B8073 to Dervaig.

Baliscate Guest House, Salen Road (☎01688/302495). Imposing whitewashed Victorian guest house, with a large garden, set back from the road to Salen, just outside Tobermory. ②.

Failte Guest House, Main Street (☎01688/302495). Very comfortably and pleasantly furnished en-suite rooms, some of which have views out over the harbour. ②. Open March–Oct.

Glengorm Castle, near Tobermory (☎01688/302321). Rambling Baronial mansion in a superb, secluded setting, four miles northwest of Tobermory, overlooking the sea. Guests get use of the castle's huge public rooms; self-catering cottages are available, too. ⑥.

Harbour Guest House, Main Street (☎01688/302209). Spacious, clean rooms, some great views and big breakfasts. ①.

Highland Cottage, Breadalbane Street (☎01688/302030). Superior guest house, plushly furnished, fully en suite and boasting excellent home-cooking. ⑤.

Western Isles Hotel (☎01688/302012, *wihotel@aol.com*). Tobermory's most distinguished hotel, a grandiose Scottish Baronial pile high above the harbour, with terrific views. ⑤.

The Town

The harbour – known as **Main Street** – is one long parade of multicoloured hotels, guest houses, restaurants and shops, and you could happily spend an hour or so pottering around: Mull Pottery and the Mull Silver Company are both worth a browse, as is The Gallery, a converted church more of interest for its architecture than the tartan and shortbread on sale. One of Tobermory's endearing features is the incessant chiming of its diminutive **Clock Tower**, erected by the author Isabella Bird in 1905 in memory of her sister, who died of typhoid on the island in 1880. Close by is a polychrome watery cherub, donated by the local water-supply contractors in 1883.

A recent arrival on Main Street is the **Hebridean Whale and Dolphin Trust** (April–Oct Mon–Fri 10am–6pm, Sat & Sun 11am–5pm; Nov–March Mon–Fri 11am–5pm; free), run by a welcoming bunch of enthusiasts. The small office has lots of information on how to identify marine mammals, and on recent sightings. They're very child-friendly, too, and will keep kids amused for an hour or so with computer marine games, word searches and a bit of artwork. Sea Life Surveys (☎01688/302787), who offer a variety of whale- and dolphin-watching **tours**, are run from the same office.

Another good wet weather retreat is the **Mull Museum** (Easter to mid-Oct Mon–Fri 10.30am–4pm, Sat 10am–1pm; £1), further along Main Street, which packs in a great deal of information and artefacts (including a few objects salvaged

THE TOBERMORY TREASURE

The most dramatic event in Tobermory's history was in 1588, when a ship from **the Spanish Armada** sank in mysterious circumstances while having repairs done to its sails and rigging in the town harbour. The story goes that one of the MacLeans of Duart was taken prisoner, but when the ship weighed anchor he made his way to the powder magazine and blew it up. However, several versions of the story exist, and even the identity of the ship has been hotly disputed: for many years it was thought to be the treasure-laden Spanish galleon *Almirante di Florencia*, but it now seems more likely that it was the rather more prosaic troop-carrier *San Juan de Sicilia*. Nevertheless, the possibility of precious sunken booty at the bottom of Tobermory harbour has fired the greed of numerous lairds and kings – in the 1950s Royal Navy divers were engaged by the Duke of Argyll in the seemingly futile activity of diving for treasure, and in 1982 another unsuccessful attempt was made.

from the *San Juan*) in one tiny room. Alternatively, there's the minuscule **Tobermory Distillery** (Easter–Oct Mon–Fri 10.30am–4pm; £2.50) at the south end of the bay, founded in 1795 but closed down three times since then. Today, it's back in business and offers a guided tour (every 30min), rounded off with a tasting.

A stiff climb up Back Brae will bring you to the island's new arts centre, **An Tobar** (Tues–Sat 10am–4pm; free), housed in a converted Victorian schoolhouse. The centre hosts exhibitions, a variety of live events, and contains a café with comfy sofas set before a real fire. The rest of the upper town is laid out on a classic grid-plan, and merits a stroll, if only for the great views over the bay.

Eating and drinking

Main Street is heaving with **places to eat**. You can get inexpensive fry-ups and fish and chips at *Gannets* or huge bar meals in the lounge bar at the *Mishnish*. For more imaginative local seafood and meat dishes, however, you need to go to *Back Brae* (evenings only), which does filling, moderately expensive set menus, or to the *Western Isles Hotel*, which serves superior bar food in the conservatory overlooking the Sound of Mull, as well as more expensive à la carte dishes in the dining room. Fresh fish and seafood is available from the Tobermory Fish Mart shop, on Main Street, and would do for **picnic** fodder, supplemented, perhaps, by bread and goodies from the excellent Island Bakery, also on the harbourfront.

WALKS AROUND TOBERMORY

There are a couple of none-too-strenuous **walks** from Tobermory, which will transport you in a matter of minutes into the Scottish countryside. The first is an hour-long coastal walk to the **lighthouse** (a mile to the north of town) and back. The path begins just behind the tourist office, and takes you through mixed woodland, some 50ft above the sea, before descending to the shore. The second, also an hour long, takes you in the opposite direction, starting in the car park by the distillery and heading southeast along the coast to **Aros Park**, the former grounds of the now demolished Aros House, currently owned by the Forestry Commission and basically a municipal park. The rhododendrons are spectacular in early summer, as are the park's two impressive waterfalls, especially after a few days' rain.

If you want to know what there is in the way of **entertainment** in Tobermory (or anywhere else on Mull), be sure to pick up the free monthly newsletter *Round & About*, and/or buy a copy of *Am Muileach*, the monthly island newspaper. The lively bar of the *Mishnish Hotel* has been the most popular local drinking hole for many years, and features live music at the weekend, It's also the focus of Mull's annual **Traditional Music Festival**, a feast of Gaelic folk music held on the last weekend in April. Unfortunately, the *Mishnish* lost much of its character (and some of its custom) after a recent facelift, after competition arrived in the shape of *MacGochan's*, a purpose-built, though pleasant enough, pub, which also offers occasional live music, on the opposite side of the harbour near the distillery. Mull's other major musical event, after the folk festival, is the annual **Mendelssohn on Mull Festival**, held over ten days in early July, which commemorates the composer's visit here in 1829.

Dervaig and Calgary

The gently undulating countryside west of Tobermory, beyond the freshwater Mishnish lochs, provides some of the most beguiling scenery on the island. Added to this, the road out west, the B8073, is exceptionally dramatic, with fiendish switchbacks much appreciated during the annual Mull Rally, which takes place each October.

The only village of any size is **DERVAIG**, which nestles beside narrow Loch Chumhainn, just eight miles southwest of Tobermory, distinguished by its unusual pencil-shaped church spire and dinky whitewashed cottages set in twos along its main street. Dervaig is best known as the home of **Mull Theatre**, one of the smallest professional theatres in the world, which puts on an adventurous season of plays adapted for a handful of resident actors (April–Sept; booking recommended ☎01688/400245). The theatre lies within the grounds of the Victorian *Druimard Country House* (☎01688/400345; ⑦; late March–Oct), which has a decent bar, and offers top-class, expensive pre-theatre dinners. A cheaper spot of refreshment is available from *Coffee and Books*, which offers just that (and a few provisions) from its premises opposite the *Bellacroy Hotel*, whose bar is a great place to shelter for the day in bad weather.

Dervaig has a wide choice of **places to stay**, aside from the aforementioned *Druimard*. The best of the B&Bs are the vegetarian-friendly *Glen Bellart House* (☎01688/400282; ①; Easter–Oct), in one of the whitewashed houses on the main street; *Glenview* (☎01688/400239; ②; April–Oct), a really lovely 1890s house on the edge of the village; the excellent *Cuin Lodge* (☎01688/400346; ②; March–Oct), northwest of the village overlooking the loch; or *Balmacara* (☎01688/400363; ③), a modern and extremely luxurious hillside house. A little beyond Dervaig, the **Old Byre Heritage Centre** (Easter–Oct daily 10.30am–6.30pm; £2) is better than many of its kind, with a video on the island's history, and a passable tearoom. **Wildlife tours** of the island are operated out of the village by Explore Mull Wildlife (☎01688/400209), while Inter-Island Cruises (☎01688/400264) go to Staffa and the Treshnish Isles.

The road continues cross-country to **CALGARY**, once a thriving crofting community, now an idyllic holiday spot boasting Mull's finest sandy bay, backed by low-lying dunes and machair, with wonderful views over to Coll and Tiree. There's just one hotel, the delightful *Calgary Farmhouse* (☎01688/400256; ④; April–Oct), whose excellent, moderately priced restaurant, *The Dovecote*, is

WHALES AND DOLPHINS

Watching whales, dolphins and porpoises – collectively known as cetaceans – is a growing tourist industry, and one which, if managed carefully, should eventually make it more lucrative to help preserve cetaceans rather than kill them. The Moray Firth (see p.211) is one of the best places in the UK to watch **bottlenose dolphins**, but the waters around the Inner Hebrides have, if anything, a wider variety of cetaceans on offer. Although there are several operators who offer whale-watching boat trips from Oban (see p.74), Dervaig (see opposite) and Tobermory (see p.82), it is quite possible to catch sight of marine mammals from the shore, or from a ferry. The chief problem is trying to identify which cetacean you've seen.

The most common sightings are of **harbour porpoises**, the smallest of the marine mammals, which are about the size of an adult human and have a fairly small dorsal fin. Porpoises are easily confused with dolphins; however, if you see the creature leap out of the water, then you can be sure it's a dolphin, as porpoises only break the surface with their backs and fins. If you spot a whale, the likelihood is that it's a **minke whale**, which grows to about thirty feet in length, making it a mere tiddler in the whale world, but a good four or five times bigger than a porpoise. Minkes are baleen whales, which is to say they have no teeth; instead, they gulp huge quantities of water and sift their food through plates of whalebone. Whales do several things dolphins and porpoises can't do, such as blowing water high into the air, and breaching, which is when they launch themselves out of the water and belly-flop down. The two other whale species regularly seen in Hebridean waters are the **killer whale** or orca, distinguished by its very tall, pointed, dorsal fin, and the **pilot whale**, which is even smaller than the minke, has no white on it, and no throat grooves.

(unsurprisingly) housed in a converted dovecote. The south side of the beach is a favourite spot for **camping** rough, though the only facilities are the public toilets. For the record: the city of Calgary in Canada does indeed take its name from this little village, though it was not so named by Mull emigrants, but by one Colonel McLeod of the North West Mounted Police, who once holidayed here.

Salen and around

SALEN, on the east coast halfway between Craignure and Tobermory, lies at the narrowest point on the island. As such it makes a good central base for exploring the island, though it has none of Tobermory's charm. There are, however, several decent places to stay, ranging from the **hostel** accommodation of *Arle Farm Lodge* (☎01680/300343; ②), a well-equipped modern lodge on a working farm, four miles up the A848, to the pretty Victorian *Gruline Home Farm* **B&B** (☎01680/300380; ③), four miles to the southwest. Those with more substantial means should head three miles west to the shores of the Loch na Keal, where the award-winning *Killiechronan Hotel* (☎01680/300403; ⑦; March–Oct) offers dinner and B&B only; a set-menu dinner for non-residents is £25 a head. Salen itself has only a couple of very ordinary eating options, though it does have **bike rental** from *On Yer Bike* (☎01680/300501), who also have child trailers to rent. The nearest **campsite** is the well-equipped site at *Balmeanach Park* (☎01680/300342; March–Oct), five miles southeast by the Sound of Mull at Fishnish.

The most unusual sight near Salen is the **MacQuarie Mausoleum**, a simple buttressed tomb, set within a walled clearing surrounded by pine trees and rhododendrons, and lovingly maintained by the National Trust for Scotland, on behalf of the National Trust of Australia. Within lies the body of Lachlan MacQuarie (1761–1824), the "Father of Australia", who, as the effusive epitaph explains, was appointed by the British as Governor of New South Wales in 1809, to replace the unpopular William Bligh, formerly of the *Bounty*. However, the enlightened MacQuarie was equally unpopular with the Aussie settlers, primarily for instituting liberal penal reforms, and also had to be recalled in 1820.

Isle of Ulva

A chieftain to the Highlands bound
Cries "Boatman, do not tarry!
And I'll give thee a silver pound
To row us o'er the ferry!"
"Now who be ye, would cross Lochgyle
This dark and stormy water?"
"O I'm the chief of Ulva's isle,
An this, Lord Ullin's daughter."

Lord Ullin's Daughter, Thomas Campbell (1777–1844)

Around the time poet laureate Campbell penned this tragic poem, **Ulva**'s population was a staggering 850, sustained by the huge quantities of kelp which were exported for glass and soap production. That was before the market for kelp collapsed and the 1846 potato famine hit, after which the remaining population was brutally evicted. Nowadays barely thirty people live here, and the island is littered with ruined crofts, not to mention a church, designed by Thomas Telford, which would once have seated over three hundred parishioners. It's great walking country, however, with several clearly marked paths crisscrossing the rocky heather moorland interior – and you're almost guaranteed to spot some of the abundant wildlife: at the very least deer, if not buzzards, golden eagles and even sea eagles, with seals and divers offshore. Those who like to have a focus for their wanderings should head for the ruined crofting villages, and basalt columns similar to those on Staffa; along the island's southern coastline, for the island's highest point, Beinn Chreagach (1027ft); or along the north coast to Ulva's tidal neighbour, Gometra, off the west coast.

To **get to Ulva** (from the Norse *ulv øy*, or "wolf island") which lies just a hundred yards or so off the west coast of Mull, follow the signs for "Ulva Ferry" from Salen – if you've no transport, a postbus can get you there, but not back. From **Ulva Ferry**, a small bicycle-passenger-only ferry is available on demand (Mon–Fri 9am–5pm; June–Aug also Sun; at other times by arrangement on ☎01688 500226; £2.50 return); look out for the ferryman's dog, who is famous for his cartwheels. *The Boathouse*, near the ferry slip on Ulva, serves as a licensed **tearoom** selling cakes, snacks, Guinness and Ulva oysters. You can learn more about the history of the island from the **Heritage Centre** exhibition upstairs, soon to be supplemented with more displays in nearby **Sheila's Cottage**, a newly restored thatched crofthouse. There's no accommodation, but with permission from the present owners (☎01688/500264, *ulva@zetnet.co.uk*) you can **camp** rough overnight.

Isle of Staffa and the Treshnish Isles

Five miles southwest of Ulva, **Staffa** is the most romantic and dramatic of Scotland's many uninhabited islands. On its south side, the perpendicular rock-face features an imposing series of black basalt columns, known as the Colonnade, which have been cut by the sea into cathedralesque caverns, most notably **Fingal's Cave**. The Vikings knew about the island – the name derives from their word for "Island of Pillars" – but it wasn't until 1772 that it was "discovered" by the world. Turner painted it, Wordsworth explored it, but Mendelssohn's *Die Fingalshöhle*, inspired by the sounds of the sea-wracked caves he heard on a visit here in 1829, did most to popularize the place – after which Queen Victoria gave her blessing, too. The geological explanation for these polygonal basalt organ pipes is that they were created by a massive subterranean explosion some sixty million years ago. A huge mass of molten basalt ejaculated onto land and, as it cooled, solidified into what are, essentially, crystals. Of course, confronted with such artistry, most visitors have found it difficult to believe that their origin is entirely natural – indeed, the various Celtic folk tales, which link the phenomenon with the Giant's Causeway in Ireland, are certainly more appealing.

To **get to Staffa**, join one of the many boat trips from Oban, Dervaig, Ulva Ferry or Fionnphort, weather permitting. Staffa-only trips start at £10 per person on the *Iolaire* (☎01681/700358; £10 return), which sails out of Fionnphort, and with Turus Mara (☎01688/400242, *turus.mara@dial.pipex.com*), operating out of Ulva Ferry. However, Inter-Island Cruises (☎01688/400264), which run from Dervaig, are worth the extra money.

Several outfits, such as Turus Mar and the whale-watching Sea Life Surveys (based in the offices of Tobermory's Hebridean Whale and Dolphin Trust, see p.82), also offer **boat trips** around the archipelago of uninhabited volcanic islets that make up the **Treshnish Isles** northwest of Staffa. None of them are more than a mile across, the most distinctive being **Bac Mór**, shaped like a Puritan's hat and popularly dubbed the Dutchman's Cap. Most trips include a stopover on **Lunga**, the largest island, and a nesting place for hundreds of seabirds, in particular guillemots, razorbills (mid-May to July) and puffins (late April to mid-Aug), as well as a breeding ground for common seals (June) and Atlantic greys (early Sept). The two most northerly islands, **Cairn na Burgh More** and **Cairn na Burgh Beag**, have the remains of ruined castles, the first of which served as a lookout post for the Lords of the Isles and was last garrisoned in the Civil War; Cairn na Burgh Beag hasn't been occupied since the 1715 Jacobite uprising.

Ben More and the Ardmeanach peninsula

From the southern shores of Loch na Keal, which almost splits Mull in two, rise the terraced slopes of **Ben More** (3169ft) – literally "big mountain" – a mighty extinct volcano, and the only Munro in the Hebrides outside of Skye. It's most easily climbed from Dhiseig, halfway along the loch's southern shores, though an alternative route is to climb up to the col between Beinn Fhada and A'Chioch, and approach via the mountain's eastern ridge. Further west along the shore the road carves through spectacular overhanging cliffs before heading south past the Gribun rocks which face the tiny island of **Inch Kenneth**, where Unity Mitford lived until her death in 1948. There are great views out to Staffa and the

UNITY MITFORD ON INCH KENNETH

Born in 1914, **Unity Valkyrie Mitford** was the youngest of the so-called Mitford Sisters, the daughters of Lord Redesdale. The family became notorious in the 1930s, after Unity's older sister, Diana, became involved with (and eventually married) Howard Mosley, leader of the British Union of Fascists. One of the other daughters, Jessica, was a lifelong Communist, who fought in the Spanish Civil War. However, it was Unity who went on to gain the greatest infamy due to her close relationship with Hitler, which began after she moved to Germany in 1934. For a while, she became one of Hitler's closest companions, accompanying him on official functions, and even addressing Nazi rallies. On the day that Britain declared war on Germany, Unity attempted to kill herself with a pistol given to her by the *Führer*, but only succeeded in lodging a bullet in her head. Nine days later she was brought back to Britain, where the press clamoured for her internment. Instead, she was allowed to retire to the island of **Inch Kenneth**, which the family had bought in 1937. She lived there as an invalid, with her mother, Lady Redesdale, eventually dying in an hospital in Oban in 1948. The cause of death was meningitis, brought on by a cerebral abscess caused by the bullet, which was still lodged in her head. Another of the daughters, Nancy, became a novelist and satirized the family in her first two novels, *The Pursuit of Love* and *Love in a Cold Climate*.

Treshnish Isles as the road leaves the coast behind, climbing over the pass to Loch Scribain, where it eventually joins the equally dramatic Glen More road (A848) from Craignure.

If you're properly equipped for walking, however, you can explore the **Ardmeanach peninsula**, to the west of the road, on foot. On the north coast, a mile or so from the road, is **Mackinnon's Cave** – at 100ft high, one of the largest caves in the Hebrides, and accessible only at low tide. As so often, there's a legend attached to the cave, which tells of an entire party, led by a lone piper, who were once devoured here by evil spirits. Starting from the south coast, it's a longer, rougher six-mile hike from the road to **MacCulloch's Tree**, a 40-foot-high fifty-million-year-old fossil tree trunk embedded in the cliffs at Rubha na h-Uambha at the western tip of the peninsula. You'll need a good map and, again, you need to time your arrival with low tide; the area is NTS-owned and you should call in at Burg Farm on the way to make your presence known (and to get directions).

The Ross of Mull

Stretching for twenty miles west as far as Iona is Mull's rocky southernmost peninsula, the **Ross of Mull**, which, like much of Scotland, appears blissfully tranquil in good weather, and desolate and bleak in bad climes. Most visitors simply drive through the Ross en route to Iona, but if you have the time it's definitely worth considering exploring, or even staying, in this little-visited part of Mull.

The most scenic spots on the Ross are hidden away on the south coast. If you're approaching the Ross from Craignure, the first of these is signposted even before you've negotiated the splendid Highland pass of Glen More, which brings you to the Ross itself. **LOCHBUIE**, situated above a peaceful, sandy bay six miles off the main A849, is dominated by the fifteenth-century ivy-strewn ruins of **Moy Castle**, an old MacLean stronghold. North of the castle is one of the few **stone circles** in the west of Scotland, with eight stones all about 6ft high and dating from the second century BC. The best-value accommodation in the vicinity is at *Barrachandroman* (☎01680/814220, *spelve@aol.com*; ②), a converted barn overlooking Loch Spelve, a couple of miles east of Lochbuie.

A popular and fairly easy walk is the five-mile hike west along the coastal path to the tiny village of **CARSAIG**, where the Inniemore School of Painting enjoys an idyllic setting, at the end of a dead-end road, three miles south of Pennyghael (see below), on the A849. An even finer walk is possible to the west of Carsaig, where the coastal path takes you past, first the **Nun's Cave**, where nuns from Iona are alleged to have hidden during the Reformation, and then, after four miles or so, at Malcolm's Point, the spectacular **Carsaig Arches**, formed by eroded sea caves, which are linked to basalt cliffs.

The main A849 road, single-track (for the most part) and plagued by the large number of coaches that steam down it en route to Iona, hugs the northern coastline of the Ross. The welcoming and comfortable *Pennyghael Hotel* (☎01681/704288; ③; Easter–Oct), which has a good restaurant and a decent bar, overlooks Loch Scridain and Ben More, from the hamlet of **PENNYGHAEL**. However, if your budget stretches to it, there are two much more exceptional hotels near **BUNESSAN**, the largest village on the peninsula, roughly two-thirds of the way along the Ross. The *Assapol House Hotel* (☎01681/700258; ⑥; Easter–Oct) is a former eighteenth-century manse overlooking its own freshwater loch, two miles southeast of Bunessan; room prices include dinner and breakfast. Two miles west of Bunessan stands *Ardfenaig House* (☎01681/700210; ⑥; April–Oct), an old shooting lodge with its own jetty and a self-catering converted coach house.

Bunessan itself has a few useful shops, plus the remarkable **Angora Rabbit Farm** (Easter–Oct daily except Sat 11am–5pm; £2), just east of town on the A849. Here, an eccentric couple keep comical, long-haired bunnies in order to harvest their incredibly soft fleeces as yarn. Whatever time you arrive, you'll get a guided tour, and the kids will get to stroke the rabbits, but if you arrive at noon you can watch their fur being clipped, and at 3pm you can observe a spinning demonstration. If the weather's good, it might be worth heading off for the two adjacent sandy beaches, at **UISKEN** and neighbouring **ARDALANISH**. Either of these can be enjoyed by staying at *Uisken Croft* (☎01681/700307; ①; April–Oct) or at *Ardalanish Farm* (☎01681/700265; ①), both of which are highly recommended.

The road ends at **FIONNPHORT**, facing Iona, probably the least attractive place to stay on the Ross, though it has a nice sandy bay backed by pink granite rocks to the north of the ferry slipway. Partly to ease congestion on Iona, and to give their neighbours a slice of the tourist pound, Fionnphort was chosen as the site for the **Columba Centre** (mid-May to Sept Mon–Sat 10am–6pm, Sun 11am–6pm; £2), which opened in 1997 on the 1400th anniversary of the saint's death; inside, a small museum tells the story of Columba's life (for more on which, see p.90) using a combination of special effects and original artefacts.

If you're in need of a bed in Fionnphort, try the granite-built *Seaview* (☎01681/700235; ②), or the whitewashed *Staffa House* (☎01681/700677; ②), both of which are close to the ferry, and have views over to Iona. The basic *Fidden Farm* campsite (☎01681/700427; April–Sept), a mile south along the Knockvologan road by Fidden beach, is the nearest to Iona. Fidden beach looks out to the **Isle of Erraid**, accessible across the sands at low tide. Robert Louis Stevenson is believed to have written *Kidnapped* (its hero, David Balfour, gets shipwrecked here) in one of the island's cottages, overlooking the Torran Rocks, out to sea to the south, where his father and uncle built the Dubh Artach lighthouse in 1862. The island is now in Dutch ownership, and cared for by the Findhorn Community.

Isle of Iona

> *Ross: Where is Duncan's body?*
> *Macduff: Carried to Colme-kill,*
> *The sacred storehouse of his predecessors,*
> *And guardian of their bones.*
>
> *Macbeth* (Act II, Scene IV), William Shakespeare

Less than a mile off the southwest tip of Mull, **IONA** – just three miles long and not much more than a mile wide – has been a place of pilgrimage for several centuries, and a place of Christian worship for more than 1400 years. For it was to this flat Hebridean island that St Columba fled from Ireland in 563 and established a monastery which was responsible for the conversion of more or less all of pagan Scotland as well as much of northern England. This history and the island's splendid isolation have lent it a peculiar religiosity; in the much-quoted words of Dr Johnson, who visited in 1773, "that man is little to be envied . . . whose piety would not grow warmer among the ruins of Iona". Today, however, the island can barely cope with the constant flood of day-trippers, so to appreciate the special atmosphere and to have time to see the whole island, including the often overlooked west coast, you should plan on staying at least one night.

Some history

Legend has it that **St Columba** (Colum Cille), born in Donegal some time around 521, was a direct descendant of the semi-legendary Irish king, Niall of the Nine Hostages. A scholar and soldier priest, who founded numerous monasteries in Ireland, he is thought to have become involved in a bloody dispute with the king when he refused to hand over a copy of the *Book of Psalms* copied illegally from the original owned by St Finian of Moville. This, in turn, provoked the Battle of Cúl Drebene (Cooldrumman) – also known as the **Battle of the Book** – at which Columba's forces won, though with the loss of over 3000 lives. The story goes that, repenting this bloodshed, Columba went into exile with twelve other monks, eventually settling on Iona in 563, allegedly because it was the first island he encountered from which he couldn't see his homeland. The bottom line, however, is that we know very little about Columba, though he undoubtedly became something of a cult figure after his death in 597. He was posthumously credited with miraculous feats such as defeating the Loch Ness monster – it only had to hear his voice and it recoiled in terror – and banishing snakes (and, some say, frogs) from the island. He is also famously alleged to have banned women and cows from Iona, banishing them to Eilean nam Ban (Woman's Island), just north of Fionnphort, for, as he believed, "where there is a cow there is a woman, and where there is a woman there is mischief".

Whatever the truth about Columba's life, in the sixth and seventh centuries, Iona enjoyed a great deal of autonomy from Rome, establishing a specifically **Celtic Christian** tradition. Missionaries were sent out to the rest of Scotland and parts of England, and Iona quickly became a respected seat of learning and artistry; the monks compiled a vast library of intricately **illuminated manuscripts** – most famously the *Book of Kells* (now on display in Trinity College, Dublin) – while the masons excelled in carving peculiarly intricate crosses. Two factors were instrumental in the demise of the Celtic tradition: a series of Viking raids, the worst of which was the massacre of 68 monks on the sands of Martyrs' Bay in 806; and relentless pressure from the established Church, beginning with the Synod of Whitby in 664, which chose Rome over the Celtic Church, and culminated in the suppression of the Celtic Church by King David I in 1144.

In 1203, Iona became part of the mainstream church with the establishment of an **Augustinian nunnery** and a **Benedictine monastery** by Reginald, son of Somerled, Lord of the Isles. During the Reformation, the entire complex was ransacked, the contents of the library burnt and all but three of the island's 360 crosses destroyed. Although plans were drawn up at various times to turn the abbey into a Cathedral of the Isles, nothing came of them until in 1899, when the (then) owner, the eighth duke of Argyll, donated the abbey buildings to the **Church of Scotland**, who restored the abbey church for worship over the course of the next decade. Iona's modern resurgence began in 1938, when **George MacLeod**, a minister from Glasgow, established a group of ministers, students and artisans to begin rebuilding the remainder of the monastic buildings. What began as a mostly male, Gaelic-speaking, strictly Presbyterian community is today a lay, mixed and ecumenical retreat. The entire abbey complex has been successfully restored, and the island, apart from the church land and a few crofts, now belongs to the NTS.

Baile Mór

The passenger ferry from Fionnphort drops you off at the island's main village, **BAILE MÓR** (literally "large village"), which is in fact little more than a single terrace of cottages facing the sea. Just inland lie the extensive pink granite ruins of the **Augustinian nunnery**, disused since the Reformation. A beautifully maintained garden now occupies the cloisters, and if nothing else the complex gives you an idea of the state of the present-day abbey before it was restored. Across the road to the north, housed in a manse built, like the nearby parish church, by the ubiquitous Thomas Telford, is the **Iona Heritage Centre** (April–Oct Mon–Sat 10.30am–4.30pm; £1.50), with displays on the social history of the island over the last 200 years, including the Clearances, which nearly halved the island's population of 500 in the mid-nineteenth century. At a bend in the road, just south of the manse and church, stands the fifteenth-century **MacLean's Cross**, a fine late medieval example of the distinctive, flowing, three-leaved foliage of the Iona school.

Iona Abbey

At the main entrance to the **abbey complex**, there's a small information hut, where you're asked to give a £2 donation and can pick up a plan of the abbey. No buildings remain from Columba's time: the present abbey dates from the arrival of the Benedictines in around 1200, was extensively rebuilt in the fifteenth and sixteenth centuries, and restored virtually wholesale this century. Iona's oldest building, the plain-looking **St Oran's Chapel**, lies south of the abbey, to your right, and boasts a Norman door dating from the eleventh century. Legend has it

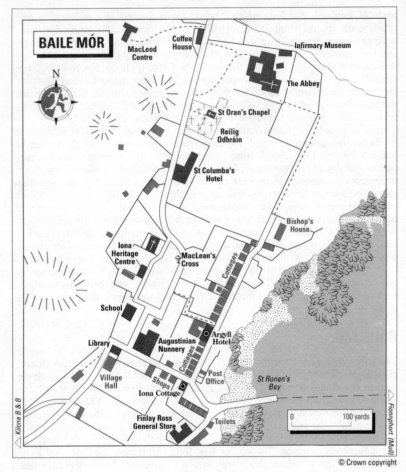

BAILE MÓR

MacLeod Centre

Coffee House

Infirmary Museum

The Abbey

St Oran's Chapel

Reilig Odhráin

St Columba's Hotel

Bishop's House

Iona Heritage Centre

MacLean's Cross

Cottages

School

Library

Augustinian Nunnery

Cottages

Argyll Hotel

Post Office

St Ronan's Bay

Village Hall

Shops

Iona Cottage

Finlay Ross General Store

Toilets

Kilona B & B

Fionnphort (Mull)

0   100 yards

© Crown copyright

that the original chapel could only be completed through human sacrifice. Oran, one of the older monks in Columba's entourage, apparently volunteered to be buried alive, and was found to have survived the ordeal when the grave was opened a few days later. Declaring that he had seen hell and it wasn't all bad, he was promptly reinterred for blasphemy.

Oran's Chapel stands at the centre of Iona's sacred burial ground, **Reilig Odhráin** (Oran's Cemetery), which is said to contain the graves of sixty kings of Norway, Ireland, France and Scotland, including Duncan and Macbeth. The best of the early Christian gravestones and medieval effigies which once lay in the Reilig Odhráin have unfortunately been removed to the Infirmary Museum, behind the abbey (see opposite), and to various other locations within the complex. The graveyard is still used as a cemetery by the island, however, and the grave that many visitors now head for is that of the short-lived leader of the

Labour Party, **John Smith** (1938–94), who was a frequent visitor to Iona, though he himself was born in the town of Ardrishaig.

Approaching the abbey itself, from the main entrance, you cross an exposed section of the evocative medieval **Street of the Dead**, whose giant red marble cobbles once stretched from the abbey, past St Oran's Chapel, to the village. Beside the road stands the most impressive of Iona's Celtic high crosses, the eighth-century **St Martin's Cross**, smothered with figural scenes – the Virgin and Child at the centre, Daniel in the lion's den, Abraham sacrificing Isaac and David with musicians in the shaft below. The reverse side features Pictish serpent-and-boss decoration. Standing directly in front of the abbey are the base of St Matthew's Cross (now in the Infirmary Museum) and, to the left, a replica cast of the eighth-century **St John's Cross**, decorated with serpent and boss and Celtic spiral ornamental panels. Before you enter the abbey, take a look inside **St Columba's Shrine**, a small steep-roofed chamber to the left of the main entrance. Columba is believed to have been buried either here or under the rocky mound to the west of the abbey, known as Tórr an Aba.

The **Abbey** itself has been simply and sensitively restored, to incorporate the original elements. You can spot many of the medieval capitals in the south aisle of the choir and in the south transept, where the white marble effigies of the eighth Duke of Argyll and his wife, Ina, lie in a side chapel – an incongruous piece of Victorian pomp in an otherwise modest and tranquil place. The finest pre-Reformation effigy is that of John MacKinnon, the last abbot of Iona, who died around 1500, and now lies on the south side of the choir steps. For reasons of sanitation, the **cloisters** were placed, contrary to the norm, on the north side of the church (where running water was available); entirely reconstructed in the late 1950s, they now shelter lots of medieval grave slabs, a useful historical account of the abbey's development, and the abbey bookshop. There are free daily guided tours of the abbey (the times are posted up inside the west door). If you want to see some more medieval grave slabs from Reilig Odhráin, the rest of St Matthew's Cross and the original fragments of St John's Cross, you should walk round the back of the abbey to the **Infirmary Museum**, which also contains the stone pillow allegedly used by Columba himself.

Practicalities

There's no **tourist office** on Iona, and as demand far exceeds supply you should organize **accommodation** well in advance. Of the island's two **hotels**, the stone-built *Argyll* (☎01681/700334; ⑤; April–Oct), in the terrace of cottages overlooking the Sound of Iona, is by far the nicest. As for **B&Bs**, *Iona Cottage* (☎01681/700569; ①; Easter–Oct) is an attractive whitewashed cottage right by the pier; for a more secluded location, try *Kilona* in Sithean (☎01681/700362; ①), a mile from the ferry, on the peaceful west side of the island. **Camping** is not permitted on Iona, and there is no youth hostel. If you want to stay with the **Iona Community**, contact the *MacLeod Centre* (☎01681/700404, *ionacomm@iona.org.uk)*, popularly known as the "Mac". Hostel accommodation is provided and you must be prepared to participate fully in the daily activities, prayers and religious services.

Visitors are not allowed to bring cars onto the island, but **bikes** can be rented from the Finlay Ross general store (☎01681/700357). **Food** options are limited: the eclectic bar menu of the *Argyll* is probably your best option or, for something lighter, head for the *Coffee House*, run by the Iona Community, just west of the abbey, which serves home-made soup and delicious cakes.

WALKS ON IONA

In many ways the landscape of Iona – low-lying, treeless with white sandy coves backed by machair – is more reminiscent of the distant islands of Coll and Tiree than it is of neighbouring Mull. Few tourists bother to stray from Baile Mór, yet in high season there is no better way to appreciate Iona's solitary beauty.

Perhaps the easiest jaunt is up **Dún I**, Iona's only real hill, which rises to the north of Iona Abbey to a height of 300ft – a great place to wander at dawn or dusk. The west coast has some great sandy beaches; the **Camus Cúl an t-Saimh** (Bay at the Back of the Ocean) by the golf course is the longest. More sheltered is the tiny bay on the south coast, **Port a' Churaich**, thought to be where Columba first landed in a coracle (*curaich*) made with tarred cowhides. The fifty-odd small cairns are said to have been piled up by the monks as a penance for their sins. A short distance to the east is the **disused marble quarry** at Rubha na Carraig Geire, on the southeasternmost point of Iona. Quarried intermittently for several centuries, it was finally closed down in 1914; much of the old equipment is still visible, rusting away by the shore.

Coll and Tiree

Coll and **Tiree** are among the most isolated of the Inner Hebrides, and if anything have more in common with the outlying Western Isles than with their closest neighbour, Mull. Each is roughly twelve miles long and three miles wide, both are low-lying, treeless and exceptionally windy, with white sandy beaches and the highest sunshine records in Scotland. Like most of the Hebrides, they were once ruled by Vikings, and didn't pass into Scottish hands until the thirteenth century. Coll's population peaked at 1440, Tiree's at a staggering 4450, but both were badly affected by the Clearances, which virtually halved their populations in a generation. Coll was fortunate to be in the hands of the enlightened MacLeans, but they were forced to sell in 1856 to the Stewart family, who sold two-thirds of the island to a Dutch millionaire in the 1960s. Tiree was ruthlessly cleared by its owner, the Duke of Argyll, who sent in the marines in 1885 to evict the crofters. After the passing of the Crofters' Act the following year, the island was divided into crofts, though it remains a part of the Duke of Argyll's estate. Both islands have strong Gaelic roots, but the percentage of English-speaking newcomers is rising steadily.

The CalMac **ferry** from Oban calls at Coll (2hr 40min) and Tiree (3hr 40min) every day except Thursdays and Sundays throughout the year. Tiree also has an **airport** with daily flights (Mon–Sat) to and from Glasgow. The majority of visitors on both islands stay for at least a week in self-catering accommodation (see p.34), though there are B&Bs and hotels on the islands. However, choice is limited, so it's as well to book as far in advance as possible (and that goes for the ferry crossing, too). The only **public transport** is on Tiree, which has an infrequent postbus service (Mon–Sat only), plus a shared taxi system (☎01879/220311 or 220419).

Isle of Coll

The fish-shaped rocky island of **Coll** (population 175) lies less than seven miles off the coast of Mull. The CalMac ferry drops off at Coll's only real village, **ARINAGOUR**, whose whitewashed cottages dot the western shore of Loch Eatharna.

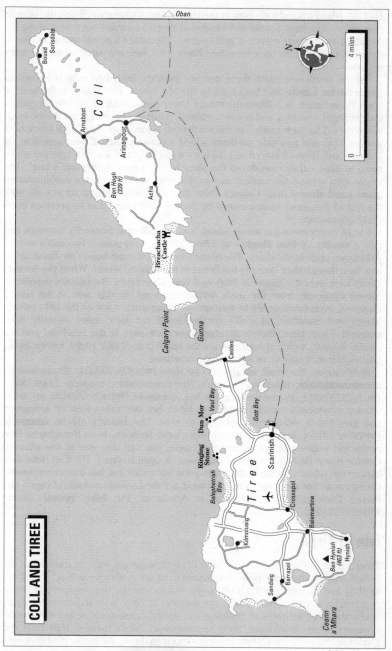

COLL AND TIREE

Oban

Coll

Bousd
Sorisdale
Arnabost
Arinagour
Ben Hogh
(339 ft)
Acha
Breachacha
Castle
Calgary Point
Gunna

Caoles
Vaul Bay
Dun Mor
Gott Bay
Ringing
Stone
Scarinish
Balephetrish
Bay
Tiree
Crossapol
Balemartine
Kilmoluaig
Ben Hynish
(463 ft)
Hynish
Sandaig
Barrapol
Ceann
a Mhara

N

4 miles

0

Half the island's population lives in the village, and it's here you'll find the island's post office, churches, school and handful of shops; two miles northwest along the Arnabost road, there's even a golf course. The island's petrol pump is also in Arinagour, and is run on a volunteer basis – it's basically open when the ferry arrives.

On the southwest coast there are two edifices, both confusingly known as **Breachacha Castle**, and both built by the MacLeans. The oldest, at the head of Loch Breachacha, is a fifteenth-century tower house with an additional curtain wall, recently restored, and is now a training centre for Project Trust overseas aid volunteers. The "new castle", to the northwest, is made up of a central block built around 1750 and two side pavilions added a century later. It was here that Dr Johnson and Boswell stayed in 1773 after a storm forced them to take refuge en route to Mull – they considered the place to be "a mere tradesman's box". The whole area around the castles, and to the west where a strip of rabbit-infested **giant sand dunes** links Calgary Point (the southwesternmost tip of Coll) with the rest of the island, is now owned by the RSPB on account of its precious corn-crake population.

For an overview of the whole island, you can follow in Boswell's footsteps and take a wander up **Ben Hogh** – at 339ft, Coll's highest point – two miles west of Arinagour, close to the shore. The island's northwest coast boasts the finest sandy beaches, though they take the full brunt of the Atlantic winds. When the Stewart family took over the island in 1856, and raised the rents, the island's population moved wholesale from the more fertile southeast, to this part of the island. However, overcrowding led to widespread emigration; a few of the old crofts in Bousd and Sorisdale, at Coll's northernmost tip, have more recently been restored. From here, there's an impressive view over to the headland and the islands beyond, which in turn obscure the small crop of tidal rocks, known as the Cairns of Coll, a mile or so north of the headland.

In Arinagour, the small, family-run *Coll Hotel* (☎01879/230334; ③) can provide **accommodation**; otherwise, there's the comfortable, modern *Taigh Solas* (☎01879/230333; ①), overlooking the bay. *Achamore* (☎01879/230430; ①), a traditional nineteenth-century farmhouse B&B, lies two miles west of Arinagour, and also has a self-catering caravan to rent. The island's official **campsite** (☎01879/230374; April–Oct), which offers basic facilities, is on Breachacha Bay, in the old walled gardens of the new castle; you can also stay in the adjacent *Garden House* B&B (phone as for campsite; ③; open all year). The *Coll Hotel* doubles as the island's social centre, does good bar meals and has a more expensive dining room. For a change from hotel **food**, try the *Lochside* restaurant (April–Oct closed Tues lunch & Sun), also in Arinagour. For **bike rental**, phone ☎01879/230382.

Isle of Tiree

Tiree, as its Gaelic name *tir-iodh* (land of corn) suggests, was once known as the breadbasket of the Inner Hebrides, thanks to its acres of rich machair. Nowadays crofting and tourism are the main sources of income for the resident population of around 800. One of most distinctive features of Tiree is its architecture, in particular the large numbers of "pudding" or "spotty" houses, where only the mortar is painted white. In addition, there are numerous "white houses" (*tigh geal*) and traditional "blackhouses" (*tigh dubh*); for more on these, see p.286. Wildlife lovers can also have a field day on Tiree, with lapwings, wheatears, redshank, greylag geese and large, laid-back brown hares in abundance. And, with no shortage of wind, Tiree's sandy beaches attract large numbers of windsurfers for the Tiree Wave Classic every October.

The CalMac ferry calls at Gott Bay Pier, close to the village of **SCARINISH**, home to a post office, a supermarket, a butcher's and a bank, with a petrol pump back at the pier; to the east is **Gott Bay**, backed by a two-mile stretch of sand. It's just one mile across the island from Gott to Vaul Bay, on the north coast, where the well-preserved remains of a drystone broch, **Dun Mor** – dating from the first century BC – lie hidden in the rocks to the west of the bay. From here it's another two miles west along the coast to the *Clach a'Choire* or **Ringing Stone**, a huge glacial boulder decorated with mysterious prehistoric markings, which when struck with a stone gives out a metallic sound. The story goes that, should the Ringing Stone ever be broken in two, Tiree will sink beneath the waves. A mile further west you come to the lovely **Balephetrish Bay**, where you can watch waders feeding in the breakers, and look out to sea to Skye and the Western Isles.

The most intriguing sights, however, lie in the bulging western half of the island, where Tiree's two landmark hills rise up. The highest of the two, **Ben Hynish** (463ft), is unfortunately occupied by a "golf-ball" radar station, which tracks incoming transatlantic flights; the views from the top, though, are great. Below Ben Hynish, to the east is **HYNISH**, with its recently restored **harbour**, designed by Alan Stevenson in the 1830s to transport building materials for the magnificent 140-foot-tall **Skerryvore Lighthouse**, which lies on a sea-swept reef some twelve miles southwest of Tiree. The harbour features an ingenious reservoir to prevent silting, and up on the hill behind, beside the row of light-keepers' houses, a stumpy granite signal tower. The tower, whose signals used to be the only contact the lighthouse keepers had with civilization, now houses a **museum** telling the history of the Herculean effort required to erect the lighthouse; weather permitting, you can see the lighthouse from the tower's viewing platform.

On the other side of Ben Hynish, a mile or so across the golden sands of Balephuil Bay, is the spectacular headland of **Ceann a'Mhara** (pronounced "Kenavara"). The cliffs here are home to thousands of seabirds, including fulmars, kittiwakes, guillemots, razorbills, shags and cormorants, with gannets and terns feeding offshore; the islands of Barra and South Uist are also visible on the northern horizon. In the scattered west coast settlement of **SANDAIG**, to the north of Ceann a'Mhara, three thatched white houses in a row have been turned into the **Thatched House Museum** (June–Sept Mon–Fri 2–4pm), which gives an insight into how the majority of islanders lived in the last century.

Practicalities

From the **airport**, about three miles west of Scarinish, you can either catch the postbus, phone for a shared taxi the night before (see p.94), or arrange for your hosts to collect (most will). Transport around the island is limited, though the postbus calls at all the main settlements; **bike rental** is available at the *Tiree Lodge*. Of the island's two **hotels**, the *Tiree Lodge* (☎01879/220368; ②), a mile or so east of Scarinish along Gott Bay, is preferable to the *Scarinish* (☎01879/220308; ②), overlooking the old harbour. Better than both the above, however, are *Kirkapol House* (☎01879/220729; ②), just beyond the *Tiree Lodge*, a great B&B in a converted kirk, and *The Glassary* (☎01879/220684; ③), over on the west coast in Sandaig. *The Sheiling* (☎01879/220503; ①; April–Oct) is a simple B&B that's convenient for the airport. There are no official campsites, but **camping** is allowed with the local crofter's permission.

As for **eating**, apart from bar snacks or à la carte at the *Tiree Lodge*, the best option is *The Glassary* (phone as on p.97) over in Sandaig, an unpretentious, moderately priced restaurant that serves good food, much of it locally produced. The island seriously lacks a tearoom of any description, and the only place you can be sure of getting a cuppa is at *Glebecraft*, off the main road to the north of Scarinish – it's an experience not to be missed, and they've got Jacob sheep to look at out back. For a map of the island and the daily papers, you need to go to the supermarket at Crossapol.

Isle of Colonsay

Isolated between Mull and Islay, the Isle of **Colonsay** – eight miles by three at its widest – is nothing like as bleak and windswept as Coll or Tiree. Its craggy, heather-backed hills even support the occasional patch of woodland, plus a bewildering array of plant and birdlife, wild goats and rabbits, and one of the

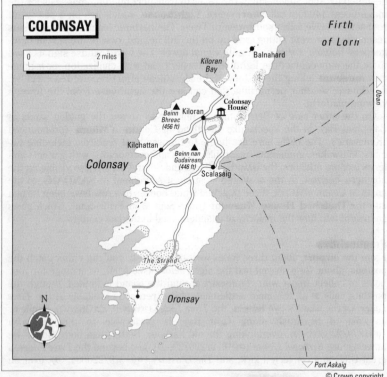

© Crown copyright

finest quasi-tropical gardens in Scotland. That said, the population is precariously low, at around 100, down from a pre-Clearance peak of just under 1000, and the ferry links with the mainland are infrequent: three a week from Oban (Wed, Fri & Sun; 2hr 15min); one a week from Kennacraig via Islay (Wed; 3hr 35min), when a day-trip is possible, giving you around six hours on the island. There's a large number of self-catering cottages, but, with no camping or caravanning and just one hotel, a couple of B&Bs and a bunkhouse, there's no fear of mass tourism taking over.

The CalMac ferry terminal is at **SCALASAIG**, on the east coast, where there's a post office/shop, a petrol pump, a restaurant and the island's hotel. Right by the pier, the old waiting room now serves as the island's heritage centre and is usually open when the ferry docks. Two miles north of Scalasaig, inland at **KILORAN**, is **Colonsay House**, built in 1722 by Malcolm MacNeil. In 1904, the island and house were bought by Lord Strathcona, who made his fortune building the Canadian Pacific Railway (and whose descendants still own the island). He was also responsible for the house's lovely gardens and woods, which are slowly being restored to their former glory. The house and gardens are still off limits, but the outbuildings are now holiday cottages and you're free to wander round the woodland garden to the south, and inspect the strange eighth-century **Riasg Buidhe Cross**, to the east of the house, decorated with an unusually lifelike mug shot (possibly of a monk) east of the house.

To the north of Colonsay House, where the road ends, you'll find the island's finest sandy beach, the breathtaking **Kiloran Bay**, where the breakers roll in from the Atlantic. There's another unspoilt sandy beach backed by dunes at Balnahard, two miles northeast along a rough track; en route, you might spot wild goats, choughs, and even a golden eagle. The island's west coast forms a sharp escarpment, quite at odds with the gentle undulating landscape that characterizes the rest of the island. Due west of Colonsay House around **Beinn Bhreac** (456ft), the cliffs are at their most spectacular and in their lower reaches provide a home to hundreds of seabirds, among them kittiwakes, cormorants and guillemots in spring and early summer.

Isle of Oronsay

Whilst on Colonsay, most folk take a day out to visit the **Isle of Oronsay**, which lies half a mile to the south and contains the ruins of an Augustinian priory. The two islands are separated by "The Strand", a mile of tidal mud flats which act as a causeway for two hours either side of low tide (check locally for timings); you can drive over to the island at low tide, though most people park their cars and walk across. Although legends (and etymology) link SS Columba and Oran with both Colonsay and Oronsay, the ruins actually only date back as far as the fourteenth century. Abandoned since the Reformation and now roofless, you can, nevertheless, still make out the original church and tiny cloisters. The highlight, though, is the **Oronsay Cross**, a superb example of late medieval artistry from Iona which stands to the west of the chapel, and the beautifully carved grave slabs in the Prior's House. It takes about an hour to walk from the tip of Colonsay across the Strand to the priory (wellington boots are a good idea). If you don't have your own picnic, you can get tea, cakes and more substantial food from the *Barn Café* (summer daily except Sat) on the Colonsay side of the Strand.

Practicalities

The island's only **hotel**, the *Isle of Colonsay* (☎01951/200316; ⑨), is a cosy eighteenth-century inn at heart, within easy walking distance of the pier in Scalasaig; it serves very decent bar snacks and acts as the island's social centre. The best alternative is to stay at the superb *Seaview* **B&B** (☎01951/200315; ②; April–Oct), run by the charming Lawson family in Kilchattan on the west coast. The budget option is to sleep in the newly established *Backpackers' Lodge* **hostel**, in Kiloran, run by the Colonsay Estate (☎01770/200312). Most people who visit the island, however, stay in **self-catering accommodation**, the majority of which is run by the aforementioned Colonsay Estate (phone as above), who offer a huge choice of cottages and a wide price range. It's also possible to book self-catering places for just a couple of nights, through *Island Lodges* (☎01951/200320; ②).

An alternative to **eating out** at the hotel bar is *The Pantry* (closed Sun), above the pier in Scalasaig, which offers simple home-cooking as well as teas and cakes (ring ahead if you want to eat in the evening; ☎01951/200325). All accommodation (and ferry crossings) need to be booked well in advance for the summer; self-catering cottages tend to be booked from Friday to Friday, because of the ferries. The hotel, *Seaview* and A. McConnel (☎01951/200355) will rent out **bikes**, and there's a limited **bus** and **postbus** service (Mon–Sat only) for those without their own transport. If you need a map or any books on the Highlands and Islands, go to the very well-stocked **bookshop** (and tearoom) right by the hotel.

Mid-Argyll

Mid-Argyll is a vague term which loosely describes the central wedge of land south of Oban and north of Kintyre. **Lochgilphead**, on the shores of Loch Fyne is the chief town in the area, though it has little to offer beyond its practical use – it has a tourist office, a good supermarket and is the regional transport hub, though, on the whole, public transport is thin on the ground. The highlights of this gently undulating scenery lie along the sharply indented west coast, in particular the rich Bronze Age and Neolithic remains in the Kilmartin valley, one of the most important prehistoric sites in Scotland.

The Slate Islands and the Garvellachs

Just eight miles south of Oban, a road heads off the A816 west to a small group of islands commonly called the **Slate Islands**, which at their peak in the mid-nineteenth century quarried over nine million slates annually. Today many of the old slate villages are sparsely populated, and an inevitable air of melancholy hangs over them, but their dramatic setting amid crashing waves makes for a rewarding day-trip.

Isle of Seil

The most northerly of the Slate Islands is **Seil**, a lush island, now something of an exclusive enclave (Princess Diana's mother, Mrs Shand-Kydd, is a resident). It's separated from the mainland only by the thinnest of sea channels and spanned by Thomas Telford's elegant humpback **Clachan Bridge**, built in 1793 and popularly known as the "Bridge over the Atlantic". The pub next door to the bridge is the *Tigh na Truish* (House of the Trousers), where kilt-wearing islanders would change into trousers to conform to the post-1745 ban on Highland dress.

The main village on Seil is **ELLENABEICH**, its neat white terraces of workers' cottages – featured in the film *Ring of Bright Water* – crouching below black cliffs on the westernmost tip of the island. This was once the tiny island of Eilean a'Beithich (hence "Ellenabeich") separated from the mainland by a slim sea channel until the intensive slate quarrying succeeded in silting it up. Confusingly, the village is often referred to by the same name as the nearby island of Easdale, since they formed an interdependent community based exclusively around the slate industry.

Isle of Easdale

Easdale remains an island, though the few hundred yards that separate it from Ellanabeich have to be dredged to keep the channel open. On the eve of a great storm on November 23, 1881, Easdale, less than a mile across at any one point, supported an incredible 452 inhabitants. That night, waves engulfed the island and flooded the quarries. The island never really recovered, slate quarrying stopped in 1914, and by the 1960s the population was reduced to single figures.

Recently many of the old workers' cottages have been restored: some as holiday homes, others sold to new families (the present population stands at over thirty). One of the cottages now houses the interesting **Easdale Folk Museum** (April–Oct daily 10.30am–5.30pm; £2), near the main square, selling a useful historical map of the island, which you can walk round in about half an hour. The **ferry** from Ellenabeich runs partly to schedule, partly on demand (April–Sept Mon–Sat 7.15am–8.50pm, Sun 9.30am–5.50pm; Oct–March check at Oban tourist office, see p.71), and there's *The Puffer* **bar/restaurant**, plus a cosy, little whitewashed **B&B** at no. 22 (☎01852/300438; ①).

Isle of Luing

To the south of Seil, across the narrow, treacherous Cuan Sound lies **Luing** (pronounced "Ling"), a long, thin, fertile island which once supported more than 600 people. During the Clearances, the population was drastically reduced to make way for cattle; Luing is still renowned for its beef and for the crossbreed named after it. A car **ferry** (Mon–Sat 8am–6pm; mid-June to Aug also Fri & Sat 7.30–10.30pm) crosses the Cuan Sound every half-hour or so, though foot passengers can cross until later in the evening (Mon–Thurs 8am–10pm, Fri & Sat 8am–11.30pm, Sun 11am–6pm). There's a **postbus** service on Luing itself (Mon–Sat only).

CULLIPOOL, the pretty main village with its post office and general store, lies a mile or so southwest; quarrying ceased here in 1965, and the place now relies on tourism and lobster fishing. Luing's only other village, **TOBERONOCHY**, lies on the more sheltered east coast, three miles southeast of Cullipool. Its distinctive white cottages, built by the slate company in 1805, nestle below a ruined church, which contains a memorial to the fifteen Latvian seamen who drowned off the nearby abandoned slate island of **Belnahua** during a hurricane in 1936. Other than self-catering cottages, the only **accommodation** available on the island is at *Bardrishaig Farm* (☎01852/314364; ①; mid-Jan to mid-Dec), on the road to Cullipool. For **bike rental**, ring ☎01852/314256 in the evening.

Isle of Scarba and the Garvellachs

Scarba is the largest of the islands around Luing, a brooding 1500-foot hulk of slate, not much more than a couple of miles across, inhospitable and wild – most of the fifty or so inhabitants who once lived here had left by the mid-nineteenth century. To the south, between Scarba and Jura, the raging **Gulf of Corrievrechan** is the site of one of the world's most spectacular whirlpools, thought to be caused by a rocky pinnacle below the sea. It remains calm only for an hour or two at high and low tide; between flood and half-flood tide, accompanied by a southerly or westerly wind, water shoots deafeningly some 20ft up in the air. Inevitably there are numerous legends about the place – known as *coire bhreacain* (speckled cauldron) in Gaelic – concerning *Cailleach* (Hag), the Celtic storm goddess. The best place from which to view it is the northern tip of Jura (see p.130).

The string of uninhabited islands visible west of Luing are known collectively as the **Garvellachs**, after the largest of the group, **Garbh Eileach** (Rough Rock), which was inhabited as recently as fifty years ago. The most northerly, **Dún Chonnuill**, contains the remains of an old fort thought to have belonged to Conal of Dalriada, and **Eileach an Naoimh** (Holy Isle), the most southerly of the group, is where the Celtic missionary Brendan the Navigator founded a community in 542, some twenty years before Columba landed on Iona (see p.90). Nothing survives from Brendan's day, but there are a few ninth-century remains, among them a double-beehive cell and a grave enclosure. One school of thought has it that the island is Hinba, Columba's legendary secret retreat, where he founded a monastery before settling on Iona.

If you're interested in taking a **boat trip** to Corrievrechan or the Garvellachs, contact Ruby Cruises (☎01852/500616), who operate out of Ardfern (see below), Gemini Cruises (☎01546/830238), who operate from Crinan (see p.106), or Porpoise Charters (☎01852/300203), who are based at Balvicar, just south of the Clachan Bridge.

Arduaine and Craignish

Probably the finest spot at which to stop and have a bite to eat on the main road from Oban to Lochgilphead is the *Loch Melfort Hotel* (☎01852/200233, *lmhotel@aol.com*; ⑤), in **ARDUAINE**, where you can enjoy great bar snacks, sitting out on the hotel lawn, with views over Asknish Bay and out to the islands of Shuna, Luing, Scarba and Jura. Beside the hotel are the **Arduaine Gardens** (daily 9.30am–dusk; £2.50; NTS), which enjoy the same idyllic lochside location. Gifted as recently as 1992, the gardens are stupendous, particularly in May and June, and have the feel of a intimate private garden, with pristine lawns, lily-strewn ponds, mature woods and spectacular rhododendrons and azaleas. The gardens' disgruntled former owners, the Wright brothers, still live next door and have an equally lovely adjacent garden. Below the hotel and gardens, *Arduaine Caravan and Camping Park* is a lovely lochside **campsite** (☎01852/200331; Easter–Oct).

A couple of miles south, on the far side of Asknish Bay is the slightly surreal **CRAOBH HAVEN**, a planned holiday village and marina that's reminiscent of a bad film set. There's a fine walk to be had, however, from Craobh Haven along the spine of the **Craignish peninsula** to the southernmost tip some five miles away. Heading back up the single-track road that runs along the shores of Loch Craignish, stop off at the *Galley of Lorne* in yachty **ARDFERN**, a real pub and a great place to quench your thirst. There's accommodation close to Craobh Haven, either in the luxurious log-cabin-style *Buidhe Lodge* (☎01852/500291; ②), or in the rambling Baronial pile of *Lunga* (☎01852/500237; ①), run by an eccentric laird.

Kilmartin Glen

The chief sight on the road from Oban to Lochgilphead is the **Kilmartin Glen**, the most important prehistoric site on the Scottish mainland. The most remarkable relic is the **linear cemetery**, where several cairns are aligned for more than two miles, to the south of the village Kilmartin. These are thought to represent the successive burials of a ruling family or chieftains, but nobody can be sure. The best view of the cemetery's configuration is from the Bronze Age **Mid-Cairn**, but the Neolithic **South Cairn**, dating from around 3000 BC, is by far the oldest and the most impressive, with its large chambered tomb roofed by giant slabs.

Close to the Mid-Cairn, the two **Temple Wood stone circles** appear to have been the architectural focus of burials in the area from Neolithic times to the Bronze Age. Visible to the south are the impressively cup-marked **Nether Largie standing stones** (no public access), the largest of which looms over 10ft high.

© Crown copyright

Cup- and ring-marked rocks are a recurrent feature of prehistoric sites in the Kilmartin Glen and elsewhere in Argyll. There are many theories as to their origin: some see them as Pictish symbols, others as primitive solar calendars, and so on. The most extensive markings in the entire country are at **Achnabreck**, off the A816 towards Lochgilphead.

Kilmartin

Situated on high ground to the north of the cairns is the tiny village of **KILMARTIN**, where a new interpretive centre, **Kilmartin House** (daily 10am–5.30pm; £3.90), is housed in the old manse adjacent to the village church. The fifteen-minute audiovisual is not half as interesting as the excellent museum, which is both enlightening and entertaining. Not only can you learn about the various theories concerning prehistoric crannogs, henges and cairns, but you can practise polishing an axe, examine different types of wood and fur, and listen to a variety of weird and wonderful sounds (check out the Gaelic bird imitations). The **café/restaurant** is equally enticing, with local (often wild) produce on offer, which you can wash down with heather beer.

The nearby church is worth a brief reconnoitre, as it shelters the badly damaged and weathered **Kilmartin crosses**, while a separate enclosure in the graveyard houses a large collection of medieval grave slabs of the Malcolms of Poltalloch. Kilmartin's own castle is ruined beyond recognition; head instead for the much-less-ruined **Carnasserie Castle**, on a high ridge a mile up the road towards Oban. The castle was built in the 1560s by John Carswell, an influential figure in the Scottish church, who published the first ever book in Gaelic, *Knox's Liturgy*, which contained the doctrines of the Presbyterian faith. Architecturally, the castle is interesting, too, as it represents the transition between fully fortified castles and later mansion houses, and has several original finely carved stone fireplaces, doorways, as well as numerous gun-loops and shot holes.

Mòine Mhór and Dunadd

To the south of Kilmartin, beyond the linear cemetery, lies the raised peat bog of **Mòine Mhór** (Great Moss), now a nature reserve and home to remarkable plant, insect and birdlife. To get a close look at the sphagnum moss and wetlands, head for the newly laid-out Tileworks Walk, just off the A816, which includes a short boardwalk over the bog.

Mòine Mhór is best known as home to the Iron Age fort of **Dunadd**, one of Scotland's most important Celtic sites, occupying a distinctive 176-foot-high rocky knoll once surrounded by the sea but currently stranded beside the winding River Add. It was here that Fergus, the first King of Dalriada, established his royal seat, having arrived from Ireland in around 500 AD. Its strategic position, the craggy defences and the view from the top are all impressive, but it's the **stone carvings** between the twin summits which make Dunadd so remarkable: several lines of inscription in ogam (an ancient alphabet of Irish origin), the faint outline of a boar, a hollowed-out footprint and a small basin. The boar and the inscriptions are probably Pictish, since the fort was clearly occupied long before Fergus got there, but the footprint and basin have been interpreted as being part of the royal coronation rituals of the kings of Dalriada. It is thought that the Stone of Destiny was used at Dunadd before being moved to Scone Palace, then to Westminster Abbey in London, where it languished until it was returned to Edinburgh in 1996.

Practicalities

Great-value **B&B** is available at *Tibertich* (☎01546/810281; ①; March–Nov), a working sheep farm in the hills to the north of Kilmartin, off the A816. Otherwise, you're best off basing yourself in Crinan rather than Lochgilphead (see p.106 and below). Alternatively, you could hole up in the excellent *Cairnbaan Hotel* (☎01546/603668; ⑥), an eighteenth-century coaching inn overlooking the Crinan Canal; it has a great restaurant and bar meals featuring locally caught seafood – to whip up an appetite you can nip up to the cup- and ring-marked stone behind the hotel. The aforementioned café/restaurant at Kilmartin House is a great lunchtime **eating** option; alternatively, *The Cairn* (☎01546/510254; March–Oct), opposite the church in Kilmartin, is also open in the evening, and features moderately expensive Scottish and Mediterranean dishes.

Lochgilphead

The unlikely administrative centre of Argyll & Bute, **LOCHGILPHEAD**, as the name suggests, lies at the head of Loch Gilp, an arm of Loch Fyne. It's a planned town in the same vein as Inveraray, though nothing like as picturesque. If you're staying in the area, however, you're bound to find yourself here at some point, as Lochgilphead has the only bank and supermarket (not to mention swimming pool) for miles. If you're desperate for something to do in wet weather, you could pay a visit to Highbank Pottery, a short distance up the Oban road (A816), where they make grotesque ceramic animals and offer guided tours of the premises (Mon–Fri 10.30am & 2pm; nominal fee). A better idea, in fine weather, is to head for **Castle Riding Centre** (☎01546/603274) at Brenfield Farm, three miles south, which runs highly enjoyable riding courses lasting from a day to a week, plus trekking and pub rides, and even **rents out bikes** and golf equipment. Another fine-weather option is to stroll round **Kilmory Woodland Park**, a couple of miles up the A83 to Inveraray, with its Iron Age fort, bird hide and lochside views, and take in the gardens laid out in 1830 around Kilmory Castle (now headquarters of the Argyll & Bute District Council).

The **tourist office**, 27 Lochnell St (April & mid-Sept to Oct Mon–Fri 10am–5pm, Sat & Sun noon–5pm; May & June Mon–Sat 10am–5pm, Sun 11am–5pm; July to mid-Sept Mon–Sat 9.30am–6pm, Sun 10am–5pm; ☎01546/602344), will help find you **accommodation**, though really you'd be better off in Crinan (see p.106). If you are looking yourself, the *Stag Hotel* (☎01546/602496; ④) on the main street is the safest option, though it's no bargain. You can also **camp** at the pristinely maintained *Lochgilphead Caravan Park*, a short distance west of town in Bank Park (☎01546/602003; April–Oct); bike rental is available, too. As for **food**, the *Smiddy*, on Smithy Lane (closed Sun), does simple well-cooked grub – for high-class picnic fare, call in at the *Alba Smokehouse* in Kilmory, a mile out of town on the Inveraray road in the industrial estate.

Knapdale

Forested **Knapdale** – from the Gaelic *cnap* (hill) and *dall* (field) – forms a buffer zone between the Kintyre peninsula and the rest of Argyll, bounded to the north by the Crinan Canal and to the south by West Loch Tarbert and consisting of three fingers of land, separated by Loch Sween and Loch Caolisport.

Crinan Canal

In 1801 the nine-mile-long **Crinan Canal** opened, linking Loch Fyne, at Ardrishaig south of Lochgilphead, with the Sound of Jura, thus cutting out the long and treacherous journey around the Mull of Kintyre. John Rennie's original design, although an impressive engineering feat, had numerous faults, and by 1816 Thomas Telford was called in to take charge of the renovations. The canal runs parallel to the sea for quite some way before cutting across the bottom of Mòine Mhór and hitting a flight of locks either side of **CAIRNBAAN** (there are fifteen in total); a walk along the towpath is both picturesque and pleasantly unstrenuous.

There are usually one or two yachts passing through the locks, but the most relaxing place from which to view the canal in action is **CRINAN**, the pretty little fishing port at the western end of the canal. Crinan's tiny harbour is, for the moment at least, still home to a small fishing fleet; a quick burst up through Crinan Wood to the hill above Crinan will give you a bird's-eye view of the sea-lock and its setting. Every room in the *Crinan Hotel* (☎01546/830261; ⑧) looks across Loch Crinan to the Sound of Jura – one of the most beautiful views in Scotland, especially at sunset when the myriad islets and the distinctive Paps of Jura are reflected in the waters of the loch. If the *Crinan* is beyond your means, try one of the secluded **B&Bs**, such as *Tigh-na-Glaic* (☎01546/830261; ③), perched above the harbour, also with views out to sea. Bar **meals** at the *Crinan* are moderately expensive, but recommended, as is the hotel's expensive seafood restaurant, *Lock 16*, on the third floor, which commands a panoramic view; there's only one sitting, at 8pm, so booking is advisable. Down on the lockside there is a cheaper, cheerful **café** (Easter–Oct), serving mouthwatering home-made cakes and wonderful clootie dumplings. If you want to go on one of the **boat trips** organized by Gemini Cruises (☎01546/830238), however, you need to go to Crinan's other harbour, half a mile further along the coast; from here the waymarked three-mile **Crinan Walk** takes you through the nearby Forestry Commission plantation, with excellent views out to sea.

Knapdale Forest and Loch Sween

South of the canal, **Knapdale Forest**, planted in the 1930s, stretches virtually uninterrupted from coast to coast, across hills sprinkled with tiny lochs. The Forestry Commission has set out several lovely **walks**, the easiest of which is the circular, mile-long path which takes you deep into the forest just past **Achanamara** (five miles south of Crinan). The three-mile route around **Loch Coille-Bharr**, which begins from a bend in the B8025, to Tayvallich, is fairly gentle; the other walk, although half a mile shorter, is more strenuous, starting from the B841 (halfway between Crinan and Lochgilphead), which runs along the canal, and ascending the peak of **Dunardry** (702ft). There are several good cycle routes, from easy to tough, in this area – all clearly waymarked.

Continuing down the western finger of Knapdale you come to the pretty, sheltered village of **TAYVALLICH**, after which the peninsula splits again. The western arm leads eventually to the medieval **Chapel of Keills**, newly roofed, with a display of late medieval carved stones, and the remains of a small port where cattle used to be landed from Ireland. There is also a fine view of the **MacCormaig Islands**, the largest of which, Eilean Mór (currently owned by the Scottish National Party), was previously a retreat of the seventh-century St Cormac, but is now a breeding ground for seabirds. The other arm, the **Taynish peninsula**, is a

National Nature Reserve and has one of the largest remaining oak forests in Britain, boasting over twenty species of butterfly. If you want to eat round here, then head for the *Tayvallich Inn* for good local food.

Six miles south of Achanamara, on the eastern shores of **Loch Sween**, is the "Key of Knapdale", the eleventh-century **Castle Sween**, the earliest stone castle in Scotland, but in ruins since 1647. The tranquillity and beauty of the setting is spoilt by the nearby caravan park, an eyesore which makes a visit pretty depressing. You're better off continuing south to the thirteenth-century **Kilmory Chapel**, also ruined but with a new roof protecting the medieval grave slabs and the well-preserved MacMillan's Cross, an eight-foot fifteenth-century Celtic cross showing the crucifixion on one side and a hunting scene on the other.

The easternmost finger of Knapdale is isolated and fairly impenetrable, but it's worth persevering the twenty miles of single-track road in order to reach **KIL-BERRY**, where you can **camp** at the *Port Ban Caravan Park* (☎01880/770224; April–Oct), and enjoy the fantastic sunsets, or **stay the night** in comfort at the *Kilberry Inn* (☎01880/770223; ④; Easter to Oct), which guarantees peace and quiet, plus excellent home-cooking (Mon–Sat). There's also a church worth viewing in Kilberry and a small collection of carved medieval graveslabs, while the western shores of West Loch Tarbert are usually replete with birdlife.

Kintyre

But for the mile-long isthmus between West Loch Tarbert and the much smaller East Loch Tarbert, **KINTYRE** (from the Gaelic *ceann tire*, "land's end") would be an island. Indeed, in the eleventh century, when the Scottish king, Malcolm Canmore, allowed Magnus Barefoot, King of Norway, to lay claim to any island he could circumnavigate by boat, Magnus succeeded in dragging his boat across the Tarbert isthmus and added the peninsula to his Hebridean kingdom. After the Wars of the Covenant, when the vast majority of the population and property was wiped out by a combination of the 1646 potato blight coupled with the destructive attentions of the Earl of Argyll, Kintyre became a virtual desert until the earl began his policy of transplanting Gaelic-speaking Lowlanders to the region. They probably felt quite at home here, as the southern half of the peninsula lies on the Lowland side of the Highland Boundary Fault.

Getting around Kintyre without your own transport is a slow business, though services have improved. There are regular daily **buses** from Glasgow to Campbeltown, via Tarbert and the west coast, and even a skeleton service down the east coast. Bear in mind, though, if you're driving, that the new west coast road is extremely fast, whereas the single-track east coast road takes more than twice as long. Campbeltown has an **airport**, with regular flights from Glasgow, which is only forty miles away by air, compared to over 120 miles by road, and there's now a **ferry link with Northern Ireland** from Campbeltown to Ballycastle.

Tarbert

A distinctive rocket-like church steeple heralds the fishing village of **TARBERT** (in Gaelic *An Tairbeart*, meaning "isthmus"), sheltering an attractive little bay backed by rugged hills. Tarbert's herring industry was mentioned in the Annals of Ulster as far back as 836 AD, though right now the local fishing industry is down to its lowest level ever, due to the strict EU quota system. Ironically, it was local Tarbert fishermen, who, in the 1830s, pioneered the method of herring-fishing known as trawling, seining or ring-netting, which eventually wiped out the Loch Fyne herring stocks. Tourism is now an increasingly important source of income, as is the money that flows through the town during the last week in May, when the yacht races of the famous Scottish Series take place.

Of Robert the Bruce's fourteenth-century **castle** above the town to the south, only the ivy-strewn ruins of the keep remain, though the view from the overgrown rubble makes a stroll up here worthwhile. There are steps up to the castle from beside the excellent Ann Thomas bookshop and gallery on the harbourfront, and, at the far end of the road, a lovely shell beach. Tarbert's main formal tourist attraction, though, is the **An Tairbeart Heritage Centre** (Easter–Dec daily 10am–5pm; free), five minutes' walk up the Campbeltown road. In addition to a shop selling local produce and a tearoom, there are temporary exhibitions on local history and a child-centred, educative **woodland walk** that gives you the chance to get close to the local wildlife, and takes you to Maggie's House, a nineteenth-century crofthouse, last inhabited in the 1960s, and now slowly being restored. A whole range of activities such as wood turning and sheepshearing are on offer, too, at the centre.

Tarbert's **tourist office** (April Mon–Fri 10am–5pm, Sat & Sun noon–5pm; May & June Mon–Sat 10am–5pm, Sun 11am–5pm; July to mid-Sept Mon–Sat 9.30am–6pm, Sun 10am–5pm; mid-Sept to Oct Mon–Sat 10am–5pm, Sun noon–5pm; ☎01880/820429) is on the harbour. If you need to **stay**, there's no shortage of B&Bs, though none are outstanding – try *Springside* B&B on Pier Road (☎01880/820413; ①). Highly recommended, however, are the wonderfully Victorian *Columba Hotel* further along Tarbert waterfront (☎01880/820808; ④), and, two miles up the A83 to Lochgilphead, *Stonefield Castle Hotel*, a handsome Victorian mansion set in magnificent grounds overlooking Loch Fyne (☎01880/820836; ⑦). The nearest **campsite** is *West Loch Tarbert Caravan Park* (☎01880/820873; April–Oct), two miles south of Tarbert on the A83. **Bike rental** is available from Mr Leitch (☎01880/820287), on the opposite side of the harbour from the tourist office.

The best bar **food** is to be had at the *Victoria Hotel*, where you can sit in the conservatory and look out across the harbour. For some excellent fish and seafood, head for the pricey *Anchorage* (☎01880/820881; May–Sept daily; Oct–April Tues–Sat eves only), on the opposite side of the harbour, unforgettable not least for its eccentric proprietor.

FERRY CONNECTIONS IN AND AROUND TARBERT

One reason you might find yourself staying in Tarbert is its proximity to no fewer than four **ferry terminals**. The small CalMac ferry, which connects Kintyre with **Portavadie** on the Cowal peninsula, leaves from Tarbert's Pier Road; the busiest terminal, however, is at **Kennacraig**, five miles south along the A83, which runs daily sailings to Islay and a once-weekly service to Colonsay. From Kennacraig, the B8001 cuts across the peninsula to **Claonaig**, where a summer car ferry (April to mid-Oct) runs to Lochranza on Arran; and finally, south of Kennacraig on the A83, the Gigha ferry departs from **Tayinloan**.

Isle of Gigha

Gigha (pronounced "Geeya", with a hard "g") is a low-lying, fertile island, just three miles off the west coast of Kintyre, reputedly occupied for 5000 years. The island's Ayrshire cattle produce over a quarter of a million gallons of milk a year, despite the fact that Gigha's creamery closed down in the 1980s; the island also produces the distinctive fruit-shaped goat's cheese which is one of the main exports. Like many of the smaller Hebrides, Gigha was sold by its original lairds, the MacNeils, and has been put on the market numerous times in recent years, causing great uncertainty amongst the 140 or so inhabitants.

The ferry from Tayinloan, 23 miles south of Tarbert, deposits you at the island's only village, **ARDMINISH**, where you'll find the post office and shop and the all-denominations island church with some interesting stained-glass windows, including one to Kenneth Macleod, composer of the well-known ditty *Road to the Isles*. The main attraction on the island is the **Achamore Gardens** (daily 9am–dusk; £2), a mile and a half south of Ardminish. Established by the first post-war owner, Sir James Horlick of hot drink fame, they are best seen in early summer, ablaze with rhododendrons and azaleas. To the southwest of the gardens, the ruins of the thirteenth-century **St Catan's Chapel** are floored with intricately carved medieval gravestones; the ogam stone nearby is the only one of its kind in the west of Scotland. The real draw of Gigha, however, apart from the peace and quiet, are the white sandy beaches, including one at Ardminish itself, that dot the coastline.

Gigha is so small – six miles by one mile – that most visitors come here just for the day. There is no camping allowed, and no hostel, but it is possible **to stay** either with the McSporrans at the *Post Office House* (☎01583/505251; ①) or at the *Gigha Hotel* (☎01583/505254; ⑤; March–Oct), which also runs self-catering flats dotted over the island. The *Gigha Hotel* is also the place to go for tea and cakes, and for bar meals. **Bike rental** is available from the post office, and there's a nine-hole **golf course**.

The west coast

Kintyre's bleak **west coast** ranks among the most exposed stretches of coastline in Argyll. Atlantic breakers pound the shoreline, while the persistent westerly wind forces the trees against the hillside. However, when the weather's fine and the wind not too fierce, there are numerous deserted sandy beaches to enjoy with great views over to Gigha, Islay, Jura and even Ireland.

There are several **campsites** to choose from along the stretch of coast around **TAYINLOAN**, ranging from the big *Point Sands Caravan Park* (☎01583/441263; April–Oct), two miles to the north, near a long stretch of sandy beach, or the smaller, more informal *Muasdale Holiday Park*, three miles to the south (☎01583/421207; April–Oct). Other **accommodation** options along the coast include the late Victorian *Balinakill Country House* at Clachan (☎01880/740206; ③), north of Tayinloan, and the *Argyll Hotel* (☎01583/421212, *wmacken759@aol.com*; ③), a clean, fully modernized old Victorian inn overlooking a sandy beach in Bellochantuy. For **food** along the coast, try the *Tayinloan Inn*, a cosy pub offering better-than-average bar meals, or the *North Beachmore Farm*, signposted off the A83, just south of Tayinloan, with superb views over the coast, and good, low-priced meals, tea and cakes.

Two-thirds of the way down the coast you can visit **Glenbarr Abbey** (Easter–Oct daily except Tues 10am–5.30pm; £2.50), an eighteenth-century laird's house filled with tedious memorabilia about the once-powerful MacAlister clan, now reduced to augmenting their income by giving personal guided tours of their house to the trickle of tourists that pass this way. Still, there are plenty of musty old sofas to lounge around in, a tearoom, and attractive grounds which provide a brief respite from the Atlantic winds. If you're up for spot of **horse riding**, get in touch with the nearby Barrglen Equitation Centre, based at Arnicle Farm (☎01583/421397), which offers lessons and longer rides for "the good, the bad and the wobbly".

The only major development along the entire west coast is **MACHRIHANISH**, at the southern end of Machrihanish Bay, the longest continuous stretch of sand in Argyll. There are two approaches to the **beach**: from Machrihanish itself, or from Westport, at the north end of the bay, where the A83 swings east towards Campbeltown; either way, the sea here is too dangerous for swimming. Machrihanish itself was once a thriving salt-producing and coal-mining centre – you can still see the miners' cottages at neighbouring Drumlemble – but now survives solely on tourism. The main draw, apart from the beach, is the exposed championship **golf links** between the beach and Campbeltown airport on the nearby flat and fertile swath of land known as the Laggan. There's also a tiny **seabird observatory** at Uisaed Point, ten minutes' walk west of the village, though it's best visited in the winter months, when it provides a welcome shelter for ornithologists trying to spot a rare bird blown off course.

Several of the imposing, detached Victorian town houses overlooking the bay in Machrihanish, such as *Ardell House* (☎01586/810235; ④; March–Oct), offer **accommodation**; there's also a large, fully equipped and very exposed **campsite** (☎01586/810366; March–Sept) overlooking the golf links. For **nightlife**, *The Beachcomber* bar is the liveliest place in Machrihanish.

Campbeltown

CAMPBELTOWN's best feature is its setting, in a deep bay sheltered by Davaar Island and the surrounding hills. With a population of 6500, it is also one of the largest towns in Argyll and, if you're staying in the southern half of Kintyre, its shops are by far the best place to stock up on supplies. Originally known as Kinlochkilkerran (*Ceann Loch Cill Chiaran*), the town was renamed in the seventeenth century by the Earl of Argyll – a Campbell – when it became one of the main points for immigration from the Lowlands. As is evident from the architecture, Campbeltown's heyday was the Victorian era, when shipbuilding was going strong, coal was shipped by canal from Drumlemble, the fishing fleet was vast and Campbeltown Loch was said to be made of whisky. The decline of all its old industries has left the town permanently depressed, though its geographical isolation has been tempered by the new car ferry link with Ballycastle in Northern Ireland.

The Town

Nineteenth-century visitors to Campbeltown frequently found the place engulfed in a thick fog of pungent peat smoke from the town's 34 **whisky distilleries**. Today, only Glen Scotia and Springbank are left to maintain this regional sub-group of single malt whiskies which is distinct from Highland, Islay or Lowland varieties (see p.37 for more on whisky). The family-owned Springbank distillery, off Longrow, offers tours by appointment (☎01586/552085; £2.50), and you can buy a guide to Campbeltown's former distilleries from the tourist office; aficionados should also peruse the huge range of whiskies for sale at Eaglesome on Longrow South.

The town's one major sight is the **Campbeltown Cross**, a fourteenth-century blue-green cross with figural scenes and spirals of Celtic knotting, which presides over the main roundabout on the quayside. Until the last war, it used to be rather more impressive in the middle of the main street outside the **Town Hall**, with its distinctive eighteenth-century octagonal clock tower. Back on the palm-tree-dotted waterfront is the **"Wee Picture House"**, a dinky little Art Deco cinema on Hall Street, built in 1913 and now doubling as a bingo hall (Fri), and movie house. Next door is the equally delightful **Campbeltown Museum and Library** (Wed, Fri & Sat 10am–1pm & 2–5pm, Tues & Thurs 10am–1pm & 2–7.30pm; free), built in 1897 in the local sandstone, crowned by a distinctive lantern, and decorated on its harbourside wall with four relief panels depicting each of the town's main industries at the time. Inside, there's a timber-framed ceiling and etched glass partitions to admire, not to mention a rather unusual brass model of the Temple of Solomon (as it might have looked). The museum itself, which you enter through the library, provides a less remarkable rundown on local history; for a more enlightening version, head to the Heritage Centre (described below).

It used to be said that Campbeltown had almost as many churches as it did distilleries, and even today the townscape is dominated by its church spires – in particular, the top-heavy crown spire of **Longrow Church**, on the road to Machrihanish. The former Lorne Street Church, known locally as the "Tartan Kirk", partly due to its Gaelic associations and its stripy bell-cote and pinnacles, has now become the **Campbeltown Heritage Centre** (April–Oct Mon–Sat noon–5pm, Sun 2–5pm; £2). A beautiful wooden skiff from 1906 stands where the main altar once was, and there's plenty on the local whisky industry and St Kieran, the sixth-century "Apostle of Kintyre", who lived in a cave – which you can get to at low tide – not far from Campbeltown. A dedicated ascetic, he would only eat bread mixed with a third sand and a few herbs; he wore chains, had a stone pillow and slept out in the snow – unsurprisingly, at the age of 33, he died of jaundice.

One of the most popular day-trips is to **Davaar Island**, linked to the peninsula at low tide by a mile-long shoal, or *dóirlinn* as it's known in Gaelic. Check the times of the tides from the tourist office before setting out; you have around six hours in which to make the return journey from Kildalloig Point, two miles or so east of town. Davaar is uninhabited and used for grazing (hence no dogs are allowed); its main attraction, besides the wealth of rock flora, is the cave painting of the Crucifixion executed in secret by local artist Archibald MacKinnon, in 1887, and touched up by him after he'd owned up in 1934; a year later, aged 85, he died.

Practicalities

Campbeltown's **tourist office** is currently on the Old Quay (April Mon–Sat 10am–5pm; May & June Mon–Sat 9am–5pm, Sun noon–5pm; July to mid-Sept Mon–Sat 9am– 6.30pm, Sun noon–5pm; mid-Sept to Oct Mon–Fri 10am–5pm, Sun 10am–4pm; Nov–March Mon–Fri 10am–4pm; ☎01586/552056); the new pier for the **ferry** to Ballycastle lies just to the south and the **airport** lies three miles west, towards Machrihanish (there's a bus connection). There's no shortage of **accommodation**, the delightful family-run *Ardshiel Hotel*, on Kilkerran Road (☎01586/552133; ③), being by far the best choice; it's situated on a lovely leafy square, just a block or so back from the ferry terminal, and has a cosy bar, serving food, and a more expensive à la carte restaurant. Another excellent choice is the *Balegreggan Country House Hotel* (☎01586/552062; ④), a fine detached Victorian villa, in the hills to the north of town, off the A83. For a cheap, simple, central B&B, head for *Eagle Lodge*, 56 High St (☎01586/551359; ①; Feb–Nov).

As for **places to eat**, the *Locarno Café* on Longrow South is a period-piece greasy spoon, one of many in Campbeltown. The best bar meals and restaurant are to be found at the aforementioned *Ardshiel Hotel*, while the *Commercial Inn* on Cross Street is a good drinking hole. You can **rent bikes** at The Bike Shop, Longrow (☎01586/554443). If you're here in the middle of August, be sure to check out the **Mull of Kintyre Music & Arts Festival**, which features some great traditional Irish and Scottish bands.

Southend and the Mull of Kintyre

The bulbous, hilly end of Kintyre, to the south of Campbeltown, features some of the most spectacular scenery on the whole peninsula, mixed with large swaths of Lowland-style farmland. **SOUTHEND** itself, a bleak, blustery spot, comes as something of a disappointment, though it does have a wide sandy beach. Below the cliffs to the west of the beach, a ruined thirteenth-century chapel marks the alleged arrival point of St Columba prior to his trip to Iona, and on a rocky knoll nearby a pair of footprints carved into the rock are known as **Columba's footprints**, though only one is actually of ancient origin. Jutting out into the sea at the east end of the bay is **Dunaverty Rock**, where a force of 300 Royalists was massacred by the Covenanting army of the Earl of Argyll in 1647, despite having surrendered voluntarily. A couple of miles out to sea from Dunaverty lies **Sanda Island**, which contains the remains of St Ninian's chapel, plus two ancient crosses, a holy well. a lighthouse and lots of seabirds, including puffins; it's now a holiday retreat with self-catering cottages available (☎01586/553134; April–Sept). Back on the mainland, there are even nicer beaches further west at Carskiey Bay, and at Macharioch Bay, three miles east, looking out to distant Ailsa Craig in the Firth of Clyde.

Most people venture south of Campbeltown to make a pilgrimage to the **Mull of Kintyre** – the nearest Britain gets to Ireland, whose coastline, just twelve miles away, appears remarkably close on fine days. Although the Mull was made famous by the mawkish number-one hit by sometime local resident Paul McCartney, with the help of the Campbeltown Pipe Band, there's nothing specifically to see in this godforsaken storm-racked spot but the view. The roads up to the **"Gap"** (1150ft) – where you must leave your car – and particularly down to the lighthouse, itself 300ft above the ocean waves, are terrifyingly tortuous. It's about a mile from the "Gap" to the lighthouse (and a long haul back up), though there's a strategic viewpoint just ten minutes' walk from the car park.

There are few places to **stay** in this remote region. Southend's only hotel has been closed for some time and cuts a forlorn figure, set back from the bay; try *Ormsary Farm* (☎01586/830665; ①; April–Sept) instead, a small dairy farm up Glen Breakerie, or the **campsite** at *Machribeg Farm* (☎01586/830249; Easter–Sept), right by the beach. If you're interested in **horse riding**, call the

Mull of Kintyre Equestrian Centre at Homeston Farm (☎01586/552437), sign-posted off the B842 to Southend.

The east coast

The **east coast** of Kintyre is gentler than the west, sheltered from the Atlantic winds and in parts strikingly beautiful, with stunning views across to Arran. However, be warned that bus services are very limited up the east coast and, if you're driving the thirty or so miles up to Skipness on the slow, winding, single-track B842, you'll need a fair amount of time.

The ruins of **Saddell Abbey**, a Cistercian foundation thought to have been founded by Somerled in 1160, lie ten miles up the coast from Campbeltown, set at the lush, wooded entrance to Saddell Glen. The abbey fell into disrepair in the six-teenth century, and, though the remains are not exactly impressive, they do shel-ter a collection of medieval grave slabs decorated with full-scale relief figures of knights. Standing by the privately owned shoreline there's a splendid memorial to the last Campbell laird to live at Saddell Castle, which he built in 1774.

Further north lies the fishing village of **CARRADALE**, the only place of any size on the east coast and "popular with those who like unsophisticated resorts", as one 1930s guide put it. The village itself is rather drab, but the tiny, very pret-ty harbour with its small fishing fleet, and the wide, sandy beach to the south, make up for it. On the east side of the beach is **Carradale Point**, a wildlife reserve with feral goats and a good example of a **vitrified fort** built more than two thousand years ago on a small tidal island off the headland (best approached from the beach). There are several pleasant walks with good views across to Arran laid out in the woods around Carradale, for which the best starting point is the car park at Port na Storm on the road into the village. The best wet-weather option is **Network Carradale Heritage Centre** on the outskirts of the village (Easter to mid-Oct Mon–Sat 10.30am–5pm, Sun 12.30–4pm; £1), which traces the demise of the local herring fleet; it's small in scale but informative, and there's good home-baking to be had in the tearoom.

Accommodation is available at the *Carradale Hotel* (☎01583/431223; ③), whose bar is the hub of village social life (and whose food is good). There are sev-eral **B&Bs**, the best of which is the big Victorian *Dunvalanree Guest House* (☎01583/431226; ③), overlooking the sheltered little bay of Port Righ, towards Carradale Point; you can also stay at *Mains Farm* (☎01583/431216; ①; April–Oct), a working farm adjacent to *Carradale Bay* **campsite** (☎01583/431665; Easter–Sept), right by the sandy beach. Carradale also boasts a real baker – try the treacle scones or cookie pudding (bread and butter pudding south of the bor-der). Close by, a little to the south, above a seal-strewn soft shingle beach, the imposing Victorian pile, *Torrisdale Castle*, offers **self-catering** in castle or cottage (☎01583/431233).

Five miles further up the coast road is **Grogport Tannery** (daily 9am–6pm; free), which produces naturally coloured, organically tanned, fully washable sheepskins (gloves and slippers, too). The B842 ends seven miles north of Grogport at **CLAONAIG**, little more than a slipway for the small summer car ferry to Arran. Beyond here, a dead-end road winds its way along the shore a few miles further north to the tiny village of **SKIPNESS**, where the considerable ruins of the enormous thirteenth-century **Skipness Castle** and a chapel look out across the Kilbrannan Sound to Arran. You can sit outside and admire both, whilst enjoying fresh oysters, delicious queenies, mussels and home-baked cakes from the excellent **seafood cabin** (late May to Sept) at *Skipness House*, which also offers **accommodation** in a family home (☎01880/760207; ⑤). There are several gentle walks laid out in the nearby mixed woodland, up the nearby glen.

Isle of Arran

Shaped like a kidney bean, **Arran** is the most southerly (and therefore the most accessible) of all the Scottish islands. The Highland–Lowland dividing line passes right through its centre – hence the tourist board's aphorism about it being like "Scotland in miniature" – leaving the northern half sparsely populated, mountainous and bleak, while the lush southern half enjoys a much milder climate. Despite its immense popularity, the tourists, like the population of around 4500 – many of whom are incomers – tend to stick to the southeastern quarter of the island, leaving the west and the north relatively undisturbed.

There are two big crowd-pullers on Arran: **geology** and **golf**. The former has fascinated rock-obsessed students since Sir James Hutton came here in the late eighteenth century to confirm his theories of igneous geology. A hundred years later, Sir Archibald Geikie's investigations were a landmark in the study of Arran's geology, and the island remains a popular destination for university and school field trips. As for golf, Arran boasts seven courses, including three of the eighteen-hole variety at Brodick, Lamlash and Whiting Bay, and a unique twelve-hole course at Shiskine, near Blackwaterfoot.

Although tourism is now by far its most important industry, Arran, at twenty miles in length, is large enough to have a life of its own. While the island's post-1745 history and the Clearances (set in motion by the local lairds, the dukes of Hamilton) are as depressing as elsewhere in the Highlands, in recent years Arran has not suffered from the depopulation which has plagued other, more remote islands. Once a county in its own right (along with Bute), Arran has been left out of the new Argyll and Bute district in the latest county boundary shake-up, and is coupled instead with mainland North Ayrshire, with which it enjoys year-round transport links, but little else.

Transport on Arran itself is pretty good: daily **buses** circle the island (Brodick tourist office has timetables) and there are two **ferry services** – a year-round one from Ardrossan in Ayrshire to **Brodick**, and a smaller ferry from Claonaig on the Kintyre peninsula to **Lochranza** in the north (April to mid-Oct).

Brodick

Although the resort of **BRODICK** (from the Norse *breidr vik*, "broad bay") is a place of little charm, it does at least have a grand setting in a wide, sandy bay set against a backdrop of granite mountains. Its development as a tourist resort was held back for a long time by its elitist owners, the dukes of Hamilton, though nowadays, as the island's capital and main communication hub, Brodick is by far the busiest town on Arran.

Brodick's sights, such as they are, are clustered on the north side of the bay, a couple of miles from the ferry terminal. The **Arran Heritage Museum** (Easter–Oct Mon–Sat 11am–5pm; £2) is a somewhat dry collection of old tools and furniture in a converted eighteenth-century crofter's farm, and is really only

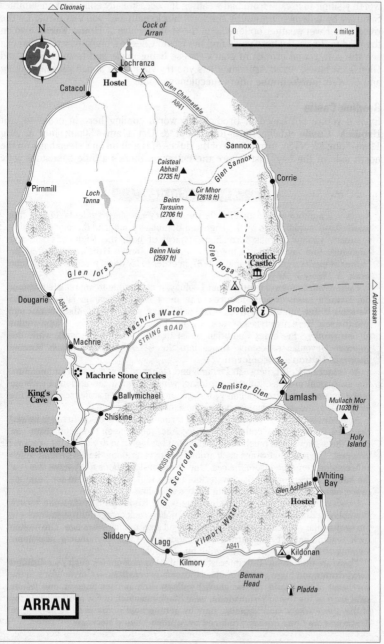

△ *Claonaig*

N

Cock of Arran

0   4 miles

Lochranza

Hostel

Catacol

Glen Chalmadale

A841

Sannox

Caisteal Abhail (2735 ft) ▲

Corrie

Pirnmill

Loch Tanna

Cir Mhor (2618 ft) ▲

Glen Sannox

Beinn Tarsuinn (2706 ft) ▲

▲

Beinn Nuis (2597 ft) ▲

Glen Rosa

Brodick Castle 🏛

Glen Iorsa

Dougarie

A841

Machrie Water

Brodick ℹ

△ *Ardrossan*

Machrie

STRING ROAD

Machrie Stone Circles

Benlister Glen

King's Cave 🏕

Ballymichael

Lamlash

Mullach Mor (1030 ft) ▲

Shiskine

Holy Island

Blackwaterfoot

ROSS ROAD

Glen Scorrodale

Glen Ashdale

Whiting Bay

Hostel

Kilmory Water

Sliddery

Lagg

A841

Kildonan

Kilmory

Bennan Head

Pladda

ARRAN

© Crown copyright

worth visiting to escape from bad weather. It's occasionally enlivened on summer Sundays by a demonstration by the local blacksmith and you can picnic by the river. Other wet-weather options lie in the visitor centre at **Home Farm**, also on the road to the castle; here you'll find the Island Cheese Company, where you can see the soft, round crotins of goat's cheese being made and taste Brodick and Glenshant blues; Arran Aromatics lets you try your hand at natural-soapmaking and *Creelers* **smokehouse** offers succulent seafood.

Brodick Castle

Even if you're not based in Brodick, it's worth coming here in order to visit **Brodick Castle** (daily: April–June, Sept & Oct 11am–4.30pm; July & Aug 11am–5pm; £5; NTS), former seat of the dukes of Hamilton on a steep bank on the north side of the bay. Just before the entrance, there's a little sandstone jetty

---

ARRAN GEOLOGY

Arran is a number-one destination for the country's geology students. Firstly, this small island is split in two by the Highland Boundary Fault, and therefore contains a superb variety of rock formations, typical of both the Highlands and the Lowlands. And, secondly, it is the place where **Sir James Hutton** (1726–97), the "father of modern geology" came in 1787, in order to lay down research for his epic work, *A Theory of the Earth*.

Even if you know very little about geology, it is possible to appreciate some of the island's more obvious features. The most famous location is just beyond **Newton Point** , on the north shore of Loch Ranza, where Allt Beithe stream runs into the sea. Here, two types of rocks by the shore are set virtually at right angles to one another, the older Cambrian schist dipping towards the land, while the younger Devonian sandstone slopes into the sea. This phenomenon became known as **Hutton's unconformity**.

At **Imacher Point**, between Pirnmill and Dougarie, you can view in miniature the geological process known as **folding**, which affected the ancient Cambrian schist around a hundred million years ago, and, on a larger scale, resulted in the formation of mountain ranges such as those of North Arran.

Another classic, more recent geological formation to be seen on Arran is **raised beaches**, formed at the end of the last Ice Age, some fifteen thousand years ago, when the sea level was much higher, and then left high and dry when the sea level dropped. The road that wraps itself around Arran runs along the flat ground which subsequently emerged from the sea. One of the best locations to observe this is at the **King's Cave**, north of Blackwaterfoot (see p.120), where you can see huge sea caves, stranded some distance from today's shoreline.

Down on the south coast, the shoreline below **Kildonan** reveals some superb examples of **dolerite dykes**, formed when molten rock erupted through cracks in the sedimentary sandstone rocks above around sixty million years ago. The molten rock solidified and, being harder, now stands above the surrounding sandstone, forming strange rocky piers jutting out into the sea.

There are numerous other interesting features to look out for, such as **solidified sand dunes** and huge granite boulders, known as **erratics**, on Corrie beach in the northeast of the island, classic **glacial valleys** such as Glen Sannox, and **felsite sills** such as the one at Drumadoon, near Blackwaterfoot, in the southwest. If any of the above whets your appetite, start by getting hold of the geological booklet, *Arran and the Clyde Islands*, produced by Scottish Natural Heritage.

where the duke's wine and ice from Canada was landed. It used to serve the village, but the eleventh duke thought the tenants unsightly and had them moved out of sight round the bay. He also closed the barytes mine at Sannox, a vital source of employment for the islanders, on the grounds that it "spoilt the solemn grandeur of the scene".

The bulk of the castle was built in the nineteenth century, giving it a domestic rather than military look, and the **interior** – once you've fought your way past the 87 stags' heads on the stairs – is comfortable but undistinguished. Don't miss the portrait of the eleventh duke's faithful piper, who injured his throat on a grouse bone, was warned never to pipe again but did so and died. Probably the most atmospheric room is the copper-filled Victorian kitchen, which conjures up a vision of the sweated and sweating labour required to feed the folk upstairs.

Much more attractive, however, are the walled **gardens** (daily 9.30am–dusk; gardens and country park only £2.50) and extensive grounds, a treasury of exotic plants and trees enjoying the favourable climate (including one of Europe's finest collections of rhododendrons), and commanding a superb view across the bay. There is an adventure playground for kids, but the whole area is a natural playground with waterfalls, a giant pitcher plant that swallows thousands of midges daily, and a maze of paths. Buried in the grounds there is a bizarre Bavarian-style **summerhouse** lined entirely with pine cones, one of three built by the eleventh duke to make his wife, Princess Marie of Baden, feel at home. For the energetic there is also a **country park** with eleven miles of scenic trails, starting from a small informative, hands-on nature centre. In summer there are guided walks with the rangers, but at any time you can be surprised by red squirrels, nightjars and the abundance of fungi. The excellent castle **tearoom** serves traditional food with a local flavour and is highly recommended.

Practicalities

Brodick's **tourist office** (May–Sept Mon–Sat 9am–7.30pm, Sun 10am–5pm; Oct–April Mon–Sat 9am–5pm; ☎01770/302140) is by the CalMac pier, and has reams of information on every activity from pony trekking to paragliding. Unless you've got to catch an early-morning ferry, however, there's little reason to stay in Brodick. Should you do so, the best **rooms** close to the ferry terminal are at the excellent *Dunvegan House Hotel* (☎01770/302811; ④), the Art Deco *Invercloy Hotel* (☎01770/302225, *invercloyhotel@s.i.co.uk*; ②; March–Oct), or the good-value *Belvedere Guest House* (☎01770/302397, *brachure@visionunltd.force9.co.uk*; ①); closer to the castle is the sandstone *Glen Cloy Farm House* (☎01770/302351, *mvpglencloy@compuserve.com*; ②; March–Nov), which has real fires and a warm welcome. For those in search of leisure facilities, the *Auchrannie Country House Hotel* (☎01770/302234, *auchrannie@btinternet.com*; ④), former home of the dowager Duchess of Hamilton, has the lot, including a huge indoor pool, sauna, steam room and gym, all of which are open to non-residents, too. Offering nothing so vulgar as a swimming pool is the tasteful *Kilmichael Country House Hotel* (☎01770/302219; ⑥), originally built in the seventeenth century and still retaining lots of period features; dinner here is very expensive and very formal, but it's one of the best you'll get on the island. The nearest **campsite** is *Glenrosa* (☎01770/302380), a lovely farm site two miles from town off the B880 to Blackwaterfoot.

For **food**, apart from dinner at the aforementioned *Kilmichael Country House Hotel*, the only place that really stands out is the moderately expensive seafood

---

OUTDOOR ACTIVITIES ON ARRAN

Arran has a highly developed tourist industry, and there are a number of outfits ready and willing to help you enjoy the great outdoors. For **hiking** in the mountains in the northern half of the island, all you need is a good map and the right gear – see p.46 for safety in the hills, while the walks are described in more detail on p.121. The Forestry Commission has laid out several more gentle **woodland walks** in its various plantations, as well as an eleven-mile cycle route from Lamlash to Kilmory; Forest Enterprise (☎01770/302218) also organizes various guided forest walks in the summer. **Bike rental** is available from Brodick Cycles (☎01770/302460), opposite the village hall, and from the Balmichael Visitor Centre in Shiskine (☎0700/292538), which offers guided cycling tours, departing daily at 10am from the Centre. **Horse riding**, from half-hour rides for the kids to full-day treks for experienced riders, can be sorted out at Brodick Riding Centre in Corriegills (☎01770/302800), a couple of miles southeast of the town, or at Cairnhouse Riding Centre in Blackwaterfoot (☎01770/860466). For **boat rental**, contact either Brodick Boat Hire (☎01770/302868), on Bordick Beach, or Lamlash Boat Hires, who are based on the pier in Lamlash. Finally, for the truly mad, there's the chance to go **paragliding** with Flying Fever (☎01770/820292).

---

restaurant *Creelers* (☎01770/302810; mid-March to Oct), by the Arran Heritage Museum on the road to the castle; there are above-average bar meals at *Brodick Bar & Brasserie* (☎01770/302169) by the post office; the bar snacks (lunchtime only) at *Duncan's Bar* in the *Kingsley Hotel* make a cheaper option and there's real ale too; while, the *Douglas Hotel* features regular **live music** sessions on Sundays. If you want to find out about any other events taking place on Arran, pick up a copy of the island's **weekly newspaper**, the *Arran Banner*.

The south

The **southern half of Arran** is less spectacular, and less forbidding than the north; it's more heavily forested and the land is more fertile, and for that reason the vast majority of the population lives here. The tourist industry has followed them, though with considerably less justification.

Lamlash, Holy Island and Whiting Bay

With its distinctive Edwardian architecture and mild climate, **LAMLASH** epitomizes the sedate charm of southeast Arran. Lamlash Bay has in its time sheltered King Hakon's fleet in 1263 and, more recently, served as a naval base in both world wars. Its major drawback for the visitor, however, is that it is made not of sand but of boulder-strewn mud flats. The monument on the village green marks the spot on which a farewell sermon was given to the eleven families, victims of the Clearances, who, in 1829, sailed from here to Canada.

The best reason for coming to Lamlash is to visit the slug-shaped hump of **Holy Island**, which shelters the bay, and is now owned by a group of Tibetan Buddhists who have set up a meditation centre – providing you don't dawdle, it's possible to scramble up to the top of Mullach Mór (1030ft), the island's highest point, and still catch the last ferry back. En route, you might well bump into the island's most numerous residents: feral goats, Highland cattle and rabbits. The Holy Island ferry runs more or less hourly (☎01770/600998; £6 return); alternatively, you might prefer to go **mackerel fishing** – booking essential, from the caravan on the pier (☎01770/600349).

If you want to **stay** in style in Lamlash, head for the *Glenisle Hotel* (☎01770/600559; ③; closed Jan), or the comfortable *Lilybank* (☎01770/600230; ②; March–Oct), which does good home-made food. You can **camp** at the fully equipped *Middleton Camping Park* (☎01770/600255; April–Oct), just five minutes' walk south of the centre. Lamlash's best **restaurant** is undoubtedly the *Carraig Mhor* near the pier (☎01770/600453; Mon–Sat eves only), which offers an exclusive and expensive menu featuring fresh local game, fish and seafood. There are a few cheaper options, such as the **bar meals** at the *Pier Head Tavern*, or at the friendly *Drift Inn* by the shore; there's even a Chinese takeaway behind the post office. On the subject of eating, it was a Lamlash man, Donald McKelvie, who made Arran potatoes world-famous, breeding in the rich soil of the island, Arran Pilot, Arran Chief and Arran Victory, of which Maris Piper is a modern descendant.

An established Clydeside resort for over a century now, **WHITING BAY**, four miles south of Lamlash, is actually pretty characterless. However, it's a good base for walking in the southern half of Arran and there are some excellent **places to stay**, including *The Royal* (☎01770/700286; ②; March–Oct), the *Argentine House Hotel*, run (confusingly) by a Swiss couple (☎01770/700662; *argentine.hotel.arran@dial.pipex.com*; ③; closed mid-Jan to mid-Feb), and the *Burlington Hotel* (☎01770/700255; *burlhotel@aol.com*; ③; Easter–Oct), all on Shore Road. At the lower end of the price range, *Norwood* (☎01770/700536; ①; March–Oct), on Smiddy Brae, is the best choice. Whiting Bay also boasts a **youth hostel** (☎01770/700339; March–Oct), at the southern end of the bay. **Eating** options are limited outside of the hotels; the best dining room is at the *Argentine House Hotel*, but it's expensive. Otherwise, you're limited to the snacks at the *Coffee Pot* on the seafront, or the bar meals at the *Cameronia Hotel*. For **bike rental**, go to Whiting Bay Hires (☎01770/700382) on the jetty.

Kildonan to Lagg

Access to the sea is tricky along the south coast, but worth the effort, as the sandy beaches here are among the island's finest. One place you can get down to the sea is at **KILDONAN**, an attractive small village south of Lamlash, set slightly off the main road, with a good sandy beach which you share with the local wildlife and, at its east end, a ruined castle looking out to the tiny island of Pladda. Those with kids might like to drop in at the nearby **South Bank Farm Park** (Easter–Sept daily 10am–5pm; £2), to see rare breeds and the occasional sheepdog demonstration (Tues & Thurs 2pm). You can also camp in Kildonan, at the *Breadalbane* **campsite** (☎01770/820210), right on the shore.

KILMORY, four miles west of Kildonan, is the home of the prizewinning **Torrylinn Creamery** (daily 10am–4pm), which produces a cheddary cheese called Arran Dunlop, and where you can watch the whole process from a viewing window. Next door to Kilmory is the picturesque village of **LAGG**, nestling in a tree-filled hollow by Kilmory Water. The friendly village stores has an excellent **tearoom**; those feeling flush should **stay** at the comfortable *Lagg Country House Hotel* (☎01770/870255; ⑤), an eighteenth-century inn set in acres of woodland; for a nice family **B&B**, go for the converted seventeenth-century flax mill of *Kilmory House* (☎01770/870342; ①). Scotland's only naturist beach is half a mile west of Lagg, down a rough track at Cleat shore.

Blackwaterfoot and Machrie

BLACKWATERFOOT, on the western end of String Road, which bisects the island, is dominated, not to say somewhat spoilt, by the presence of the island's largest hotel. In every other way, Blackwaterfoot is a beguiling little place, which boasts the only twelve-hole golf course in the world. A gentle two-mile walk north along the coast will bring you to the **King's Cave**, one of several where Robert the Bruce is said to have encountered the famously patient arachnid, while hiding during his final bid to free Scotland in 1306 If you want **to stay**, the Victorian *Blackwaterfoot Hotel* (☎01770/860202; ⑤; March–Dec) is the place to hole up, though there are even better B&Bs just up the road in **SHISKINE**; in particular, *The Old House* (☎01770/860302; ②; April–Nov).

North of Blackwaterfoot, the wide expanse of **Machrie Moor** boasts a wealth of Bronze Age sites. No fewer than six **stone circles** sit east of the main road, and, although many of them barely break the peat's surface, the tallest surviving monolith is over eighteen feet high. The most striking configuration is at Fingal's Cauldron Seat, with two concentric circles of granite boulders; legend has it that Fingal tied his dog to one of them while cooking at his cauldron. If you're feeling peckish, the Machrie golf course **tearoom** (April to mid-Oct) is a welcome oasis in this sparsely populated area.

The north

The desolate **north half of Arran** – effectively the Highland part – features bare granite peaks, the occasional golden eagle and miles of unspoilt scenery, within reach only to those prepared to do some serious hiking. Arran's most accessible peak is also the island's highest, **Goat Fell** (2866ft) – take your pick from the Gaelic, *goath*, meaning "windy", or the Norse, *geit-fjall*, "goat mountain" – which can be ascended in just three hours from Brodick (return journey 5hr), though it's a strenuous hike (for the usual safety precautions, see p.46). From Goat Fell, experienced walkers can follow the horseshoe of craggy summits and descend either from the saddle below Beinn Tarsuinn (2706ft) or from Beinn Nuis (2597ft) itself.

Corrie and Sannox

Another good base for hiking is the pretty little seaside village of **CORRIE**, six miles north of Brodick, where a procession of pristine cottages lines the road to Lochranza. You can **stay** at *Tigh-na-Achaidh* (☎01770/810208; ③), Corrie's finest B&B, or, if it's full, the much larger, traditional seafront *Blackrock House* (☎01770/810282; ④; March–Oct). A good budget option is the *North High Corrie Croft* **bunkhouse** (☎01770/302203), above the village on a raised beach; it has one large room for group bookings, and an annexe with eight beds (advance booking advisable). **Bike rental** is available from The Spinning Wheel (☎01770/810640). Corrie Golf Club, confusingly in Sannox, offers good-value **meals** all day in summer.

At **SANNOX**, two miles north, the road leaves the shoreline and climbs steeply, giving breathtaking views over to the scree-strewn slopes around Caisteal Abhail (2735ft). If you make this journey around dusk, be sure to pause in **Glen Chalmadale**, on the other northern side of the pass, to catch a glimpse of the red deer that come down to pasture by the water. Another possibility is to turn off to North Sannox, where you can park and walk along the shore to the **Fallen Rocks**, a major rock-fall of Devonian sandstone.

WALKING IN NORTH ARRAN

Ordnance Survey Landranger map no. 69.

The ferociously jagged and barren outline of the mountains of **north Arran** is on a par with that of the Cuillin of Skye. None of the peaks are Munros, but they are spectacular, nevertheless, partly because they rise up so rapidly from sea level, and, in fine weather, hand out such wonderful views over sea and land.

One of the most popular walks is to is the circuit of peaks that surround Glen Rosa. The walk begins with the relatively straightforward ascent of **Goat Fell** (2866ft), which is normally approached from the grounds of Brodick Castle, to the south. From Goat Fell, you can follow a series of rocky ridges that spread out in the shape of an "H". In order to keep to the crest of the ridge, head north to the next peak of **North Goat Fell** (2657ft), and then make the sharp descent to The Saddle, a perfect spot for refuelling, before making the ascent of **Cir Mhor** (2618ft), by far the most exhilarating peak in the whole range, and the finest viewpoint of all. The next section of the walk, southwest across the knife's-edge ridge of **A'Chir**, is quite tricky due to the Bad Step, a lethal gap in the ridge, which you can avoid by dropping down slightly on the east side. Beyond A'Chir, the ascent of **Beinn Tarsuinn** (2706ft) and **Beinn Nuis** (2597ft) are relatively simple. A path leads down from the southeast face of Beinn Nuis to Glen Roas and back to Brodick. If you don't fancy attempting A'Chir, or if the weather closes in, you can simply descend from the Saddle, or from the southwest side of Cir Mhor, to Glen Rosa.

The walk described above covers a total distance of eleven miles, with over 4600ft of climbing, and should take between eight and ten hours to complete. All walks should be approached with care, and the usual **safety precautions** should be observed (see p.46).

Lochranza

On fair Lochranza streamed the early day,
Thin wreaths of cottage smoke are upward curl'd
From the lone hamlet, which her inland bay
And circling mountains sever from the world.

The Lord of the Isles, Sir Walter Scott

The ruined castle which occupies the mud flats of the bay, and the brooding north-facing slopes of the mountains which frame it, make for one of the most spectacular settings on the island – yet **LOCHRANZA**, despite being the only place of any size in this sparsely populated area, attracts far fewer visitors than Arran's southern resorts. Lochranza now boasts the island's first legal whisky **distillery** for more than 150 years, which offers guided tours ending with a free sample (daily 10am–6pm; £2.50), but won't begin to offer its first single malt until 2001; it's housed in an elegant building and boasts the moderately expensive *Harolds* **restaurant**, a state-of-the-art place which is not to be missed (☎01770/830264; closed Wed eve). If you're just passing through, you can always get a filling snack at the *Pier Tearoom* by the ferry, serving breakfast, lunch, dinner and takeaways from its licensed restaurant, with a magnificent view across to Kintyre.

The finest **accommodation** is to be had at the superb *Apple Lodge* (☎01770/830229; ③), which does excellent home-cooking, or at the *Lochranza Hotel* (☎01770/830223; *george@lochranza.co.uk*; ②), whose bar is the centre of the local social scene; the most intriguing of the **B&Bs** is the welcoming *Castlekirk* (☎01770/830202; ①; closed Jan & Dec) in a converted nineteenth-century church opposite the castle. Lochranza also has a **youth hostel** (☎01770/830631; closed Jan) overlooking the castle, and a well-equipped **campsite** (☎01770/830273, *camp@lochgolf.demon.co.uk*; Easter to mid-Oct) beautifully situated by the golf course on the Brodick Road.

Catacol and Pirnmill

An alternative to staying or drinking in Lochranza is to continue a mile or so southwest along the coast to **CATACOL**, and stay or drink at the friendly *Catacol Bay Hotel* (☎01770/830231, *davecath@aol.com*; ②). It takes the prize as the island's best pub by far, serving good, basic food (with several veggie options) and great beer on tap; there's a small adjoining **campsite**, and seals and shags to view on the nearby shingle. The pub also puts on live music most weeks, and hosts a week-long **folk festival** in early June.

Just past the pub there is a row of striking black-and-white cottages, known as the **Twelve Apostles**, built by the eleventh Duke of Hamilton, and intended to house tenants displaced to make way, not for sheep, but for deer (thanks to Queen Victoria's passion for stalking them), though no one could be persuaded to live in them for two years. You can stay close by at *Fairhaven Guest House* (☎01770/830237; ②; closed Christmas & New Year), a **B&B** with a homely air at the start of the path up Glen Catacol.

From here to the String Road it's very bleak, but ideal for spotting wildlife, on hillside and at sea. The next village of any size is neat and tidy **PIRNMILL**, so called because they used to make "pirns" or bobbins for the mills of Paisley here (until they ran out of trees). In summer you can get a snack in the *Anvil Tearoom*.

Isle of Islay

The fertile, largely treeless island of **ISLAY** (pronounced "eye-la") is famous for one thing – single malt **whisky**. The smoky, peaty, pungent quality of Islay whisky is unique, recognizable even to the untutored palate, and all six of the island's distilleries will happily take visitors on a guided tour, ending with the customary complimentary tipple. Yet, despite the fame of its whiskies, Islay remains relatively undiscovered, much as Skye and Mull were some twenty years ago. Part of the reason, no doubt, is that it takes an expensive, two-hour ferry journey from Kennacraig on Kintyre to reach the island and, once there, you'll find no luxury hotels or fancy restaurants. If you do make the effort, however, you'll be rewarded with a genuinely friendly welcome from islanders proud of their history, landscape and Gaelic culture.

In medieval times, Islay was the political centre of the Hebrides, with **Finlaggan**, near Port Askaig, the seat of the MacDonalds, Lords of the Isles. The picturesque, whitewashed villages you see on Islay today, however, date from the planned settlements founded by the Campbells in the late eighteenth and early nineteenth centuries. Apart from whisky and solitude, the other great draw is the **birdlife**, in particular the scores of white-fronted and barnacle geese who winter here in their thousands. A good time to visit is in late May/early June, when the **Islay Festival** (*Feis Il*), takes place, with whisky tasting, pipe bands, folk dancing and other events celebrating the island's Gaelic roots.

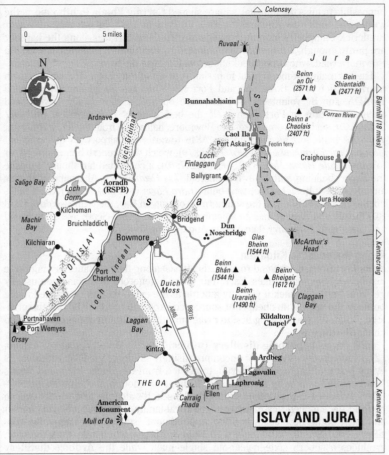

Colonsay

Ruvaal

J u r a

Bunnahabhainn

Beinn
an Oir
(2571 ft)

Bein
Shiantaidh
(2477 ft)

Corran River

Beinn a'
Chaolais
(2407 ft)

Ardnave

Caol Ila
Port Askaig

Feolin ferry

Barnhill (18 miles)

Craighouse

Loch
Finlaggan

Saligo Bay

Ballygrant

Aoradh
(RSPB)

I s l a y

Loch
Gorm

Jura House

Kilchoman

Bruichladdich

Machir
Bay

Bridgend

Dun
Nosebridge

Bowmore

Kilchiaran

McArthur's
Head

Glas
Bheinn
(1544 ft)

Kennacraig

Beinn
Bhán
(1544 ft)

Port
Charlotte

Duich
Moss

Beinn
Bheigeir
(1612 ft)

Beinn
Uraraidh
(1490 ft)

Claggain
Bay

Portnahaven
Port Wemyss

Laggan
Bay

Kildalton
Chapel

Orsay

Kintra

THE OA

Ardbeg

Lagavulin

Laphroaig

Port
Ellen

American
Monument

Carraig
Fhada

Mull of Oa

Kennacraig

ISLAY AND JURA

0   5 miles

N

© Crown copyright

Public transport, in the form of buses and postbuses, will get you from one end of the island to the other, but it's as well to know that there is one solitary bus on a Sunday; pick up an island transport guide from the Islay tourist office in **Bowmore**. The **airport**, which lies between Port Ellen and Bowmore, has regular flights to and from Glasgow, and the local bus or postbus will get you to either of the above villages. For a local point of view and news of up-coming events, pick up a copy of the fortnightly *Ileach* or visit their Web site (*www.ileach.co.uk*).

Port Ellen and around

Laid out as a planned village in 1821 by Walter Frederick Campbell, and named after his wife, **PORT ELLEN** is the busiest port on Islay, with the island's largest fishing fleet, and main CalMac ferry terminal. Arriving at Port Ellen by boat, it's impossible to miss the unusual, square-shaped **Carraig Fhada lighthouse**, at the western entrance to Kilnaughton Bay, erected in 1832, in memory of Walter Frederick Campbell's aforementioned wife. The neat terraces along the harbour are pretty enough, but the bay is dominated by the modern maltings, just off the Bowmore road, whose powerful odours waft across the town.

There's really not much point in basing yourself in Port Ellen. The island's main **tourist office** is in Bowmore, and Port Ellen has just an ad hoc office called KOADA, run by volunteers, and therefore open only sporadically. If you need **accommodation** in Port Ellen itself, the best place is *Tighcargaman* (☎01496/ 302345; ①), set back from the road to Bowmore, half a mile from the ferry. However, you'd be better off heading up the A846 towards the airport, to the excellent *Glenmachrie Farmhouse* (☎01496/302560; ③), which does superb home-cooking, or to *Glenegedale House Hotel* (☎01496/302147; ③), a converted farmhouse opposite the airport building, with its own restaurant, *The Heather Hen*. Alternatively, there's an independent **hostel** at the stone-built *Kintra Farm* (☎01496/302051), three miles northwest of Port Ellen, at the southern tip of Laggan Bay; the farm also does B&B (①) in July and August, has an adjoining **campsite** (April–Sept), and serves food and drink at *The Granary* (late May to Aug evenings only).

Along the coast to Kildalton

From Port Ellen, a dead-end road heads off east along the coastline, passing three distilleries in as many miles. Each tour offers a generous dram, and you usually get your entry fee back if you buy a bottle at the end – though be warned that a bottle of the stuff is no cheaper at source, so expect to pay over £20 for the privilege. Whatever you do, ring first to make sure there's a tour running, as times do change frequently.

First comes **Laphroaig distillery** (☎01496/302418; Mon–Fri 10am & 2.15pm; £2), which produces the most uncompromisingly smoky of the Islay whiskies. As every bottle of Laphroaig tells you, translated from the Gaelic the name means "the beautiful hollow by the broad bay", and, true enough, the whitewashed distillery is indeed in a gorgeous setting by the sea. It's also the first whisky ever to be officially supplied to a member of the royal family (Prince Charles, of course) and each bottle now bears the "By Appointment" stamp. The **Lagavulin distillery** (☎01496/302400; Mon–Fri 10.30am & 2.30pm; £2), a mile down the road, produces a superb sixteen-year-old single malt, while the **Ardbeg distillery** (☎01496/302244; Mon–Fri 10am–4pm; June–Aug also Sat; £2), another mile on, sports the traditional pagoda-style roofs of the malting houses, and has recently been brought back to life by Glenmorangie.

Armed with a bottle of your choice, you could do worse than head down to the shoreline just beyond Lagavulin and have a tot or two beside **Dunyvaig Castle** (*Dún Naomhaig*), a romantic ruin on a promontory looking out to the tiny isle of Texa. There are a handful of **B&Bs** along the rapidly deteriorating road – *Tighna-Suil* (☎01496/302483; ①) has a lovely secluded position. A mile beyond this, the simple thirteenth-century **Kildalton Chapel** boasts a wonderful eighth-century Celtic ringed cross made from the local "bluestone", which is, in fact, a rich bottle-green. The quality of the scenes matches any to be found on the crosses carved by the monks in Iona: the Virgin and Child are on the east face, with Cain murdering Abel to the left, David fighting the lion on the top, and Abraham sacrificing Isaac on the right; on the west side amidst the serpent-and–boss work are four elephant-like beasts.

The Oa

The most dramatic landscape on Islay is to be found in the nub of land to the southwest of Port Ellen known as **The Oa** (pronounced "O"), a windswept and inhospitable landscape, much loved by illicit whisky distillers and smugglers over the centuries. Halfway along road, a ruined church is visible to the south, testament to the area's once large population dispersed during the Clearances. The chief target for most visitors to the Oa is the gargantuan **American Monument**, built in the shape of a lighthouse on the clifftop above the Mull of Oa. It was erected by the American National Red Cross in memory of those who died when the *Tuscania* was torpedoed seven miles offshore in February 1918, and when the *Otranto* was shipwrecked off Kilchiaran (see p.127) in October of the same year. The memorial is inscribed with the unusual sustained metaphor: "On Fame's eternal camping ground, their silent tents are spread, while glory keeps with solemn round, the bivouac of the dead." If you're driving, you can park in a car park, just before Upper Killeyan farm, and follow the duckboards across the soggy peat. En route, look out for choughs, golden eagles and other birds of prey, not to mention feral goats and, down on the shore, basking seals; for a longer walk, follow the coast round to or from Kintra (see above).

Bowmore

At the northern end of the seven-mile-long Laggan Bay, across the monotonous peat bog of Duich Moss, lies **BOWMORE**, Islay's administrative capital, with a population of around 900. It was founded in 1768 to replace the village of Kilarrow, which was deemed by the local laird to be too close to his own residence. It's a striking place, laid out in a grid-plan rather like Inveraray, with the whitewashed terraces of Main Street climbing up the hill in a straight line from the pier on Loch Indaal to the town's crowning landmark, the **Round Church**, whose central tower looks uncannily like a lighthouse. Built in the round, so that the devil would have no corners in which to hide, it has a plain, wood-panelled interior, with a lovely tiered balcony and a big central mushroom pillar.

A little to the west of Main Street is **Bowmore distillery** (☎01496/810441; Easter–Sept Mon–Fri 10.30am, 11.30am, 2pm & 3pm, Sat 10.30am; Oct–Easter Mon–Fri 10.30am & 2pm; £2), the first of the legal Islay distilleries, founded in 1779, and still occupying its original whitewashed buildings by the loch. One of the distillery's former bonded warehouses is now the **MacTaggert Leisure Centre**, whose pool is partially heated by waste heat from the distillery; if you're camping or self-catering, it's as well to know that it has a very useful, minuscule laundrette.

Islay's only official **tourist office** is in Bowmore (April Mon–Sat 10am–5pm; May & June Mon–Sat 9.30am–5pm, Sun 2–5pm; July to mid-Sept Mon–Sat 9.30am–5.30pm, Sun 2–5pm; mid-Sept to Oct Mon–Sat 10am–4.30pm; Nov–March Mon–Fri noon–4pm; ☎01496/810254); it can help you find **accommodation** anywhere on Islay or Jura. Like Port Ellen, Bowmore itself is, in fact, not the best place to stay. If you must, however, you're probably better off in one of the town's better B&Bs, such as *Lambeth House* (☎01496/810597; ①), centrally located on Jamieson Street, or *Sheiling* (☎01496/810634; ①), on Flora Street. Of the hotels, the *Lochside Hotel* (☎01496/810390, *alistair@whisky4u.co.uk*; ②), on Shore Street, is reasonable, and has a stupendous array of single malts in the bar. If you're looking for more character and comfort, head out to the *Bridgend Hotel*

(☎01496/810960; ⑤), a couple of miles up the road, positioned by the main road junction, but also close to the island's finest patch of deciduous woodland.

Bowmore's cosiest **pub**, however, is the *Harbour Inn* on Main Street, where you can warm yourself by a peat fire; you can get breakfast, lunch or dinner at the inn's outstanding **restaurant**, though it's advisable to book in the evening (☎01496/810330). *The Cottage* (closed Sun) is a cheap and friendly greasy spoon, further up on the same side of the street. Somewhat incredibly there's no fish-and-chip shop in Bowmore, though there is an excellent **bakery**, again on Main Street.

Loch Gruinart

If you're visiting Islay between mid-September and the third week of April, it's impossible to miss the island's staggeringly large wintering population of **barnacle** and **white-fronted geese**. During this period, the geese dominate the landscape, feeding incessantly off the rich pasture, strolling by the shores, and flying in formation across the winter skies. In the spring, the geese hang around just long enough to snap up the first shoots of new grass, in order to give themselves enough energy to make the 2000-mile journey to Greenland, where they breed in the summer. Understandably, many local farmers are not exactly very happy about the geese feeding off their land, and they now receive compensation for the inconvenience.

You can see the geese just about anywhere on the island – there are an estimated 20,000 here (and rising) – though they are at their most concentrated in the fields between Bridgend and Ballygrant. In the evening, they tend to congregate in the tidal mud flats and fields around **Loch Gruinart**, which is now an **RSPB nature reserve**. The nearby farm of Aoradh (pronounced "oorig") is now run by the RSPB, and one of its outbuildings contains a **visitor centre** (daily 10am–5pm; free), housing an observation point with telescopes and a CCTV link with the mud flats; there's also a hide across the road looking north over the salt flats at the head of the loch. From the hide, you're more likely to see pintail, widgeon, teal and other waterfowl than geese.

The road along the western shores of Loch Gruinart to Ardnave is a good place to spot **choughs**, members of the crow family, distinguished by their curved red beaks and matching legs. Halfway along the road, there's a path off to the ruins of **Kilnave Chapel**, whose working graveyard contains a very weathered, eighth-century Celtic cross. The road ends at Ardnave Loch, beyond which lie numerous sand dunes, where seals often sun themselves, while otters sometimes fish offshore. Nature-lovers and twitchers should hole themselves up in *Loch Gruinart House* (☎01496/850212; ①), by the reserve, or at the rudimentary *Craigens Farm* **campsite** by the head of the loch (☎01496/850256; April–Oct).

Port Charlotte and the Rinns of Islay

PORT CHARLOTTE, founded in 1828 by Walter Frederick Campbell and named after his mother, is generally agreed to be Islay's prettiest village. Known as the "Queen of the Rinns" (derived from the Gaelic word for a promontory), its immaculate whitewashed cottages hug a sandy cove overlooking Loch Indaal. On the northern fringe of the village, in a whitewashed former chapel, the imaginative **Museum of Islay Life** (Easter–Oct Mon–Sat 10am–5pm, Sun 2–5pm; £2), has a children's corner, a good library of books about the island, and tantalizing snippets about eighteenth-century illegal whisky distillers. Close by the museum is the spanking-new **Islay Cheese Company** (Mon–Fri 10am–4pm, Sat 10am–2pm; free), which has a shop, explanatory panels and a viewing window from which you can see the long curd table where the Dunlop cheese is turned to remove the whey. The **Wildlife Information Centre** (Easter–Oct Mon, Tues, Thurs & Fri 10am–3pm, Sun 2–5pm; £1.80), housed in the former distillery warehouse, is also worth a visit for anyone interested in the island's fauna and flora. Tickets are valid for a week, allowing you to go back and identify things that you've seen on your travels.

Port Charlotte is the perfect place in which to base yourself on Islay. The welcoming *Port Charlotte Hotel* (☎01496/850360, *carl@portcharlottehot.demon.co.uk*; ⑤) has the best **accommodation**, and a good (only moderately expensive) restaurant specializing in seafood. For B&B, you're actually better off going for *Octofad Farm* (☎01496/850225; ①; April–Oct), a dairy farm a few miles down the road beyond Nerabus. Port Charlotte itself is also home to the SYHA Islay **hostel** (☎01496/850385; mid-March to Oct), housed in an old bonded warehouse next door to the Wildlife Information Centre. The *Croft Kitchen* (☎01496/850230; mid-March to mid-Oct), opposite the museum, serves simple **food**, such as sandwiches and cakes, as well as inexpensive seafood, including oysters. The bar of the *Port Charlotte* is very easy-going, while the local crack (and occasional live music) goes on at the *Lochindaal Inn*, down the road.

The main coastal road culminates seven miles south of Port Charlotte at **PORTNAHAVEN**, a fishing and crofting community since the early nineteenth century. The familiar whitewashed cottages wrap themselves prettily around the steep banks of a deep bay, where seals bask on the rocks in considerable numbers; in the distance, you can see Portnahaven's twin settlement, **PORT WEMYSS**, a mile south. The communities share a little whitewashed church, located above the bay in Portnahaven, with separate doors for each village. A short way out to sea are two islands, the largest of which, Orsay, sports the **Rinns of Islay Lighthouse**, built by Robert Louis Stevenson's father in 1825; ask around locally if you're keen to visit the island.

Those in search of still more solitude should head for the isolated west coast of the Rinns, which is peppered with sandy beaches. The finest of these is the lovely golden beach of **Machir Bay**, backed by great white sand dunes, with an old wreck that's visible at low tide. The sea here has dangerous undercurrents, however, and is not safe to swim in (the same goes for the much smaller Saligo Bay, to the north). **Kilchiaran church**, set back from the bay, beneath low rocky cliffs, is in a sorry state of disrepair, but its churchyard contains a beautiful fifteenth-century cross, decorated with interlacing on one side and the Crucifixion on the other; at its base there's a wishing stone that should be turned sunwise when wishing. Across a nearby field towards the bay lies the **sailors' cemetery**, containing 75 graves of those drowned when HMS *Otranto* sank in a storm in October 1918; they lie in three neat rows, from the cook to the captain, who has his own much larger gravestone.

Finlaggan and Port Askaig

Just beyond Ballygrant, on the road to Port Askaig, a narrow road leads off north to **Loch Finlaggan**, site of a number of prehistoric crannogs (artificial islands) and, for four hundred years from the twelfth century, headquarters of the Lords of the Isles, semi-autonomous rulers over the Hebrides and Kintyre. The site is evocative enough, but there are, in truth, very few remains beyond the foundations. Remarkably, the palace that stood here appears to have been unfortified, a testament perhaps to the prosperity and stability of the islands in those days. Unless you need shelter from the rain, or are desperate to see the head of the commemorative medieval cross found here, you can happily skip the **visitor centre** (Easter & Oct Tues, Thurs & Sun 2–4pm; May–Sept daily except Sat 2.30–5pm; £2), to the northeast of the loch, and simply head on down to the site itself (access at any time), which is dotted with interpretive panels. Duckboards allow you to walk out across the reed beds of the loch and explore the main crannog, **Eilean Mor**, where several carved gravestones can be seen among the ruins, which seem to support the theory that the Lords of the Isles buried their wives and children, while having themselves interred on Iona. Further out into the loch is another smaller crannog, **Eilean na Comhairle**, originally connected to Eilean Mor by a causeway, where the Lords of the Isles are thought to have held meetings of the Council of the Isles.

Islay's other ferry connection with the mainland, and its sole link with Colonsay and Jura, is from **PORT ASKAIG**, a scattering of buildings which tumble down a little cove by the narrowest section of the Sound of Islay (*Caol Ila*). The only real reason to come here is to catch one of the ferries or go to the hotel bar; if you've time to kill, you can wander round the island's **RNLI lifeboat station** or through the nearby woods of Dunlossit House. Whisky fanatics might want to head half a mile north of Port Askaig to the **Caol Ila distillery** (☎01496/840207; Easter–Sept Mon, Tues, Thurs & Fri 10.30am, 11.15am, 1.30pm & 2.45pm, Wed 10.30am & 11.15am; £2), or the **Bunnahabhainn distillery** (☎01496/840646; tours by appointment Mon–Fri), a couple of miles further on; both enjoy idyllic settings, overlooking the Sound of Islay, though they are no beauties in themselves.

Easily the most comfortable **place to stay** is the lovely whitewashed *Kilmeny Farmhouse* (☎01496/840668; ④), southwest of Ballygrant, a place which richly deserves all the superlatives it regularly receives. A more modest alternative is a room at the secluded B&B at *The Kennels* (☎01496/840237; ①). The *Ballygrant Inn* is a good **pub** in which to grab a pint, as is the bar of the *Port Askaig Hotel*, which enjoys a wonderful position by the pier at Port Askaig, with views over to the Paps of Jura.

Isle of Jura

Twenty-eight miles long and eight miles wide, the long whale-shaped island of **Jura** is one of the wildest and most mountainous of the Inner Hebrides, its entire west coast uninhabited and inaccessible except to the dedicated walker. The distinctive **Paps of Jura** – so called because of their smooth breast-like shape, though there are in fact three of them – seem to dominate every view off the west coast of Argyll, their glacial rounded tops covered in a light dusting of quartzite scree. The island's name derives from the Norse *dyr-oe* (deer island) and, appropriately enough, the current deer population of five thousand outnumbers the two hundred humans 25:1. With just one road, which sticks to the more sheltered eastern coast of the island, and only one hotel and a smattering of B&Bs, Jura is an ideal place to go for peace and quiet and some great walking.

WALKING THE PAPS OF JUPA

Perhaps the most popular of all the hillwalks on Jura is an ascent of any of the island's famous **Paps of Jura**: Beinn an Oir (2571ft), Beinn a'Chaolais (2407ft) and Beinn Shiantaidh (2477ft), which cluster together in the south half of the island. It's possible to do a round trip from Craighouse itself, or from the Feolin Ferry, but the easiest approach is from the three-arched bridge on the island's main road, three miles north of Craighouse. From the bridge, keeping to the north side of the Corran River, you eventually reach Loch an t'Siob. If you only want to climb one Pap, then simply climb up to the saddle between Beinn an Oir and Beinn Shiantaidh and choose which one (Beinn an Oir is probably the most interesting), returning to the bridge the same way. The trip to and from the bridge should take between five and six hours; it's hard going and care needs to be taken, as the scree is unstable.

If you want to try and bag all three Paps, you need to attack Beinn Shiantaidh via its southeast spur, leaving the loch at its easternmost point. This makes for a more difficult ascent, as the scree and large lumps of quartzite are tough going. Descending to the aforementioned saddle, and climbing Beinn an Oir is straightforward enough, but make sure you come off Beinn an Oir via the south spur, before climbing Beinn a'Chaolais, as the western side of Beinn an Oir is dangerously steep. Again, you can return via the loch to the three-arched bridge.

Every year, in the last bank holiday weekend in May, hundreds of masochists take part in a fell race up the Paps, which the winner usually completes in three hours. Given the number of deer on Jura, it's as well to be aware of the **stalking season** (Aug–Oct), during which you should check with the the *Jura Hotel* before heading out. At all times of year, you should take all the usual **safety precautions** (see p.46); beware, too, of adders, which are quite numerous on Jura.

If you're just coming over for the day from Islay, and don't fancy climbing the Paps, you could happily spend the day in the lovely wooded grounds of **Jura House** (daily 9am–5pm; £2), five miles up the road from Feolin Ferry, where the car ferry from Port Askaig arrives. Pick up a booklet at the entrance to the grounds, and follow the path which takes you down to the sandy shore, a perfect picnic spot in fine weather. Closer to the house itself, there's an idyllic **walled garden**, divided in two by a natural rushing burn that tumbles down in steps. The garden specializes in Antipodean plants, which flourish in the frost-free climate; in season, you can buy some of the garden's organic produce or take tea in the tea tent.

Anything that happens on Jura happens in the island's only real village, **CRAIGHOUSE**, eight miles up the road from Feolin Ferry. The village enjoys a sheltered setting, overlooking Knapdale on the mainland – so sheltered, in fact, that there are even a few palm trees thriving on the seafront. There's a shop/post office, the island hotel and a tearoom, plus the tiny **Craighouse distillery** (☎01496/820240; tours by appointment), which welcomes visitors.

The family-run *Jura Hotel* in Craighouse is the island's one and only **hotel** (☎01496/820243; ④), not much to look at from the outside, but warm and friendly within, and centre of the island's social scene. The hotel does inexpensive bar meals, and has a shower block and laundry facilities round the back for non-residents. For **B&B**, try Mrs Boardman at 7 Woodside (☎01496/820379; ①; April–Sept). There's an infrequent **minibus service** on the island (phone ☎01496/820314 to find out when it's running). The **ferry** from Port Askaig occasionally fails to run if there's a strong northerly or southerly wind, so bring your toothbrush if you're coming for a day-trip.

GEORGE ORWELL ON JURA

In April 1946, Eric Blair (better known by his pen name of **George Orwell**) intending to give himself "six months' quiet" in which to complete his latest novel, moved to a remote farmhouse called **Barnhill**, on the northern tip of Jura, which he had visited for the first time the previous year. He appears to have relished the challenge of living in Barnhill, fishing almost every night, shooting rabbits, laying lobster pots, and even attempting a little farming. Along with his adopted 3-year-old son Richard, and later his sister Avril, he clearly enjoyed his spartan existence. The book Orwell was writing, under the working title *The Last Man in Europe*, was to become *1984* (the title was arrived at by simply reversing the last two digits of the year in which it was finished – 1948). During his time on Jura, however, Orwell was suffering badly from tuberculosis, and eventually he was forced to return to London, where he died in January 1950.

Barnhill, 23 miles north of Craighouse, is as remote today as it was in Orwell's day. The road deteriorates rapidly beyond Lealt, and, after two miles, is closed to all vehicles, so pilgrims need to walk the last two or three miles to the house itself. Orwell wrote most of the book in the bedroom (top left window as you look at the house) – at present, there is no public access. If you're keen on making the journey out to Barnhill, you might as well combine it with a trip to the nearby **Gulf of Corrievrechan** (see p.102), which lies between Jura and Scarba, to the north. Orwell nearly drowned in the **whirlpool** during a fishing trip in August 1947, along with his three companions (including Richard): the outboard motor was washed away, and they had to row to a nearby island and wait for several hours before being rescued by a passing fisherman. The best time to see the water whirling is between flood and half-flood tide, with a southerly or westerly wind.

travel details

TRAINS

Glasgow (Queen St) to: Arrochar & Tarbert (4 daily; 1hr 15min); Dalmally (3 daily; 2hr 15min); Helensburgh Central (every 30min; 45min); Helensburgh Upper (4 daily; 45min); Oban (3 daily; 3hr).

MAINLAND BUSES (NOT INCLUDING POSTBUSES)

Arrochar to: Carrick Castle (Mon–Sat 3 daily; 1hr); Garelochhead (Mon–Fri 2 daily; 20min); Inveraray (Mon–Sat 5 daily, Sun 2 daily; 35min); Lochgilphead (Mon–Sat 3 daily, Sun 2 daily; 1hr 30min); Lochgoilhead (Mon–Sat 3 daily; 40min).

Campbeltown to: Campbeltown airport (Mon–Fri 2 daily; 10min); Carradale (Mon–Sat 3–4 daily, Sun 2 daily; 45min); Machrihanish (Mon–Sat 9–11 daily, Sun 3 daily; 15min); Saddell (Mon–Sat 3–4 daily, Sun 2 daily; 25min); Southend (Mon–Sat 5–6 daily, Sun 2 daily; 23min).

Colintraive to: Dunoon (Mon–Fri 1–3 daily, Sat 3 daily; 40min); Tighnabruaich (Mon–Thurs 1–2 daily; 35min).

Dunoon to: Colintraive (Mon–Fri 1–3 daily, Sat 3 daily; 40min); Inveraray (Mon–Fri 5 daily, Sat 3 daily; 1hr 15min); Lochgoilhead (Mon–Fri 0–3 daily; 1hr 15min).

Glasgow to: Arrochar (Mon–Sat 6 daily, Sun 3 daily; 1hr 10min); Campbeltown (Mon–Sat 3 daily, Sun 2 daily; 4hr 25min); Dalmally (Mon–Sat 4 daily, Sun 2 daily; 2hr 20min); Inveraray (Mon–Sat 6 daily, Sun 3 daily; 1hr 45min); Kennacraig (Mon–Sat 2 daily, Sun 1 daily; 3hr 30min); Lochgilphead (Mon–Sat 3 daily, Sun 2 daily; 2hr 40min); Oban (Mon–Sat 4 daily, Sun 2 daily; 3hr); Tarbert (Mon–Sat 3 daily, Sun 2 daily; 3hr 15min); Taynuilt (Mon–Sat 4 daily, Sun 2 daily; 2hr 45min).

Inveraray to: Dalmally (Mon–Sat 3 daily, Sun 1 daily; 25min); Dunoon (Mon–Fri 5 daily, Sat 3 daily; 1hr 15min); Lochgilphead (Mon–Sat 3 daily, Sun 2 daily; 40min); Oban (Mon–Sat 3 daily, Sun 1 daily; 1hr 5min); Tarbert (Mon–Sat 3 daily, Sun 2 daily; 1hr 30min); Taynuilt (Mon–Sat 3 daily, Sun 1 daily; 45min).

Kennacraig to: Claonaig (Mon–Sat 3 daily; 15min); Skipness (Mon–Sat 3 daily; 20min).

Lochgilphead to: Campbeltown (Mon–Sat 4 daily, Sun 2 daily; 1hr 25min); Crinan (Mon–Fri 1–3 daily, Sat 2 daily; 20min); Inveraray (Mon–Sat 3 daily, Sun 2 daily; 40min); Kilmartin (Mon–Sat 1–5 daily; 15–40min); Oban (Mon–Sat 1 daily; 1hr 30min); Tarbert (2–4 daily; 30min).

Oban to: Appin (Mon–Sat 4 daily, Sun 1 daily; 30min); Benderloch (Mon–Sat 10–14 daily, Sun 6 daily; 20min); Ellenabeich (Mon–Sat 2–4 daily; 45min); Kilmartin (Mon–Sat 1 daily; 1hr 10min); Lochgilphead (Mon–Sat 1 daily; 1hr 30min).

Tarbert to: Campbeltown (Mon–Sat 4 daily, Sun 2 daily; 1hr 10min); Claonaig (Mon–Sat 3 daily; 30min); Kennacraig (Mon–Sat 5 daily, Sun 1 daily; 15min); Skipness (Mon–Sat 3 daily; 35min).

Tighnabruaich to: Portavadie (Mon–Sat 3–4 daily; 25min); Rothesay (Mon–Thurs 1–2 daily; 1hr).

ISLAND BUSES (NOT INCLUDING POSTBUSES)

Arran

Brodick to: Blackwaterfoot (Mon–Sat 16–19 daily, Sun 5 daily; 30min–1hr 20min); Corrie (Mon–Sat 5–6 daily, Sun 4 daily; 20min); Kildonan (Mon–Sat 4–5 daily, Sun 4 daily; 40min); Lagg (Mon–Sat 4–5 daily, Sun 4 daily; 55min); Lamlash (Mon–Sat 12–13 daily, Sun 4 daily; 10min); Lochranza (Mon–Sat 5–6 daily, Sun 4 daily; 45min); Pirnmill (Mon–Sat 5–6 daily, Sun 4 daily; 1hr); Whiting Bay (Mon–Sat 12–13 daily, Sun 4 daily; 25min).

Bute

Rothesay to: Kilchattan Bay (Mon–Sat 4 daily, Sun 3 daily; 30min); Mount Stuart (1 daily except Tues & Thurs every 45min; 15min); Rhubodach (Mon–Sat 1–2 daily; 20min).

Colonsay

Scalasaig to: Kilchattan (Mon–Fri 2–4 daily; 30min); Kiloran Bay (Mon–Fri 2–3 daily; 12min); The Strand (Mon–Fri 1 daily).

Islay

Bowmore to: Port Askaig (Mon–Sat 8–10 daily, Sun 1 daily; 30–40min); Port Charlotte (Mon–Sat 4–6 daily; 30min); Port Ellen (Mon–Sat 5–7 daily, Sun 1 daily; 20–30min); Portnahaven (Mon–Sat 5–7 daily; 50min).

Mull

Craignure to: Fionnphort (Mon–Sat 4 daily, Sun 1 daily; 1hr 10min); Fishnish (Mon–Sat 4 daily, Sun 3 daily; 10min); Salen (Mon–Sat 4 daily, Sun 2 daily; 25min); Tobermory (Mon–Sat 4 daily, Sun 3 daily; 50min).

Tobermory to: Calgary (Mon–Fri 3–6 daily, Sat 2 daily; 45min); Dervaig (Mon–Fri 3–6 daily, Sat 2 daily; 30min); Fishnish (Mon–Sat 4 daily, Sun 3 daily; 40min).

CAR FERRIES (SUMMER TIMETABLE)

To Arran: Ardrossan–Brodick (Mon–Sat 5–6 daily, Sun 4 daily; 55min); Claonaig–Lochranza (10 daily; 30min).

To Bute: Colintraive–Rhubodach (frequently; 5min); Wemyss Bay–Rothesay (every 45min; 30min).

To Campbeltown: Ballycastle (Northern Ireland)–Campbeltown (2 daily; 3hr).

To Coll: Oban–Coll (1 daily except Thurs & Sun; 2hr 40min).

To Colonsay: Kennacraig–Colonsay (Wed 1 daily; 3hr 40min); Oban–Colonsay (Wed, Fri & Sun 1 daily; 2hr 10min); Port Askaig–Colonsay (Wed 1 daily; 1hr 20min).

To Dunoon: Gourock–Dunoon (hourly; 20min); McInroy's Point–Hunter's Quay (every 30min; 20min).

To Gigha: Tayinloan–Gigha (hourly; 20min).

To Islay: Colonsay–Port Askaig (Wed 1 daily; 1hr 20min); Kennacraig–Port Askaig (Mon–Sat 1–2 daily; 2hr); Kennacraig–Port Ellen (1–2 daily except Wed; 2hr 10min); Oban–Port Askaig (Wed 1 daily; 4hr).

To Jura: Port Askaig–Feolin Ferry (Mon–Sat 16 daily, Sun 6 daily; 10min).

To Kintyre: Portavadie–Tarbert (hourly; 25min).

To Lismore: Oban–Lismore (Mon–Sat 2–4 daily; 50min).

To Luing: Cuan Ferry (Seil)–Luing (every 30min; 5min).

To Mull: Kilchoan–Tobermory (Mon–Sat 7–8 daily; July & Aug also Sun 5 daily; 35min); Lochaline–Fishnish (Mon–Sat every 50min, Sun hourly; 15min); Oban–Craignure (Mon–Sat 6 daily, Sun 4–5 daily; 40min).

To Tiree: Oban–Tiree (1 daily except Thurs & Sun; 3hr 40min).

PASSENGER-ONLY FERRIES (SUMMER TIMETABLE)

To Helensburgh: Kilcreggan–Helensburgh (Mon–Sat 3 daily; 25min); Gourock–Helensburgh (Mon–Sat 4 daily; 40min).

To Iona: Fionnphort–Iona (Mon–Sat frequently, Sun hourly; 5min).

To Lismore: Port Appin–Lismore (daily every 2hr; 5min).

FLIGHTS

Glasgow to: Campbeltown (Mon–Fri 2 daily; 35min); Islay (Mon–Fri 2 daily, Sat 1 daily; 40min); Tiree (Mon–Sat 1 daily; 45min).

CHAPTER TWO

THE CENTRAL HIGHLANDS

The **Central Highlands** lie in the heart of Scotland, bounded by the country's two major geological fissures, the **Highland Fault**, which runs along a line drawn approximately from Arran to Aberdeen and marks the southern extent of Scotland's Highlands, and the **Great Glen**, the string of lochs that runs on a similar southwest–northeast axis between Fort William and Inverness. The appeal of the region is undoubtedly its landscape, a concentrated mix of mountain, glen, loch and moorland that responds to each season with a dramatic blend of colour and mood, from benign beauty to malevolent hostility – sometimes swinging between the two in the course of a single day. The call of the outdoors – from leafy riverside strolls to an ice-climb in training for a Himalayan expedition – is a strong one here. Yet shuffled into the landscape is a rich history stemming in large part from the fact that along the geological divide of north and south is a significant cultural and social shift, and it is no surprise that the region is littered with castles, battlefields and monuments that hark back to centuries of power struggle of Highlander with Sassenach or lowlander, whether from Scotland or south of the border.

Northwest of Glasgow, the elongated teardrop of **Loch Lomond** marks the western boundary of the region with Argyll. The magnificent scenery around the loch continues east into the fabled mountains, glens, lochs and forests of the **Trossachs**, an area that caught the imagination of **Sir Walter Scott**, who took so much delight in the tales of local clansman **Rob Roy MacGregor**, the notorious seventeenth-century outlaw, that he set them down in his novel of the same name. Thanks to Scott, and also to William and Dorothy Wordsworth's effusive praise, Queen Victoria decided to visit, placing the area firmly on the tourist map. Today, however, the trappings of tourism – evident in twee shops and tearooms in every small town – don't impinge too much on the experience, particularly if you're ready to explore deeper into the landscape itself on foot or by bike.

North of the Trossachs, **lochs Earn**, **Tay** and **Rannoch** lie stacked up across the centre of the region, each surrounded by impressive hills and increasingly rugged countryside. Beyond Rannoch, across the moor of the same name and north into the hills around **Loch Ericht**, is a vast tract of land visited only by determined walkers and mountain bikers who are prepared to leave public roads well behind them. Further to the east, across the string of passes followed by the main A9 trunk road and railway between Perth and Inverness, a similar pattern is followed: the southernmost hills, grouped around the **Angus glens**, are renowned for their prettiness and easily accessible, but to the north the more

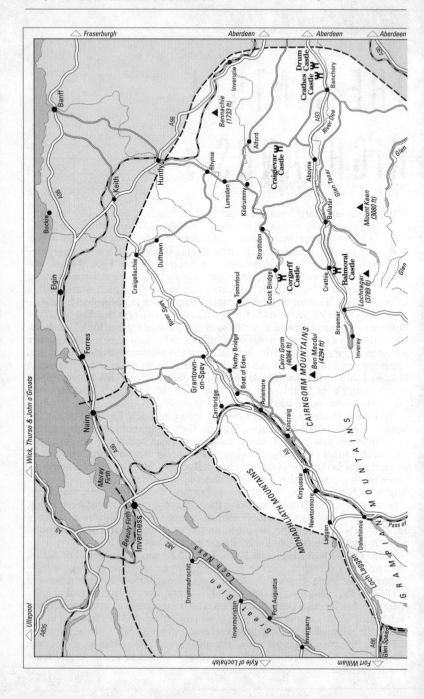

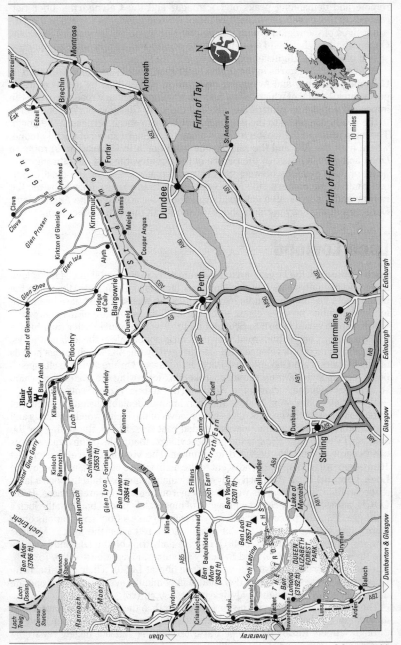

N

Firth of Tay

Firth of Forth

10 miles

0

Fettercairn
Montrose
Brechin
Arbroath
Esk
Edzell
Forfar
St Andrew's
Glens
Dykehead
Clova
Clova
Glen Prosen
Kirriemuir
Glamis
Dundee
Glen Isla
Kirkton of Glenisle
Meigle
Coupar Angus
Alyth
Glen Shee
Bridge of Cally
Blairgowrie
Perth
Spittal of Glenshee
Dunkeld
Pitlochry
Crieff
Dunfermline
Blair Castle
Blair Atholl
Aberfeldy
Strath Earn
Edinburgh
Killiecrankie
Loch Tummel
Kenmore
Comrie
Edinburgh
Drumochter Glen Garry
Kinloch Rannoch
Schiehallion
(3553 ft)
Fortingall
St Fillans
Ben Vorlich
(3201 ft)
Dunblane
Glasgow
Loch Rannoch
Glen Lyon
Ben Lawers
(3984 ft)
Loch Earn
Callander
Stirling
Loch Ericht
Rannoch Station
Killin
Lochearnhead
Ben Ledi
(2857 ft)
Lake of
Menteith
Dumbarton & Glasgow
Ben Alder
(3766 ft)
Loch Ossian
Ben Balquhidder
Ben More
(3943 ft)
Loch Katrine
QUEEN
ELIZABETH
FOREST
PARK
Drymen
Loch Treig
Corrour Station
Rannoch Moor
Crianlarich
Ardlui
inversnaid
Tarbet
Ben Lomond
(3192 ft)
Rowardennan
Luss
Aberfoyle
Balloch
Arden
Tyndrum
Oban
Inveraray
THE TROSSACHS

© Crown copyright

remote and demanding peaks of **Lochnagar** and the **Cairngorms** offer rich rewards to those prepared to explore them. Beyond these, the eastern and northern fringes of the region are no less emotive for being on the margin; for many, Queen Victoria's beloved **Deeside** and the whisky trail of **Speyside** are quintessential parts of the Highland experience.

With no sizeable towns in the region other than useful service centres such as Callander, Pitlochry and Aviemore, **orientation** is best done by means of transport routes – many of which follow historic trading or military roads between the important population centres the edges of the area: Glasgow, Stirling and Perth to the south, Aberdeen to the east, and Fort William and Inverness to the north. The main route on the **western** side is along the western shore of Loch Lomond, where both the A82 and the railway line wind north to Crianlarich en route to Oban and Fort William. In the **centre** of the country, the A84 cuts through the heart of the Trossachs between Stirling and Crianlarich, while the most important route to the **eastern** side is between Perth to Inverness, follwed by the the railway and the busy A9 trunk road. Also useful for accessing the Angus glens, Deeside and the Cairngorms is the A93 from Perth through to Aberdeen.

Loch Lomond

Loch Lomond is the largest stretch of fresh water in Britain (about 24 miles long and up to five miles wide), and is almost as famous as Loch Ness, thanks to the ballad about its "bonnie, bonnie banks". The song was said to be have been written by a Jacobite prisoner captured by the English, who, sure of his fate, wrote that his spirit would return to Scotland on the low road much faster than his living compatriots on the high road. However, all is not bonnie at the loch nowadays, especially on its overdeveloped west side, fringed by the A82 which brings hoards of day-trippers from Glasgow, just thirty miles away. On the water itself, speedboats tear up and down on summer weekends, destroying the tranquillity which so impressed Queen Victoria, the Wordsworths and Sir Walter Scott.

Nevertheless, the west bank of the loch is an undeniably beautiful stretch of water and, despite the crowds, gives better views of the loch's wooded islands and surrounding peaks than the heavily wooded east side. **LUSS**, the setting for the Scottish TV soap *High Road*, is the prettiest village, though its picturesque streets can become unbearably crowded in summer. The **visitor centre** (Easter–Oct 10am–6pm; ☎01436/860601), adjacent to the main village car park, and run by the **Loch Lomond Park Authority**, gives a fascinating glimpse into the loch's landscape, wildlife and history as well as the environmental pressures it faces. **BALLOCH**, a brash holiday resort with a glut of moderately priced hotels at the loch's southern tip, is the place to head for if you want to take a **boat trip**. Various operators offer cruises around the 33 islands scattered near the shore: Mullens Cruises, Riverside (☎01389/751481), operate daily trips on the Lomond Duchess and the Lomond Maid (£5); and Sweeney's Cruises, Riverside (☎01389/752376), run one-hour cruises departing hourly (starting at £4.50). Their daily Balloch–Luss cruise leaves at 2.30pm (£7), and ninety-minute evening cruises operate daily during July and August only, leaving at 7.30pm (£6).

The tranquil east bank is far better for walking than the west, and is traversed in its entirety by the West Highland Way footpath, from where you can head on through **Queen Elizabeth Forest Park**, or take the stiff but hugely rewarding

---

BEN LOMOND

Ordnance Survey Landranger map no. 56

Ben Lomond (3192ft), the most southerly of the "Munros", is one of the most frequently climbed hills in Scotland, its commanding position above Loch Lomond affording amazing views of both the Highlands and Lowlands. You should allow five to six hours for the climb.

The tourist route starts in Rowardennan, at the car park at the rear end of the public road just beyond *Rowardennan Hotel*. The route rises through forest and crosses open moors to gain the southern ridge, which leads to the final pyramid. The path zigzags up, then rims the crags of the northeast corrie to reach the summit.

You can return the same way or start off westwards, then south, to traverse the subsidiary top of Ptarmigan down to the youth hostel in Rowardennan (see below) and then along the track to the start.

---

three-hour hike from **ROWARDENNAN** to the summit of Ben Lomond, the subject of the Scottish proverb "Leave Ben Lomond where it stands" – just let things be.

Practicalities

The West Highland **train** – the line from Glasgow to Mallaig, with a branch line to Oban – joins Loch Lomond seventeen miles north of Balloch at **TARBET**, and has one other station further on at **ARDLUI**, at the mountain-framed head of the loch. There are plenty of **buses** along the shore from Balloch.

Loch Lomond's **tourist office** (daily: April–June, Sept & Oct 10am–5pm; July & Aug 9.30am–7.30pm; ☎01389/753533) is above the marina in Balloch. They'll reserve a room for you without charge at one of the many local **hotels** and **B&Bs**, such as the comfortable *Balloch Hotel*, Balloch Road (☎01389/752579; ④), which also has a decent restaurant, or the friendly *Gowanlea Guest House* on Drymen Road (☎01389/752456; ②). A couple of miles up the west side of the loch at minuscule **ARDEN** is Scotland's most beautiful **youth hostel**, a turreted building complete with ghost (☎01389/850226). Caravan parks abound on the west side of the loch, and in Balloch itself there's the year-round *Tullichewan Caravan Park*, Old Luss Road (☎01389/759475), which also rents out **bikes**; tents are best pitched at the secluded Forestry Commission **campsite** (☎01360/870234; April–Oct), two miles south of Rowardennan at Cashel on the eastern shore of the loch.

Passenger ferries cross between Inverbeg and Rowardennan, where there's an eponymous **hotel** (☎01360/870273; ⑤) and a wonderfully situated **youth hostel** (☎01360/870259; March–Oct), right on the West Highland Way. On the northeast shore of the loch is the *Inversnaid Lodge* (☎01877/386254; ⑥); once the hunting lodge of the Duke of Montrose, it now has a photography centre with instruction and workshops from guest tutors. There is no road from Rowardennan up the east of the loch to Inversnaid; you have to take the B829 west from Aberfoyle. From Inversnaid you can take the mile-long lochside walk to Rob Roy's cave, a hide-out which is said to have given shelter to both Rob Roy and Robert the Bruce.

As for **eating**, on the west side of the loch the *Inverbeg Inn* (signposted off the A82) is the most convenient place to stop, with bar snacks and outdoor seating from which to view the loch, as well as a few comfortable **rooms** (☎01436/860678; ⑦). On the east side, there's little option but to take a picnic.

The Trossachs

Often described as the Highlands in miniature, the **Trossachs** area boasts a magnificent diversity of scenery, with dramatic peaks and mysterious, forest-covered slopes that live up to all the images ever produced of Scotland's wild land. This is Rob Roy country, where every waterfall, hidden cave and barely discernible path was once frequented by the seventeenth-century Scottish outlaw who led the Clan MacGregor. Strictly speaking, the name "The Trossachs", normally translated as either "bristly country" or "crossing place", originally referred only to the wooded glen between **Loch Katrine** and **Loch Achray**, but today it is usually taken as being the whole area from **Callander** in the east to **Queen Elizabeth Forest Park** in the west, right up to the eastern banks of Loch Lomond.

This is fabulous walking territory. **Ben Venue** and **Ben A'an**, by the southern end of Loch Katrine, and **Ben Ledi**, just northwest of Callander, especially, offer challenging climbs and, on clear days, stunning views. The **weather**, however, is

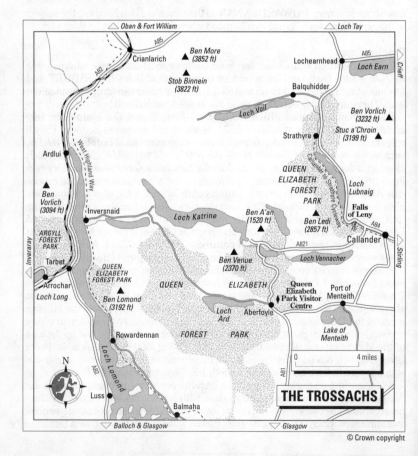

© Crown copyright

unpredictable, and every year there are fatalities in the Trossachs Mountains, so be sure to follow the necessary safety precautions (see p.46). Less taxing walks can be made from the **Queen Elizabeth Park Visitor Centre**, on the A821 north of Aberfoyle. It's a good idea to consult the Bartholomew guide *Walk Loch Lomond and the Trossachs*, which grades walks according to difficulty. The **Trossachs Trundler** (June–Sept daily except Sat; contact any tourist office for details) is a gleaming vintage bus which takes a circular route linking Callander, Loch Katrine and Aberfoyle, stopping at various points en route. The bus is timed to connect with sailings of the SS *Sir Walter Scott* on Loch Katrine, and costs £4.50 for a day pass or £7.40, including the bus fare from Stirling to Callander.

The Trossachs' high tourist profile was largely attributable in the early days to Sir Walter Scott, whose *Lady of the Lake* and *Rob Roy* were set in and around the area. Since then, neither the popularity – nor beauty – of the region have waned, and in high season the place is jam-packed. Autumn is a better time to come, when the hills are blanketed in rich, rusty colours and the crowds are thinner. In terms of where to stay, **Aberfoyle** has a slightly dowdy air, even at the height of summer, so it is better to opt for the romantic seclusion of the **Lake of Menteith**, or the handsome country town of **Callander**.

Aberfoyle and the Lake of Menteith

Like Brigadoon waking once a year from a mist-shrouded slumber, each summer the sleepy little town of **ABERFOYLE**, twenty miles west of Stirling, dusts itself down for the annual influx of tourists. Its position in the heart of the Trossachs is ideal, with **Loch Ard Forest** and **Queen Elizabeth Forest Park** stretching across to **Ben Lomond** and **Loch Lomond** to the west, the long curve of Loch Katrine and **Ben Venue** to the northwest, and **Ben Ledi** to the northeast.

Don't come here for lively nightlife or entertainment, but for a good, healthy blast of the outdoors. The town itself is well equipped to lodge and feed visitors (though booking is recommended), and is an excellent base for walking and pony trekking, or simply wandering the hills. You might like to wander to Doon Hill to the north of Aberfoyle; cross the bridge over the Forth, continue past the cemetery and then follow signs to the **Fairy Knowe** (knoll). A toadstool marker points you through oak and holly trees to the summit of the Knowe, where there is a pine tree, said to contain the unquiet spirit of the Reverend Robert Kirk, who studied local fairy lore and published his enquiries in *The Secret Commonwealth* (1691). Legend has it that, as punishment for disclosing supernatural secrets, Robert Kirk was forcibly removed to fairyland where he has languished ever since, although his mortal remains can be found in the nearby graveyard. This short walk should preferably be made at dusk, when it is at its most atmospheric.

About four miles east of Aberfoyle towards Doune, the **Lake of Menteith** is a superb fly-fishing centre and Scotland's only lake (as opposed to loch), so named due to a historic mix-up with the word *laigh*, the Scots for 'low-lying ground', which applied to the whole area. To rent a **fishing boat**, contact the Lake of Menteith Fisheries (☎01877/385664; April–Oct). From the northern shore of the lake you can take a little ferry (April–Sept Mon–Sat 9.30am–6.30pm, Sun 2–6.30pm; £3) to the **Island of Inchmahome**, and explore the lovely ruin of the Augustine abbey. Founded in 1238, **Inchmahome Priory** (HS) is perhaps the most beautiful island monastery in Scotland, its remains rising tall and graceful above the trees. The masons employed to build the priory are thought to be those who built Dunblane

Cathedral; certainly the western entrance there resembles that at Inchmahome. The nave of the church is roofless, but in the choir are preserved the graves of important families from the surrounding area. Most touching is a late thirteenth-century double effigy depicting Walter, the first Stewart Earl of Menteith, and his Countess Mary who, feet resting on lion-like animals, turn towards each other and embrace. Also buried at Inchmahome is Robert Bontine Cunninghame Graham (1852–1936), the adventurer, scholar, socialist and Scottish nationalist, who was Liberal MP for northwest Lanarkshire for 25 years and the first president of the National Party of Scotland. A pal of Buffalo Bill in Mexico as well as an intimate friend of the novelist Joseph Conrad, Cunninghame Graham had a ranch in Argentina, where he was affectionately known as "Don Roberto".

Five-year-old **Mary, Queen of Scots** was hidden at Inchmahome in 1547 before being taken to France; there's a knot garden in the west of the island known as Queen Mary's bower, where, legend has it, the child Queen played. Traces remain of a orchard planted by the monks, but the island is thick now with oak, ash and Spanish chestnut. On a nearby but inaccessible island is the ruined castle of **Inchtalla**, the home of the earls of Menteith in the sixteenth and seventeenth centuries.

Seven miles east of Aberfoyle on the A873 to Callander, the **Farm Life Centre** (April–Oct daily 10am–6pm; £3.50) makes an entertaining stop for children on a rainy day. Kids can pet a host of animals, make oatcakes, milk goats and ride tractors on this converted farm; there's also a picnic area, tearoom and small museum.

Practicalities

Regular **buses** from Stirling to Aberfoyle pull into the car park on Main Street. The **tourist office**, directly next door, has full details of local accommodation, sights and outdoor activities (daily: March–June, Sept & Oct 10am–5pm; July & Aug 9.30am–7pm; ☎01877/382352). The nearby **Scottish Wool Centre** (daily: Easter–Oct 9.30am–6pm; Nov–Easter 10am–4.30pm) sells all the usual sweaters and woolly toys as well as featuring shows of sheepshearing and sheepdog trials, and is a popular stopoff point with tour buses.

For **accommodation**, there are scores of **B&B**s in Aberfoyle, including the comfortable Tudor-style *Craigend*, 1 Craighuchty Terrace (☎01877/382716; ②; March–Oct), and many dotted around the surrounding countryside, among them *Creag-Ard House* (☎01877/382297; ②) in the pretty village of Milton, two miles west of Aberfoyle. It looks out on Ben Lomond and Loch Ard, to which it has fishing and boating rights. At Kinlochard, five miles west of Aberfoyle, is the deluxe *Forest Hills Hotel* (☎01877/387277; ⑦), set in 25 acres of woodland, with excellent food and a leisure centre. More atmospheric than Aberfoyle, the **Lake of Menteith** is a beautiful place to stay – the *Lake Hotel and Restaurant* (☎01877/385258; ⑥) at Port of Menteith has a lovely lakeside setting next to the Victorian Gothic parish church, and a classy restaurant, or there are the handsome *Lochend Chalets* (☎01877/385268) on the lake, which sleep four to six people, and cost £240–650 per week in summer.

A couple of miles south of Aberfoyle on the edge of Queen Elizabeth Forest Park, *Cobleland Campsite* (☎01877/382392; April–Oct), run by the Forestry Commission, covers five acres of woodland by the River Forth (little more than a stream here). Further south, the excellent family-run *Trossachs Holiday Park* (☎01877/382614; April–Oct) is twice the size and has **bikes** for rent.

One of Scotland's best **restaurants**, the *Braeval Old Mill* (☎01877/382711; dinner Wed–Sat, lunch Thurs–Sun), lies just east of Aberfoyle on the road to Stirling. Plain on the outside and pleasingly austere inside, it serves delicious and exquisitely presented gourmet food for around £30 per head. For those on a smaller budget, there's a range of decent eating places in the centre of Aberfoyle; try the *Forth Inn* (☎01877/382372) or *The Coach House* (☎01877/382822), both on Main Street.

Duke's Pass

Even if you have to walk it, don't miss the twelve-mile trip from Aberfoyle to Callander, which for part of the way takes you along the **Duke's Pass** (so called

HIKING AND BIKING IN THE TROSSACHS

Ordnance Survey Landranger map no. 57

The 75,000 acres of the **Queen Elizabeth Forest Park**, a spectacular tract of wilderness bordering **Loch Lomond** and incorporating **Loch Ard**, **Loch Achray** and **Loch Lubnaig**, as well as **Ben Venue**, **Ben A'an** and **Ben Ledi**, offers a vast playground of well-marked forest trails, sheltered picnic spots and seductive viewpoints.

Walks in the forest range from gentle riverside strolls to stiff climbs to the hilltops, where on a good day the views of the width of central Scotland are unsurpassed. On each side of Callander, pleasant and less-than-arduous walks wind north through a wooded gorge to the **Falls of Leny** and **Bracklinn Falls** – both distances of only a mile or so. Most of the best of the longer walks in Queen Elizabeth Forest Park are in the **Achray** and **Loch Ard** forests – the visitor centre in Aberfoyle (see opposite) is a good base for both. Of the peaks, **Ben A'an** (1520ft) offers the best value for the least elevation required: start from the old *Trossachs Hotel* on the north bank of Loch Achray, then follow the well marked path through the woods, emerging just under the summit crags, which the path then skirts to bring you to the top. A rather more challenging climb is to the summit of **Ben Ledi** (2857ft), the distinctive peak that can be seen all the way along the A84 between Stirling and Callander. Start at the car park near the Stank at the southern end of Loch Lubnaig; various forest roads wind up the hillside at leisurely angles, but stick to the more direct footpath that emerges from the trees under a daunting band of crags on the hill's eastern face. The path passes to the left of these, climbs to the long southern spur and then follows this ridge to the summit. At just under 3000ft, Ben Ledi doesn't quite qualify as a "Munro": to pick off a couple of these, head for **Stuc a'Chroin** (3199ft) and **Ben Vorlich** (3232ft), both a few miles northeast of Ben Ledi, and from the Trossachs side best approached along Glen Ample, starting from the north shore of Loch Lubnaig. There's also a long approach from Callander, beginning at the car park for Bracklinn Falls (see above).

The Trossachs are a popular place for **mountain-bikers**, with the network of good-quality forest tracks of the Queen Elizabeth Forest Park offering a challenge to most levels of off-road adventurers. As with the walking trails, the best routes are along the colour-coded trails of Achray and Loch Ard forests around Aberfoyle. For those looking for a less arduous and more scenic ride, the six-mile **Callander to Strathyre Cycleway**, part of the network of cycleways between the Highlands and Glasgow, follows part of the old Caledonian train line to Oban, which closed in 1965. From Callander it goes through the narrow Pass of Leny to the foot of Ben Ledi, where it runs along the quieter western side of Loch Lubnaig to Strathyre. You can extend the ride along the quiet road which runs along west side of River Balvag, which after a couple of miles swings west towards Loch Voil and **Balquhidder** (see p.143), where you can visit Rob Roy's grave.

because it once belonged to the Duke of Montrose), as it weaves through the **Queen Elizabeth Forest Park** to just south of Loch Katrine.

The A821 twists up out of Aberfoyle, following the contours of the hills and snaking back on itself in tortuous bends. About halfway up is the park's excellent **visitor centre** (April–Oct daily 10am–6pm; Nov–March Sat & Sun only 10am–4pm; ☎01877/382258; car park fee £1), which gives details on the local fauna and flora. From here various marked paths wind through the forest, giving splendid views over the lowlands and surrounding hills. About five miles further on, a track to the right marks the start of the **Achray Forest Drive**, a worthwhile excursion by car, foot or mountain bike, which leads through the forest and along the western shore of **Loch Drunkie**, before rejoining the main road. After another couple of miles, a road branches off to the left, leading to the southern end of **Loch Katrine** at the foot of **Ben Venue** (2370ft, a strenuous walk), from where the historic steamer, the SS *Sir Walter Scott*, has been plying the waters since 1900, chugging up the loch to Stronachlachar and the wild country of Glengyle (April–Oct Mon–Fri & Sun 4 daily, Sat 2 daily; £3.70).

The final leg of the pass is along the tranquil shores of **Loch Venachar** at the southern foot of Ben Ledi. Look out for the small **Callander Kirk** in a lovely setting at the edge of the loch, where services are still held on the first Sunday of each month at 3pm – presumably because it takes all morning to get there.

Callander and around

CALLANDER, on the eastern edge of the Trossachs, sits quietly on the banks of the River Teith roughly ten miles north of Doune, at the southern end of the **Pass of Leny**, one of the key routes into the Highlands. Larger than Aberfoyle, it is an even more popular summer holiday base and a convenient springboard for exploring the surrounding area. Its wide main street recalls the influence of the military architects who designed the town after Bonnie Prince Charlie's Jacobite Rebellion of 1745.

Callander first came to fame during the "Scottish Enlightenment" of the eighteenth and nineteenth centuries, when the glowing reports given by Sir Walter Scott and William Wordsworth prompted the first tourists to venture into the wilds by horse-drawn carriage. Development was given a boost when Queen Victoria chose to visit, and then by the arrival of the train line – long since closed – in the 1860s.

The present community has not been slow to capitalize on the town's appeal, establishing a plethora of restaurants and tearooms, antique shops, secondhand bookshops, and shops selling local woollens and crafts. The chief formal attraction is the **Rob Roy and Trossachs Visitor Centre** at Ancaster Square on the main street (Jan & Feb Sat & Sun only 11am–4.30pm; March–May & Oct–Dec daily 10am–5pm; June daily 9.30am–6pm; July & Aug daily 9.30am–10pm; Sept daily 10am–6pm; £2.50), which gives an entertaining and partisan account of the life of the diminutive redhead.

Practicalities

Callander's **tourist office** is in the Rob Roy and Trossachs Visitor Centre (same times; ☎01877/330342), and can book **accommodation**. The best options include *The Priory*, on Bracklinn Road (☎01877/330001; ③), a highly recommended Victorian house in its own gardens with good views; the handsome Victorian

ROB ROY

"Rob Roy, hero or villain?" ponders the tourist literature, in the great spirit of enquiry. Given that Rob Roy's clan, the MacGregors, may be the source of the term "blackmail" (from the levying of black meal through protection rackets), and that Rob Roy himself achieved fame through cattle-rustling and thieving, the evidence seems to point to the "villain" thesis. His life, though, dramatizes the clash between the doomed clan culture of the Gaelic-speaking Highlanders, and the organized feudal culture of lowland Scots, which effectively ended with the defeat of the Jacobites at Culloden in 1746.

Rob Roy (meaning "Red Robert" in Gaelic) was born in 1671 in Glengyle, just north of Loch Katrine ,and started life as a cattle farmer, supported by the powerful Duke of Montrose. When the duke withdrew his support, possibly having been robbed of £1000 by Rob Roy, the latter became a bankrupt and a brigand, plundering the rich carse land and avenging himself on the duke. He was present at the Battle of Sherrifmuir in 1715, ostensibly as a Jacobite but probably as an opportunist – the chaos would have made cattle raiding easier. Eventually captured and sentenced to transportation, Rob Roy was pardoned and returned to Balquhidder, where he remained until his death in 1734. His grave there, a simple affair found behind the ruined church, is one of the main events on the unofficial Rob Roy trail, though the peaceful site is mercifully underdeveloped and free of tourist trappings. His life has been much romanticized, from Sir Walter Scott's 1818 version of the story in his novel *Rob Roy*, to the 1995 film of the same name, starring Liam Neeson.

Brook Linn Country House, Leny Feus (☎01877/330103; ③; March—Nov), set above the town; and the family-run *Ben A'an Guest House* (☎01877/330317; ③), 158 Main St. A couple of miles out of town – cross the river at Bridge Street, follow the A81, turn right at the Invertrossachs Junction and continue for a mile – you'll find *Trossachs Backpackers* (☎01877/331200, *trosstel@aol.com*), a sparkling new thirty-bed **hostel** and activity centre with self-catering dorms, family rooms and **bike rental** (☎01877/331100). For more luxury, try the *Roman Camp Country House Hotel*, signposted off the main street (☎01877/330003; ⑧), a turreted and romantic seventeenth-century hunting lodge in twenty-acre gardens on the River Teith, or the *Invertrossachs Country House* (☎01877/331126; ⑥), west of Callander on the southern shores of Loch Venachar, a plush Edwardian mansion offering superior B&B. Despite its popularity, there are few **restaurants** worth recommending in Callander. The best place is in the *Roman Camp Hotel*, which serves splendid Scottish produce in refined surroundings. For good pub food, try the *Myrtle Inn* on the eastern edge of Callander, or the *Lade Inn* in Kilmahog, two miles west of the town.

Loch Earn

North of Callander, the A84 speeds along the side of Loch Lubnaig to **LOCHEARNHEAD**, at the western end of **Loch Earn**. This wide tranquil expanse is ideal for **watersports**, and particularly good for beginners. Lochearnhead Watersports (☎01567/830330) organizes and teaches a wide variety of activities, including waterskiing, windsurfing, Canadian canoeing and kayaking. Lochearnhead is also a good base for **walking**, and the watersports centre runs "heritage rambles". For **accommodation**, try the *Clachan Cottage Hotel* (☎01567/830247; ③), or the cheaper *Earnknowe* B&B (☎01567/830238; ②), both on Lochside, Lochearnhead. There are also some good **self-catering** options in the area: from *Earnknowe*, you can rent attractive stone cottages close to Lochearnhead village (2–6 people; £120–355 per week). In addition, there are some Scandinavian-style wooden chalets with good facilities (☎01567/830211; 6 people; £280–355 per week), or a nice little whitewashed cottage in St Fillans (☎0131/313 0467 or 01764/670004; 2–4 people; £240 per week). Perhaps the best choice for the area as a whole, though, is the chalet-like *Four Seasons Hotel* (☎01764/685333; ⑤) in St Fillans, with its wonderful lochside location. It's also the best choice for **eating**; indeed, there are few other options in the area.

Breadalbane and Loch Tay

North of Lochearnhead, the A85 moves into **Glen Dochart**, a long glen surrounded by the **mountains of Breadalbane** (pronounced "Bread-*al*bane"), named after the earls of Breadalbane. At the eastern end of the glen the same mountain range also looms over fourteen-mile-long, freshwater **Loch Tay**, starting point of the river that winds through Perth and empties into the North Sea by Dundee. The villages of **Killin** and **Kenmore** are situated at either end of the loch, with the grand Ben Lawers range rising between them on the loch's northern side. The largest town in the area, **Aberfeldy**, straddles the River Tay a few miles further east of Kenmore and has a number of easy, attractive walks.

In Glen Dochart, at **CRIANLARICH**, the main road swings east to join the A82, the busy Glasgow–Fort William trunk road, an important staging post on various transport routes, including the main railway lines from Oban and Fort William as they head south and the West Highland Way long-distance footpath. Otherwise there's little reason to stop here, unless you're keen on tackling some of the steep-sided hills that rise up from the glen. Five miles further north from here on the A82, the village of **TYNDRUM** owes its existence to a minor (and very short-lived) nineteenth-century gold rush, but today is dotted with some rather ugly hotels and service stations, including the famous **Green Welly Shop** (☎01838/400271), where you can purchase a pair of the old dependables from the vast selection of clothing, boots and other outdoor gear on display, or simply stop for a cup of tea and watch coach parties loading and unloading in the car park. At Tyndrum both the road and rail routes north split, one branch heading due west towards Oban, the other carrying on north over Rannoch Moor to Glen Coe and Fort William.

Killin

At the western end of Loch Tay, some twelve miles east of Crianlarich, is the small town of **KILLIN**, where the River Dochart comes rushing out of the hills and down the frothy **Falls of Dochart**, before disgorging into Loch Tay. There's little to do in Killin itself, but it makes a convenient base for some of the area's best walks. The **tourist office** is located by the falls (Nov, Dec & Feb Sat & Sun 10am–4pm; March–May & Oct daily 10am–5pm; June & Sept daily 9.30am–6pm; July & Aug daily 9am–6pm), next to the **Breadalbane Folklore Centre** (same times as tourist office; £1). The centre explores the history and mythology of

Breadalbane and holds the 1300-year-old "healing stones" of St Fillan, an early Christian missionary who settled in Glen Dochart.

Killin is littered with B&Bs, but one of the more unusual places **to stay** is the *Dall Lodge Hotel*, Main Street (☎01567/820217, *wilson@dalllodgehotel.co.uk*; ⑤), which is filled with all manner of exotic Far Eastern bits and pieces, and has a dining room serving fine local produce. There is also a **youth hostel** (☎01567/820546; April–Oct), in a fine old country house just beyond the northern end of the village, with views out over the loch.

Kenmore

On a slight promontory at Loch Tay's northern end and overlooking the River Tay, **KENMORE**'s whitewashed houses and well-tended gardens cluster around the gate to **Taymouth Castle** – built by the Campbells of Glenorchy in the early nineteenth century and now a private golf club. Also in Kenmore, the **Scottish Crannog Centre** (April–Oct Mon–Fri 10am–5pm, Sat & Sun 10am–6pm; £2.80), perched above the loch on stilts, is an authentic reconstruction of a Bronze Age defensive house complete with sheepskin rugs and wooden bowls. There are various **boat rental** places around this end of the loch, as well as **Croft-na-Caber** (☎01887/830588), an impressive **outdoor pursuits** complex on the southern bank of the loch, where you can try waterskiing, fishing, hill walking, cross-country skiing, river sledging, rafting and jet biking. The complex also offers comfortable **accommodation** either in its own hotel (☎01887/830236; ④) or in well-equipped chalets overlooking the loch (2–6 people; £210–590 per week). You don't have to stay here to use the facilities, however, and tuition or equipment rental is available by the hour, half-day, full day or longer. As an example of prices, a day's sailing or windsurfing instruction costs around £50. You can also stay at the overwhelmingly Scottish *Kenmore Hotel*, in the village square (☎01887/830205; ⑤), a descendant of Scotland's oldest inn, established here in

---

CLIMBING THE BEN LAWERS GROUP

Ordnance Survey Landranger map no. 51

On the northern side of Loch Tay is moody **Ben Lawers** (3984ft), Perthshire's highest mountain; from the top there are incredible views towards both the Atlantic and the North Sea. The ascent – which, despite the well-marked footpath, should not be tackled without all the right equipment (see p.46) – takes around three hours from the NTS **visitor centre** (mid-April to Sept daily 10am–5pm; ☎01567/820397), which is reached by a signposted road off the A827. The centre has an audiovisual show, slides of the mountain flowers – including the rare Alpine flora found here – and a nature trail with accompanying descriptive booklet.

The Ben Lawers range offers rich pickings for Munro-baggers, with nine hills over 3000ft in close proximity. The whole double-horseshoe-shaped ridge from Meall Greigh in the east to Meall a'Choire Leith in the northwest is too much for one day, though the eastern section from Meall Greigh (3284ft) to Beinn Ghlas (3619ft), taking in Ben Lawers, can be walked in eight to ten hours in good conditions. Standing on its own a little to the east is perhaps the prettiest of the lot, Meall nan Tarmachan ("the hill of the ptarmigan"); at 3427ft, a less arduous but rewarding climb from the roadside a mile or so further on from the visitor centre.

1572, or at *Ben Lawers Hotel* (☎01567/820436; ③), about halfway between Kenmore and Killin, where the food is particularly good. Meanwhile, *Mrs Jolly's B&B* (☎01567/830353; ②), Lower Dualin Croft, is another good place to sample traditional Scottish hospitality in a tranquil location.

North of Loch Tay

Beyond Breadalbane, the mountains tumble down into **Glen Lyon** – at 34 miles long, it is the longest enclosed glen in Scotland – where, legend has it, the Celtic warrior Fingal built twelve castles. Access to the glen is usually impossible in winter, but the narrow roads are passable in summer. You can either take the road from Killin up past the **Ben Lawers Visitor Centre**, four miles up Loch Tay, and continue going, or take the road from Fortingall, which is a couple of miles north of the loch's northern end. The two roads join up, making a round-trip possible, but bear in mind that there is no road through the mountains to Loch Rannoch further north. **FORTINGALL** itself is little more than a handful of thatched cottages, although locals make much of their 3000-year-old yew tree – believed (by them at least) to be the oldest living thing in Europe. The village also lays claim to being the birthplace of **Pontius Pilate**, reputedly the son of a Roman officer who was stationed here.

Aberfeldy

A largely Victorian town six miles or so further on from Kenmore, **ABERFELDY** makes a good base for exploring the area. The **tourist office** at The Square in the town centre (April–June, Sept & Oct Mon–Sat 9.30am–5.30pm, Sun noon–4pm; July & Aug Mon–Sat 9am–7pm, Sun 11am–6pm; Nov–March Mon–Fri 9.30am–5pm, Sat 9.30am–1.30pm; ☎01887/820276) gives details of the so-called Locus Project, a local initiative whereby a series of looped trails has been devised to take in all the main sights.

Aberfeldy sits at the point where the Urlar Burn – lined by the silver birch trees celebrated by Robert Burns in his poem *The Birks of Aberfeldy* – flows into the River Tay. The Tay is spanned by **Wade's Bridge**, built by General Wade in 1733 during his efforts to control the trouble in the Highlands, and, with its humpback and four arches, regarded as one of the general's finest remaining crossing points. Overlooking the bridge from the south end is the **Black Watch Monument**, a pensive, kilted soldier, erected in 1887 to commemorate the peacekeeping troop of Highlanders gathered together by Wade in 1739.

The small town centre is a busy mixture of craft and tourist shops, its main attraction the superbly restored early nineteenth-century **Aberfeldy Water Mill** (Easter–Oct Mon–Sat 10am–5pm, Sun 11am–5pm; £2), which harnesses the water of the Urlar to turn the wheel that stone-grinds oatmeal in the traditional Scottish way.

One mile west of Aberfeldy, across Wade's Bridge, **Castle Menzies** (April to mid-Oct Mon–Sat 10.30am–5pm, Sun 2–5pm; £2.30) is an imposing, Z-shaped, sixteenth-century tower house, which until the middle of this century was the chief seat of the Clan Menzies. With the demise of the Menzies line, the castle was taken over by the Menzies Clan Society, which since 1971 has been involved in the lengthy process of restoring it. Now the interior, with its wide stone staircase, is refreshingly free of fixtures and fittings, restored to authentic austerity.

If you want to **stay** in Aberfeldy, head for *Moness House Hotel and Country Club*, Crieff Road (☎01887/820446, *moness@btinternet.com*; ④), a whitewashed country house which also offers luxurious **self-catering** cottages (2–6 people; £245–500 per week), as well as fishing, golf and watersports. Alternatively, there's *Guinach House*, by the Birks (☎01887/820251, *100127.222@compuserve.com*; ⑤), a tastefully decorated place in pleasant grounds near the famous silver birches, with a good dining room, or *Farleyer House* (☎01887/820332; ⑧), a mile out of Aberfeldy on the B846, which is highly recommended as a hotel and **restaurant**. For B&B, try *Novar*, 2 Home St (☎01887/820779; ①), or *Mavisbank*, Taybridge Drive (☎01887/820223; ①; March–Oct), both attractive stone cottages.

Loch Tummel, Loch Rannoch and Loch Ericht

North of Loch Tay and west of Pitlochry (see p.149), the B8019/B846 twists and turns along the Grampian mountainsides, overlooking **Loch Tummel** and then **Loch Rannoch**. These two lochs, celebrated by Harry Lauder in his famous song *The Road to the Isles*, are joined by Dunalastair Water, which narrows to become the River Tummel at the western end of the loch of the same name. This is a spectacular stretch of countryside and one which deserves leisurely exploration. **Queen's View** at the eastern end of Loch Tummel is a fabulous vantage point, looking down the loch across the hills to the misty peak of Schiehallion (3520ft) or the "Fairy Mountain", whose mass was used in early experiments to judge the weight of the Earth. The Forestry Commission's **visitor centre** (April–Oct daily 10am–6pm; ☎01350/727284) interprets the fauna and flora of the area, and also has a café.

Beyond Loch Tummel, marking the eastern end of Loch Rannoch, the small community of **KINLOCH RANNOCH** is popular with backpackers, who stock up at the local store before taking to the hills. You can **stay** here in the converted eighteenth-century croft *Cuilmore Cottage* (☎01882/632218; ②), with a rustic atmosphere and delicious food, or try *Bunrannoch House* (☎01882/632407; ②), a Victorian former shooting lodge with lovely views. The road follows the loch to its end and then heads six miles further into the desolation of **Rannoch Moor**, where **Rannoch Station**, a lonely outpost on the Glasgow–Fort William West Highland train, marks the end of the route. The only way back is by the same road as far as Loch Rannoch, where it's possible – but not always advisable, depending on conditions – to return on a (very) minor road along the south side of the lochs. The round-trip is roughly seventy miles.

After Rannoch Station, the next stop on the train line north is **Corrour**, an outpost at 1340ft above sea level with little more to it than the station and vast acres of open moorland and mountainscape. There's no public road within ten miles, so to get here and away you need to be well acquainted with the train timetable or properly prepared for a long walk. For film (rather than outdoor) aficionados, Corrour is the spot where Renton and his gang make their futile attempt to enjoy the great Scottish outdoors in the film *Trainspotting*. If you're inclined to be a bit less cynical, there are two **places to stay** here, *Corrour Station Bunkhouse* (☎01397/732236), which has fourteen beds (bedding included) and a restaurant/café attached, and the more basic *Loch Ossian Youth Hostel* (☎01397/732207 or central reservations ☎0541 553255; mid-March–Oct), a mile from the station in a pretty setting on the shores of Loch Ossian, named after a legendary Gaelic hero and poet.

Corrour is one of the jumping-off points if you're aiming for the remote hills grouped around mighty **Ben Alder** (3766ft), another of Bonnie Prince Charlie's hide-outs after Culloden, and **Loch Ericht**, a dark and often forbidding loch that stretches from north of Loch Rannoch to Dalwhinnie, an alternative way into the area, which lies on the A9 between Pitlochry and Aviemore.

Dunkeld, Pitlochry and Blair Atholl

The main route into the Highlands on the eastern side of the country is the A9 between Perth and Inverness, a busy and accident-prone road that can be difficult to pass after snowfalls in winter. The railway follows the same winding course through the mountains, offering good links from the central belt to the Cairngorms (see p.168) and Inverness.

Dunkeld and Birnam

DUNKELD, twelve miles on from Perth up the A9 (trains from Perth to Inverness stop here; buses #23 and #27, Sun #22), was proclaimed Scotland's ecclesiastical capital by Kenneth MacAlpine in 850. Its position at the southern boundary of the Grampian Mountains made it a favoured meeting place for Highland and Lowland cultures, but in 1689 it was burnt to the ground by the Cameronians – fighting for William of Orange – in an effort to flush out troops of the Stuart monarch, James VII. Subsequent rebuilding, however, has created one of the area's most delightful communities, and it's well worth at least a brief stop to view its whitewashed houses and lovely cathedral. The **tourist office** is at The Cross in the town centre (April–June, Sept & Oct Mon–Sat 9.30am–5.30pm, Sun 11am–4pm; July & Aug Mon–Sat 9am–7.30pm, Sun 11am–7pm; Nov & Dec Mon–Sat 9.30am–1.30pm; ☎01350/727688).

Dunkeld's partly ruined **cathedral** is on the northern side of town, in an idyllic setting amid lawns and trees on the east bank of the Tay. Construction began in the early twelfth century and continued throughout the next two hundred years, but the building was more or less ruined at the time of the Reformation. The present structure, in Gothic and Norman style, consists of the fourteenth-century choir and the fifteenth-century nave. The choir, restored in 1600 (and several times since), now serves as the parish church, while the nave remains roofless apart from the clock tower. Inside, note the leper's peep near the pulpit in the north wall, through which lepers could receive the sacrament without contact with the congregation. Also look out for the great effigy of "The Wolf of Badenoch", Robert II's son, born in 1343. The wolf acquired his name and notoriety when, after being excommunicated from the Church for leaving his wife, he took his revenge by burning the towns of Forres and Elgin and sacking Elgin cathedral. He eventually repented, did public penance for his crimes and was absolved by his brother Robert III.

Dunkeld is linked to its sister community, **BIRNAM**, by Thomas Telford's seven-arched bridge of 1809. This little village has a place in history thanks to Shakespeare, for it was on "Dunsinane Hill" to the southeast of the village that

Macbeth declared, "I will not be afraid of death and bane/Till Birnam Forest come to Dunsinane", only to be told by a messenger:

> *As I did stand my watch upon the Hill,*
> *I look'd toward Birnam, and anon me thought*
> *The Wood began to move . . .*

The **Perthshire Visitor Centre** just south of Birnam, down the A9 at Bankfoot (March–Oct daily 9am–8pm; Nov–Feb Mon–Fri 9am–7pm, Sat & Sun 9am–7.30pm; £2) offers "The Macbeth Experience", which documents – on film and through talking dummies – the true story of Macbeth, who in real life was quite the opposite of Shakespeare's scheming villain. Several centuries later, another literary personality, Beatrix Potter, drew inspiration from the area, recalling her childhood holidays here when penning the *Peter Rabbit* stories. The **Beatrix Potter Garden** in Birnam celebrates the connection.

There are several large **hotels** in Dunkeld, including the *Atholl Arms Hotel*, Tay Terrace (☎01350/727219; ④), the *Royal Dunkeld*, Atholl Street (☎01350/727322; ④), and the Victorian Gothic *Birnam House Hotel* on Perth Road (☎01350/727462; ⑤). Just to the north, the luxurious *Stakis Dunkeld* (☎01350/727771; ⑨) is set at the end of a long drive which winds through the hotel's lush estate, where you can fish, shoot, cycle and stroll. For **B&B**, try the non-smoking *Bheinne Mhor* (☎01350/727779; ②), Birnam Glen, Dunkeld, or the friendly *Heatherbank* (☎01350/727413; ①), on St Mary's Road in Birnam. There are a few mediocre **eating places** on Dunkeld's main street; the best food options are lunch at the *Atholl Arms* or a more expensive dinner at the *Stakis Dunkeld*.

Driving north on the A9 to Pitlochry, you can stop off and walk the mile and a half to **The Hermitage** (buses from Perth to Pitlochry stop near here), set in the wooded gorge of the River Braan. This pretty eighteenth-century folly, also known as Ossian's Hall, was once mirrored to reflect the water, but the mirrors were smashed by Victorian vandals and the folly was more tamely restored. The hall, appealing yet incongruous in its splendid setting, neatly frames a dramatic waterfall.

Pitlochry

Surrounded by hills just north of the confluence of the Tummel and Tay rivers at Ballinluig, **PITLOCHRY** spreads gracefully along the eastern shore of the Tummel, on the lower slopes of Ben Vrackie (see box on p.151). Even after General Wade built one of his first roads through here in the early eighteenth century, Pitlochry remained little more than a village. Queen Victoria's visit in 1842 helped put the area on the map, but it wasn't until the end of the century that Pitlochry established itself as a popular holiday centre.

Today the busy main street is a constant flurry of traffic, both locals and tourists. Beyond the train bridge at the southern end of the main street (Atholl Road leading to Perth Road) is Bells' **Blair Atholl Distillery**, Perth Road (Oct–Easter Mon–Fri 9am–5pm; Easter–Sept also Sat 9am–5pm, Sun noon–5pm; tours every 10min; £3 including tastings), where the excellent visitor centre illustrates the process involved in making the Blair Atholl Malt. Whisky has been produced on this site since 1798, in which time production has been stepped up to around two million litres a year, making this a medium-sized distillery.

A perfect contrast to Blair Atholl is the **Edradour Distillery** (March–Oct Mon–Sat 9.30am–5pm, Sun noon–5pm; Nov & Dec Mon–Sat 10am–4pm; Dec group bookings only), Scotland's smallest, in an idyllic position tucked into the hills a couple of miles east of Pitlochry on the A924. A whistle-stop audiovisual presentation covering more than 250 years of production precedes the tour of the distillery itself.

On the western edge of Pitlochry, just across the river, lies Scotland's renowned "Theatre in the Hills", the **Pitlochry Festival Theatre** (☎01796/472680; Easter–early Oct). Set up in 1951, the theatre started in a tent on the site of what is now the town curling rink, before moving to the banks of the river in 1981. Backstage tours, covering all aspects of theatre production (generally Thurs & Fri 2pm; £3; booking essential), are on offer during the day, while a variety of productions – both mainstream and offbeat – are staged in the evening.

A short stroll upstream from the theatre is the **Pitlochry Power Station and Dam**, a massive concrete wall which harnesses the water of the man-made Loch Faskally, just north of the town, for hydroelectric power. Although the visitor centre (April–Oct daily 10am–5.30pm; £1.90) explains the ins and outs of it all, the main attraction here, apart from the views up the loch, is the **salmon ladder**, which the salmon leap up on their annual migration – a sight not to be missed.

Practicalities

Access to Pitlochry is easy by public transport, thanks to its position on the main train line to Inverness, and regular buses running from Perth. The **bus** stop and the **train** station are on Station Road, at the north end of town, ten minutes' walk from the centre and the **tourist office**, 22 Atholl Rd (March to mid-May & Oct Mon–Sat 9am–6pm, Sun noon–6pm; mid-May to Sept daily 9am–8pm; Nov–April Mon–Fri 9am–5pm, Sat 9am–1.30pm; ☎01796/472215). The office gives out an informative free guide of walks in the surrounding area, and also offers an **accommodation** booking service.

Birchwood Hotel, East Moulin Road (☎01796/472477, *birchwoodhotel@msn.com*; ⑤), occupies a lovely Victorian country house at the top of town, set in four acres of grounds, and has a particularly good restaurant. South of the hotel, the magnificent and much pricier *Pitlochry Hydro*, Knockard Road (☎01796/472666; ⑦), looks out over the Tummel Valley. Five miles west of Pitlochry on the B8019, at Strathtummel, the *Queens View Hotel* (☎01796/473291, *queensviewhotel @compuserve.com*; ⑤) has lovely views, good bar meals and a fine restaurant. In the town centre, there are a number of cheaper hotels along the main street, including the comfortable *McKays Hotel*, 138 Atholl Rd (☎01796/473888; ④), and many guest houses and **B&Bs**. Try *Craigroyston House*, 2 Lower Oakfield (☎01796/472053; ③); *Comar House*, Strathview Terrace (☎01796/473531; ②); or *Ferryman's Cottage* (☎01796/473681; ②), Port-na-Craig, in a beautiful position next to the River Tummel. The **youth hostel** (☎01796/472308) is a fine stone mansion on Knockard Road at the top of town.

Pitlochry is the domain of the tearoom and pitifully short of **restaurants** and pubs; the best option is the *Killiecrankie Hotel* (☎01796/473220, *killiecrankie.hotel@btinternet.com*; ⑤), at Killiecrankie, three miles north on the A9, where the meals are hearty and well priced. In town, try the popular restaurant at the Festival Theatre, or the nearby *Port-na-craig Inn & Restaurant*, both of which have beautiful riverside locations. For a pub lunch with spectacular views over the water, it's worth driving ten miles west to the *Loch Tummel Inn*

WALKS AROUND PITLOCHRY

Ordnance Survey Landranger maps nos. 43 & 52

Pitlochry is surrounded by good walking country. The biggest lure has to be **Ben Vrackie** (2733ft), which provides a stunning backdrop for the Festival Theatre and deserves better than a straight up-and-down walk; however, the climb should only be attempted in settled weather conditions, with the right equipment and following the necessary safety precautions (see p.46). A good circular walk goes via the quiet Loch Faskally to **Killiecrankie Visitor Centre** (refreshments available) and then heads up the hill by a seldom-used route before returning via Moulin. Allow a full day for the complete walk.

Head through Pitlochry northwards and branch off to pass the *Green Hotel* to reach attractive Loch Faskally. You could walk right round it, but for the purposes of this walk follow the shore and take the signs up the River Garry to go through the **Pass of Killiecrankie**. This is looked after by the NTS, which has a visitor centre with interpretive displays, books and souvenirs for sale. To get this far takes a couple of hours.

From the NTS centre walk north up the old A9 and branch off on the small tarred road signposted **Old Faskally**, which twists up under the new A9 and past a house and the gates of Old Faskally. Keep on the tarred road until you reach a diversion sign which leads up the embankment above the road onto a lesser track and through a kissing gate at the top of the field. Continue from here until you finally leave the cultivated land through the hill dyke.

The track zigzags up heathery pasture to an old wall and a gate in a fence just beyond: go through the gate then bear right across the open hillside, crossing the **Allt Eachainn**, the burn that drains this corrie, before heading up the hill opposite in another series of bends, clearly seen from below. Also visible from below is a footpath bearing off left as the slope gets steeper, which you should follow through the heather towards the pass. It goes over the saddle of a dark heathery prow and, a couple of hundred yards beyond, brings you to the pass looking down on **Loch a' Choire**. The track from Pitlochry/Moulin crosses below the dam on the loch and heads directly up the peak. This steep track can be seen from the col; skirt north of the loch to join it. As Ben Vrackie is an isolated summit, the weather can change quickly and clouds render route-finding difficult, so Loch a' Choire may be a better place to picnic. The descending path from Loch a' Choire is clear and runs across the moors to reach forest level. A stile crosses the fence into the birch and pine woods that lead down to a small car park. Follow the minor road from it down to the hamlet of **Moulin** and on to Pitlochry.

(☎01882/634272; ④), halfway along Loch Tummel. Its restaurant is also highly recommended and booking ahead is essential for dinner.

Blair Atholl to Dalwhinnie

Four miles north of Pitlochry, the A9 cuts through the **Pass of Killiecrankie**, a breathtaking wooded gorge which falls away to the River Garry below. This dramatic setting was the site of the **Battle of Killiecrankie** in 1689, when the Jacobites quashed the forces of General Mackay. Legend has it that one soldier of the Crown, fleeing for his life, made a miraculous jump across the eighteen-foot **Soldier's Leap**, an impossibly wide chasm halfway up the gorge. Queen Victoria, visiting here 160 years later, contented herself with recording the beauty of the area in her diary. Exhibits at the slick NTS **visitor centre** (April–Oct daily 10am–5.30pm; ☎01796/473233; £1) recall the battle and examine the gorge in detail.

Before leading the Jacobites into battle, Graham of Claverhouse, Viscount ("Bonnie") Dundee, had seized **Blair Castle** (April–Oct daily 10am–6pm; £6), three miles up the road at **Blair Atholl**. Seat of the Atholl dukedom, this whitewashed, turreted castle, surrounded by parkland and dating from 1269, presents an impressive sight as you approach up the drive. A piper may be playing in front of the castle: he is one of the Atholl Highlanders, a select group retained by the duke as his private army – a privilege afforded to him by Queen Victoria, who stayed here in 1844. Today the duke is the only British subject allowed to maintain his own force.

A total of 32 rooms are open for inspection, and display a selection of paintings, furniture and plasterwork that is sumptuous in the extreme, although the vast number of stuffed animals may not be to everyone's liking. The Tapestry Room, on the top floor of the original Cumming's Tower, is hung with Brussels tapestries and contains an outrageous four-poster bed, topped with vases of ostrich feathers which originally came from the first duke's suite at Holyrood Palace in Edinburgh. The Ballroom, also, with its timber roof, antlers and melange of portraits, is Baronial Scotland at its best.

Highland cows graze the ancient landscaped grounds and peacocks strut in front of the castle. There is a **riding stable** from where you can take treks, and formal woodland walks have been laid out – don't miss the neglected, walled Japanese water garden. There is also a well-equipped **caravan park** (☎01796/481263) in the grounds.

Beyond Blair Atholl, the A9 follows the line of **Glen Garry** and the River Garry through the Grampian Mountains. The road climbs continuously, sweeping past the eastern end of **Glen Errochty**, on towards the barren **Pass of Drummochter** and to the bleak little village of **Dalwhinnie** at the northern end of Loch Ericht. The scenery is marvellous all the way, but there is literally nothing here apart from the mountains and moors.

The Angus glens

Immediately north of Dundee, the low-lying Sidlaw Hills divide the city from the rich agricultural region of Strathmore, whose string of tidy market towns lies on a fertile strip along the southernmost edge of the heather-covered lower slopes of the Grampian Mountains. These towns act as gateways to the **Angus glens** – or "Braes o' Angus", a series of tranquil valleys penetrated by few roads and offering some of the most rugged and majestic landscapes of northeast Scotland. It's a rain-swept, wind-blown, sparsely populated area, whose roads become impassable with the first snows, sometimes as early as October, and in the summer there are ferocious midges to contend with. Nevertheless, most of the glens, particularly **Glen Clova**, are well and truly on the tourist circuit, with the rolling hills and dales attracting hikers, birdwatchers and botanists in the summer, grouse shooters and deer hunters in autumn and a growing number of skiers in winter. The most useful road through the glens is the A93, which cuts through **Glen Shee** to Braemar on Deeside (see p.162). It's pretty dramatic stuff, threading its way over Britain's highest main road pass – the **Cairnwell Pass** (2199ft). Public transport in the region is limited: to get up the glens you'll have to rely on the **postbuses** from Blairgowrie (for Glen Shee) and Kirriemuir (for glens Clova and Prosen).

SKIING IN THE ANGUS GLENS

For information on **skiing** in the Angus glens, call Ski Glenshee (☎013397/41320), who also offer ski rental and lessons. In addition, lessons, skis and boards are available from Cairnwell Mountain Sports (☎01250/885255), at the Spittal of Glenshee. **Ski rental** starts at around £12 a day, while lessons are around £10 for two hours. **Lift passes** cost £17.50 per day or £70 for a five-day (Mon–Fri) ticket. For the latest snow and weather conditions, phone the Ski Hotline (☎0891/654656).

Glen Shee

The most dramatic and best known of the Angus glens, **Glen Shee** is dominated by its ski fields, ranged over four mountains above the Cairnwell mountain pass. During the winter season – December to March – skiers, predominantly from central Scotland, brave the ridiculously cold temperatures and bitter winds. Ski lifts and tows give access to gentle beginners' slopes, while experienced skiers can try the more intimidating Tiger run. In summer it's all a bit sad, with lifeless chairlifts and bare, scree-covered slopes, although hang-gliders take advantage of the crosswinds between the mountains and there are some excellent hiking and mountain-biking routes.

The well-heeled town of **BLAIRGOWRIE** (officially Blairgowrie and Rattray), little more than one main road set among raspberry fields on the glen's southernmost tip, is as good a place as any to base yourself – and is particularly useful in winter if you plan to ski. Set right on the river, the town's only claim to fame is that St Ninian once camped at Wellmeadow, a pleasant grassy triangle in the town centre. If you've time to kill here, wander up the leafy river bank to **Keathbank Mill** (daily May–Oct 10.30am–5pm; £3.50), a huge old jute mill with an 1862 steam turbine driven by the largest working water wheel in Scotland. Also housed within the complex are some absorbing workshops where the country's largest heraldic crests are carved.

Blairgowrie **tourist office** (Easter–June, Sept & Oct Mon–Sat 9.30am–5.30pm, Sun 11am–4pm; July & Aug Mon–Sat 9am–7pm, Sun 10am–6pm; Nov–Easter Mon–Fri 9.30am–5.30pm, Sat 10am–2pm; ☎01250/872960), on the high side of the Wellmeadow, can help with **accommodation**. Over the bridge spanning the fast-flowing River Ericht, Blairgowrie melts into its twin community of **Rattray**, where, on the main street (Boat Brae), you'll find the excellent *Ivy Bank House* B&B (☎01250/873056; ①), offering sweeping views of the river and surrounding hills, as well as use of a floodlit tennis court. Alternatively, there's the opulent, ivy-covered *Kinloch House* (☎01250/884237; ⑦), one of the area's most prestigious hotels, set in its own vast grounds three miles west of town on the A923, while, at the other end of the scale, **camping** is available at the year-round *Blairgowrie Holiday Park* on Rattray's Hatton Road (☎01250/872941). The town boasts plenty of places to **eat**: *Cargills* by the river on Lower Mill Street (☎01250/876735; closed Mon) is the best bet for a formal meal, while, for lighter meals and takeaways, there's the *Dome Restaurant*, just behind the tourist office, which has been run by two local Italian families since the 1920s. For good **pub** grub, try the *Brig o'Blair* on the Wellmeadow, or head six miles out of town on the A93 to the delightfully situated *Bridge of Cally Hotel* (☎01250/886231; ③), which also has rooms. **Bikes** can be rented from the *Blairgowrie Holiday Park* (see above), and from

Mountains and Glens (☎01250/874206), 300yd from the tourist office on Railway Road.

Nearly twenty miles north of Blairgowrie, the **SPITTAL OF GLENSHEE**, though ideally situated for skiing, is little more than a tacky service area, only worth stopping at for a quick drink or bite to eat. However, it does boast an excellent bunkhouse run by Cairnwell Mountain Sports, on the A93 (☎01250/885255), which rents out skis, bikes and even offers hang-gliding lessons. In addition, it's handily close to one of the nicest places to stay in the area, *Dalmunzie House* (☎01250/885224; ⑤), a gorgeous, turreted, Highland sporting lodge, reflecting the peace and tranquillity of the rugged scenery. From the Spittal the road climbs another five miles or so to the ski centre at the crest of the Cairnwell Pass.

Blairgowrie is well linked by **bus** to both Perth and Dundee by the hourly #57; to get up Glen Shee, however, you'll have to rely on the **postbus**, which leaves town (Mon–Sat) at 9.05am and returns from the Spittal of Glenshee at 2.15pm.

Glen Isla

Running parallel to Glen Shee, and linked to it via the A926, is **Glen Isla**, dominated by Mount Blair (2441ft). A lot less dramatic than its sister glens, it suffers from an excess of angular conifers alongside great bald chunks of hillside waiting to be planted. Heading north into the glen along the B954 from the tiny village of **MEIGLE**, fifteen miles north of Dundee and home to the **Meigle Museum** (April–Sept daily 9.30am–6pm; £1.80; HS), Scotland's most important collection of early Christian and Pictish inscribed stones, the River Isla narrows and then plunges some 60ft into a deep gorge to produce the classically pretty waterfall of **Reekie Linn**, or "smoking fall", so called because of the water mist produced when the fall hits a ledge and bounces a further 20ft into a deep pool known as the Black Dub. The glen cheers up enormously north of the tiny hamlet of **KIRKTON OF GLENISLA**, ten miles or so up the glen. Here, the cosy *Glenisla Hotel* (☎01575/582223; ④) is great for eating and drinking, as well as being a good base for walking. In the nearby Glenisla forest there are some trails for hiking, while, just before Kirkton, a turnoff on the right-hand side leads to the Glenmarkie Riding Centre (☎01575/582341), which offers pony trekking and a wonderfully isolated B&B (②).

Transport connections into the glen are limited: the plain Strathmore town of Alyth, three miles north of Meigle, is on the main bus routes linking Blairgowrie with Dundee and Kirriemuir, while the hourly #57 bus from Dundee to Perth passes through Meigle. The only transport up to Kirkton is a postbus, which leaves Alyth at 7.40am (Mon–Sat).

Glens Prosen, Clova and Doll

The sandstone town of **KIRRIEMUIR**, known locally as Kirrie, is set on a hill six miles northwest of Forfar on the cusp of glens Clova and Prosen. Despite the influx of hunters up for the "season", it's still a pretty special place, a haphazard confection of narrow closes, twisting wynds and steep braes. In the nineteenth century it was made famous by a local handloom-weaver's son, J.M. Barrie, the creator of Peter Pan. **Barrie's birthplace**, a plain little whitewashed cottage at 9 Brechin Rd (Easter weekend & May–Sept Mon–Sat 11am–5pm, Sun 1.30–5pm; Oct Sat 11am–5pm, Sun 1.30–5pm; £2; NTS), displays his writing desk, photos and newspaper clippings.

Kirrie's helpful **tourist office** is in Cumberland Close (April–June & Sept Mon–Sat 10am–5pm; July & Aug Mon–Sat 9.30am–5.30pm; ☎01575/574097), in the new development behind *Visocchi's* in the main square. **Accommodation** is available at *Crepto B&B*, Kinnordy Place (☎01575/572746; ①), or the respectable *Airlie Arms*, St Malcolm's Wynd (☎01575/572487; ③). *Visocchi's* is great for daytime **snacks** and ice cream, while the *Airlie*, and *Thrums Hotel*, on Bank Street, both serve good food in the evening. Of the **pubs**, the *Kilt and Clogs*, behind the tourist office, is the most lively. **Postbuses** into glens Clova and Prosen leave from the main post office, on Reform Street, at 8.30am (Mon–Sat). A second Glen Clova bus leaves around 3pm (Mon–Fri), but only goes as far as Clova village before returning to Kirriemuir. Hourly buses connect with Forfar for onward travel.

Glen Prosen

Five miles north of Kirrie, the low-key hamlet of **DYKEHEAD** marks the point where glens **Prosen** and Clova divide. **Accommodation** is available here at the *Royal Jubilee Arms Hotel* (☎01575/540381; ③), an old inn scarred by a grim modern conversion that, nonetheless, provides excellent all-day food, drink and Sunday-night **ceilidhs**. A mile or so up Glen Prosen, you'll find the house where Captain Scott and fellow explorer Dr Wilson planned their ill-fated trip to Antarctica in 1910–11, with a roadside **stone cairn** commemorating the expedition. From here, Glen Prosen proper unfolds before you. Little has changed since Scott's time, and it remains essentially a quiet wooded backwater, with all the wild and rugged splendour of the other glens but without the crowds. To explore the area thoroughly you need to go on foot, but a good road circuit can be made by crossing the river at the tiny village of **GLENPROSEN** and returning to Kirriemuir along the western side of the glen via Pearsie.

The best walk in the area is the reasonably easy four-mile **Minister's Path** (so called because the local minister would walk this way twice every Sunday to conduct services in both glens), connecting Prosen and Clova. Take the footpath between the kirk and the bridge in Glenprosen village, then the right fork where the track splits, and continue over the colourful burnt moorland down into Clova. As there is no afternoon return service by postbus from Prosen to Kirriemuir, you either have to stay the night or follow the path to its end, **Wester Eggie**, and pick up the Clova village postbus (Mon–Fri 3.30pm).

Glen Clova and Glen Doll

Of all the Angus glens, **Glen Clova** – which in the north becomes Glen Doll – with its stunning cliffs, heather slopes and valley meadows, is the firm favourite of many. Although it can get unpleasantly congested in peak season, the area is still remote enough so you can leave the crowds with little effort. Wildlife is abundant, with deer on the mountains, wild hares and even grouse and the occasional buzzard. The meadow flowers on the valley floor and arctic plants (including great splashes of white and purple saxifrage) on the rocks also make it something of a botanist's paradise.

The B955 from Dykehead and Kirriemuir divides at the Gella bridge over the swift-coursing River South Esk (unofficially, road traffic is encouraged to use the western branch of the road for travel up the glen, and the eastern side going down). Six miles north of Gella, the two branches of the road join up once more at the hamlet of **CLOVA**, little more than the hearty *Clova Hotel* (☎01575/550222; ③), which also has a simple outside bunkhouse (£5 per night), and hosts regular

WALKS FROM GLEN DOLL

These walks are some of the main routes across the Grampians from the Angus glens to Deeside, many of which follow well-established old drovers' roads. A number of them cross the royal estate of Balmoral, and Prince Charles's favourite mountain – Lochnagar – can be seen from all angles. The walks should always be approached with care; make sure to follow the usual safety precautions.

Capel Mounth to Ballater (15 miles; 7hr). Head across the bridge from the car park, turning right after a mile when the track crosses the Cald Burn. Out of the wood, the path zigzags its way up fierce slopes before levelling out on the moorland plateau. Soon descending, the path crosses a scree near the eastern end of Loch Muick. With the loch to your left, walk down along the scree till you reach the River Muick, crossing the bridge to take the quiet track along the river's northern shore to Ballater.

Capel Mounth round trip (15 miles; 8hr). Follow the above to Loch Muick, then follow the path down to loch level and double back on yourself along the loch's southern shore. When the track crosses the Black Burn, either take the steep left fork or continue along the shore for another mile, heading up the dramatic Streak of Lightning path that follows Corrie Chash. Both paths meet at the ruined stables below Sandy Hillock. Just beyond, take the path to the left, descending rapidly to the waterfall by the bridge at Bachnagairn, where a gentle burn-side track leads the three miles back to Glen Doll car park.

Jock's Road to Braemar (14 miles; 7hr). Take the road north from the car park past the youth hostel. After almost a mile, follow the signposted Jock's Road to the right, keeping on the northern bank of the burn. Pass a barn, Davey's Shelter, below Cairn Lunkhard and continue onto a wide ridge towards the path's summit at Crow Craigies (3018ft). From here, the path bumps down over scree slopes to the head of Loch Callater. Go either way round the loch, and follow the Callater Burn at the other end, eventually hitting the main A93 two miles short of Braemar.

barbecues, ceilidhs and even helicopter and balloon flights. Meals and real ale are available in the lively *Climbers' Bar* at the side of the hotel. An excellent, if fairly strenuous, four-hour walk from behind the old school at the back of the hotel leads up into the mountains and around the lip of **Loch Brandy**, which legend predicts will one day flood and drown the valley below.

North from Clova village, the road turns into a rabbit-strewn lane coursing along the riverside for four miles to the car park and informal **campsite** in **Glen Doll**, a useful starting point for numerous superb **walks** (see box). From the car park, it's only a few hundred yards further to the **youth hostel** (☎01575/550236; mid-March to Oct), a cheerful restored hunting lodge that boasts a squash court along with the usual facilities.

Edzell and Glen Esk

Travelling around Angus, you can hardly fail to notice the difference between organic settlements and planned towns built by paranoid landowners who forcibly rehoused local people in order to keep them under control, especially after the Jacobite uprisings. One of the better examples of this phenomenon, **EDZELL**, along the B966 five miles north of Brechin (and linked to it by buses #21, #29 and #30), was cleared and rebuilt with Victorian rectitude a mile to the west of its original site in the 1840s. The long, wide and ruler-straight main street is lined with prim nineteenth-century buildings, now doing a roaring trade as genteel teashops and antique emporia.

The original village (identifiable from the cemetery and surrounding grassy mounds) lay immediately to the west of the wonderfully explorable red sandstone ruins of **Edzell Castle** (April–Sept daily 9.30am–6pm; Oct–March Mon–Wed & Sat 9.30am–4.30pm, Thurs 9.30am–noon, Sun 2–4.30pm; £2.50; HS), itself a mile west of the planned village. The main part of the old castle is a good example of a comfortable tower house, whose main priority became luxurious living rather than defence, with some intricate decorative corbelling on the roof, a vast fireplace in the first-floor hall and numerous telltale signs of building from different ages.

It is, however, the **pleasance garden** overlooked by the castle tower that makes a visit to Edzell essential, especially in late spring and early to midsummer. The garden was built in 1604, at the height of the optimistic Renaissance, by Sir David Lindsay, and its refinement and extravagance are evident. The walls contain sculpted images of erudition: the Planetary Deities on the east side, the Liberal Arts (including a decapitated figure of Music) on the south, and, under floods of lobelia, the Cardinal Virtues on the west wall. In the centre of the garden, low-cut box hedges spell out the family mottoes and enclose voluminous beds of roses.

Four miles southwest of Edzell, lying either side of the lane to Bridgend – which can be reached either by carrying on along the road past the castle, or by taking the narrow road at the southern end of Edzell village – are the **Caterthuns**, twin Iron Age hillforts that were probably occupied at different times. The surviving ramparts on the White Caterthun (978ft) – easily reached from the small car park below – are the most impressive, and this is thought to be the later fort, occupied by the Picts in the first few centuries AD. Views from both, over the mountains to the north and the plains and foothills to the south, are stunning.

Just north of Edzell, a fifteen-mile road climbs alongside the River North Esk to form **Glen Esk**, the most easterly of the Angus glens and, like the others, scarcely populated. Ten miles along the Glen, the excellent **Glenesk Folk Museum** (Easter–May Mon, Sat & Sun noon–6pm; June to mid-Oct daily noon–6pm; £2) brings together records, costumes, photographs, maps and tools from the Angus glens, depicting the often harsh way of life for the inhabitants. The museum is housed in a lovely old shooting lodge known as The Retreat, and is run independently and enthusiastically by the local community. Inside there's also a craft shop and a noted tearoom – due reward for those who have endured the winding glen road. There are some excellent **hiking** routes further up the glen, including one to Queen Victoria's Well in Glen Mark and another up Mount Keen, Scotland's most easterly Munro.

If you want to stay in Edzell, there's decent **B&B** at *Elmgrove*, Inveriscandye Road (✆01356/648266; ①), while the most attractive of the hotels in town, the *Panmure Arms* (✆01356/648950; ③), at the far end of the main street near the turnoff to the castle, has recently been smartened up and offers rooms and meals. Further up the glen, you can **camp** one and a half miles north of the village at the *Glenesk Caravan Park* (✆01356/648565; April–Oct), while at Invermark, near the head of the Glen and a good jumping-off point for various hiking routes, is *The House of Mark* (✆01356/670315; ②), a former manse in a lovely setting, which serves evening meals by arrangement.

Deeside

More commonly known as **Royal Deeside**, the land stretching west of the coast along the River Dee revels in its connections with the royal family, who have regularly holidayed here, at **Balmoral**, since Queen Victoria bought the estate. Eighty thousand Scots turned out to welcome her on her first visit in 1848, but some weren't so charmed – one local journalist remarked that the area was about to be "desolated by cockneys and other horrible reptiles". Today, however, most locals are fiercely protective of the royal connection.

Many of Victoria's guests weren't as enthusiastic about Deeside as she was: Count von Moltke, then aide-de-camp to Prince Frederick William of Prussia, observed, "It is very astonishing that the Royal Power of England should reside amid this lonesome, desolate, cold mountain scenery", while Tsar Nicholas II whined, "The weather is awful, rain and wind every day and on top of it no luck at all – I haven't killed a stag yet." However, the Queen adored the place, and the woods were said to remind Prince Albert of Thuringia, his homeland.

Deeside is undoubtedly handsome in a fierce, craggy Scottish way, and the royal presence has helped keep a lid on any unattractive mass development. The villages strung along the A93, the main route through the area, are well heeled and the facilities for visitors are first-class, with a number of bunkhouses and youth hostels, some outstanding hotels and plenty of castles and grounds to snoop around. It's also an excellent area for **outdoor activities**, with hiking routes into both the Grampian and Cairngorm mountains, and good mountain-biking, canoeing and skiing.

Bluebird **bus** #201 from Aberdeen regularly chugs along the A93, serving most of the towns on the way to **Braemar**, past Balmoral to the west.

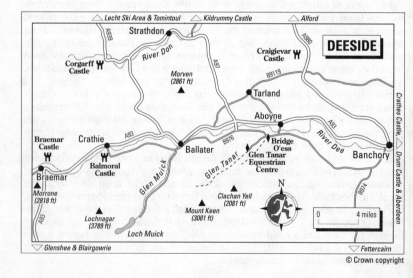

© Crown copyright

Drum Castle, Crathes Castle and Banchory

West of Aberdeen is low-lying land of mixed farming, forestry and suburbs. Easily reached from the main road are the castles of **Drum** and **Crathes**, both interesting fortified houses with pleasant gardens, while the uneventful town of **Banchory** serves as gateway to the heart of Royal Deeside.

Drum and Crathes castles

Ten miles west of Aberdeen on the A93, **Drum Castle** (Easter weekend & May–Sept daily 1.30–4.45pm; Oct Sat & Sun 1.30–4.45pm; £4.40; NTS) stands in a clearing in the ancient **woods of Drum**, made up of the splendid pines and oaks that once covered this whole area before the shipbuilding industry precipitated mass forest clearance (the grounds are open 10am–6pm on the same days as the castle; £2 grounds only). The castle itself combines a 1619 Jacobean mansion with Victorian extensions and the original, huge thirteenth-century keep which has recently been restored and reopened. Given in 1323 by Robert the Bruce to his armour-bearer, William de Irvine, for services rendered at Bannockburn, the castle remained in Irvine hands for 24 generations until the NTS stepped in in 1976. To get a sense of the medieval atmosphere of the place, ascend the Turnpike Stair, above the Laigh Hall, where a 700-year-old window seat gives views of the ancient forest.

Further along the A93, three and a half miles east of Banchory, **Crathes Castle** (April–Oct daily 11am–4.45pm; £2.10 or £5 including grounds and walled garden; NTS) is a splendid sixteenth-century granite tower house adorned with flourishes such as overhanging turrets, gargoyles and conical roofs. Its thick walls, narrow windows and tiny rooms loaded with heavy old furniture make Crathes rather claustrophobic, but it is saved by some wonderfully painted ceilings, either still in their original form or sensitively restored; the earliest dates from 1602. Don't miss the Room of the Nine Nobles, where great heroes of the past, among them Julius Caesar, King David and King Arthur, are skilfully painted on the beams. More intriguing still is the Green Lady's Room, where a mysterious child's skeleton was found beneath the floor and the ghost of a young girl, sometimes carrying a child, is said to have been spotted – most recently in the 1980s. The Muses Room, with portrayals of the nine Muses and seven Virtues, is also impressive. Beware the "trip stair", originally designed to foil seventeenth-century burglars.

By the entrance to Crathes, a cluster of restored stone cottages houses an interesting crafts shop, pottery and the *Milton Restaurant* (☎01330/844566), which serves high-class food, including a well-priced supper menu between 5pm and 7pm.

Banchory

BANCHORY, meaning "fair hollow", is really just a one-street town, and there's not much to see, though it can be a useful place to stay. The small local **museum** on Bridge Street, behind High Street (June–Sept Mon–Sat 10am–1pm & 2–5pm, Sun 2–6pm; April & May Sat only, Oct Sat only 11am–5pm; free), may warrant half an hour or so if you're a fan of local boy James Scott Skinner, renowned fiddler and composer of such tunes as *The Bonnie Lass o' Bon Accord*. Alternatively, you can watch salmon leap at the little footbridge where the Dee joins the Feugh River to the south of town.

The **tourist office**, in the museum (Easter–May & Oct Mon–Sat 10am–1pm & 2–5pm; June & Sept Mon–Sat 10am–1pm & 2–6pm, Sun 1–6pm; July & Aug Mon–Sat 9.30am–7pm, Sun 1–7pm; ☎01330/822000), can provide information on walking and fishing in the area. There are several reasonable places **to stay** here and in the surrounding countryside. In town, the *Burnett Arms Hotel*, 25 High St (☎01330/824944, *burnett@msn.com.uk*; ⑤), a friendly former coaching inn, does Banchory's best pub grub, while *Primrose Hill*, on North Deeside Road on the eastern outskirts of town (☎01330/823007; ②), is a decent B&B. Outside Banchory on the Inchmarlo road, the smart *Tor-Na-Collie Hotel* (☎01330/822242, *tornacoille@btinternet.com*; ⑥) was once a retreat for Charlie Chaplin and his family, and serves splendid Scottish salmon, venison and malt whisky in its upscale restaurant. More affordable escapism is available year-round at the *Wolf's Hearth* bunkhouse, ten miles northwest of Banchory, just outside Tornaveen on the B9119 (☎013398/83460). A converted farm building in a beautiful rural setting, it makes a great base for walking, cycling or skiing, and also offers a variety of creative activities such as painting and pottery. Evening meals are available here if you make arrangements beforehand.

EXPLORING GLEN TANAR

Ordnance Survey Landranger map no. 44

Lying to the south of the Deeside town of Aboyne, the easily navigated forest tracks of **Glen Tanar** offer a taste of the changing landscape of the northeastern Highlands, passing through relatively prosperous farmland along the River Dee, through ancient woodland and then to remote grouse moors and bleak hillsides in the heart of the Grampian mountains. Flatter than, and without the vehicle traffic, of Glen Muick to the west, Glen Tanar is a great place to explore on mountain bikes, although there is plenty of opportunity for walking and there's also an **equestrian centre** (☎013398/86448) in the glen, offering riverside and forest horse trails from around £45 for a half-day.

Leave the south Deeside road (B976) at **Bridge o' Ess**, one and a half miles from Aboyne. Here you can enter the forest on the south side of the Water of Tanar, or carry on along a tarred road on the north side for two miles to a car park. Immediately across the river from this is a **ranger information point**, where you can pick up details on the various routes in the glen, as well as some background on the flora and fauna of the area. If you're on **foot**, the best idea is to strike out from here along the forest tracks that follow both sides of the river, connected at various points by attractive stone bridges, allowing for easy round-trips. Most of the time you are surrounded by superb old pine woodland, some of which is naturally seeded remnants of ancient Caledonian forest, with broadleafs in evidence along the river, and wild flowers and fungi when in season. If you're on a **bike**, stick to the track on the north side of the river: not far past the small wooden shelter known as Half Way Hut, you emerge from the forest, with the glen-sides closing in, and **Mount Keen** (3081ft), the most easterly of Scotland's 3000-foot mountains, looming ahead. The end of the glen, at **Shiel of Glentanar**, is eight miles from the car park, from where you can either retrace your path or take to the hills by following the steep track round the back of Clachan Yell. It should take around six hours return, following the main track, or eight hours going via Clachan Yell. The more ambitious can pick up the Mounth road (see p.156) at Shiel of Glentanar, which heads up and over Mount Keen to Invermark at the head of Glen Esk (see p.156).

Ballater and Balmoral

Heading west from Banchory on the A93, after twelve miles you'll come to the workaday town of **ABOYNE**, notable only for the excellent *Black Faced Sheep* coffee shop just off the main road, and the *White Cottage* restaurant (☎013398/86265), a couple of miles before Aboyne on the Banchory side, which specializes in high-quality Scottish cooking made with fresh local produce. Another ten miles beyond Aboyne is the neat and ordered town of **BALLATER**, attractively hemmed in by the river and fir-covered mountains. The town was dragged from obscurity in the nineteenth century, when it was discovered that the local waters were useful in curing scrofula. Although scrofula is no longer a problem, Ballater spring water is back in fashion and on sale around town.

It was in Ballater that Queen Victoria first arrived in Deeside by train from Aberdeen back in 1848 – she wouldn't allow a station to be built any closer to Balmoral, eight miles further west. Although the line has long been closed, you can still visit the elegant **train station** in the centre of town, which now houses a tearoom. The local shops, having provided the royals with household basics, also flaunt their connections, sporting oversized crests above their doorways.

Ballater is an excellent base for local **walks and outdoor activities**. There are numerous hikes from Loch Muick (pronounced "Mick"), nine miles southwest of town, including the Capel Mounth drovers' route over the mountains to Glen Doll (see p.156), and a well-worn but strenuous all-day trek up and around **Lochnagar** (3789ft), the mountain much painted and written about by the current Prince of Wales. The starting point for all these walks is the Balmoral Rangers' **visitors centre**, on the shores of the loch (☎013397/55059 for opening hours), which also offers a series of free guided nature walks. Good quality **bikes** can be rented from Wheels and Reels (☎013397/55864), at 2 Braemar Rd, just over the railway bridge from Station Square, while, for canoeing and ski equipment and guides for a range of **outdoor activities**, contact Dave Latham (☎013308/50332). Other outdoor equipment, as well as local guidebooks, a full range of OS maps and good advice about heading to the local hills, is available at the friendly Lochnagar Leisure outdoor shop on Station Square (daily 9am–5.30pm).

Ballater practicalities

The **tourist office** is opposite the station in Station Square (Easter–May & Oct Mon–Sat 10am–1pm & 2–5pm, Sun 1–5pm; June & Sept Mon–Sat 10am–1pm & 2–6pm, Sun 1–6pm; July & Aug Mon–Sat 9.30am–7pm, Sun 1–7pm; ☎013397/55306). There are plenty of reasonable **B&Bs** in town, including the excellent no-smoking *Inverdeen House*, on Bridge Square (☎013397/55759; ②), which offers a choice of six breakfasts, many involving piles of Canadian pancakes. Other places to try include two options on Braemar Road – the welcoming *Deeside Hotel* (☎013397/55420; ②), or *The Green Inn Restaurant*, 9 Victoria Rd (☎013397/55701; ⑤ for dinner, bed and breakfast), which has three very comfortable rooms. A few miles out of town on the road to Tomintoul (see p.167) is *Gairnshiel Lodge* (☎013397/55582; ②). In a remote but beautiful setting, it's a great base for walking or cycling. For **camping**, the *Anderson Road Caravan Park* (☎013397/55727; Easter–Oct), down towards the river, has around sixty tent pitches. There are numerous **places to eat**, from smart hotel restaurants to bakers and coffee shops: the award-winning *Green Inn* is pricey but excellent quality, while *Bruno's Restaurant* (☎013397/55346; April–Sept Wed–Sun), 34 Victoria Rd, is an unexpectedly authentic, if over-the-top, Italian in a family house. For **drinking** with locals, try the back bar (entrance down Golf Street) of the *Prince of Wales*, which faces the main square.

Balmoral Estate and Crathie Church

Originally a sixteenth-century tower house built for the powerful Gordon family, **Balmoral Castle** (mid-April to May Mon–Sat 10am–5pm; June & July daily 10am–5pm; £4) has been a royal residence since 1852, when it was converted to the Scottish Baronial mansion that stands today. The royal family traditionally spend their summer holidays here, but despite its fame it can be something of a disappointment even for a dedicated royalist. For the three months when the doors are nudged open, the general riffraff are permitted to view only the ballroom and the grounds; for the rest of the year, it is not even visible to the paparazzi who converge en masse when the royals are in residence here in August. With so little of the castle on view, it's worth making the most of the grounds and larger estate by following some of the country walks or joining a two-hour **pony trek** (daily 10am & 2pm; for details ☎013397/42334; £20).

Opposite the castle's gates on the main road, the otherwise dull granite church of **CRATHIE**, built in 1895 with the proceeds of a bazaar held at Balmoral, is the royals' local church. A small **tourist office** operates in the car park by the church on the main road in Crathie (daily: April 10am–5pm; May–Aug 9.30am–6pm; Sept & Oct 10am–5.30pm; ☎013397/42414).

Braemar

Continuing for another few miles, the road rises to 1100ft above sea level to the upper part of Deeside and the village of **BRAEMAR**, situated where three passes meet and overlooked by an unimposing **castle** (Easter–Oct daily except Fri 10am–6pm; £2.50) of the same name. Signs as you enter Braemar boast that it's an "Award Winning Tourist Village", which just about sums it up, as everything seems to have been prettified to within an inch of its life or have a price tag on it. That said, it's an invigorat-

---

MORRONE-BRAEMAR'S BEACON

Ordnance Survey Landranger map no. 43

Late August and through autumn, when the mountain is plush with extravagant colours, is the best time to ascend **Morrone**. In winter, it can be a spectacular viewpoint but very exposed. Allow four hours for the walk.

Make your way up Chapel Brae at the west end of Braemar, passing a car park and pond, then Mountain Cottage, and swinging left up through fine birch woods (a nature reserve). Keep right of the fences and house. The track bears right (west), and at a fork take the left branch up to the Deeside Field Club view indicator. Skirt the crags above this to the left and the path is obvious thereafter. The summit provides a fantastic sweeping view of the Cairngorms. You can descend by the upward route, but an easy continuation is to head down by the Mountain Rescue post's access path, which twists along and then down into Glen Clunie. Turn left along the minor road back to Braemar; the walk finishes by heading through the local golf course. In summer, you can take a Land-Rover safari up Morrone: contact the tourist office in Braemar for details.

ing, outdoor kind of place, well patronized by committed hikers, although probably best known for its Highland Games, the annual **Braemar Gathering** (first Saturday of September). Games were first held here in the eleventh century, when Malcolm Canmore set contests for the local clans in order to pick the bravest and strongest for his army. Since Queen Victoria's day, successive generations of royals have attended, and the world's most famous Highland Games have become rather an overcrowded, overblown event. You're not guaranteed to get in if you just turn up; tickets can be bought in advance from February 1, from the Bookings Secretary, BRHS, Coilacriech, Ballater AB35 5UH (☎013397/55377).

A pleasant diversion from Braemar is to head six miles west to the end of the road and the **Linn of Dee**, where the river plummets savagely through a narrow rock gorge. From here there are countless **walks** into the surrounding country-side or up into the heart of the Cairngorms (see p.168). There's a very basic **youth hostel** just before the falls at Inverey (mid-May to early Sept; book through the Braemar hostel on ☎013397/41659, or central reservations ☎0541/553255).

Practicalities

Braemar's **tourist office** is in the modern building known as the Mews in the middle of the village on Mar Road (Jan–May & Sept–Dec Mon–Sat 10am–1pm & 2–5pm, Sun noon–5pm; June daily 10am–6pm; July & Aug daily 9am–7pm, Sept daily 10am–1pm & 2–6pm; ☎013397/41600). **Accommodation** is scarce in Braemar in the lead-up to the Games, but at other times there's a wide choice. *Clunie Lodge Guest House*, Clunie Bank Road (☎013397/41330; ②), on the edge of town, is a good **B&B** with lovely views up Clunie Glen, and there's a large **youth hostel** at Corrie Feragie, 21 Glenshee Rd (☎013397/41659 or central reservations ☎0541/553255). Alternatively, the cheery *Rucksacks*, an easy-going bunkhouse well equipped for walkers and backpackers, is just behind the Mews complex (☎013397/41517). The *Invercauld Caravan Club Park* (☎013397/41373), just south of the village off the Glenshee Road, has fifteen **camping** pitches. Standard and fairly pricey hotel **food** is available from the bars of the various large hotels, or for some cheap stodge there's the *Braemar Takeaway* by the river bridge. For **drinking**, the *Invercauld Arms* in the middle of town is a youthful hangout with a pool table. For advice on **outdoor activities**, as well as ski, mountain-bike and

---

DEESIDE HIGHLAND GAMES

Royal Deeside is the home of the modern **Highland Games**, claiming descent from gatherings organized by eleventh-century Scottish king Malcolm Canmore to help him recruit the strongest and fittest clansmen for his army. The most famous of the local games is undoubtedly the **Braemar Gathering**, held on the first Saturday in September, which can see crowds of 15,000 and usually a royal or two as guest of honour. Vying for celebrity status in recent years has been the **Lonach** gathering in Strathdon, held the weekend before Braemar, where local laird Billy Connolly dispenses drams of whisky to marching village men and has been known to invite some Hollywood chums along – Steve Martin arrived dressed in kilt and jacket, while Robin Williams competed in the punishing hill race. For a true flavour of the spirit of Highland gatherings, however, try to get to one of the events that take place in other local towns and villages at weekends throughout July and August, where locals outnumber tourists and the competitions are guaranteed to be hard-fought and entertaining.

climbing equipment rental, head to Braemar Mountain Sports (open daily 8.30am–7pm), opposite the *Takeaway*.

The Don Valley and the Lecht

The quiet countryside around the **Don Valley**, once renowned for its illegal whisky distilleries and smugglers, used also to be a prosperous agricultural area. As the region industrialized, however, the population drifted towards Dundee and Aberdeen, and nowadays little remains of the old farming communities but the odd deserted crofter's cottage. From Aberdeen, the River Don winds northwest through **Inverurie**, where it takes a sharp turn west to **Alford**, then continues past ruined castles through the **Upper Don Valley** and the heather moorlands of the eastern Highlands. This remote and undervisited area is positively littered with ruined castles, Pictish sites, stones and hillforts, all of which it is impossible to cover here. There are some excellent free leaflets in the Grampian Archeology series (available from all tourist offices), which give far more detail, and the well-signposted **Castle Trail** takes in the area's main castles. The Lecht Road, from Corgaff to the hilltop town of **Tomintoul**, rises steeply, making the area around it, simply known as the **Lecht**, an ideal skiing centre.

Inverurie is served by the regular Aberdeen to Inverness **train** and various **bus** services up the A96. Bluebird buses #215 and #220 link Alford with Aberdeen, but getting as far as Strathdon is much harder and public transport links with Tomintoul are all but nonexistent.

Inverurie and around

Some seventeen miles from Aberdeen, the prosperous granite farming town of **INVERURIE** makes a convenient base for visiting the numerous relics and castles in the area. The **tourist office** (July & Aug Mon–Sat 9.30am–6pm, Sun 1–5pm; Sept–June Mon–Sat 9.30am–5pm; ☎01467/625800) shares space with a bookshop at 18 High St, not far from the station, and is a good place to stop in if before setting off to find the local sites, many of which are tucked away and confusingly signposted. While you're in Inverurie, don't miss the **Thainstone Mart**, just off the A96 south of town, one of Europe's largest and most impressive livestock sales (Mon & Wed–Fri around 10am).

Bennachie and Archaeolink

The granite hill **Bennachie**, five miles west of Inverurie, is possibly the site of Mons Graupius, Scotland's first ever recorded battle in 84 AD when the Romans defeated the Picts. At 1733ft, this is one of the most prominent tors in the region, with tremendous views, and makes for a stiff two-hour walk. The best route starts from the Bennachie Centre (April–Oct Tues–Sun 10am–5pm, Nov–March Wed–Sun 10am–5pm), a mile past **Chapel of Garioch** (pronounced "Geery"), itself a couple of miles off the A96. Immediately west of here is one of the most notable Pictish standing stones in the region, the **Maiden Stone**, a ten-foot slab inscribed with marine monsters, an elephant-like beast, and the mirror and comb for which the stone is named.

A further four miles from Chapel of Garioch, the **Archaeolink Prehistory Park**, on the B9002 at Oyne (April–Oct daily 10am–5pm; £3.90), gives an insight into the area's Pictish heritage. The brand-new park includes a reconstructed Iron Age farm, a hillside archeological site, and an innovative building containing lively audiovisual displays designed to bring prehistory (anything from six thousand years ago to the Battle of Mons Graupius) to life. Although it's a clear attempt to capture the imagination of young people, adults will be just as enthralled, partly because the experience is spread across a hillside with short walks, impressive views and interesting archeological projects.

Fyvie Castle

Some thirteen miles north of Inverurie stands the huge, ochre mansion of **Fyvie Castle** (May, June & Sept daily 1.30–4.45pm; July & Aug daily 11am–4.45pm; Oct Sat & Sun 1.30–4.45pm; £4.40; NTS). Scottish Baronial to the hilt, Fyvie's fascinating roofscape sprouts five curious steeples, one for each of the families who lived here from the thirteenth to the twentieth century. Beginning life as a typical courtyard castle, with a protective wall more than 6ft thick, over the ensuing centuries the place met with considerable architectural expansion. The Chancellor of Scotland bought Fyvie in 1596 and was probably responsible for the elaborate south front with its gables and turrets; his grandson sympathized with the Jacobites and, following his exile, the estate was confiscated and handed over to the Gordons. In 1889 the castle was sold to the Forbes-Leith, a local family who had made a fortune in America and were responsible for the grand Edwardian interior. The exquisite dining room is nowadays rented out for corporate entertaining by oil companies who hobnob among the Flemish tapestries, Delft tiles and the fine collection of paintings that includes feathery Gainsborough portraits and twelve works by Sir Henry Raeburn.

Alford and around

ALFORD, 25 miles west of Aberdeen, only exists at all because it was chosen, in 1859, as the terminus for the Great North Scotland Railway. The best of the sights is the **Grampian Transport Museum** on Main Street (April–Oct daily 10am–5pm; £3.50), a large display of transport through the ages. Unusual exhibits include the *Craigevar Express*, a strange, three-wheeled steam-driven vehicle developed by the local postman for his rounds before the invention of the engine, and, incongruously, a beautiful Art Deco Belgian dance organ with over four hundred pipes and a full set of drums.

Practically next door is the terminus for the **Alford Valley Railway** (April, May & Sept Sat & Sun 1–4.30pm; June–Aug daily 1–4.30pm; ☎019755/62326), a two-foot narrow-gauge train that runs for about a mile from Alford Station through wooded vales to the wide open space of **Murray Park**; the return journey takes an hour. The station is also home to the neat **tourist office** (April–June, Sept & Oct Mon–Sat 10am–5pm, Sun 1–5pm; July & Aug Mon–Sat 10am–6pm, Sun 1–6pm; ☎019755/62052).

Craigievar Castle

Six miles south of Alford on the A980, **Craigievar Castle** (guided tours only: May–Sept daily 1.30–4.45pm; ☎013398/83635; £6; NTS) is a fantastic pink confection of turrets, gables, balustrades and cupolas bubbling over from the top three storeys. It was built by a Baltic trader known as Willy the Merchant in 1626, who evidently allowed his whimsy to run riot. The castle's massive popularity, however – it features on everything from shortbread tins to tea towels all over Scotland – has been its undoing, and the sheer number of visitors has caused interior damage. The NTS is currently limiting the number of people entering the house by keeping the guided tours small, but in any case the best part of the castle is its external appearance, which you can see free from the well-kept **grounds** (all year 9.30am–sunset; free).

Lumsden and Rhynie

The A944 heads west from Alford, meeting the A97 just south of the tiny village of **LUMSDEN**, a surprising centre for Scottish sculpture. A contemporary **Sculpture Walk** – heralded by a fabulous skeletal black horse at its southern end – runs parallel to the main road, coming out near the premises of the **Scottish Sculpture Workshop** (Mon–Fri 9am–5pm or by arrangement; ☎01464/861372), very much an active workshop, rather than a gallery, at the northern end of village.

The village of **RHYNIE**, folded beautifully into the hills three miles further north up the A97, is for ever associated with one of the greatest Pictish memorials, the **Rhynie Man**, a remarkable six-foot boulder discovered in 1978, depicting a rare whole figure, clad in a tunic and holding what is thought to be a ceremonial axe. The original can be seen in the foyer of the regional council's headquarters at Woodhill House in Aberdeen, but there's a cast on display at the school in Rhynie, across the road from the church; if you want to see it, contact Bill Inglis on ☎01464/861398. A further claim to fame for the village is that the bedrock lying deep beneath it, known as **Rhynie Chert**, contains plant and insect fossils up to 400 million years old, making them some of the earth's oldest fossils. A mile or so from the village, along the A941 to Dufftown, a car park gives access to the **Tap O'Noth**, Scotland's second-highest Pictish hillfort (1847ft), where substantial remnants of the wall around the lip of the summit show evidence of vitrification (fierce burning), probably to fuse the rocks together.

Rhynie is a reasonable – if very quiet – place **to stay**. The cheapest and the best choice is the *Gordon Arms Hotel*, on Main Street (☎01464/861615; ①).

The Upper Don Valley

Ten miles west of Alford stand the impressive thirteenth-century stone ruins of **Kildrummy Castle** (April–Sept Mon–Sun 9.30am–6pm; £1.80; HS), site of some particularly hideous moments of conflict. During the Wars of Independence, Robert the Bruce sent his wife and children here for their own protection, but the castle blacksmith, bribed with as much gold as he could carry, set fire to the place and it fell into English hands. Bruce's immediate family survived, but his brother was executed and the entire garrison hung, drawn and quartered. Meanwhile, the duplicitous blacksmith was rewarded for his help by having molten gold poured down his throat. Other sieges took place during the subsequent centuries: Balliol's forces attacked in 1335, Cromwell took over in 1654 and the sixth Earl of Mar used the castle as the headquarters of the ill-fated Jacobite risings in 1715. Following John Erskine's withdrawal, Kildrummy became redundant and it was abandoned as a fortress and residence and fell into ruin. Beside the ruins is a Scottish Baronial-style castle built in 1901, now the grand *Kildrummy Castle Hotel* (☎019755/71288; ⑦), superbly endowed with wood-panelled rooms, Victorian furniture and a raised terrace on which you can enjoy afternoon tea overlooking the castle.

Ten miles further west, the A944 sweeps round into the parish of **STRATH-DON**, little more than a succession of occasional buildings by the roadside. However, four miles from here, up a rough track leading into Glen Nochty, lies the unexpected **Lost Gallery** (Mon & Wed–Sun 11am–5pm; ☎019756/51287), which shows work by some of Scotland's leading modern artists in a wonderfully remote and tranquil setting. Heading west again on the A944, past the much-photographed signs to the village of Lost, you'll come to **Candacraig Gardens** (May–Sept Mon–Fri 10am–5pm; Sat & Sun 10–6pm; free), the walled grounds of Candacraig House, Highland retreat of comedian Billy Connolly, who recently starred as John Brown in the award-winning film *Mrs Brown*, set at nearby Balmoral Castle (see p.162). The house is private, but the gardens, an exuberant display of colour and energy, are open to the public. In the old laundry on the other side of the main house, *No. 3 Candacraig Square* (☎019756/51472, *no3@buchanan.co.uk*; ②) is a stylish B&B with wooden floors, piles of books and a promise of fresh fish for breakfast.

A further eight miles on, just beyond the junction of the Ballater road, lies **Corgarff Castle** (Jan–March & Dec Sat 9.30am–4pm, Sun 2–4pm; April–Sept daily 9.30am–6pm; Oct & Nov Mon–Wed & Sat 9.30am–4pm, Thurs 9.30am–2pm, Sun 2–4pm; £2.50; HS), an austere tower house with an unusual star-shaped curtain wall and an eventful history. Built in 1537 – the wall was added in 1748 – it was first attacked in 1571, during a religious feud between the Forbes, family of the laird of the castle, and the Gordons, who torched the place, killing the laird's wife, family and servants. In 1748, in the aftermath of Culloden, the Hanoverian government turned Corgarff into a barracks in order to track down local Jacobite rebels and, finally, in the mid-nineteenth century, the English Redcoats were stationed here with the unpopular task of trying to control whisky smuggling. Today there's little to see inside, but the place has been restored to resemble its days as a barracks, with stark rooms and rows of hard, uncomfortable beds – authentic touches which extend to graffiti on the walls and peat smoke permeating the building from a fire in the first floor. One unexpected bonus here, if you're from far-flung parts, is the chance to hear the history of the castle in one of the nineteen languages the keeper has recorded it in over the years, ranging from Thai to Icelandic.

Leading to the castle from the south is the old military road, which, unusually, hasn't been covered over by the present road and is fairly clear for about three miles. A mile or so along this from the castle, approached from the main road by the track beside Rowan Tree Cottage, is *Jenny's Bothy* at Dellachuper (☎019756/51449), a beautifully remote and simple **bunkhouse**, surrounded by empty scenery and wild animals. You'll have to bring your own supplies if you're coming here, but it's a great base for hiking, biking or skiing, or just detaching yourself from the madding crowd for a day or two.

Tomintoul

Just past Corgarff, at Cock Bridge, the road leaps up towards the ski slopes of the Lecht and, four miles further on, **TOMINTOUL** (pronounced "*Tom*-in-towel"); at 1150ft, the highest village in the Scottish Highlands. Tomintoul owes its existence to the post-1745 landowners' panic when, as in other parts of the north, isolated inhabitants were forcibly moved to new, planted villages, where a firm eye could be kept on everybody. Its long, thin layout is reminiscent of a Wild West frontier

---

SKIING THE LECHT

The Lecht offers dry ski-slope-skiing all year, and the recent introduction of snow-making equipment should help extend the snow season beyond January and February. While the gentle slopes are good for beginners, experienced skiers won't find much to tax them, though there is a Snowboard Fun Park, with specially built jumps and ramps. Lift passes cost £12 a day for adults; ski and boot rental costs £12 a day from the ski school at the base station (☎019756/51440), which also provides tuition for £6 an hour. For **information** on skiing and road conditions here, call the base station or the Ski Hotline (☎0891/654654).

---

town; Queen Victoria, passing through, wrote that it was "the most tumble-down poor looking place I ever saw". That said, it makes a good base for **skiing** the Lecht area in winter, and there's some terrific **walking** hereabouts, with Tomintoul marking the end of the long-distance Speyside Way (see p.177).

Practicalities

In the central square, the **tourist office** (April, May & Oct Mon–Sat 10am–1pm & 2–5.30pm, Sun 2–5pm; June & Sept Mon–Sat 10am–1pm & 2–5.30pm, Sun 2–5.30pm; July & Aug Mon–Sat 10am–7pm, Sun 1–7pm; ☎01807/580285) also acts as the local **museum**, with mock-ups of an old farm kitchen and a smithy (same hours as tourist office; free). Information about the extensive Glenlivet Crown Estate, its wildlife (including reindeer), and numerous paths and bike trails, is available from the **ranger's office** (☎01807/580283 for opening hours) at the far end of the long main street.

If you need a place **to stay**, the *Tomintoul Bunkhouse*, immediately beside the tourist office, is plain, but friendly and useful; contact the neighbouring *Gordon Hotel* (☎01807/580206) to make bookings or call in at the hotel reception. There's also a basic SYHA hostel on Main Street (☎01807/580282 or central reservations ☎0541/553255). Of the B&Bs, try *Conglass Hall*, on Main Street (☎01807/580291 ①), or *Milton Farm*, half a mile out of town on the B9008 to Dufftown (☎01807/580288; ①). Of the hotels gathered around the main square, the *Glenavon* (☎01807/580218; ①) is the most convivial for a drink, and serves ale made in the local Tomintoul Brewery, while the best bet for something to **eat** is a pub meal here or at the *Gordon Hotel*.

Strathspey and the Cairngorms

Rising high in the heather-clad hills above Loch Laggan, forty miles due south of Inverness, the **River Spey**, Scotland's second longest river, drains northeast towards the Moray Firth through one of the Highlands' most spellbinding valleys. Famous for its **ski slopes**, **salmon fishing** and **ospreys**, Strathspey forms a broad cleft between the mighty Monadhliath mountains in the north and the ice-sculpted Cairngorm range to the south. Outdoor enthusiasts flock here year round to take advantage of the superb hiking, watersports and winter snows, but the valley is also a major transport artery connecting Inverness and the northern highlands with the south.

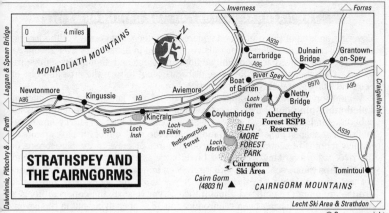

© Crown copyright

Of Strathspey's scattered settlements, **Aviemore** absorbs the largest number of visitors, particularly in midwinter, when it metamorphoses into the UK's busiest ski resort. The village itself isn't up to much, but the 4000-foot-summit plateau of the Cairngorm is often snowcapped, providing stunning mountain scenery on a grand scale. Sedate **Kingussie**, further up the valley, is an older-established holiday centre, popular more with anglers and grouse hunters than canoeists and climbers, while the Georgian town of **Grantown-on-Spey**, jumping-off point for **Loch Garten**, makes another good base for exploring the area. Most of upper Strathspey is privately owned by the Glen More Forest Park and Rothiemurchus Estate, who provide between them a plethora of year-round outdoor facilities, with masses of accommodation of all types. Both bodies actively encourage the recreational use of their land, which gives you the freedom to go virtually anywhere you want.

Aviemore

AVIEMORE was first developed as a resort in the mid-1960s, as the towering concrete **Aviemore Centre** bears witness: a shabby assortment of cavernous concrete buildings and incongruous high-rise hotels presently undergoing a much-needed redevelopment. The village proper, a sprawling jumble of traditional stone houses and tacky tourist shops set in a sea of car and coach parks, isn't much better. That said, Aviemore is by far the most important service centre in the area, with a wide range of facilities, an advantage which outweighs its lack of aesthetic appeal.

Winter sports

Scottish **skiing** on a commercial scale first really took off in Aviemore. By continental European and North American standards it's all on a tiny scale, but occasionally snow, sun and lack of crowds coincide and you can have a great day. February and March are usually the best times, but in some years the snow may still be good until April. Lots of places – not just in Aviemore itself – sell or rent equipment; for a rundown of ski schools and rental facilities in the area, check out the tourist office's *Ski Scotland* brochure.

THE NATURAL HISTORY OF THE CAIRNGORMS

Covering an area of three hundred square miles, the Cairngorms are the largest mountainscape in the UK and the only large plateau in the country over 2500ft. As such, they harbour an array of unique flora and fauna and, though presently protected as a National Nature Reserve, plans are afoot to turn the area into one of Scotland's first gazetted National Parks.

Vegetation in the area ranges from one of the largest tracts of ancient **Caledonian pine and birch forest** remaining in Scotland, at Rothiemurchus, to subarctic tundra on the high plateau, where alpine flora such as **starry saxifrage** and the star-shaped pink flowers of **moss campion** peek out of the pink granite in the few months of summer that the ground is free of snow. In the pine forests of the river valleys strikingly coloured **birds** such as **crested tits**, **redwings** and **goldfinches** can be seen, along with rarely seen **mammals** such as the **red squirrel** and **pine marten**. On the heather slopes above the forest, **red** and **black grouse** are often encountered, though their larger relative, the **capercaillie**, is a much rarer sight, having been reintroduced in 1837 after dying out in the seventeenth century. Of birds of prey, the area is well-known now for its **osprey**, best seen at the osprey observation centre (see p.174) at Loch Garten or fishing on the lochs around Aviemore, though **golden eagles** and **peregrine falcons** can very occasionally be seen higher up. Those venturing up to the plateau have the chance of seeing the shy **ptarmigan**, another member of the grouse family, which nests on bare rock and has a white plumage during winter, or even the **dotterel** and **snow bunting**, rare visitors from the Arctic, along with **mountain (blue) hares**, which also turn white in winter and are best seen in spring as they scurry across patches of brown hillside where the snow has melted.

The **Cairngorm Ski Area**, about eight miles southeast of Aviemore, above Loch Morlich in Glen More Forest Park, is well served by buses from Aviemore. You can rent skis and other equipment from the Day Lodge at the foot of the ski area (☎01479/861261), which also has a shop, a bar and restaurant, and sells tickets for the year-round chairlift. A highly controversial plan to replace the chair lift with a **funicular railway** has recently been passed – while debates rage between environmentalists, developers and tourism bodies, don't expect too much to change, for even once construction begins it's likely to be a few years before the project is completed.

If there's lots of snow, the area around **Loch Morlich** and into the **Rothiemurchus Estate** provides enjoyable cross-country skiing through lovely woods, beside rushing burns and even over frozen lochs. If you really want to know about survival in a Scottish winter, you could try a week at *Glenmore Lodge* (☎01479/861276) in the heart of the Glenmore Forest Park at the east end of Loch Morlich. This superbly equipped and organized centre, run by Sports Scotland, offers winter courses in hillwalking, mountaineering, alpine ski-mountaineering, avalanche awareness and much besides, including an array of less serious recreational courses in kayaking, abseiling and the like. To add to the winter scene, there's a herd of **reindeer** at Loch Morlich, and the Siberian Husky Club holds its races in the area.

Summer sports

In summer, the main activities around Aviemore are **watersports**, and there are two centres that offer sailing, windsurfing and canoeing. The Loch Morlich

Watersports Centre (☎01479/861221), five miles or so east of Aviemore at the east end of the loch, rents equipment and offers tuition in a lovely setting with a sandy beach, while, upvalley, the Loch Insh Watersports Centre (☎01540/651272) offers the same facilities in more open and less crowded surroundings. It also rents mountain bikes, boats for loch fishing, and gives ski instruction on a 164-foot dry slope.

Riding and **pony trekking** are on offer up and down the valley: try Alvie Stables at Alvie near Kincraig (☎01540/651409, mobile ☎0831/495397), or the Carrbridge Trekking Centre, Station Road, Carrbridge, a few miles north of Aviemore (☎01479/841602).

Fishing is very much part of the local scene: you can fish for trout and salmon on the River Spey, and the Rothiemurchus Estate has a stocked trout-fishing loch at **Inverdruie**, where success is virtually guaranteed. Instruction and rod rental is available from the centre beside the loch. Fishing permits cost around £5–15 per day to fish a stocked loch and £25 on the Spey itself, and are sold at Speyside Sports in Aviemore a mile down the road toward the ski grounds from the tourist office, and at Loch Morlich Watersports Centre (see above), which also rents rods and tackle.

The area is also a great one for **mountain-biking**, with both Rothiemurchus and Glenmore estates more progressive in their attitude to the sport than many. The Rothiemurchus visitor centre at Inverdruie has route maps, and you can also rent bikes here, while Bothy Bikes (☎01479/810787), in the Aviemore Shopping Centre beside the train station on Grampian Road, rents out good-quality mountain bikes with front suspension, as well as offering friendly advice on different grades of local routes.

Information, accommodation and eating

Aviemore's **tourist office** is just south of the train station on the main drag, Grampian Road (April–October Mon–Fri 9am–6pm, Sat 10am–5pm, Sun 10am–4pm; Nov–March Mon–Fri 9am–5pm, Sat 10am–5pm; ☎01479/810363). It offers an accommodation booking service, free maps and endless leaflets on local attractions. There's no shortage of **accommodation** in the area. On Grampian Road, *MacKenzies Hotel* (☎01479/810672; ②) and *Ver Mont Guest House* (☎01479/810470; ③) are both good value, and there are also plenty of **B&Bs**; try Mrs Clark at *Sonas* (☎01479/810409; ①). However, the nicest place in the area is *Corrour House Hotel* at Inverdruie, two miles southeast of Aviemore (☎01479/810220; ⑤). As for **hostel** accommodation, Aviemore's large SYHA hostel (☎01479/810345 or central reservations ☎0541/553255), is close to the tourist office, while the brand-new *Aviemore Independent Bunkhouse* (☎01479/811137) on Dalfaber Road is also very central and has good facilities, including four-bed bunk rooms and a decent drying room. There are also two more low-price options near the village of Kincraig, six miles south of Aviemore: the *Loch Insh Watersports Centre* (☎01540/651272; ①), beautifully sited beside the loch, has en-suite B&B and self-catering chalets, and the *Glen Feshie Hostel* at Balachroick (☎01540/651323), where the all-in price includes bed linen and as much porridge as you like for breakfast. There's no shortage of **campsites** either: two of the best are the *Campgrounds of Scotland* site at Coylumbridge (☎01479/812800) and the *Forestry Enterprise* one at Glenmore (☎01479/861271).

All the hotels serve run-of-the-mill bar **food**, but for a more interesting option head to *The Old Bridge Inn* on the east side of the railway, below the bridge, which

---

WALKS AROUND AVIEMORE

Ordnance Survey Landranger map no. 36

Walking is an obvious attraction in the Aviemore area, but always follow the usual safety rules (see p.46). If you want to walk the high tops, take either the service road and summit path or the chairlift up from the Day Lodge (see p.170). However, as well as the high mountain trails, there are some lovely **low-level walks** around Aviemore. It takes an hour or so to complete the gentle circular walk around pretty **Loch an Eilean** in the Rothiemurchus Estate, beginning at the end of the signposted back road that turns east off the B970 two miles south of Aviemore. The estate visitor centres at the lochside and by the roadside at Inverdruie provide more information on the many woodland trails that crisscross this area. A longer walk starts at the near end of **Loch Morlich**. Cross the river by the bridge and follow the dirt road, turning off after about a mile to follow the signs to Aviemore. The path goes through beautiful pine woods and past tumbling burns, and you can branch off to Coylumbridge and Loch an Eilean. Unless you're properly prepared for a 25-mile hike, don't take the track to the **Lairig Ghru**, which eventually brings you out near Braemar. The routes are all well marked and easy to follow and, depending on what combination you put together, can take anything from two to five hours.

Another good shortish (half-day) walk leads along well-surfaced forestry track from Glenmore Lodge up towards the **Ryvoan Pass**, taking in An Lochan Uaine, known as the "Green Loch" and living up to its name, with amazing colours that range from turquoise to slate grey depending on the weather. The track narrows once past the loch and leads east towards Deeside, so retrace your steps if you don't want a major trek. The Glenmore Forest Park Visitor Centre by the roadside at the turnoff to *Glenmore Lodge* has information on other trails in this section of the forest.

serves delicious meals and real ales in a mellow, cosy setting, or *Café Mambo*, in Aviemore Shopping Centre on Grampian Road, which attracts a younger crowd with its bright, funky decor and extensive, contemporary menu. Further afield, the Loch Insh Watersports Centre (see p.170) has a particularly pleasant restaurant overlooking the loch, with snacks available during the day and filling meals in the evening.

Kingussie

KINGUSSIE (pronounced "King*yoos*ee") lies twelve miles south of Aviemore and is far cosier, stacked around a single main street. Beyond its usefulness as a place to stay, the chief attraction here is the excellent **Highland Folk Museum** (May–Aug Mon–Fri 9.30am–5.30pm, Sat & Sun 1–5pm; April, Sept & Oct guided tours only Mon–Fri 10.30am–4.30pm; £3, combined entry with Newtonmore £4). The museum is split into two complementary parts: the Kingussie section contains an absorbing collection of artefacts typical to traditional Highland ways of life, as well as a farming museum, an old smokehouse, a mill, a Hebridean "blackhouse", and a traditional herb and flower garden; most days in summer there's a demonstration of various traditional crafts. The larger site at **Newtonmore** (same hours; £3, combined entry with Folk Museum £4), three miles south of Kingussie on the A86, tries to create more of a living history museum, with reconstructions of a working croft, a church where recitals on traditional Highland instruments are given through the summer months, and a small village of blackhouses being constructed using only authentic tools and materials.

Kingussie is also notable for the ruins of **Ruthven Barracks** (free access), standing east across the river on a hillock. The best-preserved garrison built to pacify the Highlands after the 1715 rebellion, it makes for great exploring by day and is stunningly floodlit at night. Taken by the Jacobites in 1744, Ruthven was blown up in the wake of Culloden to prevent it from falling into enemy hands. It was also the place from where clan leader Lord George Murray dispatched his acrimonious letter to Bonnie Prince Charlie, holding him personally responsible for the string of blunders that had precipitated their defeat.

At nearby **Kincraig**, between Kingussie and Aviemore on the B9152, there are a couple of unusual encounters with animals which offer a memorable diversion if you're not setting off on various strenuous outdoor pursuits. While the style of the **Highland Wildlife Park** (daily: April, May, Sept & Oct 10am–6pm; June–Aug 10am–7pm, Nov–March 10am–4pm; last entry two hours before closing; entry may be restricted in snowy conditions: phone ☎01540/651270; £6.30), with its various captive animals, may not appeal to everyone, it is accredited to the Royal Zoological Society of Scotland and offers a chance to see exotic foreigners such as wolves and bison, as well as many rarely seen natives, including pine martens, capercaillie, wildcat and eagles. Nearby, the excellent **Working Sheepdogs** show at Leault Farm (open daily; phone ☎01540/651310 to find out when demonstrations are being held; £3.50) offers the opportunity to see a champion shepherd demonstrate how to herd a flock of sheep with up to eight dogs, using whistles and other commands. The hour-long display also includes geese-herding, a chance to see traditional hand-shearing, and displays on how collie pups are trained.

Practicalities

Kingussie's **tourist office** is in the same building as the entrance to the Highland Folk Museum, on Duke Street (same hours as museum; ☎01540/661297). If you want to base yourself here, try *Greystones* (☎01540/661052, *greystones@lineone.net*; ①) on Acres Road, off Ardbroilach Road, which has good facilities for walkers and cyclists and serves meals. Other good options are *Ruthven Farm House* (☎01540/661226; ①), a pleasant **B&B** overlooking the barracks; *St Helens* (☎01540/661430; ②), on Ardbroilach Road, noted for its great breakfasts; and the very central *Bhuna Monadh* (☎01540/661186; ②), 85 High St. Of the **hotels**, *Scot House* on Newtonmore Road (☎01540/661351; ④) is a comfortable place, where you can get imaginative meals at reasonable prices. There are also a couple of decent **hostels** in the area: *The Laird's Bothy* (☎01540/661334) is right on the High Street beside the *Tipsy Laird* pub, while the *Pottery Bunkhouse* (☎01528/544231) is attached to Caoldair Pottery at Laggan Bridge, eleven miles west of Kingussie on the A86.

The most ambitious **food** in the area is served at *The Cross* restaurant, in a converted tweed mill on Tweed Mill Brae (☎01540/661166; March–Nov & Christmas; daily except Tues). Its pricey meals make interesting use of local ingredients and there's a vast wine list; they also have several rooms (⑧ including dinner). Cheaper food is available at several cafés and pubs on the High Street. The *Royal Hotel* serves standard bar meals, with some vegetarian options, a good choice of cask ales and some 250 malts, while *The Tipsy Laird* also does real ales as well as bistro-style meals. *Café Volante* does great cheap-and-cheerful fish and chips and, during the day, *La Cafetière* has excellent coffee, with good home-baking, soup, toasties and baked potatoes; it closes at 5pm.

Carrbridge

Worth considering as an alternative to Aviemore – particularly as a skiing base – **CARRBRIDGE** is a pleasant, quiet village about seven miles northeast. Its **Landmark Heritage Park** (daily: April to mid-July 9.30am–6pm; mid-July to Aug 9.30am–8pm; Sept–Oct 9.30am–5.30pm; Nov–March 10am–5pm; £6.40, families from £20.10) combines multimedia presentations on history and natural history with forest walks, nature trails, a maze and fun rides; it's more tastefully done than some places of this kind and an excellent place for children to let off steam. There are some decent accommodation options, including the friendly *Cairn Hotel* (☎01479/841212; ②), the immaculate *Fairwinds Hotel* (☎01479/841240; ③) and, more basic, the tiny but cosy *Carrbridge Bunkhouse* (☎01479/841250, *christian.j@virgin.net*), half a mile or so north of the village on the Inverness road.

Grantown-on-Spey

Buses run from Aviemore and Inverness to the tiny Georgian town of **GRANTOWN-ON-SPEY**, about fifteen miles northeast of Aviemore, which, if you've got your own transport, makes another good base for exploring Strathspey and the Cairngorm area. Activity is concentrated around the attractive central square, including a small **museum** (Tues–Sat 10am–4pm; £3) on Burnfield Avenue which tells the story of the people and the building of the town. The **tourist office** is on High Street (April–Oct daily 9am–6pm; ☎01479/872773), and there's a wide choice of **accommodation**: *Speyside Backpackers* (☎01479/873514) at 16 The Square has dorms and basic double rooms (①), while, if you're after something more upmarket, head for the large seventeenth-century *Garth Hotel*, at the north end of the square (☎01479/872836; ③), or the slightly less pricey *Tyree House Hotel* (☎01479/872615; ③) on its west side. Both are open all year round and have good **restaurants** that serve Scottish specialities.

Loch Garten

The **Abernethy Forest RSPB Reserve** on the shore of **LOCH GARTEN**, eight miles south of Grantown-on-Spey (or seven miles north of Aviemore), is famous as the nesting site of one of Britain's rarest birds. A little over fifty years ago, the **osprey**, known in North America as the "fish hawk", had completely disappeared from the British Isles. Then, in 1954, a single pair of these exquisite white-and-grey eagles mysteriously reappeared and built a nest in a tree half a mile or so from the loch. Although efforts were made to keep the exact location secret, one year's eggs fell victim to a gang of thieves, and thereafter the area became the centre of an effective high-security operation. Now the birds are well established not only here but elsewhere, and there are believed to be up to 130 pairs nesting across the Highlands. The best time to visit is during the nesting season, between late April and August, when the RSPB opens an **observation centre** (daily 10am–6pm; £2.50) complete with powerful telescopes and television monitoring of the nest. This is the place to come to get a glimpse of osprey chicks in their nest; you'll be luckier to see the birds perform their trademark swoop over water to pluck a fish out with their talons, though nearby Loch Garten itself, as well as Loch Morlich and Loch Insh, are good places to stake out in the hope of a sighting, while one of the best spots is the Rothiemurchus trout loch at Inverdruie. The reserve is also home to several other species of rare birds and animals, including the Scottish crossbill, capercaillie, whooper swan and red squirrel – **guided walks** leave from the observation centre at 9.30am on Wednesdays.

Loch Garten can be difficult to reach without your own transport; check with one of the tourist offices in the area about inclusive tours combining a trip on the popular **Strathspey Steam Railway** from Aviemore to Boat of Garten, with a bus journey to the reserve. If you want to **stay** in Boat of Garten, there are a couple of good options: *Fraoch Lodge* (☎01479/831331, *info@scotmountain.co.uk*; ③), at 15 Deshar Rd, is run by mountaineers and has a bunkhouse as well as comfortable B&B, along with good facilities and local advice for outdoor enthusiasts; alternatively, *Glenavon House* (☎01479/831213; ④) is a smarter but still charming guest house, with five rooms.

Speyside

Strictly speaking, **Speyside** is the region surrounding the Spey River, but to most people the name is synonymous with the **whisky triangle**, stretching from just north of **Craigellachie** down towards Tomintoul in the south, and west to Huntly. Indeed, there are more whisky distilleries and famous brands (including Glenfiddich and Glenlivet) concentrated in this small area than in any other part of the country. Running through the heart of the region is the River Spey, whose clean clear waters play such a vital part in the whisky industry and are home to thousands of salmon. At the centre of Speyside, the quiet market town of **Dufftown** makes a good base for a tour of the distilleries, while the only other settlement of any interest is **Huntly**, being well served by road (A96) and rail links with Aberdeen and Elgin.

Dufftown and Craigellachie

The cheery community of **DUFFTOWN**, founded in 1817 by James Duff, the fourth Earl of Fife, proudly proclaims itself "Malt Whisky Capital of the World", and indeed it exports more of the stuff than anywhere else in Britain. Approaching the town from the south along the A941, you'll see the gaunt hilltop ruins of **Auchindoun Castle**. Although you can't go inside, it's enjoyable to wander along the track from the main road to this three-storey keep encircled by Pictish earthworks.

Following the A941 through the town brings you to the **Glenfiddich Distillery** (see p.178), past the old Dufftown train station, currently being restored for a steam line through to Keith. Behind the distillery, the ruin of the thirteenth-century **Balvenie Castle** (April–Sept daily 9.30am–6pm; £1.20; HS) sits on a mound overlooking vast piles of whisky barrels. The castle was a Stewart stronghold,

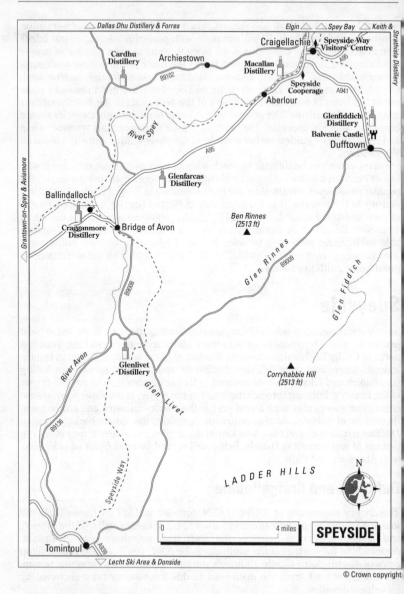

which was abandoned after the 1745 uprising, when it was last used as a government garrison.

Four miles north of Dufftown, the small settlement of **CRAIGELLACHIE** sits above the confluence of the sparkling waters of the Fiddich and the Spey. From the village, you can look down on a beautiful iron bridge over the Spey built by

THE SPEYSIDE WAY

The core of the seventy-mile-long **Speyside Way** follows the River Spey from its mouth at Spey Bay on the Moray Firth south to Aviemore (see p.169), with branches linking it to Buckie on the Moray Firth coast, Dufftown and Tomintoul, on the edge of the Cairngorm Mountains. The whole thing is a five- to seven-day walk, or a long day's cycle ride, but its proximity to main roads and small villages means that it is excellent for shorter walks, especially in the heart of distillery country between Craigellachie and Glenlivet. The path uses disused railway lines for much of its length, and there are simple campsites and good B&Bs at strategic points along the route.

Thomas Telford in 1815. By the River Fiddich on the A95 Huntly road, there's a **visitor centre** for the Speyside Way (generally open Easter–Oct daily 9am–5pm; ☎01340/881266), which sells maps of the route and gives advice on what to look for along the way.

Practicalities

Dufftown's four main streets converge on Main Square. For maps and informa-tion on the **whisky trail**, head straight to the **tourist office** inside the hand-some clock tower at the centre of the square (April, May & Oct Mon–Sat 10am–1pm & 2–5pm; June & Sept Mon–Sat 10am–1pm & 2–6pm, Sun 1–6pm; July & Aug Mon–Sat 10am–7pm, Sun 1–7pm; ☎01340/820501). There's a good range of places **to stay** in Dufftown itself, as well as in the surrounding coun-tryside. In town, *Morven*, on Main Square (☎01340/820507; ①), offers good, cheap B&B, while there's a tiny hostel, *Whisky Capital Backpackers* (☎01340/821069 or 821066), a mile out of town on the Huntly road. In Craigellachie, the most comfortable option is the extremely welcoming and homely B&B attached to the *Green Hall Gallery* on Victoria Street (☎01340/871010, *stewart.johnston@dial.pipex.com*; ①). For unquestionable style and luxury, head to *Mimore House* (☎01807/590378; April–Oct; ⑥), the former home of Glenlivet owner George Smith, which sits right beside the distillery on a quiet hillside above the Livet Water, while in Archiestown, a few miles west of Craigellachie, the *Archiestown Hotel* (☎01340/810218; ⑤) is filled with an eclec-tic collection of odd artefacts but is a good base for walking or cycling and serves great seafood.

The *Glenfiddich Café* just beyond the tourist office on Church Street does simple **meals** and takeaways, while the popular *Taste of Speyside* on Balverie Street, just off the square, serves classier (and pricier) Scottish food. Nine miles out of town along the B9009 towards Glenlivet, the *Croft Inn* is a cosy roadside **pub** with well-priced local dishes and beautiful views over Ben Rinnes, while the best selection of malts is at the *Grouse Inn* at Cabrach, ten miles out along the A941 to Rhynie. In Craigellachie, the tiny *Fiddichside Inn*, on the A95 Huntly road, is a wonderfully original and convivial pub with a gar-den by the river, while the busy *Highlander Inn* (☎01340/881446; ②) on Victoria Street serves good pub grub and also has rooms. The best place for takeaways of the liquid kind is The Whisky Shop, on Dufftown's main square, which stocks a superb range of whiskies and hosts occasional tastings. **Bikes** can be rented from Clarke's Cycle Hire (☎01340/881525), beside the *Fiddichside Inn* at Craigellachie.

THE MALT WHISKY TRAIL

Speyside's **Malt Whisky Trail** is a clearly signposted seventy-mile meander around the region via eight distilleries, although there are others not on the official trail that you can visit by prior arrangement: The Macallan at Craigellachie (☎01340/871471), and Cragganmore at Ballindalloch (☎01807/500202) are both worth trying. Unless you're seriously interested in whisky, it's best to just pick out a couple that appeal, perhaps choosing one for the whisky and another for its setting. All the distilleries offer a guided **tour** (some are free, and some charge an entry fee, then give you a voucher which is redeemable against a bottle of whisky from the distillery shop) with a tasting to round it off – if you're driving, you'll be offered a miniature to take away with you. Indeed, most people travel the route by car, though you could cycle it, or even walk using the Speyside Way (see p.177).

Cardhu, on the B9102 at Knockando (March–Nov Mon–Fri 9.30am–4.30pm; July–Sept also Sat 9.30am–4.30pm, Sun 11am–4pm; Jan, Feb & Dec 10am–4pm; £2 with voucher). This distillery was established over a century ago when the founder's wife was nice enough to raise a red flag to warn local crofters when the authorities were on the lookout for their illegal stills. Sells rich, full-bodied whisky which has distinctive peaty flavours, in an attractive bulbous bottle.

Dallas Dhu, Mannachie Road, Forres (April–Sept daily 9.30am–6pm; Oct–March Mon–Wed & Sat 9.30am–4pm, Thurs 9.30am–noon, Sun 2–4pm; £2.50). Located apart from the others, this classic Victorian distillery no longer makes whisky, but all the old equipment is in place and you can look around freely with an audioguide handset.

Glenfiddich, on the A941 just north of Dufftown (April to mid-Oct Mon–Sat 9.30am–4.30pm, Sun noon–4.30pm; mid-Oct to March Mon–Fri 9.30am–4.30pm; free). Probably the best known of the malt whiskies, and the biggest and slickest of all the distilleries. It's a lighter, sweet whisky which comes in familiar triangular shaped bottles. Uniquely, Glenfiddich is bottled on the premises – an interesting process to watch. Informative (and free) tours, though the place is thronged with tourists.

Glenlivet, on the B9008, ten miles north of Tomintoul (April–Oct Mon–Sat 10am–4pm, Sun 12.30–4pm; July & Aug last tour 5pm; £2.50 with voucher). With a famous name and a lonely hillside setting, this was the first licensed distillery in the Highlands, following the 1823 Act of Parliament which aimed to reduce illicit distilling and smuggling. The Glenlivet twelve-year-old malt is a floral, fragrant medium-bodied whisky.

Speyside Cooperage, Craigellachie, four miles north of Dufftown (Mon–Fri 9.30am–4.30pm; Easter–Sept also Sat 9.30am–4pm; £2.95). Gain an insight into the ancient and skilled art of cooperage, and watch the oak casks for whisky being made and repaired.

Strathisla, Keith (Feb & March Mon–Fri 9.30am–4pm; April–Nov Mon–Sat 9.30am–4pm, Sun 12.30–4pm; £4, with a £2 voucher). A small old-fashioned distillery claiming to be Scotland's oldest (1786); it's certainly one of the most attractive, situated in a highly evocative highland location on the strath of the Isla River. The malt itself has a rich (almost fruity) taste and is pretty rare, but is used as the heart of the better-known Chivas Regal blend.

Ben Nevis and Aonach Mhor Massif, from Caledonian Canal

Glenturret Distillery

Shinty match, Fort William

Glengorm Castle, Mull

MICHAEL JENNER

Ruthven Barracks, Kingussie

ROB HUMPHREYS

FOTOGRAFF/M. HANNAFORD

Tobermory harbour, Mull

Marine flora, Staffa

PAUL HARRIS

Corgarff Castle

MICHAEL JENNER

Port Askaig, Islay

Loch Gamhna, Rothiemurchus Estate, Strathspey

Common dolphins, off Mull   CalMac ferry leaving Oban

Aonach Eagach Ridge, Glencoe

travel details

Trains

Aberdeen to: Dundee (every 30min; 1hr 15min); Edinburgh (1–2 hourly; 2hr 35min); Glasgow (1–2 hourly; 2hr 35min); Insch (1–2 hourly; 35min); Inverness (1–2 hourly; 2hr 25min).

Aviemore to: Edinburgh (Mon–Sat 8 daily, Sun 3 daily; 3hr); Inverness (Mon–Sat 8 daily, Sun 4 daily; 40min); Newtonmore (Mon–Sat 6 daily, Sun 4 daily; 20min).

Crianlarich to: Corrour (4 daily; 1hr); Glasgow (4 daily; 1hr 45min); Rannoch (4 daily; 50min).

Inverness to: Aberdeen (1–2 hourly; 2hr 25min); Edinburgh (5 daily; 3hr 30min); Glasgow (3 daily; 3hr 25min); Insch (1–2 hourly; 1hr 35min).

Newtonmore to: Aviemore (Mon–Sat 6 daily, Sun 4 daily; 20min); Inverness (Mon–Sat 6 daily, Sun 4 daily; 55min).

Perth to: Aberdeen (hourly; 1hr 40min); Dundee (hourly; 25min); Edinburgh (9 daily; 1hr 25min); Glasgow Queen Street (hourly; 1hr 5min); Pitlochry (8 daily; 30min).

Pitlochry to: Edinburgh (5 daily; 2hr); Glasgow Queen Street (3 daily; 1hr 45min); Perth (8 daily; 30min); Stirling (3–5 daily; 1hr 15min).

Stirling to: Aberdeen (hourly; 2hr 15min); Dundee (hourly; 1hr); Edinburgh (hourly; 1hr); Glasgow Queen Street (hourly; 30min); Inverness (3–5 daily; 3hr); Perth (hourly; 30min); Pitlochry (3–5 daily; 1hr 15min).

Buses

Aberdeen to: Ballater (hourly; 1hr 45min); Banchory (hourly; 55min); Braemar (4–6 daily; 2hr 10min); Crathie (for Balmoral) (4–6 daily; 1hr 55min); Dufftown (2 weekly; 2hr 10min); Dundee (hourly; 2hr); Inverness (hourly; 3hr 40min); Nairn (hourly; 2hr 50min).

Aviemore to: Grantown-on-Spey (6–9 daily; 35min); Fort William (2 daily; 1hr 30min); Inverness (15 daily; 40min); Newtonmore (8 daily; 20min); Perth (15 daily; 1hr 50min).

Ballater to: Crathie (for Balmoral) (June–Sept 1 daily; 15min).

Banchory to: Ballater (June–Sept 1 daily; 45min); Braemar (June–Sept 1 daily; 1hr 20min); Crathie (for Balmoral) (June–Sept 1 daily; 1hr).

Crianlarich to: Edinburgh (2 daily; 2hr 30min); Glasgow (4 daily; 1hr 45min); Stirling (2 daily; 1hr 20min).

Perth to: Edinburgh (hourly; 1hr 20min); Glasgow (20 daily; 1hr 35min); Inverness (10 daily; 2hr 30min); London (4 daily; 9hr); Stirling (20 daily; 50min).

Pitlochry to: Edinburgh (7 daily; 2hr 15min); Glasgow (9 daily; 2hr 20min); Perth (17 daily; 40min); Stirling (6 daily; 1hr 25min).

Stirling to: Aberfoyle (4 daily; 45min); Callander (11 daily; 45min); Dundee (12 daily; 1hr 30min); Edinburgh (hourly; 1hr 35min); Glasgow (34 daily; 1hr 10min); Inverness (12 daily; 3hr 30min); Lochearnhead (2 daily; 1hr 40min); Perth (20 daily; 50min); Pitlochry (2 daily; 1hr 30min).

CHAPTER THREE

THE GREAT GLEN

T he **Great Glen**, a major geological fault-line cutting diagonally across the Highlands from Fort William to Inverness, is the defining geographic feature of the the north of Scotland. A huge rift valley was formed when the northwestern and southeastern sides of the fault slid against each other for more than sixty miles, the present landscape was shaped by glaciers that only retreated around 8000 BC. The glen is impressive more for its sheer scale than its great beauty, but its imposing barrier of loch and mountain means that no one can travel into the northern Highlands without passing through it, and with the two major service centres of the Highlands at either end it makes an obvious and rewarding route between the west and east coasts.

Of the Great Glen's four elongated lochs, by far the most famous and most touristy is **Loch Ness**, home to the mythical beast and linked to the other three, **lochs Oich, Lochy** and **Linnhe** (a sea loch) by the **Caledonian Canal**. This begins at **Corpach**, a satellite of **Fort William**, a well-located but largely disappointing town squeezed in between the shores of Loch Linnhe and the slopes of **Ben Nevis**, Britain's highest point. The area around Fort William is filled with opportunities for great walking, climbing, mountain-biking and numerous other

LOTS AND LOTS OF LOCHS AND LOCKS

Surveyed by James Watt in 1773, the **Caledonian Canal** was completed in the early 1800s by Thomas Telford to enable ships to pass between the North Sea and the Atlantic without having to navigate Scotland's treacherous northern coast. There are sixty miles between the west coast entrance to the canal at Corpach, near Fort William, and its exit onto the Moray Firth at Inverness, although strictly speaking only 22 miles of it are bona fide canal – the other 38 exploit the Great Glen's natural string of **freshwater lochs** of Lochy, Oich and Ness.

The most famous piece of canal engineering in Scotland is the series of eight **locks** at Benavie, about a mile from the entrance at Corpach, known as Neptune's Staircase (see p.188). While the canal was originally built for freight-carrying ships and large passenger steamers, these days it is almost exclusively used by small yachts and pleasure boats. Good spots to watch their leisurely progress are Neptune's Staircase and Fort Augustus, where four locks take traffic through the centre of the village into Loch Ness.

If you're interested in the **history of the waterway**, there's the small Caledonian Canal Heritage Centre (see p.197) in Ardchattan House, beside the locks in Fort Augustus. For more active encounters with the canal, you can set off along a section of the Great Glen Way footpath or Great Glen cycle way, both of which follow the **canal towpath** for part of their length (see box on p.182), or you can take to the water on a **kayak** from Scottish Voyageurs (see p.198), based at Fort Augustus, or join a five-day guided trip along the length of the canal in a **Canadian canoe** with Alfresco Adventures (see p.196), based near Fort William.

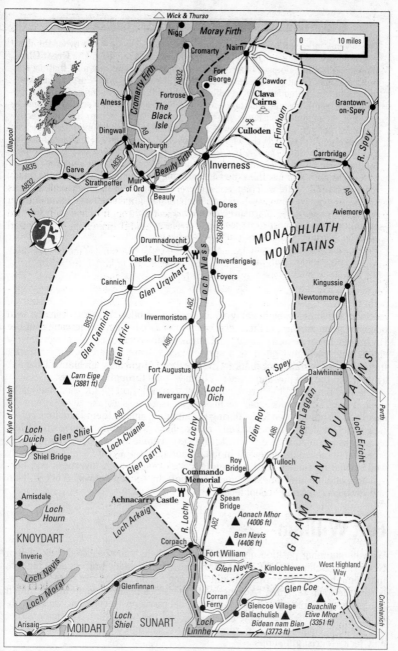

THE GREAT GLEN WAY AND CYCLE ROUTE

The seventy-mile cleft of the Great Glen is the most obvious – and by far the flattest – way of traversing northern Scotland from west to east coast. The **Great Glen Way** long-distance footpath is a relatively undemanding five day hike that uses a combination of canal towpath and forest- and hill-tracks between Fort William and Inverness. Accommodation is readily available all the way along the route in campsites, youth hostels, bunkhouses and B&Bs, though in high season it's worth booking ahead and if you know you're going to arrive late somewhere it's worth checking that you can still get a meal where you're staying or somewhere nearby. The maps you'll need to do the whole thing are Ordnance Survey Landranger maps 41, 34 and 26, while *The Great Glen Way* by Heather Connon and Paul Roper (Mainstream; £9.99) is a comprehensive guidebook describing the route.

A **cycle path** also traverses the Glen, offering a tranquil alternative to the hazardous A82. The path, which shares some of its route with the footpath but also utilises stretches of minor roads, is well signposted and can be managed in one long day or two easier days. Alternatively, bikes can be rented at Fort William, Benavie, Fort Augustus, Drumnadrochit and Inverness, from where you can tackle shorter sections. A leaflet outlining the route is available from tourist offices, or direct from Forest Enterprise, Strathoich, Fort Augustus PH32 4BT (☎01320/366322).

The suggested **direction** for both routes is from west to east – the direction of the prevailing southwesterly wind.

outdoor activities, most notably in Glen Coe, Scotland's most dramatic and poignant glen. At the northeastern end of the Great Glen is the capital of the Highlands, **Inverness**, a pleasant and unrushed town with a couple of worthwhile sights but used most often as a springboard to remoter areas further north. Inevitably, most transport links to the northern Highlands, including Ullapool, Thurso and the Orkney and Shetland Islands, pass through Inverness.

The traditional and most rewarding way to travel through the glen itself is by **boat**. A flotilla of kayaks, small yachts and pleasure vessels take advantage of the canal and its old wooden locks during the summer, among them Jacobite Cruises (see p.203 for details). Alternatively, an excellent **cycle path** traverses the Glen, as well as a long-distance footpath, the seventy-mile **Great Glen Way**, which takes five to seven days to walk in full. In addition, the Great Glen is reasonably well served by **buses**, with several daily services between Inverness and Fort William, and a couple of extra buses covering the section between Fort William and Invergarry during school terms.

Fort William

With its stunning position on Loch Linnhe and the snow-streaked bulk of Ben Nevis rising behind, **FORT WILLIAM**, known by the many walkers and climbers that come here as "Fort Bill", should be a gem. Sadly, the lack of taste that nearly saw the town renamed "Abernevis" in the 1950s is also evident in the ribbon bungalow development and an ill-advised dual carriageway complete with a grubby pedestrian underpass, which have wrecked the waterfront. The main street and the little squares off it are more appealing, though occupied by some decidedly tacky tourist gift shops.

THE WEST HIGHLAND WAY

Opened in 1980, the spectacular **West Highland Way** was Scotland's first long-distance footpath, stretching some 95 miles from Milngavie (six miles north of central Glasgow), to Fort William, where it reaches the foot of Ben Nevis, Britain's highest mountain.

The route follows ancient drove roads, along which Highlanders herded their cattle and sheep to market in the lowlands, as well as military roads built by troops to control the Jacobite insurgence in the eighteenth century, old coaching roads and even disused railway lines. In addition to the stunning scenery, increasingly dramatic as the path heads north, walkers may see some of Scotland's rarer wildlife, including red deer, feral goats – ancestors of those left behind after the Highland clearances – and, soaring over the highest peaks, golden eagles.

Passing through the lowlands north of Glasgow, the West Highland Way crosses the Highland Boundary Fault Line near the southern end of Loch Lomond, then follows the famously bonnie banks of the loch north to Crianlarich. From here, it traverses open heather moorland across the wilderness of Rannoch moor, entering the spectacular eastern end of Glencoe before zigzagging up 1000ft over the Devil's Staircase to Kinlochleven. From here it's an inspiring final leg round the Mamore Mountains and into Glen Nevis, which leads into Fort William.

Though this is emphatically not the most strenuous of Britain's long-distance walks – it passes between lofty mountain peaks, rather than over them – a moderate degree of fitness is required as there are some steep ascents. In places the landscape is empty and exposed, so as well as making sure you've got good footware you should be well prepared for sudden and extreme weather changes. If you're looking for an added challenge, you could work a climb of Ben Lomond or Ben Nevis into your schedule. You might choose to walk individual sections of the Way – the section from Inverarnan to Tyndrum (thirteen miles) is relatively easy and has good transport connections at either end, while the climb from Glencoe up the Devil's Staircase to Kinlochleven (eight miles) is more spectacular, and the final leg from Kinlochleven to Fort William (fourteen miles) can be done in a day, starting from Fort William if you catch an early bus to Kinlochleven – but to tackle the whole thing you need to set aside at least seven days. Also, avoid a Saturday start from Milngavie and you'll be less likely to be walking with hordes of people, plus there'll be less pressure on accommodation. Most walkers tackle the route from south to north (the scenery gets better each day) and manage between ten and fourteen miles at a time, staying at hotels, B&Bs and bunkhouses en route. Camping is only permitted at recognized sites.

Although the path is clearly waymarked, you may want to check the official guide, published by the HMSO, which includes Ordnance Survey maps as well as descriptions of the route, with detailed cultural, historical, archeological and wildlife information. It's available from bookshops or from the HMSO, 72 Lothian Rd, Edinburgh EH3 9AZ. Further details about the Way, including an accommodation list, can be obtained from the West Highland Way ranger, Balloch Castle, Balloch, Dunbartonshire G53 8LX (☎01389/758216), or from the very useful West Highland Way Web site at *www.west-highland-way.co.uk*. As well as giving comprehensive accommodation listings, the Web site has links to tour companies and transport providers, who will take your luggage from one stopping point to the next.

For all its modern foibles, however, Fort William and its surrounding area has a turbulent and bloody **history**, not surprising given its strategic position at one end of the Great Glen. The garrison, originally named Inverlochy but later re-named in honour of William III, was founded in 1654 on the orders of Oliver Cromwell and was successfully held by government troops during both of the Jacobite risings. The fort itself, however, didn't survive the arrival of the West Highland Railway, which built a station on the site.

Arrival and information

Fort William is easily reached by **bus** from Inverness, and by **train** (the stations are next door to each other at the north end of High Street) direct from Glasgow via the famous, scenic **West Highland Railway** (see p.226). If you're driving, **parking** can be a nightmare: a free shuttle bus (mid-May to Sept) runs the short distance into town from both the West End Car Park down beside the loch, at the southwest end of town, and the An Aird Car Park beside the train station. The **tourist office**, on Cameron Square, just off High Street (April & May Mon–Sat 9am–5pm, Sun 10am–4pm; June, Sept & Oct Mon–Sat 9am–6pm, Sun 10am–5pm; July & Aug Mon–Sat 9am–8.30pm, Sun 9am–6pm; Nov–March Mon–Fri 9am–5pm, Sat 10am–4pm; ☎01397/703781), hands out free town maps and can help arrange onward transport to many of the less-visited areas of the west coast.

You'll find a host of outdoor-activity specialists in town. High-spec **mountain bikes** are available for rent at Off Beat Bikes (☎01397/704008) on the High Street; they also know the best local routes and are involved with building a down-hill mountain-bike course at the Nevis Range lower gondola station (see p.190), where they have another branch (July & Aug only) – good for exploring forest

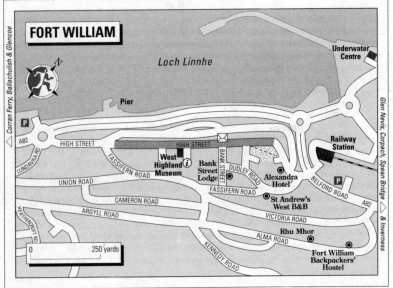

© Crown copyright

tracks in that area. The Underwater Centre (☎01397/703786), at the water's edge beyond the train station, rents out **diving** equipment, run Padi Courses, charter dive boats and offer guided dives; and local **mountain guides** include Alan Kimber of *Calluna* (see p.186) and Donald Watt (see box on p.189).

Accommodation

Fort William's plentiful **accommodation** ranges from large luxury hotels to budget hostels and bunkhouses. Numerous B&Bs are also scattered across the town, many of them in the suburb of Corpach, where there are also a couple of good hostels; it's on the other side of Loch Linnhe, three miles along the Mallaig road, and served by a regular bus service from Fort William. Note that a wide array of places to stay in this area may be reserved through the tourist office for a £1 booking fee, or you can ask for its free *Visitors Guide* and phone around yourself.

Hotels and B&Bs

Alexandra Hotel, The Parade (☎01397/702241, *sales@miltonhotels.com*). Established hotel right in the town centre, with well-appointed rooms and a restaurant. ⑤.

Bank Street Lodge, Bank Street (☎01397/700070). New and slightly characterless lodge with neat doubles, twin and family rooms, all with TVs, and a very central location. Also has a couple of rooms used as four or eight-bed dorms (£11 per night). ①.

Distillery House, North Road, just north of the town centre near the junction for Glen Nevis (☎01397/700103). Very comfortable and well-equipped upper-range B&B. ③.

Glenloy Lodge Hotel, about six miles from Fort William on the minor road running north from Banavie (☎01397/712700). Comfortable, friendly and secluded small hotel with views across to Ben Nevis. ④.

The Grange, Grange Road (☎01397/705516). Top-grade accommodation in a striking old stone house, with four luxurious en-suite doubles and a spacious garden. Vegetarian breakfasts on request; non-smoking. April–Oct. ⑤.

Inverlochy Castle, two miles north of Fort William on the A82 (☎01397/702177). A grand country house hotel set in wooded parkland, two miles north of Fort William; exceptional levels of service and outstanding food – but at a price. ⑨.

Rhiw Goch, beside Neptune's Staircase, Banavie (☎01397/772373). Non-smoking modern villa with three twin rooms in a great situation beside the canal looking over to Ben Nevis. ①.

Rhu Mhor, 42 Alma Rd (☎01397/702213). Congenial B&B a 10min walk from the town centre, offering good breakfasts; vegetarians and vegans are catered for by arrangement. ①.

ACCOMMODATION PRICE CODES

Throughout this book, accommodation **prices** have been graded with the codes below, according to the cost of the least expensive double room in high season. Price codes are not given for campsites, most of which charge under £10 per person. Almost all hostels charge less than £10 a night for a bed – the few exceptions to this rule have the prices quoted in the text. For a full account of the accommodation price codes, see p.32.

① under £40	④ £60–70	⑦ £110–150
② £40–50	⑤ £70–90	⑧ £150–200
③ £50–60	⑥ £90–110	⑨ £200 and over

St Andrews West, Fassifern Road (☎01397/703038). Comfortable and extremely central B&B in an attractive converted granite church with various inscriptions and stained-glass windows remaining. ①.

Hostels and campsites

Ben Nevis Bunkhouse, Achintee Farm, Glen Nevis (☎01397/702240, *achintee.accom@ glennevis.com*). A more civilized option than the nearby SYHA place, with hot showers, self-catering kitchen and TV room. Located just over the river from the Ben Nevis Visitor Centre – get to it by following the Ben path across the river or by taking Achintee Road along the north side of the River Nevis from Claggan.

Calluna, Heathcroft (☎01397/700451, *mountain@guide.u-net.com*). Central, small family-run budget self-catering flat with standard facilities, but tricky to find: head up Lundavra Road from the roundabout, then double back left along Connochie Road. The owner, Alan Kimber, is one of the area's top mountain guides, so there's plenty of good outdoor advice available.

Farr Cottage, on the main A830 as it goes through Corpach (☎01397/772315, *farrcottage@sol.co.uk*). One of the liveliest of the local backpacker hostels, with everything from pizza feasts to whisky tastings going on in the evenings. Accommodation, in medium-sized dorms, is slightly more expensive than others locally.

Fort William Backpackers, Alma Road (☎01397/700711). A big house 5min walk up the hill from town, with great views and large communal areas, though some of the facilites are a bit ropy. Part of the Macbackpackers chain, so minibus tours pull in at regular intervals.

Glen Nevis Caravan and Camping Park, two miles up the Glen Nevis road (☎01397/702191). Good facilities include hot showers, a shop and restaurant.

Glen Nevis SYHA Hostel, two and a half miles up the Glen Nevis road (☎01397/702336 or central reservations ☎0541/553255). Large, but best avoided in midsummer, when it's chock-full of teenagers. Handy for the Ben Nevis path but a long walk from town.

The Smiddy Bunkhouse, Station Road (☎01397/772467, *smiddy@snowgoose.prestel.co.uk*). A cosy twelve-bed hostel right next to Corpach train station at the entrance to the Caledonian Canal. Part of the Snowgoose Mountain Centre (see p.190), offering year-round mountaineering, kayaking and other outdoor activities.

The Town

Fort William's downfall started in the nineteenth century, when the original fort, which gave the town its name, was demolished to make way for the train line. Today, the town is a sprawl of dual carriageways, and there's little to detain you except the splendid and idiosyncratic **West Highland Museum**, on Cameron Square, just off High Street (April–Oct Mon–Sat 10am–5pm; July & Aug also Sun 2–5pm; Nov–March Mon–Sat 10am–4pm; £2). Its collections cover virtually every aspect of Highland life and the presentation is traditional, but very well done, making a refreshing change from state-of-the-art heritage centres. There's a good section on Highland clans and tartans and, among interesting Jacobite relics, a secret portrait of Bonnie Prince Charlie, seemingly just a blur of paint that resolves itself into a portrait when viewed against a cylindrical mirror. Look out, too, for the long Spanish rifle used in the assassination of a local factor (the landowner's tax-collector-cum-bailiff) – the murder that subsequently inspired Robert Louis Stevenson's novel, *Kidnapped*. You'll also see a 550-kilogram slab of aluminium, the stuff that's processed locally into silver foil.

Excursions from town include the popular day-trip to Mallaig (see p.227) on the **Jacobite Steam Train** (mid-June to Sept Mon–Fri; also Sun during Aug; depart Fort William 10.20am, depart Mallaig 2.10pm; day return £19.75; bookings

☎01463/239026). Heading along the north shore of Loch Eil to the west coast via historic Glenfinnan (see p.224), the journey takes in some of the region's most spectacular scenery. Several **cruises** also leave from the town pier every day, offering the chance to spot the marine life of Loch Linnhe, including seals, otters and seabirds.

Eating

Fort William has a reasonable range of places **to eat**. On the High Street, the *Grog and Gruel* serves an eclectic mix of pizzas, pasta and Mexican dishes with real ale, while the *Great Food Stop* at the *Alexandra Hotel* does inexpensive grills, fish and pasta dishes. *McTavish's Kitchen*, an American/Scottish restaurant on High Street, has a predictable menu of moderately priced steaks and seafood, with several vegetarian options; in summer, it also hosts nightly Scottish entertainment sessions (8.30–11.30pm). The pick of the bunch, though, is the *Crannog Seafood Restaurant*, an elegantly converted bait store on the pier, where oysters, langoustines, prawns and salmon are cooked with flair. The wine list is also excellent, although the prices make it best kept for a treat. Out of town, the *Old Pines* near Spean Bridge (☎01397/712324) is worth trying, or you can dine very well indeed in the more formal setting of *Inverlochy Castle* (☎01397/702177), though here the bill for two will probably run into three figures. A good place for **picnic food** as well as a snack is the *Café Chardon*, up a lane off High Street next to AT Mays; they do excellent baguettes, croissants and pastries to eat in or take away.

Around Fort William

Any disappointment you harbour about the dispiriting flavour of Fort William itself should be offset against the wealth of scenery and activities in its immediate vicinity. Most obvious – on a clear day, at least – is **Ben Nevis**, the most popular, though hardly the most rewarding, of Scotland's high peaks, the path up which leaves from **Glen Nevis**, itself a starting point for excellent walks of various lengths and elevations. The mountain abutting Ben Nevis is **Aonach Mhor**, home of Scotland's most modern ski resort, while some of the best views of both can be had from **Corpach**, a small village opposite Fort William which marks the start of the **Caledonian Canal**.

The main road travelling up the Great Glen from Fort William towards Inverness is the A82, ten miles along which is the small settlement of **Spean Bridge**, a good waypoint for getting to various remote and attractive walking areas, notably **glens Spean** and **Roy**, found along the A86 trunk road, which links across the central highlands to the A9 and the Speyside region (see p.175).

Glen Nevis

A ten-minute drive out of Fort William, **Glen Nevis** is indisputably among the Highlands' most impressive glens: a classic U-shaped glacial valley hemmed in by steep bracken-covered slopes and swaths of blue-grey scree. Herds of shaggy Highland cattle graze the valley floor, where a sparkling river gushes through glades of trees. With the forbidding mass of Ben Nevis rising steeply to the north, it's not surprising this valley has been chosen as the location for scenes in sever-

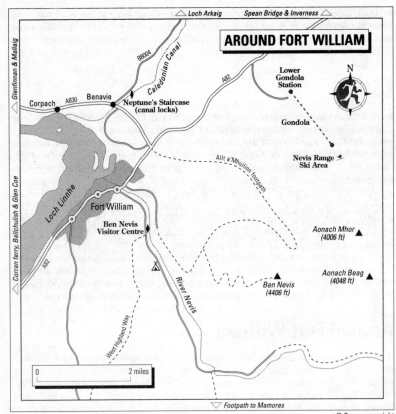

© Crown copyright

al **movies**, such as *Rob Roy* and *Braveheart*. Apart from its natural beauty, Glen Nevis is also the starting point for the ascent of Scotland's highest peak, and you can rent **mountain equipment** and **mountain bikes** at the trailhead. Highland Country **bus** #42 runs from An Aird, Fort William, approximately hourly through the day as far as the youth hostel; less frequently, the service carries on another two and a half miles up the glen to the car park by the Lower Falls (mid-May to Sept only; 10–20 min).

Neptune's Staircase and Corpach

Three miles from the centre of Fort William along the A830 northwards to Mallaig at the suburb of Benavie, the Caledonian Canal climbs 64ft in less than half a mile via a punishing but picturesque series of eight locks known as **Neptune's Staircase**. There are stunning views from here of Ben Nevis and its neighbours, and it's a popular point from which to walk or cycle along the canal towpath. Bikes can be rented from Caledonian Activity Breaks (☎01397/772373),

GLEN NEVIS AND BEN NEVIS: WALKS AND HIKES

Harvey's Ben Nevis Walkers Map and Guide

The above **map** is available in the the the Fort William tourist office and several shops around town. Anyone keen to do some serious **planned walking** should contact Donald Watt (☎01397/704340), the leader of the Lochaber Mountain Rescue Team, who organizes half- and whole-day walks.

Of all the walks in and around **Glen Nevis**, the ascent of **Ben Nevis**, Britain's highest summit, inevitably attracts the most attention. In high summer, the trail is teeming with hikers, whatever the weather. However, this doesn't mean the mountain should be treated casually. It can snow round the summit any day of the year and more people perish here annually than on Everest, so take the necessary precautions (see p.46); in winter, of course, the mountain should be left to the experts.

The most obvious **route to the summit**, a Victorian pony path up the whaleback south side of the mountain which was built to service the observatory that once stood on the top, starts from the **Ionad Nibheis Visitor Centre** (Easter–Oct daily 9am–5pm; free), a mile and a half southeast of Fort William (reached by bus #42 from An Aird in Fort William). From the centre, which has background information on the mountain and a daily weather forecast on the board outside, cross the footbridge over the River Nevis. Follow the the well-marked path for about twenty minutes until it joins a path leading directly down to the Glen Nevis SYHA Hostel (see p.186 for details), continuing upwards over two aluminium bridges, swinging onto a wide saddle with a small loch before veering right to cross the Red Burn. A series of seemingly endless zigzags rises from here over boulderfields onto a plateau, which you cross to reach the summit, marked by cairns, a shelter and a trig point. Return via the same route or, if the weather is settled and you're confident enough, make the side-trip from the saddle mentioned earlier into the **Allt a'Mhuilinn glen** for spectacular views of the great cliffs on Ben Nevis's north face. The Allt a'Mhuilinn may be followed right down to valley level as an alternative route off the mountain, reaching the distillery on the A82 a mile north of Fort William. Allow a full day for the climb, as it will take around eight hours.

If you don't fancy a hike up the mountain, a great **low-level walk** runs from the end of the road at the top of the glen. The good but very rocky path leads through a dramatic gorge with impressive falls and rapids, then opens out into a secret hanging valley, carpeted with wild flowers, with a high waterfall at the far end. It's a pretty place for a picnic and if you're really energetic you can walk on over **Rannoch Moor** to **Corrour Station**, where you can pick up one of four daily trains to take you back to Fort William.

based at Rhiw Goch, one of the cottages backing onto the canal at the top of the sequence of locks.

Another mile along the road is the suburb of **Corpach**, the point where the canal enters from Loch Linnhe. The site of a mothballed paper mill, the main event here is the unexpectedly absorbing **Treasures of the Earth** exhibition (daily: Feb–June & Sept–Dec 10am–5pm, July & Aug 9.30am–7pm; £3), which has a dazzling array of rocks, crystals, gemstones and fossils, with detailed explanations about where they come from and how they get their different colours. Some of the displays are quite entertaining, with a recreated mine showing how the stones are discovered and a UV-lit chamber revealing the psychedelic colours hid-

---

THE NEVIS RANGE SKI STATION

The **Nevis Range Ski Station** (☎01397/705825), seven miles northeast of Fort William on the A82, boasts Scotland's only cable-car system (daily: July & Aug 9.30am–8pm; Sept to mid-Nov & mid-Dec to June 10am–5pm; £6.50 return), in the **Aonach Mhor** ski area – a popular attraction during both winter and the summer off-season period. Built in 1989 with a hefty grant from the regional council, the one-and-a-half mile gondola ride (15min) gives an easy approach to some high-level walking, but for most tourists it simply provides an effortless means to rise 2000ft and enjoy the spectacular views from the terrace of the self-service restaurant at the top. In July and August, you can also ski on the Nevis Range's 246-foot **dry slope** (July & Aug Mon–Thurs & Sun 11.30am–1pm; £9 including ski rental and group instruction), while a two-mile championship-grade **downhill mountain-bike course** starting from the top gondola station is presently under construction. Highland County bus #41 from Fort William runs here four times a day (June–Oct).

---

den inside different gemstones. Also in Corpach, The **Snowgoose Mountain Centre** (☎01397/772752, *info@snowgoose.prestel.co.uk*), set beside the *Smiddy Bunkhouse* (see p.186), offers instruction, rental and residential courses including hillwalking, mountaineering and canoeing.

Glen Roy and Loch Laggan

Shortly after the Commando Memorial (see box opposite), the A82 dips into the village of Spean Bridge, where it's met by the A86 trunk road to Dalwhinnie on the A9 and Kingussie in Speyside (see p.172). The countryside here is attractive but relatively untrammelled, with some good hiking routes leading to a generous sprinkling of pretty glens and Munros. At **Roy Bridge**, three miles along the road from Spean Bridge, a minor road turns off which runs up **Glen Roy**. A couple of miles along the glen, you'll see the so-called "parallel roads": not roads at all, but ancient beaches at various levels along the valley sides which mark the shorelines of a loch confined here by a glacial dam in the last ice age. Back on the A86, two miles beyond Roy Bridge, *Aite Cruinnichidh*, 1 Achluachrach (☎01397/712315, *gavin@achluachrach.prestel.co.uk*), is a comfortable bunkhouse in a beautiful setting, with good facilities and local advice for climbers, walkers and cyclists. The West Highland Railway line runs right past the hostel, fringing the river Spean and the spectacular **Monassie Gorge**, which you can view from a footpath leading down from the roadside. Other good local contacts for outdoor activities include Jimmy Couts (☎01397/712812, *info@ fishing-scotland.co.uk*), in Roy Bridge, who offers **fly fishing** guiding and tuition, plus Highland Icelandic Horses (☎01397/712427), based on a farm near Achnacarry Castle, who do well-run day- and half-day treks or three- to seven-day **horse-riding trails**.

The railway line and road part company at Tulloch, a few miles further east, where trains swing south to pass Loch Treig and cross Rannoch Moor (see p.147). The station building at Tulloch is a brand-new bunkhouse, *Station Lodge* (☎01397/732333, *stationlodge@renwscot.demon.co.uk*), again with good facilities for walkers and climbers. Further east, the A86 runs alongside the artificial **Loch Laggan**, raised in 1934 to provide water for the aluminium works at Fort William;

THE COMMANDO TRAIL

From 1942 until the end of World War II, the Lochaber district around the southern part of the Great Glen was used as a training area by the elite **commando** units of the British Army. A striking **memorial** depicting a group of bronze soldiers, sculpted in 1952 by Scott Sutherland, stands overlooking an awesome sweep of moor and mountain beside the A82 just to the north of Spean Bridge. Nearby, in a room at the back of the *Spean Bridge Hotel*, the proudly assembled **Commando Exhibition** (June–Sept daily 10am–5.30pm; £2) shows a twenty-minute video of the commandos during their time in the area, along with displays of photos, medals and memorabilia.

The soldiers' base was at **Achnacarry Castle**, hereditary seat of the Clan Cameron, around which there's an interesting five-mile **walk** retracing many of the places used by them during their training. To get here, follow the minor B8004 beside the memorial which branches down to Gairlochy, by the canal side at Loch Lochy's southern tip, then follow the signs for the small **Clan Cameron museum** (Easter to mid-Oct daily 11am–5.30pm), located in the old post office opposite the castle. The museum tells the clan history, including its involvement in the 1745 rebellion, plus memorabilia relating to the commando's residency. You can park your car here and walk to the the eastern end of **Loch Arkaig**, one of Scotland's most ruggedly wild and remote stretches of water, then walk down the tree-lined **Mile Dorcha**, or **Dark Mile**. Around here there are various caves and small bothies used by **Bonnie Prince Charlie** when he was on the run after Culloden, dodging government troups, putting trust in only a few loyal companions, and desperately hoping for the arrival of a French ship to carry him to safety. The road leads to the shores of **Loch Lochy**, where the commandos would practise opposed landings, often using live ammunition to keep them on their toes. After a mile by the lochside, turn right back along the road which leads to the museum. A **leaflet** giving a fuller description of the trail and the commandos' activities in the area can be obtained from tourist information offices in the area.

the water travels in tunnels of up to 15ft in diameter carved through miles of solid rock. To the north of the loch is the **Creag Meagaidh National Nature Reserve**, where a hill track leads up through changing bands of mountain vegetation to **Lochan a Choire**. Right by the nature reserve car park, you can see several small herds of red deer, kept here for scientific study.

Glen Coe and around

Despite its long-standing fame and popularity, **Glen Coe**, half an hour's drive south of Fort William on the main A82 road to Glasgow, can still fairly claim to be one of Scotland's most inspiring places. Arriving from the south across the desolate reaches of Rannoch Moor, the start of the glen, with **Buachaille Etive Mór** to the south and **Beinn a'Chrùlaiste** to the north, is little short of forbidding. By the heart of the glen, with the three huge rock buttresses known as the **Three Sisters** on one side and the Anoach Eagach ridge on the other combining to close up the sky, it's little wonder that most visitors feel compelled to stop simply to take it all in. Added to the heady mix is the infamous **massacre** of 1692, nadir of the long-standing enmity between the clans MacDonald and Campbell. At its western end, Glen Coe meets Loch Leven: the main road goes west and over the bridge at

Ballachulish en route to Fort William, while at the eastern end of the loch is the neglected settlement of **Kinlochleven**, best known now as a waypoint on the **West Highland Way** long-distance footpath (see p.183), but also a handy spot for getting deep into the mountains that surround the town on all sides.

Glen Coe

Breathtakingly beautiful, **Glen Coe** (literally "Valley of Weeping"), sixteen miles south of Fort William on the A82, is one of the best-known Highland glens: a spectacular mountain valley between velvety-green conical peaks, their tops often wreathed in cloud, and cascades of rock and scree. In 1692 it was the site of a notorious **massacre**, in which the MacDonalds were victims of a long-standing government desire to suppress the clans. Fed up with what they regarded as unacceptable lawlessness, and a groundswell of Jacobitism and Catholicism, the government offered a general pardon to all those who signed an oath of allegiance to William III by January 1, 1692. When clan chief **Alastair MacDonald** missed the deadline, a plot was hatched to make an example of "that damnable sept", and **Campbell of Glenlyon** was ordered to billet his soldiers in the homes of the

---

WALKS AROUND GLEN COE

Ordnance Survey Landranger map no. 41

Flanked by sheer-sided Munros, Glen Coe offers some of the Highlands' most challenging **hiking** routes, with long steep ascents over rough trails and notoriously unpredictable weather conditions that claim lives every year. The walks outlined below number among the glen's less ambitious routes, but still require a map. It's essential that you take the proper precautions (see p.46) and stick to the paths, both for your own safety and the sake of the soil, which has become badly eroded in places.

A good introduction to the splendours of Glen Coe is the half-day hike over the **Devil's Staircase**, which follows part of the old military road that once ran between Fort William and Stirling. The trail, a good option for families and less-experienced hikers, starts at the village of **Kinlochleven**, due north across the mountains from Glen Coe at the far eastern tip of Loch Leven (take the B863): head along the single-track road from the British Aluminium Heritage Centre to a wooden bridge, from where a gradual climb on a dirt jeep track winds up to Penstock Farm. The path, a section of the **West Highland Way**, is marked from here onwards by thistle signs, and is therefore easy to follow uphill to the 1804-foot pass and down the other side into Glen Coe. The Devil's Staircase was named by four hundred soldiers who endured severe hardship to build it in the seventeenth century, but in fine settled weather the trail is safe and affords stunning views of Loch Eilde and Buachaille Etive Mhor. A more detailed account of this hike features in the *Great Walks: Kinlochleven* leaflet (no. 4), on sale at most tourist offices in the area.

Another leaflet in the Great Walks series (no. 5: *Glen Coe*) gives a good description of the **Allt Coire Gabhail** hike, another old favourite. The trailhead for this half-day route is in Glen Coe itself, at the car park opposite the distinctive Three Sisters massif on the main A82 (look for the giant boulder). From the road, drop down to the floor of the glen and cross the River Coe via the wooden bridge, where you have a choice of two onward paths; the easier route, the less worn one, peels off to the right. Follow this straight up the Allt Coire Gabhail for a couple of miles

MacDonalds, who for ten days entertained them with traditional Highland hospitality. In the early morning of February 13, the soldiers turned on their hosts, slaying between 38 and 45 and causing more than 300 to flee in a blizzard, some to die of exposure.

Today, the glen, a property of the NTS since the 1930s, is virtually uninhabited, and provides outstanding climbing and walking. A small **NTS visitor centre** (April–Oct 9.30am–5.30pm; 50p), in the middle of the glen just off the main road, shows a short video about the massacre, and has a gift shop selling the usual books, postcards and Highland kitsch; for information about the area, the **tourist office** at Ballachulish is more useful. There is a shortish walk from the centre through the forest to Signal Rock, which unsurprisingly offers good views up and down the glen. More substantial are the informative ranger-led **guided walks** which leave from the centre (May–Aug): a high-level hike leaves at 10.30am on Thursdays (£10), and a low-level walk at 2.30pm on Tuesdays (£2).

At the eastern end of Glen Coe beyond the demanding Buachaille Etive Mhor, the landscape opens out onto the vast Rannoch Moor, dotted with small lochs and crossed by the West Highland Way, the A82 and, farther east, the West Highland Railway. From the **Glen Coe Ski Centre**, a ski lift climbs 2400ft to Meall a

---

until you rejoin the other (lower) path, which has ascended the valley beside the burn via a series of rock pools and lively scrambles. Cross the river here via the stepping stones and press on to the false summit directly ahead – actually the rim of the so-called "Lost Valley" which the Clan MacDonald used to flee to and hide their cattle in when attacked. Once in the valley, there are superb views of Bidean, Gearr Aonach and Beinn Fhada, which improve as you continue on to its head, another twenty- to thirty-minute walk. Unless you're well equipped and experienced, turn around at this point, as the trail climbs to some of the glen's high ridges and peaks.

Undoubtedly one of the finest walks in the Glen Coe area not entailing the ascent of a Munro is the **Buachaille Etive Beag** (BEB) circuit, for which you should check out the Ordnance Survey Pathfinder Guide: *Fort William and Glen Coe Walks*. Following the textbook glacial valleys of Lairig Eilde and Lairig Gartain, the route entails a 1968-foot climb in only nine miles of rough trail, and should only be attempted by relatively fit hikers. Park near the waterfall at **The Study** – the gorge part of the A82 through Glen Coe – and walk up the road until you see a sign pointing south to "Loch Etiveside". The path angles up from here, crisscrossing the Allt Lairig Eilde before the final pull to the top of the pass, a rise of 787ft from the road. The burn flowing through Glen Etive to Dalness is, confusingly, also called the Allt Lairig Eilde; follow its west-bank path until you reach a fenced-off area, and then cross the stream, using the trail that then ascends Stob Dubh (the "black peat") directly from Glen Etive to gain some height. Next, pick a traverse line across the side of the valley to the col of the Lairig Gartain, and onwards to the top of the pass – a haul of around 984ft that is the last steep ascent of this circuit. The drop down the other side towards the estate lodge of Dalness is easy. When you reach the single-track road, follow the path signposted as the "Lairig Gartain", northeast to a second pass, from where an intermittent trail descends the west (left) side of the River Coupall valley, eventually rejoining the A82. Much the most enjoyable path back northeast down the glen from here is the roughly parallel route of the old military road, which offers a gentler and safer return with superb views of the **Three Sisters** – finer than those ever seen by drivers.

Bhuiridh, giving spectacular views over Rannoch Moor and to Ben Nevis (all year; 15min; £3.75 return). At the base station, there's a tiny **Museum of Mountaineering** (daily 8.30am–5pm), where the rescue statistics make cautionary reading, and a simple but pleasant café. At the western end of the glen, **GLEN COE village** lies on the shore of Loch Leven, an inlet of Loch Linnhe.

Practicalities

There's a good selection of **accommodation** in Glen Coe and the surrounding area. Basic options include an SYHA **hostel** (☎01855/811219 or central reservations ☎0541/553255) on a back road halfway between Glen Coe village and the *Clachaig Inn*; the year-round Red Squirrel **campsite** (☎01855/811256) nearby; and a grassier NTS campsite (☎01855/811397; April–Oct) on the main road. Glen Coe village has a few comfortable **B&Bs**, such as the secluded *Scorry Breac* (☎01855/811354, *john@tajones.demon.co.uk*; ①), and the *Glencoe Guest House* (☎01855/811244; ①), while the best-known **hotel** in the area is the stark *Clachaig Inn* (☎01855/811252, *inn@glencoe-scotland.co.uk*; ③), a great place to swap stories with fellow climbers, and to reward your exertions with pints of beer and heaped platefuls of food; it's up Glen Coe, on the minor road from the village. At the other end of the glen, close to the ski area, is another well-established climber's watering hole, the *Kingshouse Hotel* (☎01855/851259; ②), a classic wayfarers' inn which always proves a welcome sight after the wide emptiness of Rannoch Moor. **Mountain bikes** and **tandems** can be rented from the *Clachaig Inn*.

Ballachulish and Kinlochleven

Two miles west of Glen Coe village, **BALLACHULISH village** was a major centre for the production of roofing slates, from 1693 to 1955, while North and South Ballachulish were once the terminals for the ferry across the mouth of Loch Leven, now crossed by a bridge. On the seaward side of the main road, the pricey **Highland Mysteryworld** (Easter–Oct daily 10am–6pm; £4.95), aimed mainly at families, attempts to conjure up some of the myths and legends of the Highlands, with the help of a crew of enthusiastic actors, animatronics and lots of smoke; it has a reasonable café and relatively kitsch-free gift shop. Much more genuine mystery is stirred up on **boat trips** (☎01855/811658 for details), which leave from the West Pier at Ballachulish and take you out to Eilean Munde, an island in Loch Leven where clan chiefs are buried; needless to say, the cruise is also a great way to take in the surrounding scenery.

At the eastern end of Loch Leven, at the foot of the spectacular mountains known as the Mamores, is the rather lifeless settlement of **KINLOCHLEVEN**, which has felt rather ignored ever since the bridge at Ballachulish ended the flow of northbound traffic detouring around the loch in preference to waiting in long ferry queues. Kinlochleven was the site of a huge aluminium smelter, established in 1904 and powered by a hydroelectric scheme that dammed the Blackwater valley above the village which at the time it was built was the largest in Europe. The story is told in **The Aluminium Story** (April–Oct Tues–Fri 10.30am–6pm, Sat & Sun 11am–3pm; free), a small series of displays in the same building as the town library, although the final chapter of the tale is that the factory is now all but closed, and despite large amounts of aid money the town is being left to its fate.

The real activity here comes from climbers heading into the Mamores, and from walkers strolling in on the **West Highland Way**, for whom the town is a con-

FORT WILLIAM AND GLEN COE OUTDOOR ACTIVITIES

In and around Fort William and Glen Coe you'll find a concentration of **outdoor activity** specialists who can help you make the most of the area's spectacular array of lochs, rivers and mountains, and we've listed specific activities below. Most of the places and people listed below offer guiding, instruction and equipment rental, and they're all good sources of advice about their particular speciality. Other good places to go for **information** and advice are outdoor equipment stores – in Fort William the best are Nevisport, at the train station end of High Street, or West Coast Outdoor Leisure, 102 High St – or backpackers and bunkhouses, many of which are run by outdoor enthusiasts. These stores, and most local bookshops and tourist information offices, also keep a good selection of **guidebooks** outlining local walks.

Climbing For rock climbing or winter mountaineering – a popular sport that ensures that the climbing community is active in this area throughout the year – contact any of the mountain guides listed below under "Walking".

Diving There are some excellent wrecks and kelp forests off the west coast. The Underwater Centre (see p.185) can provide all you need.

Fishing For fly-fishing tuition and guiding, contact Jimmy Couts (see p.190) at Roy Bridge.

Horse riding For horse-riding trails, call Highland Icelandic Horses (see p.190), at Achnacarry, near Spean Bridge.

Mountain-biking Contact Off Beat Bikes (see p.184), in Fort William, or Havoc Bikes (see p.196) in Ballachulish.

Skiing Skiing opportunites are available at the Nevis Range Ski Centre (see p.190) and the Glen Coe Ski Centre (see p.193).

Walking Some of the best routes include the Great Glen Way (see p.182), walks in Glen Nevis and on Ben Nevis see (p.189), the Commando Trail (see p.191) and walks in Glen Coe (see p.192). If you're interested in tackling the more difficult peaks, such as the Anoach Eagach ridge in Glen Coe, or want to improve your mountain skills such as navigation, it's a good idea to hire a mountain guide, normally for around £100 a day. Contact *Calluna* (see p.186), Snowgoose Mountain Centre (see p.190), or Glencoe Mountain Sport (see p.196).

Watersports For kayaking, contact Snowgoose Mountain Centre (see p.190); for its derivative, fun yakking (using inflatable two-man rafts-cum-kayaks), on local rivers, get in touch with Vertical Descents (see p.196). For canoe adventure trips, try Alfresco Adventures (see p.196).

venient overnight stop a day's walk from Fort William. The two hostels in town are the inexpensive *West Highland Lodge Bunkhouse* (☎01855/831471, *whl@cqm.co.uk*), a traditional bunkhouse with a great setting up on the hill, and the newer *Blackwater Hostel* (☎01855/831253), beside the river, decidedly upmarket, with TVs and en-suite facilities in four-bed dorms, but no communal lounge. You can also camp here, and rent mountain bikes. Welcoming B&B is available at *Edencoille Guest House* (☎01855/831358; ①), while there are two good hotels in town: *MacDonald Hotel* (☎01855/831539, *martin@macdonaldhotel.demon.co.uk*; ④), whose *Bothy Bar* is popular with walkers; and the spectacularly situated *Mamore Lodge* (☎01855/831213; ③), an old hunting lodge with attractive wood-panelled rooms and great views from the bar and restaurant.

Practicalities

Ballachulish has a useful **tourist office**, on Albert Road (April & May Mon–Sat 9am–5pm, Sun noon–4pm; June–Aug Mon–Sat 9am–6pm, Sun 10am–5pm; Sept & Oct Mon–Sat 10am–5pm, Sun 10am–4pm; ☎01855/811296), though most of the best **accommodation** is across the bridge in North Ballachulish and Onich. For a cheap bed, head to the elderly but inexpensive *Inchree Bunkhouse* (☎01855/821287) at Onich, where accommodation is also available in chalets and there's a decent real-ale pub and bistro. In Ballachulish village, *Fern Villa* (☎01855/811393; ②) is a welcoming **B&B**, while *Cuildorag House* (☎01855/821529; ②) in Onich is a particularly pleasant vegetarian and vegan B&B, renowned for its great breakfasts. **Hotels** include the *Ballachulish* (☎01855/821582; ⑥) in South Ballachulish, a grand but welcoming old place with good food, while the *Onich Hotel* (☎01855/821214; ⑤) is smart and friendly. Enthusiastic Havoc Bikes, located in a shed by the main road at Onich, is a good place to rent **mountain bikes** with all the trimmings, including helmet, rucksack and water bottle. Other outdoor activity operators include **walking** specialists Glencoe Mountain Sport(☎01855/811472; *www.glencoe-mountain-sport.co.uk*), while three- or four-day **canoe** adventure trips into the heart of wildernesses, such as Rannoch Moor and Loch Arkaig, are organized by Alfresco Adventures (☎01855/821248). Vertical Descents (☎01855/821593; mid-May to Sept; £35), also offer adrenaline-pumping canyoning trips (£30) down Inchree Falls near Corran Ferry.

Loch Ness

Travelling northeast along the Great Glen from Fort William, the first of the string of freshwater lochs you encounter is Loch Lochy, closely followed by the smaller Loch Oich. By far the largest, however, is **LOCH NESS**, probably the most eagerly scanned body of water in the world. Long and undeniably scenic, with rugged heather-clad mountains rising steeply from a wooded shoreline and some attractive valleys opening up on either side, its fame is based overwhelmingly on its legendary inhabitant, the **Loch Ness monster**, whose notoriety ensures a steady flow of hopeful visitors to the settlements dotted along the loch, in particular **Drumnadrochit**. Nearby, the impressive ruins of **Castle Urquhart** – a favourite monster-spotting location – perch atop a rock on the lochside and attract a deluge of bus parties during the summer. Almost as busy in high season is **Fort Augustus**, at the more scenic southwest tip of Loch Ness, where more visitor' centres proliferate and you can idle some hours watching queues of boats tackling one of the Caledonian Canal's longest flight of **locks**.

Although most visitors travel along the west shore of Loch Ness, on the A82, the opposite, eastern side, skirted by the sinuous single-track B862/852 (originally a military road built to link Fort Augustus and Fort George) is quieter and affords far more spectacular views. However, buses from Inverness only run as far south as **Foyers**, so – unless you take a bus tour from Inverness (see p.201) – you'll need your own transport to complete the whole loop around the loch, taking in the most impressive stretch between Fort Augustus and the high, hidden Loch Mhor, where the imposing Monadhliath range looms to the south.

NESSIE

The world-famous Loch Ness monster, affectionately known as **"Nessie"** (and by serious aficionados as *Nessiteras rhombopteryx*), has been around a long time. The first mention of her crops up in St Adamnan's seventh-century biography of **St Columba**. While on his way to evangelize the pagan inhabitants of Inverness, the saint allegedly calmed the monster after she attacked one of his monks. Present-day interest, however, is probably greater outside Scotland than from within, dating from the 1930s when the A82 was built along the loch's western shore. Recent encounters range from glimpses of ripples by anglers, to the famous occasion in 1961 when thirty hotel guests saw a pair of humps break the water's surface and cruise for about half a mile before submerging.

Several seemingly photographic evidence is showcased in the two "Monster Exhibitions" at Drumnadrochit, but the most impressive of these – including the renowned black-and-white movie footage of Nessie's humps moving across the water, and the photo of her neck and head – have been exposed as fakes. Hi-tech sonar surveys carried out over the past two decades have failed to come up with conclusive evidence, but it's hard to dismiss Nessie as pure myth. Too many locals have mysterious tales to tell, which they invariably keep to themselves for fear of ridicule by incredulous outsiders. Loch Ness also has an undeniably enigmatic air; even the most hardened cynics rarely resist the temptation to scan the waters for signs of life, just in case . . .

Fort Augustus

FORT AUGUSTUS, the tiny village at the more scenic southwestern tip of Loch Ness, was named after George II's son, the chubby lad who later became the "Butcher" Duke of Cumberland of Culloden fame; it was built as a barracks after the 1715 Jacobite rebellion. Today, it's dominated by comings and goings along the Caledonian Canal, which leaves Loch Ness here, and by its large former **Benedictine Abbey**, a campus of grey Victorian buildings founded on the site of the original fort in 1876. The abbey formerly housed a Catholic boys school and until recently was home to a small but active community of monks, but this broke up due to financial pressures and the building now lies empty.

Traditional Highland culture is the subject of **The Clansmen Centre**'s lively and informative exhibition (Easter to mid-Oct daily 10am–6pm; £3), on the banks of the canal. Guides sporting sporrans and rough woollen plaids talk you through the daily life of the region's seventeenth-century inhabitants inside a mock-up of a turf-roofed stone croft, followed by demonstrations of weaponry in the back garden, where you can be photographed in traditional Highland garb. Most of the young staff work here for fun, donning kilts on their free weekends to fight mock battles with enthusiasts from other parts of the Highlands, which must be why they are so unnervingly adept at wielding broadswords. Rather more sedate is the small **Caledonian Canal Heritage Centre** (Easter–Oct daily 10am–6pm; free), in Ardchattan House on the northern bank of the canal, where you can view old photographs and records about the building and history of the canal, and watch a black-and-white film of the days when paddle boats and large barges passed through the locks every day.

Practicalities

Fort Augustus's small **tourist office** (Mon–Sat: April–June 10am–5pm; July & Aug 9am–6pm; Sept & Oct 10am–5pm; ☎01320/366367) hands out useful free maps detailing popular walks in the area. They'll also help sort out fishing permits if you fancy trying your luck in the loch or nearby river.

The only **hostel** accommodation in town is at *Morag's Lodge* (☎01320/366289) above the petrol station on the Loch Ness side of town, where the atmosphere livens up with the daily arrival of backpackers' minibus tours. The *Old Pier* (☎01320/366418; ③) is a particularly appealing B&B, right on the loch at the north side of the village; there are log fires in the evenings – often very welcome, even in summer – and boats and horse riding are available to guests. Of the **hotels**, try the small, friendly *Caledonian* (☎01320/366256; ②), overlooking the Abbey, or the *Brae* (☎01320/366289; ④), just off the main road as you approach the village from the north, surrounded by woodland.

Eating places include the *Gondolier*, on the southern side of the village, which serves ambitious Scottish food at reasonable prices, or you can try the *Bothy Bite* beside the canal for Scottish specialities with a good range of moderately priced fish, steak and pies. The village has a lively **pub**, drawing a mixed clientele of locals, yachties and backpackers, as does *Poachers* on the main road. There's some good **cycling** routes locally, along the Great Glen cycle route and elsewhere, and you can rent mountain bikes from Scottish Voyageurs (☎01320/366666), based in the last building beside the canal on the southern side, heading towards Fort William. If you're keen to paddle rather than peddle, the same company also offer guided ten-seater Canadian canoe trips, and rent out canoes and other boats.

North from Fort Augustus: East Loch Ness

The tranquil and scenic **east side of Loch Ness** is skirted by General Wade's old military highway, now the B862/852. From Fort Augustus, this narrow single-track road swings inland through the near-deserted **Stratherrick** valley, dotted with tiny lochans and flocks of shaggy sheep, before dropping down to rejoin the loch at **FOYERS**, where there are numerous marked forest trails and an impressive waterfall. In the village, the friendly *Foyers House* (☎01456/486623; ①) makes a good place to **stay** and **eat**, with a bunkhouse offering dorms and doubles, a terrace with great views over the loch, and a restaurant serving up local salmon, venison and rabbit, as well as vegetarian options.

Three miles further north at **INVERFARIGAIG** – where a road up the beautiful, steep-sided river valley leads over to Loch Mhor – stands **Boleskine House**, former residence of the infamous Satanist and occult guru, Alastair Crowley. The self-styled "Great Beast" of black magic lived here between 1900 and 1918, amid rumours of devil worship and human sacrifice. In the 1970s, Led Zeppelin's Jimmy Page bought the place, but sold it after the tragic death of his daughter some years later. Set back in its own grounds, the house still has a gloomy air about it, and is not open to the public.

A much warmer welcome awaits visitors at the sleepy village of **DORES**, nestled at the top end of Loch Ness, where the *Dores Inn* makes a pleasant pit stop. Only nine miles from Inverness, the old pub, which serves an excellent pint of 80 shilling and inexpensive bar food, is popular with Invernessians, who trickle out here on summer evenings for a stroll along the grey-pebble beach, and some monster-spotting.

Invermoriston and Glen Moriston to Glen Shiel

Heading north from Fort Augustus along the main A82, which follows the loch's northeastern shore, **INVERMORISTON** is a tiny, attractive village just above Loch Ness, from where you can follow well-marked woodland trails past a series of grand waterfalls. Dr Johnson and Boswell spent a couple of nights here planning their journey to the Hebrides; you, too, could stay at the *Glenmoriston Arms Hotel* (☎01320/351206; ⑤), an old-fashioned inn with more than a hundred malt whiskies at the bar. Alternatively, the SYHA *Loch Ness Youth Hostel* (☎01320/351274 or central reservations ☎0541 553255; April–Oct), three and a half miles north of Invermoriston and overlooking the loch, is a more economical base.

If you're driving on from Invermoriston to the **west coast**, the roads (A887–A87) are good, as it's the main commercial and tourist route to the Skye Bridge. Rugged and somewhat awesome, the stretch through **Glen Moriston**, beside **Loch Cluanie**, has serious peaks at either side and little sign of human habitation as the road climbs. At the western end of the loch, you'll find the isolated *Cluanie Inn* (☎01463/798200; ⑤), a cosy wayside place with a very busy craft centre attached. From here, the road drops gradually down **Glen Shiel** into the superb mountainscape of **Kintail** (see p.232).

Drumnadrochit

Situated above a verdant, sheltered bay fifteen miles from Inverness, **DRUM-NADROCHIT**, practically the first chance to draw breath as you head down the A82, is the epicentre of Nessie hype, sporting a rash of tacky souvenir shops and two rival monster exhibitions whose head-to-head scramble for punters occasionally erupts into acrimonious exchanges – detailed with relish by the local press. Of the pair, the **Original Loch Ness Monster Exhibition** (daily: April–June & Sept–Nov 10am–6pm; July & Aug 9am–9pm; Dec–March 10am–4pm; £3.50) is the least worthwhile – basically a gift shop with a shoddy audiovisual show tacked on the side. If you're genuinely interested in "Nessie" lore, the **Official Loch Ness Monster Exhibition** (daily: April–June 9.30am–5.30pm; July & Aug 9am–8pm; Sept & Oct 9am–6.30pm; Nov–March 10am–4pm; £5.95), though more expensive (and no more "official" than the other), is a much better bet, offering an in-depth rundown of eyewitness accounts through the ages and mock-ups of the various research projects carried out in the loch. A recent upgrade has attempted to offer something to sceptics as well as believers by offering more scientific background to set against the various myths and sightings. **Cruises** on the loch aboard the *Nessie Hunter* can be booked at the Original Loch Ness Visitor Centre (Easter–Oct hourly 9.30am–6pm; 50min; £8), though a more relaxing alternative is to head out **fishing** with a local ghillie – the boat can take five to eight people and costs £25 for two hours; contact Bruce on ☎01456/450279 to book. If you want to turn your back on all the hype and enjoy the surrounding scenery, well-run **pony trekking** is available at the Highland Riding Centre (☎01456/450220), at Borlum Farm, just before you get to Castle Urquhart.

Castle Urquhart

Most photographs allegedly showing the monster have been taken a couple of miles further south, around the fourteenth-century ruined lochside **Castle**

Urquhart (daily: April–June & Sept 9.30am–6.30pm; July & Aug 9.30am–8.30pm; Oct–March 9.30am–4.30pm; last admission 45min before closing; £3.80). Built as a strategic base to guard the Great Glen, the castle played an important role in the Wars of Independence. It was taken by Edward I of England and later held by Robert the Bruce against Edward III, only to be blown up in 1692 to prevent it from falling to the Jacobites. It's pretty dilapidated today, but looks particularly splendid floodlit at night when all the crowds have gone. The castle receives more visitors each year than any other historic site in the Highlands, and the pressures are inevitably taking their toll: a major project is under way to create a larger car park and visitor centre built into the hillside between the main road and the castle.

Practicalities

There's a good range of accommodation around Drumnadrochit, and in the adjoining village of Lewiston. Two very welcoming **B&Bs** are *Gilliflowers* (☎01456/450641, *gillyflowers@cali.co.uk*; ①), a renovated farmhouse tucked away down a country lane in Lewiston, or the modern *Drumbuie* (☎01456/450634; ①), on the northern approach to Drumnadrochit, which has great views and a resident herd of Highland cattle. **Hotels** include the pleasant and secluded *Benleva* (☎01456/450288; ③), between Lewiston and the loch. Two miles west from Drumnadrochit along the Cannich road is a particularly relaxed country-house hotel, *Polmailly House* (☎01456/450343, *polmailyhousehotel@btinternet.com*; ⑤); it's very family-friendly and there's acres of space, a swimming pool, sauna, riding, and sailing on Loch Ness. For **hostel** beds, head to the immaculate and friendly *Loch Ness Backpackers Lodge* (☎01456/450807, *hostel@lochnessbackpackers.freeserve.co.uk*), at Coiltie Farmhouse in Lewiston; follow the sign to the left when coming from Drumnadrochit. As well as dorm beds, it has one double room (①), and excellent facilities, including boat trips and recommended walks.

All the hotels in the area serve good bar **food**; in Drumnadrochit the *Glen Café* has a short and simple menu with basic grills, while the slightly more upmarket *Fiddlers' Café Bar*, next door to the *Glen* on the village green, offers local steaks, salmon and appetizing home-baked pizza; it also rents out good-quality **mountain bikes** (☎01456/450223), and provides maps and rain capes on request.

Glen Urquhart and Glen Affric

You can head west from Drumnadrochit on the A831 through **Glen Urquhart**, a fairly open valley with farmland giving way to scrubby woodland and heather as you near **CANNICH**. The **youth hostel** here (☎01456/415244 or central reservations ☎0541/553255; April–Oct) makes a good base for exploring **Glen Affric**, claimed by many to be Scotland's loveliest valley. It's real calendar stuff, with a rushing river and Caledonian pine and birch woods opening out onto an island-studded loch that was considerably enlarged after the building of the dam, one of many hydroelectric schemes around here. Hemmed in by a string of Munros, the glen is great for picnics and pottering, particularly on a calm and sunny day, when the still loch reflects the islands and surrounding hills.

The area also offers some tremendous **hiking**. Among the most popular routes is the one winding west through Kintail to Shiel Bridge, on the west coast near Kyle of Lochalsh (about 25 miles), which takes at least two full days; a remote but recently revamped **youth hostel** (no phone; April–Oct) makes a convenient stopover halfway into the walk on the banks of the burn above Loch Affric. The trail is easy to follow, but can get horrendously boggy if there's been a lot of rain, so allow plenty of time and take adequate wet-weather gear, as well as the relevant Ordnance Survey map.

Inverness

INVERNESS, 105 miles northwest of Aberdeen on the A96 and 114 miles north of Perth on the A9, is the largest town in the Highlands – a good base for day-trips and a jumping-off point for many of the more remote parts of the region. **Buses** and **trains** leave for communities right across the far north of Scotland, and it isn't uncommon for people from as far afield as Thurso, Durness and Kyle of Lochalsh to travel down for a day's shopping here, Britain's most northerly chain-store centre. Though boasting few conventional sights, the town's setting on the leafy banks of the River Ness is appealing. Crowned by a pink crenellated **castle** and lavishly decorated with flowers – for which the town has won several awards – the compact centre has retained much of its medieval street layout (although unsightly concrete blocks overshadow the period buildings in places), while the salmon-packed River Ness, which flows through the centre, is lined with leafy parks and prosperous-looking stone houses, including the excellent **Balnain House**, where you can learn about and listen to all forms of Highland music, including whatever noise you can manage to squeeze out of the set of bagpipes left out for you to try.

Some history

Inverness's sheltered **harbour** and proximity to the open sea made it an important entrepôt and shipbuilding centre during medieval times. David I, who first imposed a feudal system on Scotland, erected a **castle** on the banks of the Ness to oversee maritime trade in the early twelfth century, promoting it to royal burgh status soon after. Bolstered by receipts from the lucrative export of leather, salmon and timber, the town grew to become the kingdom's most prosperous northern outpost, and an obvious target for the marauding Highlanders who plagued this remote border area.

A second wave of growth occurred during the eighteenth century as the Highland cattle trade flourished. The arrival of the **Caledonian Canal** and **rail** links with the east and south brought further prosperity, heralding a tourist boom that reached a fashionable zenith in the Victorian era, fostered by the British royal family's enthusiasm for all things Scottish. Over the last thirty years, the town has become one of the fastest-expanding in Britain, with its population virtually doubling due to the growing tourist industry and improved communications.

Arrival and information

Inverness **airport** (☎01463/232471) is at Dalcross, seven miles east of the town; from here the #11 **bus** (Mon–Sat every 1hr–1hr 30min, check times on ☎01343/222244; 20min; £2.50) goes into town, and a **taxi** costs around £10. The **bus station** (☎01463/233371) and **train station** (☎0345/484950) both lie just off Academy Street to the east of the town centre. The **tourist office** (June to mid-July Mon–Fri 9am–6pm, Sat & Sun 9am–5pm; mid-July to Aug Mon–Fri 9am–8.30pm, Sat & Sun 9am–6pm; Sept–May Mon–Fri 9am–5pm, Sat 10am–4pm; ☎01463/234353) is in a 1960s block on Castle Wynd, just five minutes' walk from

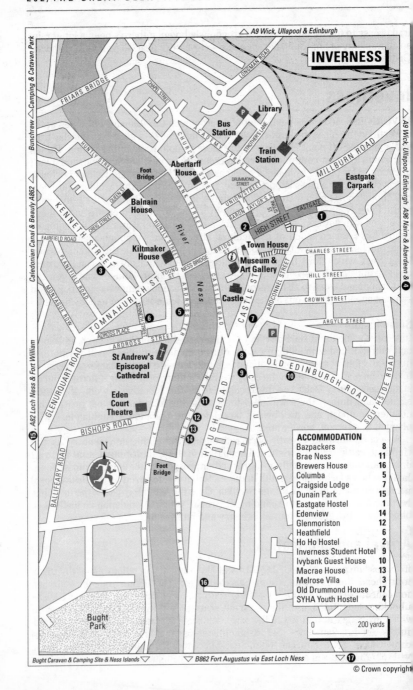

INVERNESS

A9 Wick, Ullapool & Edinburgh

Bunchrew △ Camping & Catavan Park

A9 Wick, Ullapool, Edinburgh, A96 Nairn & Aberdeen

LONGMAN ROAD

FRIARS BRIDGE

CHAPEL STREET

Library

P

Bus Station

ACADEMY ST

CHURCH STREET

STROTHERS LANE

Train Station

MILLBURN ROAD

Eastgate Carpark

HUNTLY STREET

Foot Bridge

Abertarff House

BANK STREET

DRUMMOND STREET

UNION STREET

Eastgate

Caledonian Canal & Beauly A862

Fairfield Road

KENNETH STREET

QUEEN ST

GREIG STREET

Balnain House

River Ness

BARON TAYLOR'S ST

INGLIS ST

BARON TAYLOR'S ST

HIGH STREET

EASTGATE

2

1

CHARLES STREET

HILL STREET

CROWN STREET

TOMNAHURICH ST

HUNTLY STREET

Kiltmaker House

YOUNG ST

NESS BRIDGE

BRIDGE ST

Town House

i Museum & Art Gallery

CASTLE ROAD

ARDCONNEL STREET

3

PLANEFIELD ROAD

MONTAGUE ROW

FAIRFIELD ROAD

ARDROSS STREET

Castle

5

6

ARDROSS PLACE

ARDROSS STREET

ARGYLE STREET

7

KENNETH STREET

GLENURQUHART ROAD

St Andrew's Episcopal Cathedral

NESS BANK

OLD EDINBURGH ROAD

8

9

10

SOUTHSIDE ROAD

A82 Loch Ness & Fort William

Eden Court Theatre

BISHOPS ROAD

CULDUTHEL ROAD

HAUGH ROAD

11

12

13

14

BALLIFEARY ROAD

N

Foot Bridge

LADIES WALK

NESS WALK

16

Bught Park

15

△ A82 Loch Ness & Fort William

ACCOMMODATION	
Bazpackers	8
Brae Ness	11
Brewers House	16
Columba	5
Craigside Lodge	7
Dunain Park	15
Eastgate Hostel	1
Edenview	14
Glenmoriston	12
Heathfield	6
Ho Ho Hostel	2
Inverness Student Hotel	9
Ivybank Guest House	10
Macrae House	13
Melrose Villa	3
Old Drummond House	17
SYHA Youth Hostel	4

0   200 yards

Bught Caravan & Camping Site & Ness Islands ▽   ▽ B862 Fort Augustus via East Loch Ness   ▽ **17**

© Crown copyright

TOURS AND CRUISES

Inverness is the departure point for a range of day **tours** and **cruises** to nearby attractions, including Loch Ness and the Moray Firth. Among the most popular is Guide Friday's open-topped double-decker tour of **Inverness** (May–Sept every 45min; 30min; £5), which you can hop on and off all day; the bus also goes out to **Culloden** (1hr 20min; £6.50). Tickets can be bought on the buses, which leave from Bridge Street near the tourist office, or at Guide Friday's booth in the train station (May–Oct Mon–Fri & Sun 9am–5.30pm, Sat 8.30am–5.45pm; July–Sept also Mon–Fri till 8.30pm), which also acts as a booking agent for the tours below. In addition, the useful Highland County Tourist Trail bus (every 2hr 10.15am– 4.15pm; £4.50 for hop-on, hop-off ticket) leaves from outside the tourist office, stopping at the bus station, Fort George, Cawdor Castle and Culloden, then returning to the tourist office.

There are various **Loch Ness** tours leaving from the tourist office, such as a half-day trip including a short cruise on the loch, and visits to the **monster exhibition** at **Drumnadrochit** and **Urquhart Castle** (£8.50 excluding admission fees), or a full-day trip right round the loch, including a boat ride (£13). By far the most original tour is **Gordon's Minibus** (☎01463/731202), a history and nature tour run by a charismatic doctor of marine biology, which also goes out on a boat on the loch – a day-trip (10am–4pm) costs £8.90. Longer **boat trips** on Loch Ness are run morning and afternoon by Jacobite Cruises (☎01463/233999; April–Oct) – a courtesy bus operates from the Tourist Office down to the dock at Tomnahurich Canal Bridge on Glenurquhart Road, a mile and a half south of the town centre. Meanwhile, an entertaining if slightly bizarre **Terror Tour** takes groups on foot around the town centre (daily 7pm from the tourist office; £5.50; ☎01463/768652), with grisly tales of ghosts, torture and witches told along the way.

Good outings further afield include the day-trips run by Stagecoach buses to **Ullapool**, **Lochinver**, **Durness** and **Smoo Cave**, which leaves from the tourist office and stops at several youth hostels en route (£15, or £19 if the trip is spread over four days). Finally, the Orkney Bus leaves Inverness bus station every day during the summer for a gruelling full-day whistle-stop tour of the **Orkney** islands (£42; advance bookings may be made at the tourist office or on ☎01955/611353).

See p.211 for details of **dolphin**-spotting cruises on the Moray Firth. Tickets for all tours are available from the tourist office.

the station. It stocks a wide range of literature on the area, can book local accommodation for a £1.50 fee, and the friendly staff also hand out useful free maps of the town and environs.

Accommodation

Inverness is one of the few places in the Highlands where you're unlikely to have problems finding **accommodation**, although in July and August you'll have to book ahead. You can reserve a bed through the tourist office, or in the train station concourse at the Thomas Cook booth, but bear in mind that both places levy a booking fee, and charge the hotel or guest-house owner a hefty commission, which is then passed on to you in your room tariff. Inverness boasts several good **hotels**, and nearly every street in the older residential areas of town has a sprinkling of **B&Bs**. Good places to look include both banks of the river south of the Ness Bridge, and Kenneth Street and its offshoots on the west side of the river.

There are several budget travellers' **hostels** in town, all reasonably central, and a couple of large **campsites**, one near the Ness Islands and the other further out to the west.

Hotels

Brae Ness, Ness Bank (☎01463/712266). A homely Georgian hotel overlooking the river and St Andrews Cathedral, with a non-smoking licensed restaurant for residents. April–Oct only. ③.

Columba, Ness Walk (☎01463/231391). Huge, central hotel opposite the castle and just over the bridge from the town centre, whose tariffs, which include breakfast, drop at weekends. Popular with bus parties and businesspeople. ④.

Dunain Park (☎01463/230512, *dunainparkhotel@btinternet.com*). Luxurious country-house hotel off the A82 Fort William road, about three miles from the centre of town. Excellent food and beautiful rooms. ⑧.

Glenmoriston, 20 Ness Bank (☎01463/223777). Very classy and comfortable hotel slap on the riverside, with well-appointed rooms and a topnotch Italian restaurant. ⑥.

B&Bs

Brewers House, 2 Moray Park, Island Bank Road (☎01463/235557). A welcoming B&B in a characterful old house a little further down the river than some pricier guest houses, but still an easy stroll from the centre. ①.

Craigside Lodge, 4 Gordon Terrace (☎01463/231576). Spacious rooms, great views, and close to the centre. Non-smoking. ②.

Edenview, 26 Ness Bank (☎01463/234397). Very pleasant B&B in a riverside location as good as the more expensive hotels, 5min walk from the centre; non-smoking. ②.

Heathfield, 2 Kenneth St (☎01463/230547). A very comfortable and friendly B&B at the quiet end of a street packed with B&Bs. All rooms have central heating and some are en suite; non-smoking. ①.

Ivybank Guest House, 28 Old Edinburgh Rd (☎01463/232796). A grand Georgian home just up the hill from the castle, with open fires and a lovely wooden interior. ②.

Macrae House, 24 Ness Bank (☎01463/243658). Right on the river, friendly, and with large, comfortable rooms. Non-smoking. ②.

Melrose Villa, 35 Kenneth St (☎01463/233745). Very family-friendly, with excellent breakfasts. Three singles as well as doubles and twins, with most rooms en suite. ①.

Old Drummond House, Oak Avenue (☎01463/226301). Part of a nicely renovated 200-year-old mansion at the quiet end of a suburban avenue, a mile or so from the centre. ①.

Hostels

Bazpackers, top of Castle Street (☎01463/717663). The most homely and relaxed of the town's hostels, with thirty beds including two double rooms and a twin; some dorms are mixed. Has good views and a garden, which is used for barbecues, as well as the usual cooking facilities; non-smoking.

Eastgate Hostel, Eastgate (☎01463/718756, *info@eastgatehostel.com*). Well-maintained former hotel above *Le Déja Vu* restaurant. Sleeps 38 in six-bed dorms and two twin rooms. Free tea and coffee is provided; no curfew.

Ho Ho Hostel, 23a High St (☎01463/221225). Formerly the grand Highland Club, a town base for lairds; now a large hostel with big rooms which tends to attract a partying crowd.

Inverness Student Hotel, 8 Culduthel Rd (☎01463/236556). A busy fifty-bed hostel with the usual facilities and fine views over the river. Part of the Macbackpackers group, so expect minibus tours to pull in most days.

SYHA Hostel, Victoria Drive, off Millburn Road, about three-quarters of a mile from the centre (☎01463/231771, central reservations ☎0541/553255). One of SYHA's flagship new hos els, fully equipped with large kitchens and communal areas, eco-friendly facilities and ten our-bed family rooms among the 188-bed total, but all rather soulless.

Campsites

Bught Caravan and Camping Site, Bught Park (☎01463/236920). Inverness's main campsite, on the west bank of the river near the sports centre. Good facilities, but it can get very crowded at the height of the season.

Bunchrew Caravan and Camping Park, Bunchrew, three miles west of Inverness on the A862 (☎237802). Well-equipped site on the shores of the Beauly Firth, with hot water, showers, laundry and a shop. It's very popular with families, so you'll have to contend with kids as well as midges.

The Town

The logical place to begin a tour of Inverness is the central **Town House** on High Street. Built in 1878, this Gothic pile hosted Prime Minister Lloyd George's emergency meeting to discuss the Irish crisis in September 1921, and now accommodates council offices. There's nothing of note inside, but the old **Mercat Cross** next to the main entrance is worth a look. The cross stands opposite a small square formerly used by merchants and traders and above the ancient *clach-na-cudainn*, or "stone of tubs" – so called because washerwomen used to rest their buckets on it on their way back from the river. A local superstition holds that, as long as the stone remains in place, Inverness will continue to prosper.

Looming above the Town House and dominating the horizon is **Inverness Castle** (mid-May to Sept Mon–Sat 10am–5pm; £3), a predominantly nineteenth-century red-sandstone edifice perched picturesquely above the river. The original castle formed the core of the ancient town, which had rapidly developed as a port trading with Europe after its conversion to Christianity by St Columba in the sixth century. Two famous Scots monarchs were associated with the building: **Robert the Bruce** wrested it back from the English during the Wars of Independence, destroying it in the process; and **Mary, Queen of Scots** had the governor of the second castle hanged from its ramparts after he had refused her entry in 1562. This structure was also destined for destruction, held by the Jacobites in both the 1715 and the 1745 rebellions, and blown up by them to prevent it falling into government hands. Today's edifice houses the Sheriff Court and, in summer, the **Castle Garrison Encounter**, an entertaining and noisy interactive exhibition, in which the visitor plays the role of a new recruit in the eighteenth-century Hanoverian army. At around 7.30pm during the summer, a lone piper clad in full Highland garb performs for tourists on the castle esplanade. The statue of a woman staring south from the terrace is a memorial to **Flora MacDonald**, the clanswoman who helped Bonnie Prince Charlie escape to Skye in the wake of Culloden.

Below the castle, the **Inverness Museum and Art Gallery** (Mon–Sat 9am–5pm; free) on Castle Wynd gives a good general overview of the development of the Highlands. Informative sections on geology, geography and history cover the ground floor, while upstairs you'll find a muddled selection of silver, taxidermy, weapons and bagpipes, alongside a mediocre art gallery.

Leading north from the Town House, medieval **Church Street** is home to the town's oldest-surviving buildings. On the corner with Bridge Street stands the **Steeple** (1791), whose spire had to be straightened after an earth tremor in 1816.

Further down Church Street is **Abertarff House**, reputedly the oldest complete building in Inverness and distinguished by its stepped gables and circular stair tower. It was erected in 1593 and is now owned by the NTS. The **Old High Church** (Fri noon–2pm & during services; tour at 12.30pm), founded by St Columba in 1171 and rebuilt on several occasions since, stands just along the street, hemmed in by a walled graveyard. Any Jacobites who survived the massacre of Culloden were brought here and incarcerated prior to their execution in the cemetery. If you take the guided tour, you'll be shown bullet holes left on gravestones by the firing squads.

Balnain House

One of Scotland's most novel museums stands over the footbridge that crosses the Ness just below the Old High Church. An immaculately restored, white-painted Georgian mansion, **Balnain House** (July & Aug Mon–Fri 10am–10pm, Sat & Sun 10–6pm; Sept–June Mon–Sat 10am–5pm; £2) has a modest performance space and an interactive exhibition that will appeal as much to the casual visitor as folk-music aficionados. The exhibition traces the development of Highland **music** from its prehistoric roots (ringing rocks, cast-bronze battle horns and ancient Gaelic songs) to modern electric folk-rock. CD listening posts and a short video allow you to sample snatches of numerous other musical styles from the region, including clan-gathering and spell-casting songs, complex Shetland fiddle reels and the haunting singing of the Hebrides. You can even try to play various instruments, including the bagpipes, clarsach and fiddle. There's also a congenial café downstairs where ceilidhs, music sessions and recitals take place (see p.208), and a shop selling traditional Highland instruments, CDs and cassettes.

Elsewhere on the west bank

A five-minute walk upstream (south) from Balnain House brings you to the **Kiltmaker Centre** on the corner of Huntly Street (mid-May to Sept Mon–Sat 9am–10pm, Sun 10am–5pm; Oct to mid-May Mon–Sat 9am–5.30pm; £2). Entered through the factory shop, a small visitor centre sets out everything you ever wanted to know about **tartan**. The finished products are, of course, on sale in the showroom downstairs, along with all manner of Highland knitwear, woven woollies and Harris tweed.

Rising from the west bank directly opposite the castle, **St Andrews Episcopal Cathedral** was intended by its architects to be one of the grandest buildings in Scotland. However, funds ran out before the giant twin spires of the original design could be completed, hence Inverness isn't officially a city, but a town. The interior is pretty ordinary, too, though it does claim an unusual octagonal chapterhouse.

From the cathedral, you can wander a mile or so upriver to the peaceful **Ness Islands**, an attractive, informal public park reached and linked by footbridges. Laid out with mature trees and shrubs, the islands are the favourite haunt of local anglers. Further upstream still, the river runs close to the **Caledonian Canal**, designed by Thomas Telford in the early nineteenth century as a link between the east and west coasts, joining lochs Ness, Oich, Lochy and Linnhe. Today its main use is recreational, and there are cruises through part of it to Loch Ness, while the towpath provides relaxing walks with good views.

Three miles to the west of the town, on the top of **Craig Phadrig** hill, there's a vitrified **Iron Age fort**, reputed to be where the Pictish King Brude received S

THE TRUTH ABOUT TARTAN

Tartan is big business and an essential part of the tourist industry. Every year, hundreds of visitors return home clutching tartan monsters, foreign-made souvenirs tied with foreign-made tartan ribbon, or lengths of cloth inspiringly named Loch This, Ben That or Glen Something-Else, fondly believing that they are bringing authentic history with them. The reality is that tartan is an ancient Highland art form that romantic fiction and commercial interest have enclosed within an almost insurmountable wall of myth.

Real tartan, the kind that long ago was called **"Helande"**, was a fine, hard and almost showerproof cloth spun in Highland villages from the wool of the native sheep, dyed with preparations of local plants and with patterns woven by artist-weavers. It was worn as a huge single piece of cloth, which was belted around the waist and draped over the upper body, rather like a knee-length toga. The colours of old tartans were clear but soft, and the broken pattern gave superb camouflage; unlike modern versions, whose colours are either so strong that the pattern is swamped or so dull that it has no impact.

Tartan did not become popular in the Lowlands until the beginning of the eighteenth century, when it was adopted as the anti-Union badge of **Jacobitism**, and it was not until after 1745 that the Lowlands took it over completely. The 1747 ban on wearing tartan put an end to the making of tartan in Highland glens; instead, whole villages on the Lowland fringes devoted themselves to supplying the needs of the army and emigrant Highlanders in the colonies and, after the ban was lifted in 1782, those of the home market. The wars abated and the colonies became more self-sufficient, and what had become a major industry faced hard times. At first the remedy was sought in a proliferation of new pattern, for, despite the existence of a handful with clan names, tartan was (in the main) a small-scale fashion fabric. Then Sir Walter Scott set to work glamorizing the clans, George IV visited Edinburgh in 1822 and wore a kilt, and, finally, Queen Victoria set the royal seal of approval on both the Highlands and tartan.

At about this time, the idea that every clan had its own distinguishing tartan became highly fashionable. To have the right to wear tartan, one had to belong, albeit remotely, to a clan, and so the way was paved for the "what's-my-tartan?" lists that appear in the tartan picture books and the souvenir shops. Great feats of genealogical gymnastics were performed in the concoction of these lists, but they could not include every name, so "district", "national" and "political" tartans were developed.

Columba in the sixth century. The walls of the fort were built of stone laced with timber and, when the timber was set alight, some of the stone fused to glass – hence the term "vitrified". Waymarked forest trails start from the car parks at the bottom of the hill and lead up to the fort, though only the outline of its perimeter defences are now visible. Buses #3 and #12 from the town centre (Mon–Sat every 15min) drop you to the bottom of the hill.

Eating and drinking

Inverness has lots of **eating** places, including a few excellent-quality gourmet options, while for the budget-conscious there's no shortage of **pubs**, **cafés** and **restaurants** around the town centre. **Takeaways** cluster on Young Street, just across the river, and at the ends of Eastgate and Academy Street. Good places for

picnic food include *Crumbs* on Inglis Street, *The Gourmet's Lair* on Union Street, and *Lettuce Eat* on Drummond Street.

Restaurants

Café No. 1, 75 Castle St (☎01463/226200). By far the most ambitious cooking in the town centre, with an impressive contemporary approach and good local ingredients. Moderate–expensive.

Castle Restaurant, 41 Castle St. Classic, long-established café that does a roaring trade in down-to-earth Scottish food – meat pies, chicken and fish, dished up with piles of chips. Open at 8am for breakfast. Inexpensive. Closed Sun.

Le Déja Vu, 38 Eastgate (☎01463/231075). Unpretentious, relaxed place specializing in French country cooking using game, chicken, fish and shellfish. Great food, friendly service and good-value set menus. Moderate.

Dunain Park Hotel Restaurant, Dunain Park (☎01463/230512). Award-winning Scots-French restaurant in a country-house hotel set in lovely gardens just southwest of town; a good choice for a leisurely dinner. Expensive.

Girvan's, 2–4 Stephen's Brae, at the eastern end of the High Street (☎01463/711900). Uncomplicated but decent restaurant – serving Scottish meat and fish dishes – and daytime patisserie.

Glen Mhor Hotel, 9 Ness Bank (☎01463/234308). *Nico's Bistro* at the back of the hotel specializes in well-presented Scottish cuisine (mainly local salmon, beef and game) at moderate prices. The *Riverview Restaurant* at the front is also good. Expensive.

Littlejohn's, Church Street (☎01463/713005). One of a chain, which serves a wide range of food, with many Mexican touches. Friendly and reasonable value. Moderate.

Rajah, Church Street end of Post Office Avenue (☎01463/237190). An excellent Indian restaurant, tucked away in a backstreet basement. Moderate.

Riva, 4–6 Ness Walk (☎01463/237377). Reasonably authentic modern Italian bistro/café beside the river with antipastia, decent mains and good coffee and cakes. Moderate. Upstairs, inexpensive pasta dishes can be had at *Pazzo's Pasta Bar* (evenings only; closed Mon & Sun).

River Café and Restaurant, 10 Bank St, near the Grieg Street footbridge (☎01463/714884). Healthy wholefood lunches and evening meals, with a great selection of freshly baked cakes and good coffee. Inexpensive–moderate.

Nightlife and entertainment

The liveliest **nightlife** in Inverness revolves around the pubs and the town's two main dance venues. The far end of Academy Street has a cluster of good **pubs**; the public bar of the *Phoenix* is the most original town-centre place, while the ersatz-Irish *Lafferty's* next door often has live music, as does the *Blackfriars* across the street. In a basement beside the river on the corner of Bank and Bridge streets, *Johnny Foxes* also drapes itself in shamrocks but draws eager crowds to its regular live music sessions. Over on Bridge Street, the *Gellions* is a legendary watering hole with several other congenial places in between.

The town's liveliest **nightclub** is *Mr G's* on Castle Street, which has queues of the town's youth forming outside on Fridays and Saturdays. On the north side of the bus station, the larger *Blue* hosts local and nationally known DJs, plus occasional bands. The basement café at Balnain House museum, on the east bank of the Ness, opposite Grieg Street footbridge, has informal **folk sessions** that sometimes turn into ceilidhs on Tuesday and Thursday nights through summer, and Thursday nights in winter. In addition, the museum stages regular recitals and workshops by Highland musicians and touring artists; details of all these are posted in the café, and the lobby upstairs. Balnain House also occasionally hosts "The Tickled Rib", billed as the north's best comedy club – it is, in fact, the north's only comedy club. Finally, if you crave a strong infusion of tartan and **bagpipes**, the nightly "Scottish Showtime" at the *Cummings Hotel* on Church Street is the place to be: the show has been running for years and is probably the most polished of its kind you'll find.

Listings

Airport ☎01463/232471.

Bike rental Barney's, 35 Castle St (☎01463/232249).

Bookshops Leakey's, Greyfriars' Hall, Church Street (☎01463/239947), is a great spot to browse for secondhand books, with a café inside and a warming wood stove in winter; James Thin, 29 Union St (☎01463/233500), has an excellent range of Scottish books and maps; and Waterstone's can be found at 50–52 High St (☎01463/717474).

Car rental Budget is on Railway Terrace, behind the train station (☎01463/713333); Europcar has an office at the Highlander Service Station, Millburn Road, and a desk at the airport (☎01463/235337); Hertz is in the train station and at the airport (☎01463/711479); Thrifty is at 33 Harbour Rd (☎01463/224466); and Sharps Reliable Wrecks (☎01463/236684) is based at Station Square.

Cinemas The Eden Court Theatre and the attached Riverside Screen, on the banks of the Ness, host touring theatre productions, concerts and films; La Scala on Strother's Lane, just off Academy Street, has two screens; Warner Village, on the A96 Nairn road about two miles from the town centre, boasts seven screens.

Dentist V.R. Marden, 4 Fraser St (☎01463/242344).

Exchange Try American Express agents Alba Travel, 43 Church St (Mon–Sat 9am–5pm; ☎01463/239188); the tourist office's bureau de change (same hours as tourist office) changes cash and currency for £2.50 or 2.5 percent; and Thomas Cook, 9–13 Inglis St (Mon–Fri 9am–5pm; ☎01463/711921).

Hospital Accident and emergency care is provided by Raigmore Hospital (☎01463/704000), on the southeastern outskirts of town close to the A9.

Internet Email access is available at MTC, 2 Grant St (Mon–Thurs 9am–5pm, Fri 9am–4.30pm).

Laundry 17 Young St (☎01463/242507).

Left luggage Train station lockers cost from £2 to £4 for 24hr; the left-luggage room in the bus station costs £1 per item (Mon–Sat 8.30am–6pm, Sun 10am–6pm).

Library Inverness library (☎01463/236463), housed in the Neoclassical building on the northeast side of the bus station, has an excellent genealogical research unit (Mon–Fri 10am–1pm & 2–5pm; ☎01463/220330). Consultations with the resident genealogist cost £12 per hour, but are free if shorter than 10min. An appointment is advisable.

Outdoor supplies Clive Rowland Outdoor Sports, 9 Bridge St (☎01463/238746); Graham Tiso, 41 High St (☎01463/716617).

Pharmacy Boots, Eastgate Shopping Centre (Mon–Fri 9am–5.30pm, Thurs 9am– 7pm, Sun noon–5pm; ☎01463/225167).

Post office 14–16 Queensgate (Mon–Thurs 9am–5.30pm, Fri 9.30am–5.30pm, Sat 9am–6pm; ☎0345/223344).

Public toilets Usually immaculate ones in Mealmarket Close, north side of High Street.

Sports centre Inverness sports centre and Aquadome leisure pool (Mon–Fri 7.30am–10pm, Sat & Sun 7.30am–9pm; ☎01463/667500), a mile or so south of the town centre off the A82, has a large pool, gym and other indoor sports facilities. Nearby is an ice rink (daily 2–4.30pm & 7–9.30pm).

Taxis Culloden Taxis (☎01463/790000); Rank Radio Taxis (☎01463/221111).

Around Inverness

As the capital and crux of the Highlands, Inverness lies within easy reach of some compelling scenery. Stretching southwest towards Fort William is the Great Glen, with the massed peaks of Glen Affric beyond. To the north is the huge, rounded form of Ben Wyvis, while to the east lies the **Moray Firth**, to some extent a commuter belt for Inverness, but also boasting a lovely coastline and a gentle, undulating green landscape that makes a fertile contrast to the windswept moorland and mountains that virtually surround it. The main attraction here is the battlesite at **Culloden**, where a small visitor centre and memorial stones recall the gruesome events which saw the end of Bonnie Prince Charlie's ill-fated Jacobite uprising of 1745–46. Not far from this are a couple more worthwhile historical sites, including the whimsical **Cawdor Castle**, featured in Shakespeare's *Macbeth*, and **Fort George**, one of several impressive Hanoverian bastions erected in the wake of the Jacobite rebellion. A little further east is the the low-key holiday resort of **Nairn**, with its long white-sand beaches and championship golf course.

West of Inverness, the Moray Firth becomes the **Beauly Firth**, a sheltered sea loch bounded by the Black Isle in the north and the wooded hills of the Aird to the south. The main settlement here is the village of Beauly, a sleepy spot with a ruined priory, but with most northbound traffic using the Kessock Bridge to cross the Moray Firth from Inverness this whole area is quieter, and the A862, which skirts the shoreline and the mud flats, offers a more scenic alternative to the faster A9.

Culloden

The windswept moorland of **CULLODEN** (site open all year; free; visitor centre open daily: Feb, March, Nov & Dec 10am–4pm; April–Oct 9am–6pm; £3.20; NTS), five miles east of Inverness, witnessed the last ever battle on British soil when, on April 16, 1746, the Jacobite cause was finally subdued – a turning point in the history of the Scottish nation.

The second Jacobite rebellion had begun on August 19, 1745, with the raising of the Stuarts' standard at **Glenfinnan** on the west coast (see p.225). Shortly after, Edinburgh fell into Jacobite hands, and Bonnie Prince Charlie began his march on London. The English, however, had appointed the ambitious young Duke of Cumberland to command their forces, and this, together with bad weather and lack of funds, eventually forced the Jacobites to retreat north. They ended up at Culloden, where, ill-fed and exhausted after a pointless night march, they were hopelessly outnumbered by the English. The open, flat ground of Culloden Moor was also totally unsuitable for the Highlanders' style of courageous but undisciplined fighting, which needed steep hills and lots of cover to provide the element of surprise, and they were routed. After the battle, in which 1500 Highlanders were slaughtered (many of them as they lay wounded on the battlefield), Bonnie Prince Charlie fled west to the hills and islands, where loyal Highlanders sheltered and protected him. He eventually escaped to France, leaving his erstwhile supporters to their fate – and, in effect, the end of the clan system. The clans were disarmed, the wearing of tartan and playing of bagpipes forbidden, and the chiefs became landlords greedy for higher and higher rents.

THE DOLPHINS OF MORAY FIRTH

The **Moray Firth**, a great wedge-shaped bay forming the eastern coastline of the Highlands, is one of only three areas of UK waters that supports a resident population of **dolphins**. Just over a hundred of these beautiful, intelligent marine mammals live in the estuary, the most northerly breeding ground for this particular species – the bottle-nosed dolphin (*Tursiops truncatus*) – in Europe, and you stand a good chance of spotting a few, either from the shore or a boat.

Tursiops truncatus is the largest dolphin in the world, typically growing to a length of around 13ft and weighing between 396 and 660 pounds. The adults sport a tall, sickle-shaped dorsal fin and a distinctive beak-like "nose", and usually live for around 25 years, although a number of fifty-year-old animals have been recorded. During the summer, herds of thirty to forty dolphins have been known to congregate in the Moray Firth; no one is exactly sure why, although experts believe the annual gatherings, which take place between late June and August, may be connected to the breeding cycle. Another peculiar trait of the Moray Firth school is its habit of killing porpoises. Several porpoise corpses with serrated tooth marks have been washed ashore in the area, the dolphins tossing dead or dying porpoises around in the waves as if for fun.

Both adults and calves frequently leap out of the water, "bow riding" in front of boats and performing elegant synchronized swimming routines together. This, of course, makes them spectacular animals to watch, and dolphin-spotting has become something of a craze in the Moray Firth area. One of the best places in Scotland, if not in Europe, to look for them is **Chanonry Point**, on the Black Isle (see p.263) – a spit of sand protruding into a narrow, deep channel, where converging currents bring fish close to the surface, and thus the dolphins close to shore; the hour or so before high tide is the most likely time to see them. **Kessock Bridge**, one mile north of Inverness, is another prime dolphin-spotting location. You can go all the way down to the beach at the small village of North Cessock, underneath the road bridge, where there's a decent place to have a drink at the pub in the *North Cessock Hotel*, or you can stop above the village in a car park just off the A9 at the **visitor centre** and listening post (daily 10am–5pm; ☎01463/731866; £1 for the whole season) set up by a team of zoologists from Aberdeen University studying the dolphins, where hydrophones allow you to eavesdrop on the clicks and whistles of underwater conversations.

In addition, several companies run **dolphin-spotting boat trips** around the Moray Firth. However, researchers claim that the increased traffic is causing the dolphins unnecessary stress, particularly during the all-important feeding period, when passing vessels are thought to force calves underwater for uncomfortably long periods. They have therefore devised a code of conduct for boat operators, based on the experiences of other countries where dolphin-watching has become disruptive. So if you decide to go on a spotting cruise, make sure the operator is a member of the Dolphin Space Programme's Accreditation Scheme. Operators currently accredited include Majestic Cruises, Inverness (☎01463/731661); Karl Nielsen, 21 Great Eastern Rd, Portessie, Buckie (☎01542/832289); Macaulay Charters, Inverness (☎01463/751263); Moray Firth Cruises, Shore Street, Inverness (☎01463/717900); and Dolphin Écosse, Bank House, High Street, Cromarty (☎01381/600323).

Culloden also unleashed an orgy of violent reprisals on Scotland, as unruly English troops raped and pillaged their way across the region; within a century, the Highland way of life had changed out of all recognition.

Today you can walk freely around the battle site; flags show the position of the two armies, and **clan graves** are marked by simple headstones. The **Field of the English**, for many years unmarked, is a mass grave for the fifty or so English soldiers who died. Half a mile east of the battlefield, just beyond the crossroads on the main road, is the **Cumberland Stone**, thought for many years to have been the point from where the duke watched the battle. It is more likely, however, that he was much further forward and simply used the stone for shelter. Thirty Jacobites were burnt alive outside the old **Leanach cottage** next to the visitor centre; inside, it has been restored to its eighteenth-century appearance. The **visitor centre** itself provides background information through detailed displays and a film show, as well as a short play set on the day of the battle, presented by local actors (June–Sept only; included in entry price), or you can take the evocative hour-long guided **walking tour** (June–Sept daily; £3). In April, on the Saturday closest to the date of the battle, there's a small commemorative service. The visitor centre has a reference library, and will check for you if you think you have an ancestor who died here. The site is served by Guide Friday **buses** from Bridge Street in Inverness (June–Sept 10 daily from 10.30am; last bus back to town leaves Culloden at 5.45pm; 25min) and Highland Country bus #12 from Inverness post office (Mon–Sat 8 daily), as well as Highland County's Tourist Trail circular service from outside the tourist office (June–Sept daily).

The Clava Cairns

If you're visiting Culloden with your own transport, make a short detour to the **CLAVA CAIRNS**, an impressive collection of prehistoric burial chambers clustered around the south bank of the River Nairn, a mile southeast of the battlefield. Erected some time before 2000 BC, the cairns, which are encircled by standing stones in a spinney of mature beech trees, are of two different kinds: one large and one very small **ring-cairn**; and two **passage graves**, which have a narrow passageway from edge to centre. Though cremated remains have been found in both types of structure, and unburnt remains discovered in the passage graves, little is known about the nomadic herdsmen who are thought to have built them.

Kilravock Castle

Surrounded by lawns and pine trees, **Kilravock** (pronounced "Kilrawk") **Castle** (April–Oct Wed 2–5.30pm, or by prior arrangement; ☎01667/493258; £3.50), five miles northeast of Culloden, is more like a stately home than a fortress. Dating from the fifteenth century, it is the seat of the Rose family, whose founding father, a Norman, settled here in 1190. The best-known Rose of Kilravock, however, is the one who entertained **Bonnie Prince Charlie** here on the eve of the battle of Culloden in 1745. Although not a Jacobite himself, the laird felt duty-bound by the traditional code of Highland hospitality to accommodate the rebel prince, even though he feared the consequences. According to one contemporary chronicler, the Duke of Cumberland rode out here himself on his 25th birthday to grill Rose over the affair, famously exclaiming, "I hear, sir, you've been entertaining my cousin!" He decided not to punish the Highlander, though, and for some reason left behind his knee-length **riding boots**, which are displayed in the castle, along with the bowl from which Bonnie Prince Charlie is alleged to have been served a glass of punch by his host.

Today, the Rose family maintain Kilravock as a wonderfully old-fashioned **guest house** (☎01667/493258; ②), whose spacious, well-appointed rooms are superb value if you don't mind the ban on alcohol and cigarettes, or grace being said before meals (the establishment is run according to strict Christian principles). In addition, garden enthusiasts should not miss the opportunity to visit the castle **grounds** (Mon–Sat 10am–4pm; £1.50), which harbour a tangle of woodland trails, while the castle's **restaurant** serves lunches and afternoon teas, as well as dinners (booking essential, on ☎01667/493258).

Cawdor Castle

The pretty, if slightly self-satisfied village of **CAWDOR**, eight miles east of Culloden, is the site of the **Cawdor Castle** (May to mid-Oct daily 10am–5.30pm; £5.40), apocryphally known as the setting for Shakespeare's *Macbeth* (the fulfilment of the witches' prediction that Macbeth was to become Thane of Cawdor sets off his tragic desire to be king). Though visitors descend here in their droves each summer because of the site's literary associations, the castle, which dates from the early fourteenth century, could not possibly have witnessed the grizzly historical events on which the Bard's drama was based. However, the immaculately restored monument – a fairy-tale affair of towers, turrets, hidden passageways, dungeons, gargoyles and crenellations whimsically shooting off from the original keep – is still well worth a visit.

The Cawdors have lived here for six centuries, and the castle still feels like a family home, albeit one with tapestries, pictures and opulent furniture. As you explore, look out for the Thorn Tree Room, a vaulted chamber complete with the remains of an ancient tree – carbon-dated to 1372 and an ancient pagan fertility symbol believed to ward off fairies and evil spirits. According to Cawdor family legend, the fourteenth-century Thane of Cawdor dreamed he should build on the spot where his donkey lay down to sleep after a day's wandering – the animal chose this tree, and building began immediately.

The **grounds** of the castle are possibly the best part of the visit, with an attractive walled garden, a topiarian maze, a small golf course, a putting green and nature trails. It's also worth visiting the village for a drink or meal at the traditional *Cawdor Tavern*, an old inn serving beautifully prepared local food. Highland **bus** #12 (Mon–Sat 8 daily; 35min) runs to Cawdor from Inverness post office, with the last bus back leaving the castle just after 6pm.

Fort George

Eight miles of undulating coastal farmland separate Cawdor Castle from **Fort George** (April–Sept daily 9.30am–6.30pm; Oct–March Mon–Sat 9.30am–4.30pm, Sun 2–4.30pm; £3.50), an old Hanoverian bastion considered by military architectural historians to be one of the finest fortifications in Europe. Crowning a sandy spit that juts into the middle of the Moray Firth, it was built (1747–69) as a base for George II's army, in case the Highlanders should attempt to rekindle the Jacobite flame. By the time of its completion, however, the uprising had been firmly quashed and the fort has been used ever since as a barracks; note the armed sentries at the main entrance and the periodic crack of live gunfire from the nearby firing ranges.

Apart from the sweeping panoramic **views** across the Firth from its ramparts, the main incentive to visit Fort George is the **Regimental Museum** of the

Queen's Own Highlanders. Displayed in polished glass cases is a predictable array of regimental silver, coins, moth-eaten uniforms and medals, along with some macabre war trophies, ranging from bloodstained nineteenth-century Sudanese battle robes to Iraqi gas masks gleaned in the Gulf War. The heroic deeds performed by various recipients of Victoria Crosses make compelling reading. The **chapel** is also worth a look: squat and solid outside, and all light and grace within.

Walking on the northern, grass-covered casemates, which look out into the estuary, you may be lucky enough to see the school of bottle-nosed **dolphins** (see p.211) swimming in with the tide. This is also a good spot for birdwatching: a colony of kittiwakes occupies the fort's slate rooftops, while the white-sand beach and mud flats below teem with waders and seabirds.

The easiest way to get to Fort George by public transport is by Highland **bus** #11B from Inverness post office (Mon–Sat 9 daily; 25min).

Nairn

One of the driest and sunniest places in the whole of Scotland, **NAIRN**, sixteen miles east of Inverness, began its days as a peaceful community of fishermen and farmers. The former spoke Gaelic, the latter English, allowing James VI to boast that a town in his kingdom was so large that people at one end of the main street could not understand those at the other end. Nairn became popular in Victorian times, when the train line offered a convenient link to its revitalizing sea air and mild climate, and today it still relies on tourism, with all the ingredients for a traditional seaside holiday – a sandy beach, ice-cream shops and fish-and-chip stalls. Its windy, coastal **golf course**, the Links, is one of the most popular in Scotland (☎01667/462787), and Thomas Telford's **harbour** is filled with leisure rather than fishing boats. Nearby, amid the huddled streets of old Fishertown – the town centre is known as new Fishertown – is the tiny **Fishertown Museum** (June–Aug Mon–Sat 10am–5pm; free), signposted from the town centre and the harbour. The more interesting exhibits focus on the parsimonious and puritanical life of the fishing families.

With a good map to help navigate the maze of minor roads, you can explore some pleasant countryside south of Nairn, particularly in the valley of the **River Findhorn**, with **Dulsie Bridge**, on the old military road linking Perth and Fort George, being a favourite local picnic spot. A few miles further south, the waters of **Lochindorb** surround a ruined thirteenth-century castle. The relative flatness of the land makes these roads ideal for cycling; a bike is also a great way to explore **Culbin Forest**, an unusual area of coastal forest northeast of Nairn where the trees were planted to stabilize an extensive area of sand dune. The forest, a Site of Special Scientific Interest, has a network of paths and information boards, along with picnic spots and plenty of wildlife, including an array of migrating waterfowl at the adjacent RSPB reserve of Culbin Sands.

Nairn's helpful **tourist office** is at 62 King St (Easter–May, Sept & Oct Mon–Sat 10am–5pm; June–Aug daily 9am–6pm; ☎01667/452753). For **accommodation**, try *Clifton House*, Viewfield Street (☎01667/453119; ⑥), which is stacked with antiques and paintings and hosts music and arts events, or *Greenlawns*, 13 Seafield St (☎01667/452738; ②), a spacious and friendly B&B with most rooms en suite. However, the most luxurious option is the *Golf View Hotel* (☎01667/452301; ⑥), overlooking the golf course and sea, where delicious, well-priced informal meals are served in the conservatory, also with great views. The plainer *Longhouse Restaurant* (☎01667/455532), on the corner of Harbour Street and Watson's Place, has moderately priced seafood and inexpensive light meals on its menu. **Bike rental** is available from Nairn Watersports (☎01667/455416), down by the harbour.

Beauly

The sleepy stone-built village of **BEAULY** lies ten miles west of Inverness, at the point where the Beauly River – one of Scotland's most renowned salmon-fishing streams – flows into the Firth. It's ranged around a single main street that widens into a spacious marketplace, at the north end of which stand the skeletal red sandstone remains of **Beauly Priory** (daily 9.30am–6pm; £1.20; HS). Founded in 1230 by the Bisset family for the Valliscaulian order, and later becoming Cistercian, it was destroyed during the Reformation and is now in ruins.

The locals will tell you the name Beauly was bestowed on the village by Mary, Queen of Scots, who, when staying at the priory in the summer of 1564, allegedly cried, "Ah, quelle beau lieu!" (What a beautiful place!). In fact, it derives from the Lovat family, who came to the region from France with the Normans in the eleventh century. Among the more notorious members of this dynasty was Lord Simon Lovat, whose legendary misadventures included a kidnap attempt on a 9-year-old girl, followed by forced marriage to her mother. He was outlawed for this, but went on to play an active role in the Jacobite uprisings, expediently swapping sides whenever the one he was spying for looked likely to lose. Such chicanery earned him the nickname "The Old Fox of '45", but failed to save him from the chop: Lovat was eventually beheaded in London (ironically enough, for backing the wrong side at Culloden). The Victorian **monument** in the square, opposite the Priory, commemorates the more illustrious career of one of Simon Lovat's descendants, Simon Joseph, the sixteenth Lord Lovat, who founded a fighting unit during the Boer War. If you want to find out more about the colourful Lovats and other scions of the Fraser clan, head to the restored **Wardlaw Mausoleum** at Kirkhill, about four miles east of Beauly signposted off the A862 (May–Sept Wed & Sat 2–4pm; free), which was built in 1634 but includes a fourteenth-century window from a church previously built on the site.

As a change from distilleries, you can visit a **winery** at **Moniack Castle** (March–Oct Mon–Sat 10am–5pm; Jan, Feb, Nov & Dec Mon–Sat 11am–4pm; £2), also four miles east of Beauly, just off the main Inverness road (A862), where you can taste and buy over 25 different home-made products, including silver-birch or meadowsweet wine, sloe-berry liqueur, juniper chutney and rosehip jam.

Practicalities

Beauly has a small community tourist office in a cabin beside the priory (June–Sept daily 10am–8pm), which has information on good walks in the area. The town has a surprising number of **places to stay**. The most comfortable is the modern *Priory Hotel* (☎01463/782309; ④) at the top of town, which also has a good restaurant. The *Lovat Arms Hotel* (☎01463/782313; ④), at the opposite end of the main street, is a more traditional option and hosts occasional ceilidhs. If you're looking for cheaper accommodation, try the *Heathmount Guest House* (☎01463/782411; ②), one of several pleasant **B&Bs** in a row of large Victorian houses just south of the *Lovat* on the main road.

Finding somewhere to **eat** in Beauly isn't a problem, either. Both of the town's hotels sport pricey à la carte restaurants, while the *Archdale Hotel's* cosy café, at the bottom of the square, serves a range of inexpensive snacks and main meals, including several vegetarian specialities. Otherwise, head for the *Beauly Tandoori*, which dishes up moderately priced Indian food, or the *Friary* chippy; both are on the main square.

Muir of Ord

MUIR OF ORD, a sprawling village four miles north of Beauly, is visited in huge numbers for the **Glen Ord Distillery** (March–Oct Mon–Fri 9.30am–5pm; July & Aug also Sat 9.30am–5pm, Sun 12.30–5pm; £2), on its northern outskirts. Its well-laid-out visitor centre explains the mysteries of whisky production with a tour that winds up in the cellars, where you get to sample a selection of the famously peaty Glen Ord malts, most of which find their way into well-known blends on sale in the distillery shop.

You can either visit Ord on a guided tour from Inverness (details from the tourist office), or take the infrequent Stagecoach Inverness **bus** #18 from Union Street in Inverness (Mon–Sat 3 daily); more helpfully, the **train** from Inverness stops at Muir of Ord station (Mon–Sat 6–7 daily; June–Sept also Sun 4 daily; 15min).

travel details

Trains

Fort William to: Crianlarich (Mon–Sat 3–4 daily, Sun 1–3 daily; 1hr 40min); Glasgow (Mon–Sat 3 daily, Sun 1–2 daily; 4hr); London (1 nightly; 12hr); Mallaig (Mon–Sat 4 daily, Sun 1–3 daily; 1hr 25min); Spean Bridge (Mon–Sat 4 daily, Sun 3 daily; 13min); Tulloch (Mon–Sat 4 daily, Sun 3 daily; 30min).

Inverness to: Aberdeen (Mon–Sat 11 daily, Sun 7 daily; 2hr 25min); Aviemore (Mon–Sat 8 daily, Sun 4 daily; 40min); Edinburgh (Mon–Sat 8 daily, Sun 3 daily; 3hr 30min); Glasgow (Mon–Sat 3 daily, Sun 2 daily; 3hr 35min); Kyle of Lochalsh (Mon–Sat 3–4 daily, plus Sun 2 daily in summer; 2hr 40min); London (Mon–Fri & Sun 2 daily, Sat 1 daily; 8hr 35min); Nairn (Mon–Sat 11 daily, Sun 7 daily; 15min); Thurso (Mon–Sat 3 daily, plus Sun 2 daily in summer; 3hr 45min); Wick (Mon–Sat 3 daily, plus Sun 2 daily in summer; 3hr 45min).

Buses

Fort William to: Aviemore (2 daily; 1hr 30min); Ballachulish (12 daily; 25min); Drumnadrochit (6 daily; 1hr 30min); Fort Augustus (6 daily; 1hr); Glasgow (5 daily; 3hr); Glencoe (6 daily; 30min); Inverness (6 daily; 2hr); Mallaig (1–2 daily; 2hr); Oban (4 daily; 1hr 30min).

Inverness to: Aberdeen (hourly; 3hr 40min); Aviemore (Mon–Sat 15 daily, Sun 12 daily; 40min); Cromarty (4 daily; 45min); Drumnadrochit (6 daily; 25min); Durness (May to early Oct 1 daily; 5hr); Fort Augustus (6 daily; 1hr); Fort William (6 daily; 2hr); Glasgow (7 daily; 3hr 35min–4hr 25min); Kyle of Lochalsh (3–4 daily; 2hr); Nairn (Mon–Sat hourly; 35min); Newtonmore (8 daily; 1hr 10min); Oban (Mon–Sat 2 daily; 4hr); Perth (10 daily; 2hr 35min); Portree (3–4 daily; 3hr 20min); Thurso (Mon–Sat 5 daily, Sun 4 daily; 3hr 30 min); Ullapool (2–4 daily; 1hr 25min); Wick (Mon–Sat 3 daily; 1hr 55min).

Flights

Inverness to: Amsterdam (1 daily; 1hr 35min); Edinburgh (Mon–Fri 1 daily; 50min); Glasgow (Mon–Fri 2 daily; 50min); Kirkwall (Mon–Fri 2 daily; 40min); London (4 daily; 1hr 25min); Shetland (Mon–Fri 1 daily; 1hr 50min); Stornoway (Mon–Sat 2 daily; 40min).

CHAPTER FOUR

THE NORTH AND NORTHWEST HIGHLANDS

T he northernmost part of the Scottish mainland, the area north and west of the Great Glen, holds some of the country's most spectacular scenery: a classic combination of bare mountains, remote glens, dark lochs and tumbling rivers, surrounded on three sides by a magnificently pitted and rugged coastline. The inspiring landscape and the tranquillity and space that it offers are without doubt the main attractions of the region, yet you may still be surprised at just *how* remote much of it is. The vast peat bogs in the north, for example, are among the most extensive and unspoilt wilderness areas in Europe, while a handful of the west coast's isolated crofting villages can still only be reached by boat.

Exposed to slightly different weather conditions and, to some extent, different historical and cultural influences, each of the three coastlines has its own distinct character. The **west coast**, with its jagged shoreline of sea lochs, rocky headlands

GETTING AROUND THE NORTHERN HIGHLANDS

Unless you're prepared to spend weeks on the road, the North and Northwest Highlands are simply too vast to see in a single trip. Most visitors, therefore, base themselves in one or two areas, exploring the coast or hills on foot, and making longer hops across the interior by car, bus or train. **Getting around** is obviously easiest if you've got your own transport, but with a little forward planning you can see a surprising amount using **buses** and **trains**, especially if you fill in with **postbuses** (timetables are available at most post offices).

The key road on the **east coast** is the A9, which hugs the coast from Inverness to **Wick** and **Thurso**, with its connections to Orkney. One of the Highlands' main rail lines follows broadly the same route. Connections to the **west coast** are more fragmented: the quickest way to **Ullapool**, the largest settlement in the region, is along the A835 from Inverness, though with independent transport or plenty of time the much longer approach along the coast from the south is far more scenic. Fort William is the jumping-off point for the **Ardnamurchan** peninsula and the A830, also known as the "Road to the Isles", to **Mallaig**, from where there are ferries to Skye, the Small Isles and the Outer Isles. The other main route to Skye is along the central A87 to **Kyle of Lochalsh**. Both Kyle of Lochalsh and Mallaig are also served by spectacular train lines: services to Kyle leave from Inverness, while the Fort William to Mallaig route is the final part of the famous **West Highland Railway** line (see box on p.226).

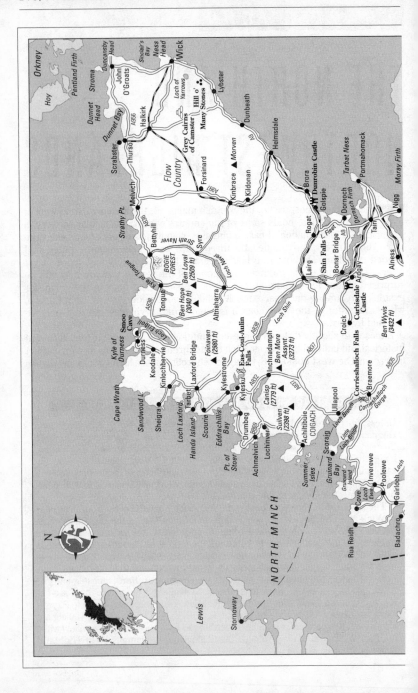

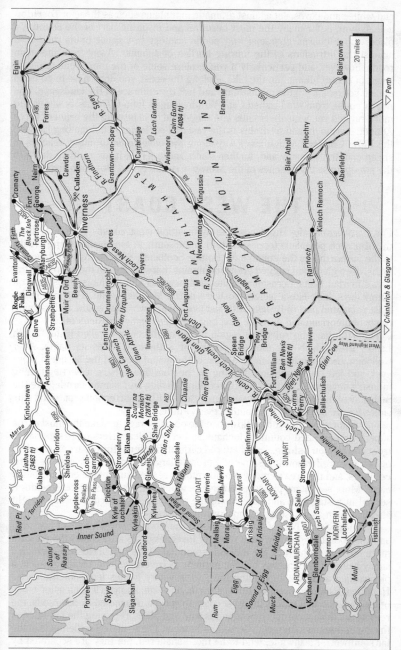

and white-sand coves, set against dramatic mountains such as those of **Torridon** and **Assynt**, is for many the most beautiful and inspiring part of the country, a place whose charm, character and poetic scenery just about holds their own against the intrusions of the touring hordes of summer. Away from the main roads, however, and particularly if you explore some of the more remote peninsulas, or set off hiking into the hills or along the coast, you don't have to go far to detach yourself from the mainstream and feel the embrace of the landscape. The **north coast**, from wind-lashed Cape Wrath along to John O'Groats, is wilder and more rugged yet, with sheer cliffs and sand-filled bays bearing the brunt of fierce Atlantic storms. Inland from this is the vast and ecologically unique bog lands of the **Flow Country**, which gives way along the **east coast** to empty reaches of sheep country, forestry and, further south, more fertile lands running down to the sweeping sandy beaches of the **Moray**, **Cromarty** and **Dornoch firths**.

THE WEST COAST

For many people, the Highlands' starkly beautiful **west coast** – stretching from the **Morvern** peninsula (opposite Mull) in the south, to wind-lashed **Cape Wrath** in the far north – is the epitome of "Bonnie Scotland". Serrated by long blue sea lochs, deep glens and rugged green mountains that sweep from the shoreline, the area's myriad islets, occasional white-sand beaches and turquoise bays can, on sunny days, look like a picture postcard of the Mediterranean. This also is the least populated part of Britain, with just two small towns, few roads, and yawning tracts of moorland and desolate peat bog between crofting settlements.

The **Vikings**, who ruled the region in the ninth century, called it the "South Land", from which the modern district of Sutherland takes its name. After Culloden, the Clearances emptied most of the inland glens of the far north, however, and left the population clinging to the coastline, where a herring-fishing industry developed. Today, tourism, crofting, fishing and salmon farming are the mainstay of the local economy, supplemented by EU construction grants and subsidies for the sheep you'll encounter everywhere.

For visitors, **cycling** and **walking** are the obvious ways to make the most of the superb scenery, and countless lochans and crystal-clear rivers offer superlative trout and salmon **fishing**. The shattered cliffs of the far northwest are an ornithologist's dream, harbouring some of Europe's largest and most diverse **seabird colonies**, and the area's craggy mountaintops are the haunt of the elusive golden eagle. More sedentary pleasure can also be found in the wonderful fresh **seafood** served in restaurants and pubs along the coastline, in particular locally caught shellfish such as mussels, scallops, prawns and lobster.

The most-visited part of the west coast is the stretch between Kyle of Lochalsh and Ullapool. Lying within easy reach of Inverness, this area boasts the region's more obvious highlights: the awesome mountainscape of **Torridon**, **Gairloch**'s sandy beaches, the famous botanic gardens at **Inverewe**, and **Ullapool** itself, a picturesque and bustling fishing town from where ferries leave for the Outer Hebrides. However, press on further north, or south, and you'll get a truer sense of the isolation that makes the west coast so special. Traversed by few roads, the remote northwest corner of Scotland is wild and bleak, receiving the full force of the north Atlantic's frequently ferocious weather. The scattered settlements of the far southwest, meanwhile, tend to be more sheltered, but they are separated by some of the most extensive wilderness areas in Britain – lonely peninsulas with evocative Gaelic names like **Ardnamurchan**, **Knoydart** and **Glenelg**.

Tempered by the Gulf Stream, the west coast's weather ranges from stupendous to diabolical. Never count on a sunny morning meaning a fine day: it can rain here at any time, and go on raining for days. Beware, too, as always in this part of the world, of the dreaded **midge**, which drives even the hardiest of locals to distraction on warm summer evenings. One often-overlooked pleasure of these northern parts, however, is the long **daylight** of summer, which in June and July can mean evenings lingering on towards midnight and spectacularly coloured sunsets filling the western sky.

Without your own vehicle, **getting around** the west coast can be a problem. There's a reasonable **train** service from Inverness to Kyle of Lochalsh and from Fort William to Mallaig, and a useful **summer bus** service connects Inverness to Ullapool, Lochinver, Scourie and Durness. However, services peter out as you venture further afield, and you'll have to rely on **postbuses**, which go just about everywhere, albeit slowly and at odd times of day. **Driving** is a lot less problematic: the roads aren't busy, though they are frequently single-track and scattered with sheep. On such routes, refuel whenever you can, as pumps are few and far between, and make sure your vehicle is in good condition, because, even if you manage to reach the nearest garage, spares may well have to be sent over from Inverness.

Morvern and Ardnamurchan

Immediately west and southwest of Fort William are two large chunks of particularly remote, sparsely populated land: the **Morvern** peninsula, with its single settlement at Lochaline and little else but big, empty hills; and the **Ardnamurchan** peninsula, further west, a wild spot often lashed by Atlantic storms but endearingly untouched and rugged. Most of the settlements here, and consequently the roads and transport links, are strung along the coast and the long sea lochs that cut deep notches into the interior. The inland areas of **Sunart** and **Moidart** are largely empty reaches of mountain and moorland separated by the beautiful Loch Shiel.

The main link to this region is the five-minute ferry crossing at **Corran Ferry** (every 15min; £4.50 for vehicles, foot passengers and bicycles free), a nine-mile drive south of Fort William. The alternative is to approach on the roads from the north, either along the long and tortuous route down the west side of Loch Linnhe, or through Moidart on the B861 from Arisaig. The few buses that head into Morvern and Ardnamurchan from Fort William connect with the Corran ferry, though you'll have to be prepared for long journey times and infrequent connections if you're planning on travelling to the most remote spots.

Morvern

Bounded on three sides by sea lochs and, in the north, by desolate Glen Tarbet, the remote southwest part of the region, known as **Morvern**, is unremittingly bleak and empty. Most visitors only travel through here to get to **LOCHALINE** (pronounced "Loch*aa*lin"), a remote community on the **Sound of Mull**, from where a small ferry chugs to **Fishnish** – the shortest crossing from the mainland.

The village, little more than a scattering of houses and a diving school (☎01967/421627) around a small pier, is a popular anchorage for yachts cruising the west coast, but holds little else to detain you. However, the easy stroll to the nearby fourteenth-century ruins of **Ardtornish Castle**, reached via a track that turns east off the main road one and a half miles north of Lochaline, makes an enjoyable detour. A further walk takes you to see the Loch Tearnait **crannog**, a defensive island dating back about 1500 years; this walk and others are detailed in the *Great Walks* series available from tourist offices in the area. If you're looking for somewhere to **stay**, try the tiny *Lochaline Hotel* (☎01967/421657; ①), which serves reasonable bar food and has a couple of small but comfortable **rooms**.

Sunart and Ardgour

The predominantly roadless regions of **Sunart** and **Ardgour** make up the country between Loch Shiel, Loch Sunart and Loch Linnhe, north of Morvern: the heart of Jacobite support in the mid-eighteenth century, and a Catholic stronghold to this day. The area's only real village is sleepy **STRONTIAN**, grouped around a green on an inlet of Loch Sunart. In 1722, lead mines here yielded the first ever traces of the element **strontium**, named after the village. Worked by French POWs, the same mines also furnished shot for the Napoleonic wars. Strontian's other claim to fame is the "**Floating Church**", which was moored nearby in Loch Sunart in 1843. After being refused permission by the local laird to found their own "kirk", or chapel, on the estate, members of the Free Presbyterian Church bought an old boat on the River Clyde, converted it into a church and then had it towed up the west coast to Loch Sunart.

Travelling by **public transport**, you can get to Strontian (Mon–Sat) on the 8am bus from Kilchoan (see opposite), or on a bus that leaves Fort William at 12.15pm and Ardgour at 12.50pm. Strontian's **tourist office** (Easter–Oct Mon–Sat 9am–5pm, Sun 10am–3pm; ☎01967/402131) will book accommodation for a small fee. *Loch View* **B&B** (☎01967/402465; ①) is excellent value, with large rooms in a fine lochside Victorian house, while *Sea View* (☎01967/402060; ②), a small and very traditional cottage next door, is friendly but more basic; it welcomes dogs. The modern *Kinloch House* (☎01967/402138; ②) is very comfortable, with stunning views down the loch. Strontian also has a couple of good **hotels**, including the *Strontian Hotel* (☎01967/402029; ②), in a splendid position near the water, and the luxurious *Kilcamb Lodge* (☎01967/402257; ⑤ including dinner; March–Nov), a restored country house set in its own grounds on the lochside, whose restaurant serves excellent food.

Ardnamurchan

A tortuous single-track road (the B8007) winds west from **Salen** along the northern shore of Loch Sunart to the wild **Ardnamurchan peninsula**, the most westerly point on the British mainland. The unspoilt landscape is relatively gentle and wooded at the eastern end, but as you travel west the trees disappear and are replaced by a wild, salt-sprayed moorland. The peninsula, which lost most of its inhabitants during the infamous Clearances, is today virtually deserted apart from the handful of tiny crofting settlements clinging to its jagged coastline. Ardnamurchan remains a naturalist's paradise, harbouring a huge variety of birds, animals, and wild flowers like thrift and wild iris.

Glenborrodale and the Glenmore Natural History Centre

An inspiring introduction to the diverse flora, fauna and geology of Ardnamurchan is the superb **Glenmore Natural History Centre** (April–Oct 10.30am–5.30pm; £2.50), nestled near the shore just west of the hamlet of **GLEN-BORRODALE**. Brainchild of local photographer Michael MacGregor (whose stunning work enlivens postcard stands along the west coast), the centre is housed in a sensitively designed timber building, complete with turf roof and wildlife ponds. TV cameras relay live pictures of the comings and goings of the surrounding wildlife, from a pine marten's nest, a heronry and from underwater pools in the nearby river, while an excellent audiovisual show features MacGregor's photographs of the area accompanied by specially composed music. The small **café** serves sandwiches and good home-baked cakes, and there's a useful bookshop. The nearby **RSPB reserve**, a mile to the east, is rich in wildlife too, being home to tree creepers, golden eagles, otters and seals, while for coastal wildlife-spotting – or trips to Tobermory on Mull or Fingal's Cave – contact Ardnamurchan Charters at Glenborrodale (☎01972/500208).

Kilchoan and Ardnamurchan Point

KILCHOAN, nine miles west of the Glenmore Centre, is Ardnamurchan's main village – a straggling but appealing crofting township overlooking the Sound of Mull. Between Easter and mid-October, a **car ferry** runs from here to Tobermory (7 daily; 35min), while in the winter a passenger ferry plies the route for school-children and shoppers. The new community centre in the village houses a **tourist office** (Easter–Oct daily 10am–6pm; ☎01972/510222), who will help with and book accommodation, though year-round the community centre will act as an informal source of local advice and assistance.

Accommodation isn't plentiful in Kilchoan, but both the *Meall mo Chridhe Hotel* (☎01972/510328; ⑤, with dinner ⑦; April–Oct), a converted eighteenth-century manse set among trees above the road, and *Doirlinn House* (☎01972/510209; ②; March–Oct), a B&B with great views, are very pleasant. Further afield, *Feorag House* (☎01972/500248; ⑦ including dinner) at Glenborrodale is an acclaimed upmarket B&B, while, a couple of miles before the Ardnamurchan Point lighthouse (see below), there's the *Sonachan Hotel* (☎01972/510211; ②), a cosy and friendly haven also offering good bar meals, and *Hillview* (☎01972/510322; ①), a traditional cottage about four miles north of Kilchoan at Achnaha (you'll need your own transport). The only direct bus to Kilchoan leaves from Corran Ferry at 12.35pm, arriving two hours later.

Beyond Kilchoan the road continues to rocky, windy **Ardnamurchan Point**, with its unmanned **lighthouse** and spectacular views west to Coll, Tiree and across to the north of Mull. You can't normally get up the tower, but the light-house buildings house a café and an enthusiastically run **visitor centre** (April–Oct 9.30am–6pm; £2.50; ☎01972/510210), whose main theme is lighthouses, their construction and the people who lived in them. About three miles north of the point, the shell-strewn sandy beach of **Sanna Bay** offers truly unforgettable vistas of the Small Isles to the north, circled by gulls, terns and guillemots.

Moidart

Back on the A861 towards the district of **Moidart**, the main settlement is **ACHARACLE**, an ancient crofting village lying at the seaward end of Loch Shiel.

Surrounded by gentle hills, it's an attractive place whose scattered houses form a real community, with several shops, a post office, and plenty of places to stay. The informal *Loch Shiel House Hotel* (☎01967/431224; ②) has nice rooms and simple but good food, including local salmon and haddock. *Belmont* (☎01967/431266; ②) is a comfortable and central B&B, as is *Mrs Crisp's* (☎01967/431318; ①), just across the road. On the south side of the village, *Ardshealach Lodge* (☎01967/431301; ②) is secluded and welcoming. You can get to Acharacle by **boat** with Loch Shiel Cruises on Wednesdays (☎01397/722235), or by **bus** on the infrequent links with Mallaig and Fort William. There are plenty of untaxing and attractive **walks** in the local area – for a book detailing these, call in at Out of Doors, a shop opposite the hotel. Beside this is the *Burger Bite*, a takeaway and bakery with good picnic fodder. Acharacle's village hall is often used for ceilidhs: look out for notices in the shops.

If you're determined to be a bit more adventurous, the Achananellan Centre (☎01967/431265) on the remote south shore of Loch Shiel has self-catering bunkhouse accommodation available, as well as bikes, canoes and sailing dinghies to rent. Bookings must be made in advance. The easiest way to get there is to arranged to be picked up by boat at the pier at Dalilea, a few miles east of Acharacle.

Loch Moidart and Castle Tioram

A mile north of Acharacle, a sideroad running north off the A861 winds for three miles or so past a secluded estuary lined with rhododendron thickets and fishing platforms to **Loch Moidart**, a calm and sheltered sea loch. Perched atop a rocky promontory in the middle of the loch is **Castle Tioram** (pronounced "cheerum"), one of Scotland's most atmospheric historic monuments. Reached via a sandy causeway, the thirteenth-century fortress, whose Gaelic name means "dry land", was the seat of the MacDonalds of Clanranald until it was destroyed by their chief in 1715 to prevent it from falling into Hanoverian hands while he was away fighting for the Jacobites. Today, the surviving walls and tower enclose an inner courtyard and a couple of empty chambers.

The Road to the Isles

Between Fort William and the busy fishing and ferry port of Mallaig is a dramatic, lonely region known as the **Rough Bounds**, its name, a translation from the Gaelic, implying a region geographically and spiritually outside current thought and behaviour. The route between the two towns, followed by both the West Highland Railway and a narrow, winding road (the A830), is known as **The Road to the Isles**, which traverses the mountains and long glens to break out onto a spectacularly scenic coast of sheltered inlets, stunning white beaches and wonderful views to the off-lying islands of Rum, Eigg, Muck and Skye.

Along the way, the road passes a number of spots closely connected with the story of the doomed Jacobite uprising of 1745 led by Bonnie Prince Charlie. At **Glenfinnan** there's a monument on the spot where his standard was raised, while towards **Arisaig** are the spots where he both landed and departed on his infamous adventure. A little further north are the beautiful beaches of **Morar**, while at **Mallaig**, one of the few substantial settlements on the whole northwest coast, there are one or two worthwhile attractions, including the chance to investigate

THE BONNIE PRINCE CHARLIE TRAIL

Along the Road to the Isles are various places which have great resonance whenever the romantic but ultimately tragic tale of **Bonnie Prince Charlie**'s failed rebellion is told. Having first landed on the Outer Isles, he first set foot on the Scottish mainland on the sparkling sands at **Borrodale** on Loch nan Uamh (Loch of Caves) near Arisaig on July 25, 1745. In his bid to claim the throne of Britain for his father, the Old Pretender, he had been promised 10,000 French troops; instead he arrived with only seven companions – the "Seven Men of Moidart", who are commemorated at **Kinlochmoidart** by a now somewhat ravaged line of beech trees, still distinctive from the roadside. Having stayed a week at Kinlochmoidart, trying to ascertain what support he might muster, the prince took the old hill route (known as the General's Road) to **Dalilea**, on the north shore of Loch Shiel, and the next day, August 19, rowed from Glenalandale to the head of the loch at **Glenfinnan**. Here, surrounded by no more than two hundred loyal clansmen, he awaited the arrival of the clans loyal to the Jacobite cause. At this point, all his ambitions hung by a thread – most of the important local chiefs had turned their back on what they regarded as a desperate enterprise, and it was only when the prince persuaded two younger chiefs to join him late in the day that eight hundred more Highlanders arrived, the standard was raised, and the famous rebellion of 1745 was under way. The tall **Glenfinnan Monument** (see p.226) at the head of Loch Shiel is a poignant memorial both to the inspiring symbolism of that day and the Highlanders who subsequently fought and died for the Prince.

If Charles' original encounter with the Arisaig and Moidart area had been filled with optimism and high ideals, his next visit was far less auspicious. By the summer of 1746 he was on the run, his armies had been routed at Culloden and a price of £30,000 was on his head. It is often noted with admiration that, despite the huge sum on offer, none of the countless Highlanders the prince called on for food, favours or hiding turned him in, and that his fortitude and bravery in those desperate months earned him much more respect than his failure as a leader of men. Fleeing from Culloden down the Great Glen, he passed through Arisaig again on his way to the Outer Isles, desperately hoping for the arrival of a French ship to rescue him. It was on South Uist that he was extracted from a tight situation by Flora Macdonald (see p.296), but still on the run he landed back on the mainland again at **Mallaigvaig**, a short walk from Mallaig. The place was swarming with soldiers, and he went on to **Borrodale** once more, this time hiding in a large cave by the shore. From here Charles set off across Lochaber, dodging patrols and hiding in caves and shelters, including some near **Loch Arkaig** (see p.191) and on the slopes of Ben Alder, by **Loch Ericht** (see p.148). It was here that he got word that a French frigate, *L'Heureux*, was off the west coast, and he made a final dash to Arisaig, departing on September 19, 1746 from a promontory in **Loch nan Uamh**, half a mile east of the spot where he'd landed fourteen months before. Today, a cairn on the shores of the loch beside the A830, between Lochailort and Arisaig village, marks the spot.

the local sealife, if you're waiting on connections out to the islands or over to Knoydart.

Glenfinnan

One doesn't need to be Scottish or to have Jacobite sympathies to appreciate the poignancy of **GLENFINNAN**, nineteen miles west of Fort William at the head of

Loch Shiel, where Bonnie Prince Charlie raised his standard to signal the start of the Jacobite uprising of 1745. A more beautiful spot could not have been chosen for a campaign that is remembered as encapsulating the bravery, romance and idealism of the Highland clans, yet it is filled with a sadness born not just for the brutal drama played out over the twelve months after the prince's arrival, but also for the fact that the rebellion was to change the Highlands for ever. The **Glenfinnan Monument**, erected near the spot where the standard was raised by Alexander Macdonald of Glenaladale in 1815, is a pilgrimage spot for anyone interested in Prince Charlie and the Jacobite cause. A **visitor centre** (daily: April, May, Sept & Oct 10am–5pm; June–Aug 9.30am–6pm; £1.50; NTS), opposite the monument, gives an account of the "forty-five" uprising through to the rout at **Culloden** eight months later (see p.210); there's also a café here. For a longer taste of the enchanting atmosphere of the spot, a one- to two-hour **boat trip** on the loch with Loch Shiel Cruises (April–Oct; £5–8; ☎01397/722235) is highly recommended; on Wednesdays they go all the way down to Acharacle and back (£15).

Glenfinnan is one of the most spectacular moments on the West Highland Railway line, not only for the glimpse it offers of the monument and graceful Loch Shiel, but also the mighty 21-arch **viaduct**, built in 1901 and one of the first large constructions made out of concrete. You can learn more of the history of this section of the railway at the **Glenfinnan Station Museum** (June–Sept daily 9.30am–5pm; 50p), set in the old booking office of the station. Right beside the station, two old railway carriages have been pressed into use as one of the most original restaurants and bunkhouses along the West Coast; the **Dining Car** (May–Sept daily 9.30am–11pm; ☎01397/722400) is open for light lunches, home-baking and excellent evening meals, while the **Sleeping Car** (open all year), a converted 1958 camping coach, sleeps ten in bunkbeds.

THE WEST HIGHLAND RAILWAY LINE

Scotland's most famous railway line, and a journey counted by many as among the world's most scenic, the brilliantly engineered **West Highland Railway** runs from Glasgow to Mallaig via Fort William. The line is in two sections: the southern part travels from Glasgow along the Clyde River and up Loch Long, before switching to the banks of Loch Lomond on its way to **Crianlaraich**. After climbing around Beinn Odhar on a unique horseshoe-shaped loop of viaducts, the line traverses desolate **Rannoch Moor**, where the track had to be laid on a mattress of tree roots, brushwood and thousands of tons of earth and ashes. By this point, the line has diverged from the road and travels through country which can only otherwise be reached by long-distance footpaths. Passing Loch Ossian at **Corrour station** (see p.147), the train then swings into Glen Roy, passing through the dramatic **Monassie Gorge** and entering Fort William from the northeast.

The second leg of the journey, from Fort William to Mallaig, is arguably even more spectacular. Shortly after leaving Fort William, it crosses the Caledonian Canal beside Neptune's Staircase by way of a swing bridge at **Benavie**, before travelling along the shores of **Locheil** and crossing the magnificent 21-arch viaduct at **Glenfinnan**, where you'll also catch a glimpse of the Jacobite Memorial (see above) at the head of Loch Shiel. At Glenfinnan station there's a small **museum** (see above) dedicated to the history of the line, a restaurant and a bunkhouse. Not long after this, the line reaches the coast, where there are unforgettable views of the Small Isles and Skye as it runs past the famous silver sands of **Morar** and up to **Mallaig**, where there are connections to the ferry, which crosses to Armadale on Skye.

Morar

Beyond Glenfinnan, the A830 runs alongside captivating Loch Eilt in the district of **Morar**, through Lochailort – where it meets the road from Acharacle – and onto a coast marked by acres of white sands, turquoise seas and rocky islets draped with orange seaweed. **ARISAIG**, scattered round a sandy bay at the west end of the Morar peninsula, makes a good base for exploring this area. There's nothing in the way of specific attractions, but if the weather's fine you can spend hours wandering along the beaches and quiet back roads, and there's a small seal colony at nearby **RHUMACH**, reached via the single-track lane leading west out of the village along the headland. A daily boat also leaves from Arisaig during the summer for the Small Isles (see p.299); contact Arisaig Marine (☎01687/450224). **Accommodation** in the village is plentiful. *Kinloid Farm House* (☎01687/450366; ②, with dinner, ⑤; March–Oct) is one of several pleasant B&Bs with sea views, while the more upmarket *Old Library Lodge* (☎01687/450651; ⑤; April–Oct) has a handful of well-appointed rooms, some of them in a 200-year-old converted stable overlooking the waterfront. The restaurant downstairs, serving moderately priced lunches and excellent à la carte dinners (reservations recommended), is renowned for adding an exotic twist to fresh local ingredients – try Mallaig cod with Moroccan marinade.

Stretching for eight miles or so north of Arisaig is a string of stunning white-sand beaches backed by flowery machair, with barren granite hills rising straight up behind, though the views are somewhat marred by the abandoned cars, rusting metal and decrepit caravans which blight this part of the coast. The next settlement of any significance is **MORAR**, where the famous beach scenes from *Local Hero* were shot. Since then, however, a bypass has been built around the village, and the white sands, plagued by the rumble of frozen-cod trucks, are no longer the unspoilt idyll Burt Lancaster paddled ecstatically around in the early 1980s. You can still find some pleasant places to stay – of the string of campsites, try *Camusdarach* (☎01687/450221), which isn't quite on the beach but is quieter and less officious than others nearby. B&B is also available in the attractive main house (①). **Loch Morar** – rumoured to be the home of **Morag**, a lesser-known rival to Nessie – runs east of Morar village into the heart of a huge wilderness area, linked to the sea by what must be one of the shortest rivers in Scotland. Hemmed in by heather-decked mountains, it featured in the movie *Rob Roy*: the cattle-rustling clansman's cottage was sited on its roadless northern shore.

Mallaig

A cluttered, noisy port whose pebble-dashed houses struggle for space with great lumps of granite tumbling down to the sea, **MALLAIG**, 47 miles west of Fort William along the A830 (regular buses and trains run this route), is not a pretty village. Before the railway reached here in 1901, it consisted of only a few cottages, but now it's a busy, bustling place and, as the main ferry stop for Skye and the Small Isles (see p.299), is always full of visitors. The continuing source of the village's wealth is its thriving **fishing industry**: on the quayside, piles of nets, tackle and ice crates lie scattered around a bustling modern market. When the fleet is in, trawlers encircled by flocks of raucous gulls choke the harbour, and the pubs, among the liveliest on the west coast, host bouts of serious drinking.

Apart from the daily bustle of the harbour, the main attraction in town is **Mallaig Marine World**, north of the train station near the harbour (June & Sept Mon–Sat 9am–7pm, Sun 10am–6pm; July & Aug Mon–Sat 9am–9pm, Sun 10am–6pm; Oct–May Mon–Sat 9am–5.30pm, Sun 11am–5pm; £2.75), where tanks of local sea creatures and informative exhibits about the port provide an unpretentious but sensitive introduction to the local waters. Alongside the train station, the **Mallaig Heritage Centre** (May–Sept Mon–Sat 11am–4pm, Sun 1–4pm; £1.80), displaying old photographs of the town and its environs, is worth a browse. In addition, there are a couple of enjoyable **walks** around the town. The trail to **Mallaigmore**, a small cove with a white-sand beach and isolated croft, begins at the top of the harbour on East Bay; follow the road north past the tourist office and turn off right when you see the signpost between two houses. The round-trip takes about an hour.

The stretch of coast **north of Mallaig** encompasses the lonely **Knoydart** and **Glenelg peninsulas**, two of Britain's last true wilderness areas, as it heads towards **Kyle of Lochalsh**, the main departure point for Skye. This whole region is also popular with Munro-baggers, harbouring a string of summits over 3000ft. The famous Five Sisters massif and Kintail Ridge, flanking the A87 a short way south of Kyle, offer some of the Highlands' most challenging **hikes** and are easily accessible by road.

Practicalities

Mallaig is a compact place, concentrated around the harbour, where you'll find both the **tourist office** (April, May, Sept & Oct Mon–Sat 10am–6.30pm; June–Aug Mon–Sat 9am–8pm, Sun 10am–4pm; Nov–March Mon, Wed & Fri 10am–2pm; ☎01687/462170), which will book accommodation for you, and the **bus** and **train stations**. The CalMac ticket office (☎01687/462403), serving passengers for Skye and the Small Isles, is also nearby, and you can arrange transport to Knoydart by telephoning Bruce Watt Cruises (☎01687/462320 or 462233), which sails to Inverie every Monday, Wednesday and Friday morning and afternoon, the later cruise continuing east along Loch Nevis to Tarbet; the loch is sheltered, so crossings are rarely cancelled. Mr Watt also operates cruises (mid-May to mid-Sept) to Loch Scavaig on Skye (see p.289) on Tuesdays and Thursdays (11am).

There are plenty of places **to stay**; the *West Highland Hotel* (☎01687/462210; ③) is pleasantly old-fashioned, if a little shabby in places, and some rooms have excellent sea views, while the *Marine* (☎01687/462217; ③) is much smarter inside than first views suggest. For **B&B**, head around the harbour to East Bay, where you'll find the immaculate *Western Isles Guest House* (☎01687/462320; ①), with the nearby *Haco Cottage* (☎01687/462434; ①) a good alternative. Budget travellers should head for *Sheena's Backpackers' Lodge* (☎01687/462764), a refreshingly laid-back independent hostel overlooking the harbour, with mixed dorms, self-catering facilities and a sitting room. For **eating**, the *Marine Hotel* serves good-value bar meals featuring fresh seafood which are well above average, while the nearby *Seafood Restaurant* (also known as the *Cabin*) has a more ambitious menu but is very popular, so booking is wise. During the day, the *Tea Garden* at *Sheena's Backpacker's Lodge* is a great place to watch the world go by while you tuck into a bowl of Cullen Skink (soup made from smoked haddock), a pint of prawns, or home-made scones.

The Knoydart peninsula

To get to the heart of the **Knoydart peninsula**, you have to catch a boat from Mallaig or Glenelg, or else hike for a couple of days across rugged moorland and mountains and sleep rough in old stone bothies (most of which are marked on Ordnance Survey maps). Either way, you'll soon appreciate why many regard this as Britain's most dramatic and unspoilt wilderness area. Flanked by Loch Nevis ("Loch of Heaven") in the south and the fjord-like inlet of Loch Hourn ("Loch of Hell") to the north, Knoydart's nobbly green peaks (three of them Munros) sweep straight out of the sea, shrouded for much of the time in a pall of grey mist. Unsurprisingly, the peninsula tends to attract walkers, lured by the network of well-maintained **trails** that wind east into the wild interior, where Bonnie Prince Charlie is rumoured to have hidden out after Culloden.

At the end of the eighteenth century, around a thousand people eked out a living from this inhospitable terrain through crofting and fishing. Evictions in 1853 began a dramatic decrease in the population, which continued to dwindle through the twentieth century as a succession of landowners ran the estate as a hunting and shooting playground, prompting a famous land raid in 1948 by a group of crofters known as the "Seven Men of Knoydart", who staked out and claimed ownership of portions of the estate. Although their bid failed, the memory of their cause was invoked when the crofters of Knoydart finally achieved control over the land they lived on in a community buyout in 1998. These days the peninsula supports around seventy people, most of whom live in the tiny hamlet of **INVERIE**. Nestled beside a sheltered bay on the south side of the peninsula, it has a pint-sized post office, a shop and mainland Britain's most remote pub, the *Old Forge*.

Practicalities

Bruce Watt Cruises' **boat** chugs into Inverie from Mallaig (Mon, Wed & Fri 10.15am & 2.15pm; also June–Aug Sat 10.30am; ☎01687/462320 or 462233). To arrange for a boat crossing from Arnisdale on Loch Hourn, contact Len Morrison (☎01599/522352) or Mr MacTavish (☎01599/522211); it costs between £8 and £25 depending on passenger numbers.

There are two main **hiking routes** into Knoydart: the trailhead for the first is Kinloch Hourn, a crofting hamlet at the far east end of Loch Hourn which you can get to by road (turn south off the A87 six miles west of Invergarry), from where a well-marked path winds around the coast to Barrisdale and on to Inverie; you can also pick up this trail by taking a boat from Arnisdale, on the north shore of Loch Hourn. The second path into Knoydart starts at the west side of Loch Arkaig, approaching the peninsula via Glen Dessary. These are both long, hard slogs over rough, desolate country, so take wet-weather gear, plenty of food, warm clothes and a good sleeping bag, and leave your name and expected time of arrival with someone when you set off.

Most of Knoydart's **accommodation** is concentrated in and around Inverie. *Torrie Shieling* (☎01687/462669, *torrreidh@aol.com*; £15 per person per night), an upmarket independent **hostel** located three-quarters of a mile east of the village on the side of the mountain, is popular with hikers and families, offering topnotch self-catering facilities, comfy wooden beds in four-person rooms, and superb views across the bay. They also have a Land-Rover and boat for ferrying guests around the peninsula, and to neighbouring lochs and islands. In Inverie village itself, *Pier House* (☎01687/462347; ②, including dinner ④), a pleasant **B&B**, serves à la carte evening meals to non-residents (three courses for around £16). If you want total isolation and all the creature comforts, book into the beautiful *Doune Stone Lodges* (☎01687/462667; ⑤ includes dinner and packed lunch), on the remote north side of the peninsula. Rebuilt from ruined crofts, this place has pine-fitted en-suite double rooms right on the shore, near the ruins of an ancient Pictish fort. They'll pick you up by boat from Mallaig if you book ahead. Most visitors **eat** at *Pier House* while in Knoydart; alternatively, try the *Old Forge*'s generous bar meals, served indoors beside an open fire. You can rent **mountain bikes** from *Pier House*, who have organized bike trails in the area; they also offer **guided mountain walks** for groups of four or more.

Glenelg and Loch Duich

Further north, the **Glenelg peninsula**, jutting out into the Sound of Sleat, is the isolated and little-known crofting area featured in Gavin Maxwell's otter novel, **Ring of Bright Water**. Maxwell disguised the identity of this pristine stretch of coast by calling it "Camusfearnà", and it has remained a tranquil backwater in spite of the traffic that trickles through during the summer for the Kylerhea ferry to Skye. You can also approach the peninsula from the east by turning off the fast A87 at Shiel Bridge on **Loch Duich**, from where a narrow single-track road climbs a tortuous series of switchbacks to the Mam Ratagan Pass (1115ft), affording spectacular views over the awesome Five Sisters massif. Following the route of an old military highway and drovers' trail, the road, covered each morning by the postbus from Kyle (departs 9.45am), drops down the other side through Glen More, with the magnificent Kintail Ridge visible to the southeast, towards the peninsula's main settlement, **GLENELG**, strewn along a pebbly bay on the Sound of Sleat. A row of little whitewashed houses surrounded by trees, the village is dominated by the rambling, weed-choked ruins of Fort Bernera, an eighteenth-century garrison for English government troops, but now little more than a shell. The *Glenelg Inn* (☎01599/522273; ⑤) has luxurious, cosy rooms overlooking the bay and an excellent à la carte restaurant, which also serves cream teas, cakes and quality coffee during the day.

The six-car **Glenelg–Kylerhea ferry** (April–Oct frequent; 5min; for more details, call ☎01599/511302) shuttles across the Sound of Sleat from a jetty northwest of the village. In former times, this choppy channel used to be an important drovers' crossing: eight thousand cattle each year were herded head to tail across from Skye to the mainland.

One and a half miles south of Glenelg village, a left turn up Glen Beag leads to the **Glenelg Brochs**, some of the best-preserved Iron Age monuments in the country. Standing in a sheltered stream valley, the circular towers – Dun Telve and Dun Troddan – are thought to have been erected around two thousand years ago to protect the surrounding settlements from raiders. About a third of each main structure remains, with the curving drystone walls and internal passages still impressively intact.

Arnisdale

A narrow back road snakes its way southwest beyond Glenelg village through a scattering of old crofting hamlets and timber forests. The views across the Sound of Sleat to Knoydart grow more spectacular at each bend, reaching a high point at a windy pass that takes in a vast sweep of sea, loch and islands. Below the road at **Sandaig** is where Gavin Maxwell and his otters lived in the 1950s: the site of his house is now marked by a cairn. Swinging east, the road winds down to the waterside again, following the north shore of Loch Hourn as far as **ARNISDALE**, departure point for the boat to Knoydart (see p.229). Arnisdale is made up of the two hamlets of **CAMUSBANE** and **CORRAN**, the former consisting of a single row of old cottages ranged behind a long pebble beach, with a massive scree slope behind, while the latter, a mile along the road, is a minuscule whitewashed fishing hamlet at the water's edge. Aside from the arrival of electricity and a red telephone box, the only major addition to this gorgeous hamlet in the last hundred years has been Mrs Nash's homely **B&B** and tea hut (☎01599/522336; ①), where you can enjoy hot drinks and home-baked cake in a "shell garden", with breathtaking views on all sides. You can get to Arnisdale on the **postbus** from Kyle of Lochalsh (daily 9.45am; 3hr 40min; the return bus leaves Arnisdale at 7.10am), or use the Diversions Glenelg service between Kyle, Ratagan Youth Hostel and Glenelg post office (Mon, Wed & Fri 11.20am; 1hr 5min; ☎01599/522233), which will also go on to Arnisdale and Corran, or meet the Inverness or Glasgow buses at Kyle, by request.

Loch Duich

Skirted on its northern shore by the A87, **Loch Duich**, the boot-shaped inlet that forms the northern shoreline of the Glenelg peninsula, features prominently on the tourist trail, with buses from all over Europe thundering down the sixteen miles from **Shiel Bridge** to Kyle of Lochalsh on their way to Skye. The most dramatic approach to the loch, however, is from the east through Glen Shiel, where the mountains known as the Five Sisters of Kintail surge up to heights of 3000ft – a familiar sight from countless tourist brochures, but an impressive one nonetheless. With steep-sided hills hemming in both sides of the loch, it's sometimes hard to remember that this is, in fact, the sea. There's a congenial SYHA **hostel** just outside Shiel Bridge at **RATAGAN** (☎01599/511243 or central reservations ☎0541/553255; Feb–Dec), popular with walkers newly arrived off the Glen Affric trek from Cannich (see p.200).

Eilean Donan Castle

After Edinburgh's hilltop fortress, **Eilean Donan Castle** (April–Oct daily 10am–5.30pm; £3.75), ten miles north of Shiel Bridge on the A87, has to be Scotland's most-photographed monument. Presiding over the once strategically important confluence of lochs Alsh, Long and Duich, the forbidding crenellated tower rises from the water's edge, joined to the shore by a narrow stone bridge and with sheer mountains as a backdrop.

The original castle was established in 1230 by Alexander II to protect the area from the Vikings. Later, during a Jacobite uprising in 1719, it was occupied by troops dispatched by the king of Spain to help the **"Old Pretender"**, James Stuart. However, when King George heard of their whereabouts, he sent frigates to weed the Spaniards out, and the castle was blown up with their stocks of gunpowder. Thereafter, it lay in ruins until John Macrae-Gilstrap had it rebuilt between 1912 and 1932. Eilean Donan has also been the setting of several major **movies**, including *Highlander*, starring Christophe Lambert, and the more recent

HIKING IN GLEN SHIEL
Ordnance Survey map no. 33

The mountains of **Glen Shiel**, sweeping southeast from Loch Duich, offer some of the best hiking routes in Scotland. Rising dramatically from sea level to over 3000ft in less than a couple of miles, they are also exposed to the worst of the west coast's notoriously fickle weather. Don't underestimate either of these two routes. Tracing the paths on a map, they can appear short and easy to follow; however, unwary walkers die here every year, often because they failed to allow enough time to get off the mountain by nightfall, or because of a sudden change in the weather. Neither of the routes outlined below should be attempted by inexperienced walkers, nor without a map, a compass and a detailed trekking guide – the *SMC's Hill Walks in Northwest Scotland* is recommended. Also make sure to follow the usual safety precautions outlined on p.46.

Taking in a bumper crop of Munros, the **Five Sisters traverse** is deservedly the most popular trek in the area. Allow a full day to complete the whole route, which begins at the first fire break on the left-hand side as you head southeast down the glen on the A87. Strike straight up from here and follow the ridge north along to Scurr na Moraich (2874ft), dropping down the other side to Morvich on the valley floor.

The distinctive chain of mountains across the glen from the Five Sisters is the **Kintail Ridge**, crossed by another famous hiking route that begins at the *Cluanie Inn* on the A87. From here, follow the well-worn path south around the base of the mountain until it meets up with a stalkers' trail, which winds steeply up Creag a' Mhaim (3108ft) and then west along the ridgeway, with breathtaking views south across Knoydart and the Hebridean Sea.

James Bond adventure *The World is not Enough* (numerous film stills are sold at the ticket office). Three floors, including the banqueting hall, the bedrooms and the troops' quarters are open to the public, with various Jacobite and clan relics also on display, though the large numbers of people passing through make it hard to appreciate them.

There are several **places to stay** less than a mile away in the hamlet of **DORNIE**, including the *Silver Fir Bunkhouse* (☎01599/555264; ①), little more than a simple hut with two bunk beds and a wood-burning stove, but friendly and characterful. Otherwise, the *Dornie Hotel*, Francis Street (☎01599/555205; ④), boasts comfortable rooms, while the *Loch Duich Hotel* (☎01599/555213; ③), has splendid doubles overlooking the loch and a small restaurant serving upmarket bar snacks and evening meals. Another good place for a bar meal is the popular *Clachan*, just along from the *Dornie Hotel*.

Kyle of Lochalsh and Plockton

KYLE OF LOCHALSH, seven miles northeast of Eilean Donan Castle, is a busy town, a transit point on the route to Skye and an important train terminal. Straggling down the hill towards the pier and train station, it's not particularly attractive – concrete buildings, rail junk and myriad signs of the fishing industry abound – and is ideally somewhere to pass through rather than linger in. Since the **Skye road bridge** was opened in 1995, traffic has little reason to stop in town before rumbling over the channel a mile to the north, leaving its shopkeepers bereft of the passing trade they used to enjoy. The new bridge, built with private-sector money, has also sparked controversy over its high tolls (£5.70 for cars), with local protesters doing battle in Dingwall Sheriff Court and Edinburgh's Court of Session.

Practicalities

Buses run to the harbour in Kyle of Lochalsh from Glasgow via Fort William and Invergarry (3 daily; 5hr 30min–6hr 15min), and from Inverness via Invermoriston (4 daily; 2hr); there's also a summer service from Edinburgh (1 daily; 7hr 15min). These routes can become very crowded, so it's wise to book in advance (☎0990/505050). All these services continue at least as far as Portree, on Skye, and a shuttle service runs across the bridge to Kyleakin every thirty minutes or so. Three or four **trains** run daily, with one or two on summer Sundays, from Inverness (2hr 30min). Curving north through Achnasheen and Glen Carron, the train line is a rail enthusiast's dream, even if scenically it doesn't quite match the West Highland line to Mallaig.

The **tourist office** (April, May, Sept & Oct Mon–Sat 9am–5pm; June & Aug Mon–Sat 9am–7pm, Sun 10am–4pm; ☎01599/534276), on top of the small hill near the old ferry jetty, will book accommodation for you, which is useful as there are surprisingly few places to stay, particularly in high summer. If you're feeling flush, splash out at the *Lochalsh Hotel* (☎01599/534202; ⑤), a wonderfully located place looking out at Skye, with fabulous seafood and an air of dated luxury. For **B&B**, try Mrs Finlayson, on Main Street (☎01599/534265; ③), ten minutes' walk up the hill from the train station, or *Crowlin View* (☎01599/534286; ①), a traditional house with views to Skye, one and a half miles north of Kyle on the Plockton road. There's a simple but neat and clean backpackers' hostel in town, *Cúchulainn's* (☎01599/534492), above a pub across the main street from the tourist information. Between Kyle and Plockton, the *Old Schoolhouse* at Erbusaig (☎01599/534369; ②) is a good-quality restaurant with inexpensive and comfortable rooms. The *Seagreen Restaurant and Bookshop* (☎01599/534388), also on the Plockton road on the edge of Kyle of Lochalsh, has excellent fresh seafood and vegetarian meals in a pleasant, unfussy setting, while the *Seafood Restaurant* at the train station is also recommended, if a little pricier.

Plockton

A fifteen-minute train ride north of Kyle at the seaward end of islet-studded Loch Carron lies unbelievably picturesque **PLOCKTON**: a chocolate-box row of neatly painted cottages ranged around the curve of a tiny harbour and backed by a craggy landscape of heather and pine. Originally known as Am Ploc, the settlement was a crofting hamlet until the end of the eighteenth century, when a local laird transformed it into a prosperous fishery, renaming it "Plocktown". Its fifteen minutes of fame came in the mid-1990s, when the BBC chose the village as the setting for three series of the television drama *Hamish Macbeth*. Though the resulting spin-off has quietened down a little, in high season it's still packed full of tourists, yachtsmen and second-home owners. The unique brilliance of Plockton's light has also made it something of an artists' hangout, and during the summer the waterfront, with its row of shaggy palm trees, even shaggier Highland cattle, flower gardens and pleasure boats, is invariably punctuated by painters dabbing at their easels.

If you want **to stay**, the friendly, cosy *Haven Hotel*, on Innes Street (☎01599/544223; ⑤), is renowned for its excellent food, while the *Plockton Inn*, also on Innes Street (☎01599/544222; ③), makes an informal and comfortable alternative. The *Plockton Hotel*, Harbour Street (☎01599/544274; ④), overlooking the harbour with some rooms in a nearby cottage, has a friendly bar and serves good seafood. Of the fifteen or so **B&Bs**, *The Shieling* (☎01599/544282; ②) has a great location on a tiny headland at the top of the harbour, the nearby *Heron's Flight* (☎01599/544220; ②) has uninterrupted views across the loch from its upstairs bedrooms, while *The Manse* on Innes Street (☎01599/544442; ②) features beautifully furnished rooms and serves generous breakfasts. There's also the attractive new *Station Bunkhouse* (☎01599/544235), built in the shape of a signal box next to the train station, which has four- and six-person dorms and a cosy open-plan kitchen and living area. An interesting **self-catering** option is to stay at the *Craig Rare Breeds Farm*, midway between Plockton and Stromeferry, where you can rub shoulders with ancient breeds of Scottish farm animals, llamas and peacocks; ask for one of the cottages on the beach (2 people, £250 per week; 6 people, £380 per week; ☎01599/544205).

You should have little difficulty finding somewhere good **to eat** in Plockton: both the *Haven* and the *Plockton Inn* have excellent seafood restaurants, while *Off the Rails*, in the train station, serves good-value, imaginative snacks by day and dinner. *The Buttery*, part of Plockton Stores on the seafront, is also open all day for snacks and inexpensive meals. For **fishing** or **seal-spotting** boat trips from Plockton, try Leisure Marine (☎01599/544306) or Sea Trek Marine (☎01599/544356).

Applecross and Torridon

The most dramatic approach to the **Applecross peninsula** (the English-sounding name is actually a corruption of the Gaelic *Apor Crosan*, meaning "estuary") is from the south, along the infamous **Bealach na Ba** (literally "Pass of the Cattle"). Crossing the forbidding hills behind Kishorn and rising to 2053ft, with a gradient and switchback bends worthy of the Alps, this route, the highest road in Scotland and a popular cycling piste, is hair-raising in places, but the panoramic views across the Minch to Raasay and Skye more than compensate. The other way in is from the north: a beautiful coast road that meanders slowly from Shieldaig on Loch Torridon, with tantalizing glimpses of the Cuillins to the south.

The sheltered, fertile coast around **APPLECROSS** village, where the Irish missionary monk Maelrhuba founded a monastery in 673 AD, comes as a surprise after the bleakness of the moorland approach. It's an idyllic place: you can wander along lanes banked with wild iris and orchids, and explore beaches and rock pools on the shore. It's also quite an adventure to get here by **public transport**: the nearest railhead is seventeen miles northeast at Strathcarron Station, near Achnasheen, which you have to reach by 9.50am to catch the postbus to Shieldaig, on Loch Torridon. From here, a second postbus leaves for Applecross at 11.30am (90min). No buses of any kind run over the Bealach na Ba. The old *Applecross Inn* (☎01520/744262; ②), right beside the sea, is the focal point of the community, with rooms upstairs and a lively bar serving snacks and tasty platefuls of local seafood. A couple of friendly **B&Bs** lie south of here towards Toscaig, with its pier and inquisitive seals: try Mrs Thompson (☎01520/744260; ①) at

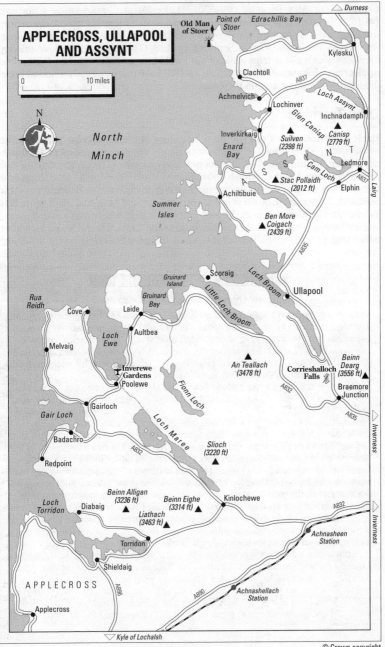

APPLECROSS, ULLAPOOL AND ASSYNT

0   10 miles

N

North

Minch

Durness

Old Man of Stoer

Point of Stoer

Edrachillis Bay

Kylesku

Clachtoll

A837

Achmelvich

Lochinver

Loch Assynt

Glen Caniso

Inchnadamph

Inverkirkaig

Enard Bay

Suilven (2398 ft)

Canisp (2779 ft)

Cam Loch

Ledmore

A837

A S S

Stac Pollaidh (2012 ft)

Elphin

Achiltibuie

Summer Isles

Ben More Coigach (2439 ft)

A835

Scoraig

Loch Broom

Ullapool

Gruinard Island

Gruinard Bay

Little Loch Broom

Rua Reidh

Cove

Laide

Aultbea

An Teallach (3478 ft)

Corrieshalloch Falls

Beinn Dearg (3556 ft)

Melvaig

Loch Ewe

Braemore Junction

Inverewe Gardens

Poolewe

Fionn Loch

A832

Laing

Inverness

Gairloch

Gair Loch

Loch Maree

Slioch (3220 ft)

Badachro

Redpoint

A832

Beinn Alligan (3236 ft)

Beinn Eighe (3314 ft)

Kinlochewe

A832

Inverness

Loch Torridon

Diabaig

Liathach (3463 ft)

Achnasheen Station

Torridon

Shieldaig

A896

A890

Achnashellach Station

APPLECROSS

Applecross

Kyle of Lochalsh

© Crown copyright

Camusteel, or Mrs Dickens (☎01520/744206; ①) at *Camusterrach*. **Camping** (☎01520/744268) is provided at the *Flowertunnel*, as you come into the village from the pass. There are a couple of options if you want to explore the area: Applecross Peninsula Visitor Services (☎01520/744262) offer half- or full-day Land-Rover or walking trips seeking out local history, wildlife and geology, while Applecross Mountain & Sea (☎01520/744393) have more rugged mountain expeditions and kayaking around the coast.

Loch Torridon

Loch Torridon marks the northern boundary of the Applecross peninsula, its awe-inspiring setting backed by the appealingly rugged mountains of **Liathach** and **Beinn Eighe**, tipped by streaks of white quartzite. The greater part of this area is composed of the reddish 750-million-year-old Torridonian sandstone, and some 15,000 acres of the massif are under the protection of the National Trust for Scotland. They run a **Countryside Centre** (May–Sept Mon–Sat 10am–5pm, Sun 2–5pm) at Torridon village at the east end of the loch, where you can call in and learn a bit more about the local geology, flora and fauna. The NTS also look after **Shieldaig Island**, which lies off the pretty village of Shieldaig on the southern

---

WALKING AROUND TORRIDON

Ordnance Survey Outdoor Leisure map no. 8

There are difficult and unexpected conditions on virtually all hiking routes around Torridon, and the weather can change very rapidly. If you're relatively inexperienced but want to do the magnificent ridge walk along the **Liathach** (pronounced "*Lee*-a-gach" or "*Lee*-ach") massif, or the strenuous traverse of **Beinn Eighe** (pronounced "Ben *Ay*"), join a National Trust Ranger Service guided hike (details from the Torridon Countryside Centre on ☎01445/791221).

For those confident to go it alone (using the above map), one of many possible routes takes you behind Liathach and down the pass, Coire Dubh, to the main road in Glen Torridon. This is a great, straightforward walk if you're properly equipped (see p.46), covering thirteen miles and taking in superb landscapes. Allow yourself the whole day. Start at the stone bridge on the Diabaig road along the north side of Loch Torridon. Follow the Abhainn Coire Mhic Nobuil burn up to the fork at the wooden bridge and take the track east to the pass (a rather indistinct watershed) between Liathach and Beinn Eighe. The path becomes a little lost in the boggy area studded with lochans at the top of the pass, but the route is clear and, once over the watershed, the path is easy to follow. At this point you can, weather permitting, make the rewarding diversion up to the Coire Mhic Fhearchair, widely regarded as the most spectacular corrie in Scotland; otherwise, continue down the Coire Dubh stream, ford the burn and follow its west bank down to the Torridon road, from where it's about four miles back to Loch Torridon.

A rewarding walk even in rough weather is the seven-mile hike up the coast from **Lower Diabaig**, ten miles northwest of Torridon village, to **Redpoint**. On a clear day, the views across to Raasay and Applecross from this gentle undulating path are superlative, but you'll have to return along the same trail, or else make your way back via Loch Maree on the A832. If you're staying in Shieldaig, the track that winds up the peninsula running north from the village makes a pleasant ninety-minute round-walk.

shore of Loch Torridon, where a heronry has been established among the tall Scots pines which cover the island; you might also have a chance of spotting a kestrel or an otter. There's an attractive small hotel by the shore in the village, *Tigh-an-Eilean* (☎01520/755251; ⑥), and also a simple campsite a little way up the hill.

The road which runs along the northern shore of the loch from **TORRIDON** village is scenic and dramatic, winding first along the shore then climbing and twisting past lochans, cliffs and gorges to the green wooded slopes of **DIABAIG**. There's a modern **youth hostel** at Torridon (☎01445/791284 or central reservations ☎0541/553255; Feb–Oct, Christmas & New Year), and one of the area's top hotels, the rambling Victorian *Loch Torridon Hotel* (☎01445/791242; ⑧), set amid well-tended lochside grounds. Next door, *Ben Damph Lodge* (☎01445/791242, *ben@lochtorridnhotel.com*; ③) is a modern conversion of an old farm steading with neat if characterless rooms and a large climber's bar. Also in Diabaig, Miss Ross (☎01445/790240; ①) has comfortable accommodation overlooking the rocky bay, and there's a good B&B, *Tigh Fada* (☎01520/755248; ①), at **DOIREANOR**, on the southwest side of Loch Shieldaig.

Loch Maree

About eight miles north of Loch Torridon, **Loch Maree**, dotted with Caledonian pine-covered islands, is one of the west's scenic highlights, best viewed from the road (A832) that drops down to its southeastern tip through Glen Docherty. It's also surrounded by some of Scotland's finest deerstalking country: the remote, privately owned *Letterewe Lodge* on the north shore, accessible only by helicopter or boat, lies at the heart of a famous deer forest. **Queen Victoria** stayed a few days here in 1877 at the wonderfully sited *Loch Maree Hotel* (☎01445/760288, *lochmaree@easynet.co.uk*; ⑤), which is comfortable and less formal than in her day.

At the southeastern end of the loch, at the junction of the A896 from Torridon and the A832 from Achnasheen, on the road from Inverness to Kyle of Lochalsh, is the small settlement of **Kinlochewe**, another good base if you're heading into the hills. There is a bunkhouse as well as B&B at the *Kinlochewe Hotel* (☎01445/760253; bunkhouse ①, B&B ②), but for little extra you're much better off heading a mile along the road towards Torridon to *Cromasaig* B&B (☎01455/760234, *cromasaig@msn.com*; ①), a great place for hillwalkers set in the forest right at the foot of the track up Beinn Eighe. In Kinlochewe itself, MORU outdoor shop at the old petrol station opposite the hotel will furnish you with maps and guidebooks, as well as equipment and sound local advice.

The A832 skirts the southern shore of Loch Maree, passing the **Beinn Eighe Nature Reserve**, the UK's oldest wildlife sanctuary. Parts of the Beinn Eighe reserve are forested with Caledonian pinewood, which once covered the whole of the country, and it is home to pine marten, wildcat, fox, badger, Scottish crossbill, buzzards and golden eagles. There's also a wide range of flora, with the higher rocky slopes producing spectacular natural alpine rock gardens. A mile north of Kinlochewe, the **Beinn Eighe Visitor Centre** (Easter & May–Sept daily 10am–5pm), on the A832, gives details of the area's rare species and sells pamphlets describing two excellent **walks** in the reserve: a woodland trail through lochside forest, and a more strenuous half-day hike around the base of Beinn Eighe. Both start from the car park a mile north of the visitor centre.

Gairloch to the Scoraig peninsula

Mostly scattered around the sheltered northeastern shore of the loch of the same name, the crofting township of **GAIRLOCH** thrives during the summer as a low-key holiday resort with several tempting sandy beaches and some excellent coastal walks within easy reach. The **Gairloch Heritage Museum** (April, May & Oct Mon–Sat 11am–4pm; June–Sept Mon–Sat 10am–5pm; for winter times phone ☎01445/712287; £2.50) has eclectic, appealing displays covering geology, archeology, fishing and farming that range from a mock-up of a croft house to an early knitting machine. Probably the most interesting section is the archive – an array of photographs, maps, genealogies, lists of place names and taped recollections, mostly in Gaelic – made by elderly locals.

The area's real attraction, however, is its beautiful **coastline**. To get to one of the most impressive stretches, head around the north side of the bay and follow the single-track B8021 beyond Big Sand (a cleaner and quieter beach than the one in Gairloch) to the tiny crofting hamlet of **Melvaig** (reachable by the 9.05am Gairloch postbus), from where a narrow surfaced track winds out to **Rua Reidh** (pronounced "Roo-a Ree") Point. The converted **lighthouse** here, which looks straight out to Harris in the Outer Hebrides, serves slap-up afternoon teas and home-baked cakes (Easter–Oct Tues, Thurs & Sun noon–5pm). You can also stay in its comfortable and relaxed **bunkhouse**, or **double rooms** (book ahead in high season on ☎01445/771263, *ruareidh@netcomuk.co.uk*; ①), or use it as a base for one of the popular walking or activity holidays organized by the folk who run the bunkhouse. Around the headland from Rua Reidh lies the secluded and beautiful **Camas Mor** beach. For a great half-day walk, follow the marked footpath inland (southeast) from here along the base of a sheer scarp slope, and past a string of lochans, ruined crofts and a remote wood to Midtown on the east side of the peninsula, five miles north of Poolewe on the B8057. However, unless you leave a car at the end of the trail or arrange to be picked up, you'll have to walk or hitch back to Gairloch, as the only transport along this road is an early-morning postvan.

A more leisurely way to explore the coast is on a wildlife-spotting cruise: Gairloch Marine Life Centre & Cruises (Easter–Oct; ☎01445/712636) at the pier run informative and enjoyable boat trips across the bay in search of dolphins, porpoises, seals and even the odd whale. You can also rent a boat for the day through Gairloch's chandlery shop (☎01445/712458), popular with sea anglers.

Badachro and beyond

Three miles south of Gairloch, a narrow single-track lane (built with the Destitution Funds raised during the nineteenth-century potato famine) winds west from the main A832, past wooded coves and inlets on its way south of the loch to **BADACHRO**, a sleepy former fishing village in a very attractive setting with a wonderful pub, the *Badachro Inn*, right by the water's edge.

Beyond Badachro, the road winds for five more miles along the shore to **Redpoint**, a minuscule hamlet with beautiful beaches of peach-coloured sand and great views to Raasay, Skye and the Western Isles. It also marks the trailhead for the wonderful coast walk to Lower Diabaig, described on p.236. Even if you don't fancy a full-blown hike, follow the path a mile or so to the exquisite beach hidden on the south side of the headland, which you'll probably have all to yourself. Redpoint is served by the Gairloch postbus (see below).

Gairloch practicalities

There's a late-afternoon bus (Mon–Sat) from Inverness to **Gairloch**, though the route and arrival time varies. Without your own transport, you'll have to depend upon postbuses to get around once there. Two postbus services (one for each side of the loch) leave from in front of the post office: one at 8.20am for Melvaig, and the other at 10.35am for Redpoint.

There's a good choice of **accommodation** in Gairloch, most of it mid-range; the central **tourist office** (April, May & mid-Sept to Oct Mon–Fri 10am–5pm, Sat 11–4pm; June Mon–Fri 9.30am–5.30pm, Sat 10am–5pm; July to mid-Sept Mon–Sat 9am–6pm, Sun noon–5pm; ☎01445/712130) will help if you have problems finding a vacancy. If you're looking for a **hotel**, try the family-run *Myrtle Bank Hotel* (☎01445/712004; ⑤), which has a good restaurant and is just above the loch. **B&Bs** are scattered throughout the area. In the village, options include the bright and pleasant *Newton Cottage* (☎01445/712007; ①), a little way up Mihol Road, and the friendly *Bains House* (☎01445/712472; ①), on the main street near the bus stop. A few hundred yards north on the Melvaig road, Gaelic-speaking Miss Mackenzie's *Duisary* (☎01445/712252; ①) is a good choice. Continuing towards Melvaig for about five miles, a little past the North Erradale junction, *Little Lodge* (☎01445/771237; ⑥ includes dinner) is outstanding, with immaculately furnished rooms, a log-burning stove, cashmere goats and dramatic sea views, as well as superb food. At Badachro, the recently built *Lochside* (☎01445/741295; ①) is spacious with a great view over the harbour and the Torridons. For **hostel** accommodation, there's a pleasant SYHA place at **Carn Dearg** two miles up the Melvaig road (☎01445/712219 or central reservations ☎0541 553255; mid-May to Sept), and the reasonable if often quiet *Badachro Bunkhouse* (☎01445/741255) overlooking Badachro harbour. **Camping** is possible at Big Sand or at Redpoint.

For **food**, Myrtle Bank's restaurant serves good meals at reasonable prices, while the fact that the chef at the *Scottish Seafood Restaurant* next to the petrol station near the pier is also the harbourmaster means that the fish and shellfish served up will be the pick of the catch. Another seafood option is *The Steading* beside the Heritage Museum. Inexpensive pasta and pricier seafood and meat are on offer at *Gino's* in the *Millcroft Hotel*, though service can be slow. For **snacks**, the *Serendipity Coffee Shop*, up the lane off the square, is a good bet, while the *Old Inn*, opposite the harbour, is a good real-ale **pub**.

Poolewe

It's a fifteen-minute hop by bus over the headland from Gairloch to the trim little village of **POOLEWE** on the sheltered south side of Loch Ewe, at the mouth of the River Ewe as it rushes down from Loch Maree. One of the area's best **walks** begins near here, signposted from the lay-by-cum-viewpoint on the main A832, a mile south of the village. It takes a couple of hours to follow the easy trail across open craggy moorland to the shores of Loch Maree, and thence to the car park at **Slatterdale**, seven miles southeast of Gairloch. If you reach Slatterdale just before 7pm on a Tuesday, Thursday or Friday, you should be able to pick up the Westerbus from Inverness back to Poolewe or Aultbea (confirm times on ☎01445/712255). Also worthwhile is the drive along the small sideroad running along the west shore of Loch Ewe to **COVE**. Here you'll find an atmospheric cave that was used by the "Wee Frees" as a church into this century; it's quite a perilous scramble up, however, and there's little to see once you're there. The route is also covered by a Poolewe **postbus** (1.55pm).

If you want **to stay** in the area, try the *Poolewe Hotel* (☎01445/781241; ③), on the Cove road; it's old-fashioned but very pleasant and serves straightforward food. From September until April they also have a bunkhouse available for hillwalkers. Rather more upscale is the *Pool House Hotel* (☎01445/781272, *poolhouse@inverewe.co.uk*; ⑤), which belonged to Osgood MacKenzie (see below); it has lovely views out over the loch and serves up tasty, if pricey, bar and restaurant meals. For **B&B** in Poolewe, *The Creagan* (☎01445/781424; ①), up the track on the village side of the campsite, is a welcoming modern house wreathed with honeysuckle. Up the Cove road, four miles north at **Inverasdale**, *Bruach Ard* (☎01445/781214; ②; April–Oct) has mostly en-suite rooms and great views to Assynt. At Cove, Mrs MacDonald (☎01445/781354; ②; April–Oct) offers upscale B&B with fine loch views. There's also an excellent **campsite** between the village and Inverewe Gardens (☎01445/781229; April–Oct). *The Bridge Cottage Coffee Shop*, just up the Cove road from the village crossroads, serves good coffee and home-baked cakes (March–Oct Mon–Sat 10.30am–5pm).

Inverewe Gardens

Half a mile across the bay from Poolewe on the A832, **Inverewe Gardens** (daily: mid-March to Oct 9.30am–9pm; Nov to mid-March 9.30am–5pm; £5; NTS), a verdant oasis of foliage and riotously colourful flower collections, form a vivid contrast to the wild, heathery crags of the adjoining coast. They were the brainchild of **Osgood Mackenzie**, who inherited the surrounding 12,000-acre estate from his stepfather, the laird of Gairloch, in 1862. Taking advantage of the area's famously temperate climate (a consequence of the Gulf Stream, which draws a warm-water current from Mexico to within a stone's throw of these shores), Mackenzie collected plants from all over the world for his walled garden, still the nucleus of the complex. Protected from Loch Ewe's corrosive salt breezes by a dense brake of Scots pine, rowan, oak, beech and birch trees, the fragile plants flourished on rich soil, brought here as ballast on Irish ships to overlay the previously infertile beach gravel and sea grass. By the time Mackenzie died in 1922, his garden sprawled over the whole peninsula, surrounded by a hundred acres of woodland. Today the NTS strives to develop the place along the lines envisaged by its founder.

Around 180,000 visitors pour through here annually, but they are easily absorbed. Interconnected by a labyrinthine network of twisting paths and walkways, more than a dozen gardens feature exotic plant collections from as far afield as Chile, China, Tasmania and the Himalayas. Strolling around the lotus ponds, palm trees and borders ablaze with exotic blooms, it's amazing to think you're at the same latitude as Hudson's Bay. Mid-May to mid-June is the best time to see the rhododendrons and azaleas, while the herbaceous garden reaches its peak in July and August, as does the wonderful Victorian vegetable and flower garden beside the sea. Look out, too, for the grand old eucalyptus in the Peace Plot, which is the largest in the northern hemisphere, and the nearby Ghost Tree (*Davidia involucrata*), representing the earliest evolutionary stages of flowering trees. You'll need at least a couple of hours to do the whole lot justice, and leave time for the **visitor centre** (mid-March to Oct daily 9.30am–5.30pm), which houses an informative display on the history of the garden. Guided walks (April–Oct) leave from here every weekday at 1.30pm. The **restaurant** at the top of the car park does good snacks and lunches.

Gruinard Bay and Little Loch Broom

Three buses each week (Mon, Wed & Sat; eastwards in the morning, westwards in the evening) run the twenty-mile stretch along the A832 from Poolewe past **Aultbea**, a small NATO naval base, to the head of **Little Loch Broom**, surrounded by a salt marsh that is covered with flowers in early summer. From **Laide**, the road skirts the shores of **Gruinard Bay**, offering fabulous views and, at the inner end of the bay, some excellent sandy beaches. During World War II, **Gruinard Island**, in the bay, was used as a testing ground for biological warfare, and for years was ringed by huge signs warning the public not to land. The anthrax spores released during the testing can live in the soil for up to a thousand years, but in 1987, after much protest, the Ministry of Defence had the island decontaminated and it was finally declared "safe" in 1990.

The road heads inland before joining the A835 at **Braemore Junction** (three Inverness–Ullapool buses stop here daily) above the head of **Loch Broom**. Just nearby, and easily accessible from the A835, are the spectacular 164-foot **Falls of Measach**, which plunge through the mile-long **Corrieshalloch Gorge**. You can overlook the cascades from a special observation platform, or from the impressive suspension bridge that spans the chasm, whose 197-foot vertical sides are draped in a rich array of plant life, with thickets of wych elm, goat willow and bird cherry miraculously thriving on the cliffs. North from the head of Loch Broom to Ullapool is one of the so-called **Destitution Roads**, built to give employment to local people during the nineteenth-century potato famines.

Hotels along here include the excellent *Old Smiddy* (☎01445/731425; ③, with dinner ⑥; April–Oct) on the main road in Laide, on the western shore of Guinard Bay and linked with Braemore and Achnasheen on the Kyle of Lochalsh railway by postbus. Crammed with travel trophies, family memorabilia, books and paintings by local artists (some on sale), the hotel has fine mountain views to the east, and serves outstanding food. Another option is *Cul-na-Mara* (☎01445/731295; ①), up the turning just past the *Sand Hotel*. At the head of Little Loch Broom, the *Dundonnell Hotel* (☎01854/633204, *selbie@dundonnellhotel.co.uk*; ⑤) is smart and comfortable and serves bar meals, while *Sail Mhor Croft* (☎01854/633224, *sailmhor@btinternet.com*) is a small independent hostel in a lovely location on the lochside a couple of miles before the *Dundonnell Hotel*.

The Scoraig peninsula

The outer part of the rugged **Scoraig peninsula**, dividing Little Loch Broom and Loch Broom, is one of the remotest places on the British mainland, accessible only by boat or on foot. Formerly dotted with crofting townships, it is now deserted apart from tiny **SCORAIG** village, where a mostly self-sufficient community has established itself, complete with windmills, organic vegetable gardens and a thriving primary school. Understandably, Scoraig's inhabitants would rather not be regarded as tourist curiosities, so only venture out here if you're sympathetic to such a community. To reach Scoraig, you have three main options: you can drive to Badrallach and walk from there, catch the occasional ferry from Ullapool to the *Altnaharrie Hotel* (see opposite) then walk, or phone the Scoraig **boat** operator (☎01854/633226), who serves the area two days a week. **Accommodation** on the Scoraig peninsula is limited to a small and particularly pleasant **campsite** at Badrallach, on the northeast shore of Little Loch Broom and a good bothy available if you've an airbed or sleeping mat (☎01854/633281).

Ullapool

ULLAPOOL, the northwest's principal centre of population, was founded at the height of the herring boom in 1788 by the **British Fisheries Society**, on a sheltered arm of land jutting into Loch Broom. The grid-plan town is still an important fishing centre, though the ferry link to Stornoway on Lewis (see p.310) means that in high season its personality is practically swamped by visitors. Even so, it's still a hugely appealing place and a good base for exploring the northwest Highlands – especially if you are relying on public transport. Regular **buses** run from here to Inverness, Durness and (May to early Oct) to the railhead at Lairg.

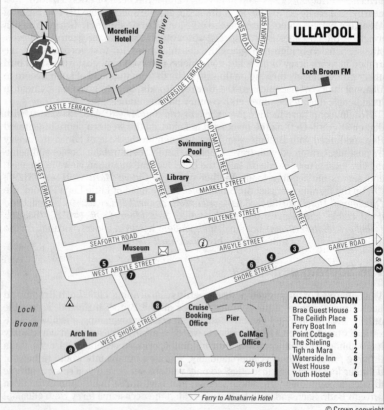

ACCOMMODATION	
Brae Guest House	3
The Ceilidh Place	5
Ferry Boat Inn	4
Point Cottage	9
The Shieling	1
Tigh na Mara	2
Waterside Inn	8
West House	7
Youth Hostel	6

▽ *Ferry to Altnaharrie Hotel*

© Crown copyright

Accommodation is plentiful and Ullapool is an obvious hideaway if the weather is bad, with cosy pubs, a new swimming pool and a lively arts centre, the *Ceilidh Place*.

Arrival and information

Forming the backbone of its grid plan, Ullapool's two main arteries are the loch-side **Shore Street** and, parallel to it, **Argyle Street**, further inland. **Buses** stop at the pier, in the town centre near the ferry dock, from where it's easy to get your bearings. The well-run **tourist office** (April–July & Sept Mon–Fri 9am–5.30pm, Sat 10am–5pm, Sun noon–5pm; Aug Mon–Sat 9am–6pm, Sun noon–6pm; Oct Mon–Fri 10am–5pm, Sat noon–4pm; Nov & Dec Mon–Fri 11am–4pm; ☎01854/612135), on Argyle Street, offers an accommodation booking service. If you're heading onto the Outer Hebrides, there are two or three daily **ferries** (Mon–Sat; 2hr 30min); for precise timings, contact CalMac on ☎01854/612358.

Accommodation

Ullapool, a popular holiday centre in summer, has all kinds of **accommodation**, ranging from one of Scotland's most expensive hotels, the *Altnaharrie*, to innumerable guest houses and B&Bs, plus a well-situated **campsite** (up the hill from the pier and turn left) and an excellent **youth hostel** on Shore Street (☎01854/612254 or central reservations ☎0541 553255; closed Jan).

Altnaharrie Hotel (☎01854/633230). A world-famous, select hotel with a very highly regarded restaurant, located across the loch from town – you're collected by launch. ⑨.

Brae Guest House, Shore Street (☎01854/612421). A great guest house in a beautifully maintained traditional building right on the loch-side. ②.

The Ceilidh Place, West Argyle Street (☎01854/612103, *reservations@ceilidh.demon.co.uk*). Tasteful and popular hotel, with the west coast's best bookshop, a relaxing first-floor lounge, a great bar/restaurant, sea views, and a laid-back atmosphere. Also has a good-value bunkhouse (May–Oct), for £15 per person in family rooms. ⑥.

Ferry Boat Inn, Shore Street (☎01854/612366). Traditional inn right on the waterfront with a friendly atmosphere and reasonable food. ③.

Point Cottage, 22 West Shore St (☎01854/612494). Very well-equipped rooms and good showers, at the quieter end of the seafront. Guests can borrow OS maps already marked up with walking routes. ②.

The Shieling, Garve Road (☎01854/612947). Outstandingly comfortable guest house overlooking the loch, with immaculate, spacious rooms (rooms 4 and 5 have the best views), superb breakfasts (try their home-made venison and leek sausages) and a sauna. ②.

Tigh Na Mara, Ardinrean (☎01854/655282). Twelve miles from Ullapool on the opposite (west) shore of Loch Broom, but worth the trip. One of Scotland's most renowned vegetarian places, offering gourmet veggie/vegan breakfasts and simple rooms in a romantic setting. The price includes dinner. ⑥.

Waterside House, 6 West Shore St (☎01854/612140). Very appealing rooms in an outstandingly pleasant, friendly B&B on the seafront. ②.

West House, West Argyle Street (☎01854/613126, *r.lindsay@btinternet.com*). Busy independent backpackers' hostel with four- to six-bed dorms and more civilized B&B on offer in a nearby house. Minibus day-tours organized and bike rental available.

The Town

Day or night, most of the action in Ullapool centres on the **harbour**, which has an authentic and salty air, especially when the boats are in. By day, attention

ULLAPOOL WALKS, HIKES AND CYCLE RIDES

Ordnance Survey maps nos. 15, 19 and 20

Ullapool is at the start of several excellent **hiking trails**, ranging from sedate shoreside ambles to long and strenuous ascents of Munros. However, the weather here can change very quickly, so take the necessary precautions (see p.46). More detailed descriptions of the **routes** outlined below are available from the youth hostel on Shore Street (30p), and are recommended; hostellers can also rent out the relevant up-to-date OS **maps** – essential for the hillwalks.

An easy half-day ramble begins at the north end of Quay Street: cross the river here and follow its bank left towards the sea until you reach a second river and cross the bridge. A single-track road leads to a hilltop lighthouse, from where you gain fine views across the sea to the Summer Isles. Return the same way or via the main road (A835).

For a harder half-day hike, head north along Mill Street on the east edge of town to Broom Court retirement home – trailhead for the Ullapool hillwalk (look for the sign next to the electricity substation). A rocky path zigzags steeply up from the roadside to the summit of **Meall Mor**, where there are great views of the area's major peaks. This is also a prime spot for botanists, with a rich array of plants and flowers, including two insect-eating species: sundew and butterwort. The path then drops sharply down the heather-clad north side of Meall Mor into **Glen Achall**, where you turn left onto the surfaced road running past the limestone quarry; the main road back to Ullapool lies a further thirty minutes' walk west. A right turn where the path meets the road will take you up to Loch Achall and the start of an old drovers' trail across the middle of the Highlands to **Croick** (see p.269). A well-maintained bothy at **Knockdamph**, eleven miles further on, marks the midway point of this long-distance hike, which should not be undertaken alone or without proper gear (see p.46).

If you're reasonably experienced and can use a map and compass, a day-walk well worth tackling is the rock path to **Achininver**, near Achiltiebuie. The route, which winds along one of the region's most beautiful and unspoilt stretches of coastline to a small **youth hostel** (mid-May to Sept; book ahead on ☎01854/622254), is easy to follow in good weather, but gets very boggy and slippery when wet. Sound footwear, a light pack and a route guide are all essential.

The warden and assistants at Ullapool hostel can also give advice on more serious mountain hikes in the area. Among the most popular is the walk to **Scoraig** (see p.241), following the old coast route over the pass to Badrallach, on the south side of the peninsula, and then northwest to Scoraig village itself. The only drawback with this rewarding route is that to get back to Ullapool you have to rely on the *Altnaharrie Hotel's* pricey and sporadic ferry boat (May–Sept; to check times, call ☎01854/633230); miss the boat and the only accommodation for miles is the ultra-expensive hotel or the bothy and campsite over at Badrallach. If you have a **mountain bike**, the return trip to Scoraig via Badrallach can be completed in a single day.

Alternatively, try the **Rhidorroch** estate track, which turns right off the A835 just past the *Mercury Hotel* (two miles out of Ullapool), and then heads past the limestone quarry mentioned earlier to Loch Achall and beyond. At the East Rhidorroch Lodge, ignore the suspension bridge and strike up the steep hill ahead onto open moorland and secluded **Loch Damph**, where there's a small bothy. A much easier but no less scenic cycle route is the tour of Loch Broom, taking in the hamlets of **Letters** and **Loggie** on the tranquil western shore, which you can get to via a quiet single-track road (off the A832 once you've cycled south and round the loch from Ullapool). At the end of this, a jeep track heads for the vitrified Iron Age fort at **Dun Lagaidh**; you have to return by the same route.

focuses on the comings and goings of the ferry, fishing boats and smaller craft, while in the evening, yachts swing on the current, the shops stay open late and customers from the *Ferry Boat Inn* line the sea wall. During summer, booths advertise trips to the **Summer Isles** – a cluster of uninhabited islets two to three miles offshore – to view seabird colonies, dolphins and porpoises, but if you're lucky you'll spot marine life from the waterfront. Otters occasionally nose around the rocks near the *Ferry Boat Inn*, and seals swim past begging scraps from the boats moored in the middle of the loch.

The only conventional "sight" in town is the **museum**, West Argyle Street (April–mid July & mid Aug–Oct Mon–Sat 9.30am–5.30pm; mid-July to mid-Aug Mon–Sat 9.30am–8pm; Nov–March Wed & Sat 11am–3pm; £2), in the old parish church, with displays on crofting, fishing, local religion and emigration. During the Clearances, Ullapool was one of the ports through which evicted crofters left to start new lives in Canada, Australia and New Zealand.

Eating and drinking

Ullapool has a wide array of places to eat and drink, ranging from the cheap-and-cheerful fish-and-chip shops on the harbourfront to one of Scotland's most expensive gourmet restaurants, at the *Altnaharrie Hotel*. The two best **pubs** are the *Arch Inn*, home of the Ullapool football team, and the *Ferry Boat Inn* (known as the "*FBI*"), where you can enjoy a pint of real ale at the lochside – midges permitting. The slightly less characterful *Seaforth*, by the pier, is the place to catch middle-of-the-road live **music**, while **live folk music** is a regular occurrence at *The Ceilidh Place* or on Thursday nights at the *FBI*.

CEILIDHS

The **ceilidh** is essentially an informal, homespun kind of entertainment, the word being Gaelic for "a visit". In remote Highland communities, talents and resources were pooled, people gathering to play music, sing, recite poems and dance. The dances themselves are thought to be ancient in origin; the Romans wrote that the Caledonians danced with abandon round swords stuck in the ground, a practice echoed in today's more sedate sword dance, where the weapons are crossed on the floor and a quick-stepping dancer skips over and around them.

Highland ceilidhs, fuelled by whisky and largely extemporized, must have been an intoxicating, riotous means of fending off winter gloom. But they have died out in their original form, like much of clan culture, which was cruelly repressed after the defeat of the Highlanders at Culloden, and the 1747 Act of Proscription, which forbade the wearing of the plaid and other expressions of Highland identity.

Ceilidhs were enthusiastically revived in the reign of tartan-fetishist Queen Victoria, although in a tamer form. The ceilidh became the preserve of the village hall and hotel, and latterly of TV, with a whole raft of Scottish "celebrities" apparently being exhumed from the grave at Hogmanay, for chirpy renditions of *Donald Where's Yer Troosers?* and other classics. More recently though, the ceilidh has thrown off some of these stale associations, and the *Ceilidh Place* in Ullapool is restoring some of its spontaneous, infectious fun. Ceilidh band music is pretty irresistible, and with simple dances like the Gay Gordons and eightsome reels – which involve you being whirled breathlessly round the room – being "called" by the bandleader, you might well be tempted to join in.

Altnaharrie Hotel (☎01854/633230). World-class cuisine by the renowned chef Gun Eriksen; superb, but steep at around £75 for dinner, and it's hard to get a table if you're a non-resident.

The Ceilidh Place, West Argyle Street (☎01854/612286). Filling snacks are served at the excellent bar, while full meals, including imaginative seafood and vegetarian dishes, are on offer in the spacious restaurant, accompanied by occasional live music. The good coffee shop does great cakes and home-made ice cream.

John MacLean's, Shore Street. A wholefood shop/deli where you can stock up on picnic-style fare, as well as a selection of freshly baked cakes.

Morefield, Morefield Lane, off North Road (☎01854/612161). Huge portions of succulent seafood, easily Ullapool's best-value, are served in the restaurant, while the bar has good fish at lower prices. It's not so great for vegetarians, and is hard to find, being improbably hidden in a modern housing estate beyond the bridge on the north side of the town.

The Scottish Larder, Ladysmith Street (☎01854/612185). Reasonably priced and filling food from local sources, specializing in interesting pies, open for lunch and dinner.

North of Ullapool

North of Ullapool, the landscape changes to consist not of mountain ranges but of extraordinary peaks rising individually from the moorland. As you head further north, the peaks become more widely spaced and settlements smaller and fewer, linked by twisting single-track roads and shore-side footpaths that make excellent hiking trails. You can easily sidestep what little tourist traffic there is by heading down the peaceful back roads, which, after twisting through idyllic crofts, invariably end up at a deserted beach or windswept headland with superb views west to the Outer Hebrides.

Ten miles north of Ullapool, a single-track road winds west off the A835 to squeeze between the northern shore of Loch Lurgainn and the lower slopes of **Cul Beag** (2523ft) and craggy Stac Pollaidh (2012ft) to reach the **Coigach** peninsula. To the southeast, the awesome bulk of **Ben More Coigach** (2439ft) presides over the district, which contains some spectacular coastal scenery including a string of sandy beaches and the Summer Isles, scattered just offshore.

Coigach's main settlement is **ACHILTIBUIE**, an old crofting village stretched above a series of white-sand coves and rocks tapering into the Atlantic, from where a fleet of small fishing boats carries sheep, and tourists, to the island pastures during the summer. The village also attracts gardening enthusiasts, thanks to the space-station-like structure overlooking its main beach. Dubbed "The Garden of the Future", the **Hydroponicum** (Easter–Sept 10am–5pm; £4; tours hourly on the hour) is a kind of glorified greenhouse that concentrates the sun's heat, while protecting the plants inside from winter cold and acidic soil. The results – exotic plants, fruit, fragrant flowers and herbs thriving in four separate "climate rooms" – speak for themselves; you can also taste its famous strawberries and other produce in the subtropical setting of the *Lily Pond Café*, which serves meals, desserts and snacks. Also worth a visit is the **Achiltibuie Smokehouse** (April–Sept Mon–Sat 9.30am–5pm; free), three miles north of the Hydroponicum at **Altandhu**, where you can see meat, fish and game being cured in the traditional way and can buy some afterwards.

The wonderful *Summer Isles Hotel* (☎01854/622282; ⑨; April–Oct), just up the road from the Achiltibuie school, enjoys a near-perfect setting above a sandy beach, with views over the islands, and is virtually self-sufficient. The hotel buys in Hydroponicum fruit and vegetables, but has its own dairy, poultry, and even runs a small smokehouse, so the food in its excellent restaurant (open to non-residents) is about as fresh as it comes. A set dinner costs about £35, while superb bar snacks and lunches feature crab, langoustines and smoked mackerel starting from £5. Of Achiltibuie's several **B&Bs**, *Dornie House* (☎01854/622271; ①) in the north of the settlement is welcoming and has particularly fine views. There's also a beautifully situated twenty-bed SYHA **hostel** (☎01854/622254 or central reservations ☎0541/553255; mid-May to Sept), three miles down the coast at Achininver, which is handy for Coigach's many mountain hikes.

Lochinver

The narrow road north from Coigach through Inverkirkaig is unremittingly spectacular, threading its way through a tumultuous landscape of secret valleys, moorland and bare rock, past the startling shapes of **Cul Beag** (2523ft), **Cul Mor** (2785ft) and the distinctive sugar-loaf **Suilven** (2398ft). A scattering of pebble-dashed bungalows around a sheltered bay heralds your arrival at **LOCHINVER**, the last sizeable village before Thurso, also with the last cash machine. It's a workaday place, with a huge fish market, from where large trucks head off to the rest of Britain. There's a better-than-average **tourist office** (April–Oct Mon–Sat 10am–5pm, July & Aug also Sun 11am–4pm; ☎01571/844330), whose **visitor centre** gives an interesting rundown on the area's geology, wildlife and history; a countryside ranger is available to advise on walks. The area is popular with **fishing** enthusiasts, and fly rods and other equipment are available for rent from the newsagent on the main road. You can get hold of permits at the tourist office, while for boat trips for sea fishing, contact Badnaban Cruises on ☎01571/844358. **Mountain bikes** are available in the village from Assynt Adventures, on the main road near the police station.

Lochinver has a range of good **B&Bs**: on the north side of the harbour, *Ardglas* (☎01571/844257; ①) has superb views, though no en-suite rooms, while nearby *Davar* (☎01571/844501; ②) is better-equipped. More central, just above the tourist office, the comfortable *Polcraig* (☎01571/844429; ②) can arrange fishing. If you're looking for **hotel** accommodation, a pleasant and relaxing option is the *Albannach* (☎01571/844407; ⑦ includes dinner; March–Dec) at Baddidarroch, an attractive nineteenth-century building set in a walled garden, and renowned for its excellent seafood, caught locally and served in a lovely wood-panelled dining room. Lochinver's most imaginative **food** can be found in the *Larder Riverside Bistro* on the main street: it has local seafood, venison and several vegetarian choices at reasonable prices. Decent bar meals are available at the *Caberfeidh* next door, which is also the most convivial place to head for a drink, while the *Seamen's Mission*, down at the harbour, is a good option for filling meals (some vegetarian) if you're on a tight budget.

Inverkirkaig Falls

Approaching Lochinver from the south, the road bends sharply through a wooded valley where a signpost for **Inverkirkaig Falls** marks the start of a long but gentle **walk** to the base of **Suilven** – the most distinctive mountain in Scotland, its huge sandstone dome rising above the heather boglands of Assynt. Serious hikers use the path to approach the mighty peak, but you can follow it for an easy three- to four-hour ramble, taking in a waterfall and a tour of a secluded loch. If you're travelling by vehicle, use the car park below the excellent Achins Bookshop near the trailhead, which is well stocked with titles on the Highlands, and has a café serving cream teas, cakes and good coffee.

East of Lochinver

The area to the **east of Lochinver**, traversed by the A837 and bounded by the gnarled peaks of the Ben More Assynt massif, is a wilderness of mountains, moorland, mist and scree. Dotted with lochs and lochans, it's also an angler's paradise, home to the only non-migratory fish in northern Scotland, the brown trout, and numerous other sought-after species, including the Atlantic salmon, sea trout, Arctic char and a massive prize strain of cannibal ferox. **Fishing** permits for the rivers in this area are like gold dust during the summer, snapped up months in

---

WALKS IN ASSYNT

Ordnance Survey Landranger map no. 15

Of Assynt's spectacular array of idiosyncratic peaks, **Stac Pollaidh** (2012ft) counts as the most accessible and popular hike. So much so, in fact, that Inverpolly National Nature Reserve have fenced off the now much-eroded main path up the mountain from the car park on the Achiltibuie road, and walkers are now requested to take the path that goes around to the northern side of the hill. You'll need a head for heights to explore the jagged summit ridge extensively, and this is one hill where you should turn back from bagging the summit if you feel uncertain doing some basic rock climbing.

Suilven (2399ft), the most memorable of the Assynt peaks, is a tough eight-hour outing, including the boggy five-mile walk to its base. From the A837 at Elphin, head round the north of Cam Loch then through the glen between Canisp and Suilven, until you pick up the path that aims for the saddle – Bealach Mor – in the middle of Suilven's summit ridge, from where the route to the top is straightforward. The return is by the same route, although at the saddle you could choose to turn southwest for the route to Inverkirkaig, while a descent down the northwestern side can lead either back to Elphin or west to Lochinver by way of Glen Canisp.

The highest peaks in Assynt are the neighbouring **Conival** and **Ben More Assynt**, though they're less distinctive than their neighbours, and generally known for their rough harshness and bleak landscape. The route follows the track up Glen Dubh from Inchnadamph, staying to the north of the river as you aim for the saddle between Conival and the peak to the north, Beinn an Fhurain. Once on the ridge, turn southeast to climb to the top of Conival, then turn east along a high, exposed ridge to top of Ben More. The entire walk, including the return to Inchnadamph, takes five to six hours.

If you're looking for something less testing, there are some classic **coastal walks** immediately north of Lochinver. From **Baddidarach**, opposite Lochinver village on the north side of the river mouth, a path with fantastic views of the Assynt peaks leads over heather slopes to Loch Dubh and down to **Achmelvich** (a 1hr walk). From here there's a sporadically signposted but reasonable path to **Clachtoll** (about 2hr) past delightful sandy coves, grassy knolls, and rocks to clamber across at low tide. At Clachtoll there's a dramatic split rock (after which the crofting hamlet is named) and an Iron Age fort. More dramatic is the ninety-minute clifftop walk from Stoer lighthouse along to the famous stack, **The Old Man of Stoer** (220ft).

advance by exclusive hunting-lodge hotels, but you can sometimes obtain last-minute cancellations (try the *Inver Lodge* on ☎01571/844496); permits for fishing lochs are easier to get hold of.

Although most of the land here is privately owned, nearly 27,000 acres are managed as the **Inverpolly National Nature Reserve**, whose visitor centre (April–Oct daily 10am–5pm; ☎01854/666254) at Knockan Cliff, twelve miles north of Ullapool on the A835, gives a thorough overview of the diverse flora and wildlife in the surrounding habitats. The theory of thrust faults was developed here in 1859 by eminent geologist James Nicol, and an interpretive **Geological Trail** shows you how to detect the movement of rock plates in the nearby cliffs. A few miles further on in the village of Knockan, the *Birchbank Holiday Lodge* (☎01854/666215; ②) is an excellent base if you're planning to hike or fish in the area; it's on a working sheep farm run by one of the area's top outdoor guides, who has a wealth of information on the best routes and places to explore.

Further north, on the rocky promontory, stand the jagged remnants of **Ardveck Castle** (free access), a MacLeod stronghold from 1597 that fell to the Seaforth Mackenzies after a siege in 1691. Previously, the Marquis of Montrose had been imprisoned here after his defeat at Carbisdale in 1650. The rebel duke, whom the local laird had betrayed to the government for £20,000 and 400 bowls of sour meal, was eventually led away to be executed in Edinburgh, lashed back to front on his horse.

The *Inchnadamph Hotel* (☎01571/822202; ④), on Loch Assynt, is a wonderfully traditional Highland retreat; inside, the walls are covered with the stuffed catches of its past guests. The hotel offers fine old-fashioned cooking, usually with good vegetarian options, in its moderately priced restaurant and bar. It's popular with anglers, who get free fishing rights to Loch Assynt, as well as several hill lochs backing onto Ben More, haunts of the infamous ferox trout. Just along the road, the Assynt Field Centre at *Inchnadamph Lodge* (☎01571/822218; ①) has basic but comfortable bunk rooms, as well as more spacious B&B accommodation. Through the year, the centre offers a variety of outdoor activity breaks and holidays, ranging from the obvious hillwalking to drystone dyke building and cookery courses focusing on local products.

North from Lochinver: the coast road

Heading **north from Lochinver**, there are two possible routes: the fast A837, which runs eastwards along the shore of Loch Assynt to join the northbound A894, or the narrow **coastal road** (the B869) that locals dub "The Breakdown Zone" because its ups and downs claim so many victims during summer. Hugging the indented shoreline, this route is the more scenic, offering superb views of the Summer Isles, as well as a number of rewarding side-trips to beaches and dramatic cliffs. **Postbuses** from Lochinver cover the route as far as Ardvar or Drumbeg (Mon–Sat). Unusually, most of the land and lochs around here are owned by local crofters rather than wealthy landlords. Helped by grants and private donations, the **Assynt Crofters' Trust** made history in 1993 when it pulled off the first ever community buyout of estate land in Scotland, and it's now pursuing a number of projects aimed at strengthening the local economy and conserving the environment. The Trust owns the lucrative fishing rights to the area, too, selling permits for £5 per day (£25 per week) through local post offices and the tourist office in Lochinver. An alternative outdoor activity is **pony trekking**, which is available through Clachtoll Trekking Centre (☎01571/855364), at Clachtoll on the road between Achmelvich and Stoer.

Heading north, the first village worthy of a detour is **ACHMELVICH**, a couple of miles along a sideroad, whose tiny bay cradles the whitest beach and most stunning turquoise water you'll encounter this side of the Seychelles. There's a noisy **campsite** and a basic forty-bed **youth hostel** (☎01571/844480 or central reservations ☎0541/553255; April–Sept) just behind the largest beach. However, for total peace and quiet there are other equally seductive beaches beyond the headlands.

The sideroad that branches north off the B869 between **Stoer** and **Clashnessie**, both of which have sandy beaches, ends abruptly by the automatic **lighthouse** at **Raffin** – built in 1870 by the Stevenson brothers (one of whom was the author Robert Louis Stevenson's dad) – but you can continue for two miles along a well-worn track to Stoer Point, named after the colossal rock pillar that stands offshore known as "**The Old Man of Stoer**". Surrounded by sheer cliffs and splashed with guano from the seabird colonies that nest on its 200-foot sides, it was climbed for the first time in 1961.

DRUMBEG, nine miles further on, is a major target for trout anglers, lying within reach of countless lochans. Permits to fish them are sold at the post office, but you'll need a detailed map and a compass to find your way in and out of this area without getting hopelessly lost. There's a lot of self-catering accommodation in the area, but few **B&Bs**. A good choice, however, is *Taigh Druimbeag* (☎01571/833209; ③; April–Oct), a comfortable old Edwardian house with period furniture and a large garden; to find it, turn off the main road at the primary school and follow the signs.

Kylesku to Kinlochbervie

KYLESKU, 33 miles north of Ullapool and around six miles west of Drumbeg, is the site of the award-winning road bridge spanning the mouth of lochs Glencoul and Glendhu. It's a pleasant place for a short stay, with plenty of good walks and a congenial hotel by the water's edge above the old ferry slipway. The family-run *Kylesku Hotel* (☎01971/502231; ④; March–Oct) has en-suite rooms, a welcoming bar popular with locals, and an excellent restaurant serving outstanding fresh seafood, including lobster, crab, mussels and local salmon (you can watch the fish being landed on the pier). Alternatively, *Newton Lodge* (☎01971/502070; ③, including dinner ⑤) is a modern, friendly and comfortable small hotel a few hundred yards up the road towards Ullapool. Cheaper accommodation is available at *Kylesku Lodges and Backpackers* (☎01971/502003), with twin rooms in a series of reasonable A-frame lodges and, inevitably, a great setting. Statesman Cruises runs entertaining boat trips (March–Oct daily 11am & 2pm; round trip 2hr; £10; ☎01571/844446) from the jetty below the hotel to the 650-foot **Eas-Coul-Aulin**, Britain's highest waterfall, at the head of Loch Glencoul; otters, seals, porpoises and minke whales can occasionally be spotted along the way.

It's also possible to reach Eas-Coul-Aulin on foot: a rough trail (3hr) leaves the A894 three miles south of Kylesku, skirting the south shore of **Loch na Gainmhich** (known locally as the "sandy loch") to approach the falls from above. Great care should be taken here, as the path above the cliffs can get very slippery when wet; the rest of the route is also difficult to follow, particularly in bad weather, and should only be attempted by experienced, properly equipped and compass-literate hikers. However, there are several less demanding walks around Kylesku if you just fancy a gentle amble: one of the most popular is the half-day low-level route along the north side of Loch Glendhu, beginning at **Kylestrome**, on the opposite side of the bridge from the hotel. Follow the surfaced jeep track east from the trailhead and turn left onto a footpath that leads through the woods. This eventually emerges onto the open mountainside, dropping down to cross a burn from where it then winds to a boarded-up old house called Glendhu, where there's a picturesque pebble beach. Several interesting side-trips and variations to this walk may be undertaken with the help of the detailed Ordnance Survey Landranger map no. 15, but you'll need a compass and wet-weather gear in case of bad weather.

Ten miles north of Kylesku, the widely scattered crofting community of **SCOURIE**, on a bluff above the main road, surrounds a beautiful sandy beach whose safe bathing has made it a popular holiday destination for families; there's plenty to do for walkers and trout anglers, too. Scourie itself has some good accommodation: try the charming *Scourie Lodge* (☎01971/502248; ②; March–Oct), an old shooting retreat with a lovely garden; the welcoming owners also do great evening meals. **UPPER BADCALL** village, three miles south of Scourie and even more remote, has a couple of B&Bs, including *Stoer View* (☎01971/502411; ①), whose clean and comfortable rooms look over Eddrachillis Bay to Stoer Point. For a little more luxury, try the nearby old-established *Eddrachillis Hotel* (☎01971/502080; ⑤, with dinner ⑥), which enjoys a spectacular situation on the bay, and serves reasonable bar food. There's also a good **campsite**, the *Scourie Caravan and Camping Park* (☎01971/502060), near the centre of the village.

Handa Island

Visible just offshore to the north of Scourie is **Handa Island**, a huge chunk of red Torridon sandstone surrounded by sheer cliffs and carpeted with machair and purple-tinged moorland. Teeming with seabirds, it's an internationally important wildlife reserve and a real treat for ornithologists, with vast colonies of razorbills and guillemots breeding on its guano-splashed cliffs during summer. From late May to mid-July, large numbers of puffins waddle comically over the turf-covered clifftops where they dig their burrows.

Apart from a solitary warden, Handa is deserted. Until midway through the last century, however, it supported a thriving, if somewhat eccentric, community of crofters. Surviving on a diet of fish, potatoes and seabirds, the islanders, whose ruined cottages still cling to the slopes by the jetty, devised their own system of government, with a "queen" (Handa's oldest widow) and "parliament" (a council of men who met each morning to discuss the day's business). Uprooted by the 1846 potato famine, most of the villagers eventually emigrated to Canada's Cape Breton; today, Handa is private property, administered as a nature sanctuary by the Scottish Wildlife Trust. If you're landing on the island, you're encouraged to make a donation of around £1.50 towards its upkeep.

You'll need about three hours to follow the footpath around the island – an easy and enjoyable walk taking in the north shore's Great Stack rock pillar and some fine views across the Minch: a detailed route guide is featured in the SWT's free leaflet available from the warden's office when you arrive. Weather permitting, boats (☎01971/502347; £7) leave for Handa throughout the day (until around 4pm) from the tiny cove of **TARBET**, three miles northwest of the main road and accessible by postbus from Scourie (Mon–Sat 1 daily; 1.50pm), where there's a small car park and jetty. Alternatively, if you want to see the island and the local coastline, with its attendant sea- and birdlife, from the sea, Laxford Cruises (☎01971/502251) offer two-hour boat trips from **FANAGMORE** (May–Sept Mon–Sat 10am, noon & 2pm; July & Aug also 4pm; £8), a mile further up the coast from Tarbet (reached by the same postbus as above). Camping is not allowed on the island, but the SWT maintains a **bothy** for birdwatchers (reservations must be made on ☎0131/312 7765, or with the warden on the island), while in Tarbet, Rex and Liz Norris (☎01971/502098; ①) run a comfortable little **B&B** overlooking the bay. For food, Tarbet's unexpected *Seafood Restaurant* (Mon–Sat noon–7pm) serves delicious, moderately priced fish and vegetarian dishes, and a good selection of home-made cakes and desserts, in its airy conservatory just above the jetty.

Kinlochbervie and beyond

North of Scourie, the road sweeps inland through the starkest part of the Highlands; rocks piled on rocks, bog and water create an almost alien landscape, and the astonishingly bare, stony coastline looks increasingly inhospitable. After about eight miles, at **Rhiconich**, you can branch off the main road to **KINLOCHBERVIE**, a major fishing port set in a rugged, rocky inlet. Trucks from all over Europe pick up cod and shellfish from the trawlers here, crewed mainly by east coast fishermen. *The Old Schoolhouse Restaurant and Guest House* (☎01971/521383; ③) provides comfortable accommodation and home-cooked meals.

Beyond Kinlochbervie, a single-track road takes you through isolated **Oldshoremore**, a working crofters' village scattered above a stunning white-sand beach, to **BLAIRMORE**, where you can park for the four-mile walk across peaty moorland to deserted **Sandwood Bay**. Few visitors make this half-day detour north, but the beach at the end of the rough track is one of the most beautiful in Scotland. Flanked by rolling dunes, and lashed by fierce gales for much of the year, the shell-white sands are said to be haunted by a bearded mariner – one of many sailors to have perished on this notoriously dangerous stretch of coast since the Vikings first navigated it over a millennium ago. Around the turn of the last century, the beach, whose treacherous undercurrents make it unsuitable for swimming, also witnessed Britain's most recent recorded sighting of a mermaid. Plans are afoot to bulldoze a motorable road up here, so enjoy the tranquillity while you can. Cape Wrath, the most northwesterly point in mainland Britain, lies a day's hike north. However, most people approach the headland from Durness on the north coast (see opposite). If you want **to camp** in the area, try the well-equipped site (☎01971/521281) at Oldshoremore, or continue through Blairmore to **Sheigra**, where the road ends, for informal camping behind the beach.

THE NORTH COAST

Though a constant stream of sponsored walkers, caravans and tour groups makes it to **John O'Groats**, surprisingly few visitors travel the whole length of the Highlands' wild **north coast**. Those that do, however, rarely return disappointed. Pounded by one of the world's most ferocious seaways, Scotland's rugged northern shore is backed by barren mountains in the west, and in the east by lochs and open rolling grasslands. Between its far ends, mile upon mile of crumbling cliffs and sheer rocky headlands shelter bays whose perfect white beaches are nearly always deserted, even in the height of summer; though, somewhat incongruously, they're also home to Scotland's best **surfing** waves. This is a great area for **birdwatching**, with huge seabird colonies clustered in clefts and on remote stacks at regular intervals along the coast; **seals** also bob around in the surf offshore, and in winter **whales** put in the odd appearance in the more sheltered estuaries of the northwest.

Getting around this stretch of coast without your own transport can be a slow and frustrating business: **Thurso**, the area's main town and springboard for Orkney, is well connected by bus and train with Inverness, but further west, after the main A836 peters into a single-track road, you have to rely on a convoluted series of postbus connections or, in peak season, a single Highland Country bus (#387).

Durness and around

Scattered around a string of sheltered sandy coves and grassy clifftops, **DURNESS**, the most northwesterly village on the British mainland, straddles the turning point on the main road as it swings east from the inland peat bogs of the interior to the north coast's fertile strip of limestone machair. First settled by the Picts around 400 BC, the area has been farmed ever since, its crofters being among the few not cleared off estate land during the nineteenth century. Today, Durness is the centre for several crofting communities and a good base for a couple of days, with some good walks. Even if you're only passing through, it's worth pausing here to see the **Smoo Cave**, a gaping hole in a sheer limestone cliff, and to visit beautiful **Balnakiel beach**, to the west. In addition, Durness is the jumping-off point for roadless and rugged **Cape Wrath**, the windswept promontory at the Scotland's northwest tip, which has retained an end-of-the-world mystique lost long ago by John O'Groats.

The Smoo Cave

A mile or so east of Durness village lies the 200-foot-long **Smoo Cave**, a natural wonder, formed partly by the action of the sea, and partly by the small burn that flows through it. Tucked away at the end of a narrow sheer-sided sea cove, guides will show you the illuminated interior, although the much-hyped rock formations are less memorable than the short rubber-dinghy trip you have to make in the second of three caverns, where the whole experience is enlivened after wet weather by a **waterfall** that crashes through the middle of the cavern. A boat trip leaves from Smoo Cave on a wildlife tour of the coast around Durness, taking in stretches of the shoreline only accessible by sea. The trip (May–Sept daily, times depending on weather and tide – ☎01971/511365 or 511284; 90min; £6.50) takes a close look at **seabird colonies**, and sightings of seals, puffins and porpoises are common.

Balnakiel

A narrow road winds northwest of Durness to tiny **BALNAKIEL**, whose name derives from the Gaelic *Baile ne Cille* (Village of the Church). The ruined **chapel** that today overlooks this remote hamlet was built in the seventeenth century, but a church has stood here for at least 1200 years. A skull-and-crossbones stone set in the south wall marks the grave of Donald MacMurchow, a seventeenth-century highwayman and contract killer who murdered eighteen people for his clan chief (allegedly by throwing them from the top of the Smoo Cave). The "half-in, half-out" position of his grave was apparently a compromise between his grateful employer and the local clergy, who initially refused to allow such an evil man to be buried on church ground. Balnakiel is also known for its **golf course**, whose ninth and final hole involves a 155-yard drive over the Atlantic; you can rent equipment from the clubhouse. The **Balnakiel Craft Village** (daily 10am–6pm; free), back towards Durness, is worth a visit. Housed in an imaginatively converted 1950s military base, the campus consists of a dozen or so workshops where you can watch painters, potters, leatherworkers, candlemakers, woodworkers, stonecarvers, knitters and weavers in action.

The white-sand beach on the east side of Balnakiel Bay is a stunning sight in any weather, but most spectacular on sunny days, when the water turns to brilliant turquoise. For the best views, walk along the path that winds north through the dunes behind it; this eventually leads to **Faraid Head** – from the Gaelic *Fear Ard* (High Fellow) – where you stand a good chance of spotting puffins from late May until mid-July. The fine views over the mouth of Loch Eriboll and west to Cape Wrath make this round-walk (3–4hr) the best in the Durness area.

Cape Wrath

An excellent day-trip from Durness begins three miles southwest of the village at **Keoldale**, where a foot-passenger ferry (June–Aug hourly 9.30am–4.30pm; May & Sept approximately 4 daily; ☎01971/511376; no motorcycles) crosses the Kyle of Durness estuary to link up with a minibus (☎01971/511287; May–Sept) that runs the eleven miles out to **Cape Wrath**. The UK mainland's most northwesterly point, the headland takes its name not from the stormy seas that crash against it for most of the year, but from the Norse word *hvarf*, meaning "turning place" – a throwback to the days when Viking warships used it as a navigation point during raids on the Scottish coast. These days, a lighthouse (another of those built by Robert Louis Stevenson's father) warns ships away from the treacherous rocks. Looking east to Orkney and west to the Outer Hebrides, it stands above the famous **Clo Mor cliffs**, the highest sea cliffs in Britain and a prime breeding site for seabirds. You can walk from here to remote Sandwood Bay (see p.252), visible to the south, although the route, which cuts inland across lochan-dotted moorland, is hard to follow in places. Hikers generally continue south from Sandwood to the trail end at Blairmore; if you hitch or walk the six miles from here to Kinlochbervie, you can (with careful planning) catch a bus back to Durness. Don't attempt this route from south to north, as, if the weather closes in, the Cape Wrath minibus stops running. Note, also, that much of the land bordering the headland is a military firing range and the area is sometimes closed – check with Durness tourist office before you set off.

Durness practicalities

Public transport in the area is sparse; the key service on the north coast is the Highland Country link (#387) to Thurso (June to mid-Sept Mon–Sat), leaving Thurso at 11.30am and Durness at 3pm. This connects at Durness with the daily Inverness Traction link (June to mid-Sept) from Inverness via Ullapool and Lochinver. Postbuses provide a more complicated year-round alternative; check at the post office, tourist office or youth hostel.

Durness has an enthusiastic **tourist office** (April–Oct Mon–Sat 10am–5pm; July & Aug also Sun 11am–4pm; Oct–March Mon–Fri 10am–1.30pm; ☎01971/511259), in the village centre, which can help with accommodation and arranges ranger-guided walks; its small visitor centre also features excellent interpretative panels detailing the area's history, geology, flora and fauna, with some good insights into the day-to-day life of the community. **Accommodation** is fairly limited in Durness itself, but there are further options along nearby Loch Eriboll (see below). Durness's best offering is the *Cape Wrath Hotel* (☎01971/511212; main hotel ④, annexe ②), which has a beautiful setting near the ferry jetty at Keoldale. Popular with walkers and fishermen, its rather austere character is offset by relaxed, friendly service and a stunning view from the dining room. Of the **B&Bs**, *Puffin Cottage* (☎01971/511208; ①) is small but pleasant, while the friendly **youth hostel** (☎01971/511244 or central reservations ☎0541/553255; mid-March to Sept), beside the Smoo Cave car park, a mile and a half east of the village, also rents out mountain bikes. There's **camping** at *Sango Sands Caravan and Camping Site*, Harbour Road (☎01971/511262), which has the added advantage of a good bar and restaurant. The other good **eating** options are the restaurants at the *Cape Wrath Hotel* and Loch Eriboll's *Port-Na-Con* guest house – in both cases, you should book in advance.

Loch Eriboll

Ringed by ghostlike limestone mountains, deep and sheltered **Loch Eriboll**, six miles east of Durness, is the north coast's most spectacular sea loch. Servicemen stationed here during World War II to protect passing Russian convoys nicknamed it "Loch 'Orrible", but if you're looking for somewhere wild and unspoilt you'll find this a perfect spot. Porpoises and otters are a common sight along the rocky shore, and minke whales occasionally swim in from the open sea.

Overlooking its own landing stage at the water's edge, *Port-Na-Con* (☎01971/511367, shm@capetech.co.uk; ②; mid-March to Oct), seven miles from Durness on the west side of the loch, is a wonderful **B&B**, popular with anglers and divers (it'll refill air tanks for £2.50). Topnotch food is served in its small restaurant (open all year, including Christmas), with a choice of vegetarian haggis, local kippers, fruit compote and home-made croissants for breakfast, and adventurous three-course evening meals for around £12; the menu always includes a gourmet vegetarian dish. Non-residents are welcome, although you'll need to book. Another good option, half a mile further south, is *Rowan House* (☎01971/511347; ①), a child-friendly place overlooking the loch with a tiny eighteen-hole golf course; fresh local oysters often feature on its menu. A further half a mile south, *Choraidh Croft* (☎01971/511235; ①; Easter–Nov) offers B&B and has a rare-breeds collection (£2), as well as a good café.

Tongue

It's a long slog around Loch Eriboll and east over the top of A Mhùine moor to the pretty crofting township of **TONGUE**. Dominated by the ruins of **Varick Castle**, the village, an eleventh-century Norse stronghold, is strewn over the east shore of the **Kyle of Tongue**, which you can either cross via a new causeway, or by following the longer and more scenic single-track road around its southern side. When the tide recedes, this shallow estuary becomes a mass of golden sand flats,

NORTH COAST WALKING AND CYCLING

Ordnance Survey Landranger maps nos. 9 and 10

An unchallenged pair of peaks rising up from the southern end of the Kyle of Tongue, Ben Hope and Ben Loyal both offer moderate to hard walks, rewarded on a decent day by vast views over the harsh north coast and empty Sutherland landscape. **Ben Hope** (3040ft), which was given its name ("hill of the bay") by the Vikings, is the most northerly of all Scotland's Munros. The best approach, a four-hour round-trip, is from the road that runs down the west side of Loch Hope. Start at a sheep shed by the roadside just under two miles beyond the southern end of Loch Hope, following the tributary of the stream that descends through an obvious break in the imposing-looking cliffline. Once on top of the cliffs, it's a relatively easy but inspiring walk along them to the summit.

Ben Loyal (2509ft), though lower, is a longer hike, at around six hours. To avoid the worst of the bogs, follow the northern spur from Ribigill Farm, a mile south of Tongue. At the end of the southbound farm track, a path emerges; follow this up a steepish slope to gain the first peak on the ridge. It's not the summit, but the views are rewarding, and from there to the top the walking is easier.

For those looking for **shorter walks** or **cycles**, there are well-marked woodland trails at **Borgie Forest**, six miles west of Tongue, and **Truderscraig Forest** by Syre, twelve miles south of Bettyhill on the B871. If you follow the signs to "**Rosal Pre-Clearance Village**", you'll find an area clear of trees with various ruins that stand as a memorial to the brutality of the Highland Clearances. Various boards provide details about the way of life of the inhabitants in the eighteenth century before the upheavals, which saw them scattered to bleak coastal settlements or onto the emigration ships leaving for Canada and America.

superb on sunny days, with the sharp profiles of **Ben Hope** (3040ft) and **Ben Loyal** (2509ft) looming large to the south.

In 1746, the Kyle of Tongue was the scene of a naval engagement reputed to have sealed the fate of Bonnie Prince Charlie's **Jacobite rebellion**. In response to a plea for help from the prince, the king of France dispatched a sloop and £13,600 in gold coins to Scotland. However, the Jacobite ship *Hazard* was spotted by the English frigate, *Sheerness*, and fled into the Kyle, hoping that the larger enemy vessel would not be able to follow. It did, though, and soon forced the *Hazard* aground. Pounded by English cannon fire, its Jacobite crew slipped ashore under cover of darkness in an attempt to smuggle the treasure to Inverness, but they were followed by scouts of the local Mackay clan, who were not of the Jacobite persuasion. The next morning, a larger platoon of Mackays waylaid the rebels, who, hopelessly outnumbered and outgunned, began throwing the gold into **Lochan Hakel**, southwest of Tongue (most of it was recovered later). The prince, meanwhile, had sent 1500 of his men north to rescue the treasure, but these too were defeated en route; historians debate whether the missing men might have altered the outcome of the Battle of Culloden three weeks later.

If you want **to stay** in Tongue, try *Rhian Cottage* (☎01847/611257; ②, with dinner ④), a pretty whitewashed house with an attractive garden, about a mile down the road past the post office, or *Woodend* (☎01847/611332; ③), a mile north on the Bettyhill road, with panoramic views of the estuary. The *Ben Loyal Hotel* (☎01847/611216; ④) and *Tongue Hotel* (☎01847/611206; ④; March–Oct) are more luxurious, and both do excellent food. There's also a beautifully situated and friendly SYHA **hostel** (☎01847/611301 or central reservations ☎0541/553255; mid-March to Oct), right beside the causeway a mile north of the village centre on the east shore of the Kyle, and two **campsites**: *Kincraig Camping and Caravan Site* (☎01847/611218) just south of Tongue post office, and *Talmine Camping and Caravan Site* (☎01847/601225), just behind a sandy beach at Talmine, five miles north of Tongue on the western side of the Kyle.

Bettyhill to Dounreay

BETTYHILL, a major crofting village, straggles along the side of a narrow tidal estuary, and down the coast to two splendid beaches. Forming an unbroken arc of pure white sand between the Naver and Borgie rivers, **Torrisdale beach** is the more impressive of the pair, ending in a smooth white spit that forms part of the **Invernaver Nature Reserve**. During summer, arctic terns nest here on the river banks, dotted with clumps of rare Scottish primroses, and you stand a good chance of spotting an otter or two. The delightful and loyally maintained **Strathnaver Museum** (April–Oct Mon–Sat 10am–1pm & 2–5pm; £1.90), housed in the old church set apart from the village near the sea, is full of locally donated bits and pieces, and includes panels by local schoolchildren telling the story of the Strathnaver Clearances. You can also see some Pictish stones and a 3800-year-old early Bronze Age beaker found in Strathnaver, the river valley south of the village, whose numerous prehistoric sites are mapped on an excellent pamphlet sold at the entrance desk.

Bettyhill's small **tourist office** (April & May Mon–Sat 1–5pm; June Mon–Sat 11am–5pm; July Mon–Sat 10am–5pm; Aug Mon–Sat 10am–6pm, Sun noon–5pm; ☎01641/521342) can book **accommodation** for you. The *Bettyhill Hotel* (☎01641/521230; ①), at the top of the hill, has character, and does good bar food. There are also several good-value B&Bs, including *Shenley* (☎01641/521421; ①; April–Oct), a grand but homely detached house in an elevated spot in the middle of the village, and *Bruachmhor* (☎01641/521265; ①; April–Oct), a small but comfortable croft house, facing south over the village.

As you move east from Bettyhill, the north coast changes dramatically as the hills on the horizon recede, to be replaced by fields fringed with flagstone walls. At the hamlet of **MELVICH**, twelve miles from Bettyhill, the A897 cuts south through Strath Halladale, the Flow Country (see p.258) and the Strath of Kildonan to Helmsdale on the east coast (see p.273). Melvich has some good accommodation, including the excellent *Sheiling Guesthouse* (☎01641/531256; ②; April–Oct) by the main road, whose impressive breakfast menu features locally smoked haddock and fresh herring.

Five miles further east, **Dounreay Nuclear Power Station**, a surreal collection of stark domes and chimney stacks marooned in the middle of nowhere, is still a fairly major local employer, though its three fast-breeder reactors were decommissioned in April 1994 and it now reprocesses spent nuclear fuel rather than generating electricity. A permanent **exhibition** (Easter–Sept daily 10am–5pm; free) in the old aircraft control tower details the processes (and, unsurprisingly, the benefits) of nuclear power, and does at least make an attempt to address issues such as the area's "leukemia cluster", and the high levels of radiation reported over the years on the nearby beaches. Free tours of the site are run from the centre, though you're not allowed out of the bus.

THE FLOW COUNTRY

The landscape of the Flow Country of Caithness – the name comes from *Flói*, an Old Norse word meaning "marshy ground" – is an acquired taste. At first sight it can seem featureless and empty, but closer study reveals a unique treasure trove of unusual vegetation, birdlife and animal life. The underlying rock is mostly a type called **Old Red Sandstone**, some of which is quarried for its slabs of stone, which are used extensively for building and paving, and even local roofing. On top of this is a thick layer of **peat**, formed over thousands of years from layers of the semi-decomposed remains of plant species lying saturated in water and building up by one or two millimetres each year. In late spring and early summer, the rich, black peat is cut, often still using traditional tools, and left in stacks to dry. In the absense of firewood, dried peat is used extensively in the Scottish Highlands and Islands – as well as in Ireland – for burning on open fires, giving off a pungent, sweet smoke. Peat fires are also commonly used in the whisky-making process to dry the grain, imparting a distinctive flavour most recognizable in the single malts from the island of Islay (see p.122), but also those from many Highland distilleries.

Among the unusual **plants** found in the Flow Country are bog asphodel, bog-bean, marsh-marigold, meadowsweet, sphagnum moss, and the insect-trapping sundew and butterwort. **Birds** found here include the rarely seen red- and black-throated divers, greenshank, as well as birds of prey including the golden eagle, hen harrier and merlin. A good place to see some of these species is the RSPB visitor centre in Forsinard (see below): here you can set out on the short **Dubh Lochan** trail; a trail leaflet points out the plants, birds, insects and mammals you might see.

South from Melvich: the Flow Country

From Melvich, you can head forty miles or so south towards Helmsdale (see p.273) on the A897, through the **Flow Country**. This huge expanse of bog land came into the news a few years ago when ecology experts, responding to plans to transform the area into forest, drew attention to the threat to this fragile landscape, described by one contemporary commentator as of "unique and global importance, equivalent to the African Serengeti or Brazil's rainforest". Some forest was planted, but the environmentalists won the day, and the forestry syndicates have had to pull out. There's an excellent RSPB Flow Country **visitor centre** (Easter–Oct daily 9am–6pm; ☎01641/571225), based in the train station at Forsinard, fifteen miles south of Melvich, which is easily accessible from Thurso, Wick and the south by train. Guided walks through the RSPB **nature reserve** leave from the visitor centre (May–Aug Tues & Thurs) and illuminate the importance of the area and its wildlife.

Thurso

Approached from the isolation of the west, **THURSO** feels like a metropolis. In reality, it's a relatively small service centre visited mostly by people passing through to the nearby port of **Scrabster** to catch the ferry to Stromness in Orkney. The town's name derives from the Norse word *Thorsa*, literally "River of the God Thor", and in Viking times this was a major gateway to the mainland. Later, ships set sail from here for the Baltic and Scandinavian ports loaded with

ACCOMMODATION
Mrs Budge's B & B   1
Mrs Oag's B & B   2
Murray House   3
Ormlie Lodge   6
Royal Hotel   4
Sandra's   5

THURSO

© Crown copyright

meal, beef, hides and fish. Much of the town, however, dates from the 1790s, when Sir John Sinclair built a large new extension to the old fishing port, "according to the most regular plan that could be contrived and in a manner not only ornamental but also positively well adapted for preserving the health and promoting the convenience of the inhabitants". The nearby Dounreay Nuclear Power Station ensured continuing prosperity after World War II, when workers from the plant (dubbed "Atomics" by the locals) settled in Thurso in large numbers. Its gradual rundown over recent years has cast a shadow over the local economy, but investment in new industries such as telecommunications has improved matters.

Traill Street is the main drag, turning into the pedestrianized Rotterdam Street and High Street precinct at its northern end. However, the shops are uninspiring, and you're better off heading to the old part of town near the harbour, to see **Old St Peter's Church**, a substantial ruin with origins in the thirteenth century, but which has been much altered over the years. Alternatively, you could visit the

Thurso Heritage Museum, High Street (Mon–Sat 10am–1pm & 2–5pm; 50p), whose most intriguing exhibit is the Pictish **Skinnet Stone**, intricately carved with enigmatic symbols and a runic cross.

Practicalities

It's a ten-minute walk from the **train station**, with services to Inverness and Wick, down Princes Street and Sir George Street, to the **tourist office** on Riverside Road (April–Oct Mon–Sat 9am–5pm; July & Aug also Sun 11am–4pm; ☎01847/892371). The bus station, close by, runs regular **buses** to John O'Groats, Wick and Inverness, and a summer service to Durness. **Ferries** operate daily from adjoining Scrabster to Orkney, which has less frequent links to Shetland and Aberdeen. You can book ahead through P&O Scottish Ferries, Aberdeen (☎01224/572615), or through any local tourist office. If you fancy a day-trip to Orkney, see "John O'Groats" (opposite). The local bus services aren't much help if you're connecting with the ferry at Scrabster – the walk is just over a mile long, or a **taxi** (☎01847/892868) will set you back £3.

Thurso is well stocked with **accommodation**, including a decent if tight-fitting hostel, *Sandra's* (☎01847/894575, *sandra's-hostel@carson.softnet.co.uk*), 24 Princes St, with four-bed bunk-rooms and drying and self-catering facilities above the lively local café. Inexpensive if tatty dorms and doubles are also available at *Ormlie Lodge* (☎01847/896888), a block of student accommodation on Ormlie Road, close to the station. Of the **B&Bs**, *Murray House*, 1 Campbell St (☎01847/895759; ③), is central, comfortable and friendly, or you could try the welcoming Mrs Oag, 9 Couper St (☎01847/894529; ③), east of High Street near the town hall, or Mrs Budge (☎01847/893205; ③), 6 Pentland Crescent, next to the beach front. The recently refurbished *Royal Hotel* (☎01847/893191; ④) on Traill Street is the main **hotel** in town and is a reasonable choice. The nearest **campsite** (☎01847/805503) is out towards Scrabster alongside the main road.

Food options include *Le Bistro*, 2 Traill St, with a reasonable-value menu of lunchtime snacks and more ambitious evening meals, and *Upper Deck*, by the harbour at Scrabster, serving large, moderately priced steaks and seafood dishes. There are several **cafés** in the town centre which offer standard, filling snacks, including *Johnston's* on Traill Street and *Sandra's* on Princes Street, while the most enjoyably rowdy **pub** is the *Central*, on Traill Street. After the pub, head to *Skinandi's Nightclub* on Sir George Street.

You can **rent bikes** at the Bike and Camping shop on the extension of High Street, beyond its junction with Couper Street, while a little further along at 57 High St, Harper's fishing shop (☎01847/893179) is the place to rent wet suits or boards, or get hold of other **surfing** supplies, before you take on the mighty north coast breaks.

Dunnet Head to Duncansby Head

Despite the plaudits that John O'Groats customarily receives, Britain's northern-most mainland point is in fact **Dunnet Head**. The headland is at the far side of Dunnet Bay, a vast sandy beach backed by huge dunes about six miles east of Thurso. The bay is popular with surfers, and even in the winter you can usually spot intrepid figures far out in the Pentland Firth's breakers. There's a **Ranger Centre** (April–Sept Tues–Fri 2–5pm, Sat & Sun 2–6pm) beside the campsite at the east end of the bay, where you can pick up information on good local history and nature walks, including a short self-guided trail into Dunnet Forest, a failed plantation which has been left to go – literally – to seed, allowing a rich range of plant and animal life to thrive. Nearby is the small village of **DUNNET**, where it's worth stopping in at **Mary-Ann's Cottage** (June–Sept Tues–Sun 2–4.30pm; £1), a farming croft vacated in 1990 by 93-year-old Mary-Ann Calder, whose grandfather had built the cottage, and maintained just as she left it, full of reminders of the three generations who lived and worked there over the last 150 years.

For Dunnet Head, turn off at Dunnet onto the B855, which runs for four miles over windy heather and bog to the tip of the headland, crowned with a Victorian lighthouse. The red cliffs below are startling, with weirdly eroded rock stacks and a huge variety of seabirds; on a clear day you can see the whole northern coastline from Cape Wrath to Duncansby Head, and across the Pentland Firth to Orkney.

John O'Groats

Familiar from endless postcards, **JOHN O'GROATS** comes as something of an anticlimax. The views north to Orkney are fine enough, but the village itself turns out to be little more than a windswept grassy slope leading down to the sea, dominated by an enormous car park that is jammed throughout the summer with tour buses. The village gets its name from the Dutchman, Jan de Groot, who obtained the ferry contract for the crossing to Orkney in 1496. The eight-sided house he built for his eight quarrelling sons (so that each one could enter by his own door) is echoed in the octagonal tower of the much-photographed *John O'Groats Hotel*, which is fast falling into disrepair but remains a good stopoff for a quick drink.

Aside from the frequent if irregular links with Land's End, maintained by a succession of walkers, cyclists, vintage-car drivers and pushers of baths, John O'Groats is connected by regular **buses** to Wick (4–5 daily; 50min) and Thurso (Mon–Fri 5 daily, Sat 2 daily; 1hr). John O'Groats Ferries (☎01955/611353) operates a daily passenger ferry across to Burwick in the Orkney Islands (May & Sept 1 daily; June–Aug 4 daily; 45min; £24 return): officially this is a foot-passenger service, but it will take bicycles and motorbikes if it isn't too busy. The company also offers a couple of whistle-stop day-tours of Orkney, as well as a more leisurely afternoon wildlife cruise round the Stacks of Duncansby and the seabird colonies of Stroma (1hr 30min; £12). The **tourist office** (April–Oct Mon–Sat 9am–5pm; ☎01955/611373) by the car park can help sort out **accommodation**: alternatively, try *Swona View* B&B (☎01955/611297; ①; April–Oct) on the road to Duncansby Head, or *Creag-Na-Mara* (☎01847/851713; ①), a welcoming B&B serving tasty evening meals at East Mey, west along the Thurso road. *Bencorragh House* (☎01955/611449; ②, with dinner ④; March–Oct) has very pleasant farmhouse accommodation at Upper Gills in Canisbay. If you're on a tight budget, head for the small **youth hostel** (☎01955/611424 or central reservations ☎0541/553255; April–Oct) at Canisbay, or one of the two local **campsites** – *Stroma View* (☎01955/611313), one mile along the Thurso road, is the more pleasant.

Duncansby Head

If you're disappointed by John O'Groats, press on a couple of miles further east to **Duncansby Head**, which, with its lighthouse, dramatic cliffs and well-worn coastal path, has a lot more to offer. The birdlife here is prolific, and south of the headland lie some spectacular 200-foot cliffs, cut by sheer-sided clefts known locally as *geos*. This is also a good place from which to view Orkney. Dividing the islands from the mainland is the infamous **Pentland Firth**, one of the world's most treacherous waterways. Only seven miles across, it forms a narrow channel between the Atlantic Ocean and North Sea, and for fourteen hours each day the tide rips through here from west to east at a rate of ten knots or more, flooding back in the opposite direction for the remaining ten hours. Combined with the rocky sea bed and a high wind, this can cause deep whirlpools and terrifying thirty- to forty-foot towers of water to form when the ebbing tide crashes across the reefs offshore. The latter, known as the "Bores of Duncansby", are the subject of many old mariners' myths from the time of the Vikings onwards.

THE EAST COAST

The **east coast** of the Highlands, between Inverness and Wick, is nowhere near as spectacular as the west, with gentle undulating moors, grassland and low cliffs where you might expect to find sea lochs and mountains. Washed by the cold waters of the North Sea, it's markedly cooler, too, although less prone to spells of permadrizzle, and midges. Although the Inverness–Thurso train line is twice forced by topography to head inland, the region's main transport artery, the A9 – slower here than in the south – follows the coast, which veers sharply northeast exactly parallel with the Great Glen, formed by the same geological fault.

From around the ninth century AD onwards, the **Norse** influence was more keenly felt here than in any other part of mainland Britain, and dozens of Scandinavian-sounding names recall the era when this was a Viking kingdom. Culturally and scenically, much of the east coast is more lowland than highland and Caithness in particular evolved more or less separately from the Highlands, avoiding the bloody tribal feuds that wrought such havoc further south and west. Later, however, the nineteenth-century **Clearances** hit the region hard, as countless ruined cottages and empty glens show. Hundreds of thousands of crofters were evicted, and forced to emigrate to New Zealand, Canada and Australia, or else take up fishing in one of the numerous herring ports established on the coast. The oil boom has brought a transient prosperity to one or two places over the past two decades, but the area remains one of the country's poorest, reliant on sheep farming, fishing and tourism.

The one stretch of the east coast that's always been relatively rich is the **Black Isle**, whose main village, **Cromarty**, is the region's undisputed highlight, with a crop of elegant mansions and appealing fishermen's cottages clustered near the entrance to the Cromarty Firth. In late medieval times, pilgrims including James IV of Scotland poured through here en route to the red-sandstone town of **Tain** to worship at the shrine of St Duthac, where the former sacred enclave has now been converted into one of the many "heritage centres" that punctuate the route north. Beyond **Dornoch**, a famous golfing resort renowned for its salubrious climate and sweeping beach, the ersatz-Loire chateau, **Dunrobin Castle**, is the main tourist attraction, a monument as much to the iniquities of the Clearances as to the eccentricity of Victorian taste. The award-winning **Timespan Heritage Centre** further north at **Helmsdale** recounts the human cost of the landlords' greed, while the area around the port of **Lybster** is littered with the remains of more ancient civilizations. **Wick**, the largest town on this section of coast, has an interesting past inevitably entwined with the fishing industry, whose story is told in another good heritage centre, but is otherwise uninspiring. The relatively flat landscapes of this northeast corner – windswept peat bog and farmland dotted with lochans and grey and white crofts – are a surprising contrast to the more rugged country south and west of here.

The Black Isle and around

Sandwiched between the Cromarty Firth to the north and the Moray and Beauly firths to the south, the **Black Isle** is not an island at all, but a fertile peninsula whose rolling hills, prosperous farms and stands of deciduous woodland make it more reminiscent of Dorset or Sussex than the Highlands. It probably gained its name because of its mild climate: there's rarely frost, which leaves the fields "black" all winter; another explanation is that the name derives from the Gaelic word for black, *dubh* – a possible corruption of St Duthus (see p.268).

The Black Isle is littered with dozens of **prehistoric sites**, but the main incentive to make the detour east from the A9 is to visit the picturesque eighteenth-century town of **Cromarty**, huddled at the northeast tip of the peninsula. A string of villages along the south coast is also worth stopping off in en route, and one of them, **Rosemarkie**, has an outstanding small museum devoted to **Pictish culture**. Chanonry Point is among the best **dolphin-spotting** sites in Europe.

Avoch, Fortrose and Rosemarkie

The most rewarding approach to Cromarty is along the south side of the Black Isle, on the A832 past the **Clootie Well**, just north of Munlochy, where coloured rags are hung on a fence to bring luck and health. Next comes the attractive harbourside fishing village of **AVOCH** (pronounced "Och"), where the *Station Hotel* serves good bar meals and real ale; there's a tiny heritage centre in the basement at the back. **FORTROSE**, a few miles further east, is another quiet village dominated by the ruins of an early thirteenth-century **cathedral**. Founded by King David I, it now languishes on a lovely yew-studded green bordered by red-sandstone and colourwashed houses, where a horde of gold coins dating from the time of Robert III was unearthed in 1880. There's also a memorial to the Seaforth family, whose demise the Brahan Seer famously predicted (see p.264).

There's a memorial plaque to the seer at nearby **Chanonry Point**, reached by a back road from the north end of Fortrose; the thirteenth hole of the golf course here marks the spot where he met his death. Jutting into a narrow channel in the Moray Firth (deepened to allow warships into the estuary during the last war), the point, fringed on one side by a beach of golden sand and shingle, is an excellent place to look for **dolphins** (see p.211). Come here around high tide, and you stand a good chance of spotting a couple leaping through the surf in search of fish brought to the surface by converging currents.

ROSEMARKIE, a one-street village north of Fortrose at the opposite (northwest) end of the beach, is thought to have been evangelized by St Boniface in the early eighth century. **Groam House Museum** (May–Sept Mon–Sat 10am–5pm, Sun 2–4.30pm; Oct–April Sat & Sun 2–4pm; £1.50), at the bottom of the village, displays a bumper crop of intricately carved standing stones (among them the famous Rosemarkie Cross Slab), and shows an informative video highlighting Pictish sites in the region. A lovely mile-and-a-half **woodland walk**, along the

THE BRAHAN SEER

Legend has it that the seventeenth-century visionary **Cùinneach Odhar** (Kenneth Mackenzie, from Uig on Skye), who lived and worked on the Seaforths' estate, derived his powers from a small white divination stone passed on to him, through his mother, from a Viking princess. With the pebble pressed against his eye, Cùinneach foretold everything from outbreaks of measles in the village to the building of the Caledonian Canal, the Clearances and World War II. His visions brought him widespread fame, but also resulted in his untimely death. In 1660, Countess Seaforth, wife of the local laird, summoned the seer after her husband was late home from a trip to France. Reluctantly – when pressurized – he told the Countess that he had seen the earl "on his knees before a fair lady, his arm round her waist and her hand pressed to his lips". At this, she flew into a rage, accused him of sullying the family name and ordered him to be thrown head first into a barrel of boiling tar. However, just before the gruesome execution, which took place near Brahan Castle on Chanonry Point, Cùinneach made his last prediction: when a deaf and dumb earl inherited the estate, the Seaforth line would end. His prediction finally came true in 1815 when the last earl died.

banks of a sparkling burn to Fairy Glen, begins at the car park just beyond the village on the road to Cromarty. Inexpensive bar food is also available at the wonderfully old-fashioned *Plough Inn*, just down the main street from the museum.

Cromarty

An ancient legend recalls that the twin headlands flanking the entrance to the Cromarty Firth, known as The Sutors (from the Gaelic word for shoemaker) were once a pair of giant cobblers who used to protect the Black Isle from pirates. Nowadays, however, the only giants in the area are Nigg and Invergordon's colossal oil rigs, marooned in the estuary like metal monsters marching out to sea. Built and serviced here for the Forties North Sea oilfield, they form a surreal counterpoint to the web of tiny streets and chocolate-box workers' cottages of **CROMARTY**, the Black Isle's main settlement. Sheltered by The Sutors at the northeast corner of the peninsula, the town, an ancient ferry crossing point on the pilgrimage trail to St Duthac's shrine in Tain, lost much of its trade during the nineteenth century to places served by the railway; a branch line to the town was begun but never completed. Although a royal burgh since the fourth century, Cromarty didn't became a prominent port until 1772, when the entrepreneurial local landlord, George Ross, founded a hemp mill here. Imported Baltic hemp was spun into cloth and rope in the mill, fuelling a period of prosperity during which Cromarty acquired some of Scotland's finest Georgian houses; these, together with the terraced fishers' cottages of the nineteenth-century herring boom, have earned the town the somewhat corny epithet, "the jewel in the crown" of Scottish vernacular architecture.

To get a sense of Cromarty's past, head straight for the award-winning **museum** housed in the old **Courthouse** on Church Street (daily: April–Oct 10am–5pm; Nov–Dec & March noon–4pm; £3), which tells the history of the town using audiovisuals and animated figures (not as dreadful as they sound, and children love them). You are also issued with a personal stereo, a tape and a map for a walking tour around the town. **Hugh Miller** (1802–52) a stonemason turned author, geologist, folklorist and Free Church campaigner, was born in Cromarty, and his **birthplace** (May–Sept Mon–Sat 11am–1pm & 2–5pm, Sun 2–5pm; £2; NTS), a modest thatched cottage on Church Street, has been restored to give an idea of what Cromarty must have been like in his day. Aside from any formal sights, Cromarty is a pleasant place just to wander around, and there's an excellent **walk** out to the south Sutor stacks. You can pick up the path by leaving town on Miller Road, and turning right when the lane becomes "The Causeway"; follow this through the woods and past eighteenth-century Cromarty House until you reach the junction at Mains Farm; a left turn here takes you across open fields and through woods to the top of the headland, from where there are superb views across the Moray Firth.

Before you move on, bear in mind that Bill Fraser of the widely respected Dolphin Écosse will take you out on half- or full-day **boat trips** to see seals, porpoises, bottle-nosed dolphins and occasionally minke whales just off the coast; you can contact him on ☎01381/600323, or visit their Dolphin Centre in Bank House on High Street, which has all sorts of background information on dolphins and whales, along with some spectacular photographs of the animals taken by clients while out on the boat. The tiny two-car Nigg–Cromarty **ferry** (May–Sept daily 9am–6pm), Scotland's smallest, also doubles up as a cruiser on summer evenings; you can catch it from the jetty near the lighthouse.

Practicalities

Nine **buses** each day run to Cromarty from Inverness (55min), returning from the stop near the playing fields on the western outskirts of town. During summer, **accommodation** is in short supply, so book ahead. Most upmarket is the traditional *Royal Hotel* (☎01381/600217; ⑥), down at the harbour, which has rather small but richly furnished rooms overlooking the Firth, and a good bar/restaurant. For **B&B**, try one of the attractive old houses on Church Street, such as Mrs Robertson's at no. 7 (☎01381/600488; ①). Above the town, Mrs Ricketts (☎01381/600308; ①) offers well-equipped rooms and good views.

The most down-to-earth place **to eat** is the *Cromarty Arms*, which serves basic, inexpensive bar meals, and a good selection of ales and malts. It also hosts a lively karaoke night and occasional country and western bands on Fridays. If you're after something a little more sophisticated, you could try the *Thistle Restaurant*, on Church Street, or the *Royal Hotel*'s restaurant, which features Scottish specialities. Cheaper meals are available in the cosy public bar or, on fine nights, on the terrace outside with great views over the Firth.

Strathpeffer

STRATHPEFFER, a Victorian spa town surrounded by wooded hills, is a congenial place to stop over. During its heyday, this was a renowned European **health resort** complete with a Pump Room, where visitors could chat while they sipped the water. Today, sadly, some of its buildings are in a sorry state, including several huge faded hotels, though plans are afoot to restore the Pavilion Ballroom to its former glory. Activity is concentrated around the main square, in the middle of which the **Water Sampling Pavilion** rekindles some of the atmosphere of the Victorian days with Bath chairs nestling against the wall and four taps carrying sulphur-laden water from various nearby sources – you are free to sample them, although for most people the rank smell more than offsets any possible benefit.

WALKS AROUND STRATHPEFFER

Ordnance Survey Landranger maps nos. 26 and 20

From the youth hostel in Strathpeffer, a two- to three-hour walk leads to the remains of a vitrified Iron Age fort at **Knock Farril**. The first part of the walk follows woodland trails; rather less than a mile further on, you can turn up onto the ridge on the right and follow it along the crest of the hill known as the Cat's Back. Past some fine old Scots pines the trees begin to thin out, and as you reach the hill-fort great views of the Cromarty Firth begin to show to the east. Along the way, look out for the unusual **Touchstone Maze**, which was built as a local arts project in 1992 and includes around eighty stones set in circles representing the major rock types from around Highlands. A path also leads directly here from near the old train station in Strathpeffer. From the fort, you can pick up a minor road and continue along the ridge to Dingwall, from where there are buses back to Strathpeffer. A shorter route drops back down from Knock Farril to the main road and then on to the village.

A little further out of the village, two miles north of Contin on the main A835 to Braemore, are the **Rogie Falls**. It's only a short walk from the car park to where the Black Water comes frothing down a long stretch of rocks and mini-gorges, in one place plunging down a 25-foot drop. Salmon can be seen leaping upriver in summer, particularly at the fish ladder built to offer an alternative route up the toughest of the rapids. A suspension bridge over the river leads to some way-marked forest trails – including a five-mile loop to **View Rock**, at a point only 160ft above sea level but which has great views of the local area.

The more ambitious hike in this area is up **Ben Wyvis**, a huge mass of mountain clearly seen from Inverness. The high point is Glas Lethad Mor (3432ft), which means, rather prosaically, "Big Greenish-Grey Slope"; the most common route is through Garbat Forest, leaving the road just south of Garbat itself, staying on the north bank of the Allt a'Bhealaich Mhoir stream to get onto the southwestern end of the long summit ridge at the minor peak of An Cabar.

Also making the most of the Victorian theme is the **Highland Museum of Childhood** (mid-March to Oct Mon–Sat 10am–5pm, Sun 2–5pm; July & Aug Mon–Fri open till 7pm; £1.50), located at the restored Victorian train station half a mile east of the main square. An attraction aimed at families, the museum looks at growing up in the Highlands, from home and school life to folklore and festivals, with some well-displayed black-and-white photographs, display cabinets with toys and games, and a colourful series of commissioned murals. In other parts of the station, there are a pleasant café and craft workshops.

Practicalities

Buses run regularly between Dingwall and Strathpeffer (Mon–Sat), dropping passengers in the square, where you'll find a small **tourist office** (April, May & Sept Mon–Fri 10am–5pm, Sat 11am–4pm; June–Aug Mon–Sat 10am–5pm, Sun 11am–4pm; ☎01997/421415) with information on points west as well as local areas. The **hotels** in the village are very popular with bus tours, but often have room: the vast *Ben Wyvis* (☎01997/421323; ④) is adequate, in nice grounds east of the main square on the Dingwall road, while north of the main square a converted Victorian villa, complete with turrets, houses the *Holly Lodge Hotel* (☎01997/421254; ②). The *Inver Lodge*, west of the main square (☎01997/421392;

①), and *Francisville*, just past the church (☎01997/421345; ①), both offer good **B&B**. If you don't mind dorms, head for the rambling fifty-bed **youth hostel** (☎01997/421532 or central reservations ☎0541 553255; April–Sept), a mile south-west of the main square up the hill towards Jameston, while those keen on tack-ling a broader range of outdoor pursuits, including canoeing, mountain-biking and assault courses, should head to the excellent Fairburn Activity Centre (☎01997/433397; ②), set in the grounds of a magnificent country estate about three miles outside the village of Marybank, south of Strathpeffer and northwest of Muir of Ord.

Dingwall and the Cromarty Firth

Most traffic nowadays takes the upgraded A9 north from Inverness, bypassing the small provincial town of **DINGWALL** (from the Norse *thing*, "parliament", and *vollr*, "field"), a royal burgh since 1226 and former port that was left high and dry when the river receded during the last century. Today, it's a tidy but dull service and market town with one long main street that's bustling all day and moribund by dinner time. Dingwall's only real claim to fame is that it was the birthplace of Macbeth, whose family occupied the now ruined castle on Castle Street.

If you need **to stay**, Castle Street is a good place to look for B&Bs: try *The Croft* (☎01349/863319; ①) at no. 25, or *St Clements* (☎01349/862172; ①) at no. 17. The smartest hotel is the stylish *Tulloch Castle*, Castle Drive (☎01349/861325; ⑤), a former Highland clan headquarters, or there's the central *Royal Hotel*, High Street (☎01349/862130; ④).

Northeast of Dingwall, the **Cromarty Firth** has always been recognized as a perfect natural harbour. During World War I it was a major **naval base**, and today its sheltered waters are used as a centre for repairing North Sea oil rigs. The A862 road from Dingwall rejoins the A9 just after the main road crosses the firth on a long causeway; shortly after this, perched on a spit between the road and the firth is the recently established **Clanland and Sealpoint** (daily: July–Sept 9.30am–8pm; Oct–June 9.30am–5.30pm; £3.50), another of the heritage centres which crop up with almost monotonous regularity through the Highland region. Each has its story to tell, however, and this one looks at the Munro Clan, along with the traditional fishing industry and some of the local wildlife, particularly the seals of the firth. Predictably, large amounts of space are given over to the café and souvenir shop, and the family-oriented exhibits mean that it can be boister-ous inside.

Rather quirkier attractions can be found not far away, notably the extraordinary edifice on the hill behind **EVANTON**, a few miles further along the A9 from Clanland. This is the **Fyrish Monument**, built by a certain Sir Hector Munro, partly to give employment to the area and partly to commemorate his own cap-ture of the Indian town of Seringapatam in 1781 – hence the design, resembling an Indian gateway. If you want to get a close-up look, it's a tough two-hour walk through pine woods to the top. An easier, but no less dramatic walk from the vil-lage, is to follow the Allt Graad River to the mile-long **Black Rock** gorge, an unex-pected chasm formed when glacial meltwaters cut a deep furrow in a band of soft-er sandstone. The gorge, a giddy 100ft deep in places but only 12–15ft wide, was reputedly once jumped by a local man, but the proximity of the surrounding wood, as well as the curtain of damp ferns and mosses which cling to the rocks, would make a repeat of this, or any close inspection of the gorge, pretty dangerous. The best approach to the gorge is along a track which leaves from *Evanton Caravan Park*, where there's also a simple but neat bunkhouse (☎01349/830917 *mlb@blackrockscot.freeserve.co.uk*), one of only two hostels on this entire stretch between Inverness and Thurso.

Around the Tain peninsula

Bounded in the south by the Cromarty Firth, and in the north by the Dornoch Firth, the hammer-shaped **Tain peninsula** can still be approached by the ancient ferry crossing from Cromarty to Nigg. The peninsula's largest settlement is **TAIN**, a small town of grand whisky-coloured sandstone buildings, and the birth-place of **St Duthus**, a missionary who inspired great devotion in the Middle Ages. His miracle-working relics were enshrined in a sanctuary here in the eleventh century, and in 1360 St Duthus Collegiate Church was built, visited annually by James IV, who usually arrived here fresh from the arms of his mistress, Jane Kennedy, whom he had conveniently installed in nearby Moray. A good place to get to grips with the peninsula's past is the **Tain Through Time** exhibition (April–Oct daily 10am–6pm; Nov–March Mon–Fri noon–4pm; £3.50), which makes creative use of three old buildings around the church and a graveyard, guiding you round using an audio guide with headphones. The ticket price also includes a tour of the church and neighbouring **museum** on Castle Brae (just off High Street), housing an interesting display of the famous Tain silver, along with mediocre archeological finds and clan memorabilia. There's not a great deal more to see in Tain, but check out High Street's castellated sixteenth-century **Tolbooth**, with its stone turrets and old curfew bell. Tain's only other attraction, the **whisky distillery** where the highly rated **Glenmorangie** malt is produced (shop open Mon–Fri 9am–5pm; June–Oct also Sat 10am–4pm; tours Mon–Fri 10.30am–3.30pm, Sat 10.30am–2.30pm; £2), lies just off the A9 on the north side of town. For **accommodation**, the *Mansfield House Hotel* (☎01862/892052 *mansfield@cali.co.uk*; £90–140), a modernized mansion-hotel in the Scots-Baronial mould, is renowned for its cooking, while the more modest *Golf View House* (☎01862/892856; ②), three minutes' drive from the town centre on Knockbreck Road, offers comfortable B&B. Good quality but still moderately priced **food** is available at the *Morangie House Hotel* to the north of town, while *Harry Gow* on the High Street (open all day) serves typical Scottish food, and classic Italian is dished up at *Café Volante*, also on the High Street, beside the Post Office.

Portmahomack

Although few people bother to explore the Tain area as far east as **Tarbat Ness** on the tip of the peninsula, if you're driving it's well worth setting aside a couple of hours to make the detour. The green, windswept village of **PORTMA-HOMACK** sprawls downhill to a sandy beach and round a bay full of sailing boats. On top of the hill, a Pictish archeological site is being excavated next to the pretty whitewashed **Tarbat Old Church**, with its odd tower and balustraded entrance at the back. There's also a **lighthouse** (one of the highest in Britain) at the gorse-covered point, reached along narrow roads running through fertile farmland. A good seven-mile walk starts here (2–3hr round-trip): head south from Tarbat Ness for three miles, following the narrow passage between the foot of the cliffs and the foreshore, until you get to the hamlet of Rockfield. A path leads past a row of fishermen's cottages from here to Portmahomack, then joins the tarmac road running northeast back to the lighthouse.

Back in Portmahomack, the *Oystercatcher* on Main Street is one of the eating highlights of this stretch of the east coast, serving delicious seafood, home-made soups and salads (open Tues–Sun 11am–6pm; also Fri & Sat evenings); they also have a few very-good-value **rooms** (☎01862/871560; ①). Otherwise, if you want to stay, you could try the *Caledonian Hotel* (☎01862/871345; ②), further along Main Street, which looks over the beach to the Dornoch Firth.

Bonar Bridge and around

Before the causeway was built across the Dornoch Firth, traffic heading along the coast used to skirt around the estuary, crossing the Kyle of Sutherland at **BONAR BRIDGE**. In the fourteenth and fifteenth centuries, the village harboured a large **iron foundry**. Ore was brought across the peat moors of the central Highlands from the west coast on sledges, and fuel for smelting came from the oak forest draped over the northern shores of the nearby kyle. However, James IV, passing through here on his way to Tain, was shocked to find the forest virtually clear-felled and ordered that oak saplings be planted in the gaps. Although now hemmed in by spruce plantations, the beautiful ancient woodland east of Bonar Bridge dates from this era.

These days there's little of note in Bonar Bridge other than the bridge itself, which has had three incarnations up to the present steel construction of 1973, all recalled on a stone plinth on the north side. However, you may want to check out the unusual **airboat** trips (book on ☎01863/766839; 30min–1hr; £8 or £15), run from the *Caledonian Hotel*. The unlikely looking craft, with a huge fan mounted on the back of a flat-bottomed launch, previously saw service in the Everglade swamps of Florida, and is used in similar fashion on the kyle to skim over shallow water and mud flats to get a closer look at the local wildlife and scenery.

Carbisdale Castle

Towering high above the River Shin, three miles northwest of Bonar Bridge, the daunting neo-Gothic profile of **Carbisdale Castle** (not open to the public) overlooks the **Kyle of Sutherland**, as well as the battlefield where the gallant Marquis of Montrose was defeated in 1650, finally forcing Charles II – if he wanted to be received as king – to accede to the Scots' demand for Presbyterianism. It was erected between 1906 and 1917 for the dowager **Duchess of Sutherland**, following a protracted family feud. After the death of her husband, the late Duke of Sutherland, the will leaving her the lion's share of the vast estate was contested by his stepchildren from his first marriage. In the course of the ensuing legal battle, the duchess was found in contempt of court for destroying important documents pertinent to the case, and locked up in Holloway prison for six weeks. However, the Sutherlands eventually recanted (although there was no personal reconciliation) and, by way of compensation, built their stepmother a castle worthy of her rank. Designed in three distinct styles (to give the impression that it was added to over a long period of time), Carbisdale was eventually acquired by a Norwegian shipping magnate in 1933, and finally gifted, along with its entire contents and estate, to the SYHA, which has turned it into what must be one of the most opulent **youth hostels** in the world, full of white Italian marble sculptures, huge gilt-framed portraits, sweeping staircases and magnificent drawing rooms alongside standard facilities such as self-catering kitchens, games rooms, TV rooms and thirty dorms, including some recently upgraded four-bed family rooms (☎01549/421232; March–Oct except first two weeks in May). The best way to get here by public transport is to take a train to nearby **Culrain** station, which lies within easy walking distance of the castle. **Buses** from Inverness (3 daily; 1hr 30min) and Tain (4 daily; 25min) only run as far as **Ardgay**, three miles south.

Croick Church

A mile or so southwest of Bonar Bridge, the scattered village of **ARDGAY** stands at the mouth of Strath Carron, a wooded river valley winding west into the heart of the Highlands. It's worth heading ten miles up the strath to **Croick Church**, which harbours one of Scotland's most poignant and emotive reminders of the **Clearances**. Huddled behind a brake of wind-bent trees, the graveyard surrounding the tiny grey chapel sheltered eighteen families (92 individuals) evicted from nearby Glen Calvie during the spring of 1845 to make way for flocks of Cheviot sheep, introduced by the Duke of Sutherland as a quick money-earner (see p.272). A reporter from *The Times* described the "wretched spectacle" as the villagers filed out of the glen " . . . in a body, two or three carts filled with children, many of them infants". An even more evocative written record of the event is preserved on the diamond-shaped panes of the chapel windows, where the villagers scratched **graffiti memorials** still legible today: "Glen Calvie people was in the churchyard May 24th 1845", "Glen Calvie people the wicked generation", and "This place needs cleaning".

Lairg

North of Bonar Bridge, the A836 parallels the River Shin for eleven miles, to **LAIRG**, a bleak and scattered place at the eastern end of lonely **Loch Shin**. On fine days, the vast wastes of heather and deergrass surrounding the village can be beautiful, but in the rain it can be a deeply depressing landscape. This workaday village is predominantly a **transport hub** and the railhead for a huge area to the northwest, and there's nothing much to see in town. However, a mile southeast on the A839, there are signs of early settlement at nearby **Ord Hill**, where archeological digs have recently yielded traces of human habitation dating back to Neolithic times. The Ferrycroft Countryside Centre and **tourist office**, on the west side of the river (April–Oct Mon–Sat 9.30am–5.30pm, Sun 10am–5pm; ☎01549/402160), hands out leaflets detailing the locations of hut circles and other sites, and is the starting point for forest walks and an archeological trail to Ord Hill. Four miles south of Lairg, on the opposite side of the river – along the A836, then the B864 – the **Falls of Shin** is one of the best places in Scotland to see **salmon** leaping on their upstream migration; there's a viewing platform, and the café by the car park does good snacks and meals. The season for salmon returning to spawn is from June to September. Every August, Lairg hosts an annual lamb sale, the biggest one-day livestock market in Europe, when sheep from all over the north of Scotland are bought and sold.

Practicalities

Lairg, at the centre of the region's **road system**, is distinctly hard to avoid: the A838, traversing some of the loneliest country in the Highlands, is the quickest route for Cape Wrath; the A836 heads up to Tongue on the north coast; and the A839 links up to the A837 to push west through lovely Strath Oykel, to Lochinver on the west coast. For non-drivers, Lairg is on the **train line** connecting

Inverness to Wick and Thurso, and is the nexus of several **postbus routes** around the northwest Highlands, including one which links Lairg with Ledmore, on the Ullapool–Durness road. Trains arrive north of the main road along the loch; buses stop right on the loch. Should you want **to stay**, *Carnbren* (☎01549/402259; ①), just south of the bridge on the Bonar Bridge road, is comfortable, as is the *Old Coach House* (☎01549/402378; ①; May–Oct), three miles south of Lairg on the B864 at Achany. *Park House* (☎01549/402208; ②), on Station Road, overlooking Loch Shin, is a welcoming spot if you're planning on doing some walking, fishing or cycling in the area.

Dornoch

DORNOCH, eight miles north of Tain, lies on a flattish headland overlooking the **Dornoch Firth**. Surrounded by sand dunes and blessed with an exceptionally sunny climate by Scottish standards, it's something of a middle-class holiday resort, with solid Edwardian hotels, trees and flowers in profusion, and miles of sandy beaches giving good views across the estuary to the Tain peninsula. The town is also renowned for its championship **golf course**, ranked eleventh in the world and the most northerly first-class course in the world.

Dating from the twelfth century, Dornoch became a royal burgh in 1628. Among its oldest buildings, which are all grouped round the spacious Square, the tiny **Cathedral** was founded in 1224 and built of local sandstone. The original building was horribly damaged by marauding Mackays in 1570, and much of what you see today was restored by the Countess of Sutherland in 1835, though her worst Victorian excesses were removed this century, when the interior stonework was returned to its original state. A later addition were the stained-glass windows in the north wall, which were endowed by the expat American-based Andrew Carnegie. Opposite, the fortified sixteenth-century Bishop's Palace, a fine example of vernacular architecture, with stepped gables and towers, has been refurbished as an upmarket hotel (see opposite). Next door, the **Old Town Jail** (Mon–Sat 10am–5pm; free) contains a mock-up of a nineteenth-century cell accessed through a gift and crafts shop.

In 1722, Dornoch saw the last burning of a **witch** in Scotland. The unfortunate old woman, accused of turning her daughter into a pony and riding her around town, ruined her chances of acquittal by misquoting the Gaelic version of the Lord's Prayer during the trial, and was sentenced to burn alive in a barrel of boiling tar – an event commemorated by the **Witch's Stone**, just south of the Square on Carnaig Street.

Practicalities

Buses from Tain and Inverness stop in the Square, where you'll also find a **tourist office** (Mon–Fri 9am–5pm; May–Oct also Sat 9am–4pm; July & Aug also Sun 11am–5pm; ☎01862/810400). There's no shortage of **accommodation**: the *Trentham Hotel* (☎01862/810551; ①), near the golf course on the northeast edge of town, is friendly and comfortable if a bit staid, while the characterful *Dornoch Castle Hotel* (☎01862/810216; ④; April–Oct), in the Bishop's Palace on the Square, has a cosy old-style bar and relaxing tea garden. Of the B&Bs, try *Trevose* (☎01862/810269; ①; March–Sept), on the Square, which is swathed in roses, or, a couple of miles out on the A949, *Evelix Farmhouse* (☎01862/810271; ①; June–Sept). Those with a tent may choose to head for the Caravan Park (☎01862/810423; April–Oct), attractively set between the manicured golf course

and the uncombed vegetation of the sand dunes which fringe the beach, althoug
the site does get busy with caravans in July and August. Expensive gourme
meals are available at the *2 Quail* restaurant (☎01862/811811; Tues–Sat) o
Castle Street, which also has tasteful rooms available (③), while both the hote
do good bar and restaurant meals, and the *Cathedral Café* is open until 9pm i
summer and serves delicious soup and snacks.

Golspie to Wick

Ten miles north of Dornoch on the A9 lies the straggling red-sandstone town o
GOLSPIE, whose status as an administrative centre does little to relieve its dul
ness. It does, however, boast an eighteen-hole **golf course** and a sandy beach
while half a mile further up the coast the **Big Burn** has several rapids and wate
falls that can be seen from an attractive **woodland trail** (beginning at th
Sutherland Arms Hotel).

Dunrobin Castle

The main reason to stop in Golspie, though, is to look around **Dunrobin Castl**
(May–Oct Mon–Sat 10.30am–4.30pm, Sun noon–4.30pm; open June–Sept ti
5.30pm; £4.80), overlooking the sea a mile north of town. Approached via a lon
tree-lined drive, this fairy-tale confection of turrets and pointed roofs – modelle
by the architect Sir Charles Berry (designer of the Houses of Parliament) on
Loire chateau – is the seat of the infamous Sutherland family, at one time Europe'
biggest landowners, with a staggering 1.3 million acres, and the principal drivin
force behind the **Clearances** in this area. The castle is on a correspondingly vas
scale, boasting 189 furnished rooms, of which the tour only takes in seventeen
Staring up at the pile from the midst of its elaborate **formal gardens**, it's wort
remembering that such extravagance was paid for by uprooting literall
thousands of crofters from the surrounding glens. Much of the extra income gen
erated by the evictions was lavished on the castle's opulent **interior**, which i
crammed full of fine furniture, paintings (including works by Landseer, Alla
Ramsay and Sir Joshua Reynolds), tapestries and *objets d'art*.

Set aside at least an hour for Dunrobin's amazing **museum**, housed in an eigh
teenth-century building at the edge of the garden. Inside, hundreds of disembod
ied animals' heads and horns peer down from the walls, alongside other mor
macabre appendages, from elephants' toes to rhinos' tails. Bagged mainly by th
fifth Duke and Duchess of Sutherland, the trophies vie for space with other fasci
nating family memorabilia, including one of John O'Groat's bones, Chinese opiun
pipes, and such curiosities as a "picnic gong from the South Pacific". There's als
an impressive collection of ethnographic artefacts acquired by the Sutherlands o
their frequent hunting jaunts, ranging from an Egyptian sarcophagus to som
finely carved Pictish stones.

The Sutherland Monument

You can't miss the 100-foot **Monument** to the first Duke of Sutherland, which
peers proprietorially down from the summit of the 1293-foot **Beinn a'Bhragaidh**
a mile northwest of Golspie. An inscription cut into its base recalls that the statu
was erected in 1834 by "a mourning and grateful tenantry [to] . . . a judicious, kin
and liberal landlord . . . [who would] open his hands to the distress of the widow

the sick and the traveller". Unsurprisingly, there's no reference to the fact that the duke, widely regarded as Scotland's own Josef Stalin, forcibly evicted 15,000 crofters from his million-acre estate – a fact which, in the words of one local historian, makes the monument "... a grotesque representation of the many forces that destroyed the Highlands". Campaigners are lobbying, so far unsuccessfully, to have the monument broken into pieces and scattered over the hillside, so that visitors can walk over the remains to a new, more appropriate memorial. However, the Sutherland estate and local council have continually resisted moves to replace it.

It's worth the wet, rocky **climb** (90min round-trip) to the top of the hill for the wonderful views south along the coast past Dornoch to the Moray Firth and west towards Lairg and Loch Shin. It's a steep and strenuous walk, however, and there's no view until you're out of the trees, about ten minutes from the top. Take the road opposite Munro's TV Rentals in Golspie's main street, which leads up the hill, past a fountain, under the railway and through a farmyard – from here, follow the Beinn a'Bhragaidh Footpath (BBFP) signs along the path into the woods. You can go back the way you came, or follow a clear track which initially goes north from the monument and then winds down through Benvraggie Wood to meet a tarred road; turn left here to link into the path of the Big Burn Glen walk (see above).

Loch Fleet

Just to the south of Golspie, the A9 fringes a tidal estuary on a causeway that was constructed in 1816 by Thomas Telford. The inlet, **Loch Fleet** (open access; free), is part of a large nature reserve harbouring some delicate coastal and woodland vegetation, including Britain's greatest concentration of one-flowered wintergreen, also known as St Olaf's candlestick, as well as a range of birdlife including greylag geese and arctic terns, and sealife such as seals and otters. You can walk in the reserve by following the minor road south out of Golspie for three miles – from Balblair Bay, a path leads into pine-forested Balblair Wood, while from Littleferry there are walks along the coastal heathland to the Moray Firth beaches.

Four miles northwest of Loch Fleet on the A839 to Lairg is one of Scotland's most unusual and imaginative **hostels**, *Rogat Railway Carriage* (☎01408/641343, *rograil@globalnet.co.uk*), where you can stay in one of two old railway carriages parked in a siding beside the station on the Inverness–Thurso line in the tiny settlement of Rogat. Each of the first-class compartments has a bunk bed on one side and the original seats on the other, while the two end compartments are used as a kitchen and common room. The owners have mountain bikes available so that you can explore the local countryside; the convivial local pub serves evening meals, and a small reduction is even offered to those arriving by train or bicycle.

Brora

BRORA, on the coast six miles north of Golspie, once boasted the only bridge in the region – thus the name, which means "River of the Bridge" in Norse. Until the 1960s, it was the only coal-mining village in the Highlands, having played host to the industry for four hundred years. These days, however, the small grey town harbours little of interest, although it's accessible by bus and train and does have *Capaldi's* on High Street, which sells brilliant home-made Italian ice cream. Three miles south of the town is the remarkably well-preserved Iron Age broch of Carn Liath, with great twelve-foot-thick walls and a number of obvious features intact, such as a staircase and entrance passage. The car park for the site is on the inland side of the A9, just before the broch if you're travelling north. A more interesting way to reach it is by walking along the coastal path which links Golspie and Brora. A mile or so north of town, the **Clynelish Distillery** (March–Nov Mon–Fri 9.30am–4.30pm; Dec–Feb by appointment, on ☎01408/623000; £2) will give you a guided tour and a sample dram.

The best **B&B** in the area is *Clynelish Farm* (☎01408/621265; ②) – turn left after the BP garage – a working Victorian stone farmhouse with en-suite rooms, built to provide employment for dispossessed crofters after the Clearances. The rooms here are spacious, with views over the fields to the Moray Firth, and evening meals are available by arrangement. Also worth considering for B&B is *Seaforth* (☎01408/621793; ①), a working croft on ten acres of land looking towards the sea.

Helmsdale

Eleven miles up the A9 from Golspie, **HELMSDALE** is an old herring port, founded in the nineteenth century to house the evicted inhabitants of Strath Kildonan, which lies behind it. Today, the sleepy-looking grey village attracts thousands of tourists, most of them to see the attractively designed **Timespan Heritage Centre**, beside the river (Easter–Oct Mon–Sat 9.30am–5pm, Sun 2–5pm; £3.50). It's a remarkable venture for a place of this size, telling the local story of Viking raids, witch-burning, Clearances, fishing and gold-prospecting through hi-tech displays, sound effects and an audiovisual programme. The centre also has an art gallery, which often has a decent show of works by Scottish artists. For a spot of light relief after the exhibition, head across the road to the sugary pink and frilly *Mirage Restaurant*. The proprietor has become something of a Scottish celebrity, modelling herself on the romantic novelist Barbara Cartland, whose shooting lodge is nearby. Photographs proudly displayed on the walls show the peroxide-blonde restaurateuse posing with her heroine, while the fittings and furnishings reflect her predilection for all things pink and kitsch, with fish tanks, fake-straw parasols, and plastic seagulls set off by the country-and-western soundtrack. She also dishes up great fish and chips, grills and puddings.

Helmsdale's **tourist office** (April–Sept Mon–Sat 10.30am–4pm; ☎01431/821640) in the Timespan centre will book accommodation for you. Most of the **B&Bs** are on the outskirts of town: *Broomhill House*, Navidale Road (☎01431/821259; ①), is the best of the bunch, with bedrooms in a turret added to the former croft by a miner who struck it lucky in the Kildonan gold rush. Alternatively, try *Torbuie* (☎01431/821424; ①), in Navidale, on the A9 less than a mile from the village, or *Eastdale*, half a mile up the A897 (☎01431/821334; ①), both of which offer comfortable rooms. There's also a small **youth hostel** (☎01431/821577; mid-May to Sept), about half a mile north of the harbour.

BAILE AN OR

From Helmsdale, the single-track A897 runs up Strath Kildonan and across the Flow Country (see p.258) to the north coast, at first following the River Helmsdale river, a strictly controlled and exclusive salmon river frequented by the royals. Some eight miles up the Strath at **BAILE AN OR** (Gaelic for "goldfield"), gold was discovered in the bed of the Kildonan Burn in 1869; a gold rush ensued, hardly on the scale of the Yukon, but quite bizarre in the Scottish Highlands. A tiny amount of gold is still found by some hardy prospectors every year: if you fancy

gold-panning yourself, you can rent the relevant equipment for £2.50 from Helmsdale's gift and fishing-tackle shop, Strath Ullie, opposite the Timespan Heritage Centre, which also sells a booklet with a few basic tips.

Dunbeath and Lybster

Just north of Helmsdale, the A9 begins its long haul up the **Ord of Caithness**. This steep hill used to form a pretty impregnable obstacle, and the desolate road still gets blocked during winter snowstorms. Once over the pass, the landscape changes dramatically as heather-clad moors give way to miles of treeless green grazing lands, peppered with derelict crofts and latticed by long drystone walls. This whole area was devastated during the Clearances; the ruined village of **BADBEA**, reached via a footpath running east off the main road a short way after the pass, is a poignant monument to this cruel era. Built by tenants evicted from nearby Ousdale, the settlement now lies deserted, although its ruined hovels show what hardship the crofters had to endure: the cottages stood so near the windy cliff edge that children had to be tethered to prevent them from being blown into the sea.

   DUNBEATH, hidden at the mouth of a small strath, twelve miles north of the Ord of Caithness, was another village founded to provide work in the wake of the Clearances. The local landlord built a harbour here in 1800, at the start of the herring boom, and the settlement briefly flourished. Today it's a sleepy place, with lobster pots stacked at the quayside and views of windswept Dunbeath Castle (closed to the public) on the opposite side of the bay. The novelist Neil Gunn was born here, in one of the terraced houses under the flyover that now swoops above the village; you can find out more about him at the **Dunbeath Heritage Centre** (Easter–Oct daily 10am–5pm; £1.50), signposted from the road. The best of the handful of modest **B&Bs** here is *Tormore Farm* (☎01593/731240; ①), a large farmhouse with four comfortable rooms, half a mile north of the harbour on the A9. Just north of Dunbeath is the simple but moving **Laidhay Croft Museum** (Easter to mid-Nov daily 10am–6pm; £1), which offers a useful perspective on the sometimes over-romanced life of the Highlander before the Clearances. A little further up the coast, obvious from the A9 between the villages of Latheron and Lybster, is the **Clan Gunn Heritage Centre and Museum** (June & Sept Mon–Sat 11am–5pm; July & Aug Mon–Sat 11am–5pm, Sun 2–5pm; £1.50), housed in an old white church surrounded by a graveyard, set against green fields and the precipitous coastline. It's mainly a place for members of the Clan Gunn and its septs – which include the more common surnames of Johnson, Thomson and Wilson, although it also doles out a bit more local history and a few titbits for those on the trail of Neil Gunn, whose most famous novels, *Highland River* and *The Silver Darlings*, were set along this coastline.

   The final stretch of road before Wick gives great views over the cliffs and out to sea to the oil rigs perched on the horizon. The planned village of **LYBSTER**, established at the height of the nineteenth-century herring boom, once had 200-odd boats working out of its harbour. Today, although still a busy fishing port, it's a grim collection of grey pebble-dashed bungalows centred on a broad main street. Most visitors head straight for the nearby **Grey Cairns of Camster**, seven miles due north and one of the most memorable sights on the northeast coast. Surrounded by bleak moorland, these two enormous prehistoric burial chambers, constructed 4000–5000 years ago, were immaculately designed, with corbelled drystone roofs in their hidden chambers, which you can crawl into through narrow passageways. More extraordinary ancient remains lie at **East Clyth**, two miles north of Lybster on the A99, where a path leads to the **"Hill o' Many Stanes"**. Some 200 boulders stand in the ground here, forming 22 parallel rows that run north to south; no one has yet worked out what they were used for, although archeological studies have shown there were once 600 stones in place. A fourteen-mile track waymarked as a cycle path leads between the two sites, entering the forest at a car park half a mile south of the Camster Cairns and emerging near the single-track road which passes the Hill o' Many Stanes and connects with the A99. Another relatively unknown historic site in the area is the **Whaligoe staircase**, ten miles north of Lybster on the A99 at the north end of the village of Ulbster. The stairway, which has 365 steps constructed out of the distinctive local slab stone, leads steeply down from the side of the house beside the car park to a natural harbour surrounded by cliffs. At the bottom you'll see a few remnants of the harbour used by herring fishermen in the last century, as well as vast numbers of seabirds, including cormorants, skuas and puffins; the daunting climb back up is made a little bit easier by the thought that, unlike the fishermen, you don't have a creel full of herring to carry all the way to the top. The stairway is steep and uneven for much of the way down, so be particularly careful if the steps are wet. To get to the stairway, turn off towards the sea at the junction signposted on its landward side to the "Cairn O'Get".

Wick

Originally a Viking settlement named *Vik* (meaning "bay"), **WICK** has been a royal burgh since 1589. It's actually two towns: Wick proper, and **Pultneytown**, immediately south across the river, a messy, rather run-down community planned by Thomas Telford in 1806 for the British Fisheries Society, to encourage evicted crofters to take up fishing.

Wick's heyday was in the mid-nineteenth century, when it was the busiest herring port in Europe, exporting tons of fish to Russia, Scandinavia and the West

---

WALKS AND CYCLES AROUND WICK

Ordnance Survey Landranger map no. 12

There's a good **clifftop walk** to the the dramatic fifteenth- to seventeenth-century ruins of **Sinclair** and **Girnigoe castles**, rising steeply from a needle-thin promontory three miles north of Wick, which functioned as a single stronghold for the earls of Caithness. In 1570 the fourth earl, suspecting his son of trying to murder him, imprisoned him in the dungeon here until he died of starvation. From the tiny fishing village of **Staxigoe**, head north from the harbour to Field of Noss farm and follow the line of the cliffs, where you'll encounter all sorts of seabirds, including puffins. At Noss Head lighthouse, head along the access road to a car park, where a path leads out to the castles on the north-facing coastline. **Cycling** is a good way to get to the castles: the roads near Noss Head are flat and straight, though you should think twice about setting off if the wind is too strong.

A longer ride (a fourteen-mile two-way-trip) is along the back roads southwest of Wick through Newton Row and Tannach to the short archeological walking trail at the **Loch of Yarrows**, which includes remains of a lochside broch, a hilltop fort and chambered cairns. A leaflet about the trail is available from Wick tourist office.

Indian slave plantations. Robert Louis Stevenson described it as "the meanest of man's towns, situated on the baldest of God's bays", and it's still a pretty grim place, in spite of a bustling shopping centre and some solid Victorian civic architecture. Pultneytown, lined with rows of fishermen's cottages, is the area most worth a wander, with the acres of largely derelict net-mending sheds, stores and cooperages around the harbour giving some idea of the former scale of the fishing trade. The town's story is told in the excellent **Wick Heritage Centre** in Bank Row, Pultneytown (June–Sept Mon–Sat 10am–5pm; £2), which contains a fascinating array of artefacts from the old fishing days, including fully rigged boats, original boat models, the old Noss Head lighthouse light and a great photographic collection dating from the 1880s.

Practicalities

The **train** station and **bus** stops are next to each other behind the hospital. Frequent local buses run to Thurso and up the coast to John O'Groats. Wick also has an **airport** (☎01955/602215), a couple of miles north of the town, with direct flights from Edinburgh, and Aberdeen, and connections further south. From the train station, head across the river down Bridge Street to the **tourist office**, just off High Street (Mon–Sat 10am–5pm; July–Sept also Sun 10am–5pm; ☎01955/602596), which can organize local **accommodation**. The best-value **B&B** in town is the welcoming *Greenvoe* on George Street (☎01955/603942; ①), looking over the river. *Wellington Guest House*, just behind the station at 41–43 High St (☎01955/603287; ②; March–Oct), is reasonable value, as is *The Clachan* B&B, South Road (☎01955/605384; ②), while The *Harbour Guest House*, on Rose Street, Pultneytown (☎01955/603276; ①), is friendly but more basic. The best of the hotels is *Mackay's*, which is by the river in the town centre (☎01955/602323, *mackays.hotel@caithness-mm.co.uk*; ③). Good-quality **bikes** can be rented from Wheels Cycle Shop (Easter–Sept Mon–Sat; ☎01955/603636) on Glamis Road.

As for **eating**, the good-value *Lamplighter Restaurant*, High Street, serves enormous helpings of imaginative food; downstairs in the same building, *Houston's Café* cheerfully churns out good burgers. *Cabrelli's*, at the east end of the High Street, opposite the bridge over to Pultneytown, is a real find, trapped in a time warp, and serving piles of fish and chips, along with authentic pizza. A few doors further on, *Carter's* serves unremarkable pub grub, while the adjoining *Camps* is among the liveliest of the **pubs** in the evenings, with occasional live music.

travel details

Trains

Dingwall to: Helmsdale (Mon–Sat 3 daily, plus Sun 2 daily in summer; 2hr); Inverness (Mon–Sat 6–7 daily, plus Sun 4 daily in summer; 25min); Kyle of Lochalsh (Mon–Sat 3–4 daily, plus Sun 2 daily in summer; 2hr); Lairg (Mon–Sat 3 daily, plus Sun 2 daily in summer; 1hr 10min); Thurso (Mon–Sat 3 daily, plus Sun 2 daily in summer; 3hr 20min); Wick (Mon–Sat 3 daily, plus Sun 2 daily in summer; 3hr 20min).

Fort William to: Arisaig (Mon–Sat 4 daily, plus Sun 3 daily in summer; 1hr 10min); Glasgow (Mon–Sat 3 daily, Sun 1–2 daily; 4hr); Glenfinnan (4 daily; 35min); London (1 nightly; 12hr); Mallaig (Mon–Sat 4 daily, Sun 1–3 daily; 1hr 25min).

Inverness to: Dingwall (Mon–Sat 6–7 daily, plus Sun 4 daily in summer; 25min); Edinburgh (Mon–Sat 8 daily, Sun 3 daily; 3hr 30min); Helmsdale (Mon–Sat 3 daily, plus Sun 2 daily in summer; 2hr 20min); Kyle of Lochalsh (Mon–Sat 3–4 daily, plus Sun 2 daily in summer; 2hr 40min); Lairg (Mon–Sat 3 daily, plus Sun 2 daily in summer; 1hr 40min); London (Mon–Fri & Sun 2 daily, Sat 1 daily; 8hr 35min); Plockton (Mon–Sat 3–4 daily, plus Sun 2 daily in summer; 2hr 15min); Thurso (Mon–Sat 3 daily, plus Sun 2 daily in summer; 3hr 45min); Wick (Mon–Sat 3 daily, plus Sun 2 daily in summer; 3hr 45min).

Kyle of Lochalsh to: Dingwall (Mon–Sat 3–4 daily, plus Sun 2 daily in summer; 2hr); Inverness (Mon–Sat 3–4 daily, plus Sun 2 daily in summer; 2hr 40min); Plockton (Mon–Sat 3–4 daily, plus Sun 2 daily in summer; 20min).

Lairg to: Dingwall (Mon–Sat 3 daily, plus Sun 2 daily in summer; 1hr 10min); Inverness (Mon–Sat 3 daily, plus Sun 2 daily in summer; 1hr 40min); Thurso (Mon–Sat 3 daily, plus Sun 2 daily in summer; 2hr 5min); Wick (Mon–Sat 3 daily, plus Sun 2 daily in summer; 2hr 5min).

Mallaig to: Arisaig (Mon–Sat 4 daily, plus Sun 3 daily in summer; 15min); Fort William (Mon–Sat 4 daily, plus Sun 3 daily in summer; 1hr 25min); Glasgow (Mon–Sat 3 daily, Sun 1–2 daily; 5hr 20min); Glenfinnan (Mon–Sat 4 daily, plus Sun 3 daily in summer; 35min).

Thurso to: Dingwall (Mon–Sat 3 daily, plus Sun 2 daily in summer; 3hr 20min); Inverness (Mon–Sat 3 daily, plus Sun 2 daily in summer; 3hr 45min); Lairg (Mon–Sat 3 daily, plus Sun 2 daily in summer; 2hr 5min).

Wick to: Dingwall (Mon–Sat 3 daily, plus Sun 2 daily in summer; 3hr 20min); Inverness (Mon–Sat 3 daily, plus Sun 2 daily in summer; 3hr 45min); Lairg (Mon–Sat 3 daily, plus Sun 2 daily in summer; 2hr 5min).

Buses

Brora to: Thurso (4–5 daily; 1hr 50min); Wick (5–6 daily; 1hr 15min).

Dornoch to: Brora (5 daily; 35min); Inverness (10 daily; 1hr 10min).

Fort William to: Acharacle (Mon–Sat 2–4 daily; 1hr 30min); Inverness (6 daily; 2hr); Mallaig (1–2 daily; 2hr).

Gairloch to: Dingwall (3 weekly; 2hr); Inverness (3 weekly; 2hr 20min); Redpoint (1 daily; 1hr 35min).

Inverness to: Aberdeen (hourly; 3hr 40min); Cromarty (4 daily; 45min); Durness (May to early Oct 1 daily; 5hr); Fort William (6 daily; 2hr); Gairloch (1 daily; 2hr 20min); Glasgow (7 daily; 3hr 35min–4hr 25min); John O'Groats (1–2 daily; 3hr 40min); Kirkwall (April–Sept 2 daily; 5hr 20min); Kyle of Lochalsh (3–4 daily; 2hr); Lairg (Mon–Sat 2 daily; 2hr); Lochinver (May to early Oct 1 daily; 3hr 10min); Oban (Mon–Sat 2 daily; 4hr); Perth (10 daily; 2hr 35min); Portree (3–4 daily; 3hr 20min); Tain (hourly; 1hr 15min); Thurso (Mon–Sat 5 daily, Sun 4 daily; 3hr 30 min); Ullapool (2–4 daily; 1hr 25min); Wick (Mon–Sat 3 daily; 1hr 55min).

Kyle of Lochalsh to: Fort William (3 daily; 1hr 50min); Glasgow (3 daily; 5hr); Inverness (3–4 daily; 2hr).

Lochinver to: Inverness (May to early Oct 1 daily; 3hr 10min).

Mallaig to: Acharacle (1–3 daily; 1hr 45min); Fort William (1–2 daily; 2hr).

Thurso to: Bettyhill (2 daily; 1hr 20min); Inverness (Mon–Sat 5 daily, Sun 4 daily; 3hr 30min); Wick (Mon–Sat 2–4 daily, Sun 1 daily; 35min).

Wick to: Inverness (Mon–Sat 3 daily; 1hr 55min); Thurso (Mon–Sat 2–4 daily, Sun 1 daily; 35min).

Ferries

To Lewis: Ullapool–Stornoway, see p.340.

To Mull: Kilchoan–Tobermory, see p.132.

To Orkney: Scrabster–Stromness, see p.245.

To Skye: Mallaig–Armadale; Glenelg–Kylerhea, see p.340.

To the Small Isles: Mallaig–Eigg, Rum, Muck and Canna, see p.340.

Flights

Inverness to: Amsterdam (1 daily; 1hr 35min); Edinburgh (Mon–Fri 1 daily; 50min); Glasgow (Mon–Fri 2 daily; 50min); Kirkwall (Mon–Fri 2 daily; 40min); London (4 daily; 1hr 25min); Shetland (Mon–Fri 1 daily; 1hr 50min); Stornoway (Mon–Sat 2 daily; 40min).

CHAPTER FIVE

SKYE AND THE WESTERN ISLES

A procession of Hebridean islands, islets and reefs off the northwest shore of Scotland, **Skye and the Western Isles** between them boast some of the country's most alluring scenery. It's here that the turbulent seas of the Atlantic smash up against an extravagant shoreline hundreds of miles long, a geologically complex terrain whose rough rocks and mighty sea cliffs are interrupted by a thousand sheltered bays and, in the far west, a long line of sweeping sandy beaches. The islands' interiors are equally dramatic, a series of formidable mountain ranges soaring high above great chunks of boggy peat moor, a barren wilderness enclosing a host of tiny lakes, or lochans.

Skye and the Western Isles were first settled by Neolithic farming peoples in around 4000 BC. They lived along the coast, where they are remembered by scores of remains, from passage graves through to stone circles – most famously at **Calanais** (Callanish) on Lewis. Viking colonization gathered pace from 700 AD onwards – on Lewis four out of every five place names is of Norse origin – and it was only in 1266 that the islands were returned to the Scottish crown. James VI (and I of England), a Stuart and a Scot, though no Gaelic-speaker, was the first to put forward the idea of clearing the Hebrides, though it wasn't until after the Jacobite uprisings, in which many Highland clans disastrously backed the wrong side, that the **Clearances** began in earnest.

The isolation of the Hebrides exposed them to the whims and fancies of the various merchants and aristocrats who caught "island fever" and bought them up. Time and again, from the mid-eighteenth century to the present day, both the land and its people were sold to the highest bidder. Some proprietors were well-meaning, but insensitive – like **Lord Leverhulme**, who had no time for crofting and wanted to turn Lewis into a centre of the fishing industry in the 1920s – while others were simply autocratic – such as **Colonel Gordon of Cluny**, who bought Benbecula, South Uist, Eriskay and Barra, and forced the inhabitants onto ships bound for North America at gunpoint – but always the islanders were powerless and almost everywhere they were driven from their ancestral homes, robbing them of their particular sense of place. However, their language survived, ensuring a degree of cultural continuity, especially in the Western Isles, where even today the mother tongue of the vast majority is **Gaelic**.

Each island has its own distinct character, though you can split the grouping quite neatly into two. **Skye** and the so-called **Small Isles** – the improbably named **Rùm**, **Eigg**, **Muck** and **Canna** – are part of the Inner Hebrides, which also include the islands of Argyll (see Argyll, Chapter 1). Beyond Skye, across the

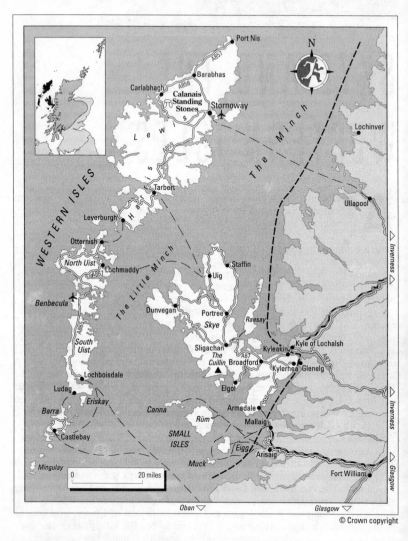

© Crown copyright

unpredictable waters of the Minch, lie the Outer Hebrides or Outer Isles, nowadays known as the **Western Isles**, a 130-mile-long archipelago stretching from **Lewis** and **Harris** in the north to **Barra** in the south.

Although this area is one of the most popular holiday spots in Scotland, the crowds only become oppressive on Skye, and even here most visitors stick to a well-trodden sequence of roadside sights that leaves the rest of the island unaffected. The main attraction, the spectacular scenery, is best explored on **foot**, following the scores of paths that range from the simplest of cross-country strolls to arduous treks. There are four obvious areas of outstanding natural beauty to aim

ACCOMMODATION PRICE CODES

Throughout this book, accommodation **prices** have been graded with the codes below, according to the cost of the least expensive double room in high season. Price codes are not given for campsites, most of which charge under £10 per person. Almost all hostels charge less than £10 a night for a bed – the few exceptions to this rule have the prices quoted in the text. For a full account of the accommodation price codes, see p.32.

① under £40	④ £60–70	⑦ £110–150
② £40–50	⑤ £70–90	⑧ £150–200
③ £50–60	⑥ £90–110	⑨ £200 and over

for: on Skye, the harsh peaks of the **Cuillin** and the bizarre rock formations of the **Trotternish** peninsula, both of which attract hundreds of walkers and mountaineers; on the Western Isles, the mountains of **North Harris** and the splendid sandy beaches that string along the Atlantic seaboard of **South Harris** and the **Uists**.

The tourist world and that of the islanders tend to be mutually exclusive, especially in the Western Isles. There are, however, ways to meet people – not so much by sitting in the pubs (they are few and far between in these parts), than by staying in the B&Bs and getting to know the owners. You could, too, join the locals at church, where visitors are generally welcome. This is a highly **religious region**, dotted with numerous tiny churches, whose denominations differ from island to island. In general terms, the south is predominantly Roman Catholic, while the Calvinist north is a stronghold of the strict Free Church of Scotland – more familiarly known as the "Wee Frees" (see p.309). Another good way to get acquainted with local life is to read the weekly *West Highland Free Press*, a refreshingly vociferous campaigning paper published in Broadford on Skye.

Travelling around Skye and the Western Isles requires some degree of forethought. The CalMac **ferries** run to a complicated timetable, and the **bus** services are patchy to say the least. It's also worth reserving space on the ferries as far in advance as possible, as they get very booked up. Also, in accordance with Calvinist dogma, the entire public transport system of Lewis and Harris closes down on **Sunday**; elsewhere, only a skeleton service remains. You should consider visiting the islands (particularly Skye) in the spring or early autumn, rather than the height of the summer, both to avoid the crowds and to elude the attentions of the pesky **midge** (see p.44).

SKYE

Justifiably **Skye** was named after the Norse word for "cloud" (*skuy*), earning itself the Gaelic moniker, *Eilean a Cheo* (Island of Mist). Yet, despite the unpredictability of the weather, tourism has been an important part of the island's economy for almost a hundred years now, since the train line pushed through to Kyle of Lochalsh in the western Highlands in 1897. From here, it was the briefest of boat trips across to Skye, and the Edwardian bourgeoisie was soon swarming over to walk its mountains, whose beauty had been proclaimed by an earlier generation of Victorian climbers.

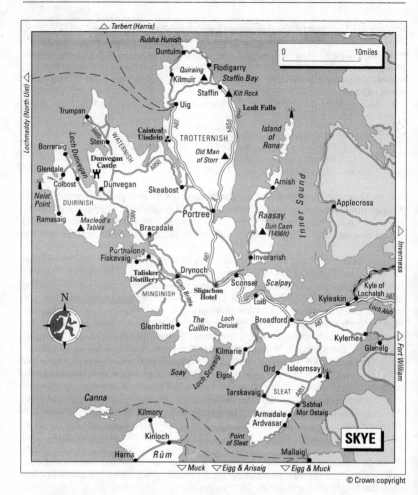

© Crown copyright

Most visitors still reach Skye from **Kyle of Lochalsh**, linked with Inverness by train via the new Skye Bridge on one of the frequent buses over to **Kyleakin**, on the western tip of the island. However, this part of Skye is pretty dull, and the more scenic approach is from the **ferry** port of **Mallaig**, further south on the Morar peninsula (see p.227). Linked by **train** with Glasgow, the Mallaig boat (up to 7 daily) takes thirty minutes to cross to **Armadale**, on the gentle southern slopes of the **Sleat peninsula**. A third option is the privately operated car **ferry** which leaves the mainland at Glenelg, south of Kyle of Lochalsh, to arrive at **Kylerhea**, from where the road heads inland towards **Portree**. If you're carrying on to the Western Isles, it's 57 miles from Armadale to the opposite end of Skye, where **ferries** leave **Uig** for Tarbert on Harris and Lochmaddy on North Uist.

Skye has several substantial **campsites**, and numerous **hostels** or bunkhouses – all of which recommend advance bookings, particularly in July and August –

plenty of B&Bs and a string of pricey, but excellent **hotels**. Most visitors arrive by car, as the **bus** services, while adequate between the villages, peter out in the more remote areas, and virtually close down on Sundays. Accommodation on the Small Isles is more limited and requires forward planning at all times of the year; formal public transport is nonexistent, but the locals will usually oblige if you have heavy baggage to shift.

Skye

Jutting out from the mainland like a giant wing, the bare and bony promontories of the **Isle of Skye** (An t-Eilean Sgiathanach) fringe a deeply indented coastline that makes the island never more than 25, and sometimes as little as 7, miles wide. This causes problems at the height of the tourist season, when the main road system begins to bottleneck with coach tours and minibuses and caravans. Yet Skye is a deceptively large island, and you'll get most out of it – and escape the worst of the crowds – if you take the time to explore the more remote parts of the island.

Though some estimate that only half the island's population are *Sgiathanachs* (pronounced "Ski-anaks"), Skye remains the most important centre for **Gaelic culture** and language outside of the Western Isles. Despite the Clearances, which saw an estimated 30,000 emigrate in the mid-nineteenth century, around forty percent of the population is fluent in Gaelic, the Gaelic college on Sleat is the most important in Scotland, and the extreme Free Sabbatarian Church (see p.309) maintains a strong presence. As an English-speaking visitor, it's as well to be aware of the tensions that exist within this idyllic island, even if you never experience them first-hand. For a taste of the resurgence of Gaelic culture, try and get here in time for the Skye and Lochalsh Festival, *Feis an Eilean*, which takes place over two weeks in mid-July.

The most popular destination on Skye is the **Cuillin** ridge, whose jagged peaks dominate the island during clear weather; to explore them at close quarters you'll need to be a fairly experienced and determined walker. Equally dramatic in their own way are the rock formations of the **Trotternish** peninsula, in the north, from which there are inspirational views across to the Western Isles. If you want to escape the summer crush, shuffle off to **Glendale** and the cliffs of Neist Point or head for the island of **Raasay**, off Skye's east coast. Of the two main settlements, **Broadford** and **Portree**, only the latter has any charm attached to it, though both have tourist offices, and make useful bases, especially for those without their own transport.

Sleat

Ferry services (Mon–Sat 6–7 daily; June to mid-Sept also Sun; 30min) from Mallaig connect with the **Sleat** (pronounced "Slate") **peninsula**, Skye's southern tip, an uncharacteristically fertile area that has earned it the sobriquet "The Garden of Skye". The CalMac ferry terminal is at **ARMADALE** (Armadal), an elongated hamlet stretching along the wooded shoreline. If you've time to kill waiting for the ferry, take a look at the huge variety of Scottish and Irish knitwear on offer at Ragamuffin by the pier, or if you need a bite **to eat**, pop into the *Pasta Shed* next door, which does a great seafood pizza (eat-in or takeaway).

Alternatively, a few hundred yards up the road, *The Gallery* café/restaurant serves inexpensive and delicious fish and seafood dishes.

If you're leaving Skye on the early-morning ferry, you may need **accommodation** in Armadale: try *Skye Batiks* B&B (☎01471/844396; ①), near the pier, or, better still, head a mile southwest to neighbouring Ardvasar, where the traditional, whitewashed *Ardvasar Hotel* (☎01471/844223; ⑤; March–Dec) has an excellent restaurant specializing in local seafood, and a lively bar. There are three **hostels** on the peninsula: *Armadale SYHA Hostel* (☎01471/844260; mid-March to Sept) is a ten-minute walk up the A851 towards Broadford and overlooks the bay; *Sleat Independent Hostel* (☎01471/844440; open all year) is two miles further up the same road, beyond Sabhal Mòr Ostaig; while *Hairy Coo Backpackers* (☎01471/833231) is another couple of miles further on, in Toravaig House by Knock Castle. The SYHA hostel **rents bikes**, as does the local petrol station (☎01471/844249), close to the pier.

Just past Armadale youth hostel, you'll find the **Clan Donald Visitor Centre** (April–Oct daily 9.30am–5.30pm; £3.80), housed in the neo-Gothic Armadale Castle, which was built by the MacDonalds as their clan seat in 1815. Part of the castle has been restored to create a touristy museum that traces the history of the Gaels, concentrating on medieval times when the MacDonalds were in their glory as the Lords of the Isles. There's a lot of fairly confusing historical text on the walls, and the romantic sound effects – the cries of seabirds and battle songs – don't really compensate for the lack of original artefacts, but the handsome forty-acre **gardens** (April–Oct daily 9.30am–5.30pm; Nov–March free) are the highlight, with guided nature walks in the grounds. There's an attractive café and a library for those who want to chase up their ancestral Donald connections.

A couple of miles up the road in an old MacDonald farm is the **Sabhal Mòr Ostaig** (☎01471/844373), a modern, independent Gaelic college of further education founded by Sir Iain Noble, an Edinburgh merchant banker, who owns a large chunk of the peninsula and is an untiring Gaelic enthusiast. The college runs a variety of extremely popular short courses in Gaelic language, music and culture, and longer full-time courses in Gaelic business, computing and media. If you're looking for a book and tape on beginners' Gaelic, the college bookshop has a good selection.

The loveliest part of the Sleat peninsula, by far, is the west coast: take the fiercely winding single-track road over to the scattered settlement of **TARSKAVAIG**, with its little sandy beach looking out over to Eigg. Further along the coast, through some ancient deciduous woods, you come to **Tokavaig**, where a stony, seaweedy beach overlooked by the ruined Dunscaith Castle boasts views over the entire Cuillin range – this, and neighbouring **ORD**, with a pleasant sandy beach, are the two best places on the whole of Skye from which to view the mountains in fine weather. There are very few places to stay in this area, but there is a B&B with great views in Ord, *Fiordhem* (☎01471/855226; ⑤; Easter–Oct).

Continuing northeast, it's another six miles to **ISLEORNSAY** (Eilean Iarmain), a secluded little village of whitewashed cottages that was once Skye's main fishing port. With the mountains of the mainland on the horizon, the views out across the bay are wonderful, overlooking a necklace of seaweed-encrusted rocks and the tidal **Isle of Ornsay**, which sports a trim lighthouse built by Robert Louis Stevenson's father. You can **stay** at another of Sir Iain Noble's enterprises, the mid-nineteenth-century *Isleornsay Hotel* – also known by its Gaelic name *Hotel Eilean Iarmain* – a pricey place with excellent service, whose **restaurant** serves great seafood (☎01471/833332; ⑤). Also based in Isleornsay is Sir Iain's Gaelic whisky company, Prabann na Linne, which markets a number of unpronounceable Gaelic-named blended and single malt whiskies; the company offers tastings at its head office (phone ☎01471/833266 for opening hours).

Kyleakin and Kylerhea

The aforementioned Sir Iain Noble is also one of the leading advocates of (and investors in) the privately financed **Skye Bridge**, which now links the tidy hamlet of **KYLEAKIN** (Caol Acain – pronounced "Ka*la*kin", with the stress on the second syllable) with the Kyle of Lochalsh (see p.232), just half a mile away on the mainland. The bridge, welcomed by the vast majority of islanders, was built entirely by Anglo-German contractors for a cool £30 million, which they are currently trying to recoup by charging around £5 each way for cars and £30 for lorries and coaches, making it the most expensive toll bridge in Europe, and no cheaper than the ferry it replaced. With a new Scottish Parliament in control, the well-orchestrated campaign by SKAT (Skye & Kyle Against Tolls), 350 of whose members have refused to pay the tolls, may yet succeed in either reducing or abolishing the fee. There's a notice board erected by SKAT just before the bridge giving you an update. Strictly speaking there are two bridges which rest on an island in the middle, **Eilean Ban**, once the home of author and naturalist Gavin Maxwell, which is set to become a wildlife sanctuary.

There's nothing much to see or do in Kyleakin, though you could have a quick look at the scant remains of **Castle Moil**, a fourteenth-century keep poking out into the straits on top of a diminutive rocky knoll, that looks romantic when floodlit. One of its earliest inhabitants, an entrepreneurial Norwegian princess, married to a MacDonald chief, hung a chain across the water and exacted a toll from every passing boat. With its ferry now defunct, Kyleakin has reinvented itself as something of a backpackers' paradise – to the consternation of many villagers – in summer, the population more than doubles. If you're intent on joining the throng, the SYHA **hostel** (☎01599/534585; open all year) is an ugly, modern building a couple of hundred yards from the old pier; nearby *Skye Backpackers* (☎01599/534510; open all year) is a more laid-back option, as is *Dun Caan Hostel* (☎01599/534087; open all year). **Bike rental** is available from Skye Bikes (☎01599/534795) on the pier. On the road to Broadford there's the cheery *Crofters Kitchen*, providing homely **food** all day with a local flavour.

You can still avoid crossing the Skye Bridge by taking the ferry service (mid-March to mid-May & Sept to mid-Oct Mon–Sat 9am–6pm; mid-May to Aug Mon–Sat 9am–8.30pm, Sun 10am–6pm; 15min) from Glenelg to **KYLERHEA** (pronounced "Kile-ray"), a peaceful little place some four miles down the coast from Kyleakin. **Seal trips**, organized by Castle Moil Seal Cruises, also set off from the ferry pier, taking you to view the seal colony on Eilean Mhal (4 daily; £5.50; ☎01599/534641). Alternatively, you can walk half an hour up the coast to the Forestry Commission **Otter Hide**, where, if you're lucky, you may be able to spot one of these elusive creatures.

Broadford

Heading west out of Kyleakin or Kylerhea brings you eventually to the island's second-largest village, charmless **BROADFORD** (An t-Ath Leathann), whose mile-long main street curves round a wide bay. Despite its rather unlovely appearance, Broadford makes a useful base for exploring the southern half of Skye, and something of a wet-weather retreat, with the unusual **Skye Serpentarium** (Easter–June, Sept & Oct Mon–Sat 10am–5pm; July & Aug also Sun; £2), full of snakes, lizards and frogs to amuse bored children. You can also go for trips in a glass-bottomed boat from the pier (check the times on ☎01471/822037). For **mountain climbing and walking**, contact Skye Highs Mountain Guiding (☎01471/822116).

More pragmatically, Broadford has a **tourist office** (April, May & Sept Mon–Sat 9.30am–5.30pm; June Mon–Sat 9am–6pm; July & Aug Mon–Sat 9am–7pm, Sun 10am–5pm; Oct Mon–Sat 9.30am–5pm; ☎01471/822361), next to the Esso garage on the main road, which also contains a laundry, small shop and bureau de change, all open 24 hours. At the west end of the village there's a bank, a bakery, a tearoom and a post office. The SYHA **hostel** is on the west shore of Broadford Bay (☎01471/822442; Feb–Dec), or there's the much smaller, more beautiful and primitive *Fossil Bothy* hostel (☎01471/822297 or 822644, *scu_h.q._mandeville@sprite.co.uk*; open all year), a mile or so east of the bay, in Lower Breakish, off the road to Kyleakin. Two **B&Bs** which stand out are the delightful old croft-house *Lime Stone Cottage*, 4 Lime Park (☎01471/822142; ①), and the modern, comfortable *Ptarmigan* (☎01471/822744; ②), on the main road, with views over the bay. Close to the *Fossil Bothy*, the pleasant *Seagull* **restaurant** (Easter–Oct eves & Sun lunch only) serves inexpensive local meat and seafood dishes, while you can **rent bikes** from the SYHA hostel or from *Fairwinds*, another good place to stay (☎01471/822270; ②; March–Oct), just past the *Broadford Hotel*.

Scalpay, Luib and The Braes

The A87 from Broadford to Portree continues to hug the coast for the next ten miles, giving out views across Loch na Cairidh to the **Isle of Scalpay**, a huge heather-backed lump that looks something like a giant scone, rising to 1298ft at the peak of Mullach na Carn. The island is part red-deer farm, part forestry plantation, and is currently owned by a merchant banker. Close by the boat slip in Ard Dorch that serves Scalpay is *The Picture House* (☎01471/822531, *holidays@ picture-house.demon.co.uk*; ①), a **B&B** with stunning views of the Inner Sound, which doubles as a photographic gallery.

As the road twists round into Loch Ainort, there's a turnoff to **Luib Folk Museum** (daily 9am–6pm; £1), a restored **blackhouse**, with a coffee shop next door. Built low against the wind, the house's thick walls are made up of an inner and outer layer of loose stone on either side of a central core of earth, a traditional type of construction which attracted the soubriquet "black house" (*tigh dubh*) around 1850, when buildings with single-thickness walls, known as "white houses" (*tigh geal*), were introduced from the mainland. The Luib museum is run by local museum magnate and restorer, Peter MacAskill, who's also responsible for two other museums in restored blackhouses on the island.

From the head of Loch Ainort, the main road takes a steep short cut across a pass to Loch Sligachan, while a prettier, minor road meanders round the coast – either way, you'll reach **SCONSER**, departure point for the car ferry to Raasay (see oppposite), and home to a nine-hole **golf course**, with superb views. There's a good **B&B** here by the shore in a croft house, *Loch Aluinn* (☎01478/650288; ②; March–Oct) or *The Old Schoolhouse* (☎01478/650313; ①; March–Dec).

On the opposite side of Loch Sligachan are the crofting communities of **The Braes**, whose inhabitants staged a successful rent strike in 1881 against their landlords, the MacDonalds. After eviction summonses were burnt by the crofters, a detachment of fifty Glasgow policemen were drafted in and took part in a "battle", which aroused a great deal of publicity for the crofters' cause (for more on which, see p.292).

Isle of Raasay

Though it takes only fifteen minutes to reach from Skye, the lovely island of **Raasay**, a nature conservancy area with great walks across its bleak and barren hills, remains well off the tourist trail. For much of its history, Raasay was the property of a branch of the Jacobite MacLeods of Lewis, and the island sent 100 men and 26 pipers to Culloden, as a consequence of which it was practically destroyed by government troops in the aftermath of the 1745 uprising. Bonnie Prince Charlie spent a miserable night in a "mean low hut" on Raasay during his flight and swore to replace the burnt turf cottages with proper stone houses (he never did). Not long after the MacLeods were forced to sell up in 1843, the Clearances started in earnest, a period of the island's history immortalized in verse by Raasay poet, Sorley MacLean (Somhairle MacGill Eathain). In 1921, seven ex-servicemen and their families from the neighbouring isle of Rona illegally squatted crofts on Raasay, and were imprisoned, causing a public outcry. As a result, both islands were bought by the government the following year. Rona, ancestral home of the family of Billy Graham, the American evangelist, is now uninhabited, and Raasay's population stands at around 160, most of them members of the Free Presbyterian Church (see p.309). Strict observance of the Sabbath – no work or play on Sundays – is the most obvious manifestation for visitors, who should respect the islanders' feelings.

The ferry docks at the southern tip of the island, an easy fifteen-minute walk from **INVERARISH**, a tiny village set within thick woods on the island's southwest coast. If your time is limited there are several walks in these woods: you can follow the miners' trail which traces the route of the railway constructed to carry iron ore to the jetty, built by German POWs in 1914, most of whom died of -influenza in 1918. The grand Georgian mansion of **Raasay House** (now an outdoor centre) was built by the MacLeods in the late 1740s, to be all but ruined by government troops a few years later. The grounds slope down to a tiny old **harbour**, overlooked by two weathered stone mermaids stuck on top of the remains of a battery armed in the Napoleonic era with several cannons. The house's stable clock stopped on the day in 1914 when 36 men of Raasay went to war – only 14 returned; also in the grounds, there are Pictish symbol stones and the charming ruined thirteenth-century Chapel of St Moluag.

The interior of Raasay is starkly barren, a rugged and rocky terrain of sandstone in the south and gneiss in the north, with the most obvious feature being the curiously truncated basalt cap on top of **Dun Caan** (1456ft), where Boswell "danced a Highland dance" on his visit to the island with Dr Johnson in 1773 – you may feel like doing the same if you're rewarded with a clear view over to the Cuillin and the Outer Hebrides. The trail to the top of the peak is fairly easy to follow, a splendid five-mile trek up through the forest and along the burn behind Inverarish. The quickest return is made down the northwest slope of Dun Caan, but – by going a couple of miles further – you can get back to the ferry along the path by the southeast shore, passing the abandoned crofters' village of Hallaig, whose steep incline led mothers to tether their children to stakes to prevent them rolling onto the shore.

If you want to explore the north of the island you really need transport and a fine day to appreciate the views across to the Skye Cuillin, Portree and the Trotternish peninsula. Where the road dips to the east coast the stark remains of **Brochel Castle** stand overlooking the shore. The last two miles of the road to Arnish is known as **Calum's Road**: in the 1960s the council refused to extend the road to the village, so Calum MacLeod decided to build it himself; it took him ten years and by the time he'd finished he and his wife were the only people left in the village. You can walk on a boggy path to the north end and onto **Eilean Tigh** at low tide, or there's a shorter walk onto **Eilean Fladday**, which is also tidal. Raasay is rich in flora and fauna and it's at the north end that you're more likely to see a golden eagle, snipe, orchids and perhaps the unique Raasay vole. Rather than walking, you could always book a guided tour with Heavy Horses Tours (☎01478/660233; Easter–Oct).

Practicalities

The CalMac **car ferry** departs for Raasay from Sconser (Mon–Sat 9–10 daily; 15min). Many visitors go for the day, since there's plenty to do within walking distance of the pier – if you do take a car, be warned there's no petrol on the island. Comfortable **accommodation** in tastefully Bohemian rooms is available at the *Raasay Outdoor Centre* (☎01478/660266, *raasay.house@virgin.net*; ①; March to mid-Oct), where Boswell and Johnson stayed; it also has a café, open to all. You can **camp** in the grounds and, for a daily cost of around £25, join in the centre's activity programme: anything from sailing, windsurfing and canoeing, to climbing and hillwalking. Close by is the likeably old-fashioned *Isle of Raasay Hotel* (☎01478/660222; ③), which serves delicious traditional Scottish food and where the view of the Cuillin surpasses any other; in the village is a pleasant Victorian guest house, *Churchton House* (☎01478/660260; ①). A rough track cuts up the steep hillside from the village to Raasay's isolated but beautifully placed SYHA **hostel** (☎01478/660240; mid-May to Sept).

The Cuillin and the Red Hills

For many people, the **Cuillin**, whose sharp snowcapped peaks rise mirage-like from the flatness of the surrounding terrain, are Skye's *raison d'être*. When the clouds finally disperse, they are the dominating feature of the island, visible from every other peninsula on Skye. There are basically three approaches to the Cuillin: from the south, by foot or by boat from Elgol; from the *Sligachan Hotel* to the north; or from Glen Brittle to the west of the mountains. Glen Sligachan is one of the most popular routes, dividing as it does the granite of the round-topped **Red Hills** (sometimes known as the Red Cuillin) to the east from the dark, coarse-grained jagged-edged gabbro of the real Cuillin (also known as the Black Cuillin), to the west. With some twenty Munros between them, these are mountains to be taken seriously, and many routes through the Cuillin are for experienced climbers only (for more on safety, see p.46).

Elgol and Loch Coruisk

The road to **ELGOL** (Ealaghol), fourteen miles southwest of Broadford at the tip of the Strathaird peninsula, is one of the most dramatic on the island, leading right

WALKING IN THE CUILLIN

For many walkers and climbers, there's nowhere in Britain to beat the **Cuillin**. The main ridge is just eight miles long, but with its immediate neighbours is made up of over thirty peaks, including eleven Munros. Those intent on doing a complete traverse of the Cuillin ridge usually start at Gars-bheinn, at the southeastern tip, and finish off at Sgurr nan Gillean (3167ft), descending on the famous *Sligachan Hotel* for a well-earned pint. The entire journey takes a minimum of fifteen hours, which either means a very long day, or two days and a bivouac. A period of settled weather is pretty much essential, and only experienced walkers and climbers should attempt it. Before setting out on any of the walks below, you should not only take note of all the usual safety precautions (see p.46), but should also be aware of the fact that **compasses** are unreliable in the Cuillin, due to the magnetic nature of the rocks.

If you're based in Glenbrittle, and simply want to bag one or two of the peaks, there are several corries that provide relatively straightforward approaches to the most central Munros. From the SYHA hostel, a path heads west along the southern bank of the stream that tumbles down from the **Coire a' Ghreadaidh**. From the corrie, you can climb up to An Dorus, the most obvious gap in the ridge ahead, from which you can either ascend Sgurr a' Mhadaidh (3012ft), to the north, or Sgurr a' Ghreadaidh (3192ft). Alternatively, before you reach Coire a' Ghreadaidh, you can head south to the **Coir' an Eich**, from which you can easily climb Sgurr na Banachdich (3166ft) via its western ridge. To the south of the youth hostel, the road crosses another stream, with another path along its southern banks. This path heads west past the impressive Eas Mór (Great Waterfall), before heading up to the **Coire na Banachdich**. The pass above the corrie is the main one over to Loch Coruisk, but also gives access to Sgurr Dearg, best known for its great view of the Inaccessible Pinnacle (3235ft), Scotland's most difficult Munro to conquer, since it requires considerable rock-climbing skills. Back at Eas Mór, paths head off for **Coire Lagan**, by far the most popular corrie thanks to its steep sides and tiny lochan. A laborious slog up the Great Stone Chute is the easiest approach if you want to reach the top of Sgurr Alasdair (3258ft).

into the heart of the Red Hills and then down a precipitous slope, with a stunning view from the top down to Elgol pier. On the way you pass the ruins of a pre-Reformation church and graveyard at Kilchrist, where there are also traces of marble quarries which flourished for a while, employing Belgian experts and running the marble on a small railway to Broadford pier. Further down the road at Torrin you'll see the modern quarry with its white gleaming gash in the hillside; the brilliance of the stone has been compared favourably with Carrara but it is too hard to work and mostly graces local driveways as chippings. In summer there's a busy stall at Elgol pier, serving burgers and seafood because the chief reason for visiting Elgol is, weather permitting, to take a boat across Loch Scavaig (March–Sept 2–4 daily), past a seal colony, to a jetty near the entrance of **Loch Coruisk** (from *coire uish*, "cauldron of water"). An isolated, glacial loch, this needle-like shaft of water, nearly two miles long but only a couple of hundred yards wide, lies in the shadow of the highest peaks of the Black Cuillin, a wonderfully overpowering landscape.

The journey by sea takes 45 minutes and passengers are dropped to spend about one and a half hours ashore; for booking (essential) and details of sailing times, ring the *Bella Jane* (☎0800/7313089). Walkers use the boat on a one-way trip simply to get to Loch Coruisk, from where there are numerous possibilities for hiking amidst the Red Hills, the most popular (and gentle) of which is the eight-mile trek north over the pass into **Glen Sligachan**. Alternatively, you could walk round the coast to the sandy bay of **Camasunary**, over two miles to the east – a difficult walk that involves a tricky river crossing and negotiating "The Bad Step", an overhanging rock with a thirty-foot drop to the sea – and either head north to Glen Sligachan, continue south three miles along the coast to Elgol, or continue east to the Am Mam shoulder, for a stunning view of mountains and the islands of Soay, Rùm and Canna. From Am Mam, the path leads down to the Elgol road, joining it at Kilmarie.

The only public transport is the **postbus** from Broadford (Mon–Fri 2 daily, Sat 1 daily), which takes two hours to reach Elgol in the morning (check with the tourist office in Broadford about connections). Rather than stay in Elgol, head for *Rowan Cottage* (☎01471/866287; ①; April–Nov), a lovely **B&B** a mile or so east in Glasnakille, or the larger, more luxurious *Strathaird House* (☎01471/866269, *jkubale@compuserve.com*; ③; April–Sept) just beyond Kilmarie, three miles up the road to Broadford. By far the most popular place to stay, though, is the **campsite** (April–Oct) by the *Sligachan Hotel* (☎01478/650204; ②) on the A87, at the northern end of Glen Sligachan. The hotel's huge *Seamus Bar* serves food for weary walkers until 10pm, and quenches their thirst with the full range of real ales produced by Skye's very own microbrewery in Uig.

Glen Brittle

Six miles along the A863 to Dunvegan from the *Sligachan Hotel*, a turning signed "Carbost and Portnalong" quickly leads to the entrance to stony **Glen Brittle**, edging the most spectacular peaks of the Cuillin; at the end of the glen, idyllically situated by the sea, is the village of **GLENBRITTLE**. Climbers and serious walkers tend to congregate at the **SYHA hostel** (☎01478/640278; mid-March to Sept) or the fairly basic **campsite** (☎01478/640404; April–Oct), a mile or so further south behind the wide sandy beach at the foot of the glen. During the summer, two buses a day (Mon–Fri; also Sat in July & Aug) from Portree will drop you at the top of the glen, but you'll have to walk the last seven miles; both the youth hostel and the campsite have grocery stores, the only ones for miles.

From the valley a score of difficult and strenuous trails lead east into the **Black Cuillin**, a rough semicircle of peaks rising to about 3000ft, which surround Loch Coruisk. One of the easiest walks is the five-mile round-trip from the campsite up **Coire Lagan**, to a crystal-cold lochan squeezed in among the sternest of rockfaces. Above the lochan is Skye's highest peak, **Sgurr Alasdair** (3258ft), one of the more difficult Munros, while Sgurr na Banachdich (3166ft) is considered the most easily accessible Munro in the Cuillin (for the usual walking safety precautions, see p.46). The Mountain Rescue Service has produced a book of walks for those who are not climbers, available locally.

Minginish

If the Cuillin have disappeared into the mist for the day, you could while away an afternoon exploring the nearby **Minginish** peninsula, to the north of Glen Brittle. One wet-weather activity is to visit the **Talisker whisky distillery** (April–June, Sept & Oct Mon–Fri 9am–4.30pm; July & Aug Mon–Sat 9am–4.30pm; Nov–March Mon–Fri 2–4.30pm; by appointment ☎01478/640314), which produces a very smoky, peaty single malt. Talisker is the island's only distillery, situated on the

Start Point Lighthouse, Sanday, Orkney

Papa Stour, Shetland

Fishing boats, Mallaig

Plockton

The Glenfinnan Monument

Calanais Standing Stones, Lewis

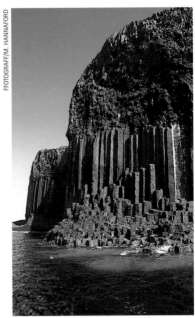

Basalt columns, Staffa

Kittiwakes nesting on cliff face

Highland Games

Kinloch Castle, Rùm

Ring of Brodgar, Orkney

Thatched bothy, Shetland

shores of Loch Harport at **CARBOST** (and not, confusingly, at the village of Talisker itself, which lies on the west coast of Minginish). Hostellers might like to know that there are three year-round **bunkhouses** in Carbost and **PORTNA-LONG**: the *Waterfront Bunkhouse* (☎01478/640005) is next to the *Old Inn* in Carbost; the *Croft Bunkhouse and Bothies* (☎01478/640254), where you can also **camp**, is signposted just before you get to Portnalong; while the *Skyewalker Independent Hostel* (☎01478/640250, *skyewalker@easynet.co.uk*) is a converted school building beyond Portnalong, en route to Fiskavaig – it also has a campsite and an excellent café which welcomes passers-by.

Dunvegan, Duirinish and Waternish

After the Portnalong and Glen Brittle turning, the A863 slips across bare round-ed hills to skirt the bony sea cliffs and stacks of the west coast twenty miles or so north to **DUNVEGAN** (Dùn Bheagain). It's an unimpressive place, strung out along the east shore of the sea loch of the same name, though it does make quite a good base for exploring two interesting peninsulas: Duirinish and Waternish.

The main tourist trap in the village is **Dunvegan Castle** (mid-March to Oct daily 10am–5.30pm; £5.20, gardens only £3.70) which sprawls on top of a rocky outcrop, sandwiched between the sea and several acres of beautifully maintained gardens. It's been the seat of the Clan MacLeod since the thirteenth century, but the present greying, rectangular fortress, with its uniform battlements and dummy pepper pots, dates from the 1840s. Inside, you don't get a lot of castle for your money and the contents are far from stunning, but there are three famous items: **Rory Mor's Horn**, a drinking vessel made from the horn of a mad bull which each new chief still has to drain at one draught "without setting down or falling down"; the **Dunvegan Cup**, made of bog oak covered in medieval silver filigree believed to have been given to Rory Mor by the O'Neils of Ulster in return for his help against England; and, most intriguing of all, the battered remnants of the **Fairy Flag** in the drawing room. This yellow silken flag from the Middle East may have been the battle standard of the Norwegian king, Harald Hardrada, who had been the commander of the imperial guard in Constantinople. Hardrada died trying to seize the English throne at the Battle of Stamford Bridge in 1066, after which his flag was allegedly carried back to Skye by his Gaelic boatmen. More fancifully, MacLeod family tradition asserts that the flag was the gift of the fairies, blessed with the power to protect the clan in times of danger – as late as World War II MacLeod pilots carried pictures of it for luck. Among the Jacobite memen-toes are a lock of hair from the head of Bonnie Prince Charlie (whom the MacLeods, in fact, fought against) and Flora MacDonald's corsets. Elsewhere there's a "virtual" consumptive in the dungeon and an interesting display on the remote archipelago of St Kilda (see p.316), long the fiefdom of the MacLeods.

From the jetty outside the castle there are regular seal-spotting **boat trips** out along Loch Dunvegan, as well as longer and less frequent sea cruises to the small islands of Mingay, Islay and Clett, which were cleared of the last crofters in 1860. Outside in the car park you can buy sandwiches from a kiosk or have a more sub-stantial snack in the castle restaurant. The estate also has a number of **holiday cottages** (☎01470/521206). On a wet day you might scrape up some enthusiasm for Dunvegan's newest tourist attraction, the **Giant Angus MacAskill Museum** (daily 10am–6pm; £1), the weakest of Peter MacAskill's three museums on Skye, housed in a restored thatched smithy. The museum's eponymous hero was, in fact, born in the Outer Hebrides in 1825 and emigrated to Nova Scotia when he was just 6. Before his untimely death of a fever at the age of just 38, he toured with the midget, Tom Thumb, who, it is said, used to dance on his outstretched hand.

Duirinish and Glendale

The hammerhead **Duirinish peninsula** lies to the west of Dunvegan, much of it inaccessible to all except walkers prepared to scale or skirt the area's twin flat-topped basalt peaks: Healabhal Bheag (1600ft) and Healabhal Mhor (1538ft). The mountains are better known as **MacLeod's Tables**, for legend has it that the MacLeod chief held an open-air royal feast on the lower of the two for James V. The main areas of habitation lie to the north, along the western shores of Loch Dunvegan, and in the broad green sweep of **Glen Dale**, attractively dotted with white farmhouses and dubbed "Little England" by the locals, due to its high percentage of "white settlers", English incomers searching for a better life. Glen Dale's current predicament is doubly ironic given its history, for it was here in 1882 that local crofters, following the example of their brethren in The Braes (see p.287), staged a rent strike against their landlords, the MacLeods. Five locals – who became known as the "Glen Dale Martyrs" – were given two-month prison sentences, and eventually, in 1904, the crofters became the first owner-occupiers in the Highlands.

All this, and a great deal more about nineteenth-century crofting, is told through fascinating contemporary news cuttings at **Colbost Croft Museum** (Easter–Oct daily 10am–6.30pm; £1), the oldest of Peter MacAskill's three Skye museums, situated in a restored blackhouse, four miles up the road from Dunvegan. A guide is usually on hand to answer questions, the peat fire smokes all day, and there's a restored illegal whisky still round the back. A little further up the shores of the loch is **Borreraig Park** (daily 9am–7pm; £1.50), an eccentric mix of a huge open-air museum of traditional horse-drawn farm machinery and a retail outlet for Skye-made crafts.

At **BORRERAIG** itself, where there was once a famous piping college, is the **MacCrimmon Piping Heritage Centre** (Easter to late May Tues–Sun 11am–5.30pm; late May to early Oct same times; £1.50), on the ancestral holdings of the MacCrimmons, hereditary pipers to the MacLeod chiefs for three centuries, until they were sent packing in the 1770s. The plaintive sounds of the *piobaireachd* of the MacCrimmons, the founding family of Scottish piping, fill this illuminating museum – to hear the real thing, go to the annual recital held in Dunvegan Castle early in August.

In the village of **GLENDALE**, at Holmisdale House, an English settler has gathered together mountains of childhood toys and games from the last hundred years, and opened a **Toy Museum** (Mon–Sat 10am–6pm; £2), whose hands-on approach manages to appeal to all ages; it's open on Sundays, too, if they're wet. Beyond Glendale, a bumpy road leads to **RAMASAIG**, and beyond for another five miles to the deserted village of Lorgill where, on August 4, 1830, life came to an end when every crofter was ordered to board the *Midlothian* in Loch Snizort to go to Nova Scotia or go to prison (those over the age of 70 were sent to the poorhouse). As a result of such Clearances, the west coast of Duirinish is mostly uninhabited now. For walkers, though, it's a great area to explore, with blustery but easy footpaths leading to the dramatically sited lighthouse on **Neist Point**, Skye's most westerly spot, which features some fearsome sea cliffs, and wonderful views across the sea to the Western Isles – you can even stay at the lighthouse, in one of the three **self-catering** cottages (☎01470/511200; sleeps 6–12 people; £495 per week). Alternatively, head north for the sheer 1000-foot cliffs of **Biod an Athair** near Dunvegan Head, though there's no path, and it's a bit of a slog.

Waternish

Waternish is a thin and little-visited peninsula to the north of Dunvegan. It's not as spectacular as either Duirinish or Trotternish, but it provides equally great views over to the Western Isles on a good day. Before you can explore the peninsula, however, you have to cross the **Fairy Bridge**, at the junction of the B886, where legend has it that a MacLeod chief, foolishly married to a fairy, was forced to say farewell when she decided to go home to her mother. More likely its significance lies in the fact that it's at the meeting of three roads and was the scene of religious assemblies of the Free Church and, later, of rebellious crofters led by John MacPherson, one of the "Glen Dale Martyrs".

Waternish's prettiest village is **STEIN**, on the west coast overlooking Loch Bay. Its row of whitewashed cottages was built in 1787 by the British Fisheries Society, but never saw success, and by 1837 the village was more or less abandoned. Today, however, it seems to be coming back to life, particularly the pub, the sixteenth-century *Stein Inn*, which is well worth a visit.

At the end of the road is **Trumpan Church**, a medieval ruin on a clifftop looking out to the Western Isles. This peaceful site was the scene of one of the bloodiest episodes in Skye history, when, in 1578, the MacDonalds of Uist set fire to the church, while numerous MacLeods were attending a service inside. Everyone perished except one young girl who escaped by squeezing through a window, severing one of her breasts in the process. She raised the alarm, and the rest of the MacLeods quickly rallied and, bearing their famous Fairy Flag (see p.291), attacked the MacDonalds as they were launching their galleys. Every MacDonald was slaughtered and their bodies were thrown in a nearby dyke. In the churchyard, along with two medieval gravestones, you can also see the **Trial Stone**, a four-foot-high pillar with a hole drilled in it. Anyone accused of a crime was blindfolded and had to attempt to put their finger in it: success meant innocence; failure, death.

Practicalities

Dunvegan is by no means the most picturesque place on Skye, but it's a useful alternative base to Portree. It has a new **tourist office** (Mon–Sat 9am–5.30pm; ☎01470/521581) and boasts several excellent **hotels** and **B&Bs** dotted along the main road, such as the converted traditional croft *Roskhill House* (☎01470/521317, *stay@roskhill.demon.co.uk*; ③). Other possibilities include the beautifully situated *Silverdale* (☎01470/521251; ①), just before you get to Colbost, or the luxurious *Harlosh House* (☎01470/521367; ⑥; April–Oct), four miles south of Dunvegan, plus *Mo Dhachaidh* (☎01470/511210; ①; Easter–Oct), in Glendale itself. There's a basic lochside **campsite** (April–Sept), a short distance west along the head of Loch Dunvegan.

The culinary mecca in the area is the expensive *Three Chimneys* **restaurant** (☎01470/511258; Mon–Sat), located beside Colbost Folk Museum, which serves sublime meals and is renowned for its marmalade pudding. More reasonably priced meals can be had at *An Strupag* in Lephin (☎01470/511204), deeper into Glen Dale. There are welcoming fires and good food at the sixteenth-century *Stein Inn* (☎01470/592362, *angus.teresa@steininn.demon.co.uk*; ②), in Stein, and outstanding seafood at the *Lochbay Seafood Restaurant* (☎01470/592235; closed Sat & Sun). Eating in Dunvegan is a little problematic, apart from obvious hotel choices, of which *Atholl House Hotel* (☎01470/521219) is probably the best for dinner. However, there is a snug **café** attached to *Dunvegan Bakery* (closed Sat afternoon & Sun) where you can also pick up sandwich components and home-made carrot cake.

Portree

Although referred to by the locals as "the village", **PORTREE** is the only real town on Skye. It's also one of the most attractive fishing ports in northwest Scotland, its deep cliff-edged harbour filled with fishing boats and circled by multicoloured restaurants and guest houses. Originally known as *Kiltragleann* (The Church at the Foot of the Glen), it takes its current name – some say – from *Portrigh* (Port of the King), after the state visit James V made in 1540 to assert his authority over the chieftains of Skye.

Information and accommodation

Hours vary enormously at Portree's **tourist office**, just off Bridge Street, so the ones here are just a guideline (April–Oct Mon–Sat 9am–5.30pm, Sun 11am–4pm; Nov–March closed Sun; ☎01478/612137). The office will, for a small fee, book **accommodation** for you – especially useful at the height of the season, when things can get very busy. Accommodation prices tend to be higher in Portree than elsewhere on the island, especially in the town itself, though B&Bs on the outskirts are usually cheaper. Of Portree's year-round **hostels**, the smartest is the *Portree Independent Hostel* (☎01478/613737, *portreeindhostel@hotmail.co.uk*) housed in the Old Post Office on the Green, though the *Portree Backpackers Hostel* (☎01478/613332), ten minutes' walk up the Dunvegan road, enjoys a more secluded location (and will pick you up from town if you ring ahead). Torvaig **campsite** (☎01478/612209; April–Oct) lies a mile and a half north of town off the A855 Staffin road.

Probably the best **hotel** is the comfortable *Cuillin Hills* (☎01478/612003; *office@cuillinhills.demon.co.uk*; ⑤), ten minutes' walk out of town along the northern shore of the bay; if the rooms are too pricey, try the reasonably-priced bar snacks with a splendid view over the harbour or afternoon tea after a walk round the nearby headland. *Viewfield House* (☎01478/612217; ⑤), on the southern outskirts of town, in the possession of the MacDonalds for over 200 years, is worth it for the Victorian atmosphere, stuffed polecats and antiques. The *Bosville Hotel* (☎01478/612846, *bosville@macleodhotels.co.uk*; ④), on Bosville Terrace, commands a good view of the harbour, and has a gourmet seafood restaurant. In the lower price range, try *Givendale Guest House* (☎01478/612183; ①; April–Oct), ten minutes' walk up the hill from the town centre on Heron Place, with good views and a warm welcome for walkers and cyclists, or *Conusg*, a B&B in a quiet spot by the *Cuillin Hills Hotel*, originally built for the coachman in the 1880s (☎01478/612426; ①; Easter–Sept). Further still out of Portree, five miles northwest in Skeabost, is the late Victorian *Skeabost House Hotel* (☎01470/532202, *skeabost@sol.co.uk* ⑤; March–Oct), which offers golf, fishing and landscaped gardens.

The Town

It's worth strolling down to the **harbour**, whose pier was built by Thomas Telford in the early nineteenth century. Fishing boats still land a modest catch, some of which is sold through Anchor Seafoods (Tues–Fri only) at the end of the pier. The harbour is overlooked by **The Lump**, a steep and stumpy peninsula with a flag-pole on it that was once the site of public hangings on the island, attracting crowds of up to 5000; it also sports a folly built by the celebrated Dr Ban, a vision-ary who wanted to make Portree into a second Oban. Up above the harbour is the spick-and-span town centre, spreading out from **Somerled Square**, built in the late eighteenth century as the island's administrative and commercial centre, and now housing the bus station and car park. The **Royal Hotel** on Bank Street occu-pies the site of the *McNab's Inn* where Bonnie Prince Charlie took leave of Flora MacDonald (see p.296), and where, 27 years later, Boswell and Johnson had "a very good dinner, porter, port and punch".

A mile or so out of town on the Sligachan road is one of Skye's most successful tourist attractions, the **Aros Centre** (daily 9am–6pm; open later in summer). Here, you can enjoy the Aros Experience (£2.50), a dramatic and unsentimental presentation of episodes of the island's history, with stunning life-size figures and special effects, ending with an audiovisual show. The centre also contains a mod-ern exhibition space, a licensed coffee bar and restaurant, and there's a special play area for small kids. If it's fine, there are waymarked forest walks and a Gaelic alphabet trail starting just outside.

For a view of the contemporary visual art scene, it's well worth seeking out **An Tuireann Arts Centre**, housed in a converted fever hospital on the Struan road (Mon–Sat 10am–6pm; free), which puts on exhibitions, stages concerts, and has an excellent small café where even the counter is a work of art, with an imagina-tive range of food on offer (Easter–Oct also Wed–Sat evenings).

Eating, drinking and nightlife

The best **food** in town is on Bosville Terrace, but it's pricey: the *Bosville Hotel*'s *Chandlery* restaurant serves excellent meals, with its sister *Bosville* restaurant being much cheaper; *Harbour View* has a seafood **restaurant** with candlelit ambience, but better is *Ben Tianavaig*, an excellent veggie and seafood place (evenings only; closed Mon; ☎01478/612152). The *Lower Deck Seafood Restaurant* on the harbour has a wood-panelled warmth to it, and is reasonably priced at lunchtime (less so in the evenings); for good **fish and chips**, pop next door to their excellent chippy. For a cuppa and a cake, there's the *Granary* bak-ery's **teashop** on Somerled Square. The *Café*, an ice-cream parlour on Wentworth Street, serves real cappuccino and espresso, plus a selection of cakes and snacks. As for **pubs**, the bar of the *Pier Hotel* on the quayside is the fishermen's drinking hole, while the bar of the *Royal Hotel* is also popular with locals.

The aforementioned Aros Centre has a striking new **theatre**, which shows films and hosts Gaelic **concerts** (for more details phone ☎01471/613649); con-certs and events also go on at An Tuireann (see above), and it's also worth check-ing out what's on at the Portree Community Centre (☎01478/613736), which hosts ceilidhs and so forth. For **bike rental**, go to Island Cycles (closed Sun; ☎01478/613121) below the Green; for **horse riding**, head for Skye Riding Centre (closed Sun; ☎01470/532233), four miles along the Uig road at Borve, or the Portree Riding and Trekking Centre off the B885 to Struan, signposted "Peiness" (open all year; ☎01478/612945). Day or half-day **boat trips** leave the pier for daily excursions to Raasay and Rona (☎01478/613718); **diving** can be organized through Hebridean Diving Services in Lochbay, towards Dunvegan

BONNIE PRINCE CHARLIE

Prince Charles Edward Stewart – better known as **Bonnie Prince Charlie** or "The Young Pretender" – was born in Rome in 1720, where his father, "The Old Pretender", claimant to the British throne, was living in exile. At the age of 25, having little military experience, no knowledge of Gaelic, an imperfect grasp of English and a strong attachment to the Catholic faith, the prince set out for Scotland on a French ship, disguised as a seminarist from the Scots College in Paris. He arrived on the Outer Hebridean island of Eriskay on July 23, 1745, and was immediately implored to return to France by the clan chiefs, who were singularly unimpressed by his lack of army. Charles was unmoved and went on to raise the royal standard at Glenfinnan, gather together a Highland army, win the Battle of Prestonpans, march on London and reach Derby before finally (and foolishly) agreeing to retreat. Back in Scotland, he won one last victory, at Falkirk, before the final disaster at Culloden in April 1746.

The prince spent the following five months in hiding, with a price of £30,000 on his head, and literally thousands of government troops searching for him. He certainly endured his fair share of cold and hunger whilst on the run, but the real price was paid by the Highlanders themselves, who risked their lives (and often paid for it with them) by aiding and abetting the prince. The most famous of these was, of course, 23-year-old **Flora MacDonald**, whom Charles met on South Uist in June 1746. Flora was persuaded – either by his beauty or her relatives, depending on which account you believe – to convey Charles "over the sea to Skye", disguised as an Irish servant girl by the name of Betty Burke. She was arrested just seven days after parting with the prince in Portree, and held in the Tower of London until July 1747. She went on to marry a local man, had seven children, and in 1774 emigrated to America, where her husband was taken prisoner during the American War of Independence. Flora returned to Scotland and was reunited with her husband on his release; they resettled in Skye and she died at the age of 68.

Charles eventually boarded a ship back to France in September 1746, but, despite his promises – "for all that has happened, Madam, I hope we shall meet in St James's yet" – never returned to Scotland, nor did he ever see Flora again. After mistreating a string of mistresses, he eventually got married at the age of 52 to the 19-year-old Princess of Stolberg, in an effort to produce a Stewart heir. They had no children, and she eventually fled from his violent drunkenness; in 1788, a none-too-"bonnie" Prince Charles died in the arms of his illegitimate daughter in Rome. Bonnie Prince Charlie became a legend in his own lifetime, but it was the Victorians who really milked the myth for all its sentimentality, conveniently overlooking the fact that the real consequence of 1745 was the virtual annihilation of the Highland way of life.

(☎01478/592219). You can collect your **email** at Gael Net Ltd on the Dunvegan road (closed Sun; ☎01478/613300).

Trotternish

Protruding twenty miles north from Portree, the **Trotternish peninsula** boasts some of the island's most bizarre scenery, particularly on the east coast, where volcanic basalt has pressed down on the softer sandstone and limestone underneath, causing massive landslides. These, in turn, have created sheer cliffs, peppered with outcrops of hard, wizened basalt, which run the full length of the peninsula. These pinnacles and pillars are at their most eccentric in the Quiraing, above Staffin Bay, on the east coast. Trotternish is best explored with your own transport, but an occasional bus service (Mon–Sat 2–4 daily) along the road encircling the peninsula gives access to almost all the coast.

The east coast

The first geological eccentricity on the **Trotternish** peninsula, six miles north of Portree along the A855, is the **Old Man of Storr**, a distinctive column of rock, shaped like a willow leaf, which, along with its neighbours, is part of a massive land-slip. Huge blocks of stone still occasionally break off the cliff face of the Storr (2358ft) above and slide downhill. At 165ft, the Old Man is a real challenge for climbers; less difficult is the half-hour trek up the new footpath to the foot of the column from the woods beside the car park.

Five miles further north, there's another turnoff to the **Lealt Falls**, at the head of a gorge which spends most of its day in shadow (and is home to a fiendish collection of midges). Walking all the way down to the falls is fairly pointless, but the views across to Wester Ross from the first stage of the path are spectacular (weather permitting). The coast here is worth exploring, however, especially the track leading to **Rubha nam Brathairean** (Brothers' Point), where the Glasgow provision boat used to put in, and where fossil hunters can also follow the road that turns off at Dunans down to the end and try their luck on the beach at low tide.

Another car park a few miles up the road gives access to **Kilt Rock**, whose tubelike, basaltic columns rise precipitously from the sea, set amongst sea cliffs dotted with nests for fulmars and kittiwakes. There is a spectacular waterfall which drops 300ft to the sea, and a small loch by the car park alive with wildlife. Close by, near the turn off to Elishader, is the slate-roofed **Staffin Museum** (sporadic opening hours; £1.25), which contains fossil finds from the area, and a dinosaur bone discovered here in 1994.

Over the brow of the next hill, **Staffin Bay**, where several fossilized dinosaur footprints were discovered in 1996, is spread out before you, dotted with whitewashed and "spotty" houses; **STAFFIN** itself is a lively, largely Gaelic-speaking community where crofts have been handed down the generations. A single-track road cuts across the peninsula from the north end of the bay, allowing access to the **Quiraing**, a spectacular forest of mighty pinnacles and savage rock formations. There are two car parks: from the first, beside a cemetery, it's a steep half-hour climb to the rocks; from the second, on the saddle it's a longer but more gentle traverse. Once you're in the midst of the rocks, you should be able to make out the Prison, to your right, and the 120-foot Needle, to your left; the Table, a great sunken platform where locals used to play shinty, lies above and beyond the Needle, another fifteen-minute scramble up the rocks; legend also maintains that a local warrior named Fraing hid his cattle there from the invading Norsemen.

The **accommodation** on the east coast is among the best on Skye, with most places enjoying fantastic views out over the sea. Just beyond the Lealt Falls there's the very welcoming and comfortable *Glenview Inn* (☎01470/562248; ③; March–Oct), with an excellent adjoining restaurant, and a **campsite** (☎01470/562213; April–Sept) south of Staffin Bay. In fine weather, you can enjoy good bar snacks on the castellated terrace of the stylish *Flodigarry Country House Hotel* (☎01470/552203; ⑥), three miles up the coast from Staffin. Behind the hotel (and now part of it) is the cottage where local heroine Flora MacDonald lived, and had six of her seven children, from 1751 to 1759. If the hotel's rooms are beyond your means, try the neat and attractive *Dun Flodigarry Backpackers' Hostel* (☎01470/552212), a couple of minutes' walk away – you can ring the hostel to arrange transport or catch the local bus.

Duntulm and Kilmuir

Beyond Flodigarry, at the tip of the Trotternish peninsula, by the road to Shulista, a public footpath leads past the ruins of a cleared hamlet to the spectacular sea stacks of **Rubha Hunish**, the most northerly point on Skye. A couple of miles further on the A855 lies **DUNTULM** (Duntuilm), whose heyday as a major MacDonald power base is recalled by the shattered remains of a headland fortress abandoned by the clan in 1732 after a clumsy nurse dropped the baby son and heir from a window onto the rocks below; on these same rocks, it is said, can be seen the keel marks of Viking longships. The imposing *Duntulm Castle Hotel* (☎01470/552213; ②; March–Nov) is close by, and provides good bar meals as well as wonderful views across the Minch to the Western Isles; the hotel also has **self-catering** cottages, including three former coastguard houses (6–10 people; £590 per week).

Heading down the west shore of the Trotternish, it's two miles to the **Skye Museum of Island Life** (Easter–Oct Mon–Sat 9.30am–5.30pm; £1.75), an impressive cluster of thatched blackhouses on an exposed hill overlooking Harris. The museum, run by locals, gives a fascinating insight into a way of life that was commonplace on Skye a hundred years ago. The blackhouse, now home to the ticket office, is much as it was when it was last inhabited in 1957, while the two houses to the east contain interesting snippets of local history. Behind the museum in the cemetery up the hill are the graves of **Flora MacDonald** and her husband. Thousands turned out for her funeral in 1790, creating a funeral procession a mile long – indeed, so widespread was her fame that the original family mausoleum fell victim to souvenir hunters and had to be replaced. The Celtic cross headstone is inscribed with a simple tribute by Dr Johnson, who visited her in 1773: "Her name will be mentioned in history, if courage and fidelity be virtues, mentioned with honour."

If you want an antidote to folk history and have a liking for puns, don't miss **Macurdie's Exhibition** just off the road in **KILMUIR**. It's unattended, open most of the time, and full of spoof artefacts and pseudo-proverbs such as "it's easier to extract a Mars bar from the gullet of a seagull than to clean your shoes with a blade of grass" – the visitors' book proves people will pay an optional 50p for anything on a wet day. The land around Kilmuir used to be called the "Granary of Skye", since every inch was cultivated: even St Columba's Loch, where there are still indistinct remains of beehive cells and a chapel, was drained and the land eagerly reclaimed by crofters. **Accommodation** is available in the attractive *Kilmuir House*, previously the old manse (☎01470/542262; *phelpskilmuirhouseskye @btinternet.com*; ①), and at the warm and friendly *Whitewave Activities* B&B (☎01470/542414; ①), in Linicro; they also organize **windsurfing**, **archery** and **canoeing**, and run a café in season.

Uig

A further four miles south of Kilmuir is the ferry port of **UIG** (Uige), which curves its way round a dramatic, horseshoe-shaped bay, and is the arrival point for CalMac ferries from Tarbet (Harris) and Lochmaddy (North Uist); if you've time to spare while waiting for a ferry, pop into Uig Pottery. The **tourist office**

(April–Oct Mon–Sat 8.45am–6.30pm; mid-July to mid-Sept also Sun 8.45am–2pm; ☎01470/542404) is inside the CalMac office on the pier. Most folk come to Uig to take the ferry to the Western Isles, but if you need an inexpensive **B&B** near the ferry terminal, head for *Braeholm* (☎01470/542396; ①; March–Oct), the **campsite** (☎01470/542360; March–Oct), by the shore near the dock, or the **SYHA hostel** (☎01470/542211; mid-March to Oct), high up on the south side of the village, with exhilarating views over the bay. The *Pub at the Pier* offers filling meals, and serves the local Skye beers, which are also on sale in the shop of the nearby brewery (Mon–Fri tours by appointment; ☎01470/542477). **Bike rental** is available from North Skye Bicycle Hire; **pony trekking**, from the *Uig Hotel* (☎01470/542205).

The prettiest place for a fair-weather stroll and picnic around Uig is the **Fairy Glen**, reached by taking the minor road up to Balnaknock. Another good walk is to the intriguing ruined castle with no door called **Caisteal Uisdein**, built by Hugh MacDonald of Sleat in the seventeenth century. Take the turning to Cuidrach and continue to the end of the road; walk through the village and then follow the posts, but you'll have to climb in through a window – in spring, the castle is filled with primroses. When Hugh's clan chief found he'd been plotting against him, he walled him up in here with a piece of salt beef and an empty water jug. Just after this, there's a signpost to the small *Glen Hinnisdal* **bunkhouse** (☎01470/552212).

THE SMALL ISLES

The history of the **Small Isles**, which lie to the south of Skye, is typical of the Hebrides: early Christianization, followed by a period of Norwegian rule that ended in 1266 when the islands fell into Scottish hands. Their support for the Jacobite cause resulted in hard times after the failed rebellion of 1745, but the biggest problems came with the introduction of the **potato** in the mid-eighteenth

---

GETTING TO THE SMALL ISLES

CalMac run passenger-only ferries to the Small Isles every day except Sunday from Mallaig (☎01687/462403). Day-trips to any one of the four islands are possible only on Saturdays, but involve catching the ferry at 5am. If you take this option, you have a choice of spending around nine hours on Canna, seven hours on Rùm, five on Muck, and just three and a half on Eigg. The CalMac ferry can currently only dock at Canna; on the other three islands, you (and all the island supplies) have to be transferred to an island tender or "flit boat". There is talk of building newer and bigger piers on the other islands in the near future.

From May to September, you can also reach Rùm, Eigg and Muck seven days a week from Arisaig with **Murdo Grant** (☎01687/450224). This is a much more pleasant way to get there, as the boat is licensed, takes you right up to the pier on all three islands and, if any marine mammals are spotted en route, the boat will pause for a bit of whale-watching. Day-trips are possible to Eigg on most days, allowing four to five hours ashore, and to Rùm and Muck on a few days, allowing two to three hours ashore. With careful studying of both CalMac and Murdo Grant timetables, you should be able to organize a visit to suit you, especially as Arisaig and Mallaig are linked by railway.

Be warned, however, that boats to the Small Isles are frequently cancelled in bad weather, so be prepared to holiday for longer than you planned.

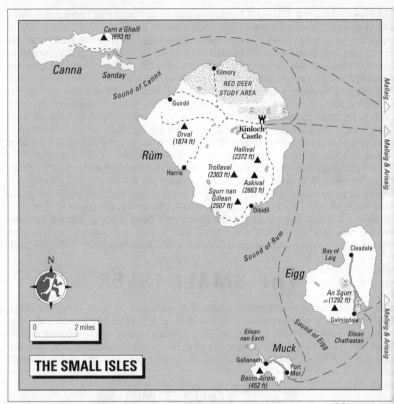

century. The consequences were as dramatic as they were unforeseen: the success of the crop and its nutritional value – when grown in conjunction with traditional cereals – eliminated famine at a stroke, prompting a population explosion. In 1750, there were just a thousand islanders, but by 1800 their numbers had almost doubled.

At first, the problem of overcrowding was camouflaged by the **kelp** boom, in which the islanders were employed, and the islands' owners made a fortune, gathering and burning local seaweed to sell for use in the manufacture of gunpowder, soap and glass. But the economic bubble burst with the end of the Napoleonic Wars and, to maintain their profit margins, the owners resorted to drastic action. The first to sell up was Alexander Maclean, who sold Rùm as grazing land for **sheep**, got quotations for shipping its people to Nova Scotia, and gave them a year's notice to quit. He also cleared Muck to graze cattle, as did the MacNeills on Canna. Only on Eigg was some compassion shown: the new owner, a certain Hugh MacPherson, who bought the island from the Clanranalds in 1827, actually gave some of his tenants extended leases.

Since the Clearances, each of the islands has been bought and sold several times, though only **Muck** is now privately owned by the benevolent laird, awrence MacEwen. **Eigg** hit the headlines in 1997, when the islanders finally managed to buy the island themselves and put an end to more than 150 years of property speculation. The other islands were bequeathed to national agencies: **Rùm**, the largest and most-visited of the group, possessing a cluster of formidable volcanic peaks and the architecturally remarkable Kinloch Castle, passed to the Nature Conservancy Council (now Scottish Natural Heritage) in 1957; and **Canna**, in many ways the prettiest of the isles with its high basalt cliffs, has been in the hands of the NTS since 1981.

Rùm

Like Skye, **RÙM** is dominated by its Cuillin, which, though only reaching a height of 2663ft at the summit of Askival, rises up with comparable drama straight up from the sea in the south of the island. The majority of the island's thirty or so inhabitants now live in **KINLOCH**, on the sheltered east coast, and most are employed by Scottish Natural Heritage (SNH), who run the island as a National Nature Reserve. SNH have been reintroducing native woodland to the island, and overseeing a long-term study of the vast red deer population. However, the organization's most notable achievement to date is the successful reintroduction of **white-tailed (sea) eagles**, whose wingspan is even greater than that of the golden eagle. These magnificent birds of prey were last known to have bred on the island of Skye in 1916. After a caesura of some seventy years, the eagles are back, and have spread from Rùm to neighbouring islands. The resident breeding population is still very small, however, and the exact location of the eyries is kept secret.

Rùm's chief formal attraction is **Kinloch Castle** (Tues & Thurs guided tours at 2pm; £3), a squat red sandstone edifice fronted by colonnades and topped by crenellations and turrets, that dominates the village of Kinloch. Completed at enormous expense in 1900 – the red sandstone was shipped in from Arran and the soil for the gardens from Ayrshire – its interior is a perfectly preserved example of Edwardian decadence, "a living memorial of the stalking, the fishing and the sailing, the tenantry and plenty of the days before 1914". From the galleried hall, with its tiger rugs, stags' heads and giant Japanese incense burners, to the "Extra Low Fast Cushion" of the Soho snooker table in the Billiard Room, the interior is packed with knick-knacks and technical gismos accumulated by **Sir George Bullough** (1870–1939), the spendthrift son of self-made millionaire, Sir John Bullough, who bought the island as a sporting estate in 1888. As such, it was only really used for a few weeks each autumn, during the "season", yet employed an island workforce of one hundred all year round. Bullough's guests were woken at eight each morning by a piper; later on, an orchestrion, an electrically driven barrel organ (originally destined for Balmoral), crammed in under the stairs, would grind out an eccentric mixture of pre-dinner tunes: *The Ride of the Valkyries* and *Ma Blushin' Rosie* among others (a demo is included in the tour). The ballroom has a sprung floor, the library features a gruesome photographic collection from the Bulloughs' world tours, but the *pièce de résistance* has to be Bullough's **Edwardian bathrooms**, whose baths have hooded walnut shower cabinets, fitted with two taps and four dials, which allow the bather to fire high-pressure water at their body from every angle.

For those with limited time or energy, there are two gentle waymarked **heritage trails**, both of which start from Kinloch, and take around two hours to com-

HIKING IN THE RÙM CUILLIN

Ordnance Survey Landranger map no. 39

Rùm's Cuillin may not be as famous as Skye's, but, if the weather's fine, there are equally exhilarating **hiking** possibilities. Whatever route you choose, be sure to take all the usual safety precautions, described on p.46.

The most popular walk is to traverse most or part of the **Cuillin Ridge**, which takes between eight and twelve hours round-trip from Kinloch. The most frequent route is up past the old dams to Coire Dubh, and then on to the saddle of Bealach Bairc-mheall. From here, you can either climb Barkeval itself, to the west, or go straight for **Hallival** (2372ft) to the southeast, which looks daunting but is no more than a mild rock scramble. South of Hallival, the ridge is grassy, but the rocky north ridge of **Askival** (2663ft) needs to be taken quite carefully, sticking to the east side for safety. Askival is the highest mountain on Rùm, and if you're thinking of heading back, or the weather's closing in, Glen Dibidil provides an easy means of descent, after which you can follow the track back to Kinloch.

To continue along the ridge, head west to the double peak of **Trollaval** (or Trallval), the furthest of which is the highest. The descent to Bealach an Fhuarain is steep, after which it's another scramble to reach the top of **Ainshval**. Depending on the time and weather, you can continue along the ridge to **Sgurr nan Gillean**, descend via Glen Dibidil and take the coastal path back to Kinloch, or skip the Sgurr and go straight on to the last peak of the ridge, **Ruinsival**, descend via the Fiachanis basin to Harris, and then slog it back to Kinloch along the road.

On your walks, look out for the island's **native ponies**, which feed mainly in Kilmory Glen and Kinloch Glen, and are used for the stag cull in July; the **Highland cattle**, who live in Harris, except during July and August, when they're moved in Guirdil; and the multicoloured **wild goats**, which stick to the coastal areas between Kilmory, Harris and Dibidil. However, if you want to see the **Manx shearwater**, which nest in burrows on Trollaval and Askival, you'll need to be there around dusk or dawn, as this is the only time the birds return to their nests.

plete. For longer walks, you must fill in route cards and pop them into the White House (Mon–Fri 9am–12.30pm), where the reserve manager can give useful advice. The island's best beach is at **KILMORY**, to the north (5hr return), though this part of the island is only open to the public on the weekend as it's given over to the study of red deer; it's also closed completely in June, during calving, and October, during rutting. When the island's human head count peaked at 450 in 1791, the hamlet of **HARRIS** on the southwest coast (6hr return) housed a large crofting community – all that remains now are several ruined blackhouses and the extravagant **Bullough Mausoleum**, built by Sir George to house the remains of his father in the style of a Greek Doric temple, overlooking the sea. This is, in fact, the second one to be constructed here: the first was lined with Italian marble mosaics, but when a friend remarked that it looked like a public lavatory Bullough had it dynamited and the current Neoclassical one erected.

Practicalities

Until Rùm passed into the hands of the SNH, it was known as the "Forbidden Isle" because of its exclusive use as a sporting estate for the rich – nowadays, visitors are made very welcome by the SNH staff. If you plan to stay the night, you do need to book in advance, as **accommodation** is fairly limited. Kinloch Castle was

SIR GEORGE BULLOUGH

Scotland has had more than its fair share of eccentric rich landlords, but few come close to **Sir George Bullough** (1870–1939), heir to a fortune accumulated by his father and grandfather, whose Lancashire factories produced textile machinery. When his father died, George was on a two-year world tour, three days short of his 21st birthday; rumour had it he'd been sent off to keep him away from his young stepmother, with whom he'd had a rather "close relationship". In 1899, at the time of the Second Boer War, Bullough, at his own expense, kitted out and staffed his recently acquired 221-foot-long steam yacht, *Rhouma*, as a hospital ship, and sent it off to South Africa. For this act of "patriotic devotion", he was rewarded with a knighthood, though rumour had it he actually received his title for agreeing to be named in the divorce proceedings between Charles Charrington and his wife, Monica, in order to avoid King Edward VII being named. There is, however, no evidence that Monica was ever the king's mistress, and once the divorce came through she and George Bullough were married.

Meanwhile, in 1897, work began on George Bullough's ultimate dream: his very own Scottish castle. For three years, 300 men were employed to build **Kinloch Castle** on Rùm – or, as George preferred it to be known, "Rhum" – and paid an extra shilling a week to wear Rùm tartan kilts; smokers were also given a daily bonus of twopence "to keep the midges away". The castle's heyday was the Edwardian era, when Rùm was fitted out with the biggest, the best and the most technologically advanced mod cons money could buy: it was double-glazed, centrally heated, was the first place in Scotland to be lit by electricity (after Glasgow) and the first private house in Scotland to have an internal telephone system. There was a nine-hole golf course, a bowling green, a huge walled garden (350ft by 200ft), with fourteen greenhouses producing exotic fruit for the guests, and six domed palmhouses, alive with hummingbirds, and fitted with heated pools stocked with giant turtles and alligators, though these were eventually removed at the insistence of the terrified staff. There were twelve full-time gardeners and fourteen full-time roadmen, whose job it was to keep Rùm's roads carefully raked so that George and his chums could race their sports cars across the island. In the bay, the Bulloughs would moor the *Rhouma*, whose band would come ashore to play from the castle ballroom's minstrels' gallery.

The outbreak of World War I signalled the end of the world of opulence in which the Bulloughs had excelled. Sir George was elevated to the baronetcy in 1916, after having loaned £50,000 interest-free to the government, but after the war, he and the family visited Rùm less and less. The house was barely used when Sir George died of a heart attack while playing golf on holiday in France in 1939. Lady Bullough eventually sold Rùm in 1957; she died ten years later, and was buried, along with her husband, in the Bullough Mausoleum in Harris.

a luxury hotel until the early 1990s, and still lets a few of its four-poster rooms – for which you pay a bit extra – but it's basically run now as an independent **hostel** (☎01687/462037), with dormitories in the old servants' quarters. SNH also run two simple mountain **bothies** (three nights maximum stay), in Dibidil and Guirdil, and basic **camping** on the foreshore near the jetty. You need to book ahead for both by contacting the reserve manager at the *White House* (☎01687/462026).

Wherever you're staying, you can either do self-catering – hostellers can use the hostel kitchen – or eat the unpretentious **food** offered in the hostel's licensed bistro, which serves full breakfasts, offers packed lunches, and charges just over £10 a head for a three-course evening meal. There is also a small shop, off-licence and post office in Kilmory. Finally, bear in mind that Rùm is the wettest of the Small Isles, and is known for having some of the worst **midges** (see p.44) in Scotland – come prepared for both.

Eigg

Eigg is without doubt the most easily distinguishable of the Small Isles from a distance, since the island is mostly made up of a basalt plateau 1000ft above sea level, and a great stump of columnar pitchstone lava, known as An Sgurr, rising out of the plateau another 290ft. It's also by far the most vibrant, populous and welcoming of the Small Isles, with a real strong sense of community. This has been given an enormous boost by the recent island buyout by the sixty-odd islanders, which ended Eigg's unhappy history of private ownership, most notoriously with the Olympic bobsleigher and gelatine heir Keith Schellenberg.

Visitors arrive in the southeast corner of the island – which measures just five miles by three – at **GALMISDALE**, where **An Laimhrig** (The Anchorage), the island's new community centre stands, housing a shop, post office, tearoom and information centre. The island minibus meets incoming ferries, and will take you to wherever you need to go on the island. Many visitors head off to **CLEADALE**, the main crofting settlement in the north of the island, where the beach, known as the "**Singing Sands**", is comprised of quartz, which squeaks underfoot when dry (hence the name). With the island's great landmark, **An Sgurr** (1292ft), watching over you wherever you go, many folk feel duty bound to climb it, and enjoy the wonderful views over to Muck and Rùm. The easiest approach is to take the path that skirts the summit to the north, and ascend from the saddle to the west; the return trip takes between three and four hours. A large colony of **Manx shearwater** nests in burrows around the summit; to view the birds, you need to be there around dawn or dusk.

The nicest place **to stay** on Eigg is *Kildonan House* (☎01687/482446; full board ③), a beautiful eighteenth-century wood-panelled house where the cooking is superb. Other B&Bs are *Lageorna* (☎01687/482405; full board ④), a croft house that also has a couple of self-catering cottages (6 people; £350 per week). As you'll probably notice, as you walk around the island, Eigg has no mains electricity, so each house has its own diesel generator.

Muck

Smallest and most southerly of the Small Isles, **Muck** is low-lying, mostly treeless and extremely fertile, and as such shares more characteristics with the likes of Coll and Tiree than its nearest neighbours. Its name derives from *muc*, the Gaelic for "pig" – or, as some would have it, *muc mara*, "sea pig" or porpoise, which abound in the surrounding water – and has long caused much embarrassment to generations of lairds who preferred to call it the "Isle of Monk", because it had briefly belonged to the medieval church.

PORT MÓR, the village on the southeast corner of the island, is where visitors arrive. The prominent memorial in the local graveyard commemorates two islanders and a visiting student who were drowned shooting shags near Eilean nan Each (Horse Island). A road, just over a mile in length, connects Port Mór with the island's main farm, **GALLANACH**, which overlooks the rocky seal-strewn skerries on the north side of the island. The nicest sandy beach is Camas na Cairidh, to the east of Gallanach. Despite being only 452ft above sea level, it really is worth climbing **Beinn Airein**, in the southwest corner of the island, for the 360-degree panoramic view of the surrounding islands; the return journey from Port Mór takes around two hours.

You can **stay** with one of the MacEwen family, who have owned the island since 1896, at *Port Mór House* (☎01687/462365; full board ③); the rooms are pine-clad and enjoy great views, and the food is delicious. Alternatively, you can stay at the island's **bunkhouse** (☎01687/462042); with permission from the landowner you may also **camp rough**, but bring supplies with you as there is no shop. The island's attempt to install wind power in the 1990s failed after the main contractor went bankrupt, but mains electricity is due to arrive in the very near future. A **tea-room** and craftshop in Port Mór springs into life when day-trippers arrive, and serves soup and sandwiches. Willow basketmaking courses are an island special-ity (contact *Port Mór House* for more details).

Canna

Measuring a mere five miles by one, and with a Catholic population of just twen-ty, **Canna** is run as a single farm by the National Trust of Scotland. The island enjoys the best harbour in the Small Isles, a horn-shaped haven at its southeast-ern corner protected by the tidal island of Sanday, now linked to Canna by a foot-bridge. For visitors, the chief pastime is walking: from the dock it's about a mile across a grassy basalt plateau to the bony sea cliffs of the north shore, which rise to a peak around Compass Hill (458ft) – so called because its high metal content distorts compasses – in the northeastern corner of the island, from where you get great views across to Rùm and Skye. The cliffs of the buffeted western half of the island are a breeding ground for both Manx shearwater and puffin; some seven miles offshore, you can see the **Heiskeir of Canna**, a curious mass of stone columns sticking up thirty feet above the water.

Accommodation is extremely limited. With permission from the National Trust for Scotland (NTS), you may **camp rough** on Canna; otherwise, the only option is **B&B** with Wendy MacKinnon (☎01687/462465; full board ⑤), or the NTS-owned *Tighard*, a **self-catering** cottage half a mile from the jetty, which sleeps a maximum of ten people. Booking forms are available from Holiday Cottages, NTS, 5 Charlotte Square, Edinburgh (☎0131/226 5922). Remember, however, that there are no shops on Canna (bar the post office), so you must bring your own supplies.

THE WESTERN ISLES

The wild and windy **Western Isles** – also known as the Outer Hebrides or the Long Isle – vaunt a strikingly hostile mix of landscapes from windswept golden sands to harsh, heather-backed mountains and peat bogs. An elemental beauty pervades each of the more than two hundred islands that make up the archipelago, only a handful of which are actually inhabited by a total of just over 30,000 people. The influence of the Atlantic Gulf Stream ensures a mild but moist climate, though you can expect the strong Atlantic winds to blow in rain on two out of every three days even in summer. Weather fronts, however, come and go at such dramatic speed in these parts that there's little chance of mist or fog settling and few problems with midges.

The most significant difference between Skye and the Western Isles is that here tourism is much less important to the islands' fragile economy, still mainly concentrated around crofting, fishing and weaving, and the percentage of "white settlers" is a lot lower. The Outer Hebrides remain the heartland of **Gaelic** culture, with the language spoken by the vast majority of islanders, though its everyday usage remains under constant threat from the national dominance of English. Its survival is, in no small part, due to the all-pervading influence of the Free Church and its offshoots, whose strict Calvinism is the creed of the vast majority of the population, with the sparsely populated South Uist, Barra and parts of Benbecula adhering to the more relaxed demands of Catholicism.

The interior of the northernmost island, **Lewis**, is mostly peat moor, a barren and marshy tract that gives way abruptly to the bare peaks of **North Harris**. Across a narrow isthmus lies **South Harris**, presenting some of the finest scenery in Scotland, with wide beaches of golden sand trimming the Atlantic in full view of the mountains and a rough boulder-strewn interior lying to the east. Further south still, a string of tiny, flatter islets, mainly **North Uist**, **Benbecula**, **South Uist** and **Barra**, offer breezy beaches, whose fine sands front a narrow band of boggy farmland, which, in turn, is mostly bordered by a lower range of hills to the east.

In direct contrast to their wonderful landscapes, villages in the Western Isles are rarely picturesque in themselves, and are usually made up of scattered, relatively modern croft houses strung out along the elementary road system. **Stornoway**, the only real town in the Outer Hebrides, is eminently unappealing. Many visitors, walkers and nature watchers forsake the settlements altogether and retreat to secluded cottages and B&Bs, though for this you really need your own transport.

Visiting the Western Isles

British Regional Airlines and Loganair operate fast and frequent **flights** (Mon–Sat only) from Glasgow and Inverness to Stornoway on Lewis, and Barra and Benbecula on North Uist. But be warned: the weather conditions on the islands are notoriously changeable, making flights prone to both delay and stomach-churning bumpiness. On Barra, the other complication is that you land on the beach, so the timetable is adjusted with the tides. CalMac **car ferries** run from Ullapool in the Highlands to Stornoway (Mon–Sat only); from Uig, on Skye, to Tarbert and Lochmaddy (Mon–Sat only); and from Oban and Mallaig to South Uist and Barra (daily). There's also an **inter-island ferry** from Leverburgh, on Harris, to Otternish, on North Uist, and between South Uist and Barra (for more on ferry services, see "Travel details" on p.340).

Although travelling around the islands is time-consuming, for many people this is part of their charm. A series of inter-island causeways makes it possible to drive from one end of the Western Isles to the other with just two interruptions – the CalMac **ferry** trip from Harris to North Uist, and the one from South Uist to Barra. The islands boast a distinctly low-key **bus** service, with no buses on Sundays. Note, however, that several local companies offer very reasonable **car**

GAELIC IN THE WESTERN ISLES

Except in Stornoway, and Balivanich on North Uist, **road signs** are now almost exclusively in **Gaelic**, a difficult language to the English-speaker's eye, with complex pronunciation (see p.467), though as a (very) general rule, the English names can often provide a rough pronunciation guide. Particularly if you're driving, it's essential to buy the bilingual Western Isles **map**, produced by the local tourist board, Bord Turasachd nan Eilean, and available at most tourist offices. To reflect the signposting, we've put the Gaelic first in the text, with the English equivalent in brackets. Thereafter we've stuck to the Gaelic names, to try to familiarize readers with their (albeit variable) spellings – the only exceptions are in the names of islands and ferry terminals, where we've stuck to the English names, partly to reflect CalMac's own policy.

---

rental – around £100 a week – though you're not permitted to take their vehicles off the Western Isles.

The islands' **hostels** are geared up for the outdoor life, occupying remote locations on or near the coast. Several of them are run by the Gatliff Hebridean Hostels Trust (GHHT), who have renovated some isolated crofters' cottages. None of these has phones, so you can't book in advance, and you really need to bring your own bedding; each has a simple kitchen, so take your own food. If you're after a little more comfort, then the islands have a generous sprinkling of reasonably priced **B&Bs** and **guest houses** – many of which are a lot more inviting than the hotels and can be easily booked over the phone, or through the tourist offices for a small fee.

Lewis (Leodhas)

Shaped rather like the top of an ice-cream cone, **LEWIS** is the largest and by far the most populous of the Western Isles and the northernmost island in the Hebridean archipelago. Most of the island's 20,000 inhabitants – two-thirds of the Western Isles' total population – now live in the crofting and fishing villages strung out along the northwest coast, between **Calanais** and **Port Nis**, in one of the most densely populated rural areas in the country. On this coast you'll also find the islands' best-preserved **prehistoric remains** – Dùn Charlabhaigh broch and Calanais standing stones – as well as a smattering of ancient crofters' houses in various stages of abandonment. The landscape is mostly flat peat bog – hence the island's name, derived from the Gaelic *leogach* (marshy) – with a gentle shoreline that only fulfils its dramatic potential around Rubha Robhanais (Butt of Lewis), a group of rough rocks on the island's northernmost tip, near Port Nis. To the south, where Lewis is physically joined with Harris, the land rises to just over 1800ft, providing a more exhilarating backdrop for the excellent beaches that pepper the isolated coastline of **Uig**, to the west of Calanais.

Most visitors use **Stornoway**, on the east coast, as a base for exploring the island, though this presents problems if you're travelling by **bus**. There's a regular service to Port Nis and Tarbert, and although the most obvious excursion – the 45-mile round trip from Stornoway to Calanais, Carlabhagh, Arnol and back – is difficult to complete by public transport, minibus tours make the trip on most days from April to October (see p.310).

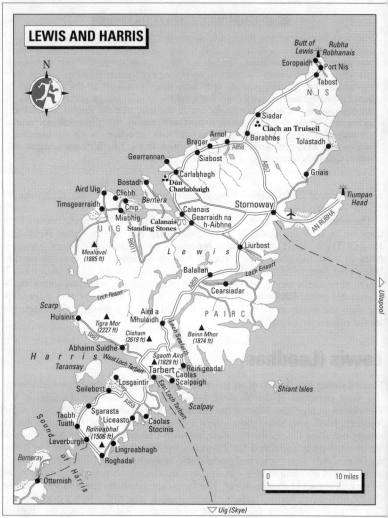

LEWIS AND HARRIS

Butt of
Lewis
Rubha
Robhanais
Eoropaidh
Port Nis
Tabost
N I S
Siadar
Clach an Truiseil
Arnol
Barabhas
Bragar
Tolastadh
Gearrannan
Siabost
A858
Carlabhagh
A857
Bostadh
Dùn
Cliobh
Charlabhaigh
Griais
Aird Uig
Bernera
Stornoway
Timsgearraidh
Cnip
Calanais
Tiumpan
Miabhig
Gearraidh na
Head
Calanais
h-Aibhne
AN RUBHA
U I G
Standing Stones
L e w i s
Liurbost
Mealisval
(1885 ft)
Balallan
Loch Erisort
B8011
Cearsiadar
Loch Resort
Scarp
Aird a
P A I R C
Huisinis
Mhulaidh
Tigra Mor
(2227 ft)
Clisham
Beinn Mhor
(2619 ft)
(1874 ft)
Abhainn Suidhe
Sgaoth Aird
H a r r i s
West Loch Tarbert
(1829 ft)
Taransay
Tarbert
Reinigeadal
Shiant Isles
Caolas
Seilebost
Losgaintir
Scalpaigh
East Loch Tarbert
A859
Scalpay
Sgarasta
Taobh
Liceasto
Tuath
Caolas
Roineabhal
Stocinis
(1506 ft)
Leverburgh
Lingreabhagh
Berneray
Roghadal
Sound
of
Harris
Otternish

0   10 miles

△ Ullapool

▽ Uig (Skye)

© Crown copyright

Some history

After Viking rule ended in 1266, Lewis became a virtually independent state, ruled over by the **MacLeod clan** for several centuries. King James VI, however, had other ideas: he declared the folk of Lewis to be "void of religion", and attempted to establish a colony, as in Ulster, by sending Fife Adventurers to attack Lewis. They were met with armed resistance by the MacLeods so, in retaliation, James VI granted the lands to their arch rivals, the MacKenzies of Kintail. In 1844, the MacKenzies sold Lewis to **Sir James Matheson**, who'd made a fortune from the

RELIGION IN THE WESTERN ISLES

It is difficult to underestimate the importance of **religion** in the Western Isles, which are sharply divided – though with little enmity – between the Catholic southern isles of Barra and South Uist, and the Protestant islands of North Uist, Harris and Lewis. Most conflicts arise from the very considerable power the ministers of the Protestant Church, or Kirk, wield in secular life in the north, where the creed of **Sabbatarianism** is very strong. Here, Sunday is the Lord's Day, and virtually the whole community (irrespective of their degree of piety) stops work – all shops close, all pubs close, all garages close and there's no public transport and, perhaps most famously of all, even the swings in the children's playgrounds are padlocked.

The other main area of division is, paradoxically, within the Protestant Church itself. Scotland is unusual in that the national church, the **Church of Scotland**, is presbyterian (ruled by the ministers and elders of the church) rather than episcopal (ruled by bishops). At the time of the main split in the Presbyterian Church – the so-called **1843 Disruption** – a third of its ministers left the Church of Scotland, protesting at the law which allowed landlords to impose ministers against parishioners' wishes, and formed the breakaway **Free Church**. Since those days there has been a partial reconciliation although, in 1893, there was another break, when a minority of the Free Church became the Free Presbyterian Church; meanwhile, others slowly made their way back to the Church of Scotland. The remaining rump of the Free Church – better known as the **"Wee Frees"** – has its spiritual heartland on Lewis. To confuse matters further, as recently as 1988 the Free Presbyterian Church split over a minister who attended a Requiem Mass during a Catholic funeral of a friend – he and his supporters have since formed the breakaway Associated Presbyterian Churches. Meanwhile, the Free Church itself is currently in crisis over the "heresies" of Professor Donald MacLeod, one of its more liberal members, who writes a regular column in the West Highland Free Press. With a minority within the church determined to force the issue, another split looks inevitable, though as MacLeod himself says, "[Scotland] needs another denomination like it needs a hole in the head".

The various brands and subdivisions of the Presbyterian Church may appear trivial to outsiders, but to the churchgoers of Lewis, Harris and North Uist (as well as much of Skye and Raasay) they are still keenly felt. In part, this is due to social and cultural reasons: Free Church elders helped organize resistance to the Clearances, and the Wee Frees have done the most to help preserve the Gaelic language. A Free Church service is a memorable experience, and in some villages it takes place every evening (and twice on Sundays): there's no set service or prayer book and no hymns; only Biblical readings, plainchant and a fiery sermon all in Gaelic; the pulpit is the architectural focus of the church, not the altar, and communion is taken only on special occasions. If you want to attend one, the Free Church on Kenneth Street in Stornoway has reputedly the largest Sunday-evening congregation in the UK, of up to 1500 people.

Chinese opium trade. Matheson invested heavily in the island's infrastructure, though, as his critics point out, he made sure he recouped his money through tax or rent. He was relatively benevolent when the island was hit by potato famine in the mid-1840s, but ultimately opted for solving the problem through eviction and emigration. His chief factor, Donald Munro, was utterly ruthless, and was only removed after the celebrated Bernera Riot of 1874 (see p.320). The 1886 Crofters Act greatly curtailed the power of the Mathesons; it did not, however, right any of the wrongs of the past. Protests, such as the Pairc Deer Raid of 1887, in which starving crofters killed 200 deer from one of the sporting estates, and the Aignish land raids of the following year, continued against the Clearances of earlier that century.

When **Lord Leverhulme**, founder of the soap empire Unilever, acquired the island (along with Harris) in 1918, he was determined to drag Lewis out of its cycle of poverty by establishing an integrated fishing industry. To this end he founded MacFisheries, a nationwide chain of retail outlets for the fish which would be caught and processed on the islands: he built a cannery, an ice factory, roads, bridges and a light railway; he bought boats, and planned to use spotter planes to locate the shoals of herring. But the dream never came to fruition. Unfortunately, Leverhulme was implacably opposed to the island's centuries-old tradition of crofting, which he regarded as inefficient and "an entirely impossible way of life". He became involved in a long, drawn-out dispute over the distribution of land to returning ex-servicemen, the "land fit for heroes" promised by the Board of Agriculture. In the end, however, it was actually financial difficulties which prompted Leverhulme to pull out of Lewis in 1923, and concentrate on Harris. He generously gifted Lews Castle and Stornoway to its inhabitants and offered free crofts to those islanders who had not been involved in land raids. In the event, few crofters took up the offer – all they wanted was security of tenure, not ownership. Whatever the merits of Leverhulme's plans, his departure left a huge gap in the non-crofting economy, and between the wars thousands more emigrated.

Stornoway (Steornabhagh)

In these parts, **STORNOWAY** is a buzzing metropolis, with some 8000 inhabitants, a one-way system, pedestrian precinct with CCTV and all the trappings of a large town. It's a centre for employment, a social hub for the island and, perhaps most importantly of all, home to the **Comhairle nan Eilean Siar** (Western Isles Council), set up in 1974, which has done so much to promote Gaelic language and culture, and try to stem the tide of anglicization. For the visitor, however, the town is unlikely to win any great praise – aesthetics are not its strong point, and the urban pleasures on offer are limited.

Information and accommodation

The best thing about Stornoway is the convenience of its services. The island's **airport** is four miles east of the town centre, a £5 taxi ride away; the swanky new octagonal CalMac **ferry terminal** is on South Beach, close to the **bus station**. You can get bus timetables, a map of the town and other useful information from the **tourist office**, near North Beach at 26 Cromwell St (April–May & Sept to mid-Oct Mon–Fri 9am–6pm, Sat 9am–5pm; June–Aug Mon, Tues, Thurs & Sat 9am–6pm & 8–9pm, Wed & Fri 9am–8pm; mid-Oct to March Mon–Fri 9am–5pm; ☎01851/703088); they also sell tickets for **minibus tours** to Calanais (Mon–Fri) and for Out and About **wildlife trips** round Lewis and Harris.

Of the **hotels**, the *Royal Hotel* on Cromwell Street (☎01851/702109; ⑤) is your best bet. Another fairly reliable choice is the *Park Guest House* (☎01851/702485; ②) on James Street; the public areas have bags of lugubrious late Victorian character; the bedrooms significantly less. Of the **B&Bs** along leafy Matheson Road, try *Ravenswood*, at no. 12 (☎01851/702673; ②). The *Stornoway Backpackers'* **hostel** is a basic affair about five minutes' walk from the ferry at 47 Keith St

(☎01851/703628, *hostel@bayble.demon.co.uk*). The nearest **campsite**, *Laxdale Holiday Park* (☎01851/703234), lies a mile or so along the road to Barabhas, on Laxdale Lane; the campsite has holiday bungalows (three nights' minimum), and a new **bunkhouse**.

The Town

For centuries, life in Stornoway has focused on its **harbour**, whose quayside was filled with barrels of pickled herring, and whose deep and sheltered waters were thronged with coastal steamers and fishing boats in their nineteenth-century heyday, when more than a thousand boats were based at the port. Today, most of the

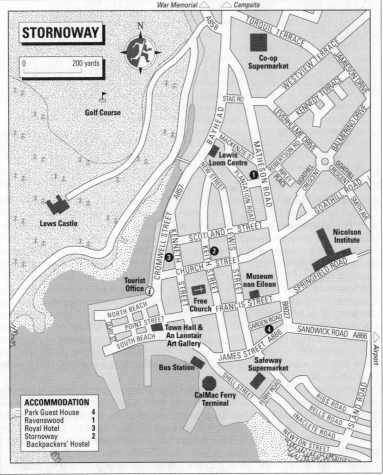

© Crown copyright

THE IOLAIRE DISASTER

Of the 6200 men from the Western Isles who served in World War I, around 1000 died. However, on New Year's Day 1919, in the single most terrible tragedy to befall Lewis, another 208 more died. On New Year's Eve some 530 servicemen were athered at Kyle of Lochalsh to return home to Lewis and their families on the mailboat. However, as there were so many of them, an extra boat was called into service, the **Iolaire**, originally built as a luxury yacht in 1881. The boat left at 7.30pm heavily overloaded, carrying 284 men, young men and veterans, friends and relatives, to cross the Minch. All went well until she was approaching the narrow entrance to Stornoway harbour, a harbour to which she had never been before, in the dark. At this point she overtook a fishing boat and it was this manoeuvre that seems to have caused the disaster. In the early hours of the morning she struck a group of rocks called Blastan Thuilm (Beasts of Holm). Families and friends had gathered at the harbour, but in the darkness it was only gradually that they realized that the ship had foundered. That same darkness prevented the men on board from seeing that they were in fact only twenty yards from the shore.

One man, a boatbuilder from Nis (Ness), a village that was to lose 21 men that night, fought his way ashore with a lifeline which saved the lives of 40 others. Another was saved by clinging to the mast for seven hours, but he lost his elder brother, who'd postponed his return so that they could come back together. Another man, when on active service, had spent 36 hours in the sea, sole survivor of his torpedoed ship; now he drowned within sight of his home. Every village in Lewis lost at least one returning loved one and this, together with the losses in the war and the mass emigration that followed, cast a shadow over life on Lewis for many years. It was the worst peacetime shipping disaster in home waters that century. The last survivor died in 1993 and the only memorials now are a monument at Rubha Thuilm (Holm Point) and the ship's bell in the Museum nan Eilean in Stornoway.

catch is landed on the mainland, and, despite the daily comings and goings of the CalMac ferry from Ullapool, the harbour is a shadow of its former commercial self. The nicest section of the harbour is Cromwell Street Quay, by the tourist office, where the remaining fishing fleet ties up for the night.

Stornoway's commercial centre, to the east, is little more than a string of unprepossessing shops and bars. The one exception is the old **Town Hall** on South Beach, a splendid Scots Baronial building, its rooftop peppered with conical towers, above which a central clock tower rises. On the first floor you'll find the **An Lanntair Art Gallery** (Mon–Sat 10am–5.30pm; free), whose exhibitions feature the work of local artists, plus a nice tearoom. Anyone remotely interested in Harris Tweed should head for the **Lewis Loom Centre** (Mon–Sat 10am–5pm; £1), run by an eccentric and engaging man and located at the far end of Cromwell Street, in the Old Grainstore off Bayhead. There's an exhibition on the cloth, a shop, and three looms, one of which is a Hattersley, which you may catch going through its paces.

Continuing up the pedestrian precinct into Francis Street, you'll eventually reach the **Museum nan Eilean** (April–Sept Mon–Sat 10am–5.30pm; Oct–March Tues–Fri 10am–5pm, Sat 10am–1pm; free), housed in the old Victorian Nicolson Institute school. The ground-floor gallery explores the island's history until the MacKenzie takeover, and is full of artefacts found during peat-cutting, including a lovely Viking dish made from alderwood. There's also a chance to view a Gaelic/English CD-ROM on the Lewis Chessmen (see p.321). The first-floor gallery includes lots of information about the herring and weaving industries, and houses an old loom shed with one of the semi-automatic looms introduced by Lord Leverhulme in the 1920s.

To the northwest of the town centre stands **Lews Castle**, a nineteenth-century Gothic pomposity built by Sir James Matheson in 1863. As the former laird's pad, it is seen as a symbol of old oppression by many: it was here, in the house's now defunct conservatory, that Lady Matheson famously gave tea to the Bernera protesters, when they marched on Stornoway prior to the riot (see p.320); when the eccentric Lord Leverhulme took up residence, he had unglazed bedroom windows which allowed the wind and rain to enter, and gutters in the floor to carry off the residue. The current plan is to make it part of the new University of the Highlands and Islands. For the moment, however, its chief attraction is its mature wooded grounds, a unique sight on the Western Isles, for which Matheson had to import thousands of tons of soil from the mainland. If you enter or exit Stornoway via Willowglen Road (A858), you'll see the town **War Memorial**, a castle tower set high above the town amidst gorse bushes, and a good place to take in the sprawl that is Stornoway.

Eating, drinking and nightlife

Decent **food** options are disappointingly limited in Stornoway. One of the best places is the *Thai Café* on Church Street, which serves inexpensive but authentic **Thai** food – as a consequence it's very popular, so book ahead (☎01851/701811). You can get snacks from the *An Lanntair* tearoom, and from *An Leabharlann*, the coffee shop in the new library on Cromwell Street. The *Golden Ocean* **Chinese** restaurant opposite is not a bad choice for lunch, early evening or takeaway, but is otherwise quite expensive. Your best bet for local food is the restaurant of the *Park Guest House*, on James Street (closed Mon & Sun), but it's expensive, unless you go for the "early bird" option. The biggest problem is that all the above places are closed on Sunday. The *Caberfeidh Hotel*, on Macauley Road, is one of the few hotels to serve Sunday lunch, while the *Stornoway Balti House*, near the bus station on South Beach, opens on Sunday evenings.

As for **pubs**, *MacNeills* on Cromwell Street is the liveliest central pub, with a mixed clientele of keen drinkers. *The Criterion*, a tiny wee pub on Point Street, is another option, as is the very pleasant bar of the *Royal Hotel*. Needless to say, all pubs are closed on Sundays, while hotel bars are open for residents only. Last, but not least, Stornoway is home to the Western Isles' only **Internet café**, *Captions*, 27 Church St (*bayble@captions.co.uk*; Mon–Sat 10am–10pm), where you can check your email and enjoy tea and home-made cakes.

Listings

Bakery Stag Bakery, Cromwell St; next door is Nature's Store, a health-food shop.

Banks The following banks all have ATMs: Bank of Scotland, Cromwell Street; Clydesdale, South Beach; Lloyds TSB, Francis Street; Royal Bank of Scotland, North Beach.

Bike rental Alex Dan's, 67 Kenneth St (closed Sun; ☎01851/704025).

Boat trips Elena C (☎01851/870537) do boat trips to the Shiant Isles and other destinations.

Bookshops Baltic Bookshop, Cromwell Street.

Car rental Lewis Car Hire, 52 Bayhead (☎01851/703760); Mackinnon Self-Drive, southeast of the town centre, at 18 Inaclete Rd (☎01851/702984).

Laundry Erica's Laundrette, Macauley Road (closed Wed & Sun; last wash 1.40pm). It's situated beyond the second roundabout out of town, and is therefore not central.

Pharmacy Boots is on the corner of Cromwell Street and Point Street.

Taxis Central Cabs, 20 MacMillan Brae (☎01851/706900).

The road to Tolastadh (Tolsta)

Given the relative paucity of attractions in Stornoway, the dead-end B895 to **TOLASTADH**, twelve miles north along the east coast, is a good road to head out on. It boasts several excellent golden beaches and marks the starting point of a lovely coastal walk to Nis.

The legacy of Lord Leverhulme's brief ownership of Lewis is recalled by the striking **Griais Memorial** to the Lewis land-raiders, situated by Griais Bridge, above Gress Sands. It was here that Leverhulme's plans came unstuck: he wanted to turn the surrounding crofting land into three big farms, which would provide milk for the workers of his fish-canning factory; the local crofters just wanted to return to their traditional way of life. Such was Leverhulme's fury at the Griais (Gress) and Col (Coll) land-raiders that, when he offered to gift the crofts of Lewis to their owners, he made sure the offer didn't include Griais and Col. The stone-built memorial is a symbolic croft split asunder by Leverhulme's interventions.

Further north, beyond Tolastadh, is probably the finest of the coast's sandy beaches, Gheardha (Garry), and the beginning of the footpath to Nis. Shortly after leaving the bay, the path crosses the "**Bridge to Nowhere**", built by Leverhulme as part of an unrealized plan to forge a new road right along the east coast. A little further along the track, there's a fine waterfall on the Abhainn na Cloich (River of Stones). The makeshift road peters out, but a path continues for another ten miles via the old sheiling village of Diobadail, to Nis (see below).

The road to Barabhas (Barvas) and Nis (Ness)

Northwest of Stornoway, the A857 crosses the vast, barren **peat bog** of the interior, an empty undulating wilderness riddled with stretchmarks formed by peat cuttings and pockmarked with freshwater lochans. The whole area was once covered by forests, but these disappeared long ago, leaving a smothering deposit of peat that is, on average, six feet thick, and is still being formed in certain places. Tourists tend to cross this barren landscape at speed, while ecologists have identified these natural wetlands as important "carbon sinks", whose erosion should be protected. For the people of Lewis, the peat represents a valuable energy resource, with each crofter being assigned a slice of the bog. The islanders spend several very sociable weeks each spring cutting the peat, turning it over and leaving it neatly laid out in the open air to dry, returning in summer to collect the dried sods and stack them outside their houses. Though tempting to take home as souvenirs, these piles are the fruits of hard labour, and remain the island's main source of domestic fuel, its pungent smoke one of the most characteristic smells of the Western Isles.

Twelve miles across the peat bog the road approaches the west coast of Lewis and divides, heading southwest towards Calanais (see p.319), or northeast through **BARABHAS** (Barvas), and a whole string of bleak and fervently Free Church crofting and weaving villages. These scattered settlements have none of the photogenic qualities of Skye's whitewashed villages: the churches are plain

---

PEAT

One of the characteristic features of the landscape of the Scottish Highlands and Islands is **peat** (*mòine*) – and nowhere is its presence more keenly felt than on Lewis. Virtually the whole interior of the island is made up of one, vast blanket bog, scarred with lines of peat banks old and new, while the pungent smell of peat smoke hits you as you drive through the villages. Essentially, peat is made up of dead vegetation that has failed to rot completely because the sheer volume of rainfall has caused the soil acidity to reach such a level that it acts as a preservative. In other words, organic matter – such as sphagnum moss, rushes, sedges and reeds – is dying at a faster rate than it is decomposing. This means, of course, that peat is still (very slowly) forming in certain parts of Scotland, at around an inch or less every fifty years. In the mostly treeless Scottish Islands, peat provided an important source of fuel, and the cutting and stacking of peats in the spring was part of annual cycle of crofting life. As a result, peat cutting remains embedded in island culture, and is still practised on a large scale in the Hebrides and Shetland. It's a social occasion as much as anything else, which heralds the arrival of the warmer, drier days of late spring.

Great pride is taken in the artistry and neatness of the peat banks and stacks. In some parts, the peat lies up to thirty feet deep, but peat banks are usually only cut to a depth of around six or seven feet. Once the top layer of turf has been removed, the peat is cut into slabs between two and four peats deep, using a traditional *tairsgeir* (pronounced "tushkar"). Since peat is ninety percent water in its natural state, it has to be carefully "lifted" in order to dry out. Peats tend to be piled up either vertically in "rooks", or crisscrossed in "windows"; either way the peat will lose around 75 percent of its water content, and shrink by about a quarter. Many folk wonder how on earth the peat can dry out when it seems to rain the whole time, but the wind helps, and eventually a skin is formed that stops any further water from entering the peats. After three or four weeks, the peats are skilfully "grieved", rather like the slates on a roof, into round-humped stacks or onto carts that can be brought home. Traditionally, the peat would be carried from the peat banks by women using "creels", baskets that were strapped on the back. Correctly grieved peats allow the rain to run off, and therefore stay dry for a year or more outside the croft.

---

and unadorned; the crofters' houses relatively modern and smothered in grey, pebble-dash rendering or harling; the stone cottages and enclosures of their forebears often lie half-abandoned in the front garden; while a rusting assortment of discarded cars and vans store peat bags and the like. Just beyond Barabhas, a signpost points to the pleasant **Morven Art Gallery** (Easter–Oct Mon–Sat 11am–5pm; free), with a handy café to hole up in during bad weather. Three miles further up the road, you pass the twenty-foot monolith of **Clach an Truiseil**, the first of a series of prehistoric sights between the crofting and weaving settlements of **BAILE AN TRUISEIL** (Ballantrushal) and **SIADAR** (Shader). Beyond Siadar, anyone with a passing interest in pottery should visit **Borgh Pottery** (Mon–Sat 9.30am–6pm; free), where you can watch the husband-and-wife team creating hand-thrown pots.

Nis (Ness)

The main road continues through a string of straggling villages, until you reach the various densely populated settlements that make up the parish of **NIS** (Ness),

OFFSHORE ISLANDS

Though three men dwell on Flannan Isle
To keep the lamp alight,
As we steer'd under the lee, we caught
No glimmer through the night.

"Flannan Isle", Wilfred Wilson Gibson

On December 15, 1900, a passing ship reported that the lighthouse on the **Flannan Isles**, built the previous year by the Stevensons some 21 miles west of the Butt of Lewis, was not working. Gibson's poem goes on to recount the arrival of the relief boat from Oban on Boxing Day, whose crew found no trace of the three keepers. More mysteriously still, a full meal lay untouched on the table, one chair was knocked over, and only two oilskins were missing. Subsequent lightkeepers doubtless spent many lonely nights trying in vain to figure out what happened, until the lighthouse went automatic in 1971.

Equally famous, but for different reasons, is the tiny island of **Sula Sgeir**, 41 miles due north of the Butt of Lewis. Every August since anyone can remember, the young men of Nis have set sail from Port Nis to harvest the young gannet or guga that nest in their thousands high up on the islet's sea cliffs. It's a dangerous activity, and one that the RSPB has tried its best to stop, but for some unknown reason boiled gannet and potato continues to be a popular Lewis delicacy, and there's never any shortage of eager volunteers for the annual cull.

Somewhat incredibly, the island of **Rona**, less than a mile across and ten miles east of Sula Sgeir, was inhabited on and off until the mid-nineteenth century. The island's St Ronan's Chapel is one of the oldest Celtic Christian ruins in the country. St Ronan was, according to legend, the first inhabitant, moving here in the eighth century with his two sisters, Miriceal and Brianuil, until one day he turned to Brianuil and said, "My dear sister, it is yourself that is handsome, what beautiful legs you have." She apparently replied that it was time for her to leave the island, and made her way to neighbouring Sula Sgeir. Rona is now in the care of Scottish Natural Heritage (☎01870/705258), from whom you must get permission before landing.

The largest of all the offshore islands is the NTS-owned **St Kilda** archipelago, roughly a hundred miles west southwest of the Butt of Lewis and over forty miles from its nearest landfall, Griminish Point on North Uist. The last 36 Gaelic-speaking inhabitants of Hirta, St Kilda's main island, were evacuated at their own request in 1930, ending several hundred years of harsh existence – well recorded in Tom Steel's book *The Life and Death of St Kilda*. Today, the island is partly occupied by the army, who have a missile-tracking radar station here linked to South Uist. The NTS (☎01870/620238) organize week-long volunteer groups, which you can apply to join, though be prepared for a rough, fourteen-hour crossing from Oban. With a calm sea and permission from the NTS – even tour operators have to negotiate long and hard – you may go ashore to visit the museum in the old village, restored by volunteers, and struggle up the massive cliffs, where the islanders once caught puffins, young fulmars and gannets.

at the northern tip of Lewis. The folk of Nis are perhaps best known for their annual culling of young gannets on Sula Sgeir (see box). For an insight into the social history of the area, take a look inside **Comunn Eachdriadh Nis** (Ness Historical Society; Mon–Sat noon–5.30pm; £2), on the left as you pass through **TABOST** (Habost). The museum, housed in an unlikely looking building, contains a huge collection of photographs, but its prize possession is a diminutive sixth- or seventh-century cross from the Isle of Rona (see box), decorated with a much-eroded nude male figure, and thought by some to have been St Ronan's gravestone. The road terminates at the fishing village of **PORT NIS** (Port of Ness), with a tiny harbour and lovely golden beach.

Shortly before you reach Port Nis, a minor road heads two miles northwest to the hamlet of **EOROPAIDH** (Europie) – pronounced "Yor-erpee". Here, by the road junction that leads to the Butt of Lewis, the simple stone structure of **Teampull Mholuaidh** (St Moluag's Church) stands amidst the runrig fields. Thought to date from the twelfth century, when the islands were still under Norse rule, but restored in 1912 (and now used once a month by the Scottish Episcopal Church for sung Communion), the church features a strange south chapel with only a squint window connecting it to the nave. In the late seventeenth century, the traveller Martin Martin noted: "they all went to church . . . and then standing silent for a little time, one of them gave a signal . . . and immediately all of them went into the fields, where they fell a drinking their ale and spent the remainder of the night in dancing and singing, etc". Church services aren't what they used to be.

From Eoropaidh, a narrow road twists to the bleak and blustery northern tip of the island, **Rubha Robhanais** – well known to devotees of the BBC shipping forecast as the **Butt of Lewis** – where a lighthouse sticks up above a series of sheer cliffs and stacks, alive with kittiwakes, fulmars and cormorants, with skuas and gannets feeding offshore, and a great place for marine mammal-spotting. The lighthouse is closed to the public, though a shop and tearoom are planned for the near future. In the meantime, you're better off backtracking half a mile or so, where there's a path down to the tiny sandy bay of **Port Sto**, a more sheltered spot for a picnic than the Butt itself. From Europaidh, you can also gain access to the dunes and machair of the nearby coastline that stretches for two or three miles to the southwest.

Practicalities

There are at least six buses a day from Stornoway to Port Nis, Sundays excepted, and one or two **accommodation** possibilities. The best place to stay is *Galson Farm Guest House* (☎01851/850492; ⑤), an eighteenth-century farmhouse in Gabhsann Bho Dheas (South Galson), halfway between Barabhas and Port Nis, with a **bunkhouse** close by (phone number as above). Another, more modest option is the modern croft of *Eisdean* (☎01851/810240; ①), in Coig Peighinnean (Five Penny Borve), four miles northeast of Barabhas, or *Cross Inn* (☎01851/810378; ①), remarkable primarily for being the only pub in the entire parish. The only **tearoom** (March–Oct; closed Sun) is *Harbour View*, in an old-boatbuilder's house overlooking Port Nis harbour; it also serves toasted sandwiches and baked potatoes. There are very few shops (other than mobile ones) in these parts, so it's as well to stock up in Stornoway before you set out.

Bru (Brue), Arnol and Siabost (Shawbost)

Heading southwest from the crossroads near Barabhas brings you to several villages that meander down towards the sea. The first is **BRU** (Brue), where you'll find the **Oiseval Gallery** (Mon–Sat 10.30am–5.30pm; free), a photographic gallery that's worth a look. In the neighbouring village of **ARNOL**, the remains of numerous blackhouses lie abandoned in the village, one of which, at the far end of the village, has been restored as a **Black House Museum** (May–Sept Mon–Fri 10am–1pm & 2–5pm, Sat 11am–1pm & 2–5pm; £1.80; HS). Dating from the 1870s and inhabited until 1964, its chimneyless roof is overlaid with grassy sods and oat-straw thatch, lashed down with fishnets and ropes. Beneath, a simple system of wooden tie beams supports the roof, which covers both the living quarters and the attached byre and barn. The postwar wallpaper inside has been removed to reveal sooty rafters above the living room, where, in the centre of the stone and clay floor, the peat fire was the focal point of the house. Today, many visitors look back with nostalgia at the old abandoned blackhouses, but it's as well to remember that they were a breeding ground for disease, and that, essentially, life in the blackhouse was pretty grim.

Returning to the main road, it's about a mile or so to **BRAGAR**, where you'll spot a stark arch formed by the jawbone of a blue whale, washed up on the nearby coast in 1920. The spear sticking through the bone is the harpoon, which only went off when the local blacksmith was trying to remove it, badly injuring him. Another two miles on at **SIABOST** (Shawbost), local schoolchildren created the appealingly amateurish **Shawbost Crofting Museum** (Mon–Sat 9am–6pm; free) in 1970. The converted church contains a real hotchpotch of stuff – most of it donated by locals – including a rare Lewis brick from the short-lived factory set up by Lord Leverhulme, an old hand-driven loom and a reconstructed living room with a traditional box bed. Behind the church is the *Eilean Fraoich* **campsite** (☎01851/710504; May–Oct). Just outside Siabost, to the west, there's a sign to the newly restored **Norse Mill and Kiln**. It's a ten-minute walk over a small hill to the two thatched bothies beside a little stream; the nearer one's the kiln, the further one's the horizontal mill. Mills and kilns of this kind were common in Lewis up until the 1930s, and despite the name are thought to have been introduced here from Ireland as early as the sixth century.

Carlabhagh (Carloway) and Calanais (Callanish)

Five miles on, the landscape becomes less monotonous, with boulders and hillocks rising out of the peat moor, as you approach the parish of **CARLABHAGH** (Carloway), with its scattering of croft houses. A mile-long road leads off north to the beautifully remote coastal settlement of **GEARRANNAN** (Garenin), where several thatched crofters' houses – the last of which was abandoned in 1973 – have been restored. One blackhouse now serves as a GHHT **youth hostel**, another is for **self-catering** (*gearrannan@lews.fc.uhi.ac.uk*; sleeps 16; £100 per night; ☎01851/643416), while another contains public toilets; **camping** is also permitted. A night here is unforgettable, and there's a beautiful stony beach from which to view the sunset.

Just beyond Carlabhagh, about 400 yards from the road, Dùn Charlabhaigh Broch perches on top of a conspicuous rocky outcrop overlooking the sea. Scotland's Atlantic coast is strewn with the remains of over 500 brochs, or fortified towers, but this is one of the best-preserved, its drystone circular walls reaching a height of more than 30ft on the seaward side. The broch consists of two concentric walls, the inner one perpendicular, the outer one slanting inwards, the two originally fastened together by roughly hewn flagstones, which also served as lookout galleries reached via a narrow stairwell. The only entrance to the roofless inner yard is through a low doorway set beside a crude and cramped guard cell. As at Calanais (see opposite), there have been all sorts of theories about the purpose of the brochs, which date from between 100 BC and 100 AD; the most likely explanation is that they were built to provide protection from Roman slave-traders.

Dùn Charlabhaigh now has its very own **Doune Broch Centre** (April–Oct Mon–Sat 10am–6pm; free), situated at a discreet distance, stone-built and sporting a turf roof. It's a good wet-weather retreat, and fun for kids, who can walk through the hay-strewn mock-up of the broch as it might have been. A mile or so beyond the broch, beside a lochan, is the *Doune Braes Hotel* (☎01851/643252, *user@doune-braes.netmedia.co.uk*; ④), a friendly, unpretentious place whose bar serves up the same tasty seafood dishes as its restaurant, only cheaper.

Calanais

Five miles south of Carlabhagh lies the village of **CALANAIS** (Callanish), site of the islands' most dramatic prehistoric ruins, the **Calanais Standing Stones**, whose monoliths – nearly fifty of them – occupy a serene lochside setting. There's been years of heated debate about the origin and function of the stones – slabs of gnarled and finely grained gneiss up to 15ft high – though almost everyone agrees that they were lugged here by Neolithic peoples between 3000 and 1500 BC. It's also obvious that the planning and construction of the site – as well as several other lesser circles nearby – was spread over many generations. Such an endeavour could, it's been argued, only be prompted by the desire to predict the seasonal cycle upon which these early farmers were entirely dependent, and indeed many of the stones are aligned with the position of the sun and the stars. This rational explanation, based on clear evidence that this part of Lewis was once a fertile farming area, dismisses as coincidence the ground plan of the site, which resembles a colossal Celtic cross, and explains away the central burial chamber as a later addition of no special significance. These two features have, however, fuelled all sorts of theories ranging from alien intervention to human sacrifice.

A blackhouse adjacent to the main stone circle has been refurbished as a **tearoom** and shop, and it's to this you should head for refreshment rather than the superfluous **Calanais Visitor Centre** (Mon–Sat: April–Sept 10am–7pm; Oct–March 10am–4pm; £1.50) on the other side of the stones (and thankfully out of view), to which all the signs direct you from the road. The centre runs a decent restaurant and a small museum on the site, but with so much information on the panels beside the stones there's little reason to visit it. You're politely asked not to walk between the stones, only along the path that surrounds them, so if you want to commune with standing stones in solitude, head for the smaller circles in more natural surroundings a mile or two southeast of Calanais, around Gearraidh na h-Aibhne (Garynahine).

If you need a place to stay, there are several inexpensive **B&Bs** in Calanais itself: try Mrs Catherine Morrison, 27 Calanais (☎01851/621392; ①; March–Sept), or an excellent B&B, which caters well for veggies and is run by Debbie Nash (☎01851/621321; ①) in neighbouring Tolastadh a Chaolais (Tolsta Chaolais), three miles north. Calanais also has a modern *Eschol Guest House* (☎01851/621357; ③), no beauty from the outside, but very comfortable within. If it's just **food** you want, *Tigh Mealros* (closed Sun), in Gearraidh na h-Aibhne, serves good, inexpensive lunches and evening meals, featuring local seafood.

Bernera (Bearnaraigh)

From Gearraidh na h-Aibhne, the main road leads back to Stornoway, while the B8011 heads off west to Uig (see p.320), and, a few miles on, the B8059 sets off north to the island of Great Bernera, usually referred to simply as **Bernera**. Joined to the mainland via a narrow bridge that spans a small sea channel, Bernera is a rocky island, dotted with lochans, fringed by a few small lobster-fishing settlements and currently owned by Comte Robin de la Lanne Mirrlees, the Queen's former herald.

Bernera has an important place in Lewis history due to the **Bernera Riot** of 1872, when local crofters successfully defied the eviction orders delivered to them by the landlord, Sir James Matheson. In truth, there wasn't much of riot, but three Bernera men were arrested and charged with assault. The crofters marched on the laird's house, Lews Castle in Stornoway, and demanded an audience with Matheson, who claimed to have no knowledge of what his factor, Donald Munro, was doing. In the subsequent trial, Munro was exposed as a ruthless tyrant, and the crofters were acquitted. A stone-built cairn now stands as a memorial to the riot, at the crossroads beyond the central settlement of **BREACLEIT** (Breaclete), which sits beside one of the island's many lochs. Here, you'll find the **Bernera Museum** (April–Sept Mon–Sat 11am–6pm; £1.50), housed in the local community centre. There's a small exhibition on lobster fishing, a St Kilda mailboat, and a mysterious 5000-year-old Neolithic stone tennis ball, but it's hardly worth the entrance fee, unless you're tracing your ancestry.

Much more interesting is the replica **Iron Age House** (Tues–Sat noon–4pm; £1) that has been built above a precious little bay of golden sand beyond the cemetery at **BOSTADH** (Bosta), three miles north of Breacleit – follow the signs "to the shore". In 1992, gale-force winds revealed an entire late Iron Age or Pictish settlement hidden under the sand; due to its exposed position, the site has been refilled with sand, and a full-scale mock-up built instead, based on the "jelly baby" houses – after the shape – that were excavated. Inside, the house is incredibly spacious, and very dark, illuminated only by a central hearth and a few chinks of sunlight. If the weather's fine and you climb to the top of the nearby hills, you should get a good view over the forty or so islands in Loch Roag, and maybe even the Flannan Isles (see p.316) on the horizon.

If you want to stay, there are a couple of comfortable, modern **B&Bs** on the island: *Kelvindale* (☎01851/612347; ①; April–Oct) in Tobson, a couple of miles northwest of Breacleit, and *Garymilis* (☎01851/612341; ①; Feb–Nov), in **Circebost** (Kirkibost).

Uig

It's a long drive along the partially upgraded B8011 to the remote parish of **Uig**, one of the areas of Lewis that suffered really badly from the Clearances, The landscape here is hillier, and more dramatic than elsewhere, a combination of myriad islets, wild cliff scenery and patches of pristine golden sand.

At the crossroads to **MIABHAIG** (Miavaig), you have a choice of either heading straight for the Uig Sands (see opposite), or veering off the main road, and heading along a dramatic little road northeast to **CLIOBH** (Cliff). The Atlantic breakers that roll onto the beach below the village are often spectacular, but make it unsafe for swimmers, who should continue another mile to **CNIP** (Kneep), to the southeast of which is **Tràigh na Beirghe**, a glorious strand of shell sand, backed by dunes and machair, in which there's a small primitive **campsite** (☎01851/672265; mid-April to mid-Sept).

The other route choice from Miabhaig is to continue along the main road through the narrow canyon of Glen Valtos (Glèann Bhaltois) to **TIMSGEAR-**

RAIDH (Timsgarry), which overlooks **Uig Sands** (Tràigh Uuige), the largest and most prized of all the golden strands on Lewis. It was in the nearby village of Eadar dha Fhadhail (Ardroil) in 1831 that a local cow stumbled across the **Lewis Chessmen**, twelfth-century Viking chesspieces carved from walrus ivory that now reside in Edinburgh's Museum of Antiquities and the British Museum in London. You can see replicas of the chessmen in the **Uig Heritage Centre** (Mon–Sat noon–5pm; £1), housed in Uig School in Timsgearraidh. As well as putting on some excellent temporary exhibitions, the museum has bits and bobs from blackhouses, and is staffed by locals, who are happy to answer any queries you have; there's also a welcome **tearoom** in the adjacent nursery during the holidays.

The most intriguing **place to stay** is *Baile na Cille* (☎01851/672241, *randjgollin@compuserve.com*; ④; April–Sept), in an idyllic setting overlooking the Uig Sands in Timsgearraidh; they also have a couple of **self-catering** cottages (6 people; £350 per week). It's an easy-going place, run by an eccentric couple, who are very welcoming to families – the Blairs have stayed here – and dish up wonderful, though expensive, set-menu dinners. An entirely different (but equally unusual) experience is to stay at the old RAF station in **AIRD UIG**, three miles north of Timsgearraidh, which is slowly being transformed by an enterprising Breton. The concrete buildings themselves are something of an eyesore, but the position, overlooking a rocky inlet beside Gallan Head, is superb. The whole complex includes **B&B** (☎01851/672474; ①), **self-catering** (5 people; £250 per week), a **hostel**, and the popular *Bonaventure* **restaurant** (closed Mon & Sun), which serves up outstanding food at bargain prices. Boat trips to Bernera and Calanais and elsewhere along the west coast are available from Sea Trek (☎01851/672464), run by Murray MacLeod from **Uigean** (Uigen), near Miabhaig.

Harris (Na Hearadh)

The "division" between Lewis and **HARRIS** – they are, in fact, one island – is embedded in a historical split in the MacLeod clan, lost in the mists of time. The border between the two was also a county boundary until 1975, with Harris lying in Inverness-shire, and Lewis belonging to Ross and Cromarty. Nowadays, the dividing line is rarely marked even on maps; for the record, it comprises Loch Resort in the west, Loch Seaforth in the east, and the six miles in between. Harris itself is more clearly divided by a minuscule isthmus, into the wild, inhospitable mountains of **North Harris** and the gentler landscape and sandy shores of **South Harris**.

Along with Lewis, Harris was purchased in 1918 by **Lord Leverhulme**, and after 1923, when he pulled out of Lewis, all his efforts were concentrated here. In contrast to Lewis, though, Leverhulme and his ambitious projects were broadly welcomed by the people of Harris. His most grandiose plans were drawn up for Leverburgh (see p.327), but he also purchased an old Norwegian whaling station in Bun Abhain Eadara in 1922, built a spinning mill at Geocrab and began the construction of four roads. Financial difficulties, a slump in the tweed industry and the lack of market for whale products meant that none of the schemes was a wholehearted success, and when he died in 1925 the plug was pulled on all of them by his executors.

Since the Leverhulme era, unemployment has been a constant problem in Harris. Crofting continues on a small scale, supplemented by the Harris Tweed

HARRIS TWEED

Far from being a picturesque cottage industry, as it's sometimes presented, the production of **Harris Tweed** is vital to the local economy, with a well-organized and unionized workforce. Traditionally the tweed was made by women, from the wool of their own sheep, to provide clothing for their families, using a 2500-year-old process. Each woman was responsible for plucking the wool by hand, washing and scouring it, dyeing it with lichen, heather flowers or ragwort, carding (smoothing and straightening the wool, often adding butter to grease it), spinning and weaving. Finally the cloth was dipped in sheep's urine and "waulked" by a group of women, who beat the cloth on a table to soften and shrink it whilst singing Gaelic waulking songs. Harris Tweed was originally made all over the islands, and was known simply as *clò mór* (big cloth).

In the mid-nineteenth century, the Countess of Dunmore, who owned a large part of Harris, started to sell surplus cloth to her aristocratic friends, thus forming the genesis of the modern industry, which serves as a vital source of employment, though demand (and therefore employment levels) can fluctuate wildly as fashions change. To earn the official Harris Tweed Association trademark of the Orb and the Maltese Cross – taken from the Countess of Dunmore's coat of arms – the fabric has to be hand-woven on the Outer Hebrides from 100 percent pure new Scottish wool, while the other parts of the manufacturing process must take place only in the local mills.

The main centre of production is now Lewis, where the wool is dyed, carded and spun; you can see all these processes by visiting the **Lewis Loom Centre** in Stornoway (see p.312). In recent years there has been a revival of traditional tweed-making techniques, with several small producers, like Anne Campbell at **Clò Mór** in Liceasto (Mon–Fri 9am–5pm; ☎01859/530364), religiously following old methods. One of the more interesting aspects of the process is the use of indigenous plants and bushes to dye the cloth: yellow comes from rocket and broom, green from heather, grey and black from iris and oak, and, most popular of all, reddish brown from crotal, a flat grey lichen scraped off rocks.

industry, though the main focus of this has shifted to Lewis. Shellfish fishing continues on **Scalpay**, while the rest of the population gets by on whatever employment is available: roadworks, crafts and, of course, tourism. There's a regular **bus** connection between Stornoway and **Tarbert**, and an occasional service which circumnavigates South Harris (see also "Travel details" on p.340).

Tarbert (Tairbeart)

The largest place on Harris is the ferry port of **TARBERT**, sheltered in a green valley on the narrow isthmus that marks the border between North and South Harris. The town's mountainous backdrop is impressive, and the town is attractively laid out on steep terraces sloping up from the dock. However, it does boast the only **tourist office** (April–Oct Mon–Sat 9am–5pm; also open to greet the ferry; winter hours variable; ☎01859/502011) on Harris, close to the ferry terminal. The office can arrange modest, inexpensive B&B **accommodation** and has a full set of bus timetables, but its real value is as a source of information on local walks.

If you wish to base yourself in Tarbert there's a **hostel**, *Rockview Bunkhouse* (☎01859/502211), on Main Street, which also offers **bike rental**. You'll need to book ahead to stay in Tarbert's two most popular **guest houses**: *Allan Cottage* (☎01859/502146; ③; April–Sept), in the old telephone exchange, and *Leachin House* (☎01859/502157; ⑤), further up the Stornoway road. Another good option is the Victorian B&B *Dunard* (☎01859/502340; ③), or there's the easy-going, old-fashioned *Harris Hotel* (☎01859/502154; ③), five minutes' walk from the ferry. The purpose-built hotel **bar** acts as the local social centre and serves low-grade bar meals; the adjacent *Crofters* **restaurant** serves moderately expensive, fairly ordinary fare. During the day, you're best off heading for the very pleasant *First Fruits* **tearoom** (April–Sept; closed Sun), behind the tourist office, housed in an old stone-built cottage and serving real coffee, home-made cakes, toasties and so forth. The only alternative is the **fish and chip shop** (April–Oct; closed Sun), next to the hostel.

North Harris (Ceann a Tuath na Hearadh)

The A859 north to Stornoway takes you over a boulder-strewn saddle between mighty **Sgaoth Aird** (1829ft) and An Cliseam or the **Clisham** (2619ft), the highest peak in the Western Isles. This bitter terrain, littered with debris left behind by retreating glaciers, offers but the barest of vegetation, with an occasional cluster of crofters' houses sitting in the shadow of a host of pointed peaks, anywhere between 1000ft and 2500ft high. These bulging, pyramidal mountains reach their climax around the dramatic shores of the fjord-like **Loch Seaforth**. Just beyond **Aird a' Mhulaidh** (Ardvourlie), at the border between Lewis and Harris, is a rare patch of woodland, much of it blighted. If you're planning on walking in North Harris, and can afford it, consider using the spectacular *Ardvourlie Castle* (☎01859/502307; ⑥; April–Oct), ten miles north of Tarbert by the shores of Loch Seaforth, as a launch pad. In nearby **Bogha Glas** (Bowglass), there's also a thatched **self-catering** cottage, *Tigh na Seileach* (4 people; £250 per week; ☎01859/502411).

A cheaper, but equally idyllic spot is the GHHT **hostel** (no phone; open all year) in the lonely coastal hamlet of **REINIGEADAL** (Rhenigdale), until recently only accessible by foot or boat. To reach the hostel without your own transport, walk east five miles from Tarbert along the road to **Caolas Scalpaigh** (Kyles Scalpay). After another mile or so, watch for the sign marking the start of the path which threads its way through the peaks of the craggy promontory that lies trapped between Loch Seaforth and East Loch Tarbert. It's a magnificent hike, with superb views out along the coast and over the mountains, but you'll need to be properly equipped (see p.46) and should allow three hours for the one-way trip.

Scalpay (Scalpaigh)

Caolas Scalpaigh looks out across East Loch Tarbert to the former island of **Scalpay** (Scalpaigh) – from the Norse *skalp-ray* (the island shaped like a boat) – now accessible via the brand-new £6-million single-track bridge. Scalpay's tightly knit prawn-fishing community is surprisingly buoyant, maintaining a relatively large population of around 400. It's a pleasant and fairly easy three-mile hike across the island to the **Eilean Glas** lighthouse, which looks out over the sea to Skye. The first lighthouse to be erected in Scotland, in 1788, the current tower was Stevenson-designed and is built out of Aberdeen granite. There are a couple of simple B&Bs on the island: *Suil-Na-Mara* (☎01859/540278; ①; April–Sept) or

WALKING IN NORTH HARRIS

Ordnance Survey Landranger map no. 13

Harris is great **walking** country. The crowds that flock to the Skye Cuillin are absent, there are no Munro-baggers, and the landscape is wonderfully lunar-esque. It's also one of the largest continuously mountainous regions in the country, made up of ancient Lewisian gneiss, one of the oldest rocks in the world formed almost 3000 million years ago. As always, if you're walking, you should take note of safety precautions (see p.46), and be particularly conscious of the weather conditions, which can change rapidly in these parts.

As the highest mountain in the Western Isles, An Cliseam or **Clisham** (2619ft) is an obvious objective for walkers, and can be easily climbed from the parking space on the A859, where the road crosses the Abhainn Mhàraig. There isn't a path as such, but if you follow the river, and approach the mountain from its southeast ridge, an ascent should be fairly straightforward (2–3hr return). Clisham forms part of a horseshoe ridge that extends from Mullach an Langa in the northwest to Tomnabhal in the east. In order to climb the whole ridge, you're better off starting off from near where the A859 crosses the Abhainn Scaladail, just before Aird a' Mhulaidh. There's an old drovers' road, half a mile before the bridge, which heads south, skirting Caisteal Ard and Cleit Ard; from the track you get a gentle approach to the southeastern ridge of Tomnabhal. At the other end of the ridge, you can return to Aird a' Mhulaidh, via Loch Mhisteam and the Abhainn Scaladail. The entire circuit of the ridge should take around five hours. If you're based in Tarbert and don't have your own transport, it's roughly an hour's walk to Bun Abhainn Eadarra.

If weather conditions are fairly poor, there are several low-level walks that take you right through the heart of the mountains of North Harris. None of them are circular, so unless you study the bus timetables carefully you'll probably have to backtrack. The first route takes the aforementioned path from Bun Abhainn Eadarra, and then continues up to Loch a' Sgàil, and, over the narrow pass into **Glen Langadale**, from which a path eventually heads east to the A859 just north of Aird a' Mhulaidh, a total distance eight miles (4hr). A longer and more rewarding ten-mile walk (5–6hr) is along **Gleann Mhiabhaig** via Loch Scourst and Loch Bhoisimid, and then east to the A859 just north of Aird a' Mhulaidh; an interesting detour can also be made to Gleann and Loch Stuladail, which are overlooked by crags. The most impressive low-level walk, however, is along **Gleann Ulladail**, where Loch Ulladail is overlooked by the overhanging headland of Sron Ulladail. There's a decent path all the way from the dam on the B887, just before Abhainn Suidhe, to Loch Ulladail, a distance of under five miles; the return journey takes four to five hours. If you've energy, and the weather's good, you can use the above low-level walk as a return route, after climbing the ridge of peaks that starts with Cleiseabhal in the south, and ends with Ullabhal in the north.

Unfortunately, the Reinigeadal GHHT hostel is too far east to use as a base for any of these walks. However, you can console yourself by climbing the nearby peak of **Toddun** (1732ft), which can be easily approached along its north or south ridge. The return trip will probably only take a couple of hours, so for a longer day's hike, you could aim for a circuit of the trio of mountains further west: Sgaoth Iosal (1740ft), Sgaoth Aird (1829ft) and Gillaval Glas (1544ft).

Seafield (☎01859/540250; ③). If you're interested in **diving**, contact Scalpay Diving Services (☎01859/540328).

The road to Huisinis (Hushinish)

The only other road on North Harris is the winding, single-track B887, which clings to the northern shores of West Loch Tarbert, and gives easy access to the awesome mountain range of the (treeless) Forest of Harris to the north. Immediately as you turn down the B887, you pass through **BUN ABHÀINN EADARRA** (Bunavoneadar), where some Norwegians established a short-lived whaling station – the slipways and distinctive red-brick chimney can still be seen. Seven miles further on, the road takes you through the gates of **Amhuinnsuidhe Castle** (pronounced "Avan-soo-ee"), built in Scottish Baronial style in 1868 by the Earl of Dunmore, and right past the front door, much to the annoyance of the castle's owners, who have tried in vain to have the road rerouted. As it is, you have time to admire the lovely salmon-leap waterfalls and pristine castle grounds.

It's another five miles to the end of the road at the small crofting community of **HUISINIS** (Hushinish), where you are rewarded with a south-facing beach of shell sand that looks across to South Harris. A slipway to the north of the bay serves the nearby island of **Scarp**, a hulking mass of rock rising to over 1000ft, once home to more than two hundred people and abandoned as recently as 1971 (it's now just a private holiday hideaway). The most bizarre moment in its history was undoubtedly in 1934, when the German scientist Gerhardt Zucher conducted an experiment with rocket mail, but the letter-laden missile exploded before it even got off the ground, and the idea was shelved.

South Harris (Ceann a Deas na Hearadh)

The mountains of **South Harris** are less dramatic than in the north, but the scenery is equally breathtaking. There's a choice of routes from Tarbert to the ferry port of **Leverburgh**, which connects with North Uist: the east coast, known as **Na Baigh** (The Bays), is rugged and seemingly inhospitable, while the **west coast** is endowed with some of the finest stretches of golden sand in the whole of the archipelago, buffeted by the Atlantic winds. Several buses set off from Tarbert, Sundays excepted, travelling out along the east coast, and returning via all points along the west coast – for more information, see "Travel details" (p.340) or contact Tarbert tourist office.

Na Baigh (The Bays)

Paradoxically, most people on South Harris live along the harsh eastern coastline of **Bays** rather than the more fertile west side. But not by choice – they were evicted from their original crofts to make way for sheep-grazing. Despite the uncompromising lunar-esque terrain – mostly bare grey gneiss and heather – the crofters managed to establish "lazybeds" (small labour-intensive raised plots between the rocks fertilized by seaweed and peat), a few of which are still in use even today. The narrow sea lochs provide shelter for fishing boats, while the interior is speckled with freshwater lochans, and the whole coast is now served by the endlessly meandering **Golden Road** (so called because of the expense of constructing it).

There are just a few places to stay along the coast, the most obvious being the **hostel** (☎01851/511255) three miles south of Tarbert in **DRINISIADAR**

(Drinishader); alternatively, there's *Hillhead* (☎01859/511226; ①; April–Oct), a good tweed-making B&B in **SCADABHAGH** (Scadabay).

Six miles beyond Liceasto at **LINGREABHAGH** (Lingarabay), the road skirts the foot of **Roineabhal** (1508ft), the southernmost mountain of the island and known as *An Aite Boidheach* (The Beautiful Place). The majority of the locals are currently fighting to prevent Redland Aggregates building one of Europe's largest superquarries here, which would demolish virtually the entire mountain over the next seventy years. Environmentalists charge that local fishing grounds would be badly affected, the devout are up in arms over the possibility of Sunday working, and the initial promise of 100 much-needed new jobs has been reduced on the evidence of a public enquiry to just 25. At the time of writing, the final outcome of the public enquiry was about to be declared.

Roghadal (Rodel)

A mile or so from Rubha Reanais (Renish Point), the southern tip of Harris, is the old port of **ROGHADAL** (Rodel), where a smattering of ancient stone houses lies among the hillocks surrounding the dilapidated harbour where the ferry from Skye used to arrive. On top of one of these grassy humps, with sheep grazing in the graveyard, is **St Clement's Church** (Tur Chliamainn), burial place of the MacLeods of Harris and Dunvegan in Skye. Dating from the 1520s – in other words pre-Reformation, hence the big castellated tower – the church was saved from ruination in the eighteenth century, and fully restored in 1873 by the Countess of Dunmore. The bare interior is distinguished by its wall tombs, notably that of the founder, Alasdair Crotach (also known as Alexander MacLeod), whose heavily weathered effigy lies beneath an intriguing backdrop and canopy of sculpted reliefs depicting vernacular and religious scenes – elemental representations of, among others, a stag hunt, the Holy Trinity, St Michael, and the devil and an angel weighing the souls of the dead. Look out, too, for the *sheila-na-gig* halfway up the south side of the church tower; unusually, she has a brother displaying his genitalia, below a carving of St Clement on the west face.

The west coast

The main road from Tarbert into South Harris snakes its way west for ten miles across the boulder-strewn interior to reach the coast. Once there, you get a view of the most stunning **beach**, the vast golden strand of **Tràigh Losgaintir**. The road continues to ride above a chain of sweeping sands, backed by rich **machair**, that stretches for nine miles along the Atlantic coast. In good weather, the scenery is particularly impressive, foaming breakers rolling along the golden sands set against the rounded peaks of the mountains to the north and the islet-studded turquoise sea to the west – and even on the dullest day the sand manages to glow beneath the waves. A short distance out to sea is the island of **Taransay** (Tarasaigh), which once held a population of nearly a hundred, but was abandoned as recently as 1974.

Nobody bothers much if you **camp** or park beside the dune-edged beach, as long as you're careful not to churn up the machair, and there's the very good B&B, *Moravia* (☎01859/550262; ①; March–Oct), overlooking the sands at **LOSGAINTIR** (Luskentyre). Just south of **BORGH** (Borve), there's a newly built **self-catering** thatched house by the beach (4 people; £330 per week; (☎01859/ 550222; *ofes@zetnet.co.uk*), and a stone-built renovated steading (6 people; £295

MACHAIR

Machair is the Gaelic term used to describe the sand-enriched coastal grasslands of the Hebrides and the Northern Isles. At first sight, machair might not look very different from your average slice of green pasture, but it is, in fact, miraculous stuff. For a start, in contrast to the links of Scotland's eastern coast, the sand blown onto the machair by the prevailing westerly wind has a very high shell content (up to eighty to ninety percent) and the calcium has a liming effect on the soil. This makes machair exceptionally rich pasture, a point not lost on settlers in these parts, who have cultivated the grasslands since Neolithic times, using seaweed as manure. Indeed, the continued small-scale cultivation of machair, such as that practised by traditional crofters, is essential for minimizing erosion and ensuring the machair's long-term fertility.

For visitors, machair is celebrated primarily for its astonishing carpet of **wild flowers** that appear each year in May, June and July. Buttercups, red and white clover, tiny eyebright, vetch, selfheal and daisies predominate in this sea of flowers, but you'll also regularly find lady's bedstraw, "eggs and bacon", ragged robin, wild thyme, bog asphodel and – if you're lucky – spotted orchids. Machair is also rich in invertebrates and, consequently, birdlife; in particular, waders such as lapwing, redshank, snipe, dunlin, ringed plover, oystercatchers, and the endangered corncrake. Almost half the Scottish machair occurs in the Western Isles, and nowhere has larger uninterrupted swaths of the stuff than the Uists and Benbecula, where shell-sand beaches extend along the entire west coast. Other places with extensive machair include Barra, Coll, Tiree, Colonsay, South Harris, and parts of Lewis, Orkney and Shetland.

---

per week); the *Borvemor* gallery/café (closed Mon, Sat & Sun) serving homemade cakes and real coffee, is attached. The choicest accommodation, though, is five miles further south in **SGARASTA** (Scarista), where one of the first of the Hebridean Clearances took place in 1828, when thirty families were evicted and their homes burnt. Here, the Georgian former manse of *Scarista House* (☎01859/550238; *ian@scaristahouse.demon.co.uk*; ⑦; May–Sept) overlooks the nearby golden sands; if you can't afford to stay, it's worth splashing out and booking for dinner, as the meat and seafood served here is among the freshest and finest on the Western Isles.

If you're intrigued by the local machair, you can go on guided walks (mid-May to mid-Sept Mon & Fri 2.30pm; £2) across a particularly magnificent stretch by the golden sands close to the village of **TAOBH TUATH** (Northton), a lovely spot overlooked by the round-topped hill of Chaipabhal at the southwesternmost tip of the island. Taobh Tuath itself is no picture postcard, with the exception of the award-winning **MacGillivray Centre** (open all year at any time), whose design was inspired by the Hebridean blackhouse. However, it's the building that clearly won the accolades and not the centre, which contains precious little information on the naturalist, William MacGillivray (1796–1852), after whom it's named, and only a little on crofting and machair.

Leverburgh (An t-Ob)

From Taobh Tuath the road veers to the southeast to trim the island's south shore, eventually reaching the sprawling settlement of **LEVERBURGH** (An t-Ob), where a series of brown clapperboard houses strikes an odd Scandinavian note. Named after Lord Leverhulme, who planned to turn the place into the largest fishing port on the west coast of Scotland, it's a place that has languished for quite some time, but has picked up quite a bit since the establishment of the CalMac **car ferry** service to Otternish on North Uist. The seventy-minute journey across the skerry-strewn Sound of Harris is one of Scotland's most tortuous ferry routes, with the ship taking part in a virtual slalom race to avoid numerous hidden rocks – it's also a great crossing from which to spot seabirds and sea mammals.

There are several **B&Bs** strung out within a two-mile radius of Leverburgh: try *Caberfeidh House* (☎01859/520276; ①), a lovely stone-built Victorian building by the turnoff to the ferry, or *Sorrel Cottage* (☎01859/520319; ①), which specializes in vegetarian and seafood cooking. A cheaper alternative is the purpose-built timber-clad *An Bothan* **bunkhouse** (☎01859/520251), which has great facilities, and is only a few minutes' walk from the ferry. On the north side of the bay, *An Clachan* co-op store has a **café** (closed Sun) upstairs, and hosts temporary local history exhibitions, while *The Anchorage* (closed Sun), overlooking the ferry slipway, is basically a greasy spoon café.

North Uist (Uibhist a Tuath)

Compared to the mountainous scenery of Harris, **North Uist** – seventeen miles long and thirteen miles wide – is much flatter and for some comes as something of an anticlimax. Over half the surface area is covered by water, creating a distinctive peaty-brown lochan-studded "drowned landscape". Most visitors come here for the trout and salmon fishing and the deerstalking, both of which (along with poaching) are critical to the survival of the island's economy. Others come for the smattering of prehistoric sites and sheer peace of this windy isle, and the solitude of North Uist's vast sandy beaches, which extend – almost without interruption – along the north and west coast.

There are two **car ferry** services to North Uist: the first is from Leverburgh on Harris to Otternish (Mon–Sat 4 daily; 1hr 10min), from where there are regular **buses** to Lochmaddy, the principal village on the east coast; the second is from Tarbert on Harris, via Uig on Skye (Mon–Sat 1–2 daily; 4hr), which docks at Lochmaddy itself. Two or three daily buses leave for Lochboisdale in South Uist along the main road, and several buses travel some way round the coastal road. There is no public transport on Sundays.

Loch nam Madadh (Lochmaddy) and around

Despite being situated on the east coast, some distance away from any beach, the ferry port of **LOCH NAM MADADH (LOCHMADDY)** – "Loch of the Dogs" – makes a good base for exploring the island. Occupying a narrow, bumpy promontory, overlooked by the brooding mountains of North Lee and South Lee to the southeast, it's difficult to believe that this sleepy settlement was a large herring port as far back as the seventeenth century. Its most salient feature now is the sixteen incongruous brown weatherboarded houses, which arrived from Sweden in 1948.

If the weather's bad or you've time to kill, take a look round **Taigh Chearsabhagh** (Mon–Sat 10am–5pm; £1), a converted eighteenth-century merchant's house, now home to an excellent local museum, arts centre and café. If

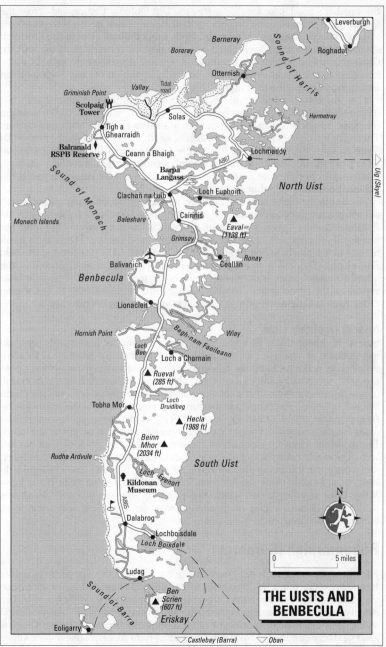

THE UISTS AND BENBECULA

© Crown copyright

the weather's good, take a walk out past the Uist Outdoor Centre, and across the footbridge that leads to the derelict Sponish House. From here a path leads east to Lochmaddy's most intriguing sight, **Both nam Faileas** (Hut of the Shadow), an ingenious drystone, turf-roofed camera obscura recently built by sculptor Chris Drury that projects the nearby land, sea and skyscape onto its back wall – take time to allow your eyes to adjust to the light, and on the way back look out for otters, who love the tidal rapids hereabouts.

The **tourist office** (mid-April to mid-Oct Mon–Fri 9am–5pm, Sat 9.30am–5.30pm; also open to greet the evening ferry; ☎01876/500321), near the quayside, has local bus and ferry timetables, and can help with **accommodation**. There are a couple of nice Victorian B&Bs, north off the main road: try the *Old Bank House* (☎01876/500275; ①). A little further north lies the *Uist Outdoor Centre* (☎01876/500480), which has **hostel** accommodation in four-person bunk rooms, and offers a wide range of outdoor activities, from canoeing round the indented coastline to "rubber tubing".

The **bar** in the *Lochmaddy Hotel* is lively and serves the usual bar meals, but it's currently not a place to recommend staying in. It is, however, a favourite with the **fishing** fraternity – there's even a set of scales in the hotel foyer – and rents out boats and sells permits for brown trout, sea trout and salmon. The island's **bank** is right by the tourist office, though it doesn't have an ATM (the nearest one is in Balivanich). There is a small **general store**, petrol and a post office, but the island's nearest large supermarket is in Solas (see opposite). The only **bike rental** on the island is from Morrison Cycle Hire (☎01876/580211), based nine miles away in **Cairinis** (Carinish), but they will deliver to Lochmaddy.

Nearby Neolithic sites

Several prehistoric sites lie within easy cycling distance of Lochmaddy (or walking distance, if you use the bus/postbus for the outward journey). The most remarkable is **Barpa Langass**, a huge chambered burial cairn a short walk from the A867, seven barren miles southwest. The stones are visible from the road and, unless the weather's good, it's not worth making a closer inspection as the chamber has collapsed and is now too dangerous to enter. A mile to the southeast, by *Langass Lodge* (☎01876/500285; ④; closed Feb), whose restaurant and bar snacks feature local seafood, a rough track leads to the small stone circle of **Pobull Fhinn**, which enjoys a much more picturesque location overlooking a narrow loch. The circle covers a large area and, although the stones are not that huge, they occupy an intriguing amphitheatre cut into the hillside. Three miles northwest of Lochmaddy along the A865 you'll find **Na Fir Bhreige** (The Three False Men), three standing stones which, depending on your legend, mark the graves of three spies buried alive or three men who deserted their wives and were turned to stone by a witch.

Bhearnaraigh (Berneray)

For those in search of still more seclusion, there's the low-lying island of **Berneray** – two miles by three, with a population of about 140 – now accessible via a brand-new causeway from **Otternish**, eight miles north of Lochmaddy. The island's main claim to fame is as the birthplace of Giant MacAskill (see p.291) and as the favoured holiday hideaway of that other great eccentric, Prince Charles, lover of Gaelic culture and royal potato-picker to local crofter, "Splash" MacKillop.

Apart from the sheer peace and isolation, the island's main draw for non-royals is a three-mile-long sandy beach on the west and north coast, backed by rabbit-free dunes and machair. The other great draw is the wonderful GHHT **hostel**, which occupies a pair of thatched blackhouses in a lovely spot by a beach, beyond Loch a Bhàigh and the main village. Alternatively you can follow in the prince's footsteps and stay (and help out) at "Splash" MacKillop's *Burnside Croft* **B&B** (☎01876/540235; ②; Feb–Nov), and enjoy "storytelling evenings"; bike rental is also available. There are several **tearooms** currently functioning along the main road, including one in the community centre at the end of the road to **Borgh** (Borve), all of which serve simple refreshments, and, with the new causeway in place, there's now a **bus** connection with Lochmaddy.

The coastal road via Solas (Sollas)

The A865, which skirts the northern and western shoreline of North Uist for more than thirty miles, takes you through the most scenic sections of the island. Once you've left the boggy east coast and passed the turning to Otternish, the road reaches the parish of **SOLAS** (Sollas), which stands at the centre of a couple of superb tidal strands – sea green at high tide, golden sand at low tide – backed by large tracts of machair that are blanketed with wild flowers in summer. A new memorial opposite the local co-op recalls the appallingly brutal Clearances undertaken by Lord MacDonald of Sleat in Solas. The current laird, Lord Granville, who owns much of North Uist, occupies the large house on the tidal island of **Vallay** (Bhalaigh), which is connected by a road that crosses the largest of the two strands. For a comfortable, friendly **B&B**, with great views across Vallay Strand, head for *Struan House* (☎01876/560282; ①; April–Sept).

Beyond Solas, the rolling hills that occupy the centre of North Uist slope down to the sea. Here, in the northwest corner of the island, you'll find **Scolpaig Tower**, a castellated folly on an islet in Loch Scolpaig, erected as a famine relief project in the nineteenth century – you can reach it, with some difficulty, across stepping stones. A tarmac track leads down past the loch and tower to Scolpaig Bay, beyond which lies the rocky shoreline of **Griminish Point**, the closest landfall to St Kilda (see p.316), which is clearly visible on the horizon in fine weather, looming like some giant dinosaur's skeleton emerging from the sea.

Roughly three miles south of Scolpaig Tower, through the sand dunes, is the **Balranald RSPB Reserve**, one of the last breeding grounds of the corncrake, among Europe's most endangered birds. Sightings are rare, partly because the birds are very good at hiding in long grass, but the males' loud "craking" is relatively easy to hear from May to July. From the excellent new **visitor centre** there's a two-hour walk along the headland, marked out by discreet white pegs, giving you ample opportunity for appreciating the wonderful carpet of flowers that covers the machair in summer, and for spotting corn buntings and arctic terns inland, and gannets and Manx shearwaters out to sea – guided walks take place throughout the summer (May–Aug Tues & Fri 2pm; ☎01878/602188).

Children might enjoy a visit to the **Uist Animal Visitor Centre** (daily 11am–7pm; £2), a farm that lies just off the main road, beyond Paible School, in **CEANN A BHAIGH** (Bayhead). Here, you can see Eriskay ponies, Highland cattle, Scottish wildcats and other rare Scottish breeds at close quarters; the centre also has a café, and **horse-drawn Romany caravans** to rent (☎01876/510223). Adults may prefer to continue a couple of miles down the main road and pop into the *Westford Inn*, a **pub** in **Claddach Chirceboist** (Claddach Kirkibost), that occasionally has live music.

Clachan to Griamsaigh (Grimsay)

At **CLACHAN NA LUIB**, by the crossroads with the A867 from Lochmaddy, there's a post office and general store. Offshore, to the south, lie two tidal dune and machair islands, the largest of which is **Baleshare** (Baile Sear), with its fantastic three-mile-long beach, connected by causeway to North Uist. In Gaelic the island's name means "east village", its twin "west village" having disappeared under the sea during a freak storm in the fifteenth or sixteenth century. This also isolated the **Monarch Islands** (sometimes known by their old Norse name of Heisgeir or Heisker), once connected to North Uist at low tide, now eight miles out to sea. The islands, which are connected with each other at low tide, were inhabited until the 1930s when the last remaining families moved to North Uist. In an isolated position, overlooking Baleshare, is *Taigh mo Sheanair* (☎01876/580246), a very welcoming, family-run **hostel**, where you can also **camp**. The hostel is clearly signposted from the main road, from which it's a good fifteen-minute walk.

On leaving North Uist the main road squeezes along a series of single-track causeways, built by the military in 1960, that cross the tidal rapids separating North Uist from Benbecula. The causeways trim the west edge of **Griomasaigh** (Grimsay), a peaceful, little-visited, rocky island that's really quite pretty, especially around **BAGH MOR** (Baymore). The main source of employment is lobster fishing, which takes place at the modern pier in **NA CEALLAN** (Kallin), where there's also a reasonable little B&B, *Glendale* (☎01870/602029; ①).

Benbecula (Beinn na Faoghla)

Blink and you could miss the pancake-flat island of **Benbecula** (put the stress on the second syllable), sandwiched between Protestant North Uist and Catholic South Uist. Most visitors simply trundle along the main road that cuts across the middle of the island in less than five miles – not such a bad idea, since nearly half the island's 1200 population are Royal Artillery personnel, working at the missile range on South Uist, and the noise on both islands can be deafening during practice sessions. Economically, the area has, of course, benefited enormously from the military presence, though the impact on the environment and Gaelic culture (with so many English-speakers around) has been less positive. There is talk of the military pulling out altogether – a devastating prospect for most islanders.

Nearly all the military personnel live in the depressing, barracks-like housing developments of **BAILE A MHANAICH** (Balivanich), the grim, grey capital of Benbecula in the northwest. The only reason to come here at all is if you happen to be flying into or out of **Benbecula airport** (direct flights to Glasgow, Barra and Stornoway), need to take money out of the Bank of Scotland ATM (the only one on the Uists), or stock up on provisions, best done at the old NAAFI store (now a Spar supermarket; open daily), to the west of the post office. There's no tourist office and, if you've got your own transport, there's no need **to stay** here, but if you're reliant on public transport try the modern **hostel** *Taigh-na-Cille* (☎01870/602522), within easy walking distance of the airport, on the road to

North Uist. The best thing about Balivanich is *Stepping Stone*, the purpose-built **café/restaurant** situated opposite the post office, a place with an ambivalent character: the café bit is cheap and cheerful, offering filled rolls and chips with everything, while the mezzanine seating area is home to *Sinteag* restaurant, where the four-course lunch for £10 is a bargain, and the evening's à la carte menu is almost twice the price. **Car rental** is available at the airport from Ask Car Hire (☎01870/602818), who are based in neighbouring Uachdar, where you'll also find *MacLean's Bakery* (closed Sun), useful for amassing a picnic.

The nearest **campsite**, *Shell Bay* (☎01870/602447; April–Oct), is in the south of the island at **LIONACLEIT** (Liniclate). Adjacent is the modern **Sgoil Lionacleit**, the only secondary school (and public swimming pool) on the Uists and Benbecula, and home to a small **museum**, which acts as a temporary exhibition space for Museum nan Eilean (Mon, Tues & Thurs 9am–4pm, Wed 9am–12.30pm & 1.30–4pm, Fri 9am–8pm, Sat 11am–1pm & 2–4pm). The island's most comfortable **hotel**, *Dark Island Hotel* (☎01870/602414; ⑤), is also next door, though it's no charmer from the outside. It serves bar meals and has a moderately expensive restaurant, featuring local specialities such as Grimsay lobsters, but you'll get better value for money at the *Orasay Inn*, just across the water in South Uist (see p.334).

South Uist (Uibhist a Deas)

To the south of Benbecula, the island of **South Uist** is arguably the most appealing of the southern chain of islands. The west coast boasts some of the region's finest machair and beaches – a necklace of gold and grey sand strung twenty miles from one end to the other – while the east coast features a ridge of high mountains rising to 2034ft at the summit of Beinn Mhor. Whatever you do, don't make the mistake of simply driving down the main A865 road, which runs down the centre of the island like a backbone. To reach the beaches (or even see them), you have to get off the main road and pass through the old crofters' villages that straggle along the west coast; to climb the mountains in the east, you need a detailed 1:25,000 map, in order to negotiate the island's maze of lochans. The only blot on South Uist's landscape is the Royal Artillery missile range, which occupies the northwest corner of the island, shattering the peace and quiet every so often.

Loch Druidibeg, Tobha Mòr (Howmore) and Kildonan Museum

The Reformation never took a strong hold in South Uist (or Barra), and the island remains Roman Catholic, as is evident from the various roadside shrines and the slender modern statue of *Our Lady of the Isles* that stands by the main road below the small hill of **Rueval**, known to the locals as "Space City" for its forest of aerials and golf balls, which help track the missiles heading out into the Atlantic. To the south of Rueval is the freshwater **Loch Druidibeg**, a breeding ground for greylag geese and a favourite spot for mute swans. The area around the loch is made up of such diverse habitats, from brackish lagoons and peaty moorland to dune and machair, that Scottish National Heritage now manage the place as a National Nature Reserve. At first glance it may not seem to be teeming with wildlife, but it's lovely countryside, and there's the chance of seeing some raptors hunting over the moorland, including hen harriers; there's a waymarked path through the reserve that begins just by the telephone box on the main road in **Stadhlaigearraidh** (Stilligarry).

One of the best places to gain access to the sandy shoreline is at **TOBHA MÒR** (Howmore), a pretty little crofting settlement with a fair number of restored houses, many still thatched, including one distinctively roofed in brown heather. A GHHT **hostel** (no phone) occupies one such house near the village church, from where it's an easy walk across the flower-infested machair to the gorgeous beach. Close by the hostel are the shattered, lichen-encrusted remains of no fewer than four medieval churches and chapels, and a burial ground now harbouring just a few scattered graves. The sixteenth-century **Clanranald Stone**, carved with the arms of the clan who ruled over South Uist from 1370 until 1839, used to lie here. It's now displayed in the nearby Kildonan Museum (see below), after it was stolen in 1990 and removed to London by a Canadian artist, Lawren Maben. It took three months before anyone noticed it had disappeared. Five years later, it was discovered by the artist's father in a bedsit near Euston Station, as he sorted out his son's belongings, following his "death by misadventure".

There's much more besides the aforementioned stone at the **Kildonan Museum** (Mon–Sat 10am–5pm, Sun 2–5pm; £1.80), on the main road five miles south of Tobha Mòr. Mock-ups of Hebridean kitchens through the ages, two lovely box beds and an impressive selection of old photos are accompanied by a firmly unsentimental yet poetic written text on crofting life in the last two centuries. Among the more unusual exhibits is a pair of ornamental shoes made of deer hooves. The museum also runs a café serving sandwiches and home-made cakes, and has a choice of historical videos for those really wet and windy days. A little to the south of the museum, the road passes a cairn that sits amongst the foundations of **Flora MacDonald**'s childhood home (see p.296); she was born nearby, but the house no longer stands.

Without doubt, the best **hotel** on the Uists is the *Orasay Inn* (☎01870/610298, *orasayinn@btinternet.com*; ③), located in a peaceful spot off the road to Loch a Charnain (Lochcarnan), in the northeastern corner of the island. It's nothing to look at from the outside, but ask for a room looking east out towards the Minch and you can enjoy a bit of birdwatching from your balcony. The bar meals are good value, the restaurant moderately expensive, and the breakfasts huge. If you're just passing along the main road and need a bit to eat, pop into the *Crofters Kitchen*, an inexpensive **café** near the causeway to Benbecula, serving not only herring in oatmeal, toasted sarnies, tatties and neaps, but also "flaky smoked salmon". This is a speciality you can also buy straight from its source, *Salar* (closed Sat & Sun), further along the road to Loch a Charnain, beyond the *Orasay Inn* turnoff.

Lochboisdale (Loch Baghasdail)

Although South Uist's chief settlement and ferry port, **LOCHBOISDALE**, occupying a narrow, bumpy promontory on the east coast, has, if anything, even less to offer than Lochmaddy, with just the *Lochboisdale Hotel* for somewhere to have a drink and a proper meal. If you're arriving here late at night on the seven-hour boat trip from Oban (or from Castlebay on Barra; 1hr 50min), you should try to book accommodation in advance; otherwise, head for the **tourist office** (Easter to mid-Oct Mon–Sat 9am–5pm; also open to meet the night ferry; ☎01878/700286). Next door to the tourist office is a useful coin-operated shower and toilet block (daily 9am–5pm). There are several small, perfectly ordinary **B&Bs** within comfortable walking distance of the dock, including *Bayview* (☎01878/700329; ②; March–Oct) and *Lochside Cottage* (☎01878/700472; ②), and a few more luxurious ones slightly further afield, such as *The Sheiling* (☎01878/700504; ①), in Gearraidh Sheile (Garryhallie), near Dalabrog (Daliburgh). The shops in Lochboisdale are pretty limited; the nearest super-market is in Dalabrog.

Perhaps the best place to hole up in this part of South Uist is the *Polochar Inn* (☎01878/700215; ④), eight miles from Lochboisdale, right on the south coast overlooking the Sound of Barra, with its own sandy beach close by. If you're head-ing for Barra you could take the passenger ferry from **Ludag jetty**, two miles east of the *Polochar Inn*, which lands at Eoligarry on Barra's north coast – and when the causeway to Eriskay is complete, in 2001, there are plans to institute a car ferry service to Barra.

Eriskay (Eiriosgaigh)

To the south of South Uist lies the barren, hilly island of **Eriskay**, famous for its patterned jerseys (on sale at the community centre), and a peculiar breed of pony, originally used for carrying peat and seaweed. The island, which measures just over two miles by one, shelters a small fishing community of about 150, and makes a great day-trip from South Uist, as long as the weather's fine. The ferry from Ludag, across the treacherously shallow waters of the Sound of Eriskay, will be made redundant when the new causeway is finished in 2001.

For a small island, Eriskay has had more than its fair share of historical head-lines. The island's main beach on the west coast, Coilleag a Phrionnsa (Prince's Cockle Strand), was where **Bonnie Prince Charlie** landed on Scottish soil on July 23, 1745 – the sea bindweed that grows there to this day is said to have sprung from the seeds Charles brought with him from France. The prince, as yet unaccustomed to hardship, spent his first night in a local blackhouse, and ate a couple of flounders, though he apparently couldn't take the peat smoke and chose to sleep sitting up rather than endure the damp bed.

Eriskay's other claim to fame came in 1941 when the 8000-ton **SS Politician** or "*Polly*" as it's fondly known, sank on its way from Liverpool to Jamaica, along with its cargo of bicycle parts, £3 million in Jamaican currency and 264,000 bottles of whisky, inspiring Compton MacKenzie's book, and the Ealing comedy (filmed on Barra in 1948), *Whisky Galore!* (released as *Tight Little Island* in the US). The real story was somewhat less romantic, especially for the 36 islanders who were charged with illegal possession by the Customs and Excise officers, nineteen of whom were found guilty and imprisoned in Inverness. The ship's stern can still be seen at low tide northwest of Calvay Island in the Sound of Eriskay, and one of the original bottles (and lots of other related memorabilia) is on show in *Am Politician*, the island's purpose-built pub near the two cemeteries on the west coast.

If you're here for the day, the best route to take is to head west from Haun jetty towards **St Michael's Church**, built in 1903 in a vaguely Spanish style on raised ground above the harbour. The most striking features of the church are the bell, which comes from the World War I battle cruiser *Derfflinger*, the last of the scuttled German fleet to be salvaged from Scapa Flow, and the altar, which is made from the bow of a lifeboat. From here, it's a short walk to the **community centre** (times according to the ferry; closed Sun), which serves tea in the summer, sells jumpers, and occasionally hosts exhibitions. The walk up to the island's highest point, **Ben Scrien** (607ft), is well worth the effort on a clear day, as you can see the whole island, plus Barra, South Uist, and across the sea to Skye, Rùm, Coll and Tiree (2–3hr return from the jetty). On the way up or down, look out for the diminutive Eriskay ponies, who roam free on the hills but tend to graze around Loch Crakavaig, the island's freshwater source.

Until the causeway is complete, there are three types of **ferry** to Eriskay from Ludag jetty on South Uist – car ferry, passenger ferry and a rigid inflatable. Which one runs depends on the tides and demand, so you need to get hold of a copy of the monthly timetable from the tourist office or phone the enquiry line (☎01878/720261). You can **camp rough** with permission, or stay (for a minimum of three nights) at the **self-catering** chalet run by Mrs Campbell (4 people; £180 per week; ☎01878/720274).

Barra (Barraigh)

Just four miles wide and eight miles long, **Barra** has a well-deserved reputation for being the Western Isles in miniature. It has sandy beaches, backed by machair, glacial mountains, prehistoric ruins, Gaelic culture, and a laid-back, welcoming Catholic population of just over 1300. Like some miniature feudal island state, it was ruled over for centuries, with relative benevolence, by the MacNeils. Unfortunately, however, the family sold the island in 1838 to Colonel Gordon of Cluny, who had also bought Benbecula, South Uist and Eriskay. The colonel deemed the starving crofters "redundant", and offered to turn Barra into a state penal colony. The government declined, so the colonel called in the police and proceeded with some of the most cruel forced Clearances in the Hebrides. In 1937, the 45th chief of the MacNeil clan bought back most of the island, and the island returned with relief to its more familiar, feudal roots.

Castlebay (Bagh a Chaisteil)

The only settlement of any size is **CASTLEBAY** (Bagh a Chaisteil), which curves around the barren rocky hills of a wide bay on the south side of the island. It's difficult to imagine it now, but Castlebay was a herring port of some significance back in the nineteenth century, with up to 400 boats in the harbour and curing and packing factories ashore. Barra's religious allegiance is immediately announced by the large Catholic church, Our Lady, Star of the Sea, which overlooks the bay; to underline the point, there's a Madonna and Child on the slopes of **Heaval** (1260ft), the largest peak on Barra, and a fairly easy hike from the bay.

As its name suggests, Castlebay has a castle in its bay, the medieval islet-fortress of **Kisimul Castle** (Mon, Wed & Sat tours at 2pm; £3; ☎01871/810336), ancestral home of the MacNeil clan. The castle burnt down in the eighteenth century, but when the 45th MacNeil chief – conveniently enough an architect by training – bought the island back in 1937, he set about restoring the castle. You can take a tour round it by catching the ferry from the slipway at the bottom of Main Street (☎01871/810449).

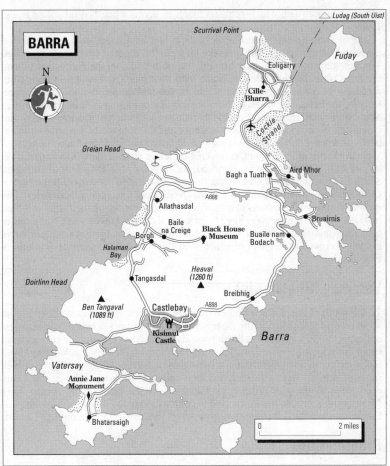

© Crown copyright

To learn more about the history of the island, and about the postal system of the Western Isles, it's worth paying a visit to **Barra Heritage Centre** (Mon–Fri 11am–5pm; £1), housed in an unprepossessing block on the road that leads west out of town.

North to Cockle Strand and Eoligarry

Following the west coast round will bring you to the island's finest sandy beaches, particularly those at Halaman Bay and near the village of **ALLATHASDAL** (Allasdale). At **BAILE NA CREIGE** (Craigston), between the two, a dead-end road leads inland to the **Black House Museum** (June–Oct Mon–Fri 11am–5pm; £1), an isolated thatched croft house, half a mile's walk from the end of the metalled road, which remains much as it was when last inhabited in the 1970s.

One of Barra's most fascinating sights is, in fact, its **airport**, on the north side of the island, where planes land and take off from the crunchy shell sands of Tràigh Mhór, better known as **Cockle Strand**; the exact timing of the flights depends on the tides, since at high tide the beach (and therefore the runway) is covered in water. As its name suggests, the strand is also famous for its cockles and cockleshells, the latter being used to make harling (the rendering used on most Scottish houses). In 1994, mechanical cockle extraction using tractors was introduced, and quickly began to decimate the cockle stocks and threaten the beach's use as an airport – as a result it has now been banned, in favour of traditional hand-raking.

To the north of the airport, connected by a thin strip of land, is the coastal village of **EOLIGARRY** (Eolaigearraidh), with a passenger ferry link to Ludag on South Uist and several sheltered sandy bays close by. To the west of the village is **Cille-Bharra**, burial ground of the MacNeils (and Compton MacKenzie). The ground lies beside the ruins of a medieval church and two chapels, one of which has been reroofed to provide shelter for several carved gravestones, some rather bizarre religious and secular objects, and a replica of an eleventh-century rune-inscribed cross, the original of which is in the National Museum of Scotland in Edinburgh.

Vatersay (Bhatarsaigh)

To the south of Barra, the island of **Vatersay** (Bhatarsaigh), shaped rather like an apple core, is now linked to the main island by a causeway – a mile or so southwest of Castlebay – to try and stem the depopulation which has brought the current head count down to just over seventy. The main settlement (also known as Vatersay) is on the south coast, and to get to it you must cross a narrow isthmus, with the golden sands of Vatersay Bay to the east, and the stones and sands of Bàgh Siar a few hundred yards to the west. Above, on the dunes of the latter, is the **Annie Jane Monument**, a granite needle erected to commemorate the 350 emigrants who lost their lives when the *Annie Jane* ran aground off Vatersay in 1853 en route to Canada.

Practicalities

If you're arriving at Eoligarry, on the passenger **ferry** from South Uist, you can rent **bikes** from Barra Cycle Hire (☎01871/810284), who will meet you at the ferry. There's also a fairly decent **bus/postbus** service which does the rounds of the island (Mon–Sat). Arriving in Castlebay by **car ferry** from Lochboisdale, Oban or Mallaig is more straightforward, and you can rent **bikes** from Castlebay Cycle Hire (☎01871/810284), half a mile east of the town centre. **Car rental** is available from Barra Car Hire (☎01871/810243), who will deliver vehicles to the airport or either ferry terminal. Barra's **tourist office** (April to mid-Oct Mon–Sat 9am–5pm; also open to greet the ferry; ☎01871/810336) is situated on Main Street in Castlebay just round from the pier, and can help book accommodation, though it's as well to book in advance for B&Bs and hotels. Those interested in a **boat trip** to the sea ccliffs on the island of **Mingulay**, south of Barra, whose last two inhabitants were evacuated in 1934, should phone Mr Campbell (☎01871/810303) or enquire at the *Castlebay Hotel*.

In Castlebay itself, the *Castlebay Hotel* (☎01871/810223; ④) is the most comfortable **place to stay**, followed by *Tigh-na-Mara* (☎01871/810304; ②; April–Oct), a guest house a couple of minutes' walk from the pier by the sea; another good choice is *Grianamul* (☎01871/810416, *ronnie.macneil@virgin.net*; ③; April–Oct). Although architecturally something of a 1970s monstrosity, the *Isle of Barra Hotel* (☎01871/810383, *barrahotel@aol.com*; ⑤; late-April to early Sept) enjoys a classic location overlooking Halaman Bay. The best option outside the *Castlebay* is *Northbay House* (☎01871/890255; ②), which is a converted school in Buaile nam Bodach (Balnabodach). There's a new GHHT **hostel** (no phone) in Breibhig (Brevig), a couple of miles east of Castlebay, where you can also **camp**; if you're camping rough you can use the toilets and shower in the CalMac office on the pier.

In contrast to the rest of the Western Isles, Castlebay is positively buzzing on a Sunday morning, when all the shops open for the folk coming out of Mass. The *Kisimul Galley* **café** serves breakfast all day every day, and specializes in cheap-and-cheerful Scottish fry-ups – try the stovies and the bridies. For more fancy fare, head to the *Castlebay Hotel*'s cosy **bar**, which regularly has cockles, crabs and scallops on its menu, and good views out over the bay. If the *Castlebay* isn't serving food, try the bar at the neighbouring *Craigard Hotel*, which serves food whenever it's open. There are two bars at the *Isle of Barra Hotel*, one of which is the locals' pub, while the other is more of a cocktail bar and lies within the hotel itself; the food here also features excellent local fish and seafood and the hotel runs an Oriental takeaway. The only two watering holes in the north of the island are the airport terminal café and the lively bar of the *Heathbank Hotel* in **Bagh a Tuath** (Northbay). **Films** are occasionally shown on Saturday evenings at the local school – look out for the posters – where there is also a swimming pool, library and sports centre, all of which are open to the general public.

In Vatersay, the friendly community centre is open daily in season for soups, snacks, tea and cakes.

travel details

TRAINS

Aberdeen to: Kyle of Lochalsh (Mon–Sat 1 daily; 5hr).

Edinburgh to: Kyle of Lochalsh (Mon–Sat 1 daily; 6hr 50min).

Fort William to: Mallaig (Mon–Sat 6 daily, Sun 3 daily; 1hr 25min).

Glasgow (Queen St) to: Mallaig (Mon–Sat 3 daily, Sun 2 daily; 5hr 10min); Oban (Mon–Sat 3 daily, Sun 2 daily; 3hr).

Inverness to: Kyle of Lochalsh (Mon–Sat 3 daily, Sun 1 daily; 2hr 30min).

BUSES

Mainland

Edinburgh to: Broadford (1 daily; 6hr 30min); Oban (1 daily; 4hr); Portree (1 daily; 7hr 40min).

Glasgow to: Broadford (3 daily; 5hr 30min); Oban (Mon–Sat 4 daily, Sun 2 daily; 3hr); Portree (3 daily; 6hr 10min); Uig (2 daily; 7hr 40min).

Inverness to: Broadford (Mon–Sat 3 daily, Sun 2 daily; 2hr 50min); Portree (Mon–Sat 3 daily, Sun 2 daily; 3hr 15min).

Kyle of Lochalsh to: Broadford (7 daily; 30min); Portree (7daily; 1hr).

Skye

Armadale to: Broadford (Mon–Sat 5 daily, Sun 2 daily; 45min); Portree (Mon–Sat 6 daily, Sun 1 daily; 1hr 20min); Sligachan (Mon–Sat 4 daily, Sun 1 daily; 1hr 10min).

Broadford to: Portree (10–12 daily; 40min).

Dunvegan to: Glendale (Mon–Sat 1–4 daily; 30min).

Kyleakin to: Broadford (Mon–Sat 12–14 daily, Sun 7 daily; 15min); Portree (Mon–Sat 6–7 daily, Sun 5 daily; 1hr); Sligachan (Mon–Sat 7–8 daily, Sun 5 daily; 45min); Uig (Mon–Sat 2 daily; 1hr 20min).

Portree to: Carbost (Mon–Fri 2–3 daily, Sat 1 daily; 35min); Duntulm (Mon–Sat 2–3 daily; 1hr); Dunvegan (Mon–Sat 4 daily; 50min); Fiskavaig (Mon–Fri 2 daily, Sat 1 daily; 50min); Staffin (Mon–Sat 3 daily; 40min); Uig (Mon–Sat 4–5 daily; 30min).

Lewis/Harris

Stornoway to: Barabhas (Mon–Fri 11–13 daily, Sat 8 daily; 25min); Calanais (Mon–Sat 5–7 daily; 40min); Carlabhagh (Mon–Sat 4–6 daily; 1hr); Leverburgh (Mon–Sat 4–5 daily; 2hr); Point (Mon–Sat hourly; 40min); Port Nis (Mon–Sat 6–9 daily; 1hr); Siabost (Mon–Sat 6 daily; 45min); Tarbert (Mon–Sat 4–5 daily; 1hr 10min); Timsgearraidh (Mon–Sat 1–2 daily; 1hr–1hr 30min); Tolsta (Mon–Sat every 90min; 40min).

Tarbert to: Scalpay (Mon–Fri 5 daily, Sat 3 daily; 20min); Huisinis (Tues, Fri & schooldays 3–4 daily; 45min); Leverburgh (Mon–Sat 8 daily; 50min); Leverburgh via the Bays (Mon–Sat 3–4 daily; 1hr 10min).

Uists/Benbecula

Lochboisdale to: Ludag (Mon–Sat 6–7 daily; 30–45min).

Lochmaddy to: Balivanich (Mon–Sat 4–5 daily; 45min–2hr); Balranald (Mon–Sat 4–5 daily; 50min); Berneray (Mon–Sat 5–6 daily; 30min); Lochboisdale (Mon–Sat 2–3 daily; 2hr).

Otternish to: Balivanich (Mon–Sat 3–4 daily; 1hr–2hr 20min); Lochmaddy (Mon–Sat 6–7 daily; 20–50min).

Barra

Castlebay to: Airport/Eoligarry (Mon–Sat hourly; 35min/45min); Vatersay (Mon–Sat 8 daily; 20min).

FERRIES (SUMMER TIMETABLE)

To Barra: Lochboisdale–Castlebay (Tues, Thurs, Fri & Sun; 1hr 40min); Mallaig–Castlebay (Sun; 3hr 45min); Oban–Castlebay (Mon, Wed, Thurs & Sat; 5hr).

To Canna: Eigg–Canna (Mon & Sat; 2hr 45min–3hr); Mallaig–Canna (Mon, Wed, Fri & Sat; 2hr 30min–4hr 15min); Muck–Canna (Sat; 2hr 15min); Rùm–Canna (Mon, Wed & Sat; 1hr–1hr 15min) .

To Eigg: Canna–Eigg (Fri & Sat; 2hr 15min–3hr); Mallaig–Eigg (Mon, Tues, Thurs & Sat; 1hr 30–1hr 50min); Muck–Eigg (Tues, Thurs & Sat; 45–50min); Rùm–Eigg (Fri & Sat; 1hr 15min–2hr).

To Eriskay: Ludag–Eriskay (at least 2 daily; 20min).

To Harris: Lochmaddy–Tarbert via Uig (Mon–Sat 1–2 daily; 4hr); Otternish–Leverburgh (Mon–Sat 4 daily; 1hr 10min); Uig–Tarbert (Mon–Sat 1–2 daily; 1hr 45min).

To Lewis: Ullapool–Stornoway (Mon–Sat 2 daily; 2hr 40min).

To Muck: Eigg–Muck (Tues, Thurs & Sat; 1hr); Canna–Muck (Sat; 2hr 15min); Mallaig–Muck (Tues, Thurs & Sat; 2hr 40min–4hr 45min); Rùm–Muck (Sat; 1hr 15min).

To North Uist: Leverburgh–Otternish (Mon–Sat 4 daily; 1hr 10min); Tarbert–Lochmaddy via Uig (Mon–Sat 1–2 daily; 4hr); Uig–Lochmaddy (1–2 daily; 1hr 50min).

To Raasay: Sconser–Raasay (Mon–Sat 9–10 daily; 15min).

To Rùm: Canna–Rùm (Wed, Fri & Sat; 1hr–1hr 15min); Eigg–Rùm (Mon & Sat; 1hr 30min–2hr); Mallaig–Rùm (Mon, Wed, Fri & Sat; 1hr 45min–3hr 30min); Muck–Rùm (Sat; 1hr 15min).

To Skye: Glenelg–Kylerhea (daily frequently; 15min); Mallaig–Armadale (Mon–Sat 6–7 daily; June to mid-Sept also Sun; 30min).

To South Uist: Castlebay–Lochboisdale (Mon, Wed, Thurs & Sat; 1hr 40min); Mallaig–Lochboisdale (Tues; 3hr 30min); Oban–Lochboisdale (daily except Tues & Sun; 5hr–6hr 50min).

FLIGHTS

Benbecula to: Barra (Mon–Fri 2 daily; 20min); Stornoway (Mon–Fri 2 daily; 35min).

Glasgow to: Barra (Mon–Fri 2 daily, Sat 1 daily; 1hr 5min); Benbecula (Mon–Sat 1 daily; 1hr); Stornoway (Mon–Sat 2 daily; 1hr).

Inverness to: Stornoway (Mon–Fri 2 daily, Sat 1 daily; 20min).

CHAPTER SIX

ORKNEY AND SHETLAND

R eaching up towards the Arctic Circle, and totally exposed to turbulent Atlantic weather systems, the Orkney and Shetland islands gather neatly into two distinct and very different clusters. Often referring to themselves first as Orcadians or Shetlanders, and with unofficial but widely displayed flags, their inhabitants regard Scotland as a separate entity; the mainland to them is the one in their own archipelago, not the Scottish mainland. This feeling of detachment arises from their distinctive geography, history and culture, in which they differ not only from Scotland but also from each other.

To the south, just a short step from the Scottish mainland, are the seventy or so **Orkney Islands**. With the major exception of **Hoy**, which is high and rugged, these islands are mostly low-lying, gently sloping and richly fertile, and for centuries have provided a reasonably secure living for their inhabitants from farming and, to a much lesser extent, fishing. In spring and summer the days are long, the skies enormous, the sandy beaches dazzling and the meadows thick with wild flowers. There is a peaceful continuity to Orcadian life reflected not only in the well-preserved treasury of Stone Age settlements, such as **Skara Brae**, and standing stones, most notably the **Stones of Stenness**, but also in the rather conservative nature of society here today.

Another sixty miles north, the **Shetland Islands** are in nearly all respects a complete contrast. Dramatic cliffs, teeming with thousands of seabirds, rise straight out of the water to rugged, heather-coated hills, while ice-sculpted sea inlets cut deep into the land, offering memorable coastal walks in Shetland's endless summer evenings. With little fertile ground, Shetlanders have traditionally been crofters rather than farmers, often looking to the sea for an uncertain living in fishing and whaling or the naval and merchant services. Today islanders enthusiastically embrace new opportunities such as fish farming and computing. Nevertheless, the past isn't forgotten; the Norse heritage is clear in every roadsign and there are many well-preserved prehistoric sites, such as **Broch of Mousa** and **Jarlshof**.

Since people first began to explore the North Atlantic, Orkney and Shetland have been stepping stones on routes between Britain, Ireland and Scandinavia, and both groups have a long history of settlement, certainly from around 3500–4000 BC. The **Norse settlers**, who began to arrive from about 800 AD, with substantial migration from around 900 AD, left the islands with a unique cultural character. Orkney was a powerful Norse earldom, and Shetland (at first part of the same earldom) was ruled directly from Norway for nearly 300 years after

ISLAND WILDLIFE

Orkney and Shetland support huge numbers of **seabirds**, particularly during the breeding season from April to August, when cliffs and coastal banks are alive with thousands of guillemots, razorbills, puffins, fulmars and, particularly in Shetland, gannets. Arctic terns are often to be found on small offshore islets or gravelly spits. On coastal heathland or moorland you should see arctic skuas, great skuas, curlews and occasionally whimbrel or golden plover, while in remoter meadows in Orkney a corncrake may be heard. Many kinds of wild duck are present, especially in winter, but eiders are particularly common. In spring and autumn, large numbers of migrants drop in on their way north or south and very rare specimens may turn up at any time of year. Fair Isle, in particular, has a long list of rarities, and Shetland's isolation has produced its own distinctive subspecies of wren. Some of the best or most accessible bird sites have been noted in the text.

The separation of the islands from the mainland has also meant that some species of **land mammal** are absent and others have developed subspecies. For instance, Shetland has no voles but Orkney boasts its own distinctive type. However, both groups have considerable populations of seals, and Shetland is probably the best place in the whole of Europe to get to see an otter. Further offshore you may well see porpoises, dolphins and several species of whale, including minke, pilot, sperm and killer. Shetland is also home to the famous Shetland pony, whose diminutive form can be seen all over the islands; now mostly domesticated, there are a few places where the ponies still run wild.

Neither of the island groups supports many **trees**, and very few are native. However, the clifftops and meadows of both Orkney and Shetland are rich with beautiful **wild flowers**, including pink thrift, the pale-pink heather-spotted orchid, red campion and, in wetter areas, golden marsh marigolds, yellow iris and insect-eating sundew. Notable **smaller plants** include the purple Scottish primrose, which grows only in Orkney and the far north of Scotland, and the Shetland (or Edmondston's) mouse-eared chickweed, with its delicate white flower streaked with yellow, which grows only on the island of Unst.

1195. The Norse legacy is clearly evident today in place names and in dialect words; neither group was ever part of the Gaelic-speaking culture of Highland Scotland, and the later Scottish influence is essentially a Lowland one.

Orkney and Shetland may share a common Norse heritage, but the modern **transport links** between the two are surprisingly poor. In the winter, there is just one ferry a week between the two, and only two a week in the height of summer. And while it's fairly common to meet a fellow visitor who's visiting both sets of islands, it's rare to find an Orcadian who's been to Shetland, or vice versa. When leaving their homeland, for whatever reason, Shetlanders tend to go to Aberdeen, while Orcadians pop over to Caithness on the Scottish mainland. Public transport is not bad, and the council-run inter-island ferries on Shetland are very cheap; Orkney's inter-island ferries, by contrast, are expensive. If you're thinking of bringing your own vehicle, it might be worth looking into renting one locally instead, given the time and cost of the car ferries from the mainland.

It's impossible to underestimate the influence of the **weather** in these parts. The one thing you can say about it is that it's interesting, frequently dramatic. More often than not, it will be windy and rainy; though, as they say in the nearby Faroes, you can have all four seasons in one day. The wind-chill factor is not to be taken

DIALECT AND PLACE NAMES

Between the tenth and seventeenth centuries, the chief language of Orkney and Shetland was **Norn**, a Scandinavian tongue close to modern Faroese and Icelandic. After the end of Norse rule and with the transformation of the church, the law, commerce and education, Norn gradually lost out to Scots and English, eventually petering out completely in the eighteenth century. Today, Orkney and Shetland have their own dialects, and individual islands and communities within each group have local variations. The **dialects** have a Scots base, with some Old Norse words; however, they don't sound strongly Scottish, with the Orkney accent – which has been likened to the Welsh one – especially distinctive. Listed below are some of the words you're most likely to hear, including some birds' names and common elements in place names. In most cases, the Shetland form is given; the Orkney terms are very similar, if not identical.

aak	guillemot	*neesick*	porpoise
alan	storm petrel	*noost*	hollow place where a boat is drawn up
ayre	beach		
böd	fisherman's store	*norie* (or *tammie-norie*)	puffin
bonxie	great skua		
bruck	rubbish	*noup*	steep headland
burra	heath rush	*peerie* (in Orkney, often *peedie*)	small
corbie	raven		
crö	sheepfold		
du	familiar form of "you"	*plantiecrub* (or *plantiecrö*)	small drystone enclosure for growing cabbages
dunter	eider duck		
eela	rod-fishing from small boats	*quoy*	enclosed, cultivated common land
ferrylouper	incomer (Orkney)	*reestit*	cured (as in *reestit* mutton)
fourareen	four-oared boat		
foy	party or festival	*roost*	tide race
geo	coastal inlet	*scattald*	common grazing land
haa	laird's house		
hap	hand-knitted shawl	*scootie alan*	arctic skua
kame	ridge of hills	*scord*	gap or pass in a ridge of hills
kishie	basket		
maa	seagull	*shaela*	dark grey
mallie (Shetland) or *mallimak* (Orkney)	fulmar petrel	*shalder*	oystercatcher
		simmer dim	summer twilight
		sixern	six-oared boat
mool	headland	*solan*	gannet
moorit	brown	*soothmoother*	incomer (Shetland)
mootie	tiny	*tystie*	black guillemot
muckle	large	*voe*	sea inlet

lightly, and there is often a dampness or drizzle in the air, even when it's not actually raining. Even in late spring and summer, when there can be long dry spells with lots of sunshine, you still need to come prepared for wind, rain and, most frustrating of all, the occasional sea fog. The one good thing about the almost constant presence of the wind is that midges are less of a problem, except on Hoy.

ORKNEY

Just a short step from John O'Groats, the **Orkney Islands** are a unique and fiercely independent grouping. In spring and summer, the meadows and clifftops are a brilliant green, shining with wild flowers, while long days pour light onto the land and sea. For an Orcadian, the "Mainland" invariably means the largest island in Orkney, rather than the rest of Scotland, and throughout their history they've been linked to lands much further afield, principally Scandinavia. In the words of the late Orcadian poet George Mackay Brown:

Orkney lay athwart a great sea-way
from Viking times onwards, and its lore
is crowded with sailors, merchants, adventurers,
pilgrims, smugglers, storms and sea-changes.
The shores are strewn with wrack, jetsam,
occasional treasure.

Small communities began to settle in the islands around 4000 BC, and the village at **Skara Brae** on the Mainland is one of the best-preserved Stone Age settlements in Europe. This and many of the other older archeological sites, including the **Stones of Stenness** and **Maes Howe**, are concentrated in the central and western parts of the Mainland. Elsewhere the islands are scattered with chambered tombs and stone circles, a tribute to the well-developed religious and ceremonial practices taking place here from around 2000 BC. More sophisticated **Iron Age** inhabitants built fortified villages incorporating stone towers known as brochs, protected by walls and ramparts, many of which are still in place. Later, Pictish culture spread to Orkney and the remains of several of their early Christian settlements can still be seen, the best at the **Brough of Birsay** in the West Mainland, where a group of small houses is clustered around the remains of an early church. In around the ninth century, **Norse** settlers from Scandinavia arrived and the islands became Norse earldoms, forming an outpost of a powerful, expansive culture which was gradually forcing its way south. The last of the Norse earls was killed in 1231, but they had a lasting impact on the islands, leaving behind not only their language but also the great **St Magnus Cathedral** in **Kirkwall**, one of Scotland's outstanding examples of medieval architecture.

After the end of Norse rule, the islands became the preserve of **Scottish earls**, who exploited and abused the islanders, although a steady increase in sea trade did offer some chance of escape. French and Spanish ships sheltered here in the sixteenth century, and the ships of the **Hudson Bay Company** recruited hundreds of Orcadians to work in the Canadian fur trade. The islands were also an important staging post in the **whaling industry** and the herring boom, which drew great numbers of small Dutch, French and Scottish boats. More recently, the naval importance of **Scapa Flow** brought plenty of money and activity during both world wars, and left the clifftops dotted with gun emplacements and the

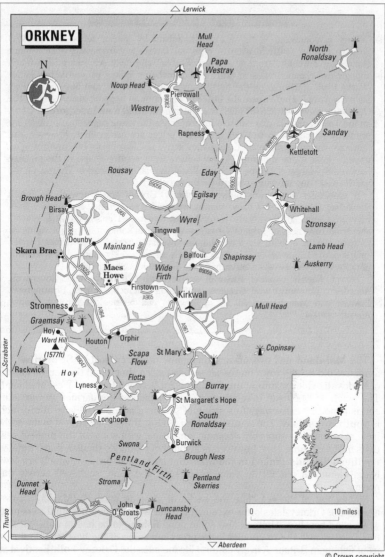

seabed scattered with wrecks, making for wonderful diving opportunities. Since the war, things have quietened down somewhat, although in the last two decades the large **oil terminal** on the island of Flotta, combined with EU funding, has brought surprise windfalls, stemming the exodus of young people. Meanwhile, many disenchanted southerners have become "ferryloupers" (incomers), moving north in search of peace and the apparent simplicity of island life.

GETTING TO ORKNEY

Orkney is connected to the Scottish mainland by several **ferry** routes. P&O Scottish Ferries (☎01856/850655) runs car ferries to **Stromness** once a week (June–Aug 2 weekly) from **Aberdeen** (8–10hr) and daily services on the much shorter and cheaper crossing (2hr) from **Scrabster**, linked by shuttle bus to the nearby town of Thurso on the north coast, which has train and bus connections from Inverness. There's also the little-known option of hopping aboard one of the Orcargo vessels (☎01856/873838) that sail into **Kirkwall** from **Invergordon** (9hr), on the Tain peninsula, just north of Inverness. As the name suggests, the ships are primarily for cargo, so facilities are basic; prices are competitive, however, and there are six sailings a week, though they arrive and leave from Invergordon at an ungodly hour in the morning. A new vehicle ferry service is also in the pipeline between St Margaret's Hope on South Ronaldsay, and Gills, east of Thurso, on the north coast (ring the tourist board for the latest).

A passenger ferry runs between **John O'Groats** and **Burwick** on South Ronaldsay (May–Sept 2–4 daily; 45min), with which the Orkney Bus service from Inverness connects; there's also a free bus service from Thurso. A day-trip is available from Inverness or John O' Groats, with a tour of some of the major sights on Orkney; details of both ferry and bus are available from John O'Groats Ferries (☎01955/611353 or 0800/731 7872). There's also a weekly (June–Aug 2 weekly; 8hr) P&O service between Stromness and **Lerwick** in Shetland.

Direct **flights** connect Kirkwall airport with Shetland, Wick, Inverness, Aberdeen, Edinburgh and Glasgow, with good connections from Birmingham, London and Manchester. All these services can be booked through British Airways (☎0345/222111).

The **Mainland** has two main settlements: the ferry port of **Stromness**, an attractive old fishing town on the far southwestern shore, and the central capital of **Kirkwall**, which stands at the dividing point between East and West Mainland. The whole of Mainland is relatively heavily populated and farmed throughout, and is joined by causeways to a string of southern islands, the largest of which is **South Ronaldsay**. The southern island of **Hoy**, the second largest in the archipelago, presents a superbly dramatic landscape, with some of the highest sea-cliffs in the country. Hoy, however, is atypical of Orkney's smaller, much quieter **northern islands** (linked to the Mainland by regular ferries), which are low-lying, elemental but fertile outcrops of rock and sand, scattered across the ocean.

Rolling out of the sea "like the backs of sleeping whales" (Mackay Brown again), the Orkney Isles offer excellent coastal **walking** and beautiful sweeping white-sand beaches. There is also some good **fishing** to be had in both salt and fresh water, with the rivers and lochs providing some of the best trout and sea-trout fishing in Britain. A lively cultural life includes the **Orkney Folk Festival** in May, and a science festival in September, both of which have events throughout the islands. June sees the **St Magnus Festival**, an arts festival based in Kirkwall, while July is peppered with several island regattas, followed by numerous agricultural shows, culminating in the County Show held in the middle of August. To find out what's on (and what the weather's going to be like), tune in to Radio Orkney on 93.7FM (Mon–Fri 7.30–8am), and buy yourself a copy of the *Orcadian*, which comes out on a Thursday.

Getting around

Bus services on the Orkney Mainland are fairly infrequent, and virtually non-existent on a Sunday, with some of the most interesting areas not served at all; on the islands, there's usually a bus service to and from the ferry terminal and that's all. However, **cycling** is cheap and, with few steep hills and modest distances, relatively easy, though the wind can make it hard going. Bikes can be rented in Kirkwall, Stromness and on most of the smaller islands. Bringing a **car** to Orkney is straightforward, if not exactly cheap; alternatively, you can rent one in Kirkwall, Stromness or on several of the islands. Especially if time is limited, it may be worth considering one of the informative bus or minibus **tours**: Wildabout Orkney Tours (☎01856/851011, *wildabout@orknet.co.uk*) offer good-value tours of the chief sights on the Mainland and Hoy.

Getting to the other islands from the Mainland isn't difficult, though it is relatively expensive: Orkney Ferries (☎01856/872044) operates several **ferries** daily to Hoy, Shapinsay and Rousay, and between one and three, depending on route and season, to all the others except North Ronaldsay, which has a weekly boat on Fridays. If you're taking a car on any of the ferries, it is sensible to book your ticket well in advance. There are also **flights** to Eday, North Ronaldsay, Westray, Papa Westray, Sanday and Stronsay, operated by Loganair (☎01856/872420), using a tiny eight-seater plane. In July and August, Loganair even offer sightseeing flights over Orkney, which are spectacular in fine weather, as well as a discounted Orkney Adventure Ticket, which allows you to visit three islands. Travel between individual islands by sea or air isn't so straightforward, but careful study of timetables can sometimes reduce the need to come all the way back to Kirkwall. It's worth enquiring from Orkney Ferries about the additional sailings on summer Sundays that often make useful inter-island connections.

Stromness

STROMNESS has to be one of the most enchanting ports at which to arrive by boat, its picturesque waterfront a procession of tiny sandstone jetties and slate roofs nestling below the green hill of Brinkie's Brae. As Orkney's main point of arrival, Stromness is a great introduction, and one that's well worth spending a day exploring, or using as a base, in preference to Kirkwall. Despite looking considerably older than Kirkwall, Stromness was actually something of a late starter, even though the natural sheltered harbour of Hamnavoe must have

---

ACCOMMODATION PRICE CODES

Throughout this book, accommodation **prices** have been graded with the codes below, according to the cost of the least expensive double room in high season. Price codes are not given for campsites, most of which charge under £10 per person. Almost all hostels charge less than £10 a night for a bed – the few exceptions to this rule have the prices quoted in the text. For a full account of the accommodation price codes, see p.32.

① under £40	④ £60–70	⑦ £110–150
② £40–50	⑤ £70–90	⑧ £150–200
③ £50–60	⑥ £90–110	⑨ £200 and over

been used since Viking times. The town really only took off in the eighteenth century, when European conflicts made it safer for ships heading across the Atlantic to travel around the top of Scotland rather than through the English Channel, many of them calling in to Stromness to take on food, water and crew. The Hudson's Bay Company made Stromness its main base from which to make the long journey across the North Atlantic, and crews from Stromness were also hired for herring and whaling expeditions, and, of course, press-ganged into the Royal Navy.

By 1842, the town boasted forty or so pubs, and reports were made of "outrageous and turbulent proceedings of seamen and others who frequent the harbour". The herring boom brought large numbers of small boats to the town, along with thousands of young women who gutted and pickled the fish before they were packed in barrels. Today Stromness remains an important harbour town and fishing port, serving as Orkney's main ferry terminal and as the headquarters of the Northern Lighthouse Board.

Information and accommodation

Arriving by ferry, you'll disembark at the new ferry terminal, which also houses the **tourist office** (April–Oct Mon–Sat 8am–6pm, Sun 9am–4pm; Nov–March Mon–Fri 9am–5pm; ☎01856/850716), where you can pick up the excellent free *Stromness Heritage Guide*, which takes you through all the buildings of interest. Unfortunately, Stromness has a fairly poor selection of **hotels**, with the venerable Victorian *Stromness Hotel* (☎01856/850610, *stromnesshotel@compuserve.com*; ⑤) – the town's first – probably your best bet. As for **B&Bs**, there's a traditional end-on waterfront house next to the museum at 2 South End (☎01856/850215; ②; April–Oct), or, further south still, *Stenigar* (☎01856/850438; ②; April–Oct), a converted boatyard which has lots of character and is situated just before the campsite on the Ness Road. Two **self-catering** options worth considering are *Pier House* (6 people; £350 per week; ☎01856/850415), a traditional end-on house at 34 Dundas Street that does weekend lets in the low season as well as week-long summer lets, or, for complete isolation, you can rent out the farmhouse on the Holms of Stromness (8 people; £390 per week; ☎01224/587278), the tidal islands in Stromness harbour (a rowing boat comes with the house).

Stromness has an SYHA **hostel** in a converted school on Helliehole Road (☎01856/850589; mid-March to Oct), signposted off the main street; it has a curfew and single-sex dorms. More laid-back is the family-run *Brown's Hostel*, 45–47 Victoria St (☎01856/850661), with bunk beds in shared rooms and kitchen facilities; it's open all year and all day, and there's no curfew. There's also a **campsite** (☎01856/873535; May to mid-Sept) in a superb setting a mile south of the ferry terminal at Point of Ness, with views out to Hoy; it's well equipped and even has its own lounge, but is extremely exposed, especially if a southwesterly is blowing.

The Town

Stromness still has a few reminders of the town's trading heyday, most notably the **Warehouse**, situated diagonally opposite the new ferry terminal. Though it may not look like it, the building was constructed in the 1760s; too late to catch the trade in American rice. More eye-catching is the **Stromness Hotel**, a tall and imposing sandstone building behind the Warehouse; during World War II, Gracie

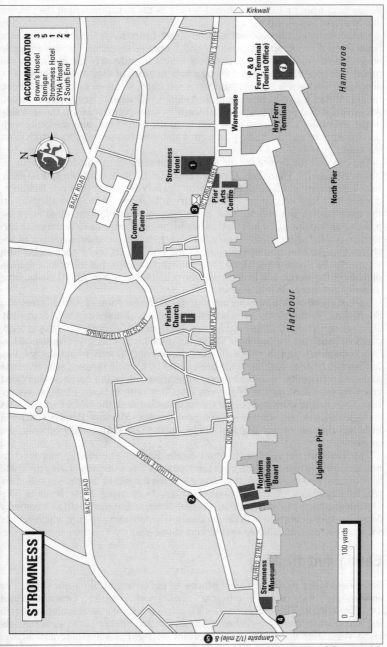

STROMNESS

△ *Kirkwall*

ACCOMMODATION	
Brown's Hostel	3
Stenigar	5
Stromness Hotel	1
SYHA Hostel	2
2 South End	4

Hamnavoe

P & O
Ferry Terminal
(Tourist Office)

Warehouse

Hoy Ferry
Terminal

North Pier

Stromness
Hotel **1**

BACK ROAD

Community
Centre

Pier
Arts
Centre

3

JOHN STREET

VICTORIA STREET

N

Harbour

Parish
Church

SPRINGFIELD CRESCENT

GRAHAM PLACE

DUNDAS STREET

HELLIHOLE ROAD

BACK ROAD

2

Northern
Lighthouse
Board

Lighthouse Pier

ALFRED STREET

Stromness
Museum

4

0   100 yards

△ *Campsite (1/2 mile) &* **5**

Fields sang from its balcony, when it served as the headquarters of the Orkney and Shetland Defence (OS Def).

Unlike Kirkwall, the old town of Stromness – famously described by Sir Walter Scott as "a dirty, straggling town" – still hugs the shoreline, its one and only street, a narrow winding affair, built long before the advent of the motor car, still paved with great flagstones and fed by a tight network of alleyways or closes. The central section, which begins at the *Stromness Hotel*, is known as **Victoria Street**, though in fact it takes on several other names – Graham Place, Dundas Street, Alfred Street and South End – as it threads its way southwards. On the east side of the street the houses are gable-end-on to the waterfront, and originally each one would have had their own pier, from which merchants would trade with passing ships.

You can visit the first of the old jetties, to the south of the modern harbour, as it now houses the **Pier Arts Centre** (Tues–Sat 10.30am–12.30pm & 1.30–5pm; July & Aug also Sun 2–5pm; free). The art gallery is spread over two buildings, divided by a lovely flagstone suntrap courtyard (access is down an alleyway off the main street): the first building hosts temporary exhibitions, often featuring painting and sculpture by local artists, while the warehouse has a remarkable permanent display of twentieth-century British art. At first it comes as a shock to see abstract works executed by members of the Cornish art scene such as Barbara Hepworth, Ben Nicholson, Terry Frost and Patrick Heron, but the marine themes of many of the works, and in particular the primitive scenes by Alfred Wallis, have a special resonance in this seaport.

Ten minutes' walk down the main street, at the junction of Alfred Street and South End, is the newly refurbished **Stromness Museum** (May–Sept daily 10am–5pm; Oct–April Mon–Sat 10.30am–12.30pm & 1.30–5pm; £2), built in 1858, partly to house the collections of the local natural history society. The natural history collection is still there – don't miss the pull-out drawers of birds' eggs, butterflies and moths – and has since been joined by a whole range of salty artefacts gathered from shipwrecks and Arctic expeditions, including barnacle-encrusted crockery from the German High Seas Fleet that sank in Scapa Flow, beaver fur hats, Cree Indian cloth and part of the torpedo that sank the HMS *Royal Oak*. As a plaque recalls, the Stromness-born poet **George Mackay Brown** (1921–96) lived out the last twenty years of his life in the house diagonally opposite the museum.

The **cannon**, further south down South End by the shore, was fired to announce the arrival of a ship from the Hudson's Bay Company. Today the trade in American rice and Canadian fur has gone, but the site of the cannon still gives magnificent views of the harbour. Further south along Ness Road is **The Doubles**, a large pair of houses on a raised platform that were built as a home by Mrs Christian Robertson with the proceeds of her shipping agency, which sent as many as 800 men on whaling expeditions in one year.

Eating and drinking

Stromness has a couple of decent **places to eat** on and off the main street. The moderately expensive *Hamnavoe Restaurant,* at 35 Graham Place (☎01856/850606; Thurs–Sun eves only), offers the town's most ambitious cooking, using local produce including shellfish, fish and beef and offering some delicious vegetarian dishes, in a very pleasant setting. For something less formal, head for the upstairs lounge bar of the *Stromness Hotel*, which does very good bar meals – go for the specials. The nearby *Coffee Shop* offers enormous breakfasts and imaginative lunches, as well as tea and cakes, though it closes at 4pm or 5pm. **Takeaway** options include the *Chip Shop* on the main street (closed Thurs eve, Sat lunch & Sun), and *Velzian's*, further south, which does thin- or thick-based pizzas and Tex-Mex. The downstairs *Flattie Bar* of the *Stromness Hotel* is a congenial place to warm yourself by the real fire, or sit outside, and have a **drink**; another popular pub is the *Ferry Inn*, opposite the hotel. *Argo's Bakery*, on Victoria Street, has a wide range of **picnic** basics, while *Orkney Wholefoods*, a few doors down, sells seafood, health food, cheese, local ice cream and delicious made-to-order sandwiches.

Listings

Banks There are branches of the Bank of Scotland and Royal Bank of Scotland on the main street, both of which have ATMs.

Bike rental *Brown's Hostel*, 45–47 Victoria St (☎01856/850661); Stromness Cycle Hire, Ferry Road (☎01856/850750).

Bookshops J.L. Broom is the best of the bookshops on the main street, and probably the best in the whole of Orkney.

Car rental Brass's Self Drive, Blue Star Garage, North End Road (☎01856/850850).

Laundry Self-service or service washes next to the *Coffee Shop* (Mon–Sat 9am–5pm).

West Mainland

The great bulk of the **West Mainland** – west of Kirkwall, that is – is fertile, productive farmland, fenced off into a patchwork of fields used either to produce crops or for cattle-grazing. Fringed by some spectacular coastline, particularly in the west, it is littered with some of the island's most impressive prehistoric sites, such as the village of **Skara Brae**, the standing **Stones of Stenness** and the chambered tomb of **Maes Howe**. Despite the intensive farming, there are still some areas which are too barren to cultivate, and the high ground and wild coastline are protected by several interesting **wildlife reserves**.

Stenness

The parish of **STENNESS**, northeast of Stromness along the main road to Kirkwall, slopes down from Ward Hill (881ft) to the lochs of Stenness and Harray, the first of which is tidal, the second of which is Orkney's most famous freshwater trout loch. The two lochs are separated by a couple of promontories, now joined by a short causeway that may well have been a narrow isthmus around 3000 BC, when it stood at the heart of Orkney's most important Neolithic ceremonial complex.

The Stones of Stenness and the Ring of Brodgar

The most visible part of the complex is the **Stones of Stenness**, originally a circle of twelve rock slabs, now just four, the tallest of which is a real monster, at over 16ft, though it's more remarkable for its incredible thinness. A broken table top

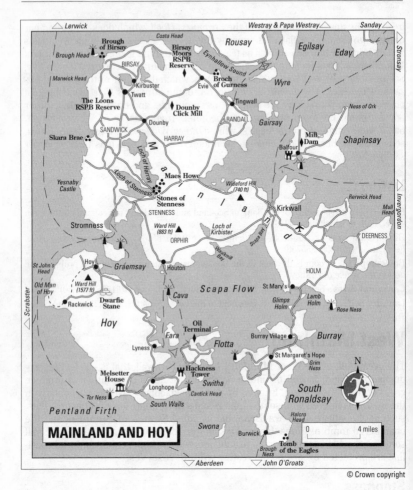

Map labels: Lerwick, Westray & Papa Westray, Sanday, Costa Head, Rousay, Egilsay, Eday, Stronsay, Brough of Birsay, Birsay Moors RSPB Reserve, Brough Head, BIRSAY, Eynhallow Sound, Broch of Gurness, Wyre, Marwick Head, Kirbuster, Evie, Twatt, Ness of Ork, The Loons RSPB Reserve, Dounby Click Mill, Tingwall, Gairsay, Shapinsay, SANDWICK, Dounby, RANDALL, Mill Dam, Balfour, HARRAY, Skara Brae, M a i n l a n d, Yesnaby Castle, Maes Howe, Wideford Hill (740 ft), Stones of Stenness, Loch of Harray, Loch of Stenness, STENNESS, Kirkwall, Rerwick Head, Mull Head, Invergordon, Stromness, Ward Hill (883 ft), Loch of Kirbister, ORPHIR, DEERNESS, Scrabster, St John's Head, Hoy, Gráemsay, Houton, Waulkmill Bay, Scapa Bay, HOLM, Old Man of Hoy, Ward Hill (1577 ft), Dwarfie Stane, Cava, Scapa Flow, St Mary's, Lamb Holm, Rose Ness, Rackwick, Hoy, Glimps Holm, Fara, Oil Terminal, Flotta, Burray Village, Burray, Lyness, St Margaret's Hope, Grim Ness, Melsetter House, Hackness Tower, Switha, South Ronaldsay, Tor Ness, Longhope, Cantick Head, Halcro Head, South Walls, Pentland Firth, Swona, Burwick, Brough Ness, Tomb of the Eagles, N, 0 4 miles, MAINLAND AND HOY, Aberdeen, John O'Groats

lies within the circle, which is surrounded by a much diminished henge, a circular bank of earth and a ditch, with a couple of entrance causeways. A path leads east from the stones to the **Barnhouse Settlement**, where the foundations of a Neolithic village contemporary with the stones have recently been excavated and remain open to the public. Less than a mile to the northwest, past the awesome Watch Stone which stands beside the road at over 18ft in height, you reach another stone circle, the **Ring of Brodgar**, a much wider circle dramatically sited on raised ground. Here there were originally 60 stones, 27 of which now stand; of the henge, only the ditch survives.

Maes Howe

There are several quite large burial mounds visible to the south of the Ring of Brodgar, but these are entirely eclipsed by one of the most impressive Neolithic burial chambers in the whole of Europe, **Maes Howe** (April–Sept daily 9.30am–6.30pm; Oct–March Mon–Wed & Sat 9.30am–4.30pm, Thurs 9.30am–noon, Sun 2.30–4.30pm; £2.50; HS), which lies less than a mile northeast of the Stones of Stenness. Dating from around 3000 BC, its incredible state of preservation is partly due to the massive slabs of sandstone it was constructed from, the largest of which weighs over three tons. The central chamber is reached down a low, long passage, one wall of which is comprised of a single immense stone. Once inside, you can stand up and admire the superb masonry of the lofty corbelled roof. Perhaps the most remarkable aspect of Maes Howe is that the tomb is aligned so that the winter solstice sun hits the top of the Barnhouse Stone, half a mile away, and reaches right down the passage of Maes Howe and alights on the ledge of one of the three cells built into the walls of the tomb. When Maes Howe was opened in 1861, it was found to be virtually empty, thanks to the work of generations of grave-robbers, who had only left behind a handful of human bones. The Vikings broke in here in the twelfth century, probably on their way to the Crusades, leaving large amounts of runic graffiti. These runes, some of which are cryptographic twig runes, are cut into the walls of the main chamber and are still clearly visible today. They include phrases such as "Many a beautiful woman has stooped in here, however pompous she might be", and "These runes were carved by the man most skilled in runes in the entire western ocean."

To enter the tomb, you must first buy a ticket from nearby **Tormiston Mill**, a converted nineteenth-century meal mill by the main road, which now houses the ticket office, toilets and interpretive display on the ground floor; a shop and some of the original mill machinery on the middle floor; and a café, which calls itself a restaurant but isn't, on the top floor. If you're planning on visiting any of Orkney's other Historic Scotland sights, it might be worth buying the joint ticket, which costs £9 and covers entry to Skara Brae, the Broch of Gurness, and the Bishop's and Earl's palaces in Kirkwall.

Practicalities

Given the density of prehistoric sites around Stenness, and its central position on the Mainland, it's not a bad area in which to base yourself. Both the **hotels** in the area attract large numbers of anglers: the *Standing Stones* (☎01856/850449, *standingstones@sol.co.uk*; ⑤), on the southern shore of the Loch of Stenness, has been pretty tastelessly modernized, though it's certainly comfortable; the *Merkister Hotel* (☎01856/771515; ③), on the northeastern shore of the Loch of Harray, has a little more character, and its bar is very popular with the locals. A more relaxing place than either of the above, however, is the carefully converted *Mill of Eyrland* (☎01856/850136, *kenandmorag@millofeyrland.demon.co.uk*; ③), in a delightful setting by a mill stream on the A964 to Orphir; it's filled with wonderful antiques, old mill machinery plus all mod cons, and serves enormous breakfasts.

Sandwick

Around seven miles north of Stromness, the parish of **SANDWICK** contains Orkney's one and only brewery, housed in what used to be Quoyloo School, and perhaps the best known of its prehistoric monuments, the Neolithic village of **Skara Brae**. Less well-known is that the cliffs to the north and south of the Bay of Skaill, where Skara Brae lies, provide some of the most spectacularly rugged **coastal walks** on Orkney's Mainland. The best place to head for is **Yesnaby**, to the south of the Bay of Skaill, where the sandstone cliffs have been savagely eroded into stacks and geos by the force of the Atlantic. Come here during a westerly gale and you'll see the waves sending sea spray shooting over the wartime buildings and the neighbouring fields. As a result, the clifftops support a unique plantlife, which thrives on the salt spray, including the rare and very small Scottish Primrose, which flowers in May and from July to late September. The walk south along the coast from here is exhilarating: the Old Man of Hoy is visible in the distance, and, after a mile and a half, you come to West Mainland's own version, known as **Yesnaby Castle**.

Skara Brae and Skaill House

The beautiful white curve of the Bay of Skaill is home to **Skara Brae** (April–Sept daily 9.30am–6.30pm; Oct–March Mon–Sat 9.30am–4.30pm, Sun 2–4.30pm; £4 in summer, £3.20 in winter), where the extensive remains of a small Neolithic fishing and farming village, dating back to 3000 BC, were discovered in 1850 after a fierce storm ripped off the dunes covering them. The village is very well preserved, its houses huddled together and connected by narrow passages which would originally have been covered over with turf. The houses themselves consist of a single, spacious living room, surrounded by a vast array of domestic detail, including dressers, fireplaces, built-in cupboards, beds and boxes, all carefully put together from slabs of stone.

Unfortunately, the sheer numbers now visiting Skara Brae mean that you can no longer explore the site properly, but only look down from the outer walls. Sadly, too, the best-preserved example, House 6, now sports a perspex roof to protect it from the elements; however, House 1, which also contains a dresser, as yet does not. Before you reach the site you must buy a ticket from the new visitor centre, which also contains a small introductory exhibition that begins with a short video. That, a few replica finds, and some hands-on stuff for kids, helps put the site in context. You then proceed to a full-scale replica of House 6, complete with a fake wood and skin roof. It's all a tad neat and tidy, with fetching up-lighting, rather than dark, smoky and smelly, but it'll give you the general idea.

In the summer months, your ticket to Skara Brae also covers entry to nearby **Skaill House**, a vast range of buildings 300 yards inland, that was once the home of the laird of Skaill. The original house was a simple two-storey block with a small courtyard, built for Bishop George Graham in the 1620s, but it has since been much extended. Guided tours are available at no extra charge, or you can simply stroll round. The house's prize possession is Captain Cook's dinner service from the *Resolution*, which was delivered after Cook's death when the *Resolution* and the *Discovery* sailed into Stromness in 1780. The last occupant of the house was Mrs Kathleen Scarth, who died in 1991; her bedroom has been left as it was, and is filled with old frocks, an ostrich feather fan and a "twist and slim exerciser".

Practicalities

With no bus service to speak of, you really need your own transport to reach Sandwick. There's no main settlement as such, though you'll find a couple of inexpensive, modern **B&Bs** in the vicinity. On the A967, overlooking the Loch of Harray, there's *Dencraigon* (☎01856/841647; ①), while northeast of the Bay of Skaill in a more secluded location is *Netherstove* (☎01856/841625; ①), with a great view over the bay, comfortable rooms and self-catering cottages available; the Georgian former manse of *Flotterston House* (☎01856/841700; ②) also enjoys great views, and does very good breakfasts. Closer to Yesnaby (and Stromness), at Kirbister, *Brettobreck Farm* (☎01856/850373; ①) is a traditional and homely Orcadian farmhouse and working dairy farm.

Birsay

Occupying the northwest corner of the Mainland, the parish of **BIRSAY** was the centre of Norse power in Orkney for several centuries, before the earls moved to Kirkwall some time after the construction of the cathedral. Today a tiny cluster of homes is gathered around the sandstone ruins of the **Earl's Palace**, which was built in the second half of the sixteenth century by Robert Stewart, Earl of Orkney, using the forced labour of the islanders, who weren't even given food and drink for their work. By all accounts, it was a "sumptuous and stately dwelling", built in four wings around a central courtyard, its upper rooms decorated with painted ceilings and rich furnishings; surrounding the palace were flower and herb gardens, a bowling green and archery butts. The palace appears to have lasted barely a century before falling into rack and ruin; the crumbling walls and turrets retain much of their grandeur, although inside there is little remaining domestic detail. By comparison, the Earl's Palace in Kirkwall seems almost humble.

Half a mile southeast of the palace, up the burn, is the **Barony Mills** (April–Sept daily 10am–1pm & 2–5pm; £1.50), Orkney's only working nineteenth-century water mill to survive into the modern era. The mill specializes in producing traditional stoneground beremeal, essential for making bere bannocks. Bere is a four-kernel barley crop with a very short growing season perfectly suited for the local climate and was once the staple diet in these parts. The miller on duty will give you a guided tour and show you the machinery going through its paces, though milling only takes place in the autumn.

Brough of Birsay

Just over half a mile northwest of the palace is the **Brough of Birsay**, a substantial Pictish settlement on a small tidal island that is only accessible during the two hours each side of high tide. Stromness and Kirkwall tourist offices have the tide times and Radio Orkney broadcasts them (93.7FM; Mon–Fri 7.30–8am). Once you reach the island, there's a small ticket office where you must pay your entrance fee (£1), and where you can see a few artefacts gathered from the site, including a game made from whalebone and an antler pin. Coastal erosion over the last eight centuries means that some of the site has disappeared off the side of the low cliffs, and concrete sea defences are currently in place to try and stem the tide.

The focus of the village was – and still is – the sandstone-built twelfth-century **St Peter's Church**, which stands higher than the surrounding buildings; the stone seating along the walls is still in place, and there are a couple of semicircular recesses for altars, and a semicircular apse. The church is thought to have stood at the centre of a monastic complex of some sort – the foundations of a courtyard and outer buildings can be made out to the west. Close by is a large complex of Viking-era buildings, including several houses, a sauna and some sophisticated stone drains.

The Brough of Birsay is a popular day-trip, partly due to the fun of dodging the tides, but few folk bother to explore the rest of the island, whose gentle green slopes, when viewed from the mainland, belie the dramatic, rugged cliffs that characterize the rest of the coastline. In winter, sea spray from the waves crashing against the cliffs can envelop the entire island. In summer the cliffs are home to various seabirds, including a fair few puffin, making the half-mile walk to the island's castellated **lighthouse**, and back along the northern coastline: well worth the effort. If you make it out here, spare a thought for the lighthouse keepers who used to man the **Sule Skerry** lighthouse – the most isolated in Britain – which lies on a piece of bare rock barely visible some 37 miles out to sea, and whose only contact with the outside world was via carrier pigeon.

Marwick Head and The Loons

The best of Birsay's coastal scenery lies to the south of Birsay Bay around **Marwick Head**. The headland itself is clearly visible on the horizon thanks to the huge castellated tower of the **Kitchener Memorial**, raised by the people of Orkney to commemorate the Minister of War, Lord Kitchener, who drowned along with all but twelve of the crew of the 11,000-ton cruiser HMS *Hampshire* when the ship struck a mine just off the coast on June 5, 1916. There has been much speculation about the incident over the years, due to the fact that Kitchener was on a secret mission to Russia to hold talks with the Tsar. As a result, salvage operations were closely controlled by the Admiralty, and the findings of the naval court of enquiry kept secret, fanning the rumours that Kitchener had been deliberately sent to his death (he was extremely unpopular at the time). In reality, it appears to have been a simple case of naval incompetence: a weather forecast from the Admiralty warning of severe northwesterly gales was ignored, as were the reports of submarine activity in the area.

Marwick Head is also an **RSPB reserve** and, during the nesting season, there are numerous fulmar, kittiwakes, guillemots, razorbills and even a few puffin in residence on the 200-foot cliffs. A mile or so inland, another RSPB reserve is centred on the wetlands of **The Loons**. There's no access to the area, but you can watch the waterfowl, snipe, curlews and even the odd short-eared owl from the hide on the northwest side of the reserve on the road to Twatt.

Kirbuster and Corrigall farm museums

Lying between the Loch of Boardhouse and the Loch of Hundland, the **Kirbuster Farm Museum** (April–Sept Mon–Sat 10.30am–1pm & 2–5pm, Sun 2–7pm; £2) offers an interesting insight into life on an Orkney farm steading in the mid-nineteenth century. Built in 1723, the farm is made up of a typical collection of flagstone buildings, though Kirbuster is more substantial than most, and boasts its own, very beautiful garden. Ducks, geese and sheep wander around the grassy open yard, which is entered through a whalebone archway. The most remarkable thing about Kirbuster, however, is that, despite being inhabited until as late as 1961, it has retained its Firehoose, in which the smoke from the central peat fire is used to dry fish fillets, and eventually allowed simply to drift up towards a hole in the ceiling; the room even retains the old neuk-beds, simple recesses in the stone walls, which would have originally been lined with wood.

The ticket for Kirbuster also covers entry to **Corrigall Farm Museum** (times as above), another eighteenth-century farmstead some five miles southeast of

Kirbuster, beyond Dounby in the parish of Harray. If you've enjoyed your time at Kirbuster – and kids almost certainly will – then it's definitely worth visiting both. There are lovely views west and south from the honeysuckle-draped ticket office, and hens and sheep scampering around the farmyard. Be sure to check out the well-preserved flagstone byre, and the stable, which has a characteristic beehive-shaped kiln for drying grain at one end.

Practicalities

It would be fair to say that there really isn't a bus service, as such, to Birsay, so you need to arrange your own transport. **Accommodation** choices are pretty limited, too, with just the *Barony Hotel* (☎01856/721327, *baronyhotel@ btinternet.com*; ②), situated on the north shore of the Loch of Boardhouse (specializing in angling holidays), and a few simple B&Bs, such as *Primrose Cottage* (☎01856/721384; ①), overlooking Marwick Bay. As for **food**, you're basically stuck with bar meals at the *Barony Hotel*, tea and cakes at the two tearooms in Birsay, or, better still, putting together your own picnic.

Evie and the Broch of Gurness

Overshadowed by the great wind turbine on Burgar Hill, the village and parish of **EVIE**, on the north coast, looks out across the turbulent waters of Eynhallow Sound towards the island of Rousay. Its chief draw is the **Broch of Gurness** (April–Sept daily 9.30am–6.30pm; £2.50; HS), the best-preserved broch on an archipelago replete with them, and one which is still surrounded by a remarkable complex of later buildings. As at Birsay, the sea has eaten away half the site, but the broch itself, dating from around 100 BC, still stands, its walls reaching a height of 12ft in places, its inner cells still intact. The compact group of homes clustered around the broch have also survived amazingly well, with much of their original and ingenious stone shelving and fireplaces still in place. The best view of the site is from the east, where you can clearly make out the "main street" leading towards the broch. The visitor centre where you buy your ticket is also worth a quick once-over, especially for those with kids, who will enjoy using the quernstone corn grinder. The broch is clearly signposted from Evie, the road skirting the pristinely white **Sands of Evie**, a perfect picnic spot in fine weather.

A large section of the hills to the southwest of Evie now form the **RSPB Birsay Moors Reserve**, whose heather-coated ground provides good hunting for kestrels, merlins and hen harriers. **Lowrie's Water**, on Burgar Hill itself, meanwhile, is regularly used as a nesting site by red-throated divers – there's an RSPB hide from which you can view the loch at the top of the rough track leading to the 3MW **aerogenerator**. The latter was built here in the 1980s, along with two others since demolished, in order to carry out research into wind power. The moor is also a source of traditional fuel, and if you take the B9057 towards Dounby you can make out the areas in which peat is cut, with small stacks often drying on the hillside.

Before you reach Dounby itself, a sign points across a field to the turf-roofed **Dounby Click Mill**, the only surviving example of a horizontal watermill in Orkney. With only limited water power available, this type of mill was a simple but effective way of grinding flour for two to three families. The mechanism inside has been fully restored, and you can see the wheel underneath the building.

Practicalities

Evie has a wide of variety of decent **accommodation**, including very possibly the best place to stay on the whole of Orkney, *Woodwick House* (☎01856/751330; ②), situated in a secluded position southeast of the main village. The house itself is beautifully decorated, and has two resident lounges, both with real fires – the food is superb, the wooded grounds are delightful, and feature a seventeenth-century doocot, and there are even occasional concerts. Non-residents can eat there for around £15 a head. At the other end of the scale, you can stay in the nicely modernized **bothy and campsite**, run by Dale Farm (☎01856/751270; April–Oct), and situated in a sheltered spot right by the junction of the road to Dounby (and not to be confused with the much tattier bothy back down the road to Kirkwall). The local shop, post office and *Mistra* **pub** are all very close by.

Orphir

The southern shores of the West Mainland, overlooking Scapa Flow, are much gentler than the rest of the coastline, and have fewer of Orkney's premier league sights. However, if you've time to spare, or you're heading for Hoy from the car ferry terminal at Houton, there are a couple of points of interest in the neighbouring parish of **ORPHIR**. Here, beside the parish cemetery, the council have built a new **Orkneyinga Saga Centre** (daily 9am–5pm; free), where a small exhibition and a fifteen-minute audiovisual attempts to give you a brief rundown of the plot of the *Orkneyinga Saga*, the bloodthirsty Viking tale written around 1200 AD by an unnamed Icelandic author, which described the conquest of the Northern Isles by the Norsemen. The Earl's Bu at Orphir features in the saga as the home of Earl Thorfinn the Mighty, Earl Paul and his son, Haakon, who ordered the murder of Earl (later St) Magnus on Egilsay (see p.374). The foundations of what is presumed to have been the Earl's Bu have been uncovered just outside the cemetery gates, while inside the cemetery is a section of the round church, built by Haakon after his pilgrimage to Jerusalem.

Further east along the A954 towards Kirkwall lies the **Hobbister RSPB reserve**, a mixture of moorland, sea cliffs, salt marsh and sand flats that's great for spotting a wide variety of birdlife and, at the sandy Waulkmill Bay, a relatively warm place in which to swim.

Kirkwall

Initial impressions of **KIRKWALL** are not always favourable. It has nothing to match the picturesque harbour of Stromness, and its urban sprawl is far less appealing. However, it does have one great redeeming feature, and that is its sandstone cathedral, without doubt the finest medieval building in the north of Scotland. In any case, if you're staying any length of time in Orkney you're more or less bound to find yourself in Kirkwall at some point, as the town is also home to the island's better-stocked shops, including the islands' only large supermarket, and is the departure point for most of the ferries to Orkney's northern isles.

Part of the reason for Kirkwall's disappointing waterfront is that today's harbour is a largely modern invention; in the mid-nineteenth century, the shoreline ran along Junction Road, and before that it was flush with the west side of main street. Nowadays, the town is very much divided into two main focal points: the

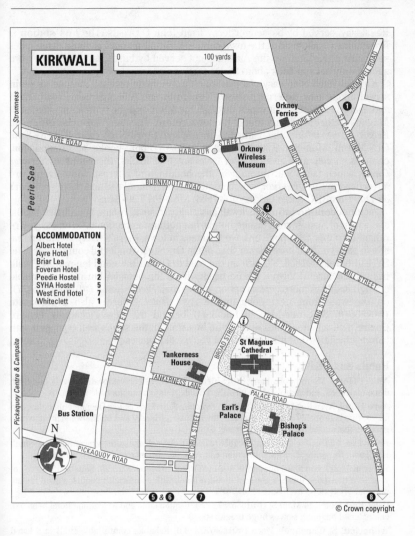

busy **harbour**, at the north end of the town, where ferries come and go all year round, and where, during the summer, launches offload smartly dressed holiday-makers from the numerous cruise ships that weigh anchor in the Bay of Kirkwall; and the flagstoned **main street**, which changes its name four times as it twists its way south from the harbour past the cathedral.

Arrival, information and accommodation

Car **ferries** docking at Stromness are met by buses to Kirkwall (40min), and there are also bus connections (45min) from the Burwick terminal on South

Ronaldsay, served by passenger ferry from John O'Groats. The **bus station** is five minutes' walk west of the town centre. Kirkwall **airport** is about three miles southeast of Kirkwall on the A960; it's not served by buses, but a taxi into town should only set you back about £6.

Kirkwall itself is an easy place in which to orientate yourself, despite its **main street** taking four different names – Bridge Street, Albert Street, Broad Street and Victoria Street – as it winds through the town, and the prominent spire of St Magnus Cathedral clearly marks the town centre. The helpful **tourist office**, on Broad Street beside the cathedral graveyard (April–Sept daily 8.30am–8pm; Oct–March Mon–Sat 9.30am–5pm; ☎01856/872856), books accommodation, changes money and gives out an excellent free leaflet, the *Kirkwall Heritage Guide*, which takes you through all the buildings of interest. Most events are advertised in the *Orcadian*, which comes out on Thursdays, and there's a *What's on Diary* on BBC Radio Orkney (93.7FM; Mon–Fri 7.30–8am).

As for **accommodation**, Kirkwall has plenty of small rooms in ordinary B&Bs, and a host of blandly refurbished hotels, but nothing exceptional, so unless you're reliant on public transport, or have business in town, there's really no strong reason to base yourself here, rather than out in Orkney's wonderful countryside. The SYHA **hostel** (☎01856/872243) on the road to Orphir is a good ten minutes' walk from the centre of town – it's no beauty from the outside, but it's comfortable enough inside. A more central option is the small *Peedie Hostel* (☎01856/875477), on the waterfront next door to the *Ayre Hotel*. There's also a **campsite** (☎01856/873535; mid-May to mid-Sept) behind the new Pickaquoy Leisure Centre, five minutes' walk west of the bus station; the site is well equipped with laundry facilities, but it's hardly what you'd call picturesque.

Hotels and B&Bs

Albert Hotel, Mounthoolie Lane (☎01856/876000). Great central location, lively bar (with disco attached), and completely refurbished inside, this is a comfortable option. ③.

Ayre Hotel, Ayre Road (☎01856/873001, *reception@ayrehotel.co.uk*) Despite outside appearances, this is probably the best option in town: smart, friendly and on the waterfront, with a good reputation for traditional live music. ⑤.

Briar Lea, 10 Dundas Crescent (☎01856/872747). Attractive nineteenth-century stone-built B&B, with its own walled garden, within easy walking distance of the town centre. ①.

Foveran Hotel, two miles out on the A964 to Orphir (☎01856/872389). Suitable if you've got your own transport, this is a pleasant modern hotel, with comfortable rooms, a good restaurant and great views over Scapa Flow. ④.

West End Hotel, 14 Main St (☎01856/872368). Comfortable and welcoming hotel in an old, characterful building; serves huge breakfasts. ③.

Whiteclett, St Catherine's Place (☎01856/874193). Reliable, comfortable B&B in a listed house right by the waterfront. ①.

The Town

Standing at the very heart of Kirkwall, **St Magnus Cathedral** (April–Sept Mon–Sat 9am–6pm, Sun 2–6pm; Oct–March Mon–Sat 9am–1pm & 2–5pm; Sunday service at 11.15am) is the town's most compelling sight. This beautiful red sandstone building was begun in 1137 by the Orkney Earl Rognvald, who decided to make full use of a growing cult surrounding the figure of his uncle Magnus, killed on the orders of his cousin Haakon in 1117 (see p.374). When

Magnus's body was buried in Birsay a heavenly light was said to have shone overhead, and his grave soon became a place of pilgrimage attributed with miraculous powers and attracting pilgrims from as far afield as Shetland. When Rognvald finally took over the earldom he built the cathedral in his uncle's honour, moving the centre of religious and secular power from Birsay to Kirkwall.

The first version of the cathedral, built using yellow sandstone from Eday and red sandstone from the Mainland, was somewhat smaller than today's structure, which has been added to over the centuries, with a new east window in the thirteenth century, the extension of the nave in the fifteenth century and a new west window to mark the building's 850th anniversary in 1987. Today the soft sandstone is badly eroded – the capitals around the main doors are reduced to knarled stumps – but it's still an immensely impressive building, its shape and style echoing the great cathedrals of Europe. Inside, the atmosphere is surprisingly intimate, the bulky sandstone columns drawing you up to the exposed brickwork arches, while around the walls is a series of mostly seventeenth-century tombstones, many carved with a skull and crossbones and other emblems of mortality, alongside chilling inscriptions calling on the reader to "remember death waits us all, the hour none knows". In the southeastern corner of the cathedral lies the tomb of the Stromness-born Arctic explorer John Rae, who went off to try and find Sir John Franklin's expedition; he is depicted asleep, dressed in moleskins and furs, his rifle and Bible by his side. Beside Rae's tomb is Orkney's own poets' corner, with memorials to, among others, George Mackay Brown, Eric Linklater, Robert Rendall and Edwin Muir. Another poignant monument is the one to the dead of HMS *Royal Oak*, which was torpedoed in Scapa Flow in 1939 with the loss of 833 men (see p.362).

To the south of the church are the ruined remains of the **Bishop's Palace** (April–Sept daily 9.30am–6.30pm; £1.80; HS), residence of the Bishop of Orkney since the twelfth century. It was here that the Norwegian King Haakon died in 1263 on his return from defeat at the Battle of Largs. Most of what you see now, however, dates from the time of Bishop Robert Reid, the founder of Edinburgh University, in the mid-sixteenth century. The walls still stand, as does the tall round tower in which the bishop had his private chambers; a narrow spiral staircase takes you to the top for a good view of the cathedral and across Kirkwall's rooftops. If you're planning on visiting any of Orkney's other Historic Scotland sights, it might be worth buying the joint ticket, which costs £9 and covers entry to Skara Brae, the Broch of Gurness and Maes Howe.

The neighbouring **Earl's Palace**, built by the infamous Earl Patrick Stewart around 1600, using forced labour, is rather better preserved, and a lot more fun to explore. With its grand entrance, fancy oriel windows, dank dungeons, massive fireplaces and magnificent central hall, it has a confident solidity, and is reckoned to be one of the finest examples of Renaissance architecture in Scotland. The roof may be missing, but many domestic details remain, including a set of toilets and the stone shelves used by the clerk to do his filing. Earl Patrick enjoyed his palace for only a very short time before he was imprisoned. The earl ordered his son, Robert, to organize an insurrection; he held out four days in the palace against the Earl of Caithness, but eventually shared the same fate as his father (see p.405).

Opposite the cathedral stands the sixteenth-century **Tankerness House**, a former home for the clergy. It has been renovated countless times over the years, most recently in the 1960s in order to provide a home for the **Orkney Museum** (Mon–Sat 10.30am–5pm; May–Sept also Sun 2–5pm; free). Among its more unusual artefacts are a collection of balls used in a traditional Orkney street game, The Ba', played at Christmas and New Year; other exhibits to look out for include the witch's spell box, and a lovely whalebone plaque from a Viking boat grave discovered on Sanday. In addition, there are a couple of rooms which have been restored as they would have been in 1820, when the building was a private home for the Baikie family. On a warm summer afternoon, the gardens (which can be entered either from the house itself or from a gate on Tankerness Lane) are thick with the buzz of bees and brilliant blooms.

At the harbour end of Junction Road, at Kiln Corner, you can browse around the tiny **Orkney Wireless Museum** (April–Sept Mon–Sat 10am–4.30pm, Sun 2–4.30pm; £2), which is packed to the roof with every sort of radio equipment, but is particularly strong on technical flotsam from the two world wars.

Highland Park, Scapa and the Grain Earth House

Further afield, a mile or so south of the town centre on the A961 to South Ronaldsay, is the **Highland Park distillery** (Easter–Oct Mon–Fri 10am–4pm; July & Aug also Sat 10am–4pm & Sun noon–4pm; Nov–March Mon–Fri tours at 2pm; ☎01856/874619; £3), billed as "the most northerly legal distillery in Scotland". It's been in operation for more than two hundred years, and still has its own maltings, although it was closed during World War II, when the army used it as a food store and the huge vats served as communal baths. You can decide for yourself whether the taste still lingers by partaking of the customary dram after one of the regular guided tours of the beautiful old buildings.

If the weather happens to be unusually good and you're moved to consider taking the plunge but are stuck in Kirkwall, do as the locals do and head one mile south of town on the B9148 to **Scapa Bay**, Kirkwall's very own sandy beach. Briefly a naval headquarters at the outbreak of World War I, Scapa's pier is now used by the council tugs and pilot launches servicing the oil tankers out in Scapa Flow. Visible from the beach is the green Admiralty wreck buoy marking the position of HMS *Royal Oak*, which was torpedoed by a German U-Boat on October 14, 1939, with the loss of 833 men (out of a total crew of around 1400). A small display shed at the eastern end of the bay tells the full story, and has photos of the wreck (still an official war grave) as it looks today.

If you've time to kill and the weather's not so good, you could search out one of Kirkwall's more unusual sights, the **Grain Earth House**, a food cellar dating back to the first millennium BC, now hidden in the industrial estate, northwest of the town centre. Collect the key (and a torch) from Ortak jewellers, at the entrance to the estate, and head round the corner. Steep steps lead down to a long, dark, curving passageway which ends at a stone-clad cellar held up by large stone pillars – now you know what it felt like to be an Iron Age bere bannock.

Eating, drinking and entertainment

Given the quality of Orkney beef, and the quantity of shellfish caught in the vicinity, Kirkwall's **food** options are pretty disappointing. *Trenabies* and the *Pomona Café*, both on Albert Street, are both venerable institutions, but the nicest **café** is the *Strynd* tearoom, up the alleyway by the tourist office. For something more substantial, there's nothing for it but to head for one of the town's hotels – the *Albert* and the *West End* are probably the best options, offering both **bar meals** and à la carte – or opt for Orkney's Indian restaurant, the *Mumutaz*, on Bridge Street. The best **fish and chips** are from *Raeburn's* at the corner of Union Street and Junction Road.

The **nightlife** scene in Kirkwall is a lot more animated. The liveliest **pub** is the *Torvhaug Inn* at the harbour end of Bridge Street; another good place to try is the *Bothy Bar* in the *Albert Hotel*, which sometimes has live music and is attached to *Matchmakers* **disco** (Thurs–Sat only). The *Ayre Hotel* has a good reputation for **traditional live music**, especially the regular Orkney Accordion & Fiddle Club nights on Wednesdays. There's also sometimes live music at the *Quoyburray Inn*, a couple of miles beyond the airport on the A960 – check the *Orcadian* entertainment listings for the latest.

Kirkwall's new Pickaquoy Leisure Centre – known locally as the "Picky" – is a short walk from the town centre, up Pickaquoy Road, past Safeway supermarket. It now serves as one of the town's main large-scale venues, and also contains the New Phoenix **cinema** (☎01856/879900). It does not, however, have a swimming pool – this is located on the other side of town on Thomas Street.

Listings

Airport ☎01856/872421.

Banks There are branches of the big Scottish banks on the main street, all with their own ATMs.

Bike rental Bobby's Cycle Hire, Tankerness Lane (☎01856/875777).

Bookshops Leonard's at the corner of Bridge Street and Albert Street are the best stocked.

Camping gear and outdoor sports Eric Kemp, 31–33 Bridge St (☎872137).

Car rental Peace's Car Hire, Junction Road (☎01856/872866); John G. Shearer, Ayre Service Station (☎01856/872950); W.R. Tullock, Castle Street and Kirkwall Airport (☎01856/876262).

Consulates Denmark and Germany, J. Robertson, Shore Street (☎01856/872961); Netherlands and Norway, J. Spence, 21 Bridge St (☎01856/872268).

Exchange In addition to the banks, the tourist office in Broad Street runs an exchange service (summer daily 8.30am–8pm).

Ferries Orcargo, Norlantic House, Grainshore, Hatston (☎01856/873838); Orkney Ferries, Shore Street (Mon–Fri 7am–5pm, Sat 7am–3pm; ☎01856/872044); P&O Passenger Terminal, Kirkwall Pier (Mon–Fri 9am–1pm & 2–5pm; ☎01856/873330).

Laundry Launderama, Albert Street (Mon–Fri 8.30am–5.30pm, Sat 9am–5pm).

Medical care Balfour Hospital, Kirkwall Health Centre and Dental Clinic, New Scapa Road (☎01856/885400).

Post office Junction Road (Mon–Fri 9am–5pm, Sat 9.30am–12.30pm).

East Mainland and South Ronaldsay

Southeast from Kirkwall, the narrow spur of the **East Mainland** juts out into the North Sea and is joined, thanks to the remarkable Churchill Barriers, to several smaller islands, the largest of which are **Burray** and **South Ronaldsay**. As with the West Mainland, the land here is densely populated and heavily farmed, but there are none of Orkney's most famous sights. Nevertheless, there are several interesting fishing villages, some good coastal walks to enjoy, and, at the **Tomb of the Eagles**, one of the most enjoyable and memorable of Orkney's prehistoric sites.

East Mainland

The northern side of the **East Mainland** consists of three exposed peninsulas that jut out like giant claws. The most intriguing peninsula is the easternmost one of **Deerness**, joined to the mainland only by a narrow, sandy isthmus. The northeastern corner around the sea cliffs of **Mull Head** boasts a large colony of nesting seabirds from May to August, including fulmars, kittiwakes, guillemots, razorbills and puffin, plus, inland, arctic terns that swoop and screech threateningly. The only way to reach Mull Head is to walk from the car park a mile or so to the south. A short walk east of the car park you can also view **The Gloup**, an impressive collapsed sea cave; the tide still flows in and out through a natural arch, making strange gurgling noises. The name stems from the Old Norse *gluppa*, or "chasm". Half a mile north of the Gloup is the **Brough of Deerness**, a grassy promontory whose narrow land bridge has collapsed, and which is now accessible only via a precipitous path – the ruins are thought to have once been a Norse or Pictish monastic site.

Visible across the sea to the north are Auskerry and Stronsay and, to the southeast, the uninhabited island of **Copinsay**, with its lighthouse, perched on yet more seabird-infested cliffs. Copinsay is now an **RSPB reserve**, with huge seabird colonies nesting on its cliffs in season; to find out about access, make enquiries with the tourist board or the RSPB (☎01856/850176).

On the south coast, just before you hit the Churchill Barriers, stands the village of **ST MARY'S**, an old fishing village whose livelihood was destroyed by the building of the causeways. Just east of St Mary's, you'll find the **Norwood Museum** (May–Sept Tues–Thurs & Sun 2–5pm & 6–8pm; also by arrangement ☎01856/781217; £3), a display of antiques collected by local stonemason Norrie Wood from the age of 13. Only about half of the collection is on display, but it's a fascinating and eccentric selection of bits and pieces from around the world, including pottery, painting, medals, furniture, cutlery, clocks, even a narwhal's tusk, all housed in a grand Orkney home.

The Churchill Barriers

To the south of St Mary's is the first of four causeways, known as the **Churchill Barriers**, since they were given the go-ahead by Churchill, when he was First Lord of the Admiralty. They were built during World War II as anti-submarine barriers, which would seal the waters between the Mainland and the string of islands to the south, and thus protect the British Navy, based in Scapa Flow at the time, from German U-boat attack. However, the Admiralty was only prompted into action by the sinking of the battleship HMS *Royal Oak* on October 14, 1939 (see p.362). Despite the presence of blockships, deliberately sunk during World War I in order to close off the eastern approaches, one German U-boat captain managed to get through and torpedo the *Royal Oak*, before returning to a hero's welcome in Germany. He claimed to have acquired local knowledge while fishing in the islands before the war. As you cross the barriers, you can still see the blockships, rusting away, an eerie reminder of Orkney's important wartime role.

The barriers – an astonishing feat of engineering when you bear in mind the strength of Orkney tides – were an incredibly expensive undertaking, costing an estimated £2.5 million even at the time. Special camps were built on the uninhabited island of Lamb Holm, in order to accommodate the 1700 men involved in the project, 1200 of whom were Italian POWs. The camps have long since disappeared, but the Italians left behind the extraordinary **Italian Chapel** on Lamb Holm. This, the so-called "miracle of Camp 60", must be one of the greatest adaptations ever, made from two Nissen huts, concrete, barbed wire and parts of a rusting blockship. It has a great false facade, and colourful trompe l'oeil decor, lovingly restored by the chapel's principal architect, Domenico Chiocchetti, who returned in 1960; Mass is still said regularly.

Burray

If you're travelling with children, you may like to stop off on the island of **Burray** in order to visit the **Orkney Fossil and Vintage Centre** (daily: April–Sept 10am–6pm; Oct 10.30am–6pm; £2), housed in a converted farm on the main road across the island. Most of the fossils on display downstairs have been found locally, so they tend to be of fish and sea creatures, since Orkney was at the bottom of a tropical sea in Devonian times. The UV room, where the rocks reveal their iridescent colours, is a particular favourite with kids. Upstairs, there's a lot of wartime memorabilia, books to read, a rocking horse to play on and a comfy chair and binoculars with which to spot the birdlife down by the shore. There's also a tearoom attached to the museum.

BURRAY VILLAGE, on the south coast of the island, expanded in the nineteenth century during the boom years of the herring industry, but was badly affected by the sinking of the blockships during World War I. The two-storey warehouse, built in 1860 in order to cure and pack the herring, has recently been converted into the *Sands Motel*, where you can get a **drink** and a bite to **eat**. The best place to stay, though, is out at *Vestlaybanks* (☎01856/731305; *vestlaybanks@btinternet.com*; ②), a very comfortable **B&B** which boasts great views over Scapa Flow.

South Ronaldsay

At the southern end of the series of four barriers is low-lying **South Ronaldsay**, which is the largest of the islands linked to the Mainland, and is, like the latter, heavily cultivated, rich farming country. It was traditionally the chief crossing point to the Scottish mainland, as it's only six miles across the Pentland Firth to Caithness. Nowadays, the car ferries arrive at Stromness, but there is still a small passenger ferry between John O'Groats and Burwick, on the southernmost tip of the island (see p.425 for details).

St Margaret's Hope

The main settlement on South Ronaldsay is **ST MARGARET'S HOPE**, which local tradition says takes its name from Margaret, the Maid of Norway, who is thought to have died here in November 1290 while on her way to marry the English King Edward II (then Prince Edward). Margaret had already been proclaimed the Queen of Scotland, and the marriage was intended to unify the two countries. Today, St Margaret's Hope – or "The Hope", as it's known locally – is a pleasing little gathering of stone-built houses overlooking a sheltered bay, and is by far the best base from which to explore the area. As is obvious from the architecture, and the piers, The Hope was once a thriving port, and local hopes are pinned on the new car ferry service link with Caithness that is due to start in the near future – in the meantime, it remains a very peaceful place in which to chill out.

The village smithy on Cromarty Square has been turned into a **Smiddy Museum** (May & Sept daily 2–4pm; June–Aug daily noon–4pm; Oct Sun 2–4pm; free), which is particularly fun for kids, who enjoy getting hands-on with the old tools, drills and giant bellows. There's also a small exhibition on the annual **Boys' Ploughing Match**, in which local boys compete with miniature hand-held ploughs. The competition, which is taken extremely seriously by all those involved, happens on the third Saturday in August, at the beautiful golden beach at the **Sands O'Right** in Hoxa, a couple of miles west of The Hope.

St Margaret's Hope has some very good **accommodation** options. First choice is the *Creel Restaurant and Rooms* (☎01856/831311; ④) on Front Road, one of the best restaurants in Scotland and winner of all sorts of awards for its superb **food** featuring local produce. It's expensive, but friendly and relaxed, and the rooms are comfortable too. More modest bar meals are available in the popular bar of the nearby *Murray Arms Hotel* (☎01856/831205; ②), and from the *Galley Inn* of *The Anchorage* B&B (☎01856/831456; ③), also on the seafront. Among the Hope's **B&Bs**, *West End House* (☎01856/831495; ②) is outstanding, with appealing rooms and a pleasant garden, as is *Bellevue Guest House* (☎01856/831294; ②), on a hill just east of the village. For more basic accommodation, head for *Wheems* **hostel**, about a mile and a half from the War Memorial in Eastside (☎01856/831537). Mattresses and ingredients for a wholesome breakfast are provided, and organic produce from the croft is on sale.

Tomb of the Eagles

One of the most enjoyable archeological sights to visit on Orkney is the ancient chambered burial cairn, at the southeastern corner of South Ronaldsay, known as the **Tomb of the Eagles** (daily: April–Oct 10am–8pm; Nov–March 10am–noon; £2.50). Discovered, excavated and still owned by a local farmer, Ronald Simpson of Liddel, a visit here makes a refreshing change from the usual interpretative centre. First off, you get to look round the family's private museum of prehistoric artefacts – this is the original "hands-on" museum, so visitors can actually touch and admire the painstaking craftsmanship of Neolithic folk, and examine a skull. Next you get a brief guided tour of a nearby Bronze Age **burnt mound**, which is basically a Neolithic rubbish dump, beside which there was a large trough, where joints of meat were boiled by throwing in rocks from the fire. Finally you get to walk out to the **chambered cairn**, by the cliff's edge, where human remains were found alongside talons and carcasses of sea eagles. To enter the cairn, you must lie on a trolley and pull yourself in using an overhead rope – something that's guaranteed to put a smile on every visitor's face. The cairn's clifftop location is spectacular, and walking along the coast in either direction is rewarding: south to the sea inlet of Ham Geo, or north to Halcro Head, and beyond to Wind Wick Bay, where seals and their pups can be seen in the autumn.

Hoy

Hoy, Orkney's second-largest island, rises sharply out of the sea to the southwest of the Mainland. The least typical of the islands, but certainly the most dramatic, its north and west sides are made up of great glacial valleys and mountainous moorland rising to the 1577-foot mass of Ward Hill, dropping into the sea off the enormous cliffs of St John's Head, and, to the south, forming the sea stack known as the **Old Man of Hoy**. This part of the island, though a huge expanse, is virtually uninhabited, with just the cluster of houses at **Rackwick** nestling dramatically in a bay between the cliffs. Meanwhile, most of Hoy's 400 or so residents live on the gentler, more fertile land in the southeast in and around the villages of **Lyness** and **Longhope**. This part of the island is littered with buildings dating from the last two world wars, when Scapa Flow served as the main base for the British Navy.

Two **ferry services** run to Hoy: a passenger ferry from Stromness to the village of Hoy (2–4 daily; 25min; ☎01856/850624), which also serves the small island of Graemsay; and the roll-on/roll-off car ferry from Houton on the Mainland to Lyness (2–5 daily; 30min–1hr; ☎01856/811397), which sometimes calls in at the oil terminal island of Flotta, and begins and ends its daily schedule at Longhope. There's no bus service on Hoy, but those arriving on the passenger ferry from Stromness should find a **minibus** waiting to take them to Rackwick.

North Hoy

Much of Hoy's magnificent landscape is embraced by the **North Hoy RSPB Reserve** (which covers most of the northwest end of the island), in which the rough grasses and heather harbour a cluster of arctic plants and a healthy population of mountain hares, as well as numerous great skuas, plus a few merlins, kestrels and peregrine falcons, while the more sheltered valleys are nesting sites for snipe and arctic skua. Walkers, arriving by passenger ferry from Stromness at Moaness Pier, near the tiny village of **HOY**, and heading for Rackwick, can either catch the minibus or take the well-marked footpath that passes Sandy Loch, and along the large open valley beyond. On the western side of this valley is the narrow gully of **Berriedale**, which supports Britain's most northerly native woodland, a huddle of birch, hazel and honeysuckle.

The minibus route to Rackwick is via the single-track road along another valley to the south. En route, duckboards head across the heather to the **Dwarfie Stane**, Orkney's most unusual chambered tomb, cut from a solid block of sandstone and dating back to 3000 BC. The sheer effort of carving out this tomb, with its two side-cells, is staggering, and as you crawl inside the marks of the tools used by the Neolithic builders on the ceiling are still visible. The tomb is also decorated with copious Victorian graffiti, the most interesting of which is to be found on the northern exterior, where Major Mouncey, a former British spy in Persia and a confirmed eccentric who dressed in Persian garb, carved his name in Latin backwards, and also in Persian the words "I have sat two nights and so learnt patience."

RACKWICK is an old crofting and fishing village squeezed between towering sandstone cliffs on the west coast. Once quite extensively cultivated, Rackwick went into a steady decline in the middle of this century: its school closed in 1953 and the last fishing boat put to sea in 1963. These days only a few of the houses are inhabited all year round (the rest serve as holiday homes), though the savage isolation of the place has provided inspiration to a number of artists and writers, including Orkney's George Mackay Brown, who wrote that "when Rackwick weeps, its grief is long and forlorn and utterly desolate". A small farm building beside the hostel serves as a tiny **museum** (open any time; free), with a few old photos and a brief rundown of Rackwick's rough history. Take the time, too, to stroll down to the beach, comprised mostly of giant sandstone pebbles washed smooth by the sea, which make a thunderous noise when the wind gets up.

Despite its isolation, Rackwick has a steady stream of walkers and climbers passing through it en route to the **Old Man of Hoy**, a great sandstone column some 450ft high, perched on an old lava flow which protects it from the erosive power of the sea. The Old Man is a popular challenge for rock climbers, and a 1966 ascent, led by Chris Bonnington, was the first televised climb in Britain. The well-trodden footpath from Rackwick is an easy three-mile walk (3hr return) – the great skuas will only divebomb you during the nesting season – and rewards you with a great view of the stack. The surrounding cliffs provide ideal rocky ledges for the nests of thousands of seabirds, including guillemots, kittiwakes, razorbills, puffins and shags. Continuing north along the clifftops, the path peters out before **St John's Head** which, at 1136ft, is one of the highest sea cliffs in the country and mostly too sheer even for nesting seabirds.

SCAPA FLOW

Apart from a few oil tankers, there's generally very little activity in the great natural harbour of **Scapa Flow**. Yet for the first half of the twentieth century, the Flow served as the main base of the British Navy, with over a hundred warships anchored here at any one time. The coastal defences required to make Scapa Flow safe to use as the country's chief naval headquarters were considerable and many are still visible all over Orkney, ranging from half-sunk blockships to the Churchill Barriers (see p.364) and the gun batteries that pepper the coastline. Unfortunately, these defences weren't sufficient to save **HMS Royal Oak** from being torpedoed by a German U-boat in October 1939 (see p.362), but they withstood several heavy German air raids during the course of 1940. Ironically, the worst disaster the Flow has ever witnessed was self-inflicted, when **HMS Vanguard** sank, on July 9, 1917, after suffering an internal explosion, taking over a thousand of her crew with her.

Scapa Flow's most celebrated moment in naval history, however, was when the entire **German High Seas Fleet** was interned here immediately after the end of World War I. A total of 74 ships was anchored off the island of Cava awaiting the outcome of the Versailles Peace Conference. At 10.30am, on Midsummer's Day, 1919, having learned that the German Navy was to be reduced to just 24 ships, the German in command, Admiral von Reuter, ordered all ships to be scuttled – by 5pm, every ship was beached or had sunk. Some still argue that the British government knew full well what von Reuter planned to do, but declined to intervene, so as to avoid the diplomatic nightmare of dividing up the fleet between the Allies.

Between the wars, the largest **salvage operation** in history took place in Scapa Flow, with the firm of Cox & Danks alone raising 24 destroyers and two huge battleships. Despite this, seven large German ships – three battleships and four light cruisers – remain on the seabed of Scapa Flow, along with four destroyers and a U-Boat. As a result, it is considered one of the world's greatest dive sites. Scapa Scuba (☎01856/851218), based in Stromness, offers one-to-one **scuba-diving** tuition for beginners, lasting three hours, diving on one of the blockships sunk by the Churchill Barriers; they also offer wreck diving for those with more experience. If you don't want to get your feet wet, Roving Eye Enterprises (☎01856/811360) run a boat fitted with an underwater camera, which does the diving for you, while you sit back and watch the video screen. The trip leaves from Houton Pier at 1.20pm, takes three hours, and includes a visit to the Scapa Flow Visitor Centre in Lyness (see opposite).

Practicalities

There are very few places to stay in North Hoy, other than the two council-run, SYHA-affiliated **hostels**, which are housed in converted schools; to book ahead, you must contact the council (☎01856/873535 ext 2404). The *Hoy Hostel* (May to mid-Sept) in Hoy village is the larger of the two, but the *Rackwick Hostel* enjoys an even better location. You can **camp** in Rackwick, either behind the hostel, down by the new, unusually attractive public toilets, or beside *Burnside Cottage* (☎01856/791316), the heather-thatched **bothy** in a beautiful setting right by the beach, which has no mattresses or kitchen facilities. **Bike rental** is available from Moaness Pier (☎01856/791225). However, there's no shop in Rackwick, so take all your supplies with you; the post office shop in Hoy only sells chocolate, but the *Hoy Inn* (closed Mon), near the post office, serves very good **bar meals**. Be warned, too, that North Hoy is probably the worst place on Orkney for midges.

Lyness and South Walls

On the opposite side of Hoy, along the sheltered eastern shore, high moorland gives way to a gentler environment similar to that on the rest of Orkney. Hoy marks the western boundary of Scapa Flow, and **LYNESS** played a major role for the British Navy during both world wars. Many of the old wartime buildings have been cleared away over the last few decades, but the harbour and hills around Lyness are still scarred with the scattered remains of concrete structures which once served as hangars and storehouses during the war, and are now used as barns and cowsheds. Among these are the remains of what was – incredibly – the largest cinema in Europe, but perhaps the most unusual remaining building is the monochrome Art Deco facade of the old **Garrison Theatre**, on the main road to the south of Lyness. Formerly the grandiose facade and foyer of a huge Nissen hut, which disappeared long ago, it's now a private home. Lyness also has a large **naval cemetery**, where many of the victims of the various disasters that have occurred in the Flow, such as the sinking of the *Royal Oak* (see p.362) now lie, alongside a handful of German graves.

The old oil pump house, which still stands opposite the new Lyness ferry terminal, has been turned into the **Scapa Flow Visitor Centre** (mid-May to June & early Sept to mid-Sept Mon–Sat 9am–4.30pm, Sun 10.30am–3.45pm; July & Aug Mon–Sat 9am–4.30pm, Sun 9.45am–6pm; mid-Sept to mid-May Mon–Fri 9am–4.30pm; £2), a fascinating insight into wartime Orkney. As well as the usual old photos, torpedoes, flags, guns and propellers, there's a paratrooper's folding bicycle, and a whole section devoted to the scuttling of the German High Seas Fleet and the sinking of the *Royal Oak*. The pump house itself retains much of its old equipment – you can even ask for a working demo of one of the oil-fired boilers – used to pump oil off tankers moored at Lyness into sixteen tanks, and from there into underground reservoirs cut into the neighbouring hillside. Every hour on the half-hour, an audiovisual on the history of Scapa Flow is shown in the sole surviving tank, which has the most incredible acoustics.

Melsetter House

The finest architecture on Hoy is to be found at **Melsetter House** (Thurs, Sat & Sun by appointment; ☎01856/791352), four miles southwest of Lyness, overlooking the deep inlet of North Bay. Originally built in 1738, it was bought by Thomas Middlemore, heir to a Birmingham leather tycoon, who commissioned the Arts and Crafts architect William Lethaby to transform the house in 1898. The charming owners will happily take you round a handful of the thoroughly lived-in rooms in the house itself, all of which are simply decorated with white wood panelling, floral plasterwork and William Morris-style fabrics, and leave you to wander freely around the house's very beautiful grounds. Don't miss the little **Chapel of St Margaret and St Colm** that Lethaby fashioned from the house's outhouses, which features some characteristic symbolic touches, and four tiny, stained-glass windows, by, among others, Ford Madox Brown and Burne-Jones. The walk back along the cliffs of the west coast to Rackwick is spectacular and takes about six hours.

South Walls

To the east, a narrow spit of sand connects the rest of Hoy with **South Walls**, a fertile peninsula which is more densely populated, with farms and homes. On the north side of South Walls is the main settlement of **LONGHOPE**, an important safe anchorage during the Napoleonic wars and World War I, but since then overshadowed by Lyness and Flotta. Longhope remains a lifeboat station, and it was the **Longhope Lifeboat** that capsized in strong gale force winds in 1969, on its way to the aid of a Liberian freighter. The entire eight-man crew was killed, leaving seven widows and ten fatherless children; the crew of the freighter, by contrast, survived. There's a gut-wrenching memorial to the men – six of whom came from just two families – in **Kirkhope Churchyard** on the road to Cantick Head Lighthouse.

Evidence of Longhope's strategic importance during the Napoleonic wars lies to the east of the village at the Point of Hackness, where the **Hackness Martello Tower** stands guard over the entrance to the bay, with a matching tower on the opposite promontory of Crockness. Built in 1815, these two circular sandstone Martello Towers are the northernmost in Britain, and were built to protect merchant ships waiting for a Royal Navy escort from American and French privateers.

FLOTTA

It comes as something of a shock when you first catch sight of the 223-foot flare stack that rises like a giant Bunsen burner from the oil terminal island of **Flotta**, east of Hoy in Scapa Flow. However, it's also a testament to the success of the local council, which, in confining the **oil industry** to the island of Flotta, has managed to minimize the impact it's had on the Mainland community. That said, it's difficult to underestimate the significance of the discovery of North Sea oil on Orkney, not only in providing several hundred well-paid jobs, but also in terms of pumping money into the local economy. Oil production has passed its peak, though it still has some years to run, and supertankers from all over the world remain a constant, slightly menacing sight in Scapa Flow.

It may seem perverse to visit an island dominated by an oil terminal, but the island does have one or two points of interest, and is very easily accessible, with frequent **car ferries** from both Hoy and the Mainland. Like Lyness, Flotta was an important naval base during both world wars, and there are a lot of **wartime relics** dotted over the island, including gun and rocket batteries, a signal station, and the huge ruin of an old YMCA, built in local stone during World War I. For a panoramic view of the island, and the whole of Scapa Flow, climb up **West Hill** (190ft), Flotta's highest point.

You can visit Hackness Tower – if it's locked, a sign will tell you where to get the key from – via a steep ladder connected to the first floor, where nine men and one officer shared the circular room. Originally a portable ladder would have been used and retracted, making the place pretty much impregnable: the walls are up to 9ft high on the seaward side, and the tower even had its own water supply. Overlooking the bay at the nearby **Hackness Battery**, positioned closer to the shore, yet more cannon were trained on the horizon.

Practicalities

There are a handful of very good, friendly **B&Bs**: *Stonequoy Farm* (☎01856/791234; ①) is a lovely 200-acre farm south of Lyness, overlooking Longhope, and the *Old Custom House* (☎01856/701358; ①) is a historic building distinguished by the miniature lions that sit atop the columns flanking the door-way, situated on the other side of the bay in Longhope. Also on this side is *Burnhouse* (☎01856/701263; ①), which also has a **self-catering** cottage available for rent. Other outstanding self-catering options include a beautifully converted outbuilding at Melsetter House (4 people; £350 per week; ☎01856/791352), and the lighthouse keepers' cottages at Cantick Head (4–6 people; £210 per week; ☎01856/701255). For **food**, there's little choice other than B&Bs, which will often provide an ample and delicious evening meal. Otherwise, the *Anchor Bar*, round the back of the ugly *Hoy Hotel* in Lyness, dishes up typical pub food; the *Scapa Flow Visitor Centre* café serves tea, coffee and snacks. There are two shops: one round the back of the *Hoy Hotel*, and one by the pier in Longhope. **Car and bike rental** is available from Halyel Car Hire in Lyness (☎01856/791240).

Shapinsay

Just a few miles northeast of Kirkwall, **Shapinsay** is the most accessible of Orkney's northern isles. A gently undulating grid-plan patchwork of rich farmland, it's a bit like an island suburb of Kirkwall. Its chief attraction for visitors is **Balfour Castle** (May–Sept Wed & Sun guided tours 3pm), the imposing Baronial pile designed by David Bryce and completed in 1848 by the Balfour family of Westray, who had made a small fortune in India the previous century. The Balfours died out in 1960 and the castle was bought by a Polish cavalry officer, Captain Tadeusz Zawadski, whose family now run the place as a hotel. The guided tours are great fun, and go down very well with children too, as they finish off with complimentary tea and home-made cakes in the servants' quarters. Before you enter the castle, you get to walk through the wooded grounds and view the vast kitchen gardens, which are surrounded by 15-foot-high walls, and once had coal-fired greenhouses to produce fruit and vegetables out of season. The castle itself is not that magnificent inside, though it has a nice lived-in feel and is pretty grand for Orkney; otters feature prominently, as they appear in the Balfour family crest.

The Balfours also reformed the island's agricultural system and built **BALFOUR** village, a neat and disciplined cottage development, to house their estate workers. The family's grandiose efforts in estate management have left some appealingly eccentric relics. Melodramatic fortifications around the harbour include the huge and ornate, if not exactly beautiful, **Gatehouse**, which is now a pub. There's also a stone-built coal-fired **Gasometer**, which once supplied castle and harbour with electricity and, southwest of the pier, the castellated **Dishan**

Tower, a seventeenth-century doocot that was converted into a cold, saltwater shower in Victorian times. The old village **Smithy** (Mon, Tues & Thurs–Sat noon–4.30pm, Wed & Sun noon–5.30pm; free) on the main street now serves as a museum of local history, with a tearoom upstairs.

Most folk visit Shapinsay on a day-trip, but if you're staying here for a few days there are one or two points of interest beyond the castle and village. One mile north of Balfour village there's the small **Mill Dam RSPB reserve**, with a hide to the west, from which you can look down on the pintail, widgeon and shovelers that breed on the wetlands. The east coast from the Foot northwards has the most interesting cliffs and sea caves, and will eventually bring you to the fairly well-preserved **Broch of Burroughston**, which is also a good spot for watching seals sunning themselves on the nearby rocks. The best stretch of sand is at the sweeping curve of **Veantro Bay** in the north.

Practicalities

Less than thirty minutes from Kirkwall by **ferry**, Shapinsay is an easy day-trip. If you want to visit the castle, before you set out you must buy an all-inclusive ticket from Kirkwall tourist office (£14.50), which includes a return ferry ticket and castle entry. The ferry for the guided tour leaves at 2.15pm, but you can catch an earlier ferry if you want to have some time to explore the rest of the island. It's also possible **to stay** in opulent style in *Balfour Castle* (☎01856/711282, *balfourcastle@btinternet.com*; ⑧); room prices include dinner, bed and breakfast, and you get use of the library and the other public rooms. More modest accommodation is available at *Girnigoe* (☎01856/711256; ①, full board ③), a very comfortable B&B close to the north shore of Veantro Bay. The only food option is the **café** in the old smithy (May–Sept), which serves teas and sandwiches.

Rousay, Egilsay and Wyre

Just over half a mile away from the Mainland's northern shore, the hilly island of **Rousay** is one of the most interesting of the smaller isles, home to a number of intriguing prehistoric sites, as well as being one of the more accessible. The group of a dozen or so houses above the ferry terminal is the only settlement of any size, but a single road runs around the edge of the island, connecting a string of small farms which make use of the more cultivable coastal fringes. Many visitors come on a day-trip, as it's easy enough to reach the main points of archeological interest on the south coast by foot from the ferry terminal. Rousay's diminutive neighbours, **Egilsay** and **Wyre**, contain a few medieval attractions of their own, which can either be visited on a day-trip from Rousay itself, or from the mainland.

Trumland House to the Knowe of Yarso

Despite its long history of settlement, Rousay is today home to little more than 200 people (many of them incomers), as this was one of the few parts of Orkney to suffer Highland-style clearances, initially by George William Traill at Quandale in the northwest. His successor, Lieutenant-General Traill-Burroughs, built the unlovely **Trumland House**, a forbidding Jacobean-style pile designed by David Bryce in 1873, hidden in the trees half a mile from the ferry terminal. Continuing

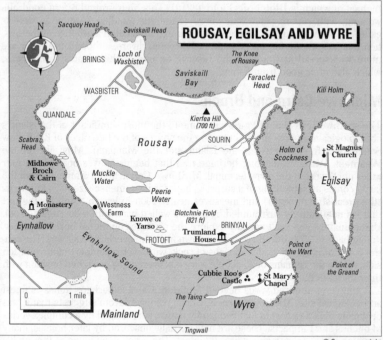

ROUSAY, EGILSAY AND WYRE

Sacquoy Head · Saviskaill Head · Loch of Wasbister · The Knee of Rousay · BRINGS · WASBISTER · Saviskaill Bay · Faraclett Head · Kili Holm · QUANDALE · Kierfea Hill (700 ft) · SOURIN · Scabra Head · *Rousay* · Holm of Scockness · St Magnus Church · Midhowe Broch & Cairn · Muckle Water · *Egilsay* · Monastery · Peerie Water · Westness Farm · Knowe of Yarso · Blotchnie Field (821 ft) · BRINYAN · *Eynhallow* · Trumland House · FROTOFT · Point of the Wart · *Eynhallow Sound* · Point of the Graand · Cubbie Roo's Castle · St Mary's Chapel · The Taing · *Wyre* · *Mainland* · Tingwall

0 — 1 mile

to substitute sheep for people, he built a wall to force crofters onto a narrow coastal strip and eventually provoked so much distress and anger that a gunboat had to be sent to restore order. You can learn a little more about the history and wildlife of the island from the well-laid-out **Trumland Orientation Centre** (Mon–Sat 7.30am–7pm; mid-May to mid-Sept also Sun), housed in a modern bungalow by the pier that doubles as a sort of waiting room for the ferry.

The first trio of archeological sights is spread out over the next couple of miles, on and off the road that leads west from the ferry terminal. **Taversoe Tuick**, the nearest chambered cairn, lies just beyond Trumland House, and was discovered by workers during the building of a Victorian viewpoint. Dating back to 3500 BC, it's unusual in that it exploits its sloping site by having two storeys, one entered from the upper side and one from the lower. A little further west is the **Blackhammar Cairn**, which is more promising inside than it looks from the outside. You enter through the roof via a ladder; the long interior is divided into "stalls" by large flagstones, rather like the more famous cairn at Midhowe (see p.374). Finally, there's the **Knowe of Yarso**, another stalled cairn dating from the same period that's a stiff climb up the hill from the road, but worth it, if only for the magnificent view. The remains of 29 individuals were found inside, with the skulls neatly arranged around the walls; the bones of 36 deer were also buried here.

A footpath sets off from beside the Taversoe Tuick tomb off into the **RSPB reserve** that encompasses a large section of the nearby heather-backed hills, the highest of which is **Blotchnie Fiold** (821ft). This high ground offers good hill-walking, with superb panoramic views of the surrounding islands, as well as excellent birdwatching. If you're lucky, you may well catch a glimpse of merlins, hen harriers, peregrine falcons and red-throated divers, although the latter are more widespread just outside the reserve on one of the island's three lochs, which also offer good trout fishing.

Midhowe Cairn and Broch

The southwestern side of Rousay is home to the most significant of the island's archeological remains, strung out along the shores of the tide races of Eynhallow Sound, which run between the island and the Mainland. Most lie on the **Westness Walk**, a mile-long heritage trail that begins at Westness Farm, four miles northwest of the ferry terminal. **Midhowe Cairn**, about a mile on from the farm, comes as something of a surprise, both for its immense size – it's known as "the great ship of death" and measures nearly 100ft in length – and for the fact that it's now entirely surrounded by a stone-walled barn with a corrugated roof. Unfortunately, you can't actually explore the roofless communal burial chamber, dating back to 3500 BC, but only look down from the overhead walkway. The central corridor is partitioned with slabs of rock, with twelve compartments on each side, where the remains of 25 people were discovered in a crouched position with their backs to the wall.

A couple of hundred yards beyond Midhowe Cairn is perhaps Rousay's finest archeological site, **Midhowe Broch**, whose compact layout suggests that it was originally built as a sort of fortified family house, surrounded by a complex series of ditches and ramparts. These are now partially obscured by later houses, many of which have shelving and stairs still intact. The broch itself looks as though it's about to collapse – it was obviously shored up with flagstone buttresses back in the Iron Age, and has more recently been given extra sea defences by Historic Scotland. The interior of the broch is divided into two separate rooms, each with their own hearth, water tank and quernstone, all of which date from the final phase of occupation around the second century AD.

From Midhowe Broch you get a good view of the nearby small island of **Eynhallow**, which is surrounded by the most ferocious tides. The island was cleared in 1851, at which point it was discovered that one of the houses was in fact a converted church, possibly part of a monastery, dating back to at least the twelfth century. Beyond Midhowe, a walk along the coast will take you past the impressive cliff scenery around **Scabra Head**, where numerous seabirds nest in summer. Inland, the heathland of Quandale and Brings provides yet more bird-watching, with arctic terns and arctic skuas in abundance.

Egilsay and Wyre

Egilsay, the largest of the low-lying islands sheltering close to the eastern shore of Rousay, makes for an easy day-trip. The island is dominated by the ruins of **St Magnus Church**, with its distinctive round tower. Built around the twelfth century in a prominent position in the middle of the island, probably on the site of a much earlier version, the roofless church is the only surviving example of the traditional round-towered churches of Orkney and Shetland. It is possible that it was built as a shrine to Earl (later St) Magnus, who arranged to meet his cousin

Haakon here in 1117, only to be treacherously killed by the latter's cook, Lifolf. A cenotaph marks the spot where the murder took place, about a quarter of a mile southeast of the church. Egilsay is almost entirely inhabited by incomers, and a large slice of the island's farmland is managed by the RSPB in order to encourage corncrakes, which you may be lucky enough to hear.

The tiny, neighbouring island of **Wyre**, to the southwest, is another possible day-trip, and is best known for **Cubbie Roo's Castle**, the "fine stone fort" and "really solid stronghold" mentioned in the *Orkneyinga Saga*, and built around 1150 by local farmer Kolbein Hruga. The castle gets another mention in *Haakon's Saga*, when those inside successfully withstood all attacks. The outer defences have survived well on three sides of the castle, which has a central keep, with walls to a height of around 6ft, its central water tank still intact. Close by the castle stands **St Mary's Chapel**, a roofless twelfth-century church founded either by Kolbein or his son, Bjarni the Poet, who was Bishop of Orkney. Kolbein's permanent residence or Bu is recalled in the name of the nearby farm, the Bu of Wyre, where the poet **Edwin Muir** (1887–1959) spent his childhood, described in detail in his autobiography. If you walk to very western tip of Wyre, known as **The Taing**, you're pretty much guaranteed to see large numbers of grey and common seals basking on the rocks.

Practicalities

Rousay makes a good day-trip from the Mainland, with regular **car ferry** sailings from Tingwall (30min), which has bus connections to and from Kirkwall. Most ferries call in at Egilsay and Wyre, but some need to be booked the day before at the Tingwall ferry terminal (☎01856/751360). Alternatively, you can join one of the very informative **minibus tours** run by Rousay Traveller (June–Aug Tues–Fri; ☎01856/821234), which connect with ferries and last between two and six hours, the longer ones allowing extended walks. **Bike rental** is available from Arts, Bikes & Crafts on Pier Road (☎01856/821398).

Accommodation on Rousay is extremely limited. The only hotel is the *Taversoe* (☎01856/821325; ②), a modern extension added onto an old croft, a couple of miles west of the terminal at Frotoft. The hotel **restaurant** offers excellent home-cooking featuring local produce, especially seafood, and vegetarian options; a bar and beer garden overlook the Eynhallow Sound. Alternatively, *Trumland Farm* (☎01856/821252), half a mile or so west of the terminal, runs a **hostel**, where you can also camp, and two self-catering cottages. As well as the *Taversoe*, the *Pier Restaurant* (☎01856/821359) right beside the terminal serves bar meals at lunchtime; if you phone in advance, they will pack you a delicious **picnic** of crab, cheese, fruit and bannock bread. In the evening, the restaurant functions as a pub.

Westray

Although exposed to the full force of the Atlantic weather in the far northwest of Orkney, **Westray** shelters one of the most tightly knit and prosperous island communities. It has a fairly stable population of 700 or so, producing superb beef, scallops, shellfish and a large catch of white fish, with its own small fish-processing factory and an organic salmon farm. Old Orcadian families still dominate every aspect of life here, giving the island a strong individual character. The landscape

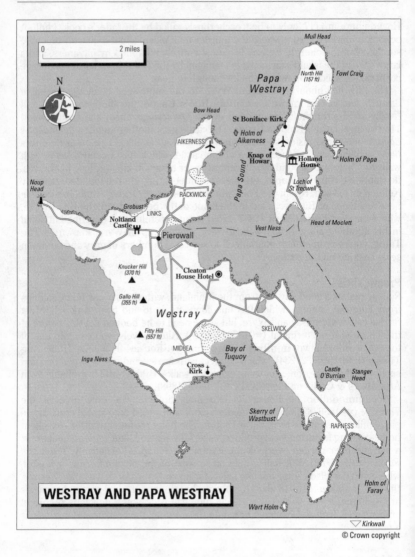

0   2 miles

N

*Papa
Westray*

Mull Head

North Hill
(157 ft)

Fowl Craig

Bow Head

St Boniface Kirk

AIKERNESS

Holm of
Aikerness

Knap of
Howar

Holland
House

Holm of Papa

Papa Sound

Loch of
St Tredwell

Noup
Head

Grobust

RACKWICK

LINKS

Noltland
Castle

Pierowall

Vest Ness

Head of Moclett

Knucker Hill
(370 ft)

Cleaton
House Hotel

Gallo Hill
(355 ft)

Westray

Fitty Hill
(557 ft)

SKELWICK

Inga Nass

MIDBEA

Bay of
Tuquoy

Cross
Kirk

Castle
O'Burrian

Stanger
Head

Skerry of
Wastbust

RAPNESS

WESTRAY AND PAPA WESTRAY

Holm of
Faray

Wart Holm

▽ *Kirkwall*

is very varied, with sea cliffs and a trio of hills in the west, and rich low-lying pastureland and sandy bays elsewhere. However, given that distances are fairly large – it's about twelve miles from the ferry terminal to the cliffs of Noup Head – and the ferry from Kirkwall takes nearly an hour and a half, Westray is an island that repays a longer stay, especially as the locals are extremely welcoming and genuinely interested in visitors.

The main village and harbour is **PIEROWALL** in the north of the island, a good eight miles from the Rapness ferry terminal on the southernmost tip of the island. For the islands, Pierowall is a place of some considerable size, with a school, several shops, a bakery (the only one not on the Mainland), and the excellent **Westray Heritage Centre** (mid-May to mid-Sept Tues–Sat 9.30am–12.30pm & 2–5pm; £2), a tiny building hidden up a lane flanked by fuchsias. If you've got children, this is a very welcoming wet-weather retreat, with a great mock-up of the sea cliffs of Noup Head (see below) and a really imaginative range of hands-on exhibits; it's also the only place on the island where you can get a cup of tea. Pierowall also boasts the **Lady Kirk**, a ruined chapel sporting a dinky little belfry, to the north of the village centre, which contains two very fine seventeenth-century tombstones.

The island's most impressive ruin, however, is the colossal sandstone husk of **Noltland Castle**, which stands above the village half a mile west up the road to Noup Head. This Z-plan castle, which is pockmarked with over seventy gun loops, was begun around 1560 by Gilbert Balfour, a shady character from Fife, who was Master of the Household to Mary, Queen of Scots and was implicated in the murder of her husband Lord Darnley in 1567. Mary was deposed before she could make her planned visit to Noltland, and Balfour, having joined an unsuccessful uprising in favour of the exiled queen, was forced to flee to Sweden. There he was found guilty of plotting to murder the Swedish king and was executed in 1576. Somewhat miraculously, the Balfour family managed to hold on to Noltland (and Westray), eventually shifting their seat to Shapinsay (see p.371). To explore the castle, you must first pick up the key, which hangs outside the back door of the nearby farm. The most striking features of the interior are the huge, carved stone newel at the top of the grand, main staircase, and the secret compartments built into the sills of two of the windows.

The northwestern tip of the island rises up sharply, culminating in the dramatic sea cliffs of **Noup Head**, which are particularly spectacular when a good westerly swell is up. The whole area is an RSPB reserve, and during the summer months the guano-covered rock ledges are packed with over 100,000 nesting seabirds, primarily guillemots, razorbills, kittiwakes and fulmars, plus a fair few puffin, too: a truly awesome sight, sound and smell. There's a great viewpoint just to the northwest of the lighthouse, and another at Lawrence's Piece, half a mile to the south, where a narrow rocky ledge juts out into the sea. The open ground above the cliffs, which is grazed by sheep, is superb maritime heath and grassland, carpeted with yellow, white and purple flowers, and a favourite breeding ground for arctic terns and arctic skuas. The coastal walk from Noup Head, south to Inga Ness, is thoroughly recommended, as is a quick ascent of Fitty Hill (57ft), Westray's highest point.

The sea cliffs in the southeast of the island, around **Stanger Head** are not quite as spectacular, but it's here that you'll find **Castle o' Burrian**, a sea stack that was once an early Christian hermitage. It's now the best place on Westray at which to see **puffins** nesting – there's even a signpost to the puffins from the main road. Also in the south of the island is the tiny **Cross Kirk** which, although ruined, retains an original Romanesque arch, door and window. It's also right by the sea, and on a fine day the nearby sandy beach is a lovely spot in which to picnic, with views over to the north side of Rousay.

Practicalities

Westray is served by car **ferry** from Kirkwall (2–3 daily; 1hr 25min; ☎01856/872044), or you can **fly** on Loganair's tiny eight-seater plane from Kirkwall to Westray (Mon–Sat 1–2 daily; 12min). **Minibus tours** of the island can also be arranged with Island Explorer (☎01857/677355), which connects with ferries. M. & J. Harcus of Meadowbank, Pierowall (☎01857/677450) run a **bus service** which will take you from Rapness to Pierowall; they also offer **car rental**. For **bike rental**, contact Sand O' Gill (☎01857/677374) or Twiness (☎01857/677319).

The finest **accommodation** on Westray is at the *Cleaton House Hotel* (☎01857/677508, *cleaton@orkney.com*; ④), a converted Victorian manse about two miles southeast of Pierowall, with great views over to Papa Westray. *Cleaton House* is also the only place on the island where you can sample Westray's organic salmon, either in the expensive hotel **restaurant** or in the hotel's congenial **bar**, washed down with a pint of draught Orkney Dark Island beer. Somewhat bizarrely, the hotel also has a **pétanque** pitch, which residents and non-residents alike are welcome to use. The *Pierowall Hotel* (☎01857/677208; ①), in Pierowall itself, is less stylish but welcoming nevertheless, with a popular bar and a reputation for excellent fish and chips. Alternatively, **B&B** is available at *Sand O' Gill* (☎01857/677374; ①), where you can also **camp** or rent the **self-catering caravan**. If you'd like to play the somewhat eccentric **golf course** on the links northwest of Pierowall, clubs can be rented from Tulloch's shop (☎01857/677373). To find out when the local **swimming pool** is available, phone Mrs Kent (☎01857/677436).

Papa Westray

Across the short Papa Sound from Westray is the neighbouring island of **Papa Westray**, known locally as "Papay". With a population hovering precariously between sixty and seventy, it has had to fight hard to keep itself viable over the last couple of decades, helped by a hefty influx of outsiders. The major points of interest are one of Orkney's best-preserved Neolithic settlements, and the RSPB reserve in the north of the island, which has a staggeringly large population of resident birds during the breeding season. As the name suggests, Papay was once a medieval pilgrimage centre, focused on a chapel dedicated to **St Tredwell**, which is now reduced to a pile of rubble, on a promontory on the loch of the same name. St Tredwell (Triduana) was a plucky young local girl who gouged out her eyes and handed them to the eighth-century Pictish King Nechtan when he attempted to rape her. By the twelfth century, the chapel had become a place of pilgrimage for those suffering from eye complaints.

The island's visual focus is **Holland House**, occupying the high central point of the island and once seat of the local lairds, the Traill family, who ruled over Papay for three centuries. The main house, with its crow-stepped gables, is still in private hands, but the current owners are perfectly happy for visitors to explore the old buildings of the home farm, on the west side of the road, which include a kiln, a doocot and a horse-powered threshing mill. An old bothy for single male servants, decorated with red horse yokes, has even been restored and made into a small **museum** (open at any time; free), filled with bygone bits and bobs, from a wooden flea trap to a box bed.

A road leads down from Holland House to the western shore, where Papay's prime prehistoric site, the **Knap of Howar**, stands overlooking Westray. Dating from around 3500 BC, this Neolithic farm building makes a fair claim to being the oldest-standing house in Europe. It's made up of two roofless buildings, linked by a little passageway; one has a hearth and copious stone shelves, and is thought to have been some kind of storehouse. Half a mile north along the coast from the Knap of Howar is **St Boniface Kirk**, a pre-Reformation church that has recently been restored. Inside, it's beautifully simple, with a bare flagstone floor, drystone walls, a little wooden gallery and just a couple of surviving box pews. The church is known to have seated at least 220, which meant they would have been squashed in, fourteen to a pew. In the surrounding graveyard there's a Viking **hogback grave**, decorated with carvings in imitation of the wooden shingles on the roof of a Viking longhouse.

The northern tip of the island around **North Hill** (157ft) is now an **RSPB reserve**. During the breeding season, you're asked to keep to the coastal fringe, where razorbills, guillemots, fulmar, kittiwakes and puffin nest, particularly around Fowl Craig on the east coast, where you can also view the rare Scottish primrose, which flowers in May and from July to late September. If you want to explore the interior of the reserve, which plays host to one of the largest arctic tern colonies in Europe as well as numerous arctic skuas, contact the warden at Rose Cottage (☎01857/644240), who does regular escorted walks.

If you're here for more than a day, it's worth considering renting a boat to take you over to the **Holm of Papay**, an even smaller island off the east coast. Despite is tiny size, the Holm boasts several Neolithic chambered cairns, one of which, occupying the highest point, is extremely impressive. Descending into the tomb via a ladder, you enter the main rectangular chamber which is nearly 70ft in length, with no fewer than twelve side-cells, each with its own lintelled entrance. To arrange a boat, contact the Community Co-operative (see below).

Practicalities

With a regular **passenger ferry** service from Pierowall (3–6 daily; 25min), Papa Westray is an easy day-trip from Westray. However, it's just as easy to stay on Papay and take a day-trip to Westray instead. On Tuesdays and Fridays, the **car ferry** from Kirkwall to Westray continues on to Papa Westray; at other times, you can catch the bus from Rapness to Pierowall to connect with the passenger ferry. Papay is also connected to Westray by the **world's shortest scheduled flight** – two minutes in duration; less with a following wind. Tickets from Loganair cost around £15 one way; you can also fly direct from Kirkwall to Papa Westray (Mon–Sat 1–2 daily). The island's Community Co-operative (☎01857/644267) has a **minibus**, which will take you from the pier to wherever you want on the island. It also runs a shop, a sixteen-bed SYHA-affiliated **hostel**, a **guest house** (②, full board ⑤) and a **self-catering cottage** (6 people; £160 per week), all housed within the old estate workers' cottages at Beltane, to the east of Holland House.

Eday

A long, thin island at the centre of Orkney's northern isles, **Eday** shares more characteristics with Rousay and Hoy than with its immediate neighbours, dominated as it is by a great block of heather-covered upland, with farmland confined to a narrow strip of coastal ground. However, Eday's hills have proved useful in their own way, providing huge quantities of peat which has been exported to the other peatless northern isles for fuel, and was even, for a time, exported to various whisky distillers. Eday's yellow sandstone has also been extensively quarried, and was used to build the St Magnus Cathedral in Kirkwall.

The island is very sparsely inhabited, has no real village as such, and is almost divided in two by the thin waist, where the island's airfield (known as London Airport) lies. The chief points of interest are all in the northern half of the island, beyond the post office, petrol pump and Eday Community Enterprises shop on the main road. This marks the beginning of the signposted **Eday Heritage Walk**, which covers all the main sights, and takes about three hours to complete. The walk initially follows the road heading northwest, past the RSPB bird hide overlooking **Mill Loch**, where several pairs of red-throated divers regularly breed.

Clearly visible to the north of the road is the fifteen-foot **Stone of Setter**, Orkney's most distinctive standing stone, weathered into three thick, lichen-encrusted fingers. The stone clearly held centre stage in the Neolithic landscape, and is visible from the other nearby prehistoric sites. From here, passing the less spectacular Braeside and Huntersquoy chambered cairns en route, climb the hill to reach Eday's finest, the **Vinquoy Chambered Cairn**, which has a similar structure to that of Maes Howe. You can crawl into the tomb through the narrow entrance – a skylight inside lets light into the main, beehive chamber, now home to some lovely ferns, but not into the four side-cells. From the cairn, continue north to the viewpoint on the summit of **Vinquoy Hill** (248ft), and on to the very northernmost tip of the island, and the dramatic red sandstone sea cliffs of **Red Head**, where guillemots, razorbills, puffins and other seabirds nest in summer.

Alternatively, simply head straight down to the east coast and **Carrick House**, the grandest home on Eday (mid-June to mid-Sept Sun 2pm; £2; ☎01857/622260). Built by the Laird of Eday in 1633, it was extended in the original style by successive owners, but is best known for its associations with the pirate **John Gow** – on whom Sir Walter Scott's novel *The Pirate* is based – who attempted to attack the house in 1725, only for his ship *The Revenge* to run aground on the Calf of Eday. He asked for help from the local laird, but was taken prisoner in Carrick House, before eventually being sent off to London where he was tortured and executed.

From Carrick House, the uninhabited island of the **Calf of Eday** is only a stone's throw away. If you're staying on Eday, it's easy enough to organize a boat to take you over to the island: try J. & H. Thomson (☎01857/622256). The island features several chambered cairns, and is home to some massive bird colonies along its eastern cliffs, including a large colony of great black-backed gulls and numerous black guillemots, as well as all the usual suspects.

Practicalities

Eday's **ferry** terminal is at Backaland pier in the south, not ideal for visiting the more interesting northern section of the island, although if you haven't got your own transport you should find it fairly easy to get a lift with someone off the ferry (2 daily; 1hr 15min–2hr). Alternatively, rent a **taxi** from Mr A. Stewart by the pier (☎01857/622206), or **bicycles** from Martin Burkett at Hamarr, in the valley below the post office (☎01857/622331). Orkney Ferries also run an **Eday Heritage Tour** every Sunday (mid-June to mid-Sept), which costs just under £30 per person, and includes return ferry tickets and a guided minibus tour around the island (including Carrick House). It's also possible to do a day-trip on the Loganair **flight** from Kirkwall to Eday on Wednesdays (☎01856/872494).

The best option when it comes to **accommodation** is the new self-catering cottages set in the hacienda-style complex around the local pub, *Pirate Gow's Inn*

(Fri–Sun only), in Calfsound (☎01700/505357; ①). All six cottages are well equipped, and can be rented out for anything from one night to a week. Friendly **B&B** is available at *Skaill Farm*, a traditional farmhouse just south of the airport (☎01857/622271; full board ③; closed April & May). The SYHA-affiliated **hostel**, situated in an exposed spot just north of the airport, is very basic and is run by Eday Community Association (☎01857/622206; April–Sept).

Stronsay

A low-lying, three-legged island to the southeast of Eday, **Stronsay** is strongly agricultural, its interior an almost uninterrupted patchwork of green pastures. Stronsay features few real sights, but the coastline has enormous appeal: a beguiling combination of sandstone cliffs, home to several seabird colonies, interspersed with wide white sands and (in fine weather) clear turquoise bays. Stronsay has seen two economic booms in the last three hundred years. The first took place in the eighteenth century, and employed as many as 3000 people; it was built on collecting vast quantities of seaweed and exporting the **kelp** for use in the chemical industry, particularly in making iodine, soap and glass. In the following century, **fishing** on a grand scale came to dominate life here, as Whitehall harbour became one of the main Scottish centres for the curing of herring caught by French, Dutch and Scottish boats. By the 1840s, up to four hundred boats were working out of the port, attracting hundreds of women herring-gutters. By the 1930s, however, the herring stocks had been severely depleted and the industry began a long decline.

   WHITEHALL, in the north of the island, remains the only real village on Stronsay, made up of a couple of rows of stone-built fishermen's cottages set between two large piers. Wandering along the tranquil, rather forlorn harbour front today, you'll find it hard to believe that the village once supported 5000 people in the fishing industry during the summer season, as well as a small army of coopers, coal merchants, butchers, bakers, several Italian ice-cream parlours and a cinema. It was said that on a Sunday, you could walk across the decks of the boats all the way to **Papa Stronsay**, the tiny island that shelters Whitehall from north, on which you can still see some of the old herring curing stations. Several houses in Whitehall are roofless and others lie empty, but the old fish market by the pier now houses a **Heritage Centre** (May–Sept daily 11am–5pm; free), with a few photos and artefacts from the herring days. It also has a small café.

   If the weather's fine, you can choose which of the island's many arching, dazzlingly white beaches to relax on. The most dramatic section of coastline, featuring great layered slices of sandstone, lies in the southeast corner of the island. Signposts show the way to Orkney's biggest and most dramatic natural arch, the **Vat of Kirbuster**. Before you reach the arch there's a seaweedy, shallow pool in a natural sandstone amphitheatre, where the water is warmed by the sun and kids and adults can safely wallow: close by is a rocky inlet for those who prefer colder, more adventurous swimming. You'll find progressively more nesting seabirds, including a few puffin, as you approach **Burgh Head**, further along down the coast. Meanwhile, at the promontory of **Lamb Head**, there are usually loads of seals, a large colony of arctic terns, and good views out to the lighthouse on the outlying island of **Auskerry**, to the south.

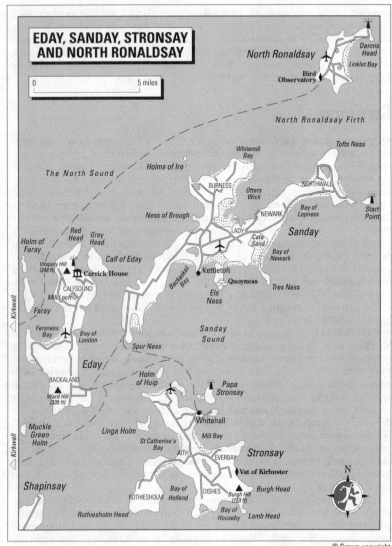

EDAY, SANDAY, STRONSAY AND NORTH RONALDSAY

0   5 miles

North Ronaldsay

Dennis Head

Linklet Bay

Bird Observatory

North Ronaldsay Firth

Tofts Ness

The North Sound

Holms of Ire

Whitemill Bay

BURNESS

Otters Wick

NORTHWALL

Start Point

Ness of Brough

NEWARK

Bay of Lopness

LADY

Sanday

Holm of Faray

Red Head

Grey Head

Calf of Eday

Cata Sand

Bay of Newark

Vinquoy Hill (248 ft)

Carrick House

Backaskail Bay

Kettletoft

Quoyness

Tres Ness

CALFSOUND

Els Ness

Mill Loch

Faray

Fersness Bay

Bay of London

Sanday Sound

Spur Ness

Eday

Holm of Huip

Papa Stronsay

BACKALAND

Ward Hill (335 ft)

Whitehall

Muckle Green Holm

Linga Holm

Mill Bay

St Catherine's Bay

AITH

EVERBAY

Stronsay

Shapinsay

Vat of Kirbuster

DISHES

Burgh Head

ROTHIESHOLM

Bay of Holland

Burgh Hill (153 ft)

Bay of Houseby

Lamb Head

Rothiesholm Head

△ Kirkwall

N

Practicalities

Stronsay is served by a regular car **ferry** service from Kirkwall to Whitehall (twice daily; 1hr 40min–2hr), and weekday Loganair **flights** (2 daily; 25min) from Kirkwall. There's no bus service, but D.S. Peace (☎01857/616335) operates taxis and **rents cars**. Of the few **accommodation** options available, a good choice is the new **hostel** in the old fish market by the pier, with a well-equipped kitchen, washing machine and comfortable bunk-bedded rooms. It's run by the folk at the *Stronsay Hotel* opposite (☎01857/616213; ①), which has seen better days – it once boasted the longest bar in the north of Scotland – but is currently undergoing a long overdue refurbishment. There's even more basic accommodation at *Torness Camping Barn* in Holland Farm (☎01857/616314), beyond Dishes, in the south of the island. Alternatively, the *Stronsay Bird Reserve* (☎01857/616363; ①) is a nicely positioned **B&B**, which also offers camping on the shores of Mill Bay. The bar in the *Stronsay Hotel* does pub **food**, and there's a takeaway along the street at *Woodlea* that's open sporadically (☎01857/616337); otherwise, you'll need to bring your own supplies and make use of the island's two shops. There's a **swimming pool** behind the school which is available for public use, but it's operated on a voluntary basis, so check first at the Heritage Centre.

Sanday

Sanday, though the largest of the northern isles, is also the most insubstantial, a great low-lying, drifting dune strung out between several rocky points. The island's sweeping aquamarine bays and vast stretches of clean white sand are the finest in Orkney, and in dry, clear weather it's a superb place to spend a day or two. The sandy soil is, in fact, very fertile, and the island remains predominantly agricultural even today, holding its very own agricultural show each year at the beginning of August.

The island has a long history as a shipping hazard, with many wrecks smashed against its shores, although the construction of the **Start Point Lighthouse** in 1802 on the island's exposed eastern tip reduced the risk for seafarers. Shipwrecks were, in fact, not an unwelcome sight on Sanday, as the island has no peat, and driftwood was the only source of fuel other than cow dung – it's even said that the locals used to pray for shipwrecks in church. The present Stevenson lighthouse, which dates from 1870, now sports very natty vertical black and white stripes. It actually stands on a tidal island, which is only accessible on either side of low tide, so ask locally for the tide times before setting out (it takes 1hr to walk there and back); phone the lighthouse keeper (☎01857/600385) in advance if you want to see inside.

The shoreline supports a healthy seal, otter and wading bird population, and behind the splendid sandy beaches are stretches of beautiful open machair and grassland, thick with wild flowers during the spring and summer. The entire coastline presents the opportunity for superb walks, with particularly spectacular sand dunes to the south of Cata Sand. Sanday is also rich in archeology, with hundreds of mostly unexcavated sites including cairns, brochs and burnt mounds. The most impressive is **Quoyness Chambered Cairn**, on the fertile farmland of Els Ness peninsula. The tomb, which dates from before 2000 BC, has been partially reconstructed, and rises to a height of around 13ft. The imposing, narrow entrance, flanked by high drystone walls, would originally have been roofed for the whole of the way into the 13-foot-long main chamber, where bones and skulls were discovered in the six small side-cells.

Unfortunately, the island's knitting factory recently closed down, but you can still visit Sanday's unusual **Orkney Angora** craft shop (☎01857/600421), in Upper Breckan in the parish of Burness. The owner will usually oblige with a quick look and a stroke of one of the comically long-haired albino rabbits who supply the wool. Close by is the stone tower of an old windmill, which belonged to the neighbouring farmstead and house of **Scar**, where you can still see the chimney from the farm's old steam-powered meal mill.

Practicalities

Ferries to Sanday arrive at the new terminal at the southern tip of the island and are met by the **minibus** (book on ☎01857/600467), which will take you to most points. The airfield is in the centre of the island and there are Loganair **flights** to Kirkwall twice daily on weekdays, and once on Saturdays. The fishing port of Kettletoft is where the ferry used to dock, and where you'll find the island's two **hotels**, neither of which is spectacularly good. Of the two, the *Belsair Hotel* (☎01857/600206; ②) has the slightly more adventurous restaurant menu, while the *Kettletoft Hotel* (☎01857/600217; ①) has a lively bar that's popular with the locals. Of the handful of **B&Bs**, try *Quivals* (☎01857/600418; ①), who can also organize car and bike rental. For a wonderful, reasonably priced **self-catering cottage** over by Start Point, contact Richard Corser (3–4 people; £150 per week; ☎01857/600403).

North Ronaldsay

North Ronaldsay – or "North Ron" as it's fondly known – is Orkney's most northerly island. Separated from Sanday by the treacherous waters of the North Ronaldsay Firth, it has a unique outpost atmosphere, brought about by its extreme isolation. Measuring just three miles by one and rising only 66ft above sea level, the island is almost overwhelmed by the enormity of the sky, the strength of wind and, of course, the ferocity of the sea – so much so that its very existence seems an act of tenacious defiance. Despite these adverse conditions, North Ronaldsay has been inhabited for centuries, and continues to be heavily farmed, from old-style crofts whose roofs are made from huge local flagstones. With no natural harbours and precious little farmland, the islanders have been forced to make the most of what they have and **seaweed** has played an important role in the local economy. During the eighteenth century, kelp was gathered here, burnt in pits and sent south for use in the chemicals industry.

The island's **sheep** are a unique, tough, goatlike breed, who feed mostly on seaweed, giving their flesh a dark tone and a rich, gamey taste, and making their thick wool highly prized. A high **drystone dyke**, completed in the mid-nineteenth century and running the thirteen miles around the edge of the island, keeps them off the farmland, except during lambing season, when the ewes are allowed onto the pastureland. North Ronaldsay sheep are also unusual in that they can't be rounded up by sheepdogs like ordinary sheep, but scatter far and wide at some considerable speed. Instead, once a year the islanders herd the sheep communally into a series of **drystone "punds"** near Dennis Head, for clipping and dipping, in what is one of the last acts of communal farming practised in Orkney.

There are very few real sights on the island, and the most frequent visitors are ornithologists, who come in considerable numbers to catch a glimpse of the rare migrants who land here briefly on their spring and autumn migrations.

The peak times of year for migrants are from late March to early June, and from mid-August to early November, although there are also many breeding species which spend the spring and summer here, including gulls, terns, waders, black guillemots, cormorants and even the odd corncrake. As on Fair Isle, there's now a permanent **Bird Observatory**, situated in the southwest corner of the island, which can give advice as to what birds have recently been sighted. The observatory was established in 1987 by adapting a croft to wind and solar power.

Holland House – built by the Traill family who bought the island in 1727 – and the island's two lighthouses at Dennis Head, are the only features to interrupt the flat horizon. The attractive, stone-built **Old Beacon** was first lit in 1789, but the lantern was replaced by the huge bauble of masonry you now see as long ago as 1809. The **New Lighthouse**, half a mile to the north, is the tallest land-based lighthouse in Britain, rising to a height of over 100ft. On a clear day you can see Fair Isle, and even Sumburgh and Fitful Head on Shetland.

Practicalities

The **ferry** from Kirkwall to North Ronaldsay only runs once a week (usually Fri; 2hr 40min–3hr), though day-trips are possible on occasional Sundays between late May and early September (phone ☎01856/872044 for details). Probably your best bet is to catch a Loganair **flight** from Kirkwall (Mon–Sat – 2 daily), which allows between five and seven hours on the island. You can **stay** overnight, either at the *North Ronaldsay Bird Observatory* (☎01857/633200, *alison@nrbo.prestel.co.uk*; ①–③), which offers full-board either in private guest rooms or in dorms. Full-board accommodation is also available at *Garso*, in the northeast (☎01857/633244, *christine.muir@virgin.net*; ③), which also has a self-catering cottage. The *Burrian Inn*, to the southeast of the war memorial, is the island's small **pub**, and does hot food. **Camping** is possible; for further information, phone ☎01857/633222.

ONWARDS TO NORWAY, THE FAROE ISLANDS AND ICELAND

Thanks to the historical ties and the attraction of a short hop to continental Europe, **Norway** is a popular destination for Shetlanders and Orcadians. Norwegians often think of Shetland and Orkney as their western isles and, particularly in west Norway, old wartime bonds with Shetland are still strong. Norwegian yachts and sail training vessels are frequent visitors to Lerwick and Kirkwall. Shetlanders can also go by ferry to the **Faroe Islands** – steep, angular shapes rising out of the North Atlantic – and from Faroe on to **Iceland**.

There are weekly **flights** between June and September from Kirkwall in Orkney (1hr 45min) and twice-weekly from Sumburgh in Shetland (1hr) to Bergen in Norway. Short inclusive breaks are available by air from Shetland; book through Hay & Co (☎01950/460661). From June to August the large, comfortable and fast Faroese car **ferry** *Nörrona* makes weekly return trips from her home port in Faroe to Shetland, Norway, Iceland and Denmark. From Shetland, Bergen in Norway and Torshavn in Faroe are thirteen hours away; to Iceland the journey takes 33 hours including a brief stop in Faroe; on the way back there's a two-day stopover in Faroe while the ship makes a return trip to Denmark.

SHETLAND

Many maps place the **Shetland Islands** in a box somewhere off Aberdeen, but in fact Bergen in Norway is a lot closer than Edinburgh, and the Arctic Circle is nearer than Manchester. The Shetland **landscape** is a product of the struggle between rock and the forces of water and ice that have, over millennia, tried to break it to pieces. Smoothed by the last glaciation, the surviving land has been exposed to the most violent weather experienced in the British Isles; it isn't for nothing that Shetlanders call the place "the Old Rock", and the coastline, a crust of cliffs with caves, blowholes and stacks, testifies to the continuing battle. Inland (a relative term, since you're never more than three miles from the sea), the terrain is a barren mix of moorland, often studded with peaty lochs of a brilliant blue (when the sun shines), and the occasional patch of green farmland, dotted with hardy, multicoloured sheep and diminutive ponies. In winter, gales are routine and Shetlanders take even the occasional hurricane in their stride, marking a calm fine day as "a day atween weathers". There are some good spells of dry, sunny weather from May to September, but it's the **"simmer dim"**, the twilight which replaces darkness at this latitude, which makes Shetland summers so memorable; in June especially, the northern sky is an unfinished sunset of blue and burnished copper. Insomniac sheep and seabirds barely settle, and golfers, similarly afflicted, play midnight tournaments.

People have lived in Shetland since **prehistoric times**, certainly from about 3500 BC, and the islands display spectacular remains, including the best-preserved broch anywhere. For six centuries the islands were part of the **Norse empire** which brought together Sweden, Denmark and Norway. In 1469, Shetland followed Orkney in being mortgaged to Scotland, King Christian I of Norway being unable to raise the dowry for the marriage of his daughter, Margaret, to King James III. The Scottish king annexed Shetland in 1472 and the mortgage was never redeemed. Though Shetland retained links with other North Sea communities, religious and administrative practice gradually become Scottish, and **mainland lairds** set about grabbing what land and power they could. Later, especially in rural Shetland, the economy fell increasingly into the hands of **merchant lairds**; they controlled the fish trade and the tenants who supplied it through a system of truck, or forced barter. It wasn't until the 1886 Crofters' Acts and the simultaneous rise of herring fishing that ordinary Shetlanders gained some security. However, the boom and the prosperity it brought were short-lived and the economy soon slipped into depression.

During the two world wars, Shetland's role as gatekeeper between the North Sea and North Atlantic meant that the defence of the islands and control of the seas around them were critical: thousands of naval, army and air force personnel were drafted in and some notable relics, such as huge coastal guns, remain. **World War II** also cemented the old links with Norway, Shetland playing a remarkable role in supporting the Norwegian Resistance (see p.405). With a rebirth of the local economy in the 1960s, Shetland was able to claim, in the following decade, that the **oil industry** needed the islands more than they needed it. Careful negotiation, backed up by pioneering local legislation, produced a substantial income from oil which has been reinvested in the community. However, it's clear that the oil boom days are over, and the islanders are having to think afresh how to carve out a living in the new millennium. **Tourism**, which has tra-

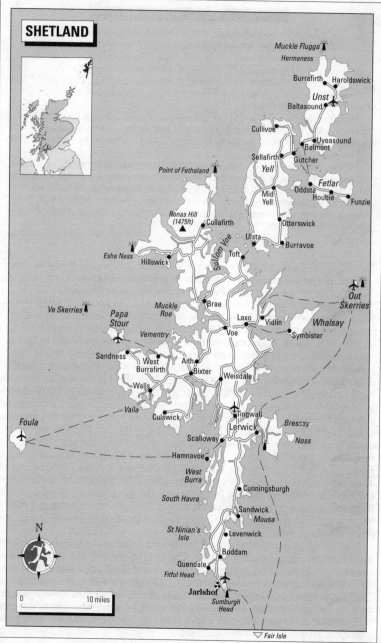

SHETLAND

Muckle Flugga
Hermaness
Burrafirth · Haroldswick
Unst
Baltasound
Cullivoe
Uyeasound
Belmont
Point of Fethaland
Sellafirth · Gutcher
Yell
Ronas Hill (1475ft) · Collafirth
Mid Yell
Oddsta
Fetlar
Houbie
Funzie
Otterswick
Ulsta
Sullom Voe
Burravoe
Esha Ness · Hillswick
Toft
Out Skerries
Muckle Roe
Brae
Ve Skerries
Laxo · Vidlin
Whalsay
Papa Stour
Voe
Symbister
Vementry
Sandness
West Burrafirth · Aith
Bixter
Walls
Weisdale
Vaila
Culswick
Tingwall
Foula
Lerwick
Bressay
Scalloway
Noss
Hamnavoe
West Burra
Cunningsburgh
South Havra
Sandwick
Mousa
St Ninian's Isle
Levenwick
Boddam
Quendale
Fitful Head
Jarlshof
Sumburgh Head

N

0   10 miles

▽ *Fair Isle*

© Crown copyright

GETTING TO SHETLAND

The **car ferry** from **Aberdeen**, P&O Scottish Ferries (☎01224/572615 or 01595/695252, *passenger@poscottishferries.co.uk*), operates a direct overnight ervice four or five times a week to Lerwick (14hr). There's also a once-weekly daytime service from **Stromness** in Orkney (8–10hr), which increases to twice weekly in summer (June–Aug); one overnight, one daytime. If you're visiting both Orkney and Shetland, be sure to check out the discounted **round-trip fares** advertised in the P&O brochure.

From mid-May to mid-September, Shetland is also directly connected to **Bergen** in Norway (13hr), **Tórshavn** in Faroe (13hr) and, via Faroe, with **Seydisfjördur** in Iceland (33hr) and **Hanstholm** in Denmark (50hr) on Smyril Line (details from P&O Scottish Ferries).

By **air**, British Airways (☎0345/222111) flies from **Edinburgh**, **Glasgow**, **Aberdeen**, **Inverness**, **Kirkwall** and **Wick**, with connections from **Birmingham**, **Manchester** and **London**. The main airport is at **Sumburgh**, 25 miles south of Lerwick, with connecting bus services to the latter. Standard fares are high, but various cheaper tickets and special offers are sometimes available if you can meet the booking conditions.

ditionally played only a minor role in the local economy, is only slowly beginning to develop. For the moment, comparatively few travellers make it out here, and those that do are as likely to be Faroese or Norwegian as British.

Whatever else you do in Shetland you're sure to find yourself, at some point or other, in the lively port of **Lerwick**, the only town of any size, and the hub of all transport and communications. Many parts of Shetland can be reached from here on a day-trip. **South Mainland**, south of Lerwick, is a narrow finger of land that runs some 25 miles to **Sumburgh Head**; this area is particularly rich in archeological remains, including the Iron Age **Mousa Broch** and the ancient settlement of **Jarlshof**. Twenty-five miles south of Sumburgh Head is the remote but thriving **Fair Isle**, synonymous with knitwear and exceptional birdlife. The **Westside** of Mainland is bleaker and more sparsely inhabited, as is **North Mainland**, although the landscape, particularly to the north, opens out in scale and grandeur as it comes face to face with the Atlantic. Off the west coast, **Papa Stour** lies just a mile from Sandness and boasts some spectacular caves and stacks; much further out are the distinctive peaks and precipitous cliffs of the remote island of **Foula**. Shetland's three **North Isles** bring Britain to a dramatic, windswept end. Their landscapes and seascapes have been shaped by centuries of fierce storms and have an elemental beauty. Nevertheless, the three islands differ markedly from one another: **Yell** has the largest population of otters in Shetland; **Fetlar** is home to the rare red-necked phalarope; north of **Unst**, there's nothing until you reach the North Pole.

Supporting an impressive array of **birds and wildlife**, the islands offer excellent birdwatching and coastal walking. The **fishing** is good, too, with lochs well stocked with brown trout, sea trout in the voes and the chance to go sea angling for ling, mackerel or even shark and halibut. **Camping** rough isn't discouraged in Shetland if done considerately and the landowner is asked first. However, make sure you're fully equipped to cope with the Shetland wind, which tests the most resilient of tents to the limit: pick a sheltered site, if possible, and use all the guy ropes you have.

Getting around

Public transport is pretty good in Shetland, with **buses** fanning out from Lerwick to just about every corner of Mainland, and even via ferries across to Yell and Unst: you can buy the full timetable (70p; includes all ferries and flights) from Lerwick tourist office. Various **tours** by bus, minibus or private car are also available; operators include John Leask & Son (☎01595/693162), Island Trails (☎01950/422408), run by Elizabeth Johnson, or the more specialist Shetland Wildlife Tours (☎01950/460254, *shetland.wildllife.tours@zetnet.co.uk*). Shetland Field Studies Trust organizes the occasional nature walk (book through the tourist office), while the Shetland Tourist Guides Association (☎01595/696671) offers tailor-made tours for groups or individuals. If you want to **rent a car** once on the islands, there are several firms to choose from (see "Listings" on p.396). **Hitching** is viable and pretty safe and **cycling** is a reasonable choice in summer, given the low level of traffic, though the wind can make some journeys very hard going.

Inter-island travel is very straightforward: the larger islands have frequent **car ferry** services throughout the day; journey times are mostly less than 30 minutes; and fares are much cheaper than those in Orkney or the Hebrides. Adults are charged around £2.50 return on most routes (around £5 to Foula, Fair Isle, Papa Stour and Out Skerries), and a car and driver cross for around £9 return. There are also British Airways **flights** linking Tingwall Airstrip (☎01595/840246), five miles west of Lerwick, to Unst and Fair Isle and less frequent Loganair flights to Whalsay, Out Skerries, Papa Stour and Foula. Some Unst and Fair Isle flights leave from Sumburgh Airport. Sample fares for these flights are £20 single Tingwall to Foula, or £36 single to Fair Isle; be sure to book well in advance, however, as the planes only take eight passengers, and be prepared to be flexible, as flights are often cancelled due to the weather. It's also possible to take **boat trips** for pleasure, to explore the coastline and spot birds, seals, porpoises, dolphins and whales; operators include Shetland Wildlife Tours (see above), and Tom Jamieson from Sandwick (for the Broch of Mousa; ☎01950/431367). Specialist services for **diving** or **sea angling** can be tracked down through the Lerwick tourist office (see p.391).

Lerwick

For Shetlanders, there's only one place to stop, meet and do business and that's "da toon", **LERWICK**. Very much the focus of Shetland's commercial life, Lerwick is home to about 7500 people, roughly a third of the islands' population. All year, its sheltered **harbour** at the heart of the town is busy with ferries, fishing boats, oil-rig supply vessels and a variety of more specialized craft including seismic survey and naval vessels from all round the North Sea. In summer, the quaysides come alive with local pleasure craft, visiting yachts, cruise liners, historic vessels such as the restored *Swan*, and the occasional tall sailing ship. Behind the old harbour is the compact town centre, made up of one long main street, Commercial Street; from here, narrow lanes, known as "**closses**", rise westwards to the late Victorian "**new town**".

Lerwick began life as a **temporary settlement**, catering to the Dutch herring fleet in the seventeenth century, which brought in as many as 20,000 men. During the nineteenth century, with the presence of ever larger Scottish,

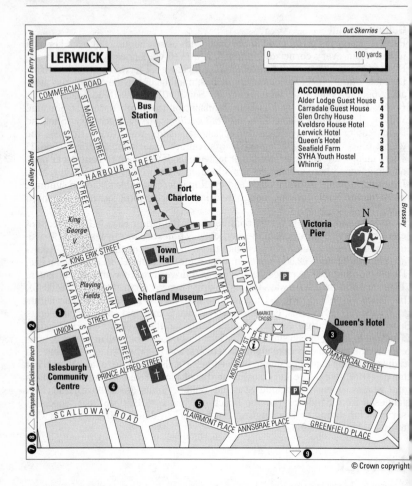

LERWICK

0   100 yards

Out Skerries

P&O Ferry Terminal

Galley Shed

Campsite & Clickimin Broch

Bressay

COMMERCIAL ROAD

ST MAGNUS STREET

MARKET STREET

Bus Station

HARBOUR STREET

SAINT OLAF STREET

Fort Charlotte

ESPLANADE

COMMERCIAL STREET

Victoria Pier

N

King George V

KING ERIK STREET

KING HARALD STREET

Town Hall

P

SAINT OLAF STREET

Playing Fields

Shetland Museum

HILLHEAD

MARKET CROSS

P

Queen's Hotel

3

❶

❷

UNION STREET

Islesburgh Community Centre

PRINCE ALFRED STREET

MOUNTHOOLY ST

i

CHURCH ROAD

COMMERCIAL STREET

❹

❺

P

❻

SCALLOWAY ROAD

CLAIRMONT PLACE

ANNSBRAE PLACE

GREENFIELD PLACE

❼❽

❾

ACCOMMODATION

Alder Lodge Guest House	5
Carradale Guest House	4
Glen Orchy House	9
Kveldsro House Hotel	6
Lerwick Hotel	7
Queen's Hotel	3
Seafield Farm	8
SYHA Youth Hostel	1
Whinrig	2

© Crown copyright

English and Scandinavian boats, it became a major fishing centre, and whalers called to pick up crews on their way to the northern hunting grounds. In 1839, the visiting Danish governor of Faroe declared that "everything made me feel that I had come to the land of opulence". Business was conducted largely from buildings known as **lodberries**, each typically having a store, a house and small yard on a private jetty. **Smuggling** was part of the daily routine, and secret tunnels – some of which still exist – connected the lodberries to illicit stores. During the late nineteenth century, the construction of the Esplanade along the shore isolated several lodberries from the sea, but further south beyond the *Queen's Hotel* are some that still show their original form. Lerwick expanded considerably at this time and the large houses and grand public buildings established then still dominate, notably the **Town Hall**, which remains the most prominent landmark. Another period of rapid growth began during the oil boom of the 1970s, with the farmland to the southwest disappearing under a suburban sprawl, the town's northern approaches becoming an industrial estate and some shopping and office development moving to new, car-friendly sites.

Arrival, information and accommodation

First impressions of Lerwick are very much dependent on the weather (and, if you arrive by boat, the crossing you've just experienced). The P&O **ferry terminal** is situated in the unprepossessing north harbour, about a mile from the town centre. If you arrive by **plane**, at **Sumburgh Airport**, you can take one of the regular buses to Lerwick; taxis (around £25) and car rental are also available. Buses stop on the Esplanade, very close to the old harbour and Market Cross, or at the Viking bus station on Commercial Road a little to the north of the town centre. Orientation within Lerwick is straightforward: the town is small and everything is within walking distance.

The **tourist office**, at the Market Cross on Commercial Street (May–Sept Mon–Fri 8am–6pm, Sat 8am–4pm, Sun 10am–1pm; Oct–April Mon–Fri 9am–5pm; ☎01595/693434), is a good source of information, and will book accommodation for a small fee. In July, August and over the Folk Festival weekend in April, accommodation is in short supply, so it's a good idea to book in advance if possible.

Shetland's best **hotels** are not to be found in Lerwick, which has been spoilt in the past by the steady supply of clientele from the oil business. The upper-range **guest houses** are usually better value for money, though you'll get closer to Shetland life in the town's simpler **B&Bs**. The **SYHA hostel** (☎01595/692114, *islesburgh@zetnet.co.uk*; April–Sept) at Isleburgh House on King Harald Street, offers unusually comfortable surroundings, and has mightily useful laundry facilities. Lerwick's *Clickimin* **campsite** (☎01595/694555; late April to Sept), enjoys the excellent facilities of the neighbouring Clickimin leisure centre, including good hot showers, but it's sheltered location, amidst Lerwick's suburbs, is far from idyllic.

BÖDS

With only one official SYHA hostel in the whole of Shetland, it's worth knowing about the islands' unique network of **camping böds**, which are open from April to September. Traditionally, a böd (pronounced "burd") was a small building beside the shore, where fishermen used to house their gear and occasionally sleep; the word was also applied to trading posts established by merchants of the Hanseatic League. The tourist board uses the term pretty loosely, however, as none of the places they run is strictly speaking a böd: they range from stone-built cottages to weatherboarded sail lofts. In order to stay at a böd, you can't simply turn up on spec, but must book in advance through Lerwick tourist office (☎01595/693434), as there are no live-in wardens. All the böds have some form of (primitive) heating system, cold water, toilets, a kitchen (though no stove or cooking utensils), and bunk beds, but (as yet) no mattresses, so a sleeping bag and bedding mat are pretty much essential. If you're camping anyway, they're a great way to escape the wind and rain for a night or two; they're also remarkably good value, at around £3 per person per night. Except in June, July and August, it's even possible to pay for exclusive use of any of the böds; prices range from £35 to £90 per night depending on the size of the böd.

Hotels, guest houses and B&Bs

Alder Lodge Guest House, 6 Clairmont Place (☎01595/695705). Converted former Victorian bank, recently refurbished, and probably the best middle-range accommodation available. ③.

Carradale Guest House, 36 King Harald St (☎01595/692251). Spacious, well-equipped guest house in a large, comfortable Victorian family home. ①.

Glen Orchy House, 20 Knab Rd (☎01595/692031). A particularly comfortable, fully modernized guest house that's almost a hotel, licensed and with good home-cooking. ④.

Kvelsdro House Hotel, Greenfield Place (☎01595/692195). Lerwick's smartest and most luxurious place, with immaculate bedrooms and a good harbour view from the bar. It's hard to find, but locals will usually oblige (note: it's pronounced "Kelro"). ⑥.

Lerwick Hotel, 15 South Rd (☎01595/692166). Modern hotel, with some good sea views, particularly favoured by business travellers. ⑤.

Queen's Hotel, Commercial Street (☎01595/692826). Right on the waterfront by the old harbour, with its feet in the sea; a beautiful old building that's undergoing badly needed refurbishment. ⑤.

Seafield Farm, off Sea Road (☎01595/693853). A very friendly B&B in a huge modern farmhouse overlooking the sea, a mile or so southwest of the town centre and therefore best for those with their own transport. ①.

Whinrig, 12 Burgh Rd (☎01595/693554). Reasonably central B&B, very comfortable and secluded. ①.

The Town

Lerwick's attractive, flagstone-clad **Commercial Street**, universally known to locals as "da Street", is still very much the core of the town. Its narrow, winding form, set back one block from the Esplanade, provides shelter from the elements even on the worst days, and is where locals meet, shop, exchange news and gossip and bring in the New Year to the sound of a harbourful of ships' sirens. The buildings exhibit a mixed bag of architectural styles, from the powerful neo-Baroque of the Bank of Scotland at no. 117 to the plainer houses and old lodberries at the south end, beyond the *Queen's Hotel*. Here, you'll find **Bain's Beach**, a small, hidden stretch of golden sand that's one of the prettiest spots in Lerwick. Further south lie the Victorian Anderson Homes and the Anderson High School, the latter's ornate, Franco-Scottish towers and dormers now unfortunately rather lost among later additions. Both were the gift of **Arthur Anderson** (1792–1868), co-founder of the Peninsular and Oriental Steam Navigation Company (P&O), for more on whom see p.394.

The Street's northern end is marked by the towering walls of **Fort Charlotte** (daily: June–Sept 9am–10pm; Oct–May 9am–4pm; free), which would once have stood directly above the beach. Begun for Charles II in 1665, during the war with the Dutch, the fort was attacked and burnt down by the latter in August 1673. In the 1780s it was repaired and given its name in honour of George III's queen. Since then, it's served as a prison, a Royal Navy training centre and, except on rare occasions when it's used by the Territorial Army, it's now open to the public. The fort affords good views from its solid battlements, and has four replica eighteenth-century cannons pointing out across Bressay Sound.

Now a desirable place to live in, it's not so long ago that the narrow lanes or "**closses**" that connect the Street to Hillhead were regarded as slumlike dens of

UP HELLY-AA

On the last Tuesday in January, whatever the weather, the Victorian "new town" of Lerwick is the setting for the most spectacular part of the Lerwick **Up Helly-Aa**, a huge fire festival, the largest of several held in Shetland from January to March. Around 900 torchbearing participants, all male and all in extraordinary costumes, march in procession behind a grand Viking longship. The annually appointed Guizer Jarl and his "squad" appear as Vikings and brandish shields and silver axes; each of the forty or so other squads is dressed for their part in the subsequent entertainment, perhaps as giant insects, space invaders or ballet dancers. Their circuitous route leads to the King George V Playing Field where, after due ceremony, all the torches are thrown into the longship, creating an enormous bonfire. A firework display follows, then the participants, known as "guizers", set off in their squads to do the rounds of more than a dozen "halls" (which usually include at least one hotel and the Town Hall) from around 8.30pm in the evening until 8am the next morning, performing some kind of act – usually a comedy routine – at each.

Up Helly-Aa itself is not that ancient, dating only from Victorian times, but it replaced an older Christmas tradition of burning tar barrels and other sorts of mischief. Around 1870, perhaps as a result of frustration at the controls increasingly imposed by the Town Council, the tar barrellers moved their activities into January, coined the name "Up Helly-Aa" and introduced both a torchlight procession and an element of disguise; it was some years, though, before the festival took on its Viking associations. Although this is essentially a community event with entry to halls by invitation only, visitors are welcome at the Town Hall, for which tickets are sold in early January; contact the tourist office well in advance. To catch some of the atmosphere of the event, check out the annual Up Helly-Aa' exhibition in the **Galley Shed** (mid-May to mid-Sept Tues & Sat 2–4pm, plus Tues & Fri 7–9pm; £2.50) on St Sunniva Street, where you can see a full-size longship, costumes, shields and photographs.

---

iniquity, from which the better-off escaped to the Victorian gridiron "new town" laid out to the west. The steep stone-flagged lanes are now fun to explore, each one lined by tall houses with trees, fuchsia, flowering currant and honeysuckle pouring over the garden walls. If you look at the street signs, you can see that all the closses were renamed in 1845, their new titles – Reform, Fox and Pitt – reflecting the liberal political culture of the period, or derived from the writings of Sir Walter Scott.

Hillhead, up in the Victorian "new town", is dominated by the splendid **Town Hall** (Mon–Fri 10am–noon & 2–3.30pm; free), a Scottish Baronial monument to civic pride, whose castellated central tower occupies the town's highest point. Built by public subscription, the many carved stone panels, coats of arms and stained-glass windows celebrate Shetland's history and, in particular, the islands' commercial and cultural links with other parts of Britain and Europe. Opposite the town hall, housed on the first floor of the desperately ugly municipal library, the **Shetland Museum** (Mon, Wed & Fri 10am–7pm, Tues, Thurs & Sat 10am–5pm; free) is full to the brim with nauticalia. More unusual exhibits include Shetland's oldest telephone, fitted with a ceramic mouthpiece, and a carved head of Goliath by Adam Christie (1869–1950), a Shetlander who spent much of his life in Montrose Asylum, and who is perhaps best known for his application to patent a submarine invisible to enemies because it would be made of glass.

Clickimin Broch and the Böd of Gremista

A mile or so southwest of the town centre on the road leading to Sumburgh, the much-restored **Clickimin Broch** stands on what was once a small island in Loch Clickimin. The settlement here began as a small farmstead around 700 BC and was later enclosed by a defensive wall. The main tower served as a castle and probably rose to around 40ft, as at Mousa (see p.399), though the remains are now not much more than 10ft high. There are two small entrances, one at ground level and the other on the first floor, which are carefully protected by outer defences and smaller walls. With the modern housing in the middle distance, it's pretty hard to imagine the original setting or sense the magical atmosphere of the place. Excavation of the site has unearthed an array of domestic goods that suggest international trade, including a Roman glass bowl thought to have been made in Alexandria around 100 AD.

In earlier times the seasonal nature of the Shetland fishing industry led to the establishment of small stores, known as **böds**, often incorporating sleeping accommodation, beside the beaches where fish were landed and dried. About a mile and a half north of the town centre, right off the A970, stands the **Böd of Gremista** (June to mid-Sept Wed–Sun 10am–1pm & 2–5pm; £2), the birthplace of **Arthur Anderson** (1792–1868). Though almost lost among the surrounding industry, the building has been beautifully restored and the displays explore Anderson's life as beach boy (helping to cure and dry fish), naval seaman, businessman, philanthropist, Shetland's first native MP and founder of Shetland's first newspaper. Built at the end of the eighteenth century for Anderson's father, the ground floor was originally used as an office and fish-curing station, while the trader and his family had permanent residence upstairs.

Eating

Shetland produces a huge harvest of fresh fish from the surrounding seas, including shellfish and salmon, and from the land there's superb lamb and even local tomatoes, cucumbers and peppers, grown under glass. The most celebrated local delicacy is *reestit* mutton: steeped in brine, then air-dried, it's the base for a superb potato soup cooked by locals around New Year. Unfortunately, the food on offer in the majority of Lerwick's hotels and pubs doesn't do these ingredients justice. It's not even possible to assemble a decent picnic, without resorting to a visit to the Safeway supermarket, situated a mile or so southwest of town, opposite the Clickimin Broch.

Faerdie-Maet, Commercial Street (by the post office). Cosy café serving generously filled rolls to eat in or take away, as well as cakes, teas, real cappuccino and good ice cream; no smoking. Closed Sun.

Fort Café, 2 Commercial St. Lerwick's best fish-and-chip shop, situated below Fort Charlotte: take away or eat inside in the small café. Closed Sun.

Great Wall, Viking Bus Station (☎01595/693988). Highly rated by the locals, this Chinese/Thai restaurant is located above the bus station.

Havly Centre, 9 Charlotte St. Spacious Norwegian lunchtime café much frequented by locals and tourists, with big comfy sofas and armchairs and a kids' corner; it offers homemade cakes, bread and pizzas. Closed Mon & Sun.

Kvelsdro House Hotel, Greenfield Place (☎01595/692195). The superior, moderately expensive bar meals or *table d'hôte*, served in the cocktail bar overlooking Bressay Sound, are your best bet.

Little Italy, 33 North Rd (☎01595/692299). Inexpensive passable pizzas and pasta in typical surroundings – does takeaway, too.

Monty's Bistro and Deli, 5 Mounthooly St (☎01595/696555). Upstairs, an unpretentious bistro offers accomplished contemporary cooking – the best in Lerwick – with friendly service and moderately expensive dishes. The downstairs deli serves inexpensive and delicious snacks, soups, salads and baked potatoes (also does takeaways). Closed Sun.

Osla's Café, Mounthooly Street. Snug, basement café with outdoor seating, decked out in bright Aztec colours, below Westwood Pine, specializing in savoury and sweet pancakes. Closed Sun.

Peerie Café, Esplanade. Funky new designer shop/gallery/café in an old lodberry, with imaginative cakes and sandwiches, and what is probably Britain's northernmost latté. Closed Sun.

Raba Indian Restaurant, 26 Commercial Rd (☎01595/695585). A consistently excellent curry house, with cheerful, efficient service and reasonable prices.

Drinking, nightlife and entertainment

At weekends or whenever the fishing fleet is confined to harbour, Lerwick's **pubs** are great social centres, packed full and brimming with atmosphere. The downstairs bar in the *Thule* on the Esplanade, is an archetypal seaport pub, usually heaving with serious drinkers. The friendliest place in town, however, is the upstairs bar in the *Lounge*, up Mounthooly Street, where local musicians usually play Saturday lunchtime and some evenings. If you're desperate to keep going until the early hours, head for the town's main dance venue, *Posers*, a small, lively and smartish nightclub at the back of the *Grand Hotel* on Commerical Street.

    Music features very strongly in Shetland life and every style has an enthusiastic following. The emphasis in traditional music is firmly instrumental, not vocal, with substantial numbers of young people learning the fiddle. In late April, musicians from all over the world converge on Shetland for the excellent **Shetland Folk Festival**, which embraces a wider range of musical styles than the title might suggest; there are concerts and dances in every corner of the islands. For details, telephone the Folk Festival office (☎01595/694757) or write to them at 5 Burns Lane, Lerwick. In mid-October, there's an **Accordion and Fiddle Festival**: similar format, same mailing address, but a different musical focus. Throughout the year, there are traditional dances in local halls all over Shetland; the whole community turns up and you can watch, or join in with, dances like the Boston Two-Step, Quadrilles or the Foula Reel. There are also gigs featuring a surprising number of accomplished local groups; rock-tinged folk styles are particularly strong. Names to catch live or recorded include Hom Bru, Drop the Box, Filska and Fiddlers' Bid. Legendary local fiddler Aly Bain (see p.446) makes occasional appearances on the islands. For details of what's on, listen in to *Good Evening Shetland* (BBC Radio Shetland, 92.7MHz FM, Mon–Fri 5.30pm), buy the *Shetland Times* on Fridays, or visit their Web site: *www.shetland-times.co.uk*. Some events are also advertised on Shetland's independent radio station, SIBC (96.2MHz FM, 24hr). If you want to pick up a CD or cassette of traditional Shetland music, head for High Level Music on the Market Cross.

    Not surprisingly, another Shetland passion is **boating and yachting**, and regattas take place most summer weekends, in different venues throughout the islands. Lately, the sport of **yoal racing** has caught on in a big way and teams from different districts compete passionately in large six-oared boats which used to serve as the backbone of Shetland's fishing industry.

Listings

Airports Tingwall Airport (☎01595/840246); Sumburgh Airport (☎01950/460654).

Banks Clydesdale, Bank of Scotland and Royal Bank of Scotland are all on Commercial Street; the Trustee Savings Bank is the gleaming and locally controversial structure on the Esplanade.

Bike rental Grantfield Garage, Commercial Road (Mon–Sat 8am–1pm & 2–5pm; ☎01595/692709).

Bookshops Shetland Times Bookshop, 73–79 Commercial St (☎01595/695531; Mon–Sat 9am–5pm).

Bus companies Leask (for Sandwick, Sumburgh Airport; Yell, Unst and Fetlar; ☎01856/693162); Shalder Coaches (for Walls and Sandness; Scalloway; ☎01595/880217); White's Coaches (for Brae and Hillswick; Vidlin and Laxo for Whalsay and Out Skerries, Walls and Sandness; ☎809443).

Car rental Bolts Car Hire, 26 North Rd (☎01595/693636); John Leask & Sons, Esplanade (☎01595/693162); Star Rent-a-Car, 22 Commercial Rd (☎01595/692075). All of these have offices at Sumburgh Airport.

Consulates Denmark, Iceland, Netherlands and Sweden at Hay and Company, 66 Commercial Rd (☎01595/692533); Finland, France, Norway and Germany at Shearer Shipping Services, Garthspool (☎01595/692556).

Laundry There is no self-service laundry in Shetland. Lerwick Laundry, 36 Market St (☎01595/693043; closed Sun), does washes, but charges individually for each item.

Medical care The Gilbert Bain Hospital (☎01595/743000) and the Lerwick Health Centre (☎01595/693201) are opposite each other on Scalloway Road.

Newspapers Daily newspapers arrive in Lerwick around noon (weather permitting); the *Shetland Times* comes out every Friday.

Post office Commercial Street (Mon–Fri 9am–5pm, Sat 9am–noon); there's a sub-post office in the Toll Clock Shopping Centre, 26 North Rd.

Sports centre There is a large, modern sports centre incorporating a superb leisure pool at the Clickimin Leisure Centre, Lochside, on the west side of town by Loch Clickimin (☎01595/694555). There's also a café and bar.

Travel agents John Leask & Son, Esplanade (☎01595/693162); Shetland Travelscope, Toll Clock Shopping Centre, 26 North Rd (☎01595/696644).

Bressay and Noss

Shielding Lerwick from the full force of the North Sea is the island of **Bressay**, dominated at its southern end by the conical Ward Hill (744ft) – "da Wart" – and accessible on an hourly car and passenger ferry from Lerwick (5min). At the end of the nineteenth century, Bressay had a population of around 800, due mostly to the prosperity brought by the Dutch herring fleet; now about 350 people live here. To find out more on the history of the island, visit the **Bressay Heritage Centre** (Tues & Fri–Sun 11am–5.30pm; ☎01595/820368), by the ferry terminal in **MARYFIELD**. A short distance to the north lies **Gardie House**, built in 1724 and, in its Neoclassical detail, one of the finest of Shetland's laird houses, where the likes of Sir Walter Scott and minor royalty once stayed.

In 1917, convoys of merchant ships would gather in Bressay Sound before travelling by naval escort across the Atlantic. Huge World War I gun batteries at Score Hill on Aith Ness in the north, and on Bard Head in the south, were constructed, and now provide a focus for a couple of interesting cliff and coastal walks. Another fine walk can be made to **Bressay Lighthouse**, three miles south of the ferry terminal at Kirkibuster Ness, built by the Stevensons in the 1850s. There are plans to turn the lighthouse and its shore station into a Marine Heritage Centre and camping böd (☎01595/694688 for the latest). Until the camping böd is open, your best bet for **accommodation** is the *Maryfield House Hotel* (☎01595/820207; ③), near the ferry terminal, which is friendly and serves good-value meals in the restaurant and cosy bar.

Noss

The chief reason most visitors pass through Bressay is in order to visit the tiny but spectacular island of **Noss** – the name means "a point of rock" – just off Bressay's eastern shore. Sloping gently into the sea at its western end, and plunging vertically from over 500ft at its eastern end, Noss has the dramatic and distinctive outline of a half-sunk ocean liner. The island was inhabited until World War II but is now a National Nature Reserve and sheep farm, partly managed by Scottish Natural Heritage (☎01595/693345), who operate an inflatable as a ferry (mid-May to Aug daily except Mon & Thurs 10am–5pm; 2min; £2.50 return). You should wait at the landing stage below the car park overlooking Noss Sound; if the weather is abnormally windy, check with the Lerwick tourist office as to whether the service is operating before setting off. If you don't have your own transport, it's a two-mile walk from the Bressay ferry terminal to Noss Sound, or you can rent bikes in Lerwick. There is also a postcar in the morning, though it takes over two hours to reach Noss Sound. Alternatively, you can join one of the daily **boat trips** (May–Aug) that set out from Lerwick to see the rock arches and caves of Bressay and the cliffs and nesting seabirds on Noss: try Shetland Wildlife Tours (☎01950/460254) or Bressaboats (☎01595/693434).

On the island, the old farmhouse or Haa of Gungstie contains a small **visitor centre** (open whenever the ferry is operating), where the warden will give you a quick briefing and a free map and guide. Nearby, there's a sandy beach, perfect for a picnic in fine weather, while behind the Haa, there's a **Pony Pund**, a square stone enclosure, built for the breeding of Shetland ponies. A stud was established here in the latter years of the nineteenth century, when the Marquis of Londonderry needed ponies to replace the women and children who had been displaced by new laws from his coal mines in County Durham. The animals were specially bred to produce "as much weight as possible and as near the ground as it can be got". The stud only lasted for about twenty years and was closed in 1899, studs in England having been established by then to supply demand at lower cost. There are no ponies on Noss today, but it's said that the influence of the breeding programme can still be seen in those roaming other parts of Shetland.

As Noss is only one mile wide, it's easy enough to do an entire circumference of the island in one day. If you do, make sure you keep close to the coast as the great skuas (locally known as "bonxies") will dive-bomb you otherwise. The most memorable feature of Noss is its cliffed coastline rising to a peak at the massive 500-foot **Noup**, from which can be seen vast colonies of cliff-nesting gannets, puffins, guillemots, shags, razorbills and fulmars: a truly wonderful sight and one of the highlights of Shetland. One of the features on the walk is the **Holm of Noss**; until 1864, it was connected to the main island by an extraordinary device called a cradle, a sort of basket suspended on ropes which was intended to allow access for the grazing of sheep. The Foula man who allegedly installed it in the seventeenth century is said to have died when, preferring to climb back down the cliffs, he fell.

SHETLAND PONIES, SHEEP AND SHEEPDOGS

Shetland is famous for its diminutive **ponies**, but it is still something of a surprise to find so many of the wee beasts on the islands. Traditionally they were used exclusively as pack animals, although a ninth-century carving on Bressay shows a hooded priest riding a very small pony, and their tails were essential for making fishing nets. During the Industrial Revolution, Shetland ponies were exported to work in the mines in England, since they were the only animals small enough to cope with the low galleries. Shetlands then became the playthings of the English upper classes (the Queen Mother is Patron of the Shetland Pony Stud Book Society) and they still enjoy the limelight at the Horse of the Year show.

It's not just the ponies that are small on Shetland, as the native **sheep** are also less substantial than their mainland counterparts. Thought to be descended from those brought by the Vikings, their wool comes in a wide range of colours, is very fine and is used to make the famous "Fair Isle" patterns and shawls so gossamer-thin that they can be passed through a wedding ring. To round up Shetland's small sheep, an even smaller **sheepdog** was bred, crossed with rough-coated collies. These dogs are now recognized as a separate breed, called "shelties", known for their gentleness and devotion as well as their working characteristics of agility and obedience. Their coat is distinctive, being long, straight and rough over a dense furry undercoat – their own thermal wear for Shetland weather conditions.

South Mainland

Shetland's **South Mainland** is a long, thin finger of land, only three or four miles wide, but 25 miles long, ending in the cliffs of **Sumburgh Head** and **Fitful Head**. The main road hugs the eastern side of the Clift Hills which form the peninsula's backbone; on the west side, there's no road between Scalloway and Maywick, except for a short spur from Easter to Wester Quarff. It's a beautiful area with wild landscapes but also good farmland, and has yielded some of Shetland's most impressive archeological treasures – in particular, **Jarlshof**.

Cunningsburgh

The view opens up to the south soon after leaving Lerwick, at the shoulder of Shurton Hill above Gulberwick. To appreciate the coastal scenery here, it's best to leave the main road at Fladdabister, a favourite haunt of local artists who come to sketch and paint among the ruins of the old crofts and where, in summer, the meadows are a mass of wild flowers. In **CUNNINGSBURGH**, the first large settlement, the best views are again from the back roads to the east through the hamlets and hay meadows of Aith and Voxter. At the south end of Cunningsburgh is the Mail Kirkyard, where a remarkable Pictish stone carved with an image of a **wolf-headed man** with an axe was found in 1992. The illustration is unusual in being secular rather than religious, which archeologists believe indicates a relatively early date. **Hostel accommodation** is available at the *Cunningsburgh Community Club* (☎01950/477241; June–Aug), which has dorm beds, good showers and a well-equipped kitchen.

Half a mile or so south of the Mail junction, the main road crosses the Catpund Burn. From the westward loop of the old road at this point, it's possible to scramble up the valley for about 300 yards to a remarkable prehistoric industrial site, the **Catpund Quarries**. In Norse times, this area was the biggest soapstone (steatite) quarry in Britain, if not the world. Products would have included various types of bowl, weights for fishing nets or for looms, and possibly items of jewellery. It's not difficult to see where vessels were carved directly from the rock. Goods from here almost certainly found their way to Norse communities in Britain, Ireland, Iceland, Faroe or mainland Europe. The small area revealed by the 1988 excavation of the site is fenced off and a board gives more information, but there's similar evidence over much of the valley floor.

Mousa

The island of **Mousa**, which lies off the east coast of South Mainland, about halfway down the peninsula, boasts the most fantastically well-preserved prehistoric broch in the whole of Scotland. Rising to more than 40ft, with its curving stonework intact, and over two thousand years old, **Mousa Broch** has a remarkable presence, and features in both *Egil's Saga* and the *Orkneyinga Saga*, contemporary chronicles of Norse exploration and settlement. In the former, a couple eloping from Norway to Iceland around 900 AD take refuge in it after being shipwrecked, while in the latter the broch is besieged by an Earl Harald Maddadarson when his mother is abducted and brought here from Orkney by Erlend the Young, who wanted to marry her. To get to the broch, simply head south from the jetty along the western coastline for about half a mile. The low entrance passage leads through two concentric walls to a central courtyard, divided into separate beehive chambers. Between the walls, a rough (very dark) staircase leads to the top parapet; a torch is provided for visitors.

To get to Mousa, take the small **passenger ferry** (mid-April to mid-Sept 1–2 daily; 15min; £5 return; ☎01950/431367) from Leebitton in the district of Sandwick, though it's best to ring ahead to check the current ferry times. Mousa is only a mile wide, but, if the weather's not too bad, it's easy enough to spend the whole day here. For a start, there are usually lots of grey and common **seals** sunning themselves on the rocks by the East and West Pool, at the southeastern corner of the island, plus black guillemots (or "tysties" as they're known in Shetland) breeding along the coast, and arctic tern colonies inland. Elsewhere, there are the remains of several buildings, some of which were inhabited until the mid-nineteenth century. From the end of May to mid-July, a large colony of around 5000 **storm petrels** breeds in the broch walls, fishing out at sea during the day, and only returning to the nests after dark; those interested in seeing the birds should enquire about the special evening trips (Wed & Sat 11pm).

Levenwick and Boddam

In Hoswick, halfway between Sandwick and Levenwick, is **Da Warp and Weft** (May–Sept Mon–Sat 10am–5pm, Sun noon–5pm; free), a visitor centre run alongside Laurence J. Smith's traditional knitwear showroom, offering an introduction to the history of local knitwear as well as teas and snacks. At Channerwick on the main road south, it's possible to cross to the west side of the Mainland for St Ninian's Isle (see p.399). Staying on the east side, the next settlement is **LEVENWICK**, where there's a lovely beach of white sand and another broch site. There's also a small, terraced **campsite** (☎01950/422207; May–Sept), run by the local community, which has hot showers, a tennis court and a superb view over the east coast.

Just beyond **BODDAM**, a back road winds around the southern shore of the nearby voe to the **Shetland Crofthouse Museum** (May–Sept daily 10am–1pm & 2–5pm; £2), housed in a thatched croft built around 1870. The museum portrays nineteenth-century crofting life with traditional furniture and fittings, including spinning wheels, high-backed Shetland chairs and baskets woven from heather fibres. **B&B**s are few and far between in these parts, but you can stay nearby at *Columbine* (☎01950/460582; ①), identified by a train signal.

St Ninian's Isle to Quendale

On the west coast, near Bigton village, a signposted track leads down to the spectacular sandy causeway (known as a tombolo) which leads to **St Ninian's Isle**. The **tombolo** – a concave strip of sand with Atlantic breakers crashing on either side – is the best example of its kind in Britain. It's usually exposed and you can walk over to the island, where there are the ruins of a church probably dating from the twelfth century but on the site of an earlier, Pictish, one. The site was excavated in the 1950s and **treasure**, a hoard of 28 objects of Pictish silver, was found hidden in a larch box beneath a slab in the earlier building's floor; the larch probably came from the European mainland, as it didn't grow in Britain at that time. The treasure included bowls, a spoon and brooches and probably dates from around 800 AD; it may have been hastily hidden during a Norse raid. Replicas are in the Shetland Museum in Lerwick and the originals can be seen in the Museum of Antiquities in Edinburgh.

South of Bigton, the coast is spectacular: cliffs alternate with beaches and the vivid greens and yellows of the farmland contrast with black rocks and a sea which may be grey, deep blue or turquoise. The **Loch of Spiggie**, which used to be a sea inlet, is an RSPB reserve known particularly for large autumn flocks of almost 400 whooper swans, but several types of duck as well as greylag geese and waders can be seen, depending on the time of year. Otters also thrive here. There's information about the reserve at the RSPB hide on the northern shore. On the other side of the road, the district of Spiggie also boasts a long but reasonably sheltered sandy beach.

A few miles south of the loch lies **QUENDALE**, overlooking a sandy south-facing bay. The village contains the beautifully restored full-size **Quendale Mill** (May–Sept daily 10am–5pm; £1.50), built in the 1860s; rarely operated now, the mill has information panels and a video. Not far from here, near the head of the rocky inlet of Cro Geo, on the other side of Garth's Ness, lies a rusting ship's bow, all that remains of the **Braer oil tanker**, a Liberian-registered, American-owned ship that ran onto the rocks here at 11.13am on January 5, 1993, a wild Tuesday morning etched in the memory of every Shetlander. Although the *Braer* released twice the quantity of oil spilt even by the *Exxon Valdez* in Alaska, the damage was less serious than it might have been, due to the oil being churned and ultimately cleansed by huge waves built by hurricane-force winds which, unusually even for Shetland, blew for most of January.

Sumburgh

From Boddam southwards, in the area known as **Dunrossness**, the landscape changes to a rolling agricultural one often compared with that of Orkney, but is still dominated from the west by the great brooding mass of Fitful Head, to the southwest. The main road, though, leads to **SUMBURGH**, whose **airport** is busy with helicopters and aircraft shuttling to and from the North Sea oilfields, and serves as Shetland's main airport for external passenger services. By the road, west of the airport, there are excavations currently under way at **Old Scatness Broch** (July & Aug Mon–Fri 10am–5pm, Sat & Sun 11am–5.30pm; free), and the Iron Age village surrounding it; those interested in having a look should phone ahead (☎01595/694688).

Jarlshof

Of all the archeological sites in Shetland, **Jarlshof** (April–Sept daily 9.30am–6.30pm; £2.50; HS; Oct–March the grounds are always open; free) is the largest and most impressive. What makes Jarlshof so amazing is the sheer size of the place, and the fact that what you see is the product of more than 4000 years of continuous occupation, with buildings dating from the Stone Age to the early seventeenth century. The name, which is misleading as it is not primarily a Viking site, was coined by Sir Walter Scott, who decided to use the ruins of the Old House in his novel *The Pirate*. However, it was only at the end of the nineteenth century that the Bronze Age, Iron Age and Viking settlements you see now were discovered, after a violent storm ripped off the top layer of turf.

The guidebook, available from the small visitor centre where you buy tickets, is very badly designed, so you might as well use the information panels instead. The Bronze Age smithy and Iron Age dwellings nearest the entrance, dating from the first and second millennia BC, are as nothing compared with the cells which cluster around the **broch**, close to the sea. Only half of the original broch survives, and its courtyard is now an Iron Age aisled roundhouse, with stone piers. However, it's difficult to distinguish the broch from the later Pictish **wheelhouses** which now surround it. Still, it's all great fun to explore, as, unlike at Skara Brae in Orkney, you're still free to roam around the cells, checking out the in-built stone shelving, water tanks, beds and so on. Inland lies the maze of grass-topped foundations marking out the **Viking longhouses**, dating from the ninth century AD and covering a much larger area than the earlier structures. Towering over the whole complex are the ruins of the laird's house, built by Robert Stewart, Earl of Orkney and Lord of Shetland, in the late sixteenth century, and the **Old House of Sumburgh**, built by his son, Earl Patrick.

Accommodation is in short supply, aside from the *Sumburgh Hotel* (☎01950/460201; ④), housed in an old Scottish Baronial laird's house, next door to Jarlshof, which is convenient for the airport, serves generous bar meals, often including local fish or shellfish, and occasionally has live music. There's also a **camping böd** in **Betty Mouat's Cottage**, a recently reconstructed traditional crofthouse that provides basic accommodation (book through Lerwick tourist office; April–Oct). Betty Mouat herself was quite a character. In January 1886, at the age of 60, she set off for Lerwick in the smack *Columbine* crewed by three local men. A storm swept the skipper overboard and the other two jumped in to try to rescue him; they failed, the skipper drowned and the two men, though they survived, lost contact with the smack. Betty and her boat were battered by the storm for nine days and nights, finally running ashore north of Aalesund in Norway. Astonishingly, she survived this experience, existing on some milk which she had with her. She returned to Shetland to become a celebrity, living into her nineties.

Sumburgh Head

The Mainland comes to a dramatic end at **Sumburgh Head**, which rises sharply out of the land only to drop vertically into the sea about a mile or so southeast of Jarlshof. The **lighthouse**, on the top of the cliff, designed by Robert Stevenson, was built in 1821, and the keepers' cottages are now rented out as self-catering accommodation (☎01387/372240). The lighthouse itself is not open to the public, but its grounds offer great views to Noss in the north and Fair Isle to the south, as well as the perfect site for watching nesting seabirds such as kittiwakes, fulmars, shags and guillemots, not to mention gannets diving for fish. This is also the easiest place in Shetland to get close to **puffins**. During the nesting season (May to mid-Aug), you simply need to look over the western wall, just before you enter the lighthouse complex, to see them arriving at their burrows a few yards below with beakfuls of sand eels or giving flying lessons to their offspring; on no account should you try to climb over the wall.

Fair Isle

Halfway between Shetland and Orkney and very different from both, **Fair Isle** supports a vibrant community of around seventy people. The north end of the island rises like a wall; the Sheep Rock, a sculpted stack of rock and grass on the east side, is one of the island's most dramatic features. The croft land and the island's scattered houses are concentrated in the east and south. Measuring just three miles by one and a half, being on Fair Isle feels a bit like being on an aircraft carrier in the middle of the Atlantic, and the weather reflects its isolated position. You can almost guarantee that it'll be windy, and most probably wet, though if you're lucky your visit might coincide with fine weather, what the islanders call "a given day".

At one time Fair Isle's population was not far short of 400, but Clearances forced emigration from the middle of the nineteenth century. By the 1950s, the population had shrunk to just 44, a point at which evacuation and abandonment of the island was seriously considered. **George Waterston**, who'd bought the island and set up a bird observatory in 1948, passed it into the care of the NTS in 1954 and rejuvenation began. Since then, islanders, the Trust and the Shetland Islands Council have invested in many improvements to housing, the harbour and basic services, including an advanced electricity system integrating wind and diesel generation, and crafts including boatbuilding, the making of fiddles, felt and stained glass have been developed.

The focus for many visitors is the **Bird Observatory**, built just above the sandy bay of North Haven where the ferry from Shetland Mainland arrives. It's one of the major European centres for ornithology and its work in watching, trapping, recording and ringing birds goes on all year. Fair Isle is a landfall for a huge number and range of migrant birds during the spring and autumn passages. Migration routes converge here and more than 345 species, including many rarities, have been noted. As a result, Fair Isle is a haven for twitchers; for more casual birdwatchers, however, there's also plenty of resident birdlife to enjoy. The high-pitched screeching that fills the sky above the airstrip comes from hundreds of arctic terns, and arctic skuas can also be seen here. Those in search of puffins should head for the cliffs around Furse, while for gannets go for the spectacular stacks of Scroo and Dronger.

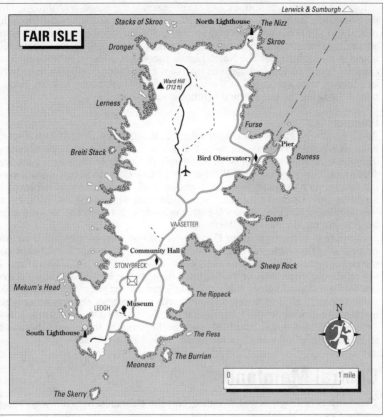

FAIR ISLE

Lerwick & Sumburgh

Stacks of Skroo
North Lighthouse
The Nizz
Skroo
Dronger
Ward Hill
(712 ft)
Lerness
Furse
Pier
Breiti Stack
Bird Observatory
Buness
Goorn
VAASETTER
Sheep Rock
Community Hall
STONYBRECK
Mekum's Head
The Rippack
LEOGH
Museum
The Fless
South Lighthouse
The Burrian
Meoness
The Skerry

N

0   1 mile

© Crown copyright

Fair Isle is, of course, even better known for its **knitting** patterns, still produced with as much skill as ever by the local knitwear cooperative, though not in the quantities which you might imagine from a walk around city department stores; there are demonstrations at the Community Hall, by the island school, from time to time (usually on a Monday, or when a cruise ship calls by). If the Hall is closed, then you'll have to make do with the samples on display at the island's **museum** (opening times vary and are advertised locally; ☎01595/760244; free), which is named after George Waterston, and situated next door to the island's Methodist Chapel. Particularly memorable are stories of shipwrecks; in 1868 the islanders undertook a heroic rescue of all 465 German emigrants aboard the *Lessing*. More famously the *El Gran Grifon*, part of the retreating Spanish Armada, was lost here in 1588 and 300 Spanish seamen were washed up on the island. Food was in such short supply that fifty died of starvation before help could be summoned from Shetland. The idea that the islanders borrowed all their patterns from the shipwrecked Spanish seamen is nowadays regarded as a patronizing myth.

Fair Isle has two **lighthouses**, one at either end of the island, both designed by the Stevenson family and erected in 1892. Before that, the Vikings used to light beacons to signal an enemy fleet advancing, and in the nineteenth century a semaphore consisting of a tall wooden pole was used – it can still be seen on the hill above South Lighthouse. The North Lighthouse was considered to be on such an exposed spot that the foghorn was operated from inside the lighthouse. Both lighthouses were automated in 1998, and the South Lighthouse had the distinction of the being the last manned lighthouse in the country.

Practicalities

Administratively, Fair Isle is connected to Shetland, as are most of its transport links. The passenger **ferry** connects Fair Isle with either Lerwick (on alternate Thurs; 4hr 30min) or Grutness, in Sumburgh (Tues, Sat & alternate Thurs; 2hr 40min); for bookings, contact J.W. Stout (☎01595/760222) in advance. The crossing can be very rough at times, so if you're at all susceptible to seasickness it might be worth considering catching a **flight** from Tingwall (Mon, Wed, Fri & Sat) or Sumburgh (Tues, Thurs & Sat); a one-way ticket costs £36, and day-trips are possible on Mondays and Wednesdays.

Camping is not permitted on Fair Isle, but if you want **to stay**, the *Fair Isle Lodge & Bird Observatory* (☎01595/760258, *birdobs@zetnet.co.uk*; ③, full board ⑤), offers full board, B&B and hostel-style dorm beds for £25 per person. Even if you're staying elsewhere, or visiting on a day-trip, the Bird Observatory offers tea, coffee and good home-cooking for lunch and dinner; you might even be able to lend a hand with the Observatory's research programme. The only other B&B options are *Schoolton* (☎01595/760250; ①, full board ③), or *Upper Lough* (☎01595/760248; ①, full board ③), both in the south of the island. There is a shop/post office in the south of the island (closed Thurs & Sun).

Central Mainland

The districts of Tingwall and Weisdale, plus the old capital of **Scalloway**, make up the **Central Mainland**, an area of minor interest in the grand scheme of things, but one which is very easy to reach from Lerwick (and vice versa). In fine weather, it's a captivating mix of farms, moors, lochs and includes Shetland's only significant woodland; the scale of the scenery ranges from the intimate to the vast, with particularly spectacular views from high points above Whiteness and Weisdale. The area also holds strong historical associations, with the Norse parliament at **Lawting Holm** and unhappy memories of Earl Patrick Stewart's harsh rule at Scalloway, and nineteenth-century Clearances at Weisdale.

Scalloway

Approaching **SCALLOWAY** from the shoulder of the **Scord**, there's a dramatic view over the town and the islands to the south and west. Once the capital of Shetland, Scalloway's importance waned through the eighteenth century as Lerwick, just six miles to the east, grew in trading success and status. Nowadays, Scalloway is very sleepy indeed, though its prosperity, always closely linked to the fluctuations of the fishing industry, has recently been given a boost with investment in new fish-processing factories, and in the impressive North Atlantic Fisheries College on the west side of the harbour.

In spite of modern developments nearby, Scalloway is dominated by the imposing shell of **Scalloway Castle**, a classic fortified tower house built with forced labour in 1600 by the infamous Earl Patrick Stewart, and thus seen as a powerful symbol of oppression. Stewart, who'd succeeded his father Robert to the Earldom of Orkney and Lordship of Shetland in 1592, held court in the castle and gained a reputation for enhancing his own power and wealth through the calculated use of harsh justice, frequently including confiscation of assets. He was eventually arrested and imprisoned in 1609, not for his ill-treatment of Shetlanders, but for his aggressive behaviour towards his fellow landowners; his son, Robert, attempted an insurrection and both were executed in Edinburgh in 1615. The castle was used for a time by Cromwell's army, but had fallen into disrepair by 1700 and is nowadays in the hands of Historic Scotland. The castle itself is well preserved and fun to explore; if the door is locked, the key can be borrowed from the Shetland Woollen Company (Mon–Sat 9am–5pm), next door to the castle.

On Main Street, the small **Scalloway Museum** (May–Sept Tues–Thurs 2–4.30pm, Sat 10am–12.30pm & 2–4.30pm; free), run by volunteers, is crammed with local relics. It explains the importance of fishing and tells the story of the **Shetland Bus** (see box). West of Scalloway, there's a pleasant if energetic walk up **Gallows Hill** (2–3hr), where alleged witches were put to death, and then on to the hamlet of Burwick, a former fishing settlement.

The best **accommodation** available in Scalloway is at the very comfortable and welcoming *Hildasay Guest House* (☎01595/880822; ②), a Hansel-and-Gretel weatherboarded house on the top of the hill above Scalloway, behind the

---

THE SHETLAND BUS

The story of the **Shetland Bus**, the link between Shetland and Norway that helped to sustain the Norwegian resistance through the years of Nazi occupation, is quite extraordinary. Constantly under threat of attack by enemy aircraft or naval action, small Norwegian fishing boats were used to run arms and resistance workers into lonely fjords. The trip took 24 hours and on the return journey brought back Norwegians in danger of arrest by the Gestapo, or those who wanted to join Norwegian forces fighting with the Allies. For three years, through careful planning, the operation was remarkably successful: instructions to boats were passed in cryptic messages in BBC news broadcasts. Although local people knew what was going on, the secret was generally well kept. Eventually, 350 refugees were evacuated, and more than 400 tons of arms, large amounts of explosives and 60 radio transmitters were landed in Norway.

Originally established at **Lunna** in the northeast of the Mainland, the service moved to **Scalloway** in 1942, partly because the village could offer good marine engineering facilities at Moore's Shipyard at the west end of Main Street, where a plaque records the morale-boosting visit of the Norwegian Crown Prince Olav. Many buildings in Scalloway were pressed into use to support the work: explosives and weapons were stored in the castle. **Kergord House** in Weisdale was used as a safe house and training centre for intelligence personnel and saboteurs. The hazards, tragedies and elations of the exercise are brilliantly described in David Howarth's book, *The Shetland Bus*; their legacy today is a closer, more heartfelt relationship between Shetland and Norway.

swimming pool. For **food**, head for *Da Haaf* (closed Sat & Sun), the unpretentious licensed restaurant in the North Atlantic Fisheries College, which serves fresh fish, simply prepared, with broad harbour views to enjoy as well.

Trondra and Burra

Southwest of Scalloway – and now connected to the Mainland by bridges – is the island of **Trondra** and, further south, the twin islands of **Burra**, which have some beautiful beaches and some fairly gentle coastal walks. The second island you come to, **West Burra**, has the largest settlement in the area, **HAMNAVOE**, a planned fishing settlement unlike any other in Shetland, established mainly in the early 1900s and still very much a working, seagoing community. Just south of Hamnavoe, a small path leads down from the road to the white sandy beach at **Meal**, deservedly popular on warm summer days. At the southern end of West Burra, at **Banna Minn**, there's another fine beach, with excellent walking nearby on the cliffs of Kettla Ness, linked to the rest of West Burra only by a slither of tombolo.

East Burra, joined to West Burra at the middle like a Siamese twin, ends at the hamlet of **HOUSS**, distinguished by the tall, ruined laird's house or Haa. From the turning place outside the cattle-grid, continue walking southwards, following the track to the left, down the hill and across the beach, and after about a mile you'll reach the deserted settlement of **Symbister**, inhabited until the 1940s. You can now see ancient field boundaries and, just south of the ruins, a **burnt mound** (an overgrown pile of Neolithic cooking stones dumped when no longer usable). Half a mile further south, the island ends in cliffs, caves and wheeling fulmars. From there, the island of **South Havra**, topped by the ruins of Shetland's only **windmill**, is just to the southwest. Once supporting a small fishing community, the island was abandoned, except for the grazing of sheep, by the last eight families in 1923; it was such a perilous existence that children as well as animals had to be tethered to prevent them from falling over the cliffs.

Tingwall

TINGWALL, the name for the loch-studded, fertile valley to the north of Scalloway, takes its name from the **Lawting** or Althing (from *thing*, the Old Norse for "parliament"), where local people and officials gathered to make or amend laws and discuss evidence from the eleventh to the sixteenth century. From the late thirteenth century, Shetland's laws were based on those of Norwegian King Magnus the Lawmender. It seems that meetings to deal with these matters took place here up to the sixteenth century, after which judicial affairs were dealt with in Patrick Stewart's new castle at Scalloway. The Lawting was situated at **Law Ting Holm**, the small peninsula at the northern end of Loch Tingwall, that was once an island linked to the shore by a causeway. Although structures on the holm have long since vanished, there's an information board which helps in visualizing the scene. At the southwest corner of the loch, a seven-foot **standing stone** by the roadside is said to mark the spot where, after a dispute at the Lawting in 1389, Earl Henry Sinclair killed his cousin and rival, Marise Sperra, together with seven of his followers.

Just north of the loch is **Tingwall Kirk**, unexceptional from the outside, but preserving its attractive late eighteenth-century interior. In the burial ground, there's a dank, turf-covered **burial aisle** from the old medieval church that was demolished in 1788. Inside are several very old gravestones, including one to a local official called a *Foud* – a representative of the king – who died in 1603. The ornate seventeenth-century sarcophagus in the graveyard was used as a social meeting point and resting place by locals who arrived early for the Sunday service.

This relatively fertile part of Shetland seems as appropriate a place as any for the **Tingwall Agricultural Museum** (June–Aug Mon–Sat 10am–1pm & 2–5pm; £1.50), about 200yd from the main crossroads at Tingwall. The enthusiastic owner has amassed a remarkable treasure trove of equipment from Shetland's crofts and farms and has an intimate knowledge of all of it.

If you're flying from **Tingwall Airstrip** (☎01595/840246), it's easy enough to get to the airstrip by taxi or car from either Lerwick or Scalloway; check-in is a laid-back affair, so if you're getting an early flight and arrive half an hour before your flight, you'll have ample time. One of the best places **to stay**, within easy striking distance of the airstrip, is at *South Haven* (☎01595/840350; ③), in Nesbister, overlooking Whiteness Voe; the proprietor couldn't be more accommodating and helpful. You can also **camp** in a tiny site beside the *Westings Hotel* (☎01595/840242; open all year), in nearby Wormadale. If you want to stay even closer to the airstrip, the modern *Herrislea House Hotel* (☎01595/840208; ④) overlooks the airstrip by the main crossroads. Its spacious **bar**, the heavily themed *Starboard Tack*, doubles as Tingwall's social centre, serves simple pub food and features occasional live traditional music.

Weisdale

WEISDALE, to the northwest of Tingwall, is notable primarily for **Weisdale Mill** (Wed–Sat 10.30am–4.30pm, Sun noon–4.30pm; free), situated up the B9075 from the head of Weisdale Voe. Built for milling grain in 1855, it is now an attractively converted arts centre, housing the small, beautifully designed **Bonhoga Gallery**, in which touring and local exhibitions of painting, sculpture and other media are shown. Don't miss the small but fascinating **Shetland Textile Working Museum** (Wed–Sat 10.30am–4pm, Sun noon–4pm; £1), in the basement, which puts on temporary exhibitions, and has pull-out drawers showing the knitted patterns unique to Shetland and Fair Isle. There's also a very pleasant café, serving soup, scones and snacks in the south-facing conservatory overlooking the stream.

Weisdale is an evocative name in Shetland, for in this valley some of the cruellest Clearances of people in favour of sheep took place in the middle of the nineteenth century. The perpetrator was David Dakers Black, a farmer from the county of Angus who began buying land in 1843. Hundreds of tenants were dispossessed and in 1850 the large **Kergord House**, then called Flemington, was built towards the northern end of the valley from the stones of some of the older houses. The ruined shells of some of the rest still stand on the valley sides; local writers, particularly John J. Graham, have recounted the period in novels (notably his *Shadowed Valley*) and drama.

Around Kergord House and on the upper valley sides there are several **tree plantations** dating mainly from around 1920 but with a later experimental addition by the Forestry Commission. An amazing range of species is present, from the sycamores and willows which thrive in many Shetland gardens to examples of chestnut, copper beech, monkey puzzle and much else besides. Along with the trees comes a woodland ecosystem, with foxgloves, Britain's most northerly rookery and a reliable cuckoo. During the war, Kergord House played a role in the Shetland Bus operation (see p.405); the saboteurs who trained here are said to have amused visitors by demonstrating booby traps and incendiary devices in the garden.

South of Kergord House and Weisdale Mill around the head of Weisdale Voe, it's possible to turn southwards along the west shore where, among trees near the voe's narrowest point, is the ruined house once occupied by **John Cluness Ross** (1786–1853). He settled in the Cocos Islands in the Indian Ocean, went into coconut farming and appointed himself king, the first of three in a family dynasty which ruled (some would say oppressed) the islanders for decades.

The Westside

The western Mainland of Shetland – known as the **Westside** – stretches west from Weisdale and Voe to Sandness. Although there are some important archeological remains and wildlife in the area, the Westside's greatest appeal lies in its outstanding **coastal scenery** and walks. At its heart, the Westside's rolling brown and purple moorland, dotted with patches of bright-green reseeded land, glistens with dozens of small, picturesque blue or silver lochs. On the west coast the rounded form of Sandness Hill (750ft) falls steeply away into the Atlantic. The coastal scenery, cut by several deep voes, is very varied; aside from dramatic cliffs, there are intimate coves and some fine beaches.

Bixter and around

The chief crossroads for the area is effectively **BIXTER**, a place of no particular consequence from where you can travel south to Skeld and Reawick, west to Walls, West Burrafirth and Sandness, or northwest along a scenic winding road towards **AITH** and eventually Voe (see p.414). There isn't a lot here, either, except a shop and school, and an attractive little harbour that serves as the base for the west of Shetland lifeboat, but you can **stay** in the refurbished *Aith Hall Camping Barn* (☎01595/810327; June–Aug), where you can either crash inside the community hall, or pitch your own tent outside and simply use the facilities. Northwest of Aith, the road ends at the farm of **Vementry**, also, confusingly, the name of the nearby island that boasts the best-preserved **heel-shaped cairn** in Shetland, right on top of the highest hill, Muckle Ward (298ft). There are also two excellently preserved **six-inch guns** from World War I on Swarbucks Head, in the north of the island. To reach the island, enquire locally or through Lerwick tourist office (see p.391).

Southwest of Bixter, on the picturesque Sandsting peninsula, there are two beautiful terracotta-coloured **sandy bays** at Reawick, and excellent **coastal walks** to be had along the coast around Westerwick and Culswick, past red granite cliffs, caves and stacks. Three miles southwest of Bixter lies the finest Neolithic structure in the Westside, dubbed the **Staneydale Temple** by the archeologist who excavated it because it resembled one on Malta. Whatever its true function, it was twice as large as the surrounding oval-shaped houses (now in ruins) and was certainly of great importance, perhaps as some kind of community centre. The horseshoe-shaped foundations measure more than 40ft by 20ft internally, with immensely thick walls, still around 4ft high, whose roof would have been supported by spruce posts (two postholes can still be clearly seen). To reach the temple, take the path marked out by black-and-white poles across the moorland for half a mile from the road. There's another significant prehistoric sight, the **Scord of Brouster**, near the Brig of Waas, where the Walls and Sandness roads divide. A helpful information board provides an explanation of the layout of various ruined houses and field boundaries, making it easier to imagine what life might have been like for the people who lived on this hillside between 3000 and 1500 BC.

Walls and Sandness

Once an important fishing port, **WALLS** (pronounced "Waas"), appealingly set round its harbour, is now a quiet village, which comes alive once a year in the middle of August for the Walls Agricultural Show, the biggest farming bash on the island. At other times, you can visit the small **Walls Museum** (Thurs–Sun 2–6pm; free), mostly of knitwear, but also displaying a typical croft interior from the turn of the century, and sundry bits of nauticalia. Walls also boasts by far the best **accommodation** options on the Westside. The beautifully restored *Voe House* (book through Lerwick tourist office; April–Oct) is the largest camping böd on Shetland; the modest price includes peat for the fires. The best B&B around is the wonderfully welcoming *Skeoverick* (☎01595/809349; ①), a lovely modern croft house which lies a mile or so north of Walls. The only hotel in the area is *Burrastow House* (☎01595/809307; ⑥), beautifully situated about three miles southwest of Walls; the house itself dates back to 1759, and has real character, with wood panelling, a traditional Victorian sit-down bathtub, and a conservatory. *Burrastow House* is also one of the best places **to eat** in the whole of Shetland, offering distinguished cooking in idyllic surroundings; meals, though expensive, are fantastic, and booking ahead is pretty much essential.

A short distance across the sea lies the island of **Vaila**, from where in 1837 Lerwick philanthropist Arthur Anderson operated a fishing station in an unsuccessful attempt to break down the system of fishing tenures under which tenants were forced to fish for the landlords under pain of eviction. The ruins of Anderson's fishing station still stand on the shore, but the most conspicuous monument is **Vaila Hall**, the largest laird's house on Shetland, originally built in 1696, but massively enlarged by a wealthy Yorkshire mill-owner, Herbert Anderton, who bought the island in 1893. Anderton also restored the island's ancient watchtower of Mucklaberry Castle, built a Buddhist temple (now sadly in ruins), and had a cannon fired whenever he arrived on the island. The island is currently owned by an eccentric young Polish woman and her partner; if you wish to visit, enquire at *Burrastow House*.

The end of the road as far as the Westside is concerned is the scattered crofting settlement of **SANDNESS** (pronounced "*Saa*ness"), which you can reach by road or by walking the coast from Walls past the dramatic Deepdale and across Sandness Hill. It's an oasis of green meadows in the peat moorland, with a nice beach, too. The modern Jamieson's **woollen spinning mill** (Mon–Fri 8am–5pm; free), at Sandness, is the only one on Shetland producing pure Shetland wool; it welcomes visitors, and you can watch how they spin the exceptionally fine Shetland wool into yarn.

Papa Stour

A mile offshore from Sandness is the quintessentially peaceful island of **Papa Stour**, created out of volcanic lava and ash which has subsequently been eroded into some of the most impressive coastal scenery in Shetland. In good weather, it makes for a perfect day-trip, but in foul weather or a sea mist it can certainly appear pretty bleak. Its name, which means "big island of the priests", derives from its early Celtic Christian connections, and it was home, in the eighteenth century, to people who were mistakenly believed to have been lepers, though in fact were suffering from a hereditary skin disease caused by severe malnutrition. The land is, in fact, very fertile, and in the nineteenth century Papa Stour supported around three hundred inhabitants, but by the early 1970s there was a population crisis: the island's school closed, and the remaining sixteen inhabitants were all past child-bearing age; worse still, it looked like the post office would close and the mailboat be withdrawn. The islanders made appeals for new blood to revive the fragile economy and managed to stage a dramatic recovery, releasing croft land to young settlers from Britain and overseas. Papa Stour was briefly dubbed "the hippie isle", but it wasn't long before some newcomers moved on, to other parts of Shetland or elsewhere, making a further appeal necessary in the early 1990s. Today the island supports a community of thirty or so.

The island's main settlement, **BIGGINGS**, lies in the west near the pier, and it was here that excavation in the early 1980s revealed the remains of a thirteenth-century Norse house, which is thought to have belonged to Duke Haakon, heir to

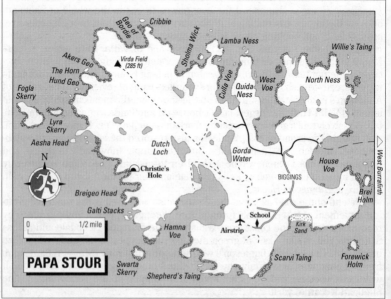

the Norwegian throne. There's an explanatory panel, but nothing much to see – in any case, the chief reason to come to Papa Stour is to go walking; to reach the best of the coastal scenery, head for the far west of the island. From **Virda Field** (285ft), the highest point on the island, in the far northwest, you can see the treacherous rocks of Ve Skerries, three miles or so northwest off the coast, where a lighthouse was erected as recently as 1979. The couple of miles of coastline from here, southeast to Hamna Voe, has some of the island's best stacks, blow-holes and natural arches. Probably the most spectacular formation of all is the **Christie's Hole**, a gloup or partly roofed cleft, which extends far inland from the cliff line, and where shags nest on precipitous ledges. Other points of interest include a couple of defunct horizontal click-mills, below Dutch Loch, and the remains of a "meal road", so called because the workmen were paid in oatmeal or flour. Several pairs of red-throated divers breed on inland lochs such as Gorda Water.

Practicalities

In summer, the passenger **ferry** runs from West Burrafirth on the Westside to Papa Stour (Mon, Wed & Fri–Sun). Always book in advance, and reconfirm the day before departure (☎01595/810460); day-trips are only possible on Friday, Saturday and Sunday. There's also a **flight** from Tingwall airport every Tuesday, and again a day-trip is feasible; tickets cost just £15 one way and the airstrip is southwest of Biggings, by the school. The only accommodation on the island is *North House* **B&B** (☎01595/873238; ①, full board ③), who can arrange boat trips around the stacks and sea caves. There's no shop, so even day-trippers should bring their own picnic with them.

Foula

Southwest of Walls, at "the edge of the world", **Foula** is without a doubt the most isolated inhabited island in the British Isles, separated from the nearest point on Mainland Shetland by about fourteen miles of often turbulent ocean. Seen from the Mainland, its distinctive mountainous form changes subtly, depending upon the vantage point, but the outline is unforgettable. Its western **cliffs**, the second highest in Britain after those of St Kilda, rise at **The Kame** to some 1220ft above sea level; a clear day offers a magnificent panorama stretching from Unst to Fair Isle. On a bad day, the exposure is complete and the cliffs generate turbulent blasts of wind known in Shetland as "flans", which tear down the hills with tremendous force.

The island has been inhabited since prehistoric times, and the people here take pride in their separateness from Shetland, cherishing local traditions such as the observance of the **Julian calendar**, officially dropped in Britain in 1752, where Old Yule is celebrated on January 6 and the New Year doesn't arrive until January 13. The folk of Foula were still using Norse udal law in the late seventeenth century, seemingly unaware that it had been superseded by Scots law in the rest of the country. Foula was also the last place that Norn, the old Norse language of Orkney and Shetland, was spoken as a first language in the eighteenth century. Likewise, the island's isolation also meant that more of the Shetland dialect survived here than elsewhere; in the late nineteenth century, Foula's people provided an enormous amount of information on the dialect and its roots in

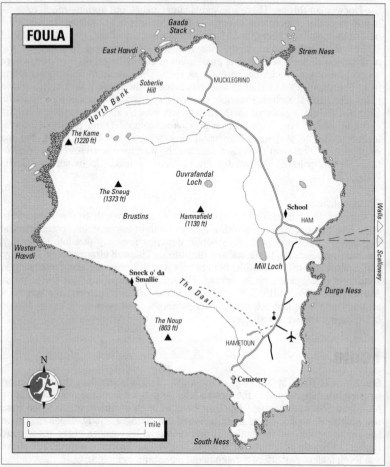

FOULA

Gaada Stack

East Hœvdi

Strem Ness

Soberlie Hill

MUCKLEGRIND

North Bank

The Kame (1220 ft)

Ouvrafandal Loch

The Sneug (1373 ft)

Brustins

Hamnafield (1130 ft)

School

HAM

Walls △ △ Scalloway

Wester Hœvdi

Sneck o' da Smallie

The Daal

Mill Loch

Durga Ness

The Noup (803 ft)

HAMETOUN

N

0   1 mile

Cemetery

South Ness

© Crown copyright

Norn for a study undertaken by the Faroese philologist Jakob Jakobsen. Foula's population, which peaked at around two hundred at the end of the nineteenth century, has fluctuated wildly over the years, dropping to three in 1720 following an epidemic of "muckle fever" or smallpox; today, the community numbers around forty.

Arriving on Foula, you can't help but be amazed by the sheer size of the island's immense, bare mountain summits. However, the gentler eastern slopes provide good crofting land, plentiful peat, and it is along this "green belt" that the island's population are scattered. The island, whose name is derived from the Old Norse for "bird island", also provides a home for a quarter of a million **birds**. Arctic terns wheel overhead at the airstrip, red-throated divers can usually be seen on

WALKING ON FOULA

Many people come to Foula intent on viewing the island's famous cliffs – though in actual fact they are very difficult to appreciate except from the air or the sea. If the weather's fine, it's worth climbing to the top of **The Sneug** (1373ft), for the views stretching from Unst to Fair Isle. From the airstrip, climb up the southeast ridge of **Hamnafield** (1130ft), and then continue along the ridge of Brustins to The Sneug itself. You can return via **The Kame** (1220ft), Foula's sheer cliff, and the North Bank to Soberlie Hill, from where you can pick up the island's road. All in all, it's only a walk of five or six miles, but it'll take three to four hours. If you're coming from the ferry at Ham, it's probably best to do the circuit in reverse, which is no bad thing, as the climb from Soberlie Hill up the North Bank is one of the most exhilarating on the island, as the edge of the hill is an ever-increasing vertical drop.

There are other more gentle walks possible on Foula, too. The coastal scenery to the north of the island, beyond Mucklegrind, features several stacks and natural arches, with the waves crashing over skerries, and seals sunning themselves. One of the easiest places to spot seabirds is from beyond the graveyard in Biggings, beyond Hametoun. The nearby hill of **The Noup** (803ft) is a relatively easy climb, compared to The Sneug, and, if you descend to the northwest, brings you to **Sneck o' da Smallie**, where there's a narrow slit in the cliffs, some 200ft high. You can return to the airstrip by heading back down the valley known as The Daal, although the bonxies are pretty thick on the ground. All Foula's cliffs are potentially lethal, especially in wet weather, and all the usual safety precautions should be taken (see p.46).

Mill Loch, while fulmars, guillemots and gannets cling to the rock ledges, but it is the island's colony of **great skuas** or "bonxies" whom you can't fail to notice. From the edge of extinction a hundred years ago, the bonxies are now thriving, with an estimated 3000 pairs on Foula, making it the largest colony in Britain. Sadly, the skuas, who eat the eggs and young of other birds, have devastated the puffin population, and, during the nesting season, they attack anyone who comes near. Although their dive-bombing antics are primarily meant as a threat, they can make walking across the island's moorland interior fairly stressful – the best advice is to stick to the coast.

Practicalities

A day-trip by **ferry** isn't possible, as the summer passenger service to Foula from Walls only runs on Tuesdays, Saturdays and alternate Thursdays (2hr 30min), with a sailing from Scalloway on remaining Thursdays (3hr); it's essential to book and reconfirm (☎01595/753232). The boat arrives at Ham, in the middle of the east coast, and has to be winched up onto the pier to protect it. There are also **flights** from Tingwall, to Foula (Mon–Wed & Fri; ☎01595/840226), with day-trips possible except on Tuesdays; tickets cost around £20 one way. If you want to stay on the island, the only **B&B** is *Leraback* (☎01595/753226; ②), near Ham, which does full board only. Even if you go to the island just for the day, bear in mind that there's no shop, so you'll need to take all your **supplies** with you. There's just one road, which runs along the eastern side of the island, and is used by Foula's remarkable fleet of unroadworthy vehicles.

North Mainland

The **North Mainland**, stretching more than thirty miles north from the central belt around Lerwick, is wilder than much of Shetland, with almost relentlessly bleak moorland and some rugged and dramatic coastal scenery. It is all but split in two by the isthmus of Mavis Grind: to the south are the districts of Delting, home to Shetland's oil terminal, Lunnasting, gateway to the islands of Whalsay and Out Skerries, and Nesting; to the north is the remote region of Northmavine, which boasts some of the most scenic cliffs in Shetland.

Voe and around

If you're travelling north, you're bound to pass by **VOE**, as it sits at the main crossroads of the North Mainland: to the east, the road leads to Vidlin and Laxo, ferry terminals for Whalsay and Out Skerries; to the northeast, the road cuts across to Toft, where the ferry departs for Yell (see p.419); to the northwest, it continues on to Brae and Northmaven. If you stay on the main road, it's easy to miss the picturesque old village, a tight huddle of homes and workshops down below the road around the pier. Set at the head of a deep, sheltered, sea loch, Voe has a Scandinavian appearance, helped by the presence of the **Sail Loft**, painted in a rich, deep red. The building was originally used by fishermen and whalers for storing their gear; later, it became a knitwear workshop, and it was here that woollen jumpers were knitted for the 1953 Mount Everest expedition. Today, the building has been converted into a large **camping böd** (book through Lerwick tourist office; April–Oct); it has hot showers, a kitchen, and a solid-fuel heater in the smaller of the bedrooms. There's a handy bakery across the road, and the *Pierhead Restaurant & Bar*, a cosy wood-panelled **pub** with a real fire and occasional live music, which offers a good bar menu and à la carte including the odd catch from the local fishing boats; phone ahead to check if the restaurant is open (☎01806/588332).

Beyond Laxo, the ferry terminal for Whalsay (see p.417), and Vidlin, the departure point for the Out Skerries (see p.419), nine miles northeast of Voe, lies **Lunna House**, with its distinctive red window surrounds, set above a sheltered harbour. The house was originally built in 1660 by the Hunter family, but is best known as the initial headquarters from which the Shetland Bus resistance operation was conducted during World War II (see p.405). Down the hill lies the little whitewashed **Lunna Kirk**, built in 1753, with a beautiful tiny interior including a carved hexagonal pulpit. Among its more peculiar features is a "lepers' squint" on the outside wall, through which those believed to have the disease could participate in the service without risk of infecting the congregation; there was, however, no leprosy here, the outcasts in fact suffering from a hereditary, non-infectious skin condition, brought on by malnutrition. In the graveyard, several unidentified Norwegian sailors, torpedoed by the Nazis, are buried.

Brae and Sullom Voe

BRAE, a sprawling settlement that still has the feel of a frontier town, was one of four expanded in some haste in the 1970s to accommodate the workforce for the huge **Sullom Voe Oil Terminal**, just to the northeast. The longest sea loch in

Shetland, Sullom Voe has always attracted the interest of outsiders in search of a deep-water harbour. During World War II it was home to the Norwegian Air Force and a base for RAF seaplanes. Although the oil terminal, built between 1975 and 1982, has passed its production peak, it is still the largest of its kind in Europe. Its size, however, isn't obvious from beyond the site boundary and few clues remain to the extraordinary scale of the construction effort, which for several years involved a workforce of 6000 accommodated in two large "construction villages" and two ships. It is still a huge source of employment, but its long-term future depends partly on whether it obtains the contracts for exploiting the new oilfields west of Shetland.

Brae may not, at first sight, appear to be somewhere to spend the night, but it does boast one of Shetland's finest **hotels**, *Busta House* (☎01806/522506; ⑤), a lovely laird's house with stepped gables that has been enlarged tastefully over the last four hundred years and which sits across the bay of Busta Voe from the modern sprawl of Brae. Even if you're not staying the night here, it's worth coming for afternoon tea in the Long Room, a stroll around the lovely wooded grounds, or for a drink and a superb bar meal in the hotel's pub-like bar. A cheaper alternative is the modern croft house B&B of *Westayre* (☎01806/522368; ①), beyond Busta, overlooking a red sandy bay on the peaceful island of Muckle Roe, which is linked to the mainland by a bridge. The nearest **campsite** (☎01806/522563), by the unattractive *Valleyfield Guest House*, on the main road a mile or so south of Brae, has all the facilities you could want, but a pitiable location.

Northmavine

Mavis Grind, the narrow isthmus at which it's said you can throw a stone from the Atlantic to the North Sea, or at least to Sullom Voe, marks the start of **Northmavine**, the northwest peninsula of North Mainland, and unquestionably one of the most picturesque areas of Shetland, with its often rugged scenery, magnificent coastline and wide open spaces. Three miles north of the isthmus, it's worth abandoning the main road to explore the remoter corners; the twisting side road west to Gunnister and Nibon travels through a wonderful tumbled landscape of pink and grey rock where abandoned fields and broken shells of croft houses provide abundant evidence of past human struggles to make a living. Where the road ends, at Nibon, you can view a jigsaw of islands and rocky headlands which, even on a relatively calm day, smash the Atlantic into streams of white foam.

Hillswick

HILLSWICK, the main settlement in the area, was once served by the steamboats of the North of Scotland, Orkney & Shetland Steam Navigation Company, and in the early 1900s the firm built the **St Magnus Hotel** to house their customers, importing it in the form of a timber kit from Norway. Despite various alterations over the years, it still stands overlooking St Magnus Bay, rather magnificently clad in black timber-framing and white weatherboarding. Nearer the shore is the much older Hillswick House and, attached to it, **Da Böd**, once the oldest pub in Shetland, said to have been founded by a German merchant in 1684, but now a rather unpredictable hippie café called *The Booth*.

It is possible **to stay** at the *St Magnus Hotel* (☎01806/503372; ②), whose foyer, dining room and bedrooms retain their original pine walls, but you can't help feeling that the place has seen better days – and the food is very ordinary. For a decent **B&B** in the vicinity of Hillswick, look no further than *Almara* (☎01806/503261; ①), a mile or two back down the road in Upper Urafirth, which will present you with good food, a family welcome and excellent views. If you're looking for a **beach** to collapse on, the nicest sandiest one is on the west side of the Hillswick isthmus, overlooking Dore Holm (see below), a short walk across the fields from the hotel.

Esha Ness

Just outside Hillswick, a sideroad leads west to the exposed headland of **Esha Ness** (pronounced "*Ay*sha Ness"), celebrated for its splendid coastline views. Spectacular red granite **cliffs**, eaten away to form fantastic shapes by the elements, are spread out before you as the road climbs away from Hillswick: in the foreground are the stacks known as **The Drongs** off the Ness of Hillswick, while in the distance, the Westside and Papa Stour are visible.

A mile or so south off the main road is the **Tangwick Haa Museum** (May–Sept Mon–Fri 1–5pm, Sat & Sun 11am–7pm; free), which, through photographs, old documents and fishing gear, tells the often moving story of this remote corner of Shetland and its role in the dangerous trade of deep-sea fishing and whaling. Kids and adults alike will also enjoy the shells, the Shetland wool and sand samples, and the prize exhibit, the Gunnister Man, who was found preserved in peat in 1951. Over 250 years old now, he's down to his bones, for the most part, but his clothes are in good condition, as is his knitted purse, which contained three coins: two Dutch and one Swedish.

Just before it finally peters out, the road divides, with the southern branch leading to the remains of **Stenness fishing station**, which was once one of the most important deep-sea or haaf-fishing stations in Shetland. The remains of a few of the böds used by the fishermen are still visible along the sloping pebbly beach where they would dry their catch. At the peak of operations in the early nineteenth century, as many as eighteen trips a year were made in up to seventy open six-oared boats, or "sixareens", to the fishing grounds thirty or forty miles to the west. A Shetland folk song, *Rowin' Foula Doon*, recalls how the crews rowed so far west that the island of Foula began to sink below the eastern horizon. Visible half a mile offshore to the south is **Dore Holm** or the "Drinking Horse", an impressive island with a natural arch.

The northern branch of the road ends at the **Esha Ness Lighthouse**, a great place to view the red sandstone cliffs, stacks and blowholes of this stretch of coast. A useful information board at the lighthouse details some of the dramatic geological features here, and, if the weather's a bit rough, you should be treated to some spectacular crashing waves. One of the features to beware of at Esha Ness are the blowholes, some of which are hidden far inland. The best example is the **Holes of Scraada**, a partly roofed cleft where the sea suddenly appears 300yd inland from the cliff line. The incredible power of the sea can be seen in the various giant boulder fields above the cliffs – these **storm beaches** are formed by rocks torn from the cliffs in storms and deposited inland.

One of the few places to stay in Esha Ness is *Johnnie Notions* **camping böd** (April–Oct; book through Lerwick tourist office; no electricity), up a turning north off the main road, in the hamlet of Hamnavoe. The house was originally the birthplace of **Johnnie "Notions" Williamson** (1740–1803). A man of many talents, including blacksmithing and weaving, his fame rests on his work in protecting several thousand of the population against **smallpox** using a serum and a method of inoculation he'd invented himself, to the amazement of the medical profession. He used a scalpel to lift a flap of skin without drawing blood, then placed the serum he'd prepared underneath, dressing it with a cabbage leaf and a bandage.

Ronas Hill

North of Ronas Voe, by the shores of Colla Firth, an unmarked road leads up **Collafirth Hill**, at the top of which are the crumbling remains of a NATO radio station. However, the natural landscape is much more impressive, with tremendous views on a clear day, and a foreground of large, scattered stones with hardly any vegetation. Though the walk isn't quite as straightforward as it looks, scale and distance being hard to judge in this setting, Collafirth Hill is the easiest place from which to approach the rounded contours of **Ronas Hill**, Shetland's highest point (1475ft). The climb, with no obvious path, is exhausting but rewarding (4hr return; see also the safety precautions on p.46): from the top you can look west to one of the most beautifully sculptured parts of the Shetland coast, as the steep slope of the hill drops down to the arching sand and shingle beach called the **Lang Ayre**, south and east over all of the Mainland, north along the coast of Yell, or out into the daunting expanse of the Atlantic. Also at the summit, among subarctic vegetation and block-fields of granite boulders formed by intense frost and wind, is a Neolithic or Bronze Age **chambered cairn**, one of the best-preserved in Shetland and useful as a shelter from the wind.

Whalsay and Out Skerries

The island of **Whalsay**, known in Shetland as the "Bonnie Isle", is a thriving and extremely friendly community of over one thousand, devoted almost entirely to fishing. The islands' crews operate a fleet of immense super-trawlers and have coped with the change and uncertainty that characterize the industry by investing huge sums in fishing further afield and catching a wider range of species, and have thus sustained a remarkable level of prosperity. The island is, in addition, extremely fertile, but crofting takes second place to fishing here; there are also plentiful supplies of peat, which can be seen in spring and summer, stacked neatly to dry out above huge peat banks, ready to be bagged for the winter.

Ferries from the Mainland arrive at the island's chief town, **SYMBISTER**, in the southwest, whose harbour is usually dominated by the presence of several of the island's sophisticated, multi-million-pound purse-netters, some over 180ft long; you'll also see smaller fishing boats and probably a few "fourareens", which the locals race regularly in the summer months. Across the busy harbour from the ferry berth stands the tiny grey-granite **Pier House** (Mon–Sat 9am–1pm & 2–5pm, Sun 2–4pm; 50p), the key for which resides in the shop opposite. This picturesque little building, with a hoist built into one side, is thought to have been a Hanseatic merchants' store, and contains a good display on how the Germans traded salt, tobacco, spirits and cloth for Whalsay's salted, dried fish from medieval times until the eighteenth century. Close by is the Harbour View house that is thought to have been a Hanseatic storehouse or booth (and is now a private house and hairdresser's). On a hill overlooking the town is the imposing Georgian mansion of **Symbister House**, built in grey granite and boasting a

Neoclassical portico. It was built in the 1830s at great expense by Robert Bruce, not because he wanted to live on Whalsay but, so the story goes, because he wanted to deprive his heirs of his fortune. Since 1940 it has served as the local school and, in the process, has lost some of its grandeur.

At the hamlet of **SODOM** – an anglicized version of Sudheim, meaning "South House" – about half a mile east of Symbister, is **Grieve House** (now a camping böd; see below), the modest former home of celebrated Scots poet, writer and republican **Hugh MacDiarmid** (1892–1978), born Christopher Grieve in the Borders town of Langholm. He stayed here from 1933 until 1942, writing about half of his output, including much of his best work: lonely, contemplative poems honouring fishing and fishermen, with whom he sometimes went out to sea. Estranged from his first wife and family and with a drink problem, MacDiarmid, practically broken, had sought temporary relief in Shetland. At first, he seems to have fallen in love with the islands, but poor physical and mental health, exacerbated (if not caused) by chronic poverty, dogged him. Eventually, unwillingly conscripted to work in a Glasgow munitions factory, he left with his new wife and young son, never to return.

Although the majority of folk live in or around Symbister, the rest of the island – which measures roughly two miles by eight – is quite evenly and fairly densely populated. Of the prehistoric remains on Whalsay, the most notable are the two **Bronze Age houses** on the northeastern coast of the island, half a mile south of Skaw, known respectively as the "Benie Hoose" and "Yoxie Biggins". The latter is also known as the "Standing Stones of Yoxie", due to the use of megaliths to form large sections of the walls, many of which still stand. The houses were clearly used over a very long period, as over 1800 tools were discovered in the Benie Hoose – the community also built the nearby chambered tomb.

Car ferries between Laxo and Whalsay (30min) run roughly every 45 minutes from early morning until late evening; if you have a car, however, it's an idea to book ahead (☎01806/566259). In bad weather, especially southeasterly gales, the service operates from Vidlin. There are also regular **flights** from Tingwall (Mon & Wed–Fri), but these are request-only, so you must book ahead; day-trips are only possible on Thursdays. A few locals do **B&B** for the odd visitor who turns up: try Mrs Jamieson (☎01806/566496; ①) in Symbister, or enquire at the post office; Mrs Simpson also has a few inexpensive self-catering options on the island (☎01806/566429). Alternatively, you can stay at the **camping böd** of *Grieve House* (April–Oct; book through Lerwick tourist office; no electricity), in Sodom. The house has lovely views overlooking Linga Sound, but is hidden from the main road, so ask for directions at the shop on the brow of the hill along the road to Huxter Loch. The island also has an eighteen-hole **golf course**, near the airstrip in Skaw, in the northeast, several shops, and a **leisure centre** with an excellent swimming pool close to the school in Symbister.

Out Skerries

Lying four miles out to sea, off the northeast tip of Whalsay, the **Out Skerries** (or "Skerries" as the locals call them), consist of three tiny low-lying rocky islands – Housay, Bruray and Grunay – the first two linked by a bridge. That people live here at all is remarkable, and that it is one of Shetland's most dynamic communities is astonishing, its affluence based on fishing from a superb, small natural harbour sheltered by all three islands, and on salmon farming in a nearby inlet. There are good, if short, walks, with a few prehistoric remains, but the majority of visitors to Skerries are divers exploring the wreck-strewn coastline, and ornithologists who come here when the wind is in the east, in the hope of catching a glimpse of rare migrants.

The Skerries' jetty and airstrip are both on the middle island of **Bruray**, which also boasts the Skerries' highest point, Bruray Wart (173ft), an easy climb, and one which brings you up close to the islands' ingenious spiral channel collection system for rainwater, which can become scarce in summer. The easternmost island, **Grunay**, is now uninhabited, though you can clearly see the abandoned lighthouse keepers' cottages on the island's chief hill; despite appearances, the lighthouse itself sits on the outlying islet of Bound Skerry. The largest of the Skerries' trio, **Housay**, has the most indented and intriguing coastline, to which you should head if the weather's fine. En route, make sure you wander through the Battle Pund stone circle, a wide ring of boulders in the southeastern corner of the island.

Ferries to and from Skerries leave from Vidlin (Mon & Fri–Sun; 1hr 30min) and Lerwick (Tues & Thurs; 2hr 30min), but day-trips are only possible from Vidlin on Fridays, Saturdays and Sundays. Make sure you book your journey by 5pm the previous evening (☎01806/515226), or the ferry might not run. You can take your car over, but, with less than a mile of road to drive along, it's hardly worth it. There are also regular **flights** from Tingwall (Mon & Wed–Fri), though a day-trip by plane is only possible on Thursdays. There is a shop, and a shower/toilet block by the pier, and **camping** is permitted, with permission. Alternatively, you can stay in *Rocklea* (☎01806/515228; ①, full board ②), a friendly **B&B** on Bruray run by Mrs Johnson.

Yell

Historically, **Yell**, the largest of Shetland's North Isles, hasn't had good write-ups. The writer Eric Linklater described it as "dull and dark", while the Scottish historian Buchanan claimed it was "so uncouth a place that no creature can live therein, except such as are born there". Certainly, if you keep to the fast main road, which links the island's two ferry terminals of Ulsta and Gutcher, you'll pass a lot of uninspiring peat moorland, but the landscape is relieved by several voes which cut deeply into it, providing superb natural harbours used as hiding places by German submarines during World War II. Yell's coastline, too, is gentler and greener than the interior and provides an ideal habitat for a large population of **otters**; locals will point out the best places to watch for them.

At **BURRAVOE**, in the southeastern corner of Yell, there's a lovely whitewashed laird's house dating from 1672, with crow-stepped gables, that now houses the **Old Haa Museum** (late April to Sept Tues–Thurs & Sat 10am–4pm, Sun 2–5pm; free), which is stuffed with artefacts, and has lots of material on the history of the local herring and whaling industry; there's a very pleasant wood-panelled café on the ground floor, too. Across the road is **St Colman's Kirk**, completed in 1900 which features three Gothic-windowed bays surmounted by a tiny little spire.

The island's largest village, **MID YELL**, has a couple of shops, a pub and a leisure centre with a good swimming pool. A mile or so to the northwest of the village, on an exposed hill above the main road, stands the spooky, abandoned

OTTERS

Otters are notoriously elusive and are probably one of the most difficult animals to catch a glimpse of. However, with an estimated population of over one thousand, Yell is one of the best places in the whole of Europe to see otters. The reason otters have thrived here is that much of the coastline is uninhabited, has good fish stocks close to the shore, plenty of freshwater for bathing, and a low-lying peaty shoreline that's easy for digging out holts. Good locations to try on Yell include Otterswick, the Ness of West Sandwick, Whalefirth and Burraness. Locals often see otters crossing the road in search of fresh water, and you're just as likely to see one when and where you least expect it. However, there are a few tips for tracking them down.

A dropping tide is thought to be best, as is a cloudy or rainy day. Dawn and dusk are good times for spotting otters, although they do feed throughout the day. Remember that they can only hold their breath for a maximum of two minutes and, on average, spend just twenty seconds underwater; they fish at sea, but need to wash the salt off their coats regularly in fresh water. Look out for otter prints in the sand – their five-toed, webbed feet are easy to distinguish from dog pawprints – or otter droppings (known as spraint), which often contain fish bones, and are usually positioned prominently on grassy hummocks. Finally, the most obvious thing is to keep quiet, be patient and, if possible, make sure you're downwind of the shore so that the otter can't smell you.

Windhouse, dating in part from the early eighteenth century; skeletons were found under the floor and in its wood-panelled walls, and the house is now believed by many to be haunted (its unhaunted lodge is a camping böd; see below). North of Windhouse, around the Loch of Lumbister, there's an **RSPB reserve** that's home to merlins, skuas and red-throated divers, and is scattered with wild flowers in summer. A pleasant walk leads along the nearby narrow gorge known as **Daal of Lumbister**, where you can see a lush growth of honeysuckle, wild thyme and moss campion.

In the north of Yell, the area around **CULLIVOE** has relatively gentle, but attractive, coastal scenery. The **Sands of Brekken** are made from crushed shells, and are beautifully sheltered in a cove a mile or two north of Cullivoe. A couple of miles to the west, the road ends at **GLOUP**, with its secretive, narrow voe. In the nineteenth century, this was one of the largest haaf-fishing stations in Shetland; a memorial commemorates the 58 men who were lost when a great storm overwhelmed six of their "sixerns" (six-oared, open rowing boats) in July 1881. This area provides some excellent walking, as does the Atlantic coast further west, where there's an Iron Age fort and field system at **Burgi Geos**.

Practicalities

Ferries to Yell are frequent and inexpensive, and taking a car over is easy, too; the Mainland ferry terminal is at Toft (daily every 20–40min; 20min). One of the best **B&Bs** on Yell is *Hillhead* (☎01957/722274; ①) in Burravoe; you can also stay with the Tullochs at Gutcher's post office (☎01957/744201; ①). A cheaper alternative is to stay in the **camping böd** at *Windhouse Lodge* (April–Oct; book through Lerwick tourist office), the (unhaunted) gatehouse on the main road near Mid Yell; it has a small wood- and peat-fired heater and hot showers. There isn't a great range of **food** options on the island, but the non-smoking café in the *Old Haa Museum*

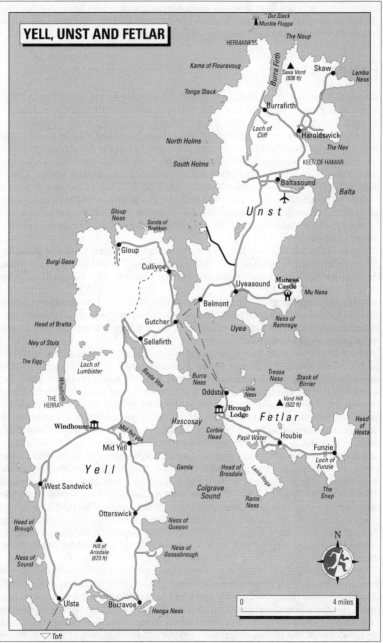

YELL, UNST AND FETLAR

Out Stack
Muckle Flugga
The Noup
HERMANESS
Kame of Flouravoug
Burra Firth
Saxa Vord (936 ft)
Skaw
Lamba Ness
Tonga Stack
Burrafirth
Loch of Cliff
Haroldswick
The Nev
North Holms
KEEN OF HAMAR
South Holms
Baltasound
Balta
Unst
Gloup Ness
Sands of Brekken
Gloup
Burgi Geos
Cullivoe
Uyeasound
Muness Castle
Mu Ness
Head of Bratta
Gutcher
Belmont
Ness of Ramnage
Ney of Stuis
Sellafirth
Uyea
The Eigg
Loch of Lumbister
Basta Voe
Burra Ness
Tressa Ness
Stack of Birrier
THE HERRA
Whalifirth
Oddsta
Une Ness
Vord Hill (522 ft)
Windhouse
Brough Lodge
Fetlar
Head of Hosta
Mid Yell Voe
Hascosay
Corbie Head
Papil Water
Houbie
Mid Yell
Funzie
Yell
Gamla
Head of Bresdale
Lamb Hoga
Loch of Funzie
West Sandwick
Colgrave Sound
The Snap
Otterswick
Ness of Queyon
Rams Ness
Head of Brough
Hill of Arisdale (673 ft)
Ness of Gossabrough
Ness of Sound
Ulsta
Burravoe
Heoga Ness
Toft

N

0   4 miles

© Crown copyright

(closed Mon & Fri) at Burravoe has soup, snacks and delicious home-baking. The *Hilltop Bar* in Mid Yell offers standard bar meals, while the *Seaview Café* at the Gutcher ferry terminal has filled rolls, snacks, soup, teas and coffees.

Fetlar

Known as "the garden of Shetland", **Fetlar** is the most fertile of the North Isles, much of it grassy moorland and lush green meadows with masses of summer flowers. Around 900 people once lived here and there might well be more than 100 now were it not for the activities of **Sir Arthur Nicolson**, who in the first half of the nineteenth century cleared many of the people at forty days' notice to make room for sheep. Nicolson's architectural tastes were rather more eccentric than some other local tyrants; his rotting but still astonishing **Brough Lodge**, a rambling castellated composition built in stone and brick in the 1820s, can be seen a mile or so south of the ferry terminal, and owes something – perhaps an apology – to Gothic, Classical and maybe even Tudor styles. Nicolson is also responsible for the nearby round-tower folly, which was built with stone taken from the abandoned croft houses.

Today Fetlar's population live on the southern and eastern sides of the island. At the main settlement, **HOUBIE**, in the centre of the island on the south coast, there's a rather less adventurously styled laird's house called Leagarth, built by Fetlar's most famous son, Sir William Watson Cheyne, who with Lord Lister pioneered antiseptic surgery. Nearby is the excellent **Fetlar Interpretive Centre** (May–Sept daily except Mon noon–5pm; free), presenting the island's history and offering information on Fetlar's outstanding birdlife through the Internet as well as by more conventional means.

Much of the northern half of the island around Fetlar's highest point, Vord Hill 522ft), is now the **RSPB North Fetlar Reserve**, which is closed from mid-May to mid-July, during which time visits are only possible with permission from the warden at Baelan, the house signposted off the main road from Brough Lodge to Houbie (☎01957/733246). As well as harbouring important colonies of arctic skuas and whimbrels, the reserve is perhaps best known for Britain's only breeding pair of **snowy owls**, which bred on Stackaberg, to the southwest of Vord Hill, from 1967 to 1975. Around twenty chicks were raised before the old male died, and since then only the female has been seen. The warden can advise you on the latest, and occasionally conducts guided walks in search of the snowy owl (phone as above). Fetlar is also one of very few places you'll see graceful **red-necked phalarope** (late May to July): the birds are unusual in that the female does the courting and then leaves the male in charge of incubation. The island boasts 95 percent of the UK population, and an RSPB hide has been provided overlooking the marshes (or mires) to the east of the **Loch of Funzie** (which, incidentally, is pronounced "Finnie"); the loch itself is a good place to look out for red-throated divers.

Of the archeological remains on Fetlar, perhaps the most remarkable is the **Funzie Girt** or Finnigirt, an ancient stone boundary of uncertain date, which divides the island into two. Its southern end has been destroyed, but it is well preserved on the western and northern slopes of **Vord Hill**, within the RSPB reserve (see above). Elsewhere on Fetlar, particularly along the remoter north coast and on Lamb Hoga, the higher moorland peninsula to the southwest, there is excellent walking. At Tresta, on the south coast, is a beautiful, sheltered, sandy beach, and the loch behind it, Papil Water, is good for fishing.

Practicalities

Ferries to Fetlar (5–6 daily; 25min) depart from both Gutcher (on Yell) and Belmont (on Unst), though they are by no means as frequent as the ferries between the Mainland, Yell and Unst. The ferry docks at Oddsta, three miles northwest of Houbie; the only public transport is an infrequent **postcar** (Mon, Wed & Fri), so if you don't have a car you should try to negotiate a lift on the ferry. If you do have a car, bear in mind that there's no petrol station on Fetlar, so fill up before you come across. Accommodation is in short supply and booking is advisable, if you wish to stay the night. Fetlar's most comfortable **B&B** is the modern *Gord* (☎01957/733227; ①), behind the island shop in Houbie, followed by *The Glebe* (☎01957/733242; ②), which is non-smoking, and is hidden among the trees above Papil Water; both will provide an evening meal. *The Garths* **campsite** (☎01957/733227; May–Sept) is in a field just to the west of Houbie, with toilets, showers and drying facilities. There's a post office, shop and **café** (closed Mon) in the middle of Houbie.

Unst

Unst has a population of around 1000, of whom 300 to 400 are connected to the RAF radar base at Saxa Vord, listening out for uninvited intruders. Much of the interior is rolling grassland – a blessed relief after the peaty moorland of Yell – but the coast is more dramatic: a fringe of cliffs relieved by some beautiful sandy beaches. As Britain's most northerly inhabited island, there is a surfeit of "most northerly" sights, which is fair enough, given that many visitors only come here in order to head straight for Hermaness, to look out over Muckle Flugga and the northernmost tip of Britain, to the North Pole beyond.

On the south coast of the island, not far from the ferry terminal, is **UYEA-SOUND**, with the stone-built Greenwell's Booth, an old Hanseatic merchants' warehouse by the pier. The house on the island of Uyea, which protects the harbour, was once the home of Sir Basil Neven-Spence, the local MP (1935–50). Further east lie the ruins of **Muness Castle**, a dinky little defensive structure, with matching bulging bastions and corbelled turrets at opposite corners. The castle was built in 1598 by the Scots incomer, Laurence Bruce, stepbrother and chief bullyboy of the infamous Earl Robert Stewart, and probably designed by Andrew Crawford, who shortly afterwards built Scalloway Castle for Robert's son Patrick. The inscription above the entrance asks visitors "not to hurt this vark aluayis", but the castle was sacked by Danish pirates in 1627 and never really re-roofed. A little to the north is a vast sandy beach, backed by the deserted crofting settlement of Sandwick.

Unst's main settlement is **BALTASOUND**, where the remains of old jetties around the bay testify to a bygone herring industry, which saw the local population of around 500 swell to as much as 10,000 during the fishing season. Nowadays, Baltasound boasts an airport, a hotel with a pub, a shop, a post office, a leisure centre with a pool, and also Britain's most northerly brewery, the **Valhalla Brewery**, which opened in 1997 and welcomes visits by appointment (☎01957/711348; £2).

From Baltasound, the main road crosses what appears to be a giant boulder field. What you see is, in fact, serpentine rock, found widely on Unst; most often it's greyish green, but it weathers to rusty orange, and in some stone walls there are pieces which are of an extraordinary deep turquoise hue. The serpentine soil is so poor it produces unusual vegetation, turning the grass bluish-grey. At the **Keen of Hamar** National Nature Reserve, east of Baltasound, numerous rare plants, including Norwegian sandwort and the unique mouse-eared Edmondston's chickweed, grow in an almost lunar landscape.

Britain's most northerly post office is over the hill to the north, at **HAROLDSWICK**, smart and eminently photogenic in its red weatherboarding. Down near the shore the **Unst Boat Haven** (May–Sept daily 2–5pm; otherwise a key is available from the adjacent shop; free), displays a beautifully presented collection of historic boats with many tools of the trade and information on fishing; most of the boats are from Shetland, with one from Norway. A little to the northeast, next door to the Methodist chapel on the road to Norwick, stands an old croft house that now houses the **Unst Heritage Centre** (May–Sept daily 2–5pm; free), where you can find out about other aspects of Unst life. The road ends at Skaw, with a beautiful beach and the very last house in Britain.

The road that heads off northwest from Haroldswick leads to the head of **Burra Firth**, a north-facing inlet surrounded by cliffs and home to Britain's most northerly golf course and rugby pitch. It is guarded to the east by the hills of **Saxa Vord** (936ft), Unst's highest point, topped by several Ministry of Defence installations. It was here that the country's unofficial wind-speed record of 177mph was recorded in 1962, before the anemometer was blown away. To the west of Burra Firth lies the bleak headland of **Hermaness**, now a National Nature Reserve and home to more than 100,000 nesting seabirds. There's an excellent **visitor centre** in the former lighthouse keepers' shore station, where you can pick up a leaflet showing the marked routes across the heather, which allow you access into the reserve. Whatever you do, stick to the path so as to avoid annoying the vast numbers of nesting great skuas.

From Hermaness Hill, you can look down over the jagged rocks of the wonderfully named Vesta Skerry, Rumblings, Tipta Skerry and **Muckle Flugga**. There are few more dramatic settings for a lighthouse, and few sites could ever have presented as great a challenge to the builders, who erected it in 1858. Beyond the lighthouse is **Out Stack**, the most northerly bit of Britain, where Lady Franklin landed in 1849 in order to pray (in vain, as it turned out) for the safe return for her husband from his expedition to discover the Northwest Passage, undertaken four years previously. The views from here are inevitably marvellous, as is the birdlife; there's a huge gannetry on one of the stacks, and puffins burrow all along the clifftops. The walk down the west side of Unst towards Westing is one of the finest in Shetland and, if the wind's blowing hard, the seascape should be pretty dramatic.

Practicalities

Ferries leave regularly from Gutcher on Yell for Belmont on Unst (every 15–30min; 10min); booking in advance is wise (☎01957/722259). **Flights** to Unst depart from Sumburgh Airport (Mon–Fri only), and arrive at the airport near Baltasound. By far the best **accommodation** on Unst is historic *Buness House* (☎01957/711315, *buness@zetnet.co.uk*; ③), a lovely old Haa in Baltasound. Another very good bet is *Prestagaard* (☎01957/755234; ①), a more modest

Victorian B&B in Uyeasound, where there's also the very handy, independent *Gardiesfauld Hostel* (☎01957/755259; April–Sept), which allows **camping**, and offers **bike rental**. The *Baltasound Hotel* serves **food** and drink to non-residents, and snacks and teas can be had at the tearoom in NorNova Knitwear just north of Muness Castle, or, often on a help-yourself basis, at the Haroldswick Shop. Shetland Wildlife Tours (☎01950/460254) offer a very popular, though expensive **boat trip** around Muckle Flugga, though you need good sea legs to enjoy it even in calm weather; the boats leave from Mid Yell, on the neighbouring island of Yell (May–Aug Wed 10am; £70).

travel details

ORKNEY

Mainland buses

Kirkwall to: Burwick (4 daily; 45min); Houton (Mon–Sat 3–5 daily; 30min); St Margaret's Hope (Mon–Fri 4 daily, Sat 2 daily; 40min); Stromness (Mon–Sat 6–8 daily; 40min); Tingwall (Mon–Sat 3 daily; 25min).

Ferries to Orkney (summer only)

Aberdeen–Stromness (2 weekly; 8–10hr); Invergordon–Kirkwall (6 weekly; 9hr); John O' Groats–Burwick (passengers only; 2–4 daily; 45min); Lerwick–Stromness (2 weekly; 8hr); Scrabster–Stromness (1–3 daily; 2hr).

Inter-island ferries (summer only)

Eday: Kirkwall–Eday (2 daily; 1hr 15min–2hr).

Egilsay: Tingwall–Egilsay (3–4 daily; 50min–1hr 45min).

Flotta: Houton–Flotta (2–5 daily; 45min).

Hoy: Houton–Hoy (2–5 daily; 30min–1hr); Stromness–Hoy (passenger-only; 2–4 daily; 25min).

North Ronaldsay: Kirkwall–North Ronaldsay (1 weekly; usually Fri; 2hr 40min–3hr).

Papa Westray: Kirkwall–Papa Westray (Tues & Fri; 2hr 15min); Pierowall (Westray)–Papa Westray (passenger-only; 3–6 daily; 25min).

Rousay: Tingwall–Rousay (6 daily; 30min).

Sanday: Kirkwall–Sanday (1–3 daily; 1hr 25min).

Shapinsay: Kirkwall–Shapinsay (5–6 daily; 45min).

Stronsay: Kirkwall–Stronsay (2 daily; 1hr 35min–2hr).

Westray: Kirkwall–Westray (2–3 daily; 1hr 25min).

Wyre: (4–5 daily; 45min–2hr 5min).

Flights to Orkney (Mon–Sat only)

Aberdeen–Kirkwall (3 daily; 45min); Edinburgh–Kirkwall (1 daily; 1hr 30min); Glasgow–Kirkwall (1–2 daily; 1hr 20min–2hr 10min); Inverness–Kirkwall (2 daily; 50min).

Inter-island flights (Mon–Sat only)

Kirkwall to: Eday (Wed 3 daily; 8–36min); North Ronaldsay (1–2 daily; 15min); Papa Westray (2 daily; 12min); Sanday (1–2 daily; 20min); Stronsay (Mon–Fri 2 daily; 25min); Westray (Mon–Sat 1–2 daily; 12min).

SHETLAND

Mainland buses

Lerwick to: Aith (Mon–Sat 1–3 daily; 45min); Brae (Mon–Fri 4–5 daily, Sat 2 daily; 45min); Hamnavoe (Mon–Sat 1–2 daily; 30min); Hillswick (1 daily except Wed & Sun; 1hr 15min); Laxo (1 daily; 40min); Sandwick (Mon–Sat 5–6 daily, Sun 3 daily; 25min); Scalloway (Mon–Sat 5–6 daily; 15min); Sumburgh (2–4 daily; 45min); Toft (Mon–Sat 1 daily; 55min); Vidlin (Mon–Sat 2 daily; 45min); Walls (Mon–Sat 1–3 daily; 45min).

Unst

Baltasound–Haroldswick (2–4 daily; 5–10min); Belmont–Baltasound (Mon–Fri school term only 1 daily; 1hr); Belmont–Uyeasound (Mon–Sat 1–3 daily; 5min).

Yell

Mid-Yell–Gutcher (1–3 daily, Sun 1 daily in school term; 25min); Ulsta–Burravoe (Mon–Sat 1 daily; 10min); Ulsta–Gutcher (Mon–Sat (1–2 daily, Sun 1 daily in school term; 30min).

Ferries to Shetland (summer only)

Aberdeen–Lerwick (4–5 weekly; 14hr); Stromness–Lerwick (1–2 weekly; 8–10hr).

Inter-island ferries (summer only)

Bressay: Lerwick–Bressay (every 30min–1hr; 5min).

Fair Isle: Lerwick–Fair Isle (alternate Thurs 1 daily; 4hr 30min); Sumburgh–Fair Isle (Tues, Sat & alternate Thurs 1 daily; 2hr 40min).

Fetlar: Belmont (Unst)–Oddsta (2–3 daily; 25min); Gutcher (Yell)–Oddsta (5–6 daily; 25min).

Foula: Scalloway–Foula (alternate Thurs 1 daily; 3hr); Walls–Foula (Tues & alternate Thurs 1 daily; 2hr 30min).

Out Skerries: Lerwick–Skerries (Tues & Thurs 1 daily; 2hr 30min); Vidlin–Skerries (Mon 1 daily, Fri–Sun 3 daily; 1hr 30min).

Papa Stour: West Burrafirth–Papa Stour (Mon, Wed & Sun 1 daily, Fri–Sat 2 daily; 45min).

Unst: Gutcher (Yell)–Belmont (every 15–45min; 10min).

Whalsay: Laxo–Symbister (14–16 daily; 30min).

Yell: Toft–Ulsta (every 20–40min; 20min).

Flights to Shetland (summer only)

Aberdeen–Sumburgh (Mon–Fri 4 daily, Sat & Sun 2 daily; 1hr); Edinburgh–Sumburgh (Mon–Sat 1 daily; 1hr 50min); Glasgow–Sumburgh (Mon–Fri 2 daily, Sat & Sun 1 daily; 2hr 25min); Inverness –Sumburgh (Mon–Sat 1 daily; 1hr 35min); Kirkwall–Sumburgh (Mon–Sat 1–2 daily; 35min); Wick–Sumburgh (Mon–Sat 1 daily; 40min).

Inter-island flights (summer only)

Sumburgh: Fair Isle (Tues, Thurs & Sat 1 daily; 15min); Unst (Mon–Fri 1 daily; 35min).

Tingwall: Fair Isle (Mon, Wed & Fri 2 daily, Sat 1 daily; 25min); Foula (Mon & Wed 2 daily, Tues & Fri 1 daily; 15min); Out Skerries, calling at Whalsay on request (Mon, Wed & Fri 1 daily, Thurs 2 daily; 20min); Papa Stour (Tues 2 daily; 10min); Unst (Mon–Fri 1 daily; 25min).

PART THREE

THE

CONTEXTS

Scottish Primrose
(Primula Scotica)

THE HISTORICAL FRAMEWORK

PREHISTORIC SCOTLAND

Scotland's first inhabitants were Mesolithic **hunter-gatherers**, who arrived as the last Ice Age retreated around 8000 BC. They lived initally in the area south of Oban, where heaps of animal bones and shells have been excavated in the caves on the Mull of Kintyre and on the plains north of Crinan. From here there is evidence of them moving onto the islands of Arran, Jura, Rum, Skye and Lewis, where the damp and relatively warm coastal climate would have been preferable to the harsher inland hills and glens. Around 4500 BC, **Neolithic farming peoples** from the European mainland began moving into Scotland. To provide themselves with land for their cereal crops and grazing for their livestock, they cleared large areas of upland forest, usually by fire, and in the process created the characteristic moorland landscapes of much of modern Scotland. These early farmers established permanent settlements, some of which, like the well-preserved village of **Skara Brae** on Orkney, were near the sea, enabling them to supplement their diet by fishing and to develop their skills as boatbuilders. The Neolithic settlements were not as isolated as was once imagined: geological evidence has, for instance, revealed that the stone used to make axeheads found in the Hebrides was quarried in Northern Ireland.

Settlement spurred the development of more complex forms of religious belief. The Neolithic peoples built large chambered burial mounds or **cairns**, such as Maes Howe in Orkney or the Clava Cairns near Inverness. This reverence for human remains suggests a belief in some form of afterlife, a concept that the next wave of settlers, the **Beaker people**, certainly believed in. They placed pottery beakers filled with drink in the tombs of their dead to assist the passage of the deceased on their journey to, or their stay in, the next world. The Beaker people also built the mysterious **stone circles**, thirty of which have been discovered in Scotland. Such monuments were a massive commitment in terms of time and energy, with many of the stones carried from many miles away, just as they were at Stonehenge in England, the most famous stone circle of all. One of the best-known Scottish circles is that of **Calanais** (Callanish) on the Isle of Lewis, where a dramatic series of monoliths (single standing stones) form avenues leading towards a circle made up of thirteen standing stones. The exact function of the circles is still unknown, but many of the stones are aligned with the position of the sun at certain points in its annual cycle, suggesting that the monuments are related to the changing of the seasons.

The Beaker people also brought the **Bronze Age** to Scotland. Bronze, an alloy of copper and tin, was stronger and more flexible than its predecessor flint, which had long been used for axeheads and knives. New materials led directly to the development of more effective weapons, and the sword and the shield made their first appearance around 1000 BC. Agricultural needs plus new weaponry added up to a state of endemic warfare as villagers raided their neighbours to steal livestock and grain. The Bronze Age peoples responded to the danger by developing a range of defences, among them the spectacular **hillforts**, great earthwork defences, many of which are thought to have been occupied from around 1000 BC and remained in use throughout the Iron Age, sometimes far longer. Less spectacular but equally practical were the **crannogs**, smaller settlements built on artificial islands constructed of logs, earth, stones and brush, such as those found on Loch Tay.

Conflict in Scotland intensified in the first millennium BC as successive waves of **Celtic** settlers, arriving from the south, increased competition for land. Around 400 BC, the Celts brought the technology of **iron** with them and, as Winston Churchill put it, "Men armed with iron entered Britain and killed the men of bronze." These fractious times witnessed the construction of hundreds of **brochs** or fortified towers. Concentrated along the Atlantic coast and in the Northern and Western Isles, the brochs were drystone fortifications (built without mortar or cement) often over 40ft in height. Some historians claim they provided protection for small coastal settlements from the attentions of Roman slave-traders. Much the best-preserved broch is on the Shetland island of **Mousa**; its double walls rise to about 40ft, only a little short of their original height. The Celts continued to migrate north almost up until Julius Caesar's first incursion into Britain in 55 BC.

At the end of the prehistoric period, immediately prior to the arrival of the Romans, Scotland was divided among a number of warring Iron Age tribes, who, apart from the raiding, were preoccupied with wresting a living from the land, growing barley and oats, rearing sheep, hunting deer and fishing for salmon. The Romans were to write these people into history under the collective name Picti, or **Picts**, meaning "painted people", after their body tattoos.

THE ROMANS

The **Roman conquest** of Britain began in 43 AD, almost a century after Caesar's first invasion. By 80 AD the Roman governor, Agricola, felt secure enough in the south of Britain to begin an invasion of the north, building a string of forts along the southern edge of the Highlands and defeating a large force of Scottish tribes at Mons Graupius. Precisely where this is remains a puzzle for historians, though most place it somewhere in the northeast, possibly on the slopes of Bennachie, near Inverurie in Aberdeenshire. The long-term effect of his campaign, however, was slight. Work on a major fort – to be the base for 5000 – at Inchtuthill, north of Perth on the Tay, was abandoned before it was finished, and the legions withdrew south. In 123 AD the **Emperor Hadrian** decided to seal the frontier against the northern tribes and built **Hadrian's Wall**,

which stretched from the Solway Firth to the Tyne and was the first formal division of the island of Britain. Twenty years later, the Romans again ventured north and built the **Antonine Wall** between the Clyde and the Forth, a clear statement of the hostility they perceived to the north. This was occupied for about forty years, but thereafter the Romans, frustrated by the inhospitable terrain of the Highlands, largely gave up their attempt to subjugate the north, and instead adopted a policy of containment.

It was the Romans who produced the first written accounts of the peoples of Scotland. In the second century AD, the Greco-Egyptian geographer Ptolemy drew up the first known map of Scotland, which identified seventeen tribal territories. Other descriptions were less scientific, compounding the mixture of fear and contempt with which the Romans regarded their Pictish neighbours. Dio Cassius, a Roman commentator writing in 197 AD, informed his readers that:

> They live in huts, go naked and unshod. They mostly have a democratic government, and are much addicted to robbery. They can bear hunger and cold and all manner of hardship; they will retire into their marshes and hold out for days with only their heads above water, and in the forest they will subsist on barks and roots.

Another Roman account, by Tacitus, also identified the first inhabitant of Scotland whose name is known, a leader of the Pictish tribes called **Calgacus**, or "swordsman", who Tacitus claimed led 30,000 men. It is telling that, just as the uncomplimentary propoganda about primitive Highlanders had hardly changed by the time of Bonnie Prince Charlie's uprising in 1745, so too the number of fighting men he might have had at his disposal – had he been able to unite them – was largely the same.

THE DARK AGES

In the years following the departure of the Romans, traditionally put at 450 AD, the population of Scotland changed considerably. By 500 AD there were four groups of people, or nations, dominant in different parts of the country. The **Picts** occupied the Northern Isles, the north and the east as far south as Fife. Today their settlements can be generally identified by place names with a "Pit" prefix, such as Pitlochry, and by the existence of carved symbol stones, like those found at Aberlemno in Angus. To the southwest, between Dumbarton and Carlisle, was a population of **Britons**. Many of the Briton leaders had Roman names, which suggests that they were a Romanized Celtic people, possibly a combination of tribes maintained by the Romans as a buffer between the Wall and the northern tribes, and peoples pushed west by the Anglo-Saxon invaders landing on the east coast. Both the Britons and the Picts spoke variations of P-Celtic, from which Welsh, Cornish and Breton developed.

On the west coast, to the north and west of the Britons (in what is now Argyll), lived the **Scotti**, Irish-Celtic invaders who would eventually give their name to the whole country. The first Scotti arrived in the Western Isles from Ireland in the fourth century AD, and about a century later their great king, Fergus Mor, moved his base from Antrim to Dunadd, near Lochgilphead, where he founded the kingdom of Dalriada. The Scotti spoke Q-Celtic, the precursor of modern Gaelic. On the east coast, the Germanic **Angles** had sailed north along the coast to carve out an enclave around Dunbar in East Lothian.

Within three centuries another non-Celtic invader was making significant incursions. From around 795 AD, **Norse** raids began on the Scottish coast and Hebrides, soon followed by the arrival of settlers, mainly in the northern isles and along the Caithness and Sutherland coastline. In 872 AD, the King of Norway set up an earldom in **Orkney**, from which **Shetland** was also governed, and for the next six centuries the Northern Isles took a path distinct from the rest of Scotland, becoming a base for raiding and colonizing much of the rest of Britain and Ireland – and a link in the chain that connected Faroe, Iceland, Greenland and, more tenuously, North America.

The next few centuries saw almost constant warfare among the different groups. The main issue was land, but this was frequently complicated by the need of the warrior castes, who dominated all of these cultures, to exhibit martial prowess. Military conquests did play their part in bringing the peoples of Scotland together, but the most persuasive force was **Christianity**. Many of the Britons had been Christians since Roman times and it had been a Briton, St Ninian, who conducted the first missionary work among the Picts at the end of the fourth century. Attempts to convert the Picts were resumed in the sixth century by St

Columba, who, as a Gaelic-speaking Scotti, demonstrated that Christianity could provide a bridge between the different tribes.

Christianity proved attractive to pagan kings because it seemed to offer them extra supernatural powers. As St Columba declared, when he inaugurated his cousin Aidan as king of Dalriada in 574, "Believe firmly, O Aidan, that none of your enemies will be able to resist you unless you first deal falsely against me and my successors." This combination of spiritual and political power, when taken with Columba's establishment of the island of **Iona** as a centre of Christian culture, opened the way for many peaceable contacts between the Picts and Scotti. Intermarriage became commonplace, and the Scotti king Kenneth MacAlpine, who united Dalriada and Pictland in 843, was the son of a Pictish princess – the Picts traced succession through the female line. Similarly, MacAlpine's creation of the united kingdom of **Alba**, later known as **Scotia**, was part of a process of integration rather than outright conquest, though it was the Scots' religion, Columba's Christianity, and their language (Gaelic) that were to dominate the merger, allowing many aspects of Pictish life, including their language, to fall forgotten and untraceable into the depths of history. Kenneth and his successors gradually extended the frontiers of their kingdom by marriage and force of arms until, by 1034, almost all of what we now call Scotland – on the mainland, at least – was under their rule.

THE MIDDLE AGES

By the time of his death in 1034, **Malcolm II** was recognized as the king of Scotia. He was not, though, a national king in the sense that we understand the term, as under the Gaelic system kings were elected from the *derbfine*, a group made up of those whose great-grandfathers had been kings. The chosen successor, supposedly the fittest to rule, was known as the *tanist*. By the eleventh century, however, Scottish kings had become familiar with the principle of heredity, and were often tempted to bend the rules of *tanistry*. Thus, the childless Malcolm secured the succession of his grandson **Duncan** by murdering a potential rival *tanist*. Duncan, in turn, was killed by **Macbeth** near Elgin in 1040. Macbeth was not, therefore, the villain of Shakespeare's imagination, but simply an ambitious Scot of royal blood acting in a relatively conventional way.

The victory of **Malcolm III**, known as Canmore (Bighead), over Macbeth in 1057, marked the beginning of a period of fundamental change in Scottish society. Having avenged his father Duncan, Malcolm III, who had spent the previous seventeen years at the English court, sought to apply to Scotland a range of ideas he had brought back with him. He and his heirs established a secure dynasty based on succession through the male line and introduced **feudalism** into Scotland, a system that was diametrically opposed to the Gaelic system, which rested on blood ties: the followers of a Gaelic king were his kindred, whereas the followers of a feudal king were vassals bought with land. The Canmores successfully feudalized much of southern and eastern Scotland by making grants to their Norman, Breton and Flemish followers; they preferred to make their capital in Edinburgh, and in these regions, Scots – a northern version of Anglo-Saxon – pushed out Gaelic as the lingua franca. They also began to reform the **Church**, a development started with the efforts of Margaret, Malcolm III's English wife, who brought Scottish religious practices into line with those of the rest of Europe and was eventually canonized.

The policies of the Canmores laid the basis for a **cultural rift** in Scotland between the Highland and Lowland communities. Factionalism between various chiefs tended to distract the Highland tribes from their widening differences with the rulers to the south, while the ever-present Viking threat also served to keep many of the clans looking to the west and north rather than the south.

In 1098, a **treaty** between Edgar, King of Scots, and Magnus Bareleg, King of Norway, ceded soverignty of all the islands to the Norwegians – Magnus even managed to include Kintyre in his swag by being hauled across the isthmus at Tarbet sitting in a boat, thus proving it an "island", as it could be circumnavigated. In practice, however, power in the western islands was in the control of local chiefs, lieutenants of a king on the Isle of Man who was himself subordinate to the King of Norway. By marrying the daughter of one of the Manx kings and skilful raiding of neighbouring islands, **Somerled**, King of Argyll, established himself and his successors as Lords of the Isles.

Their natural ally was to the Scottish rather than the Norwegian king, and when **Alexander III** (1249–86), Scotland's strongest king in two centuries, sought to buy back the Hebrides from King Haakon of Norway in 1263, the offended Norwegian king sent a fleet to teach the Scots a lesson and drag the islands back into line. Initally the bullying tactics worked, but the fleet lingered too long, was battered by a series of autumnal storms, and retreated back to Orkney in disarray following a skirmish with Alexander's army at **Largs** on the Clyde coast. While in Orkney. King Haakon died, and three years later the **Treaty of Perth** of 1266 returned the Isle of Man and the Hebrides to Scotland in exchange for an annual rent.

In 1286 **Alexander III** died, and a hotly disputed succession gave Edward I, the king of England, an opportunity to subjugate Scotland. In 1291 Edward presided over a conference where the rival claimants to the Scottish throne presented their cases. Edward chose John Balliol in preference to Robert the Bruce, his main rival, and obliged John to pay him homage, thus turning Scotland into a vassal kingdom. Bruce refused to accept the decision, thereby continuing the conflict, and in 1295 Balliol renounced his allegiance to Edward and formed an alliance with France – the beginning of what is known as the "**Auld Alliance**". In the conflict that followed, the Bruce family sided with the English, Balliol was defeated and imprisoned, and Edward seized control of almost all of Scotland.

Edward had shown little mercy during his conquest of Scotland – he had, for example, had most of the population of Berwick massacred – and his cruelty seems to have provoked a truly national resistance. This focused on **William Wallace**, a man of relatively lowly origins from southwest Scotland who forged an army of peasants, lesser knights and townsmen that was fundamentally different to the armies raised by the nobility. Figures like Balliol, holding lands in England, France and Scotland, were part of an international aristocracy for whom warfare was merely the means by which they struggled for power. Wallace, by contrast, led proto-nationalist forces drawn from both Lowlands and Highlands determined to expel the English from their country. Probably for that very reason Wallace never received the support of the nobility and, after a bitter ten-year campaign, he was betrayed and executed in London in 1305.

With Wallace out of the way, feudal intrigue resumed. In 1306 **Robert the Bruce**, the erstwhile ally of the English, defied Edward and had himself crowned king of Scotland. Edward died the following year, but the unrest dragged on until 1314, when Bruce decisively defeated a huge English army under Edward II at the Battle of **Bannockburn**. At last Bruce was firmly in control of his kingdom, and in 1320 the Scots asserted their right to independence in a successful petition to the pope, now known as the **Declaration of Arbroath**.

In the years following Bruce's death in 1329, the Scottish monarchy gradually declined in influence. The last of the Bruce dynasty died in 1371, to be succeeded by the "Stewards", hence **Stewarts**, but thereafter a succession of Scottish rulers, culminating with James VI in 1567, came to the throne when still children. The power vacuum was filled by the nobility, whose key members exercised control as Scotland's regents while carving out territories where they ruled with the power, if not the title, of kings. The more vigorous monarchs of the period, notably **James I** (1406–37), did their best to curb the power of such dynasties, but their efforts were usually nullified at the next regency. **James IV** (1488–1513), the most talented of the early Stewarts, might have restored the authority of the crown, but his invasion of England ended in a terrible defeat for the Scots – and his own death – at the Battle of Flodden Field.

Meanwhile, the shape of modern-day Scotland was completed when the Northern Isles were gradually wrested from Norway, which had united with Sweden under the Danish crown in the fourteenth century. In 1469, a marriage was arranged between Margaret, daughter of the Danish king, Christian I, and the future **King James III** (1460–88) of Scotland. Short of cash for her dowry, Christian mortgaged Orkney to Scotland in 1468, followed by Shetland in 1469; neither pledge was ever successfully redeemed. The laws, religion and administration of the Northern Isles became Scottish, though their Norse heritage is still very evident in place names, dialect and culture. Meanwhile, the MacDonald Lords of the Isles had become too unruly for the more unified vision of James IV, and in 1493 the title revert-

ed to the Crown. It still remains there: the current Lord of the Isles is Prince Charles.

THE RELIGIOUS WARS

In many respects the **Reformation** in Scotland was driven as much by the political intrigue of the reign of **Mary, Queen of Scots** (1542–67) as it was by religious conviction. Although in later years the hard-line Presbyterianism of the Highlands and Western Islands would triumph over political expediency, the revolutionary thinking of **John Knox** and his Protestant diehards initially made little impact in the north. If some of the Lowland lords were still inclined to see religious affiliation as a negotiable tool in the quest for power and influence, the loyalty – if not, perhaps, the piety – of many of the Highland chiefs to both their monarch and the Catholic faith was much more solid.

James VI (1567–1625), who in 1603 also became James I of England, disliked Presbyterianism because its quasi-democratic structure – particularly the lack of royally appointed bishops – appeared to threaten his authority. In 1610 he restored the Scottish bishops, leaving a legacy that his son, **Charles I** (1625–49), who was raised in Episcopalian England, could not handle. He had little understanding of Scottish reformism and, by attempting to impose a new prayer book on the Kirk in 1637, laying down forms of worship in line with those favoured by the High Anglican Church, provoked the **National Covenant**, a religious pledge that committed the signatories to "Labour by all means lawful to recover the purity and liberty of the Gospel as it was established and professed".

Charles declared all the "**Covenanters**" to be rebels, a proclamation endorsed by his Scottish bishops. Consequently, when the king backed down from military action and called a General Assembly of the Kirk, the assembly promptly abolished the Episcopacy. Charles pronounced the proceedings illegal, but lack of finance stopped him from mounting an effective military campaign – whereas the Covenanters, well financed by the Kirk, assembled a proficient army under Alexander Leslie. In desperation, Charles summoned the English Parliament, the first for eleven years, hoping it would pay for an army. But, like the calling of the General Assembly, the decision was a disaster and Parliament was much keener to criticize his policies than to raise taxes. In response Charles declared war on Parliament in 1642.

Until 1650, Scotland was ruled by the Covenanters and the power of the Presbyterian Kirk grew considerably. Laws were passed establishing schools in every parish and, less usefully, banning trade with Catholic countries. The only effective opposition to the theocratic state came from the **Marquis of Montrose**, who had initially supported the Covenant but lined up with the king when war broke out. Montrose was a gifted campaigner whose army was drawn from the Highlands and islands, where the Kirk's influence was still weak, and included a frightening rabble of islanders and Irishmen under the inspiration of Colonsay chief Alasdair MacDonald, or **Colkitto**, whose appetite for the fray was fed by Montrose's willingness to send them charging into battle at the precise moment they could inflict most damage. For a golden year Montrose's army roamed the Highlands undefeated, scoring a number of brilliant tactical victories over the Covenanters, but the reluctance of his troops to stay south of the Highland Line made it impossible for him to capitalize on his successes and, as the clansmen dispersed with the spoils of victory back to their lands, Montrose was left weak and exposed. Unfailingly loyal to a king who was unwilling to take the same risks for his most gifted general, Montrose was eventually captured and executed in 1650.

Although the restoration of **Charles II** (1660–85) brought bishops back to the Kirk, they were integrated into an essentially presbyterian structure of Kirk sessions and presbyteries, though the General Assembly was not re-established. Over 300 clergymen, a third of the Scottish ministry, refused to accept the reinstatement of the bishops and were edged out of the Church, forced to hold open-air services, called **Conventicles**, which Charles did his best to suppress. Religious opposition inspired military resistance and the Lowlands witnessed scenes of brutal repression as the king's forces struggled to keep control in what was known as "The Killing Time". In the southwest, a particular stronghold of the Covenanters, the government imported Highlanders, the so-called "Highland Host", to root out the opposition, which they did with great barbarity.

Charles II was succeeded by his brother **James VII** (James II of England), whose ardent Catholicism caused a Protestant backlash in England. In 1689, he was forced into exile in France and the throne passed to **Mary**, his Protestant daughter, and her Dutch husband, **William of Orange**. In Scotland there was a brief flurry of opposition to William when **Graham of Claverhouse**, known as "Bonnie Dundee", united the Jacobite clans against the government army at the Pass of Killiekrankie, just north of Pitlochry. However, the inspirational Claverhouse was killed on the point of claiming a famous victory, and again the clans, leaderless and unwilling to press south, dissipated and the threat passed. William and Mary quickly consolidated their position, restoring the full presbyterian structure in Scotland and abolishing the bishops, though they chose not to restore the political and legal functions of the Kirk, which remained subject to parliamentary control. It was sufficient, however, to bring the religious wars to a close, essentially completing the Reformation in Scotland and establishing a platform on which political union would be built.

THE UNION

One thing that lingered, however, was Highland loyalty to the Stewart line, something both William and the political pragmatists saw as a significant threat. In 1691, William offered pardons to those Highland chiefs who had opposed his accession, on condition that they took an oath of allegiance by New Year's Day 1692. Alasdair MacDonald of Glencoe had turned up at the last minute, but his efforts to take the oath were frustrated by the king's officials, who were determined to see his clan, well-known for their support of the Stewarts, destroyed. In February 1692, Captain Robert Campbell quartered his men in Glencoe and, two weeks later, in the middle of the night, his troops acted on their secret orders and carried out the infamous **massacre of Glencoe**. Thirty-eight MacDonalds died, and the slaughter caused a national scandal, especially among the clans, where "Murder under Trust" – killing those offering you shelter – was considered a particularly heinous crime.

The situation in Scotland was further complicated by the question of the succession. Mary died without leaving an heir and, on William's death in 1702, the crown passed to her sister **Anne**, James II's second daughter, who was also childless. In response, the

THE HIGHLAND CLANS

The term "**clan**", as it is commonly used to refer to the quasi-tribal associations found in the Highlands of Scotland, only appears in its modern usage in the sixteenth century. In theory, the clan bound together blood relatives who shared a common ancestor, a concept clearly derived from the ancient Gaelic notion of kinship. But in practice, many of the clans were of non-Gaelic origin – such as the Frasers, Sinclairs and Stewarts, all of Anglo-Norman descent – and it was the mythology of a common ancestor, rather than the actuality, that cemented the clans together. Furthermore, clans were often made up of people with a variety of surnames, and there are documented cases of individuals changing their names when they swapped allegiances.

At the upper end of Highland society was the **clan chief** (who might have been a minor figure, like MacDonald of Glencoe, or a great lord, like the Duke of Argyll, head of the Campbells), who provided protection for his followers: they would, in turn, fight for him when called upon to do so. Below the clan chief were the **chieftains of the septs**, or subunits of the clan, and then came the **tacksmen**, major tenants of the chief to whom they were frequently related. The tacksmen sublet their land to **tenants**, who were at the bottom of the social scale. The Highlanders wore a simple belted plaid wrapped around the body – rather than the kilt – and not until the late seventeenth century were certain **tartans** roughly associated with particular clans. The detailed codification of the tartan was produced by the Victorians, whose romantic vision of Highland life originated with George IV's visit to Scotland in 1822, when he appeared in an elaborate version of Highland dress, complete with flesh-coloured tights (for more on tartan, see p.207).

English Parliament secured the Protestant succession by passing the **Act of Settlement**, which named the Electress Sophia of Hanover, a granddaughter of James VI (James I of England), as the next in line to the throne. The Act did not, however, apply in Scotland, and the English feared that the Scots would invite James Edward Stewart, the son of James II by his second wife, back from France to be their king. Consequently, Parliament appointed commissioners charged with the consideration of "proper methods towards attaining a union with Scotland". The project seemed doomed to failure when the Scottish Parliament passed the **Act of Security**, in 1703, stating that Scotland would not accept a Hanoverian monarch unless they had first received guarantees protecting their religion and their trade.

Nevertheless, despite the strength of anti-English feeling, the Scottish Parliament passed the **Act of Union** by 110 votes to 69 in January 1707. Some historians have explained the vote in terms of bribery and corruption. This certainly played a part (the Duke of Hamilton, for example, switched sides at a key moment and was subsequently rewarded with an English dukedom), but there were other factors. Scottish politicians were divided between the Cavaliers – Jacobites (supporters of the Stewarts) and Episcopalians – and the Country party, whose presbyterian members dreaded the return of the Stewarts more than they disliked the Hanoverians. To the Highlands and Islands, however, the shift of government five hundred miles further south from Edinburgh, itself distant enough for many, was to make relatively little difference to their lives for the the best part of the rest of the century.

The country that was united with England in 1707 contained three distinct cultures: in south and east Scotland, they spoke Scots; in Shetland, Orkney and much of the northeast, the local dialect, though Scots-based, contained elements of Norn (Old Norse); in the rest of north and west Scotland, including the Western Isles, Gaelic was spoken. These linguistic differences were paralleled by different forms of social organization and customs. The people of north and west Scotland were mostly pastoralists, moving their sheep and cattle to Highland pastures in the summer, and returning to the glens in the winter. They lived in single-room dwellings, heated by a central peat fire and sometimes shared with livestock, and in hard times they would subsist on cakes made from the blood of their live cattle mixed with oatmeal. Highlanders supplemented their meagre income by raiding their clan neighbours and the prosperous Lowlands, whose inhabitants regarded their northern compatriots with a mixture of fear and contempt. In the early seventeenth century, Montgomerie, a Lowland poet, suggested that God had created the first Highlander out of horseshit. When God asked his creation what he would do, the reply was, "I will doun to the Lowland, Lord, and thair steill a kow." It was an attitude little improved from the days of the Roman chroniclers.

THE JACOBITE RISINGS

When James VII/II was deposed, he had fled to France, where he planned the reconquest of his kingdom with the support of the French king. When James died in 1701, the hopes of the Stewarts passed to his only son, James Edward Stewart, the "Old Pretender" ("Pretender" in the sense of having pretensions to the throne; "Old" to distinguish him from his son Charles, the "Young Pretender"). After the accession to the British throne of the Hanoverian George I, son of Sophia, Electress of Hanover, the first major **Jacobite uprising** occurred in 1715. Its timing appeared perfect. Scottish opinion was moving against the Union, which had failed to bring Scotland any tangible economic benefits. The English had also been accused of bad faith when, contrary to their pledges, they attempted to impose their legal practices on the Scots. Neither were Jacobite sentiments confined to Scotland. There were many in England who toasted the "King across the water" and showed no enthusiasm for the new German ruler. In September 1715, the fiercely Jacobite John Erskine, Earl of Mar, raised the Stewart standard at Braemar Castle. Just eight days later, he captured Perth, where he gathered an army of over 10,000 men, drawn mostly from the Episcopalians of northeast Scotland and from the Highlands. Mar's rebellion took the government by surprise. They had only 4000 soldiers in Scotland, under the command of the Duke of Argyll, but Mar dithered until he lost the military advantage. There was an indecisive battle at Sheriffmuir in November, but by the time the Old Pretender arrived the following month 6000 veteran Dutch troops had reinforced Argyll. The rebellion disintegrated rapidly and James slunk back to exile in France in February 1716.

Though better known, the **Jacobite uprising of 1745**, led by James's dashing son, Charles Edward Stewart (Bonnie Prince Charlie), had even less chance of success than the rising of 1715. In the intervening thirty years, the Hanoverians had consolidated their hold on the English throne, Lowland society had become uniformly loyalist, access into the Highlands for both trade and internal peacekeeping had been vastly improved by the military roads built by General Wade, and even among the clans regiments such as the Black Watch were recruited which drew on the Highlanders' military tradition but formed part of the government's standing army. The rebellion had a shaky start, with Charles landing on the west coast with only seven companions and no firm promises of clan support, and however romantically inspired, it was a fated enterprise. He only attracted less than half of the potential 30,000 clansmen who could have marched with him, and promises of support from the French and English Jacobites failed to materialize. Nevertheless, after a decisive victory over government forces at Prestonpans, near Edinburgh, Charles made a spectacular advance into England, getting as far as Derby. London was in a state of panic: its shops were closed and the Bank of England, fearing a run on sterling, slowed withdrawals by paying out in sixpences. But Derby was as far south as Charles got. On December 6, threatened by superior forces, the Jacobites decided to retreat to Scotland. The Duke of Cumberland was sent in pursuit and the two armies met on **Culloden Moor**, near Inverness, in April 1746. It was to be the last set-piece battle on British soil, the last time a claymore-wielding Highland charge would be set against organized ranks of musket-bearing troops, and the last time a Stewart would take up arms in pursuit of the throne. As with so many of the other critical points in the campaign, the Jacobite leadership at Culloden was divided and ill-prepared. When it came to the fight, the Highlanders were in the wrong place, exhausted after a forced overnight march, and seriously outnumbered and outgunned. They were swept from the field, losing over 1200 men compared to Cumberland's 300 plus. After the battle, many of the wounded Jacobites were slaughtered, an atrocity that earned Cumberland the nickname "Butcher". Charles took flight, living the next few months as a fugitive as he dodged redcoat patrols across the Highlands and Islands, famously escaping from the outer isles to Skye in the company of Flora MacDonald. Eventually a French ship came to his rescue and he returned to the Continent, where he lived out the rest of his life in drunken exile.

In the aftermath of the uprising, the wearing of tartan, the bearing of arms and the playing of bagpipes were all banned. Rebel chiefs lost their land and the Highlands were placed under military occupation. Most significantly, the government prohibited the private armies of the chiefs, thereby effectively destroying the clan system. Within a few years more Highland regiments were recruited for the British army, and by the end of the century thousands of Scots were fighting and dying for their Hanoverian king against Napoleon.

THE HIGHLAND CLEARANCES

Once the clan chief was forbidden his own army, he had no need of the large tenantry that had previously been a vital military asset. Conversely, the second half of the eighteenth century saw the Highland population increase dramatically after the introduction of the easy-to-grow and nutritious potato. Between 1745 and 1811, the population of the Outer Hebrides, for example, rose from 13,000 to 24,500. The clan chiefs adopted different policies to deal with the new situation. Some encouraged emigration, and as many as 6000 Highlanders left for the Americas between 1800 and 1803 alone. Other landowners saw the economic advantages of developing alternative forms of employment for their tenantry, mainly fishing and kelping. **Kelp** (brown seaweed) was gathered and burnt to produce soda ash, which was used in the manufacture of soap, glass and explosives. There was a rising market for soda ash until the 1810s, with the price increasing from £2 a ton in 1760 to £20 in 1808, making a fortune for some landowners and providing thousands of Highlanders with temporary employment. Fishing for **herring** – the "silver darlings" – was also encouraged, and new harbours and coastal settlements were built all around the Highland coastline. Other landowners developed **sheep runs** on the Highland pastures, introducing hardy breeds like the black-faced Linton and the Cheviot. But extensive sheep farming proved incompatible with a high peasant population, and many landowners decided to clear their estates of tenants, some of whom were forcibly moved to tiny plots of marginal land, where they were to farm as **crofters**.

The pace of the **Highland Clearances** accelerated after the end of the Napoleonic wars in 1815, when the market price for kelp, fish and cattle declined, leaving sheep as the only profitable Highland product. The most notorious Clearances took place on the estates of the Countess of Sutherland, who owned a million acres in northern Scotland. Between 1807 and 1821, around 15,000 people were thrown off her land, evictions carried out by **Patrick Sellar**, the estate factor, with considerable brutality. Those who failed to leave by the appointed time had their homes burnt in front of them, and one elderly woman, who failed to get out of her home after it was torched, subsequently died from burns. The local sheriff charged Sellar with her murder, but a jury of landowners acquitted him – and the sheriff was sacked. Not all the Clearances were as brutal, but the consequences of overpopulation were again highlighted as a potato famine followed in 1846, forcing large-scale emigration to America and Canada and leaving the huge uninhabited areas found in the region today.

The crofters eked out a precarious existence, but they hung on throughout the nineteenth century, often by taking seasonal employment away from home. In the 1880s, however, a sharp downturn in agricultural prices made it difficult for many crofters to pay their rent. This time, inspired by the example of the Irish Land League, they resisted eviction, forming the **Highland Land Reform Association** and the **Crofters' Party**. In 1886, in response to the social unrest, Gladstone's Liberal government passed the **Crofters' Holdings Act**, which conceded three of the crofters' demands: security of tenure, fair rents to be decided independently, and the right to pass on crofts by inheritance. But Gladstone did not attempt to increase the amount of land available for crofting, and shortage of land remained a major problem until the **Land Settlement Act** of 1919 made provision for the creation of new crofts. Nevertheless, the population of the Highlands continued to fall into the twentieth century, with many of the region's young people finding city life more appealing.

For all the hardships of Highland life, however, the region was undergoing a re-evaluation. particularly in the eyes of the well-educated and wealthier urban classes. In 1773 the famous London literary figure **Samuel Johnson** took a tour of the Highlands and Islands with his biographer, Edinburgh-born

James Boswell; it was less than thirty years after Culloden – the pair even met Flora MacDonald in Skye – and travel was by no means easy, but the pair's descriptions of the noble wildness of the Highlands captured the imagination of British society (see p.459). The epic poems describing the exploits of the Celtic warrior Fingal, ostensibly penned by the third-century bard Ossian but in fact an elaborate and brilliant hoax by **James MacPherson**, further established the romantic idyll of the Highlands, a process taken to fruition by the novels of **Walter Scott**, who in 1822 orchestrated the state visit of George IV to Scotland, even dressing the monarch in a stylized version of the tartan plaid which had been worn by the pretender to his great-grandfather's throne. Meanwhile roads improved, railways and canals were built and, as access improved, so tourism grew. **Queen Victoria** fell in love with the Highlands, buying an estate at Balmoral, and the huge tracts of moorland owned by the Highland lairds became **sporting estates** for shooting grouse and deer, or fishing for salmon.

TWENTIETH-CENTURY SCOTLAND

Depopulation of an all-too-familiar kind was present in the early decades of the twentieth century, with Highland regiments at the vanguard of the British Army's infantry offensives in both the Anglo-Boer wars at the turn of the century and **World War I**. Few Highland communities were left untouched by the carnage of the trenches, with one particularly tragic episode taking place on New Year's Day 1919, when the steamer *Iolaire*, packed with returning servicemen, foundered on rocks at the entrance to Stornoway harbour, drowning over two hundred local men as their families looked on helpless from the pier. The months after hostilities ended also saw one of the most remarkable spectacles in Orkney's long seafaring history, when the entire German naval fleet of over two hundred vessels, lying at anchor in Scapa Flow having surrendered to the British at the armistice, was scuttled by the skeleton German crews that remained aboard.

The same harbour was quickly involved in **World War II**, when a German U-boat breached the defences around Orkney in October 1939 and torpedoed HMS *Royal Oak*, with the loss of 833 men. Many more ships and lives were lost in the waters off the Hebrides during the hard-fought Battle of the Atlantic, when convoys carrying supplies and troops were constantly harried by German U-boats. Various bases were established in the west Highlands and Islands, including a flying-boat squadron at Kerrera, by Oban, with Air Force bases on Islay, Benbecula, Tiree and Lewis, and a Royal Naval anchorage at Tobermory; on the mainland, commandos were trained in survival skills and offensive landings in the area around lochs Lochy and Arkaig, near Fort William. Though men of fighting age again left the Highlands to serve in the forces, the war years were not altogether bleak, as the influx of servicemen ensured a certain prosperity to the places they were based at, and the need for the country to remain self-sufficient meant that farms and crofts – often worked by the women and children left behind – were encouraged to keep production levels high.

Even before the war, efforts had been made to recognize the greater social and economic needs of the Highlands and Islands with the establishment of the **Highlands and Islands Medical Service**, a precursor to the National Health Service introduced by the first postwar Labour government. Other agencies were set up in the 1940s, including the **North of Scotland Hydro Electric Board** and the **Forestry Commission**, both of which were served to improve the local infrastructure and create state-sponsored employment. In later decades the various **ferry** companies running to the Islands were coalesced into the state-subsidized Caledonian MacBrayne (or "CalMac", for short), and, partly benefiting from runways built in wartime, regular **airline** services to the islands started up. After Britain joined the EEC in 1972, the Highlands and Islands were identified as an area in need of special assistance, and in harness with the **Highlands and Islands Development Board**, significant investment was made the area's infrastructure, including roads, schools, medical facilities and harbours. European funding was also used to support the increased use and teaching of **Gaelic**, and the encouragement of Gaelic broadcasting, publishing and education, hand in hand with a flourishing of Gaelic culture, from the annual National Mod to the nationwide success of folk-rock bands such as Runrig and Capercaille, means that the indigenous language and culture of the Highlands and Islands is as healthy now as it has been all century.

The strength of cultural identity – even in its more clichéd forms – has always been a vital aspect of the Highlands and Islands' attraction as a **tourist** destination. Tourism remains the dominant industry in the region, despite the furrowed brows of, on the one hand, operators suffering a bad season and, on the other, conservationists concerned by the impact increased numbers are having. Meanwhile the main traditional industries, **farming** and **fishing**, continue with European support to struggle against European comptetition, while others, such as **whisky** and **tweed making**, remain prominent in certain pockets althogh they have never, in fact, been large-scale employers. New industries have arrived with the twentieth century, and while few have quite fulfilled the initial hopes raised of them, most remain to contribute to the economic diversity of the region. **Forestry**, for example, has seen large tracts of the Highlands planted, more sensitively now than in the past; North Sea **oil** has brought serious economic benefits not just to the northeast coast but also Orkney and Shetland; **salmon farming** has become widespread, tainting many otherwise idyllic west coast scenes, but long accepted as a vital part of many coastal communities; and various set-piece industrial developments have made their mark, from the now-disused aluminium smelter at **Kinlochleven** to the **Dounreay** nuclear reactor and reprocessing plant near Thurso. Among the most recent arrivals on the economic map is the phenomenon of "**cyber-crofting**" – essentially the operation of Internet-based businesses or services from remoter areas. The possibilities thrown up by the communications revolution have also led to proposals to establish a **University of the Highlands**, with various colleges linked to each other and to outlying students by computer.

As remote living is made more viable, however, it is not just the indigenous population who benefit, and **immigration** into the Highlands now matches the long-term trend of emigration, with Inverness presently the fastest growing urban area in Britain. The incomers – invariably called "white settlers" –

are now an established aspect of Highland life, often providing economic impetus in the form of enthusiastically run small businesses, though their presence can still rankle in the intimate lives of small communities. Any prejudicial control from outside the region is looked on suspiciously, not least in the question of **land ownership**, which remains one of the keys to Highland development – some would say the most important of all. Some of the largest Highland estates continue to be owned and managed from afar, with little regard to local needs or priorities; while two-thirds of the private land in Scotland is owned by a mere 1250 people, many of them aristocrats. However, the success of groups of crofters in buying estates in Assynt and Knoydart, as well as the purchase of the island of Eigg by its inhabitants, hints at a broadening of land ownership, which many hope the land reforms brought in by the new Scottish Parliament will do more to promote.

With so many unique issues to tackle, it is perhaps not surprising that the Highlands and Islands has always maintained an independent and generally restrained voice in Scottish **politics**. Despite the unshakable Scottishness of the region, it has remained largely ambivalent to the surges of nationalism seen in other parts of the country. In local government, large numbers of independents are regularly returned, while in British, and more recently Scottish, elections, the tendency has always been towards strong, recognizable characters – mainly Liberals, with pockets of support for the SNP (Scottish National Party) in the east and Labour in the Outer Isles.

The issue of **devolution** was long regarded with suspicion by Highlanders and Islanders for the likelihood of any Scottish Parliament being dominated by the politics of the Central Belt. Now that it has arrived, however, with the election of the **Scottish Parliament** in 1999, the presence of government closer and more sensitive to the issues that matter to the Highlands and Islands is, as it is for the rest of Scotland, cause for optimism and heightened expectation. After centuries of what has often seemed like ostracism from the rest of Scotland, the Highlands and Islands have good reason to believe that, as the nation steps into the new millennium, they are partners in the dance.

THE WILDLIFE OF THE HIGHLANDS AND ISLANDS

A comprehensive account of the Highlands and Islands wildlife would take a whole book to cover: what follows is a general overview of the effects of climate and human activity on the country's flora and fauna.

CLIMATE

Scotland's mountains are high enough to impose harsh conditions, especially in the Highlands, and the **Cairngorm plateau** (the largest area of high ground in the whole of Britain) is almost Arctic even in summer. Despite this, however, since the easing of the Ice Age about 10,000 years ago, Scotland has developed a rather complex climate, and some areas of the country are quite mild.

The warmish water of the Gulf Stream tempers conditions on the west coast, so that at **Inverewe**, for example, you'll find incongruously lush gardens blooming with subtropical plants. Inland, the weather becomes more extreme, but what restricts plantlife on many Scottish hills is not the cold so much as the stress of wind and gloomy cloud cover. **Ben Nevis**, for example, is clouded and whipped by 50mph gales for more than two-thirds of the year and, as a result, the tree line – the height to which trees grow up the slopes – may be only 150ft above sea level near the west coast, but up to over 2000ft on some of the sheltered hillsides inland.

A BRIEF HISTORY

After the Ice Age, "arctic" and "alpine" plants abounded, eventually giving way to woody shrubs and trees, notably the **Scots pine**. Oak and other hardwood trees followed in some places, but the Scots pine remained the distinctive tree, spreading expansively to form the great **Caledonian Forest**. Parts of this ancient forest still remain, miraculously surviving centuries of attack, but it is only comparatively recently that attempts at positive conservation have been made.

Early **settlement**, from the Picts to the Norsemen, led to clearance of large areas of forest, and huge areas were burnt during the clan wars. When centuries of unrest ended with the Jacobite defeat at Culloden in 1746, the glens were ransacked for timber, which was floated downriver to fuel iron-smelting and other industries. The clansmen had had a free-booting cattle economy, but during the infamous **Clearances** both the cattle and the defeated Highlanders were replaced by the more profitable sheep of the new landlords. As also happened on the English downland and moorland, intensive sheep grazing kept the land open, eventually destroying much woodland by preventing natural regeneration.

In Victorian times, **red deer** herds, which also graze heavily, provided stalking, and when rapid-firing breech-loading guns came into general use around the 1850s, **grouse shooting** became a passion. It's strange to think of birds changing the scenery, but grouse graze heather and thus large areas are burnt to encourage fresh green growth. No tree saplings survive and the open moorland is maintained.

The flatter **Lowlands** are now dominated by mechanized farming; barley, beef, turnips and potatoes conspire against wildlife, and pollution and development are as damaging here as elsewhere. Even the so-called "**wilderness**" is under threat. Its own popularity obviously holds dangers, and the unique flora of the Cairngorm peaks, for example, is in danger of being stamped out under the feet of the summer visitors using the ski lifts. But even more damaging than tourism is **conifer planting**. In recent decades, boosted (if not caused) by generous grant aid and tax dodges, large areas of open moorland have been planted with tightly packed monocultural ranks of foreign conifers, forbidding to much wildlife. Coniferization is particularly threatening to large areas of bogland in the "Flow Country" of Caithness and elsewhere, areas that are as unique a natural environment as the tropical rainforests. For these and other similar habitats, registration as an **SSSI** – a Site of Special Scientific Interest – has proved barely adequate, and the only real safeguard is for such areas to be owned or managed by organizations such as Scottish Natural Heritage (the national agency) or the Scottish Wildlife Trust, the Royal Society for the Protection of Birds and similar voluntary groups.

WILD FLOWERS

Relic patches of the Scots-pine Caledonian Forest, such as the Black Wood of Rannoch and Rothiemurchus Forest below the Cairngorms, are often more open than an oak wood, the pines, interspersed with birch and juniper, spaced out in hilly heather. These woods feature some wonderful wild flowers, such as the **wintergreens** which justify their name, unobtrusive **orchids** in the shape of creeping lady's tresses and lesser twayblade and, in parts of the northeast especially, the rare beauty of the **twinflower**, holding its paired heads over the summer needle litter.

You'll also find old oak woods in some places, especially in the lower coastward lengths of the southern glens. Here the Atlantic influence encourages masses of spring flowers including **wood anemone** and **wild hyacinth**, the Scottish term for what in England is called a bluebell. (In Scotland the name "bluebell" describes the summer-flowering English harebell that grows on more open ground.) Scotland, or at least lowland Scotland, has many flowers found further south in Britain – **maiden pink**, orchids, **cowslip** and others in grassy areas. Roadside flowers, such as **meadowsweet** and **meadow buttercup**, **dog rose**, **primrose** and **red campion**, extend widely up through Scotland, but others, such as the **white field rose** and mistletoe, **red valerian**, **small scabious**, **cuckoo pint** and **traveller's joy** (and the elm tree), reach the end of their range in the Scottish Central Lowlands.

Scotland's mountains, especially where the rock is limey or basic in character, as on Ben Lawers, for example, are dotted with arctic-alpine plants, such as mountain **avens**, with their white flowers and glossy oak-like leaves, and handsome **purple saxifrage**, both of which favour a soil rich in calcium. Here as elsewhere, the flowers are to be found on ledges and rockfaces out of reach of the sheep and deer. Other classic mountain plants are **alpine lady's mantle** and **moss campion**, which grows in a tight cushion, set with single pink flowers.

Higher up on the bleak wind-battered mountaintops, there may be nothing much more than a low "heath" of mosses and maybe some tough low grasses or rushes between the scatterings of rubble. Because this environment encourages few insects, such plants are generally self-fertilizing and some even produce small plants or "bulbils" in their flower heads instead of seed.

A variety of ferns shelter in the slopes amid the tumbled rock screes or in cracks in the rock alongside streams. In Scotland's damp climate, you'll also see many ferns on lower ground, but some, the **holly fern** for one, are true mountain species. **Lichens**, too, are common on exposed rocks, and in the woods bushy and bearded lichens can coat the branches and trunks.

Bogs are a natural feature of much of the flatter ground in the Highlands, often extending for miles. Scottish bogland comprises an intricate mosaic of domes of living bog moss (sometimes bright green or a striking orange or yellow), domes of drier, heathery peat, and pools dotted in between. The wettest areas give rise to specialized plants such as **cranberry**, **bearberry** and also the **sundews**, which gain nutrients in these poor surroundings by trapping and absorbing midges with the sticky hairs on their flat leaves.

At sea level, the rivers spawn estuaries; these and some sea lochs are edged with **salt marshes**, which in time dry out into "meadows" colourful with **sea aster** and other flowers. On the west coast, you may find **spring squill** shimmering blue as soon as the winter eases, or **Scots lovage**, a celery-scented member of the cow parsley family. A relic of arctic times, the **oysterplant**, with blue-grey leaves and pink bell flowers, also grows here, as it does on the shores of Iceland and Scandinavia.

Scotland has some wonderful **sand dune** systems, which on the back shores harden into grassy patches often grazed by rabbits to create a fine turf.

BIRDLIFE

It might seem unexpected to find birds nesting at over 3000ft, but in Scotland the wind is strong enough to blow patches of icy ground clear of snow, enabling birds to make their homes on the mountains. The **dotterel**, a small wader with a chestnut stomach, is a rare summer visitor to the Cairngorms and other heights – in the Arctic it nests down to sea level. Even rarer is the **snow bunting**: the male, black and white; the female, brownish – perhaps only ten pairs nest on Scotland's mountains, although they are seen much more widely around the coasts in winter, when the male also becomes brown. The **snowy owl**, at the southern limit of its range, is a regular visitor to Shetland.

More common on the heights is the **ptarmigan**, shy and almost invisible in its summer coat, as it plays hide-and-seek amongst the lichen-patched boulders – you're most likely to see it on the Cairngorms, as it ventures out for the sandwich crusts left by the summer visitors using the ski lifts. It is resident up here, and moults from mottled in summer to pure white in winter.

The ptarmigan's camouflage helps protect it from the **golden eagle**. This magnificent bird ranges across many Highland areas – there are perhaps three hundred nesting pairs on Skye, the Outer Hebrides, above Aviemore and Deeside, and in the Northwest Highlands, each needing a territory of thousands of acres over which to hunt hares, grouse and ptarmigan. The **raven** also has strong links with the mountains, tumbling in crazy acrobatics past the rock faces. After nearly seventy years' absence, the **white-tailed (sea) eagle**, whose wingspan is even greater than that of the golden eagle, has been successfully reintroduced to Rùm. The resident breeding population is still very small, however, and the exact location of the eyries is kept secret.

Where the slopes lessen to moorland, the domain of the **red grouse** begins. This game bird not only affects the landscape but also, via the persecution of gamekeepers, threatens eagles and other birds of prey, although they are all theoretically protected. The **cuckoo** might be heard as far north as Shetland – one of its favourite dupes, the **meadow pipit**, is fairly widespread on any rough ground up to 3000ft. Dunlin and other waders nest on the wet moorlands and boglands, where the soft land allows them to use their delicate bills to probe for insects and other food.

You'll come across many notable birds where pine woods encroach onto open moor. One such is the **black grouse**, with its bizarre courtship rituals, where both sexes come together for aggressive, ritualistic display in a small gathering area known as a "lek". The **capercaillie**, found deeper in the forest and perhaps floundering amongst the branches, is an unexpectedly large, turkey-like bird, about 3ft from bill to end of tail, which also has a flamboyant courting display. A game bird, it was shot to extinction but reintroduced into Scotland from Europe in 1837. Other birds that favour the pine woods are the **long-eared owl**, many of the tit family (including the **crested tit** in the Spey Valley), the **siskin** and the **goldcrest**. The Speyside woods, especially, are a stronghold of the **crossbill**, which uses its overlapping bill to prise open pine cones.

Scottish **lochs** are as rich in birdlife as the moorlands that embrace them. After fifty years of absence, the **osprey** returned and more than a hundred pairs now breed; the best site to see them is near Loch Garten on Speyside. In addition to common species such as **mallard** and **tufted duck**, you might also see **goosander**, **red-breasted merganser** and other wildfowl. The superbly streamlined fish-eating **red-** and **black-throated divers** nest in the northwest, while the **great northern diver**, with its shivery wailing call, is largely a winter visitor to the coasts, although one or two pairs may occasionally nest.

Scotland is also strong on **coastal birds**. **Eider duck** gather in their thousands at the mouth of the Tay, and the estuaries are also a magnet for **waders** and **wild geese** in winter: the total population of barnacle geese from the Arctic island of Spitsbergen winters in the Solway estuary and on the farmland alongside. Other areas to head for if you're interested in seabirds are remote cliffs which, although often little more than bare rock, attract vast colonies that fish the sea around them. Some have their own speciality – **Manx shearwaters** have vast colonies on Rùm, for example, while the Shetland isle of Foula has about one third (three thousand pairs) of all the **great skuas** breeding in the northern hemisphere. Remote St Kilda is also stunning, with snowstorms of **gannets, puffins, guillemots, petrels** and **shearwaters**.

In addition to Scotland's resident bird population, and the winter and spring migrants, the western coasts and islands often see transatlantic "accidentals" blown far off course, which give rise to inbred **subspecies**. St Kilda is of particular interest to specialists, not only for its sheer numbers of resident birds but also for the St Kilda wren, a distinct subspecies. Fair Isle also sees large numbers of migrant and vagrant birds from both sides of the Atlantic. In northern and parts of eastern Scotland, the English all-black carrion crow is replaced by the "hoodie" or **hooded crow**, also found around the Mediterranean, with its distinctive grey back and underparts. Where the ranges of carrion crow and hoodie overlap, they interbreed, producing offspring with some grey patches of plumage.

MAMMALS

By the mid-eighteenth century, much of Scotland's wild animal life – including the Scottish **wolf**, **beaver**, **wild boar** and **elk** – had already disappeared (though the beaver is now being reintroduced). The indigenous **reindeer** was wiped out in the twelfth century, but more recently a semi-wild herd of Swedish stock was reintroduced to the slopes of the Cairngorms above Aviemore. Of two other semi-wild species, **Highland cattle** and **Shetland ponies**, the former is a classic case of breeding fitting conditions (they can survive in snowy conditions for fifty days a year), while the latter, the smallest British native pony, probably arrived in the later stages of the Ice Age when the ice was retreating but still gave a bridge across the salt water. There are feral goats in some places, but probably the most interesting of such animals is the Soay sheep of St Kilda. This, Britain's only truly wild sheep, notable for its soft brown fleece, can be seen as a farm pet and in wildlife parks – and is even used to graze some nature reserves in the south of Britain.

Although there are **sika** and **fallow deer** in places, and **roe deer** are widespread, Scotland is the stronghold of wild **red deer** herds, which, despite culling, stalking for sport and harsh winters, still number more than quarter of a million head. By origin a woodland animal, they might graze open ground – of necessity when the forest has been cleared – but they also move up to high ground in summer to avoid the biting flies and the tourists, and to graze on heather and lichens. They're most obvious in the snowy depths of winter, when, forced downhill in search of food, large numbers may be seen by road or rail travellers on Rannoch Moor or between Blair Atholl and Drumochter Pass.

The **fox** is widespread, as are the **mole** and **hedgehog**, but the **badger** is rather more rare. The **wildcat** and **pine marten** live in remote areas, hiding away in the moors and forests. The former, despite its initial resemblance to the family pet, is actually quite different – larger, with longer, striped fur, and a blunt-ended bushy tail that is also striped. The agile cat-sized pine marten, although hunted by gamekeepers, is maintaining reduced numbers, preying on squirrels and other small animals.

Native red **squirrels** are predominantly found in the Highlands, where they are still largely free from competition from the greys, which began to establish themselves about a century ago and now have a strong presence in many Lowland areas. **Rabbit** and **brown hare** are widespread, as are the **blue** or **mountain hare** in the Highlands, usually adopting a white or patchy white coat in winter. The north Scottish **stoat** also dons a white winter coat, its tail tipped with black, when it is known as ermine. Although Scotland is too far north for the dormouse and the harvest mouse, **shrews, voles** and **fieldmice** abound and, though there are few bats, the related **pipistrelle** is quite widely seen.

You may also be lucky enough to encounter the **otter**, endangered in the rest of Britain. In Scotland, the otter is found not only in the rushing streams but more often along the west coast and in the Northern and Western Isles, where it hunts the seashore for crabs and inshore fish. The otter is not to be confused with the feral **mink**, escaped from fur farms to take up life in the wild; these mink are a scourge in some areas, destroying birds.

Whales and their kin are frequent visitors to coastal waters and **seals**, including the shy grey seal, are quite common. However, in the hitherto virgin sea lochs of the west coast, both the seals and the coastal otters are under threat from the spread of **fish farms** (for salmon and sea trout). Not only are they poisoned by the chemicals used to keep the trapped fish vermin-free, but they also face the threat of being shot by the fish-farm owners when they raid what is to them simply a natural larder.

FISH, REPTILES AND INSECTS

Quite apart from the Loch Ness monster, Scotland has a rich water life. The Dee and other rivers are fished when **salmon** swim upstream to breed in their ancestral gravel headwaters. The fish leap waterfalls on the way, and many rivers which have been dammed for hydroelectric-power generation have "salmon ladders" to help them – these make great tourist attractions. The **sea trout** is also strongly migratory, the **brown** or **mountain trout** less so, although river or stream dwellers do move upstream, and loch dwellers up the incoming rivers, to spawn. Related to these game fish is the **powan** or **freshwater herring**, found only in the poorer northern basins of Loch Lomond, and possibly a relic from Ice Age arctic conditions. The richer southern waters of Loch Lomond and similar lakes contain **roach**, **perch** and other "coarse" fish.

Although the **adder** is common, the grass snake is not found in Scotland. Both **lizards** and the snake-like **slowworm** (in fact a legless lizard) are widespread, as are the **frog** and **toad**; the natterjack toad, however, is rarely seen this far north.

Scottish boglands are notable for their **dragon flies**, which prefer acid water, and **hawkers, darters** and **damselflies** feature in the south. One Scottish particular is the **blue hawker**, common in parts of the western Highlands. As for **butterflies**, some of the familiar types from further south – common blue, hairstreaks and others – are scattered in areas where conditions are not too harsh. One species with a liking for the heights is the **mountain ringlet**, only seen elsewhere in the English Lake District and in the Alps, which flies above 1500ft in the Grampians. Adapted to quite harsh conditions, it is clearly a relic of early post-glacial times. Another mountain butterfly, the **Scotch argus**, no longer found in England or Wales, is widespread in Scotland, and the **elephant hawk moth** can be seen in the Insh marshes below the Cairngorms.

MUSIC

Scottish music is in better health than for decades, with a bedrock of Celtic groups – the likes of The Boys of the Lough, Silly Wizard, Tannahill Weavers and Runrig – storming through traditional material in a blaze of bagpipes and flying fiddles. This new new roots culture seems to have finally shaken off the image of Andy Stewart and Jimmy Shand, with their accordions and sentimental songs of the Highlands.

Scotland through the 1980s and 1990s saw an explosion of roots and dance music, and, at the same time, a renewal and revisiting of traditions that had seemed perilously close to the edge. As the 1990s close, there are a half a dozen Scottish labels devoted entirely to local music; there's a monthly roots magazine, the aptly titled **Living Tradition**, and a real sense of a scene – from Glasgow right up to the Shetlands. A new generation of bands and musicians can wear their Scottishness on their sleeves, confident that this is a music at last commanding as much respect as the traditions of Ireland.

That Scots music had been troubled in the years of Anglo pop and rock dominance was due in part, perhaps, to its nature. A precision is required in traditional Scottish performance – especially in piping – that irons out much of the individual flair of a solo player. But the broadening of the music in the new roots scene, with "non-traditional" influences coming from Ireland in particular, and from the folk scene in general, has allowed the virtuosity of individual artists to come through.

THE CELTIC FOLK BAND ARRIVES

As in much of northern Europe, the story of Scotland's roots scene begins amid the **"folk revival"** of the 1960s – a time when folk song and traditional music engaged people who did not have strong family links with an ongoing tradition. For many in Scotland, traditional music had skipped a generation and they had to make a conscious effort to learn about it. At first, the main influences were largely American – skiffle music and people like Pete Seeger – but soon people started to look to their own traditions, taking inspiration from the Gaelic songs of **Cathy-Ann McPhee**, then still current in rural outposts, or the old **travelling singers** – people like the **Stewarts of Blairgowrie**, **Isla Cameron**, **Lizzie Higgins** and, the greatest of them all, Lizzie's mother, **Jeannie Robertson**.

On the instrumental front, there were fewer obvious role models despite the continued presence of a great many people playing in **Scottish dance bands**, **pipe bands** and **Strathspey and Reel Societies** (fiddle orchestras). In the 1960s the action was coming out of Ireland and the recorded repertoire of bands like The Chieftains became the core of many a pub session in Scotland. Even in the early 1970s, folk fiddle players were rare, although **Aly Bain** (see box on p.446) made a huge impression when he came down from Shetland and, soon after, Shetland Reels started to creep into the general folk repertoire.

The "Celtic Folk Band" was a creation of the 1960s. Previously, the art of a traditional musician was essentially a solo one. These days, however, there is a more or less standard formula, with a melody lead – usually fiddle or pipes – plus guitar, bouzouki and a singer. The singer is often just another sound in the band whereas before it was the song that was the focus. Instrumental in these developments was a Glasgow folk group, **The Clutha**, who, in a folk scene dominated by singers and guitarists, boasted not one but two fiddlers, along with a concertina, and four strong singers – including the superb **Gordeanna McCulloch**.

The Clutha were hugely influential and became even more successful when **Jimmy Anderson** introduced a set of chamber pipes into the lineup. Jimmy was not only a great piper but was also a pipe maker and he "invented" a set of pipes to be played in the key of D,

ALY BAIN AND SHETLAND MAGIC

Aly Bain has been a minor deity among Scottish musicians for three decades. A fiddle player of exquisite technique and individuality, he has been the driving force of one of Scotland's all-time great bands, Boys of the Lough, throughout that time, while latterly diversifying roles as a TV presenter and author. In these guises, he has been instrumental in spreading the wings of Scottish music to an even greater extent. First and foremost, though, Bain is a Shetlander and his greatest legacy is the inspiration he has provided for a thriving revival of fortunes for Shetland's own characteristic tradition.

Aly was brought up in the capital of Shetland, Lerwick, and was enthused to play the fiddle by Bob Duncan – who endlessly played him records by the strathspey king Scott Skinner – and later the old maestro Tom Anderson. Duncan and Anderson were the last of an apparently dying breed, and the youthful Aly was an odd sight, dragging his fiddle along to join in with the old guys at the Shetland Fiddlers Society. Players like Willie Hunter Jnr and Snr, Willie Pottinger and Alex Hughson were legends locally, but they belonged to another age and the magic of Shetland fiddle playing – one inflected with the eccentricity of the isolated environment and the influence of nearby Scandinavia.

By the time the teenage Aly was persuaded to leave for the mainland, Shetland was changing by the minute, and the discovery of North Sea oil altered it beyond redemption, as the new indus-trial riches trampled its unique community spirit and sense of tradition. The old fiddlers gradually faded and died, and Shetland music seemed destined to disappear too.

That it didn't was largely down to Aly. After a spell with Billy Connolly (then a folk artist) on the Scottish folk circuit, Aly found himself working with blues iconoclast Mike Whellans, and then the two of them tumbled into a link-up with two Irishmen, Robin Morton and Cathal McConnell, in a group they called Boys of the Lough. The last thing Aly Bain imagined was that he'd spend the next quarter of a century answering to this name. But he did, and his joyful artistry, unwavering integrity and unquenchable appetite and commitment to the music of his upbringing kept Shetland music alive in a manner he could never have imagined. Even more importantly, it stung the imagination of the generation that followed.

These days, Shetland music is buzzing again, with its own annual festival a treat of music-making and drinking. There are young musicians pouring out of the place, and a plethora of bands of all styles, including pop-oriented groups such as Rock, Salt & Nails and, more recently, Red Vans. The pick of the roots players, currently, is Catriona MacDonald – who was also taught by Tom Anderson, in his last days. She is adept at classical music, and is fast becoming an accomplished mistress of Norwegian music, and her mum went to school with Aly Bain – which in Shetland these days counts for an awful lot.

which sounded much quieter than the Highland pipes. This was essential at that time, as virtually all the venues were acoustic and sound systems were not up to the job of balancing out the sounds of pipes, fiddle and voices. Such a development was to come later, in the late 1970s, with bands like Battlefield Band, The Tannahill Weavers and Ossian.

Key, too, to developments were **The Boys of the Lough**, a Scots-Irish group led by the Shetland fiddler **Aly Bain** (see box) and **The Whistlebinkies**. Developing in the Glasgow folk scene alongside The Clutha, both these groups took a strong instrumental line, rather than The Clutha's song-based approach. These two bands were in many ways Scotland's equivalent of The Chieftains and, through their musical ability and recognition outside the folk clubs, played an important part in breaking down musical barriers.

The Whistlebinkies were notable for employing only traditional instruments, including fine clarsach (Celtic harp) from **Judith Peacock**. However, the most important, and definingly Scottish, element of all three of these bands was the presence of **bagpipes**. Clutha had piper **Jimmy Anderson**, the Whistlebinkies featured **Rab Wallace**, who had a firm background in the Scots piping scene, while The Boys also had an experienced piper in **Robin Morton**. They were pioneers for what was to become a revolution.

PIBROCH: SCOTS PIPES

Bagpipes are synonymous with Scotland, yet they are not a specifically Scots instrument. The pipes were once to be found right across Europe, and pockets remain, across the English border in Northumbria, all over Ireland, in Spain and Italy, and in eastern Europe, where bagpipe festivals are still held in rural areas. In Scotland, bagpipes seem to have made their appearance around the fifteenth century, and over the next hundred years or so they took on several forms, including quieter varieties (small pipes), both bellows and mouth-blown, which allowed a diversity of playing styles.

The Highland bagpipe form known as **pibroch** (*piobaireachd* in Gaelic) evolved around this time, created by clan pipers for military, gathering, lamenting and marching purposes. Legend among the clan pipers of this era were the MacCrimmons (they of the famous *MacCrimmon's Lament*, composed during the Jacobite rebellion), although they were but one of several important piping clans, among which were the MacArthurs, MacKays and MacDonalds, and others. In the seventeenth and eighteenth centuries, through the influence of the British army, reels and strathspeys joined the repertoire and a tradition of military pipe bands emerged. After World War II they were joined by civilian bands, alongside whom developed a network of piping competitions.

The bagpipe tradition has continued uninterrupted, although for much of this century under the domination of the military and the folklorists Piobaireachd Society. Recently, however, a number of Scottish musicians have revived the pipes in new and innovative forms. Following the lead of Clutha, The Boys of the Lough and The Whistlebinkies, a new wave of young bands began to feature pipers, notably **Alba** with the then-teenage **Alan McLeod**, the **Battlefield Band**, whose arrangements involve the beautifully measured piping of **Duncan McGillivray**, and **Ossian** with **Iain MacDonald**. These players redefined the boundaries of pipe music using notes and finger movements outside of the traditional range. They also showed the influence of Irish Uillean pipe players (particularly Paddy Keenan of the Bothy Band) and Cape Breton styles which many claim is the original, pre-military Scottish style.

In 1983 Robin Morton released **A Controversy of Pipers** on his Temple Records label, an album featuring six pipers from folk bands who were also top competitive players in the piping world. Up until this point, pipers in a folk band could be considered second class by some in the piping establishment. This recording made a statement and soon the walls began to crumble . . .

Alongside all this came a revived interest in traditional piping, and in particular the strathspeys, slow airs and reels, which had tended to get submerged beneath the familiar military territory of marches and laments. The century's great bagpipe players, notably **John Burgess**, received a belated wider exposure. His legacy includes a masterful album and a renowned teaching career to ensure that the old piping tradition marches proudly into the next century.

FOLK SONG AND THE CLUB SCENE

Whilst the folk bands were starting to catch up on the Irish and integrating bagpipes, **folk song** was also flourishing. The song tradition in Scotland is one of the strongest in Europe and in all areas of the country there were pockets of great singers and characters. In the 1960s the common ground was the folk-club network and the various festivals dotted around the country.

The great modern pioneer of Scots folk song, and a man who it is perhaps no exaggeration to say rescued the whole British tradition, was the great singer and songwriter **Ewan MacColl**, born in Perthshire in 1915. He recorded the seminal **Scottish Popular Ballads** as early as 1956, and founded the first folk club in Britain. After MacColl, another of the building blocks of the 1960s folk revival were the Aberdeen group, **The Gaugers**. Song was the heart of this group – Tam Speirs, Arthur Watson and Peter Hall were all good singers – though they were also innovative in using instrumentation (fiddle, concertina and whistle) without a guitar or other rhythm instrument to tie the sound together.

Other significant Scots groups on the 1960s scene included the **Ian Campbell Folk Group**, Birmingham-based but largely Scots in character (and including future Fairport Daves, Swarbrick and Pegg, as well as Ian's sons, Aly and Robin, who went on to form UB40). They flirted with commercialism and pop sensibilities – as virtually every folk group of the era was compelled to do – and were too often unfairly bracketed with England's derided Spinners as a result. So too were **The Corries**, although they laced their blandness with enterprise, inventing their own instrumentation and writing the new unofficial national anthem, *Flower of Scotland*.

Other more adventurous experiments grew out of the folk and acoustic club scene in mid-1960s Glasgow and Edinburgh. It was at *Clive's Incredible Folk Club*, in Glasgow, that **The**

Incredible String Band made their debut, led by **Mike Heron** and **Robin Williamson**. They took an unfashionable glance back into their own past on the one hand, while plunging headlong into psychedelia and other uncharted areas on the other. Their success broke down significant barriers, both in and out of Scotland, and in their wake came a succession of Scottish folkrock crossover musicians. Glasgow-born **Bert Jansch** launched folk supergroup Pentangle with Jacqui McShee, John Renbourn and Danny Thompson, and the flute-playing **Ian Anderson** found rock success with Jethro Tull. Meanwhile, a more traditional Scottish sound was promoted by the likes of **Archie**, **Ray** and **Cilla Fisher**, who sang new and traditional ballads, individually and together.

The great figure, however, along with MacColl, was the singer and guitarist **Dick Gaughan**, whose passionate artistry towers like a colossus above three decades. He started out in the Edinburgh folk-club scene with an impenetrable accent, a deep belief in the socialist commitment of traditional song, and a guitar technique that had old masters of the art hanging onto the edge of their seats. For a couple of years in the early 1970s, he played with Aly Bain in The Boys of the Lough, knocking out fiery versions of trad Celtic material. Gaughan became frustrated, however, by the limitations of a primarily instrumental (and fiddle-dominated) group and subsequently formed **Five Hand Reel**. Again playing Scots-Irish traditional material, they might have been the greatest folk-rock band of them all if they hadn't just missed the Fairport/Steeleye Span boat.

Leaving to pursue an independent career, Gaughan became a fixture on the folk circuit and made a series of albums exploring Scots and Irish traditional music and reinterpreting the material for guitar. His **Handful of Earth** (1981) was perhaps the single best solo folk album of the decade, a record of stunning intensity with enough contemporary relevance and historical belief to grip all generations of music fans. And, though sparing in his output, and modest about his value in the genre, he's also become one of the best songwriters of his generation.

Crucial contributions to folk song came, too, from two giants of the Scottish folk scene who were probably more appreciated throughout Europe than at home – the late **Hamish Imlach**

and **Alex Campbell** – and from **song collectors** and academics such as **Norman Buchan**, with his hugely influential songbook, *101 Scottish Songs*, and **Peter Hall**, with *The Scottish Folksinger*.

GAELIC ROCKING AND FUSIONS

Scottish music took an unexpected twist in 1978 with the low-key release of an album called **Play Gaelic**. It was made by a little-known ceilidh group called **Runrig**, who took their name from the old Scottish oilfield system of agriculture, and worked primarily in the backwaters of the Highlands and Islands. The thing, though, that stopped people in their tracks was the fact that they were writing original material in Gaelic. This was the first time any serious Scottish working band had achieved any sort of attention with Gaelic material, although Ossian were touching on it around the same time, as were Nah-Oganaich.

Runrig have since marched on to unprecedented heights, appearing in front of rock audiences at concert halls around the world where only a partial proportion of the audience are jocks in exile. Their Gaelic input is marginal these days, but they started a whole new ball rolling, chipping away at prejudices, adopting accordions and bagpipes, ever sharper arrangements, electric instruments, full-blown rock styles, surviving the inevitable personnel changes and the continuous carping of critics accusing them of selling out with every new market conquered. They even made a concept album, *Recovery*, which related the history of the Gael in one collection, provoking unprecedented interest in the Gaelic language after years of it being regarded in Scotland as moribund and defunct.

Of course, not everyone applauds. Critics point out that many singers using the language are not native Gaelic speakers and only learn the words phonetically, while further controversy has been caused by the "sampling" of archive recordings for use in backing tracks. For many people these songs are important and personal and, in the case of some of the religious singing, they felt very strongly that this use was in bad taste.

Nonetheless, the popularity of Gaelic roots bands undeniably paved the way for "purer" Scots musicians and singers: clarsach player **Alison Kinnaird**, for instance; singers **Savourna Stevenson**, **Christine Primrose**,

CEILIDHS, FESTIVALS AND CONTACTS

Scottish dances thrived for years under the auspices of the RSCDS, the Royal Scottish County Dance Society. Their events tended to be fairly formal, with dancers who were largely skilled, but in the 1970s and 1980s more and more Scottish dances, or ceilidhs, adopted the (English barn dance) practice of a "caller" to call out the moves. Nowadays there are two types of traditional dance events: **ceilidh** dances, usually with a caller and perhaps a more folky band, and **Scottish Country Dances**, usually with a more traditional Scottish dance-band lineup and an expectation that the dancers will know the dance forms.

Scottish **music festivals** range from the Celtic Connections Festival, held in Glasgow in January, where you can catch many of the top names in the Celtic music world in a comfortable concert setting, to lots of smaller festivals offering a mix of concert, ceilidh and informal sessions. In recent years there has been an increase in the number of festivals where teaching takes a central role. Many of these are in the Highlands and Islands, where the Feisean movement has introduced thousands of people to traditional music-making.

Scottish bands such as Capercaillie and Runrig feed the notion that folk music can be exciting, electric and diverse, without losing sight of its roots. However, the survival of traditional music depends on support from young players: they need to play it, listen to it, and take it forward. In

Scotland, change is coming from a grassroots **Feisean Movement** (*feis* is Gaelic for "festival"). These festivals, held during summer months and school holidays, involve children receiving tuition in traditional music, drama, art, dance and Gaelic singing, with evening gigs in local venues. The teachers (and performers) are often leading musicians.

The idea began on the island of Barra, in the southern Hebrides, in 1981, and has spread to many parts of the Highlands and Islands. Its results have been remarkable. Beginners on the fiddle, clarsach, guitar, tin whistle or accordion have now begun to form bands and teach others. And the sheer numbers of young people coming through the Feis throughout the Highlands has resulted in more and more communities holding workshops and ceilidhs. In small communities there are great economic spin-offs for instrument makers, music shops and for teachers of traditional music.

Tuition projects have not been limited to the Highlands. In Edinburgh, Stan Reeves has made remarkable progress with the **Scots Music Group** within The Adult Learning Project, leading to several hundred people learning traditional instruments and an annual festival of fiddle music. In Glasgow, the **Glasgow Fiddle Workshop**, under the guidance of Ian Fraser, has made similar progress and is starting to widen its brief beyond fiddle tuition.

CONTACTS

Adult Learning Project/Scots Music Group 184 Dalry Rd, Edinburgh EH11 2EP (☎0131/337 5442, fax 337 9316).

Balnain House (Scotland's Centre for Traditional Music) 40 Huntly St, Inverness IV3 5HR (☎01463/715757, music@balnain.com). An excellent museum with listening posts, a shop, and a café hosting regular ceilidhs and get-togethers.

Feisean Nan Gaidheal Nicolson House, Somerled Square, Portree, Isle of Skye IV51 9EJ (☎01478/613355, fax 613399).

The Living Tradition PO Box 1026, Kilmarnock, Ayrshire KA2 0LG (☎01563 571220, *living.tradi-tion@almac.co.uk*). A traditional-music magazine published from Ayrshire. It covers music from Britain and Ireland, with a focus, obviously, on Scotland. They also run a mail-order service for traditional recordings.

The Piping Centre 32 McPhater St, Glasgow (☎0141 353 0220, fax 353 1570). The place to visit for anybody with an interest in piping. They have an exhibition, a teaching programme, concert space, café and even a hotel.

Flora McNeill, **Cathy-Ann MacPhee**, **Heather Heywood** and **Jock Duncan**; and the **Wrigley sisters** from Orkney – who started out as teenagers playing traditional music with technical accomplishment and attitude and who are now the core of the band **Seelyhoo**.

And among the ranks of the roots or fusion bands, each with their own agendas and styles, have passed many – perhaps most – of Scotland's finest contemporary musicians. **Silly Wizard**, especially, featured a singer of cutting quality in **Andy M. Stewart** (and did he need that M!), while **Phil and Johnny Cunningham** have gone on to display a pioneering zeal in their efforts to use their skills on accordion and fiddle to knit Scottish traditional music with other cultures.

Mouth Music, too, were innovative: a Scots-origin (but recently Canadian) duo of **Martin Swan** and **Talitha MacKenzie**, who mixed Gaelic vocals (including the traditional "mouth music" techniques of sung rhythms) with African percussion and dance sounds. Talitha MacKenzie later went solo, radically transforming traditional Scottish songs, which she clears from the dust of folklore with wonderful multitracked vocals and the characteristic Mouth Music African rhythms.

Another development was the fusion of traditional music and **jazz** by bands such as **The Easy Club** and the duo of piper **Hamish Moore** and jazz saxophonist **Dick Lee**. Moore has since come full circle, now taking his inspiration from a parallel Scottish culture which has developed in **Cape Breton**. Scottish interest in Cape Breton music has also led to the more-or-less-lost tradition of Scottish step-dancing being reintroduced.

At the beginning of the new century, however, the two most interesting Scottish roots groups are surely **Capercaillie** and Shooglenifty. The former, based on the arrangements of **Manus Lunny** and the gorgeous singing of **Karen Mattheson**, rose from Argyll pub sessions to flirt with mass commercial appeal, reworking Gaelic and traditional songs from the West Highlands. **Shooglenifty**, meanwhile, captured the imagination of a new audience with a style they described with their tongues in their cheeks as "acid croft".

DISCOGRAPHY

In addition to the discs reviewed below, see the box opposite for details of the remarkable Scottish Tradition Series of CDs and cassettes. For more information, check out the "Scottish Music Links" at *www.netreal.co.uk* – a wonderful site with links to many label and artist pages.

GENERAL COMPILATIONS

The Caledonian Companion (Greentrax, Scotland). A 1975 live recording of four of Scotland's most respected northeast musicians – Alex Green, Willie Fraser, Charlie Bremner

and John Grant – featuring solo fiddle, mouth organ, whistle and diddling.

The Rough Guide to Scottish Music (World Music Network, UK). A terrific compilation, this is strongest on the new roots bands – with good selections from Battlefield Band, Capercaillie and Wolfstone, among others – but it also delves into folk (Dick Gaughan) and traditional singing (Catherine-Ann McPhee, Heather Heyward).

The Nineties Collection (Greentrax, Scotland). Sixteen artists, including four pipers and well-known names such as Aly Bain and Phil Cunningham, play all-new tunes in a traditional style. Also available is a companion book containing over two hundred tunes (Canongate Books, Scotland).

TRADITIONAL SINGERS

Jock Duncan Duncan is an authentic bothy ballad singer from Pitlochry who gets to the heart of any song. He made his recording debut aged 70 on the album below, backed by musicians including his son, the piper Gordon Duncan. *Ye Shine Whar Ye Stan'* (Springthyme, Scotland). Some of the traditional singing on this album is truly remarkable and the production from Battlefield Band founder Brian McNeill is impressive, too, creating an atmosphere that only falls a little short of the experience of a live performance.

Heather Heywood Heywood, from Ayrshire, is reckoned by many Scotland's foremost traditional singer of her generation. She performs largely core Scottish ballads and songs. *By Yon Castle Wa'* (Greentrax, Scotland). A 1993 disc of epic ballads and contemporary songs, produced by Battlefield Band founder Brian McNeill. Heywood's forte is traditional song which she usually sings a cappella. McNeill makes the album accessible, without compromising the basic style, with the addition of accompaniment, including pipes – something which is difficult to do in live performance. This was a landmark recording in the traditional area.

Catherine-Ann MacPhee from Barra, has a warm yet strong voice and her Gaelic has the soft pronunciation of the southern islands of the Outer Hebrides. *Canan Nan Gaidheal* (*The Language of the Gael*; Greentrax, Scotland). This superb 1980s recording, rereleased on CD,

THE SCOTTISH TRADITION SERIES

Scottish traditional music – in its deepest, darkest manifestations – has been superbly documented in a series of archive recordings produced by Peter Cooke and others at Edinburgh University's School of Scottish Studies. The highlights of this collection have found their way onto a series of a couple of dozen cassettes and/or CDs, which, if you're seriously interested in the roots of many of the musicians covered in this box, are nothing less than a treasure trove.

The first volume in the series, **Bothy Ballads**, is one of the most important and fascinating. These narrative songs were composed, sung and passed around the unmarried farmworkers accommodated in bothies or outhouses in late Victorian and Edwardian days. The songs were often comic or satirical, such as warnings about skinflint farmers to be avoided at the hiring markets. Under the bothy system, workers would move on from farm to farm after six-month "fees", so the songs were in constant circulation and reinvention. They include some gorgeous ballads and instrumentals.

Music from the Western Isles (Volume 2) is another intriguing disc: **Gaelic songs** recorded in the Hebrides, including some great examples of "**mouth music**", the vocal dance music where sung rhythms are employed to take the place of instruments. There are *pibroch* songs on this disc, too – the vocal equivalent of the pipers' airs and laments. On Volume 3, *Waulking Songs from Barra*, you enter another extraordinary domain,

that of Gaelic **washing songs**, thumped out by women to the rhythms of their cloth-pounding. If you were played this blind, you could imagine yourself to be thousands of miles from Scotland. More amazing vocal traditions are unleashed on Volume 6, *Gaelic Psalms from Barra*, with their slow, fractured unison singing.

An equally compelling vocal tradition is that of the Scottish **Travelling Singers**, showcased on Volume 5, *The Muckle Sangs*. This is a delight, including virtually all the greats, Jeannie Robertson, Lizzie Higgins and the Stewarts of Blairgowrie among them.

Fiddle music is also outstandingly represented in the series, with several volumes devoted to the art. Volume 4, *Shetland Fiddle Music*, features classic players such as Tom Anderson and George Sutherland, who were to exert such influence on the likes of Aly Bain and Catriona MacDonald. Volume 9, *The Fiddler and His Art*, is a fine overall compilation, showing the different styles prevalent around the country.

Finally, as you'd expect, the Scottish Tradition has recordings of some of the finest **pibroch pipers**, among them George Moss (Volume 15), and pipe majors William MacLean, Robert Brown and R.B. Nicol (volumes 10, 11 and 12).

The Scottish Tradition Series recordings are available on CD and cassette from the Scottish label Greentrax (Cockenzie Business Centre, Edinburgh Road, Cockenzie, East Lothian EH32 0HL; ☎01875/814155).

---

shows mature traditional singing from one of the best of the current generation of Gaelic singers.

Gordeanna McCulloch The lead singer of seminal 1960s band, The Clutha, Gordeanna McCulloch is another of the great voices of the Scottish Folk revival. *In Freenship's Name* (Greentrax, Scotland). Gordeanna's voice is a strong, sweet and flexible instrument, capable of a variety of tones. Here, she is at home among some great Scots songs, all traditional, bar one, and backed by some of Scotland's top musicians.

Jim Reid With Arbroath's Foundry Bar band, Jim Reid was for many years a well-known face at festivals and ceilidhs throughout Scotland. One of the country's finest singers. *I Saw the Wild Geese Flee* (Springthyme, Scotland). A

selection of songs ranging from his own compositions to traditional ballads. Just Jim's version of *I Saw the Wild Geese Flee* makes this re-issued album a classic.

Margaret Stewart and Allan MacDonald Lewis-born Margaret Stewart is a talented Gaelic singer; Allan MacDonald is one of the famous piping family from Glenuig – his brother was the piper with Ossian and Battlefield Band. *Fhuair Mi Pog* (Greentrax, Scotland). This is a fascinating CD of music and Gaelic songs that works as terrific entertainment; lovely singing and great tunes, some of the best written by Allan himself.

Jane Turriff Turriff is a legendary song carrier. Born into the Aberdeenshire Stewart family in 1915, she grew up in a travelling family. *Singin is Ma Life* (Springthyme, Scotland). A must for anyone interested in traditional song style. Content ranges from the "big" ballads, such as *Dowie Dens of Yarrow*, through to the classic C&W song *Empty Saddles*.

Sheena Wellington Broadcaster and radio presenter, Sheena Wellington is Fife Council's Traditional Arts development officer and one of Scotland's leading traditional singers. *Strong Women* (Greentrax, Scotland). A live recording showing off what Sheena does best: communicating traditional song to an audience.

Mick West Well-known as a session singer, West is now rated at home and abroad as one of the country's finest traditional singers. *Fine Flowers & Foolish Glances* (KRL, Scotland). One of the most successful albums using jazz musicians with a strong traditional singer. It may prove to be a classic.

INSTRUMENTALISTS

Aly Bain Shetland-born Aly Bain (see box on p.446) is one of the great movers in Scottish music's revival, through his band Boys of the Lough (see opposite), and a panoply of solo and collaborative ventures. *Aly Bain and Friends* (Greentrax, Scotland). One of the best-selling Scottish albums of modern times, compiled from a TV series Bain produced on traditional Scottish music. The friends include Boys of the Lough, Capercaillie, Hamish Moore and Dick Lee, and zydeco star Queen Ida and her Bonne Temps band. **Tom Anderson and Aly Bain:** *The Silver Bow: The Fiddle Music of Shetland* (Topic, UK). This collection of Shetland fiddle tunes was notable for bringing together Bain with his old teacher, Tom Anderson. They played both individually and together on the album and the effect is never less than enthralling. **With Phil Cunningham:** *The Pearl* (Whirlie, Scotland). Bain teams up with Scotland's finest accordion player for some fabulous tunes, from slow airs to Shetland reels, reflecting the incredible range of styles which this duo have mastered. Phil composed almost half of the tracks and he plays five of the six instruments featured.

John Burgess The century's greatest exponent of traditional bagpipes. *King of the Highland Pipers* (Topic, UK). The maestro demonstrates his art to devastating effect through *piobaireachd*, strathspeys, hornpipes, reels and marches. Not for the faint-hearted!

Pete Clarke A great fiddle player whose skills with slow air playing also makes him in great demand as a song accompanist. *Fiddle Case* (Smiddymade, Scotland). An hour of topnotch traditional music – not all Scottish fiddle, though – there are tunes from Europe and the US and even a couple of songs. There's a classical feel to some of the pieces which works well, with cello and flute parts.

Gordon Duncan Gordon Duncan, the son of bothy singer Jock, is one of Scotland's younger generation of pipers, who is stretching the boundaries with some breathtaking solo piping. *The Circular Breath* (Greentrax, Scotland). As well as performing on the Great Highland Bagpipe, Gordon plays the practice chanter and low whistle. He is joined by banjo player Gerry O'Connor, Ian Carr on guitar, Ronald MacArthur on bass guitar, Jim Sutherland playing clay pots and Andy Cook on Ugandan harp.

Alasdair Fraser A master fiddler, renowned for his slow airs and now for his leading of The Skyedance Band, whose members provided music for the film *Braveheart. Dawn Dance* (Culburnie, Scotland). An album of completely self-penned tunes in the traditional style which bounces along, defying you to sit still while you listen. Fraser has a rare clarity of playing, without sacrificing the feel and enthusiasm essential to traditional music.

Willie Hunter and Violet Tulloch Willie Hunter was one of the all-time greats of the Shetland fiddle and Violet Tulloch is one of Shetland's leading piano accompanists. *The Willie Hunter Sessions* (Greentrax, Scotland). A set of recordings made over several years including Scots and Shetland strathspeys, reels and slow airs. "Traditional chamber music" of the highest order.

William Jackson Billy Jackson is one of Scotland's best-known traditional composers. He wrote some – and arranged most – of the music for folk band Ossian, and now works solo. *Inchcolm* (Linn Records, Scotland). This album brings Billy's harp playing to centre stage. It is a collection of largely unrelated tracks with some Orchestral interludes and forays into early and Eastern musics.

Iain McLachlan Iain McLachlan is a well-known and respected accordion player who also plays fiddle and melodeon. *An Island Heritage* (Springthyme, Scotland). From the writer of *The Dark Island*, real traditional music from the Western Isles played on accordion, fiddle, melodeon and pipes.

Mac-Talla In 1994, this "Gaelic supergroup" made a small number of concert appearances and one spectacular recording before settling back into their own individual paths having "made the statement". Mac-Talla's members included singers Arthur Cormack, Christine Primrose and Eilidh MacKenzie, plus Alison Kinnaird on clarsach, and ex-Runrig musician Blair Douglas. *Mairidh Gaol is Ceol* (Temple, Scotland). Glorious harmony and solo singing, accordion and harp — you can hear the spirit even if you don't understand the language.

Hamish Moore One of Scotland's finest contemporary pipers, Hamish Moore plays Border pipes, Scottish Small pipes and the great Highland Bagpipe. *Stepping on the Bridge* (Greentrax, Scotland). Inspired by the Scottish culture he discovered in Cape Breton, Moore plays Scottish pipes with Cape Breton accompanists to produce a lively glimpse of what piping may have been like before it became regimented.

Scott Skinner Skinner was a legendary fiddler — formidably kilted and moustachioed. *Music of Scott Skinner* (Topic, UK). An essential roots album, featuring rare and authentic recordings by the elusive genius of the fiddle — and the weird strathspey style in particular — dating from 1908. Some of the quality is understandably distorted, though the collection is supplemented by modern interpretations by Bill Hardie.

"NEW ROOTS" GROUPS

Battlefield Band The Battlefield Band have been one of the enduring top groups of the last thirty years. Evolving lineup changes have kept a continued freshness, with the constant being skilled musicianship and excellent songwriting. *Rain, Hail or Shine* (Temple, Scotland). All the Battlefield Band trademarks are here in force — distinctive keyboard playing, well-chosen pipe tunes, guitar and bouzouki injecting excitement and tension, fine singing — and John McCusker's sharp fiddle playing is a joy throughout.

Boys of the Lough With the virtuoso talents of Shetland fiddler Aly Bain and singer/flautist Cathal McConnell at the heart of the band, The Boys have been a benchmark of taste for thirty years. *The Boys of the Lough* (Shanachie, US). This was the group's 1973 debut — and remains one of their strongest sets, powered by contributions from Dick Gaughan and piper Robin Morton. *The Day Dawn* (Lough Records, Scotland). Quality, taste, superb singing and the relaxed easy style that comes from skilled musicians with years of experience. Along with the concertina and mandola of Dave Richardson, Aly on fiddle and Cathal on flute, whistle and vocals, this album features singer and uillean piper Christy O'Leary.

Capercaillie The hugely influential and successful Capercaillie have taken Gaelic music to a worldwide audience in a modern contemporary style from a traditional base. They have in Karen Mattheson one of the best singers around today. *Beautiful Wasteland* (Survival Records, Scotland/GreenLinnet, US). Flute, whistle and uillean pipes pop up all over the place and a whole host of things are happening with fiddles, bouzoukis, keyboards and percussion, too.

Ceolbeg Ceolbeg were not a full-time band but produced some of the finest albums of the genre, featuring some fabulous songs from their singer, Davy Steele. *An Unfair Dance* (Greentrax, Scotland). An impressive collection of tunes played on a huge variety of instruments, with a great sense of light and shade.

Deaf Shepherd Following in the footsteps of the Battlefield Band, Deaf Shepherd are a passionate 1990s band, rooted in the Scottish tradition, and getting more skilled all the time. *Synergy* (Greentrax, Scotland). A really varied album, including traditional and new material, and jumps from reels to jigs and back, involving vigorous fiddle playing and powerful bouzouki. Poignant guitar, fiddle and whistle countermelodies blend smoothly with the vocals.

The Easy Club An admirably ambitious and sadly underrated group, The Easy Club took the baton from the more thoughtful Scots bands of the 1970s and ran with it at a pace, injecting traditional rhythms with a jazz sense. *Essential* (Eclectic, Scotland). Essential it is. MacColl's *First Time Ever I Saw Your Face* never sounded like this before.

Mouth Music Gaelic nonsense songs – *puirt-a-beul* – met ambient dance, funk keyboards and African sampling in Talitha MacKenzie and Martin Swan's Mouth Music. *Mouth Music* (Cooking Vinyl, UK). Talitha MacKenzie has gone on to a solo career but this first Mouth Music disc remains her finest hour – one of the best Celtic fusions committed to disc, featuring stunning rhythms, funk, Gaelic sea shanties and *puirt-a-beul*.

Ossian This ground-breaking band, formed in the mid1970s, have recently reformed with a new lineup featuring Iain MacInnes on pipes and Stuart Morison on fiddle alongside founder members Billy Jackson on harp and Billy Ross on guitar and dulcimer. *The Carrying Stream* (Greentrax, Scotland). A fine album, signalling the welcome return of Ossian's quintessentially Scottish sound. This is a collection of terrific tunes – first-rate jigs and reels, both traditional and contemporary, blended with songs in English, Scots and Gaelic.

Runrig This band of Gaelic rock pioneers were formed in North Uist, Outer Hebrides, in 1973 by brothers Rory (bass, vocals) and Calum MacDonald (drums/vocals), with singer Donnie Munro joining the following year. They worked their way up, over fifteen years, from ceilidhs to stadiums, going Top 10 in the UK charts in 1991. They are perhaps at their very best live, with memorable tunes and vocals and well-honed, subtle musicianship. *Alba* (Pinnacle, UK). An excellent "best of" compilation of this most dynamic Gaelic band.

Seelyhoo The Wrigley sisters from Orkney have made their own statement with their own recordings. On this album they are joined by several other musicians in a band which came out of the Edinburgh session scene. *Leetera* (Greentrax, Scotland). A really fresh approach to traditional tunes and Gaelic song using fiddle, guitar, bass guitar, accordion, whistle, keyboard and percussion. Vibrant music from some of Scotland's young rising stars.

Shooglenifty Shooglenifty are a brilliant, innovative band who have made their mark well beyond the Scottish roots scene with their grafting of Scottish trad motifs and club culture trance-dance. Live, they are unstoppable. *A Whisky Kiss* (Greentrax, Scotland). The album that coined the term "acid croft", with elements of traditional music and house. A sound here, a

strange sound there, a sequence played in an odd way. There's nothing else like it.

Silly Wizard Silly Wizard were a key roots band, featuring Andy M. Stewart (vocals/bouzouki/guitar), Phil (accordion, etc) and Johnny Cunningham (fiddle). Their albums are full of fresh, lively takes on the whole traditional repertoire. *Live Wizardry* (Green Linnet, US). The band at their zenith in 1988, playing traditional and self-composed dance tunes and narrative ballads.

Andy M. Stewart, Phil Cunningham and Manus Lunny *Fire in the Glen* (Shanachie, US). Two former members of Silly Wizard combine with an Irishman in a formidable celebration of Scottish traditional music. Phil Cunningham's brilliance as an accordion player is demonstrated on any number of albums, but it's especially impressive placed against the wonderful, wonderful singing of Andy M. Stewart.

The Whistlebinkies One of the founding folk groups in Scotland – often dubbed the "Scottish Chieftains" – the Binkies are still playing music with a difference. *A Wanton Fling* (Greentrax, Scotland). An album that has all the freshness of early Whistlebinkies recordings – a combination of Lowland pipes, clarsach, flute, concertina and fiddle.

Wolfstone Wolfstone play folk-rock from the Highlands – "stadium rock meets village-hall ceilidh", said one reviewer – full of passion and fire. *The Half Tail* (Green Linnet, Scotland). This is a more subdued progressive sound than usual for Wolfstone, featuring amongst other tracks, a classic whaling song *Bonnie Ship the Diamond*, *The Last Leviathan* and catchy instrumental sets.

FOLK/SINGER-SONGWRITERS

Eric Bogle Bogle emigrated from Scotland to work in Australia as an accountant but when he returned home he was hailed for writing one of the great modern folk songs, *The Band Played Waltzing Matilda*. *Something of Value* (Sonet, UK/Philo, US). Bogle's singing doesn't quite match his songwriting, but he has all-star support. Includes the number above.

Archie and Cilla Fisher The Fisher family – Archie, Ray and Cilla – were mainstays of the 1960s/1970s Scottish folk club scene, reviving old ballads and creating new ones. **Archie**

Fisher: *The Man with a Rhyme* (Folk Legacy, US). Archie's finest hour – fourteen tracks from 1976 with the Fisher voice and guitar backed by concertina, banjo, dulcimers, cello, fiddle and flute. **Cilla Fisher and Artie Trezise**: *Cilla and Artie* (Greentrax, Scotland). Released in 1979, this still retains an ease and freshness – and Cilla's imperious rendition of the late Stan Rogers' *The Jeannie C* is in itself worth the acquisition.

Dick Gaughan Singer/guitarist/songwriter, Gaughan is one of the most charismatic of Scottish performers – an artist who can make you laugh, cry and explode with anger with every twist and nuance of delivery. His new material is still up there with his classic albums of the 1980s. *Handful of Earth* (Sonet, UK/Philo, US). This is the Gaughan classic: a majestic album of traditional and modern songs, still formidable a decade on. When *Folk Roots* magazine asked its readers to nominate the album of the 1980s, it won by a street – and deservedly so.

Robin Laing Robin Laing is one of the best songwriters and performers to emerge out of the Scottish folk scene in the 1990s. *Walking In Time* (Greentrax, Scotland). Includes four re-workings of traditional songs, three by other writers and seven of Laing's own songs, accompanied by his own Spanish guitar. Producer Brian McNeill's multi-instrumental talents are also in evidence on most of the tracks.

Ewan MacColl MacColl was, simply, one of the all-time greats of British folk song. *In Black and White* (Cooking Vinyl, UK/Green Linnet, US). This posthumous compilation, lovingly compiled by his family, showcases MacColl's superb technique as a singer, his gift for choruses (*Dirty Old Town*), his colourful observation as a lyricist (*The Driver's Song*), and his raging sense of injustice (*Black and White*) written after the Sharpeville Massacre of 1963. A fitting epitaph.

Dougie MacLean One-time member of The Tannahill Weavers, Dougie MacLean is now carving out a successful solo career as a singer-songwriter. *The Dougie MacLean Collection* (Putumayo, US). A good selection from Dougie's extensive recorded output, including perhaps his most famous song, *Caledonia*.

Adam McNaughtan Adam McNaughtan has written many songs rich in Glasgow wit including one which has travelled the world – *Oor Hamlet*, a condensed version of Shakespeare's *Hamlet* to the tune of *The Mason's Apron*. He has a deep understanding of the tradition and is one of Scotland's national treasures. *Last Stand at Mount Florida* (Greentrax, Scotland). Adam's comic songs are masterpieces and here he is in excellent voice, accompanied by fellow Stramash members – Finlay Allison, Bob Blair and John Eaglesham.

Brian McNeill A man of amazing talents, the one-time fiddling founder of the Battlefield Band is a multi-instrumentalist and a songwriter of some substance. *No Gods* (Greentrax, Scotland). An album showing the broadening of McNeill's writing talent both in song and tunes. He is joined by ten backing musicians, including masterful guitarist Tony MacManus.

Pete Heywood and Colin Irwin
(Taken from the *Rough Guide to World Music*)

BOOKS

Wherever a book is in print, the UK publisher is given first in each listing, separated, where applicable, from the US publisher by an oblique slash. Where books are published in only one of these countries we have specified which one; when the same company publishes the book in both, its name appears just once. Out of print titles are indicated as o/p – these should be easy to track down in secondhand bookshops.

ART, ARCHITECTURE AND HISTORIC SITES

J. Gifford *Highlands and Islands* (Penguin). Part of a series of definitive guides that are well illustrated, knowledgeable and readable.

Graham Ritchie & Mary Harman *Exploring Scotland's Heritage* (UK The Stationery Office). Detailed, beautifully illustrated series with the emphasis on historic buildings and archeological sites. Recently updated titles cover Orkney, Shetland, the Highlands, Aberdeen and Northeast Scotland and Argyll and the Western Isles.

Andrew Gibbon Williams & Andrew Brown *The Bigger Picture: A History of Scottish Art* (UK BBC Books). Originally published to accompany a TV series, this is a richly illustrated survey of Scottish art from 1603 to the present day. Suitable for the lay reader.

HISTORY, POLITICS AND CULTURE

Adamnan (trans. by John Marsden) *The Illustrated Life of Columba* (UK Floris Books). The original story of the life of St Columba,

annotated and accompanied by beautiful photos of the places associated with him, in particular the Hebridean island of Iona.

Ian Adams & Meredith Somerville *Cargoes of Despair and Hope* (UK John Donald Publishing). Riveting mixture of contemporary documents and letters telling the story of Scottish emigration to North America from 1603 to 1803.

Joni Buchanan *The Lewis Land Struggle* (UK Acair). A history of crucial encounters between the crofters of Lewis and their various landlords, written from the crofters' point of view using contemporary sources.

David Daiches (ed.) *The New Companion to Scottish Culture* (Polygon/Subterranean). A dense if wide-ranging tome with more than 300 articles on Scottish culture in its widest sense, from eating to marriage customs to the Scottish Enlightenment.

G. Donaldson & R.S. Morpeth (eds) *A Dictionary of Scottish History* (UK John Donald). A very useful book, listing dates, facts and potted biographies.

Diana Henderson *Highland Soldier: A Social History of the Highland Regiments 1820–1920* (UK John Donald). Detailed history of the ten highland regiments and the lives of their officers and men.

W.S. Hewison *Scapa Flow in War and Peace* (UK Bellavista Publications) Very straightforward and readable quick rundown of Scapa Flow's wartime role, written by an ex-serviceman and *Orcadian* journalist.

David Howarth *The Shetland Bus* (UK Shetland Times). Wonderfully detailed story of the espionage and resistance operations carried out from Shetland by British and Norwegian servicemen, written by someone who was directly involved.

Historic Scotland (UK The Stationery Office). A series of books covering many aspects of Scotland's history and prehistory, including the Picts, Vikings, Romans and Celts. All are colourful, accessible and well presented. Available at many Historic Scotland sites as well as bookshops.

Michael Lynch *Scotland: A New History* (UK Pimlico). Probably the best available overview of Scottish history, taking the story up to 1992.

Fitzroy Maclean *Bonnie Prince Charlie* (Canongate). Very readable and more or less definitive biography of Scotland's most romantic historical figure written by the "real" James Bond.

Ann McSween & Mick Sharp *Prehistoric Scotland* (Batsford o/p/New Amsterdam Books). Thematic introductory guide to many of Scotland's prehistoric sites, with atmospheric black-and-white photographs and imaginative illustrations.

John Marsden *Sea-road of the Saints: Celtic Holy Men in the Hebrides* (UK Floris Books). Famous early Christian saints, such as Columba and Brendan the Voyager, appear in the context of the remains that still exist in the islands.

Timothy Neat *The Summer Walkers* (Canongate). The less-publicized wandering population of the northwest Highlands – tinkers, horse traders and pearl fishers – reveal something of their lives.

Orkneyinga Saga (Penguin). Probably written about 1200 AD, this is a Norse saga which sheds light on the connection between Norway and the Northern Isles which is still felt strongly today; contains history of the early earls of Orkney, and is incidentally a stirring, blood-thirsty thriller.

John Prebble *Glencoe* (Penguin), *Culloden* (Penguin) and *The Highland Clearances* (Penguin). Emotive and subjective accounts of key events in Highland history which are very readable.

John Purser *Scotland's Music* (Mainstream). Comprehensive overview of traditional and classical music in Scotland – thorough and scholarly, but readable.

Anna Ritchie *Prehistoric Orkney* (UK Batsford). Orkney is an island so rich in prehistoric sites that even the most casual visitor will feel the need for a book like this, which helps to paint a picture of the life of the early inhabitants.

Iain Crichton Smith *Towards the Human* (UK Macdonald). Selected essays, ranging widely over poetry and poets, language and community. He explores the writing of Hugh MacDiarmid, the vital role of Gaelic in Scottish culture and his own childhood in Lewis with perceptive intelligence.

Ronald Williams *The Lords of the Isles: The Clan Donald and the Early Kingdom of the Scots* (UK House of Lochar). A book which covers the history of the early kingdom centred on Argyll and the islands from 500 AD to Robert the Bruce. It's a complicated period but the narrative carries you through.

GUIDES AND PICTURE BOOKS

Laurie Campbell & Roy Dennis *Golden Eagles* (UK Colin Baxter) Second only to the stag as a symbol of the Highlands of Scotland, the eagle is captured in this book in magnificent photographs.

Colin Baxter & Jim Crumley *Shetland – Land of the Ocean* (UK Colin Baxter) Best known for his ubiquitous postcards, Baxter's photographs succeed in capturing the grandeur of Scotland's moody landscapes.

George Mackay Brown *Portrait of Orkney* (UK John Murray). A personal account by the famous Orcadian poet of the island, its history and way of life, illustrated with photographs and drawings.

Collins Gem Scots Dictionary (UK HarperCollins). Handy, pocket-sized guide to the mysteries of Scottish vocabulary and idiom.

Collins Guide *Scottish Wild Flowers; Scottish Birds* (UK Harpercollins). Well-illustrated and informative small guides. Also in the guide series are *Clans and Tartans* and *Scottish Surnames*, which are a first step on the road to genealogy.

Derek Cooper *Skye* (UK Birlinn). A gazetteer and guide, and an indispensable mine of information; although first written in 1970, it has been revised where necessary.

Sheila Gear *Foula, Island West of the Sun* (UK Gollancz). An attempt to convey what it is like to live far out in the sea on an island of savage beauty.

James Shaw Grant *Discovering Lewis & Harris* (UK John Donald). Anecdotal and informative book by former editor of the *Stornoway Gazette*.

Hamish Haswell-Smith *The Scottish Islands* (UK Canongate). An exhaustive and impressive gazetteer with maps and absorbing information on all the Scottish islands. Filled with attractive sketches and paintings, the book is breathtaking in its thoroughness and lovingly gathered detail.

Mairi Hedderwick *Eye on the Hebrides* (Canongate). The author of the Katie Morag children's books knows the Hebrides well and with her enchanting watercolours takes you to meet all sorts of people in an affectionate look at the islands.

Charles Maclean *St. Kilda* (Canongate). Traces the social history of the island from its earliest beginnings to the seemingly inevitable end of the community with moving compassion.

Magnus Magnusson *Rùm: Nature's Island* (UK Luath Press). A detailed history of Rùm from earliest times up to its current position as a National Nature Reserve.

Gunnie Moberg & George Mackay Brown *Orkney – Pictures and Poems* (UK Colin Baxter Photography). A book to treasure, with a wonderfully evocative combination of poetry and photographs.

N.S. Newton *The Life and Times of Inverness* (UK John Donald). Inverness has a long history because of its crucial position at the head of the Great Glen.

Pevensey Island Guides (UK David & Charles). A surprisingly informative series with individual books on many of the islands, whose real strength lies in the colour photographs.

Colin Prior & Magnus Linklater *Highland Wilderness* (UK Constable). After looking at the magnificent photographs of the mountains, you'll be won over by the plea for their conservation.

Michael Russell *A Poem of Remote Lives: Images of Eriskay 1934* (UK Neil Wilson). An intriguing combination of photographs of the island taken in 1934 and the story of the German photographer, Werner Kissling, who took them.

FOLKLORE AND LEGEND

Alan J. Bruford & Donald Archie McDonald (eds) *Scottish Traditional Tales* (Polygon). A huge collection of folk stories from all over Scotland, taken from tape archives.

Alexander Mackenzie & Elizabeth Sutherland *The Prophecies of Brahan Seer* (UK Constable). These prophecies, which have received as much publicity as those of Nostradamus, were originally passed down orally in Gaelic from a mysterious figure who is

said to have come from the Isle of Lewis. They were collected and written down in 1877. This edition tells you how far they've been fulfilled.

Neil Philip (ed.) *The Penguin Book of Scottish Folk Tales* (UK Penguin). A collection of over a hundred folk tales from all over Scotland.

Nigel Tranter *Tales and Traditions of Scottish Castles* (UK Neil Wilson). The myths and legends of some of Scotland's more famous castles.

MEMOIRS AND TRAVELOGUES

George Mackay Brown *For the Islands I Sing: An Autobiography* (UK John Murray). Published posthumously at his own request, this autobiography not only provides an insight into one of the most influential Scottish poets but also into his native Orkney.

David Craig *On the Crofter's Trail* (UK Pimlico). Using anecdotes and interviews with descendants, Craig conveys the hardship and tragedy of the Highland Clearances without being mawkish.

Jim Crumley *Gulfs of Blue Air – A Highland Journey* (Mainstream). Recent travelogue mixed with nature notes and references to Scottish poets such as MacCaig and Mackay Brown. *Among Islands* (Mainstream). Superbly illustrated, this book takes you to the outer fringes of islands from Shetland to St Kilda in poetic mood.

David Duff (ed.) *Queen Victoria's Highland Journals* (UK Hamlyn). The daily diary of the Scottish adventures of "Mrs Brown" – Victoria's writing is detailed and interesting without being twee, and she lovingly conveys her affection for Deeside and the Highlands.

Elizabeth Grant of Rothiemurchus *Memoirs of a Highland Lady* (Canongate). Hugely readable recollections, written with wit and perception at the turn of the eighteenth century, charting the social changes in Edinburgh, London and particularly Speyside.

Mike Hughes *The Hebrides at War* (Canongate). This book demonstrates how crucial the Western Isles were to the defence of the Atlantic convoys against German U-boats. Excellent photographs from the period.

James Hunter *Scottish Highlanders* (Mainstream). Attempts to explain the strong sense of blood ties held by people of Scottish descent all over the world; lots of history and good photographs.

Samuel Johnson & James Boswell *A Journey to the Western Isles of Scotland* and *The Journal of a Tour to the Hebrides* (UK Penguin). Lively accounts of a famous journey around the islands taken by the noted lexicographer, Dr Samuel Johnson, and his biographer and friend.

Osgood Mackenzie *100 Years in the Highlands* (UK Birlinn). First published in 1921, this has become a classic social history of the Highlands in Victorian times.

Edwin Muir *Highland Journey* (Mainstream). A classic travelogue written in 1935 by the troubled Orcadian writer on his return to Scotland from London.

F.G. Rea *A School on South Uist* (UK Birlinn). A personal account of the life of a Hebridean schoolmaster from 1890 to 1913.

Sir Walter Scott *The Voyage of the Pharos* (Scottish Library Association). In 1814 Scott accompanied Stevenson senior on a tour of the northern lighthouses, visiting Shetland, Orkney, the Hebrides and even nipping across to Ireland; he wrote a lively diary of their adventures, including dodging American privateers.

Mike Tomkies *A Last Wild Place* (UK Jonathan Cape). Written by a journalist who lived in a derelict croft in Northwest Scotland for twenty years, this is a perceptive and loving account of the natural world around him.

FOOD AND DRINK

Annette Hope *A Caledonian Feast* (UK Mainstream). Authoritative and entertaining history of Scottish food and social life from the ninth to the twentieth century. Lots of recipes.

Michael Jackson *Malt Whisky Companion* (UK Dorling Kindersley). An attractively put-together tome, considered by many to be the "bible" on malt-whisky tasting.

G.W. Lockhart *The Scots and Their Fish* (UK Birlinn). Tells the history of fish and fishing in Scotland, and ends with a selection of traditional recipes.

Claire Macdonald *The Claire Macdonald Cookbook* (UK Bantam). Lady Claire Macdonald

of Macdonald has become widely known and respected in Scottish cookery circles. She promotes the use of native food and runs a successful hotel on Skye.

Charles McLean *Pocket Guides: Scotch Whisky* and **Charles McLean & Jason Lowe** *Malt Whisky* (UK Mitchell Beazley, o/p). The first is a small, thorough, fact-filled book covering malt, grain and blended whiskies, plus whisky-based liqueurs. The second is an attractive coffee-table book with inspiring photographs of the places whisky comes from, as well as detailed background information.

Nick Nairn *Wild Harvest/Wild Harvest 2* (UK BBC Books). Glossy TV tie-ins by an engaging young Scottish chef, who takes up the challenge of gathering and eating from the wild. Both books have fascinating, if difficult to recreate, recipes. His latest addition is *Island Harvest* (UK BBC Books).

J. Redding & T. Weston *Rainbows and Wellies* (UK Findhorn Press). Scotland is not noted for its vegetarianism, but this is a vegan book with some really gourmet recipes that's gained wide popularity.

Alison Warner *A House by the Shore* and *Scarista Style* (UK Warner). The story of how an old house on Harris was converted into the present prestigious hotel, with many of the recipes used there.

FICTION

George Mackay Brown *Beside the Ocean of Time* (UK Flamingo). A child's journey through the history of an Orkney island, and an adult's effort to make sense of the place's secrets in the late twentieth century. *Magnus* (Canongate) is his retelling of the death of St Magnus, with parallels for modern times.

George MacDonald Fraser *The General Danced at Dawn* (Fontana/Acacia), *McAuslain in the Rough* and *The Sheikh and the Dustbin* (Fontana/HarperCollins). Touching and very funny collections of short stories detailing life in a Highland regiment after World War II.

Christine Marion Fraser *Kinvara* (UK Hodder & Stoughton). Born in Glasgow, her family sagas are set in the Hebrides and in Argyll; her latest novel is centred on a lighthouse keeper on the west coast of Scotland.

Lewis Grassic Gibbon, *Sunset Song, Cloud Howe, Grey Granite* (Penguin/Canongate). This trilogy, known as *A Scots Quair* and set in north-east Scotland, has become a classic, telling the story of the conflict in one man's life between Scottish and English culture.

Neil M. Gunn *The Silver Darlings* (UK Faber). Probably Gunn's most representative and best-known book, evocatively set on the northeast coast and telling the story of the herring fisher-men during the great years of the industry. Other examples of his romantic, symbolic works include *The Lost Glen, The Silver Bough* and *Wild Geese Overhead* (UK Chambers).

Joyce Holmes *Foreign Body* (UK Hodder Headline). An attractive amateur duo of detectives solve murders in a closely observed small community in the Highlands. Welcome new-comer to the crime scene.

Eric Linklater *The Dark of Summer* (Canongate). Set on the Faroes, Shetland, Orkney (where the author was born) and in the-atres of war, this novel exhibits the best of Linklater's compelling narrative style, although his comic *Private Angelo* (Canongate) is better known.

Compton MacKenzie *Whisky Galore* (UK Penguin). Comic novel based on a true story of the wartime wreck of a cargo of whisky off Eriskay. Full of predictable stereotypes, but still funny.

Naomi Mitchison *Lobster on the Agenda* (UK House of Lochar). Recently republished, her novel written in 1952 about contemporary life in the West Highlands captures exactly a commu-nity which, shaken by the war, is trying to look forward while hampered by the prejudices of the past.

Neil Munro *The Complete Edition of the Para Handy Tales* (UK Pan). Engaging and witty sto-ries relating the adventures of a Clyde puffer captain as he more or less legally steers his grubby ship up and down the west coast. Despite a fond – if slightly patronizing – view of the Gaelic mind, they are enormous fun.

M. Sinclair *Hebridean Odyssey: Songs, Poems, Prose and Images* (UK Polygon). A useful anthol-ogy for getting the feel of the rich and varied culture of the Hebrides.

Iain Crichton Smith *Consider the Lilies* (UK Canongate). Poetic lament about the Highland Clearances by Scotland's finest bilingual (English and Gaelic) writer.

Sir Walter Scott *The Pirate* (UK Shetland Times). Inspired by stories of Viking raids and set in Orkney and Shetland, this novel was very popular in Victorian times.

CHILDREN'S FICTION

George Mackay Brown *Pictures in the Cave* (UK Kelpie). A collection of stories based on folk tales, told by a master poet. Suitable for 9-year-olds and over.

Kathleen Fidler *Desperate Journey* (UK Kelpie). Story of a family driven from Scotland in the Sutherland clearances across the Atlantic to Canada. *The Droving Lad* (UK Kelpie). A thriller about a boy and his first experience of driving cattle from the Highlands to the Lowlands. Suitable for 9-year-olds and over.

Mairi Hedderwick *Katie Morag and the Two Grandmothers* (Collins/Trafalgar Square). One of the many delightful stories of a little girl and the trouble she gets in on the West Coast island of Struay, beautifully illustrated by the author. Suitable for reading to under-5s.

Ted Hughes *Nessie the Mannerless Monster* (Faber). A verse story about the famous monster who goes to London to see the queen. Suitable for 5- to 8-year-olds.

Mollie Hunter *A Stranger Came Ashore* (UK Kelpie). Set in Shetland, this a tragic and grip-ping historical tale. Suitable for 10-year-olds and over.

Gavin Maxwell *Ring of Bright Water* (UK Penguin). Heart-warming true tale of a relation-ship with three otters. Suitable for 5 and upwards.

Robert Louis Stevenson *Kidnapped* (Puffin Classic/Bantam Classic). A thrilling historical adventure set in the eighteenth century, every bit as exciting as the better-known *Treasure Island* (Puffin Classic/Scholastic Paperbacks).

POETRY

George Mackay Brown *Selected Poems 1954–1992* (UK John Murray). Brown's work is as haunting, beautiful and gritty as the Orkney islands which inspire it.

Robert Burns *Selected Poems* (Penguin). Scotland's most famous bard. Immensely popular all over the world, his best-known works are his earlier ones, including "Auld lang syne" and "My love is like a red, red rose".

Norman MacCaig *Selected Poems* (UK Chatto & Windus). This selection includes some of the best work from this important Scottish poet whose deep love of nature and of the Highland landscape is always evident. *Norman MacCaig; A Celebration* (Chapman), an anthology written for his 85th birthday, includes work by more than ninety writers, including Ted Hughes and Seamus Heaney.

Sorley Maclean (Somhairle Macgill-Eain) *From Wood to Ridge: Collected Poems* (UK Vintage). Written in Gaelic, his poems have been translated into bilingual editions all over the world, dealing as they do with the sorrows of poverty, war and love.

John McQueen & Tom Scott (eds) *The Oxford Book of Scottish Verse* (UK Oxford University Press). Claims to be the most comprehensive anthology of Scottish poetry ever published.

Edwin Morgan *Selected Poems* (UK Carcanet). A love of words and their sounds is evident in Morgan's poems, which are refreshingly varied and often experimental. He comments on the Scottish scene with shrewdness and humour.

Edwin Muir *Collected Poems* (Faber). Muir's childhood on Orkney remained with him as a dream of paradise from which he was banished to Glasgow. His poems are passionately concerned with Scotland.

Tom Scott (ed.) *The Penguin Book of Scottish Verse* (UK Penguin). Good general selection.

Iain Crichton Smith *Collected Poems* (UK Carcanet). Born on the Isle of Lewis, Iain Crichton Smith wrote with feeling, and sometimes bitterness, in both Gaelic and English, of the life of the rural communities, the iniquities of the Free Church, the need to revive Gaelic culture and the glory of the Scottish landscape.

Roderick Watson (ed.) *The Poetry of Scotland* (UK Edinburgh University Press). An accessible anthology of poems in English, Scots and Gaelic (with notes and translations) from the fourteenth century to the present day.

OUTDOOR PURSUITS

Bartholomew Walks Series (UK Bartholomew). The series covers different areas of Scotland, including Perthshire, Loch Lomond and the Trossachs, Oban, Mull and Lochaber, and Skye and Wester Ross. Each booklet has a range of walks of varying lengths, with clear maps and descriptions.

Donald Bennet *The Munros*, and **Scott Johnstone et al** *The Corbetts* (UK Scottish Mountaineering Trust). Authoritative and attractively illustrated hillwalkers' guides to the Scottish peaks. SMT also publishes guides to districts and specific climbs.

Hamish Brown *Hamish's Mountain Walk and Climbing the Corbetts* (Bâton Wicks). The best of the travel narratives about walking in the Scottish Highlands.

Anthony Burton *The Caledonian Canal* (UK Aurum Press). A book for walkers, cyclists and boaters with maps and details of boat rental, accommodation, etc.

Andrew Dempster *Classic Mountain Scrambles in Scotland* (UK Mainstream). Guide to hillwalks in Scotland that combine straightforward walking with some rock climbing.

Richard Fitter, Alastair Fitter & Marhorie Blanney *Collins Pocket Guide to the Wild Flowers of Britain and Northern Europe* (UK HarperCollins). An excellent, easy-to-use field guide.

David Hamilton *The Scottish Golf Guide* (Canongate). An inexpensive paperback with descriptions of and useful information about 84 of Scotland's best courses.

John Hancox *Collins Pocket Reference – Cycling in Scotland* (UK HarperCollins). Spiral-bound edition with over fifty road routes of all grades up and down the country, each with a useful route map. For more off-road mountain-bike routes, try **Harry Henniker** *101 Bike Routes in Scotland* (UK Mainstream).

Philip Lusby & Jenny Wright *Scottish Wild Plants* (UK The Stationery Office). Beautifully produced book about the rarer plants of Scotland, their discovery and their conservation, produced in conjunction with the Royal Botanic Gardens of Edinburgh.

Michael Madders & Julia Welstead *Where to Watch Birds in Scotland* (UK Christopher Helm). Region-by-region guide with maps, details on access and habitat, and notes on what to see when.

Magnus Magnusson & Graham White (eds) *The Nature of Scotland – Landscape, Wildlife and People* (Canongate). Glossy picture-based book on Scotland's natural heritage, from geology to farming and conservation. Good section on crofting.

Ian Mitchell *Mountain Days and Bothy Nights* (UK Luath Press). A slim but highly entertaining volume describing the characters and experiences of modern-day hill-climbing.

Jenny Parke *Ski & Snowboard: Scotland* (UK Luath Press). Informative book about where to go to get to the best slopes, with loads of useful advice.

Pastime Publications *Scotland for Game, Sea and Coarse Fishing* (UK Pastime Publications). General guide on what to fish, where to do it and for how much, along with notes on records, regulations and convenient accommodation. Published in association with the Scottish Tourist Board.

Paul Ramsay *Lochs & Glens of Scotland* (UK Collins & Brown). Informative text and stunning photographs of the Highlands that make you want to book a holiday immediately.

Ralph Storer *100 Best Routes on Scottish Mountains* (UK David & Charles). A compilation of the best day-walks in Scotland, including some of the classics overlooked by the Munroing guides.

RECIPES

Food in the Highlands and Islands has always been limited, dictated largely by natural conditions. Scotland's northerly situation means that the only cereal crops grown in any quantity have been **oats** and a very hardy form of **barley**, called "bere", still grown in Orkney. Yeasted bread was virtually unknown until the twentieth century, and today's **oatcakes**, one of Scotland's major exports, are the descendants of the unyeasted bread, cooked on a hot stone since prehistoric times. The **potato** has been a staple part of Highland diet since the late eighteenth century and, of course, **root vegetables** like the turnip/swede ("mashit tatties and neeps"), which were also used to feed the animals in winter. Shortage of pasture means that cattle have largely been kept for **milk**, **butter** and **cheese** in the Highlands rather than meat, but, of course, Scots beef (though from the Lowlands) is well-known for its excellence. Sheep, which ousted people during the Clearances, do appear on the menu now, but the oldest dishes are generally meatless. Consequently, many traditional dishes make good use of potatoes, oats and whisky, and are simple to cook. The recipes that follow are fairly simple; some of them you'll find on menus, but others have yet to be revived. For more sophisticated dishes, look under "Food and drink" in Basics (p.35).

SOUP

A good nourishing broth or soup has always been the foundation of a Scot's day in winter. **Scotch broth**, the best known, is made from meat stock, vegetables and any leftovers, but must include pearl barley, which is soaked overnight. In many households it was left on the stove for days and topped with water and titbits when the level fell.

CULLEN SKINK

More unusual than Scotch broth, this delicious soup is being found increasingly regularly on Scottish menus. It has its roots in Cullen, a small town on the Moray Firth coast, and is traditionally made from smoked fish – for the real thing, don't use the dyed variety. Serves four.

1 smoked haddock
1 onion, chopped
1pint milk
1oz butter
A little mashed potato
Salt and pepper
Chopped parsley

Skin the haddock, place in a pan and cover with water. Bring to the boil, add the chopped onion, then simmer until the fish is cooked. Remove the fish, reserving the stock, and flake it, removing the bones. In another pan, bring the milk to the boil, then add the stock and the fish, with salt to taste (you probably won't need much). Add the butter, seasoning and enough mashed potato to thicken the soup, then stir well. Serve with chopped parsley.

MAIN COURSES

In hotels and restaurants, main courses generally include roast beef, salmon and chicken and imported dishes. The main course recipes below are strictly traditional and based on the cheap fare of the peasant. They are, however, very tasty and can sometimes be found in good cafés where home-cooking is offered.

CLAPSHOT

This dish comes from Orkney, and can be served as a side vegetable or as a main course with the addition of cheese at the mashing stage. Serves four.

500g potatoes
500g swede or turnip
1 onion, finely chopped
1 tbsp chopped chives
Milk
Butter
Salt and pepper

Peel the potatoes and swede. Cut them into smallish pieces and put them in a large pan with the onion. Pour boiling water over them and simmer gently until just soft. Drain and mash thoroughly, adding the chives and enough milk and butter to make the mixture light and fluffy. Season with salt and pepper.

RUMBLEDTHUMPS

The name for this dish means "mixed together" – rumbled – and "bashed together" – thumped. This is a meatless main course but can also be served as a vegetable dish along with meat. Serves four.

1lb potatoes

1lb white cabbage, spring cabbage or kale

3oz butter

1 medium onion or two trimmed leeks, finely chopped

1 small pot of single cream

2oz mature cheddar, grated

Chopped fresh chives

Salt and black pepper

Slice the potatoes thickly and boil in a little salted water. Once cooked, drain and mash. Slice the cabbage and boil gently in salted water, being careful not to overcook. Melt the butter in a heavy bottomed pan and sauté the onions or leeks until soft. Add the potatoes and cabbage, a little cream and seasoning to taste, then beat together with the chives. Place the mixture in an ovenproof dish, cover with grated cheddar and brown under a hot grill or in a hot oven.

STOVIES

Stovies are made from potatoes, onions and leftover cooked meat. They are a good example of a peasant dish; being mainly potato, it provided energy in the form of starch and bulk to fill empty stomachs. Despite the dish's "poor" origins, it is very tasty, filling and is often served with oatcakes at ceilidhs (country dances) and evening wedding receptions. Serves four.

2 medium onions, finely chopped

2oz beef dripping or 4tbsp of sunflower oil

2lb potatoes, peeled and roughly sliced

4 tablespoons of gravy or stock

About 6oz cold roast beef, diced

Parsley, chopped

Salt and pepper

Cook the onions in the dripping until they are soft but not brown. Add the potatoes to the onions and mix well; cover and cook for about ten minutes, stirring occasionally to prevent sticking. Add the gravy, meat, salt and pepper and mix well. Cover again and cook over a low heat until the thinner potato slices are mushy and the thicker-cut ones are soft – an hour should be enough (this part of the cooking can be done in a large casserole dish in a medium oven, to give a crunchy topping). Garnish with parsley and serve with oatcakes and a glass of milk.

PUDDINGS

Puddings were something of a luxury for the Highlander and a meal was more likely to be rounded off with a dram of whisky. There are one or two traditional recipes like the ones that follow.

CLOOTIE DUMPLING

You'll find this spiced fruit pudding in many restaurants and even in tins, but, as you might expect, some are better than others. It's very filling and can be solid – a cross between a steamed pudding and a cake, it will serve either purpose. The following is just one of many variations on the recipe. Serves four.

1.5 tbsp mixed spice

750g self-raising flour

500g mixed dried fruit

1 heaped tsp baking powder

250g granulated sugar

250g suet or margarine

2 tbsp treacle or syrup

Milk

Mix the suet, flour, fruit, spice, baking powder and sugar together. Combine the treacle with a little milk and add to the mixture. Gradually stir in more milk until the mixture has a soft consistency, then place on a white square cloth that has been well floured (this is the *clout* or *cloot*). Gather the ends together, leaving room for the dumpling to expand, and tie them in a tight knot. Place it on a plate in a large pan of boiling water. Cover, and boil gently for two hours (make sure it doesn't boil dry). Turn it out of the cloth and allow it to dry out in a medium oven for ten to fifteen minutes.

CRANACHAN

Cranachan (also known as "Stapag on the Islands", where the raspberries are generally omitted) was traditionally served at harvest time, when all the ingredients were put upon the table and everyone filled their own dish and chose their own ratio of whisky to solids. It's now back on the menu and is delicious. Serves four.

50g medium oatmeal

10fl oz fresh double cream

3 tbsp heather honey

3 tbsp whisky

350g fresh raspberries

Toast the oatmeal under a grill until it's golden, and let it cool. Whip the cream until it's stiff, then mix in the oatmeal, honey and whisky. In tall glasses, layer the raspberries with the cream mixture and chill in the fridge. Serve at room temperature, decorated with raspberries.

CARRAGEEN JELLY

This recipe comes from Lewis, and you're unlikely to find it on a menu. Its main interest is historical, as carrageen is a type of seaweed found in abundance in the Western Isles. Be careful to identify it correctly, as some seaweeds can have unfortunate results. Serves four.

250g carrageen, washed and soaked for two hours, then dried

Rind of 1 lemon, grated

500ml milk

Sugar to taste

Place the seaweed in a pan with the lemon rind and cover with milk. Bring it to the boil and simmer gently for thirty minutes. Stir in the sugar and then strain into a mould and allow to cool. It should set like a jelly and can then be turned out onto a plate.

CROWDIE

A simple form of crofting cheese, anyone can make this at home. It's a very good way of using up milk that's gone sour and goes well with oatcakes.

1litre freshly sour or full cream milk

Salt

Cream

Pour the milk into a pan and place it on a slow heat until it curdles. Make sure it doesn't simmer or boil, or the curd will harden. Let the curds cool. Next, the liquid (or whey) needs to be drained off. Line a colander with muslin, put the curds in it and leave until the whey has drained away; squeeze the last bit out by hand or with the back of a spoon. You now have basic crowdie: it simply needs a little salt and cream and a rest in the fridge before consuming. It doesn't keep well, so eat it within three days.

LANGUAGE

Language is a thorny, complex and often highly political issue in Scotland. If you're not from Scotland yourself, you're most likely to be addressed in a variety of English, spoken in a Scottish accent. Even then, you're likely to hear phrases and words that are part of what is known as Lowland Scottish or Scots, which is now officially recognized as a distinct language in its own right. To a lesser extent, Gaelic, too, remains a living language, particularly in the *Gàidhealtachd* or Gaelic-speaking areas of the Western Isles, parts of Skye and a few scattered Hebridean islands. In Orkney and Shetland, the local dialect of Scots contains many words carried over from Norn, the Norse language spoken in the Northern Isles from the time of the Vikings until the eighteenth century (for more on this, see p.343).

Lowland Scottish or **Scots** is spoken by thirty percent of the Scottish population, according to the latest survey. It began life as a northern branch of Anglo-Saxon, and emerged as a distinct language in the Middle Ages. From the 1370s until the Union in 1707, it was the country's main literary and documentary language. Since the eighteenth century, however, it has been systematically repressed in preference to English. Robbie Burns is the most obvious literary exponent of the Scots language, but there has been a revival this century led by poets such as Hugh MacDiarmid. (For examples of the works by Burns, see p.460.) Only very recently has Scots enjoyed something of a renaissance, getting itself on the Scottish school curriculum in 1996, and achieving official recognition as a distinct language in 1998. Despite these enormous political achievements, many people (rightly or wrongly) still regard Scots as a dialect of English.

Scottish **Gaelic** (*Gàidhlig*, pronounced "Gallic") is one of only four Celtic languages to survive into the modern age (Welsh, Breton and Irish Gaelic are the other three). Manx, the old language of the Isle of Man, died out earlier this century, while Cornish was finished as a community language way back in the eighteenth century. Scottish Gaelic is most closely related to Irish Gaelic and Manx – hardly surprising, since Gaelic was introduced to Scotland from Ireland around the third century BC. Some folk still argue that Scottish Gaelic is merely a dialect of its parent language, Irish Gaelic, and indeed the two languages remain more or less mutually intelligible. From the fifth to the twelfth centuries, Gaelic enjoyed an expansionist phase, gradually becoming the national language, thanks partly to the backing of the Celtic church in Iona. At the end of this period, Gaelic was spoken throughout virtually all of what is now Scotland – the main exceptions being Orkney and Shetland.

From that high point onwards, Gaelic began a steady decline over the next few centuries. Even before Union with England, power, religious ideology and wealth gradually passed into non-Gaelic hands. The royal court was transferred to Edinburgh and an Anglo-Norman legal system was put in place. The Celtic Church was Romanized by the introduction of foreign clergy, and, most importantly of all, English and Flemish merchants colonized the new trading towns of the east coast. In addition, the pro-English attitudes held by the Covenanters led to strong anti-Gaelic feeling within the Church of Scotland from its inception.

The two abortive Jacobite rebellions of 1715 and 1745 furthered the language's decline, as did the Clearances that took place in the Gaelic-speaking Highlands from the 1770s to the 1820s, which forced thousands to migrate to central Scotland's new industrial belt or emigrate to North America. Although efforts were made to halt the decline in the first half of the nineteenth century, the 1872 Education Act gave no official recognition to Gaelic, and children were severely punished if they were caught speaking the language in school.

Current estimates put the number of Gaelic speakers at 86,000 (about two percent of the population), the majority of whom live in the *Gàidhealtachd*, with an extended Gaelic community of perhaps 250,000 who have some understanding of the language. In the last two decades the language has stabilized and even recovered, thanks to the introduction of bilingual primary and nursery schools, and a huge increase in the amount of broadcasting time given to Gaelic-language programmes. The success of rock bands such as Runrig has shown that it is possible to combine traditional Gaelic culture with popular entertainment *and* reach a mass audience.

GAELIC GRAMMAR AND PRONUNCIATION

Gaelic is a highly complex tongue, with a fiendish, antiquated grammar and, with only eighteen letters, an intimidating system of spelling. Pronunciation is actually easier than it appears at first glance – one general rule to remember is that the **stress** always falls on the first syllable of a word. The general rule of syntax is that the verb starts the sentence whether it's a question or not, followed by the subject and then the object; adjectives generally follow the word they are describing.

SHORT AND LONG VOWELS

Gaelic has both short and long vowels, the latter being denoted by an acute or grave accent.

a as in c**a**t; before nn and l, like the *ow* in b**ow** (of a boat)

à as in b**a**r

e as in p**e**t

é like the *ai* in r**ai**n

i like the *ee* in str**ee**t, but shorter

í like the *ee* in fr**ee**

o as in p**o**t

GAELIC GEOGRAPHICAL AND PLACE NAME TERMS

The purpose of the list below is to help with place-name derivations (from Gaelic) and with more detailed map reading. For a list of place names derived from the Norse, see p.343.

abhainn	river		**fin**, from **fionn**	white
ach or **auch**, from **achadh**	field		**gair** or **gare**, from **geàrr**	short
			garv, from **garbh**	rough
ail, **aileach**	rock		**geodha**	cove
Alba	Scotland		**glen**, from **gleann**	valley
ardan or **arden**, from **àird**	a point of land or height		**gower** or **gour**, from **gabhar**	goat
aros	dwelling		**inch**, from **innis**	meadow or island
ault, from **allt**	stream		**inver**, from **inbhir**	river mouth
bal or **bally**, from **baile**	town, village		**ken** or **kin**, from **ceann**	head
balloch, from **bealach**	mountain pass		**knock**, from **cnoc**	hill
bad	clump of trees		**kyle**, from **caolas**	narrow strait
bagh	bay		**lag**	hollow
ban	white, fair		**larach**	site of an old ruin
bàrr	summit		**liath**	grey
beg, from **beag**	small		**loch**	lake
ben, from **beinn**	mountain		**meall**	round hill
blair, from **blàr**	field, battlefield		**mon**, from **monadh**	hill
camas	bay, harbour		**more**, from **mór**	large, great
cairn, from **càrn**	pile of stones		**rannoch**, from **raineach**	bracken
cnoc	hill			
coll or **colly**, from **coille**	wood		**ross**, from **ros**	promontory
			rubha	promontory
corran	a point jutting into the sea		**sgeir**	sea rock
			sgurr	sharp point
corrie, from **coire**	round hollow in mountainside, whirlpool		**sron**	nose, prow or promontory
			strath, from **srath**	broad valley
craig, from **creag**	rock, crag		**tarbet**, from **tairbeart**	isthmus
cruach	bold hill		**tigh**	house
drum, from **druim**	ridge		**tìr** or **tyre**, from **tìr**	land
dubh	black		**torr**	hill, castle
dun or **dum**, from **dùn**	fort		**tràigh**	shore
eilean	island		**uig**	shelter
ess, from **eas**	waterfall		**uisge**	water

GAELIC PHRASES AND VOCABULARY

The choice is limited when it comes **teach-yourself Gaelic** courses, but the BBC *Can Seo* cassette and book is perfect for starting you off. Drier and more academic is *Teach Yourself Gaelic* (Hodder & Stoughton), which is aimed at bringing beginners to Scottish "O" grade standard. *Everyday Gaelic* by Morag MacNeill (Gairm) is the best phrasebook around.

BASIC WORDS AND GREETINGS

yes	*tha*	yesterday	*an-dé*
no	*chan eil*	today	*an-diugh*
hello	*hallo*	tomorrow	*maireach*
how are you?	*ciamar a tha thu?*	now	*a-nise*
OK	*tha gu math*	hotel	*taigh-òsda*
thank you	*tapadh leat*	house	*taigh*
welcome	*fàilte*	story	*sgeul*
come in	*thig a-staigh*	song	*òran*
goodbye	*mar sin leat*	music	*ceòl*
goodnight	*oidhche mhath*	book	*leabhar*
who?	*cò?*	tired	*sgìth*
where is...?	*càit a bheil...?*	food	*lòn*
when?	*cuine?*	bread	*aran*
what is it?	*dé tha ann?*	water	*uisge*
morning	*madainn*	milk	*bainne*
evening	*feasgar*	beer	*leann*
day	*là*	wine	*fion*
night	*oidhche*	whisky	*uisge beatha*
here	*an seo*	post office	*post oifis*
there	*an sin*	Edinburgh	*Dun Eideann*
this way	*mar seo*	Glasgow	*Glaschu*
that way	*mar sin*	America	*Ameireaga*
pound/s	*not/aichean*	Ireland	*Eire*
tomorrow	*a-màireach*	England	*Sasainn*
tonight	*a-nochd*	London	*Lunnain*
cheers	*slàinte*		

ò like the *a* in enth**ra**l

ó like the *ow* in b**ow** (of a boat)

u like the *oo* in sc**oo**t

ù like the *oo* in l**oo**

VOWEL COMBINATIONS

Gaelic is littered with diphthongs, which, rather like in English, can be pronounced in several different ways depending on the individual word.

ai like the *a* in c**a**t, or the *e* in p**e**t; before dh or gh, like the *ee* in str**ee**t

ao like the *ur* in s**ur**ly

ei like the *a* in m**a**te

ea like the *e* in p**e**t, or the *a* in c**a**t, and sometimes like the *a* in m**a**te; before ll or nn, like the *ow* in b**ow** (of a boat)

èa as in h**ea**r

eu like the *ai* in tr**ai**n, or the *ea* in f**ea**r

ia like the *ea* in f**ea**r

io like the *ea* in f**ea**r, or the *ee* in str**ee**t, but shorter

ua like the *ooe* in w**ooe**r

CONSONANTS

The consonants listed below are those that differ substantially from the English.

b at the beginning of a word as in **b**ig; in the middle or at the end of a word like the *p* in **p**air

bh at the beginning of a word like the *v* in **v**an; elsewhere it is silent

c as in **c**at; after a vowel it has aspiration *before* it

ch always as in lo**ch**, never as in **ch**urch

SOME USEFUL PHRASES

It's a nice day	*tha latha math ann*	Do you speak Gaelic?	*a bheil Gàidhlig agad?*
How much is that?	*dè tha e 'cosg?*	What is the Gaelic for?	*Dé a' Ghàidhlig a tha air?*
What's your name?	*dè 'n t-ainm a th'ort?*		
Excuse me	*gabh mo leisgeul*	I don't understand	*chan eil mi 'tuigsinn*
What time is it?	*dé am uair a tha e?*	I don't know	*chan eil fhios agam*
I'm thirsty	*tha am pathadh orm*	That's good	*'s math sin*
I'd like a double room	*'se rùm dùbailte tha mi'g iarraigh*	It doesn't matter	*'s coma*
		I'm sorry	*Tha mi duilich*

NUMBERS AND DAYS

1	*aon*	30	*deug ar fhichead*
2	*dà/dhà*	40	*dà fhichead*
3	*trì*	50	*lethcheud*
4	*ceithir*	60	*trì fichead*
5	*còig*	100	*ceud*
6	*sia*	1000	*mìle*
7	*seachd*	Monday	*Diluain*
8	*ochd*	Tuesday	*Dimàirt*
9	*naoi*	Wednesday	*Diciadain*
10	*deich*	Thursday	*Diardaoin*
11	*aon deug*	Friday	*Dihaoine*
20	*fichead*	Saturday	*Disathurna*
21	*aon ar fhichead*	Sunday	*Didòmhnaich/La na Sàbaid*

SURNAMES

The prefix **Mac** or **Mc** in Scottish surnames derives from the Gaelic, meaning "son of".
In Scots, Mac is used for both sexes; but in Gaelic, women are referred to as Nic. For example:

Donnchadh Mac Aodh	Duncan MacKay
Iseabail Nic Aodh	Isabel MacKay

---

cn like the *cr* in **cr**owd

d like the *d* in **d**og, but with the tongue pressed against the back of the upper teeth; at the beginning of a word before e or i, like the *j* in **j**am; in the middle or at the end of a word like the *t* in cat; after i like the *ch* in **ch**urch

dh before and after a, o or u an aspirated *g*, rather like someone gargling; before e or i like the *y* in **y**es; elsewhere silent

fh usually silent; somtimes like the *h* in **h**ouse

g at the beginning of a word as in **g**et; before e like the *y* in **y**es; in the middle or end of a word like the *ck* in so**ck**; after i like the *ch* in lo**ch**

gh at the beginning of a word as in **g**et; before or after a, o or u rather like someone gargling; after i sometimes like the *y* in ga**y**, but often silent

l after i and sometimes before e like the *l* in **l**ot; elsewhere a peculiarly Gaelic sound produced by flattening the front of the tongue against the palate

mh like the *v* in **v**an

p at the beginning of a word as in **p**et; elsewhere it has aspiration *before* it

rt pronounced as **sht**

s before e or i like the *sh* in **sh**ip; otherwise as in English

sh before a, o or u like the *h* in **h**ouse; before e like the *ch* in lo**ch**

t before e or i like the *ch* in **ch**urch; in the middle or at the end of a word it has aspiration *before* it; otherwise as in English

th at the beginning of a word like the *h* in **h**ouse; elsewhere, and in the word *thu*, silent

GLOSSARY

Auld Old.

Aye Yes.

Bairn Baby.

Blackhouse Thick-walled traditional dwelling.

Bonnie Pretty.

Bothy Primitive cottage or hut; farmworker's or shepherd's mountain shelter.

Brae Slope; hill.

Brig Bridge.

Broch Circular prehistoric stone fort.

Burn Small stream or brook.

Byre Shelter for cattle; cottage.

Cairn Mound of stones.

Carse Riverside area of flat alluvium.

Ceilidh Social gathering involving dancing, drinking, singing and storytelling.

Clan Extended family.

Covenanters Supporter of the Presbyterian Church in the seventeenth century.

Corbett Mountain between 2500ft and 3000ft high.

Corbie-stepped Architectural term; any set of steps on a gable.

Crannog Celtic lake or bog dwelling.

Croft Small plot of farmland with house, common in the Highlands.

Crow-stepped Same as *corbie-stepped*.

Dolmen Grave chamber.

Dram Literally, one-sixteenth of an ounce. Usually refers to a small measure of whisky.

Dun Fortified mound.

First-foot The first person to enter a household on *Hogmanay* (see below).

Firth Narrow inlet.

Gillie Personal guide used on hunting or fishing trips.

Glen Deep, narrow mountain valley.

Harling Limestone and gravel mix used to cover buildings.

Hogmanay New Year's Eve.

Howe Valley.

Howff Meeting place; pub.

HS Historic Scotland.

Ken Knowledge; understanding.

Kilt Knee-length tartan skirt worn by Highland men.

Kirk Church.

Laird Landowner; aristocrat.

Law Rounded hill.

Links Grassy coastal land; coastal golf course.

Lochan Little loch or lake.

Machair Sandy, grassy, lime-rich coastal land, generally used for grazing.

Manse Official home of a Presbyterian minister.

Munro Mountain over 3000ft high.

Munro-bagging Sport of trying to climb as many Munros as possible.

Peel Fortified tower, built to withstand Border raids.

Pend Archway or vaulted passage.

Presbyterian The official (Protestant) Church of Scotland, established by John Knox during the Reformation.

Sassenach English.

Shinty Simple form of hockey.

SNH Scottish Natural Heritage

SNP Scottish National Party.

Sporran Leather purse worn in front of a kilt.

Tartan Check-patterned woollen cloth, particular patterns being associated with particular clans.

Thane A landowner of high rank; the chief of a clan.

Trews Tartan trousers.

Wee Small.

Wynd Narrow lane.

Yett Gate or door.

INDEX

Stay in touch with us!

ROUGH*NEWS* **is Rough Guides' free newsletter.
In four issues a year we give you news, travel
issues, music reviews, readers' letters and the
latest dispatches from authors on the road.**

I would like to receive ROUGH*NEWS*: please put me on your free mailing list.

NAME . . . .

ADDRESS . . . .

Please clip or photocopy and send to: Rough Guides, 62–70 Shorts Gardens, London WC2H 9AB,
England or Rough Guides, 375 Hudson Street, New York, NY 10014, USA.

OPPOSING
VIEWPOINTS®
SERIES

Gentrification and
the Housing Crisis

Other Books of Related Interest

Opposing Viewpoints Series

Identity Politics
Race in America
The Wealth Gap
Uber, Lyft, Airbnb, and the Sharing Economy

At Issue Series

Green Cities
Poverty in America
The Right to a Living Wage
The Wealth Divide

Current Controversies Series

Are There Two Americas?
Homelessness and Street Crime
LGBTQ Rights
Police Training and Excessive Force

"Congress shall make no law … abridging the freedom of speech, or of the press."

First Amendment to the US Constitution

The basic foundation of our democracy is the First Amendment guarantee of freedom of expression. The Opposing Viewpoints series is dedicated to the concept of this basic freedom and the idea that it is more important to practice it than to enshrine it.